WARNER
EASTERN UNIVERSITY
ST. DAVIDS PA 19087-3696

# Taiwan

Andrew Bender, Julie Grundvig, Robert Kelly

# Contents

DS 798.965 .B46 2004
Bender, Andrew.
Taiwan

Lonely Planet books provide independent advice. Lonely Planet does not accept advertising in guidebooks, nor do we accept payment in exchange for listing or endorsing any place or business. Lonely Planet writers do not accept discounts or payments in exchange for positive coverage of any sort.

Lonely Planet 的书籍提供独立的建议。Lonely Planet 在导览书籍中不接受广告，也不接受款项来换取资料的登录或对任何地方或企业的支持。Lonely Planet 的作者不接受折扣或款项来换取任何形式的积极报导。

TAIPEI p60

NORTHERN TAIWAN p119

TAIWAN STRAIT ISLANDS p271

WESTERN TAIWAN p196

EAST COAST p159

# Destination Taiwan

Steeped in traditional Chinese culture, with influences from Japan and the island's own indigenous tribes, Taiwan is a destination full of surprises. Beyond the bustling metropolises are lush tropical landscapes, rushing rivers, hot springs and some of northeast Asia's tallest mountains. The island is a compact showcase of natural attractions and cultural jewels, with unexpected marvels around every corner.

Taiwan's varied geography offers an amazing array of environments. In the mountains are crystal-clear lakes, hidden waterfalls and plenty of opportunities for hiking and camping. The rugged east coast, with its towering granite cliffs and windswept beaches, is a must-see for any visitor. A trip out to the tiny offshore island of Matsu in the Taiwan Strait is a trip back through history, with its preserved fishing villages and beautiful temples.

Taiwan's cities are colourful and lively – a vibrant kaleidoscope of tradition and modernity. Here travellers can experience some of the finest Chinese cuisine in the world, explore bustling night markets, attend a Taiwanese opera or relax in a traditional Chinese teahouse.

However, what's really special about Taiwan is the Taiwanese, who welcome visitors to their island with amazing warmth and hospitality. Travellers will find that the Taiwanese are some of the most generous people they've encountered, offering help and friendship without reservation. The Taiwanese make travelling in Taiwan a truly unique experience, one that will be remembered for years to come.

Laughing Buddha, Paochueh Temple (p202), Taichung

MARTIN MOOS

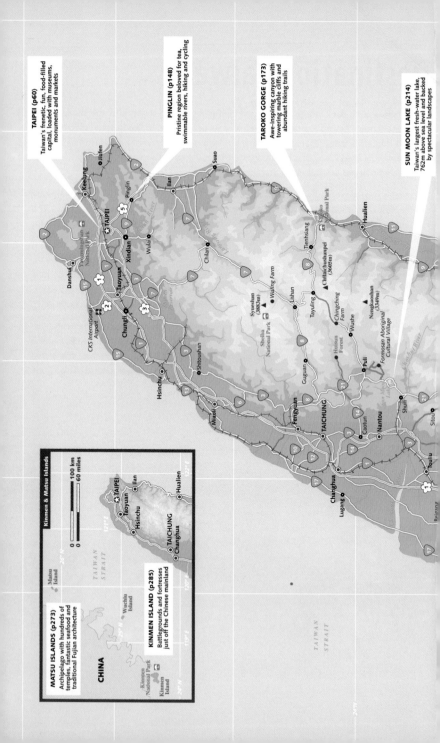

**TAIPEI (p60)**
Taiwan's frenetic, fun, food-filled capital, loaded with museums, monuments and markets

**PINGLIN (p148)**
Pristine region beloved for tea, swimmable rivers, hiking and cycling

**TAROKO GORGE (p173)**
Awe-inspiring canyon with towering marble cliffs and abundant hiking trails

**SUN MOON LAKE (p214)**
Taiwan's largest fresh-water lake, 762m above sea level and backed by spectacular landscapes

**MATSU ISLANDS (p273)**
Archipelago with hundreds of temples, fantastic seafood and traditional Fujian architecture

**KINMEN ISLAND (p285)**
Battlegrounds and fortresses just off the Chinese mainland

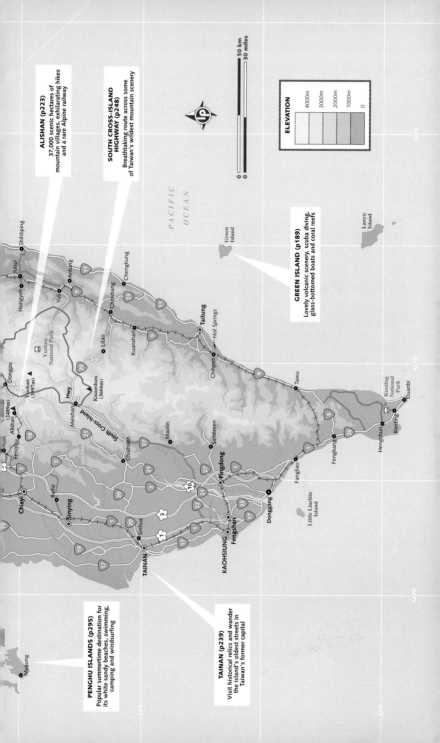

**ALISHAN (p223)**
37,000 scenic hectares of mountain villages, exhilarating hikes and a rare Alpine railway

**SOUTH CROSS-ISLAND HIGHWAY (p248)**
Breathtaking route across some of Taiwan's wildest mountain scenery

**GREEN ISLAND (p189)**
Lovely volcanic scenery, scuba diving, glass-bottomed boats and coral reefs

**PENGHU ISLANDS (p295)**
Popular summertime destination for its white sandy beaches, swimming, camping and windsurfing

**TAINAN (p239)**
Visit historical relics and wander the island's oldest streets in Taiwan's former capital

ELEVATION

4000m
3000m
2000m
1000m
0

50 km
30 miles

PACIFIC OCEAN

Shihtiping
Juisui
Hungyeh
Dongpu
Antung
Chengkung
Yuli
Litao
Yushan National Park
Chishang
Kuanshan
Taitung
Hot Springs
Chihpen
Green Island
Lanyu Island
Tawu
Yushan (3997m)
Alishan (2489m)
Kuli
Fenghu
Meishan
Kuanshan (3666m)
South Cross-Island Hwy
Chiahsien
Maolin
Sandimen
Pingdong
Hengchun
Kenting National Park
Kenting
Eluanbi
Fengkang
Fangliao
Fangshan
Donggang
Little Liuchiu Island
Chiayi
Bahe
Sinying
Sinhua
Fengshan
KAOHSIUNG
TAINAN
Makung

Many first-time visitors are surprised at the breadth of experiences Taiwan offers. People find their fancy in the treasures of Taipei's museums, cycling in the countryside, exploring temples, diving near coral reefs, climbing the peaks or snacking in the streets, and Taroko Gorge is simply not to be missed.

Brave the hairpin bends of the Suao–Hualien Hwy (p165), and admire the stunning views

MARTIN MOOS

MARTIN MOOS

Explore the 'living museum' of Lugang (p207), with its traditional buildings and old streets

Marvel at spectacular Sun Moon Lake (p214), the largest body of fresh water in Taiwan

ERIC L W

ERIC L WHEATER

Get an insight into the life of Taiwan's one-time dictator at Chiang Kai-shek Memorial Hall (p69), Taipei

MARTIN MOOS

Take in the colour and activity at Longshan Temple (p69), Taipei

Snack at one of Taipei's night markets (p105)

JOHN BORTHWICK

MARTIN

Climb Yushan (p235), the highest mountain in northeast Asia

MARTIN MOOS

Discover temples and waterfalls amid the lush vegetation of Taroko Gorge (p173)

# Getting Started

Travel in Taiwan is hardly rough going. Taipei, while an undeniably big city, is relatively easy to navigate, and much of the island is served by public transport (although you will probably want to be self-propelled in more remote regions such as the east coast). Travel by train can be very reasonable; air transport is less so, yet fares are far from larcenous by world standards.

If you plan to take on some of the island's famous mountains, be prepared with proper equipment – you can buy it in Taiwan if you need to. One thing you won't lack for is shopping. Whether it's high-end fashions or toys from the night market, there's something for everybody.

## WHEN TO GO

Sitting as it does between the Pacific and the South China Sea, Taiwan is known for changeable weather. That said, as a rule you'll find the best weather in autumn. October and November tend to be mild and dry islandwide, and especially in the southwest, though you may catch some residual typhoons from summer. In winter monsoon winds can sweep across the island from Central Asia and cool the air by 10°C or more in a matter of hours. Visiting Taiwan in spring is a craps shoot; it can be clear and dry or wet and murky. Summer is typhoon season, consistently hot and sticky, though late-afternoon showers tend to cool things down.

See Climate Charts (p312) for more information.

Maximum temperatures in the cities range from about 12°C in winter to 35°C in summer. Air conditioning is the rule in hotels and public buildings.

---

### DON'T LEAVE HOME WITHOUT...

- Tissues – many public toilets don't have paper towels or hand driers. Some visitors prefer antiseptic towels like baby wipes.
- Business cards – if you plan to do business, that is.
- Conservative business attire – ditto.
- At least one nice outfit, even if you are here to teach English to kids.
- Photocopies of diplomas, certificates, letters of reference etc if you plan on seeking employment.
- Neat socks – you'll be taking your shoes off and on as you enter homes and some teahouses, hot springs and public buildings. Unless you don't mind holey feet, invest in new socks.
- Umbrella and rain gear – weather can change very frequently!
- Tampons – if you're travelling outside Taipei.
- Shoes – if you have big feet, especially for women.
- A towel – if you are staying in cheaper hotels and wish to dry more than your hair.
- Sunscreen – expensive in Taiwan.
- Vitamins – ditto.
- Honing your chopstick skills.
- A smile. Showing anger in public will do you more harm than good.

If you're heading to the south of the island, December and January are an exceptionally good time to travel. You can still swim, bike, hike and it's hot enough – 20° to 29°C – to tan. The best thing, though, is that tourists are few, even in popular resort areas, as they are all waiting for Chinese New Year to take time off work.

Otherwise, it's best to avoid the Chinese New Year holiday – pretty much the entire country shuts down. Times *to* go are colourful festivals such as the Lantern Festival, the birth of the goddess Matsu, Dragon Boat Festival and Teachers' Day. See p316 for more details.

## COSTS & MONEY

Taiwan is a destination for all budgets.

Prices for lodging range from about NT250 for a bare-bones dorm bed in a youth hostel to NT8000 for a standard room in a luxury hotel with services such as gyms and business centres. Eating out can cost from NT25 for noodles or dumplings in a food stand, or neighbourhood or student restaurant, to NT1200 or more for something more upmarket. The typical cost for restaurant meals is NT100 to NT250.

This means that backpackers staying in hostels and eating meals at student-type restaurants or night markets can get by for under NT400 per day. For the mid-range traveller, figure on around NT2000 per person per day, assuming double occupancy. Even if you've got money to burn, you won't burn it as fast as in, say, Japan, the USA or Western

**HOW MUCH?**

Basic fare on Taipei's MRT (underground railway): NT20

Taxi ride: NT70 for the first 1.5km

Adult admission to National Palace Museum: NT100

Train fare, Taipei to Hualien (for Taroko Gorge): NT343

Motor scooter rental: NT400 per day

## TOP FIVES

### TOP HOT SPRINGS RESORTS

If you're a hot spring fan, and we hope you are, you'll find plenty of opportunities throughout Taiwan. Here are some of our favourites, but there are many more to explore.

- **Beitou** and **Yangmingshan, Taipei** (p107) So many to choose from, so close to the big city.
- **Taian Hot Springs** (p142) The Japanese chose this place 90 years ago to build a hot spring officers' club. Today it has some of the best facilities on the island and a half-dozen good hikes.
- **Wulai, Taipei County** (p150) Rough it in makeshift pools by the river or pamper yourself in resorts. Ride a gondola up past a waterfall and enjoy aboriginal cuisine and culture.
- **Chihpen Hot Springs, Taitung County** (p187) Taiwan's premier hot springs resort.
- **Chaojih Hot Springs, Green Island** (p190) Taiwan's only saltwater hot springs.

### TOP TEMPLES

Taiwan's temples exude a charm all their own, from beauty to otherworldliness.

- **Longshan Temple, Lugang** (p209) The best-preserved Qing dynasty temple in Taiwan, filled with many high-quality carvings and paintings.
- **Longshan Temple, Taipei** (p68) An important place of worship for Taipei citizens and a good spot for photographers looking for that quintessential temple atmosphere.
- **Matsu Temple, Nankan Township, Matsu Island** (p276) One of the most sacred temples in Taiwan, once thought to hold the bones of Matsu, Goddess of the Sea.
- **Tzu Hui Tang, Hualien** (p169) This elaborate temple on the outskirts of Hualien is a popular pilgrimage spot for Taoist devotees during the Lunar New Year.
- **Tzushr Temple, Sansia** (p153) A masterpiece. Restoration on this temple has been progressing steadily for over 50 years.

European capitals. Of course, this is before transport, admissions and incidentals (see 'How Much?', opposite).

In hotels it never hurts to request a discount. Either rooms can be discounted automatically, or you may have to ask for it. If you're travelling with a friend, there's often not much difference between prices for singles and twins.

While there are rarely discounts such as free museum days or discount cards typical elsewhere, admission prices are generally reasonable and sights and activities often provide discounts for seniors and students. Children's admission prices are usually based on height (eg up to 110cm). Many Chinese restaurant meals (including Taiwan's famous hotpots) are served family style and can be a great bargain when calculated per person.

**LONELY PLANET INDEX**

Litre of petrol: NT22

Can of Taiwan beer: NT30

Litre of bottled water: NT35

Skewer of fermented tofu: NT20

Chinese-style coat: NT800 and up

## TRAVEL LITERATURE

**Chiang Kai-Shek: China's Generalissimo and the Nation He Lost** by Jonathan Fenby (2003) offers insights into Taiwan's explosive and ambitious dictator. Fenby is a former editor of the *Observer* and the *South China Morning Post*.

**Formosan Odyssey** by John Ross (2002) is a personal account of one writer's journey across Taiwan just after the 21 September 1999 (921) earthquake, with dead-on descriptions of small-town life in Taiwan and excellent chapters on Taiwan's rugged history.

**Private Prayers and Public Parades** by Mark Carltonhill (2003) is written by an employee of the government information office (which also published the book). The book summarises in a lively way the many different traditions that create Taiwan's modern religious scene and explains a lot of the gods you'll find in temples.

**Taiwan: A Political History** by Denny Roy (2003) is a very readable and balanced account of Taiwan's progress towards democracy. Roy is a senior research fellow at the Asia-Pacific Center for Security Studies in Honolulu, Hawaii.

**Wild Kids** by Zhang Dachun, aka Chang Ta-Chun (English translation 2000), is an insightful story by one of Taiwan's most popular authors and centres around a Taipei teenager who gets caught up in the city's underground crime world.

**Wintry Night** by Li Qiao, aka Chiao Li (English translation 2001), is a compelling epic about the life of a Hakka family which settle in Taiwan in the 1890s.

## INTERNET RESOURCES

**Lonely Planet** (www.lonelyplanet.com) Don't forget to visit the Thorn Tree for updates from fellow Lonely Planet readers and fans.

**New Taiwan, Ilha Formosa** (www.taiwandc.org/history.htm) History from the Taiwanese perspective. This site has lots of interesting photos and a recommended reading list.

**Taiwan Cuisine** (www.sinica.edu.tw/tit/dining/0695_TaiwaneseCuisine.html) A good general overview, with pictures and restaurant suggestions.

**Taiwan E-Government** (www.gov.tw) One-stop surfing for everything from visa requirements to Taiwanese history, business, economy and the latest news.

**Tealit** (www.tealit.com) Listings for sale of goods.

**Welcome to Taiwan** (www.tbroc.gov.tw) Official website of the Tourism Board of the Republic of China.

In addition, the following websites are extremely useful for anyone looking to live or work in Taiwan and they also provide good general information.

**Forumosa** (www.forumosa.com) Online community for those with an interest in the island and its life, from visa and citizenship issues to the arts, culture and international politics.

**Zhongwen.com** (www.zhongwen.com) A nifty intro to the Chinese language.

Please refer to regional chapters for websites of local interest.

# Itineraries

## CLASSIC ROUTES

### DOWN THE EAST COAST                    Two Weeks / Taipei to Chihpen

Drive along the highway from Suao to Chihpen and you'll pass towering seaside cliffs, sand beaches, mountain hideaways and hot springs.

From Taipei head southeast to **Suao** (p162) and take a plunge into Taiwan's only cold springs. Next, it's a rollercoaster ride down the **Suao–Hualien Hwy** (p165), chiselled into cliffs that rise 450m above the crashing surf.

Turn west at Hsincheng and you'll enter **Taroko National Park** (p173). Spend two days hiking along the gorge's pristine trails before returning to the coastal highway and heading south to **Hualien** (p165). Explore this friendly city before continuing south, stopping to enjoy the stunning ocean vistas.

Next visit the Ami town of Takangkou, with a quick side trip to **Juisui** (p179). Continue south, past some unusual coastal scenery, to **Taitung** (p181), a relaxed city on the seaside. Taitung is a good jumping-off point for trips to Green and Lanyu Islands, home of the Yami aboriginal tribe. About 15km southwest of Taitung is **Chihpen** (p187), a first-class hot-spring resort where you can enjoy a soak in an outdoor pool surrounded by lush tropical scenery.

**Take two weeks and experience the indigenous culture, stunning scenery and outdoor activities described in our Down the East Coast tour.**

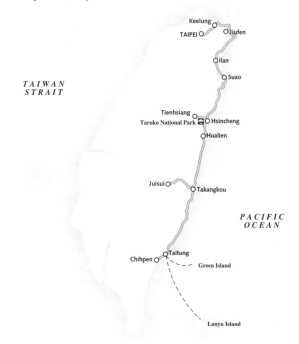

## BEEN HERE? DONE THIS?
One Month / Taipei to Green Island

No trip to Taiwan can be complete without a visit to its busy capital, Taipei. Must sees in Taipei include the **National Palace Museum** (p79), the world's foremost collection of Chinese art. Delve into Taipei's history at **Longshan Temple** (p69) and catch a performance of **Chinese opera** (p100).

You don't need to leave Taipei to explore mountains: **Yangmingshan National Park** (p110) is within the city limits and **Beitou** (p107) is a long-established hot-spring resort.

The MRT will take you as far as riverside **Danshui** (p115), from where you can head to **Bali** (p124) in the foothills of majestic Guanyinshan. Culture vultures shouldn't miss **Yingge** (p152) for ceramics, **Sanyi** (p146) for master woodcarvers or the **Juming Museum** (p124), a lovely sculpture garden. Some of these can be done as day trips from Taipei.

Down the east coast from the fishing port of **Keelung** (p125), **Taroko Gorge** (p173) is Taiwan's top destination; bike, hike or drive among sheer cliffs above roaring waters. Heading west on mountain roads via **Puli** (p220), don't miss **Sun Moon Lake** (p214), the island's largest freshwater lake and a place of startling beauty.

To the south, **Alishan National Scenic Area** (p223) is famous for a dawn trek up Chushan; and, to its east, **Yushan National Park** (p235) features northeast Asia's tallest peak and some fantastic hiking.

Finally, islands such as **Green Island** (p189) are popular for snorkelling and diving.

**From bustling Taipei to the coral reefs of Green Island and from the cliffs of Taroko Gorge to the forests around Sun Moon Lake: take one month and discover the variety on offer in Taiwan.**

# ROADS LESS TRAVELLED

## ISLAND HOPPING                              Two Weeks / Penghu to Kinmen

Head off to the remote, windswept islands of the Taiwan Strait and discover a part of Taiwan you didn't know existed.

Take a plane from Tainan to Kinmen, 280km from the coast of Taiwan. Stay in **Kincheng** (p287) and spend a day on foot exploring some of the town's historical sights and market areas. The next day, make sure to visit the **August 23rd Artillery War Museum** (p293), the battleground of the 1958 artillery war between China and Kinmen. Another worthy site is the **Mashan Observatory** (p294), Kinmen's closest point to mainland China. If the military sites are too unsettling, head to the **Shuangli Wetlands Area Centre** (p292), an excellent wetlands research area and a fine place for bird-watching.

Next, take a flight back to Tainan and get on another flight to Penghu, an archipelago of 64 islands. Sand and surf are the biggest attractions here, and during summer the place is crowded with beach enthusiasts. The city of **Makung** (p296), on the main island of Penghu, is where the hotels are, so make it your base and take a day to look around this interesting city.

For beach fun get on a ferry to **Chipei Island** (p303) north of Penghu and stay in a bungalow on the beautiful coral beach. You'll find plenty to do here – parasailing, diving and swimming are popular activities during summer.

**Our Island Hopping itinerary will introduce you to Taiwan's white-sand beaches and give you the opportunity to learn about some of the country's recent military history.**

CHINA

Kinmen Island

*TAIWAN STRAIT*

Penghu Islands

TAIWAN

Tainan

# WESTERN TAIWAN
### Two to Three Weeks / Taichung to Kenting

After some good food and nightlife in **Taichung** (p198), head to **Lugang** (p207), a sanctuary for old temples, traditional crafts and local snack food. A little south, at Ershui, catch the **Jiji Small Rail Line** (p211) and ride from the grain belt into the foothills of the Central Mountain Range. A few days cycling and hiking at the various stops along this line should leave you suitably impressed with the beauty of rural Taiwan.

For a complete change of pace head up to **Puli** (p220) for an introduction (in English) to Buddhism. Then retrace your steps back on the Jiji Line and continue south to **Chiayi** (p223). From here, you could take the small alpine train up to the mountain resort of **Alishan** (p231), or be more adventurous and rent a scooter and explore **Fenqihu** (p227), **Ruili** (p229) and other remote mountain communities in the **Alishan National Scenic Area** (p223).

After returning to Chiayi, continue south to the old capital of **Tainan** (p239) for a few days of temple- and relic-hopping. Then rent a scooter again and drive to rural **Meinong** (p257), a stronghold of Hakka culture. From there, follow the scenic highways to **Maolin** (p258), a park run by the Rukai aboriginals.

From Maolin, return to Tainan and then head south to tropical Pingdong County. Spend a day exploring the fascinating coral formations at **Little Liuchiu Island** (p262), and another day swimming or windsurfing at **Dapeng Bay** (p262). If you're tired of beaches by the time you get to **Kenting** (p264), there are museums, hikes and opportunities for nature study in protected ecological zones.

**Western Taiwan: move from the alpine to the tropical and from the old to the new with visits to soaring peaks, coral reefs, modern cities and Tainan, the old capital of Taiwan.**

# TAILORED TRIPS

## OLD TAIWAN
**Two Weeks**

Your round-the-island search for traditional Taiwan begins in **Yingge** (p152), where ceramics making has a 200-year history. At nearby **Sansia** (p153) more than 100 Qing- and Japanese-era buildings crowd together on one street. Just south in **Hsinchu** (p138), you'll find traditional glasswork, Qing-dynasty arches, houses and one perfect city gate.

Continuing south, you'll reach the woodcarving town of **Sanyi** (p146), where master craftsmen carry on a century of carving traditions. In **Lugang** (p207), time stood still for most of the 20th century, and today it is one of the best spots in Taiwan to view old streets and buildings.

In the south, don't miss **Tainan** (p239), the old capital of Taiwan. Here are Dutch-built forts and towers, and excellent traditional foods. **Meinong** (p257), to the east, preserves Hakka culture, including three-sided houses and the craft of making paper umbrellas.

Next, cross to the east coast and head north to the quaint Japanese gold mining towns of **Jiufen** (p127) and **Jinguashi** (p129). At Keelung catch a ferry to **Matsu** (p273), settled in the 1400s. In addition to traditional houses (and alcohol), you can view evidence of Taiwan's recent military history against mainland China.

## ILHA FORMOSA (A NATURE LOVER'S JOURNEY)
**One Month**

Our nature lover's journey begins in unspoiled **Taipingshan** (p134) and **Wuling Farm** (p156), home of the rare Formosan landlocked salmon. For pure scenic eye-candy head east to magnificent **Taroko Gorge** (p173).

From Taroko there's dramatic coastal scenery all the way to **Taitung** (p181). Next, head across the South Cross-Island Hwy to **Laonong** (p258). Then go south to aboriginal-run **Maolin Recreation Area** (p258). Head west through **Liugui** (p258) and stop in rural **Meinong** (p257) for a bike ride.

Go to Guanziling for the bizarre **Water Fire Cave** (p237). From **Chiayi** (p223)

visit **Alishan National Scenic Area** (p223), which has subtropical, temperate and alpine environments. Nearby **Yushan National Park** (p235) features the highest mountain in northeast Asia.

Heading north, stop in **Taian** (p142) for hiking and a hot soak. In nearby **Sheiba National Park** (p145) there are 50 peaks over 3000m to admire.

Next, head east to **Wulai** (p150) and then **Pinglin** (p148) for emerald tea fields. At the coast take the **Pingxi Branch Rail Line** (p130) to **Shifen Waterfall** (p131). Lastly, stop to view the bizarre rock formations at **Yeliu** (p121) and the sunset from **Guanyinshan** (p125).

# The Authors

### ANDREW BENDER
**Coordinating Author & Taipei**

France was closed, so after college Andy spent three years in Asia, and he's been going back and forth ever since. Yet another LP author with an MBA, this New England native eventually left the business world to do what every MBA secretly dreams of: travelling and writing about it. His work has since appeared in *Travel + Leisure*, the *Los Angeles Times*, *Men's Journal*, *Fortune* and LP titles in Europe and Asia. At home in Los Angeles he bikes at the beach, consults on cross-cultural issues in the workplace, obsesses over Chinese, Japanese and Korean food, and schemes over spoiling his nieces and nephews; he dedicates this book to Rebecca Sophia, born while he was writing it.

### Andrew & Robert's Favourite Trip

Although there's plenty to keep us happy in Taipei, we like getting out of town to explore the island's history. Fortunately Taipei's MRT allows for an easy escape to Beitou (p107), with its old-style (and modern!) hot springs, and also Danshui, home of the San Domingo (p117) and Huwei forts (p117).

Heading west from Danshui, a short ferry ride takes us across the river to Bali (p124) to view the displays at the Shihsanhang Museum of Archaeology (p124). In the other direction, we bus it to Keelung to explore two more forts, Ershawan (p127) and Baimiwang (p127). Then it's off to the old Temple Street Night Market (p127) for some of the best seafood snacks in Taiwan before heading back to Taipei.

### JULIE GRUNDVIG
**The East Coast & Taiwan Strait Islands**

Julie has been living and travelling in northeast Asia for the past 13 years. Her first introduction to Chinese culture was a two-year journey through Taiwan and mainland China where she developed a strong interest in Chinese literature and art. Later came a master's degree in Asian studies and a PhD in Chinese classical literature at the University of British Columbia. Julie has worked as editor for the *BC Asian Review* and is currently associate editor for the international journal *Yishu: Journal of Contemporary Chinese Art*. Julie lives in Vancouver, British Columbia, Canada.

### ROBERT KELLY
**Northern Taiwan & Western Taiwan**

Robert Kelly first thought to travel to Taiwan in 1986, at the time when martial law had just been lifted. He didn't make it there, however, until 1996, by which time the first presidential elections were being held. The speed with which this traditional society remodels itself never stops fascinating him. Robert, a Canadian, is married to a Taiwanese woman and has lived with her and their two cats in Taipei for the past eight years. The pleasure in writing this book came not least from discovering so many new museums, beaches, hiking trails and good restaurants. Robert has no plans to leave Taiwan now that he's seen how much this country has to offer.

## CONTRIBUTING AUTHOR

**Dr Trish Batchelor** is a general practitioner and travel medicine specialist who works at the Ciwec Clinic in Kathmandu, Nepal. She is also a medical advisor to the Travel Doctor New Zealand clinics. Trish teaches travel medicine through the University of Otago and is interested in underwater and high-altitude medicine, and in the impact of tourism on host countries. She has travelled extensively through Southeast and east Asia and particularly loves high-altitude trekking in the Himalayas.

# Snapshot

Once a tiny backwater known mainly for its production of textiles and inexpensive commercial goods, the island of Taiwan has transformed itself into an economic powerhouse, becoming a leading exporter of computer technology and an international player on the world financial market. At the crossroads of change, Taiwan continues to redefine itself, despite the looming presence of mainland China, the island's mighty neighbour to the north.

Most Taiwanese feel a strong connection to China, realising that the majority of their cultural traditions have their source in its long history. At the same time, there is a growing desire among Taiwanese to create a new history, redefined by the tumultuous events of the past 100 years.

Taiwan's troubled relationship with China remains the single biggest problem of the island. While China continues to insist that Taiwan is a renegade province of the mainland, the majority of Taiwan's younger generation, who have grown up feeling more Taiwanese than Chinese, have little desire to unify with China, a place many feel is corrupt and where the living conditions are difficult. Those of the older generation, many born on the mainland or descendants of parents who came over with the KMT (Kuomintang, or Nationalist Party) after 1949, want to keep the status quo.

Taiwan's relationship with China has left many, including the Taiwanese themselves, confused about the ambiguous status of the small island. After the KMT fled to Taiwan in 1949, Taiwan took China's seat at the UN Security Council and was recognised by most Western countries as a legitimate government. This all changed in 1971, when Taiwan lost its seat in the UN and Beijing was formally recognised (see p24). One by one, Western countries changed their allegiance to Beijing, with Taiwan left out in the cold.

Taiwan and China have attempted to establish a dialogue, but to little avail. China's desire of 'one country, two systems', giving Taiwan autonomy if it will reunify, was discussed in the early 1990s but talks broke down when President Lee Teng-hui refused China's suggestions that Taiwan and China resume direct flights and open trade. President Lee upset China even further when he changed his position on One China and declared that Taiwan and China were actually two separate countries (see p24).

The fact that the USA, despite its official support of One China, is selling arms packages to Taiwan does not help the situation. The US has been Taiwan's best ally since WWII, providing the island with military and financial support during the Cold War. The relationship was sorely tested in 1979, when President Jimmy Carter announced the USA was ending political recognition of Taiwan in favour of Beijing. To compensate, the Taiwan Relations Act ensured Taiwan that the USA would continue to provide Taiwan with defensive weapons in case of mainland invasion.

The USA strives to maintain a balance in its dealings with China and Taiwan, though China's continual threats of military force are not taken lightly by the Taiwanese or USA governments. In 1996 China conducted missile tests close to Taiwan's coast in an effort to influence Taiwan's first open elections. President Bill Clinton responded by sending Taiwan the biggest supply of nuclear weapons Asia had seen since Vietnam. China backed down, though it warned Taiwan that war and invasion

## FAST FACTS

Population: 22.5 million

Women in the workforce: 3.85 million

Infant mortality rate: seven out of 1000 live births

Population 65 or older: 8.4%

Amount spent on defence in 2000: NT353.7 million

Number of turkeys: 229,000

were probable if the island continued to show movements towards independence. The Taiwanese people appear to have become accustomed to the threats of their angry neighbour. Life goes on and most Taiwanese carry on their daily lives without fear.

The election of proindependence Democratic Progressive Party president Chen Shuibian in 2000 was Beijing's worst nightmare. President Chen has openly declared his belief that Taiwan should exist as an independent country, but will not formally declare independence unless China attacks. Over the past several years, China has refused to deal with President Chen and talks on the political front have been stifled. Amazingly, despite the animosity, China and Taiwan have managed to open limited trade on the Strait Islands via the 'Three Small Links' (p288) and the Taiwanese have invested more than $US160 billion in the mainland.

President Chen was re-elected in March 2004 but it remains unknown what the future holds for Taiwan. Undoubtedly, the people of Taiwan will move forward with the same resilience and vitality that have carried them through some of the most tremendous events in the island's history. Taiwan is a complex, rapidly changing society and shows no intention of slowing down.

# History

## EARLY HISTORY

The earliest people on Taiwan are thought to have inhabited the island around 10,000 BC, coming from southern China and Austronesia, settling in the lowlands of Taiwan's western plains and along the east coast.

Early Chinese texts contain references to Taiwan, calling the island 'Land of Yang Chou', as far back as 206 BC. Contact between China and Taiwan was erratic until the early 1400s, when boatloads of immigrants from China's Fujian province began arriving on Taiwan's shores. Disillusioned with the political instability in their homeland, they hoped to make a new start on Taiwan.

When the new immigrants arrived, they encountered two groups of aboriginals. One group made their homes on the fertile plains of central and southwestern Taiwan and the other, seminomadic, lived along the Central Mountain Range. Despite having similar ancestry, these aborigines were diverse in their languages and customs. Nowadays, these tribes are identified as the Atayal, Saisiyat, Tsou, Bunun, Rukai, Paiwan, Ami, Puyuma and Yami.

Over the next 100 years, the Fujian immigrants increased in numbers and were joined by the Hakka, another ethnic group leaving the mainland in great numbers. The Hakka, meaning 'guest', had endured persecution in China for centuries. Their ancestors had originally come from northern Hunan province and later fled south to Guangdong and Fujian provinces, where they made their living through farming and fishing.

By the early 1500s there were three categories of people on the island: Hakka, Fujianese and the aboriginal tribes, considered the first 'true' inhabitants of the island. Today Taiwan's population is mainly descended from these early Chinese immigrants, with only 2% being aboriginal.

## EUROPEAN COLONISATION

In 1544 a Portuguese fleet discovered the island and called it Ilha Formosa, meaning 'beautiful island'. The Dutch, who had established the Dutch East India Company in 1602, were anxious to trade with China and Japan and in 1603 arrived in the Penghu Islands (p295) in the Taiwan Strait.

China's Ming government was angry that the Dutch were in Penghu and immediately sent troops to throw the Dutch off the island. Indignant, the Dutch sailed to Macao, with the intent of overthrowing the Portuguese. When that failed, they returned to Penghu and in 1622 finally succeeded in establishing a colony in Makung. The remains of their presence can still be seen in the Dutch Fort ruins (p302), a few kilometres out of present-day Makung City.

The first thing the Dutch did was establish a trading route between Batavia (now Jakarta), Makung, China and Japan. For a short period of time, Dutch trade dominated the Taiwan Strait, much to the chagrin of

www.taiwandc.org /history.htm Information about Taiwanese history (from the point of view of the Taiwanese). The site has a lot of interesting photographs and an excellent recommended reading list.

| c 10,000 BC | AD 1544 |
| --- | --- |
| First human presence on Taiwan | Portuguese explorers discover Taiwan and call it Ilha Formosa |

the Ming court, who issued a decree in 1623 banning all entry of ships into the Taiwan Strait from Southeast Asia. Realising the ineffectiveness of the decree, Ming troops were sent to attack the Dutch, who gave in and agreed to remove themselves from Penghu. Oddly, the Ming allowed the Dutch to establish trading ports on mainland Taiwan instead. Understandably happy at this arrangement, the Dutch packed up and moved to Taiwan proper, where they built forts and started a prosperous trading business.

The Spanish were envious of the Dutch hold on Taiwan and the growing wealth of the Dutch East India Company. In 1626 the Spanish invaded what is now Keelung and established their territory all the way down the west coast to Danshui and eventually all over northern Taiwan. Unfortunately, Taiwan's climate took revenge and a series of catastrophes took its toll on the Spanish traders. Typhoons and malaria devastated the Spanish and attacks by local aboriginals caused them to relinquish their territory. In 1638 the Spanish withdrew from Danshui and the Dutch moved in to snatch up the remains, taking control of Keelung in 1642.

**DID YOU KNOW?**

Taiwan was once a haven for pirates, in the 15th and 16th centuries.

## UNDER THE QING DYNASTY

At the same time the Dutch were in Taiwan, China's Ming government was facing an eventual overthrow by Manchu (Qing) armies. Supporters of the Ming were forced to flee China for their lives. One staunch supporter, Cheng Cheng-kung, also known as Koxinga, had a decisive impact on Taiwanese history. As the Ming dynasty crumbled, Cheng took refuge on the small island of Kinmen (Quemoy) off China's Fujian province, vowing to eventually overthrow the Manchu and restore the Ming dynasty. In Kinmen, Cheng met a disgruntled former interpreter for the Dutch East India Company who convinced Cheng to invade Taiwan and overthrow the Dutch. Cheng agreed and somehow managed to amass an army on Kinmen, built a fleet of ships (chopping down all the island's trees in the process) and set sail for the Penghu Islands, his first stop on his way to Taiwan. Cheng and his army seized Penghu from the Dutch and moved on to Taiwan, where he was greeted by local supporters anxious to be free of Dutch rule. It didn't take long for the Dutch to realise their days in Taiwan were numbered and they soon left Taiwan.

With Cheng came 30,000 mainland Chinese, who established Taiwan island as their home. After the overthrow of the Dutch, immigration from southern China to Taiwan continued for the next 200 years. Taiwan's growing population during this time meant that the island developed rapidly, especially in the north and along the fertile plains of the west coast. To manage the fast-growing island, Cheng set up an efficient system of counties, some of which remain in use today. However, his dreams of overthrowing the Manchu remained unfulfilled; he died a year after landing on Taiwan. Many Taiwanese today regard Cheng as a hero for driving the Dutch out of Taiwan.

After Cheng's death, his son and grandson ruled the island but their ineptness caused widescale poverty and despair. In 1683, the Qing government overthrew Cheng's descendents and took over the island, placing it under the jurisdiction of Fujian province.

**1624–61**

Dutch occupation of Taiwan

**1683**

Qing forces capture Taiwan

The Qing attitude towards Taiwan was very lax, although they'd issued an imperial decree preventing passage from China to the island lest it became a safe harbour for political dissidents. This, however, did not stop the boatloads of Chinese immigrants who continued to wash up on Taiwan's shores.

Europeans continued to show an interest in Taiwan, realising its huge economic potential due to its advantageous position along the Taiwan Strait between Southeast Asia and Japan. Taiwan was also quite well known among traders, not just for its strategic location, but also as a dangerous place for shipwrecks. Traders repeatedly ran their ships into the island's unlit, rocky coastline and were tortured and beaten by the local aboriginal population. Complaints to the Qing court were futile as they dismissed the problem as inconsequential.

When the treaty for the second Opium War was signed in 1858, Taiwan was opened to trade with the West in Keelung and Suao. The southern ports of Kaohsiung and Tainan were also opened. Foreign trade increased rapidly, with Taiwan's main exports being camphor, rice, tea and opium.

## JAPANESE RULE (1894–1945)

Despite Taiwan's importance as a trading centre, the island was a wild and unruly place, with the Qing government doing little to control the frequent unrest between settlers, foreign sailors and the aboriginal population. In 1872 the crew of a shipwrecked Japanese junk was executed by an aboriginal tribe; enraged, the Japanese appealed to the Qing to inquire into the situation. Receiving only a standoffish reply, the foreign minister of Japan, Soyeshima Taneomi, was advised by the American military advisor Charles Le Gendre to attack Taiwan if the Qing did not take the situation seriously. Accompanied by Le Gendre, Soyeshima went to Beijing where he managed to obtain an audience with the emperor. The emperor admitted that the aboriginals and the constant fighting on the island were beyond his control.

Upon hearing this, Le Gendre told Japan to take the matter into its own hands; accordingly, in the spring of 1874, Japanese troops invaded Taiwan. The Qing government was shaken by Japan's aggressive tactics and promised to try to control the fighting in Taiwan and also offered to compensate the families of the dead crew members. Somewhat satisfied, the Japanese withdrew. It didn't take them long, however, to start considering the economic advantages of colonising Taiwan.

In 1894 war broke out between Japan and China over the Japanese invasion of Korea. Ships that China sent to aid Korea were sunk by the Japanese and the Chinese retaliated. China's poorly equipped navy couldn't stand up to Japan's, causing China to lose miserably in the war. Japan proposed the humiliating Treaty of Shimonoseki of 1895 that forced China to give up the Ryukyu Islands (Okinawa), Taiwan and the Penghu Archipelago.

Taiwan responded to the treaty with alarm and a group of intellectuals formed the Taiwan Democratic Republic, writing a Declaration of Independence and claiming the island as a sovereign nation. This did not deter the Japanese from their plans of turning the island into a Japanese

*Traders repeatedly ran their ships into the island's unlit, rocky coastline and were tortured and beaten by the local aboriginal population.*

| 1895 | 1945 |
|---|---|
| Treaty of Shimonoseki forces Qing to give up Taiwan to Japan | Japan is defeated in WWII and Taiwan reverts back to China's control under the leadership of Chiang Kai-shek's KMT party |

colony. After subduing the areas of Keelung and Danshui, the Japanese took over the ex-Qing governor's office in Taipei. Control over the rest of the island was not as easy as in the north and the Japanese met strong resistance as they moved further south. Employing over one-third of its army in Taiwan, the Japanese eventually overcame the Taiwanese who'd confronted the modern weapons of the invaders with bamboo spears and outdated weapons. The hopes of the Taiwan Democratic Republic were crushed, and Japan was to stay on the island for 50 years. It's believed that in the first several months after the Japanese arrived over 10,000 soldiers and civilians lost their lives.

Once the Japanese felt they had things under control they set out to modernise the island, building highways and railways to improve trade and open up formerly isolated parts, especially along the east coast, to development. They also constructed hospitals, schools and government buildings in an effort to improve the infrastructure of the island.

Despite these improvements, the Japanese rule on the island was harsh, with brutal crackdowns on political dissent. One of the main goals of the Japanese was to 'Japanicise' the island, requiring all citizens to learn Japanese and follow Japanese traditions. The Japanese rewarded obedience with financial incentives and punished the defiant.

> Mao Zedong's Communist Party was pitted against the Nationalist Party, or KMT, for control of the country.

## TAIWAN UNDER THE KMT

Taiwan remained under Japanese rule until the end of WWII. After Japan surrendered the island was restored to China on 25 October 1945, now known as Retrocession Day.

In China civil war was tearing the country apart. Mao Zedong's Communist Party was pitted against the Nationalist Party, or Kuomintang (KMT), for control of the country. Their struggle had been ongoing since the fall of the Qing, only temporarily suspended to unite against the Japanese invasion of China.

The leader of the KMT was Chiang Kai-shek, a fiery general who had participated in the overthrow of the Qing and supported the democratic vision of Dr Sun Yat-sen, who became the first president of the Republic of China (ROC) after the Qing fell. Chiang had led successful campaigns against the Japanese after the 1932 invasion of Manchuria and the 1937 invasion of Tianjin, Beijing, Shanghai and Nanjing. In 1943 Chiang Kai-shek had met American President Franklin D Roosevelt and British Prime Minister Winston Churchill in Cairo and it was decided that Manchuria and Taiwan would be returned to China after Japan's defeat.

After Japan's fall, the communists and KMT once again began to fight. Chiang Kai-shek was elected president of the Republic of China in 1948 and fought against the communists for four years, with the communists eventually establishing the People's Republic of China (PRC) in October 1949.

The Taiwanese were relieved to be rid of the Japanese but when Chiang Kai-shek, embroiled in civil war on the mainland, sent the inept general Chen Yi to be governor of Taiwan, it was a disaster. Chen Yi and his thugs plundered Taiwanese homes and shops, sending anything of value back to the mainland to help support the Nationalist fight against the communists. Riots against the KMT broke out, leading to the deaths of tens of thousands of civilians.

| 1947 | 1949 |
|---|---|
| 28 February uprising | KMT is defeated by Mao Zedong's Communist party; KMT leadership moves to Taiwan; the island is placed under martial law |

Defeated by the communists in 1949, Chiang Kai-shek fled to Taiwan that same year, followed by a steady stream of soldiers, monks, artists, peasants and intellectuals. Humiliated, Chiang vowed to recover China from communist control. One of the first things he did when he arrived in Taiwan was to send Chen Yi back to the mainland, where Chiang later had him executed for secret dealings with the communists. The KMT managed to retain the small islands of Matsu, Kinmen and Wuchiu, which to this day remain under Taiwanese control. Fearing a Chinese invasion, Chiang set Matsu and Kinmen up as military zones to rebuff any mainland attack. Scores of young Taiwanese men were sent to the islands to anticipate a mainland invasion.

**DID YOU KNOW?**

Over 80,000 Taiwanese served in the Japanese military during WWII.

On Taiwan Chiang instituted a series of land reform policies that successfully laid the foundation for Taiwan's future economic success. He also modernised the educational system and developed democratic institutions, following in the pattern of Sun Yat-sen.

Chiang initially believed that Taiwan would be a temporary base while he amassed his soldiers on the island and prepared to invade China. However, China's involvement in the Korean War delayed any such invasion and the KMT bided their time. They had plenty on their hands and under the supervision of the KMT, the island developed economically, though rule was harsh and any political dissent was quickly crushed. The 'White Terror' (p188) era of the 1950s was a frightening time in Taiwanese history, when people literally disappeared if they spoke against the government. Political dissidents were either executed or shipped to Green Island off Taiwan's east coast to serve long prison terms.

During the Korean War, the Americans were protective of Taiwan, assuring the Taiwanese that they would repel any communist attacks.

## 2-28 INCIDENT

On 27 February 1947 a trivial incident led to tragedy and became an important event in Taiwan's history. Because the government had made the sale of all tobacco a government monopoly, anyone caught selling cigarettes on the black market was punished severely. Police from the Alcohol and Tobacco Bureau seized cigarettes and money from a middle-aged widow and pistol-whipped her until she fell to the ground bleeding and unconscious. Angry crowds formed and attacked the officers, who responded by shooting into the crowd, killing an innocent bystander.

The next morning, crowds protested outside the Taipei branch of the Monopoly Bureau, attacking employees and setting the offices on fire. Later that day, crowds gathered at the governor's office demanding justice and political reforms. Military police fired on the crowds, killing dozens of protestors. In a state of emergency, all public buildings were shut down as civilians angrily took to the streets. Soon, news of the event spread throughout the entire island and riots erupted island wide. Government offices and police stations were attacked and mainland immigrants were targeted for beatings.

The KMT cracked down hard on the protestors, with executions of instigators and intellectuals who criticised the government. It's estimated that up to 30,000 Taiwanese were murdered in the weeks following the incident.

The 28 February incident evokes powerful memories even today for those who lived through the event. To commemorate those who died during the tragedy, 28 February was declared a national holiday 50 years later and Taipei New Park was renamed the 2-28 Peace Park (p68).

| 1958 | 1975 |
|------|------|
| China bombs Kinmen Island, beginning the August 23rd Artillery War; US intervention halts the shelling | Death of Chiang Kai-shek; Chiang Ching-kuo becomes chairman of KMT Central Committee |

Military outbreaks between China and Taiwan were common in the 1950s and 1960s, with Kinmen Island being subjected to regular shelling. Tragedies such as the August 23rd Artillery War (p294) and the Kuningtou War (p292) brought American military support to Taiwan.

Denny Roy's *Taiwan: A Political History* is a very readable and balanced account of Taiwan's progress towards democracy.

Despite the constant upheaval, the island prospered during the 1950s and 1960s, turning Taiwan's war-torn economy into one of the richest in Asia. At the same time, the population grew to a whopping 16 million.

In 1965 the US withdrew its financial aid and Taiwan was forced to survive financially on its own. Luckily, because of smart economic policies, Taiwan's economic progress continued, with few troubles. In 1971 Taiwan lost its seat on the UN Security Council, a precursor to the 1979 withdrawal of US recognition of Taiwan in support of the People's Republic of China. At the same time, however, the US and Taiwan signed the Taiwan's Relations Act, which promised Taiwan full military support in case of mainland attack. In 1980 Taiwan was expelled from both the International Monetary Fund and the World Bank.

Chiang Kai-shek died on 5 April 1975 at the age of 87. His son, Chiang Ching-kuo, was elected president in 1978, re-elected in 1984 and remained president until his death in 1988.

During the 1970s and 1980s, Taiwan was developing into one of the strongest economies in Asia and was a leading exporter of textiles and inexpensive commercial goods. Despite its economic success, however, the KMT kept the Taiwanese under tight control, largely because of the insecurity of the KMT mainlanders who felt like outsiders in their 'new' home.

At the time of the KMT arrival, the Taiwanese had been heavily indoctrinated by the Japanese and spoke little Mandarin. They were also accustomed to a higher standard of living than the mainland Chinese and felt an ingrained superiority towards the poorer and less well-educated immigrants, especially soldiers who often came from humble backgrounds. The KMT issued laws requiring all Taiwanese to speak Mandarin, in an attempt to 're-sinicise' the population. Of course, the Taiwanese resented the heavy-handedness of the KMT, and there were various outbreaks of rebellion and clashes with military police, the most serious being the Kaohsiung Incident in 1979.

Chiang Ching-kuo's rule over Taiwan was softer than the rule of his father. In an effort to improve relations with the Taiwanese, Chiang allowed more Taiwanese to take up political positions. Chiang was reappointed president in 1984, with Lee Teng-hui as his vice-president. Lee was the first Taiwan-born politician to hold such a high office.

One of the most important events in the 1980s occurred in 1986 with the formation of the Democratic Progressive Party (DPP). Chiang Ching-kuo, surprisingly, did not shut the party down, resulting in a large number of DPP candidates being elected to office, and culminating in the official formation of Taiwan's first opposition party. The year 1987 was another turning point for the Taiwanese when Chiang Ching-kuo announced the end of martial law, much to the joy of the Taiwanese.

In 1988, Chiang Ching-kuo passed away and Lee Teng-hui became president of Taiwan. A major dilemma he faced was what to do with mainland China, which was still continuing the same rhetoric of 40 years before, threatening the island with a military takeover. Many Taiwanese,

| 1979 | 1986–87 |
| --- | --- |
| US switches formal recognition to China; Kaohsiung Incident | Democratic Progressive Party is established as Taiwan's first opposition party; martial law is lifted |

on the other hand, had lost the fervour of the 1950s and 1960s and merely wanted to move on with their lives.

Early in his presidency, Lee Teng-hui agreed to a One China policy but later developed a proindependence stance that angered the mainland. In 1995 Lee Teng-hui visited the US in an attempt to garner US sympathy for Taiwanese independence. A year later, before Taiwan's first presidential election, China launched a series of missiles only 25km away from the Taiwanese coast. This didn't deter the Taiwanese from voting for Lee Teng-hui the following year, when he became Taiwan's first elected president.

The Chinese made very clear their stance on countries that recognised Taiwan as a sovereign nation. After Lee Teng-hui's visit to the US, China even threatened to send a nuclear missile to Los Angeles if the US kept up its communication with Taiwan.

In 1998 China softened its approach to Taiwan, offering to lift the ban on shipping and direct flights, which Lee rebuffed. He incensed the Chinese even further when he declared openly in 1999 that he believed China and Taiwan to be two separate countries.

In 2000 China once again began the aggressive military posturing as Taiwan's presidential elections loomed on the horizon. Lee Teng-hui had

### THE KAOHSIUNG INCIDENT

The Kaohsiung Incident in December 1979 was a turning point in Taiwan's progress towards becoming a democratic nation. Inspired by then US President Jimmy Carter's emphasis on human rights, many in Taiwan felt that it was time for their government to quit placing economic development over freedom. The editors of *Meilidao* (Beautiful Magazine), a liberal publication that was often critical of the government, decided to organise a rally to celebrate International Human Rights Day. The day before the rally, two organisers were arrested and beaten by police when they were caught handing out promotional flyers.

On the day of the rally, riot police blocked off the park where the rally had been planned and crowds in the tens of thousands were forced into the streets. Scuffles broke out between police and protestors and the situation turned violent, changing from a peaceful event into a full-scale riot. Eight of the organisers were arrested, including Taiwan's current vice-president Annette Lu, and sent to jail. Among the lawyers who represented the organisers was future Taiwan president Chen Shuibian. The defence lost and the organisers were sentenced to long prison terms, ranging from 12 years to life. The government shut down *Meilidao* and several other magazines, claiming they were threats to public order.

The censorship of newspapers and magazines continued throughout the 1980s, with the KMT taking a hard line against journalists who dared publish anything critical of the leadership. It wasn't until 1988 that censorship laws were overhauled, allowing for much greater freedom in the press.

The Kaohsiung Incident has had a lasting effect on the people of Taiwan. In the days following the event, the majority of the Taiwanese sympathised with the organisers of the rally and the brutal actions of the government were seen with horror. The violence brought increasing support for democratic reforms. In the years following, politicians who had been jailed for their participation in the event won political offices, often running on platforms that promised greater freedom and political openness than their predecessors. The KMT was eventually forced to make political concessions, such as lifting martial law and allowing the creation of new political parties. These actions, along with many others, have influenced the evolution of modern-day Taiwan.

| 1988 | 1996 |
|---|---|
| Chiang Ching-kuo dies; Vice-President Lee Teng-hui becomes president | Taiwan holds first full democratic elections; Lee Teng-hui is elected president |

scared off some voters with his direct stance on Taiwan and China existing as two separate countries, and DPP candidate Chen Shuibian won the
election. China was infuriated but it was a huge turning point for Taiwan
as 54 years of KMT rule finally drew to an end.

Chen's election was a disaster for the Chinese government, who were
fearful of the DPP's proindependence stance and its effects on cross-Strait
relations. Chen's challenge was to manage Taiwan's stormy relationship
with the PRC and forestall inevitable military pressure from Beijing. To
do so, Chen avoided a blatant proindependence stance and even declared
in his May 2000 inauguration speech that if China refrained from using
force against Taiwan, the DPP would not declare independence.

China was not won over by Chen's reconciliatory approach and demanded a commitment to the One China principle. Without a commitment, China insisted that it would not negotiate with Taiwan. Chen,
pledging allegiance to the DPP, could not support the One China policy
outright. As a result, cross-Strait relations made little headway the first
year of Chen's presidency. The only glimmer of improvement was the
opening of trade between China and Taiwan's offshore islands. This
'Three Small Links' policy (see p288) was officially implemented in January 2001 to much fanfare.

Despite these advances, tension between China and Taiwan remained
strained and many feel that since 2001 the DPP has done little to help
the situation. The US, under the administration of President George W
Bush, has pledged to defend Taiwan at any cost, thus fuelling even greater
resentment from China.

Chen's re-election in March 2004, preceded by a controversial assassina-
tion attempt and accusations of vote tampering, has many Taiwanese feeling that cross-Strait relations will be further strained if the island remains
under DPP control for another four-year term. As Taiwan continues on the
road to democratisation, it remains to be seen what lies ahead.

**DID YOU KNOW?**

In 2001 US President
George Bush gave Taipei
an army sales package
worth US$6 billion.

| 2000 | 2004 |
| --- | --- |
| DPP candidate Chen Shuibian elected; 54 years of KMT rule ended | President Chen Shuibian re-elected |

# The Culture

## THE NATIONAL PSYCHE

The Taiwanese have often been characterised as some of the friendliest people in northeast Asia and most travellers find this to be true. Visitors to the island will be amazed at the great lengths the Taiwanese go to make them feel comfortable. The Taiwanese pride themselves on being *hǎokè*, or 'good hosts', and will go out of their way to help foreigners feel at ease. This may be the total stranger on the bus inviting you home for dinner or the off-duty police officer who offers to take you sightseeing and then treats you to lunch afterwards. This may seem a bit off-putting to some, who aren't accustomed to such overtures, but really it's just Taiwanese friendliness and best accepted with a smile. The foundation of Chinese society is harmony and getting along with others for the sake of society as a whole is very important in a culture that has experienced such a huge amount of upheaval through the course of its history.

The concept of 'face' in Taiwan is highly regarded and can be a scary idea to those afraid of committing major social gaffes in front of their Taiwanese friends. In reality, the idea of face is very simple. All it means is not behaving in a way that would embarrass someone and cause them to lose status in front of their peers. One sure way for foreigners to make someone lose face in Taiwan is to lose their temper in public, something many Taiwanese find inexcusable. Not only will the person targeted lose face, the foreigner loses face as well for being weak and unable to control their emotions. The Taiwanese pride themselves on self-control and when flustered or embarrassed will often giggle or give an evasive response, rather than dealing with the situation directly. Of course, this does not mean the Taiwanese don't get angry, but the general rule is that self-control in dealing with people goes a long way.

Flattery is another common characteristic of the Taiwanese that some foreigners find amusing, sometimes irritating. It's really done to ease

### ETIQUETTE DOS & DON'TS

- When beckoning to someone, wave them over to you with your palm down, motioning to yourself.
- If a Taiwanese gives a gift, put it aside to open later to avoid appearing greedy.
- When someone presents you with a business card, put it aside to read later. Never put it in your wallet and then put the wallet in your back pocket. To do so implies that you want to sit on that person!
- Never write anything in red ink unless you're correcting an exam. Red ink is used for letters of protest.
- Don't give clocks as gifts. The phrase 'to give a clock' in Mandarin sounds too much like attend a funeral.
- Giving someone a handkerchief as a gift implies that they will cry soon.
- Always take your shoes off when entering a Taiwanese home.
- When meeting a Taiwanese family, greet the eldest person first as a sign of respect.
- Always present things to people with both hands, showing that what you are offering is the fullest extent of yourself.

potentially tense social situations and to create a harmonious environment. Travellers are often told how beautiful they are (even if they look and feel like Quasimodo that day) or that their Chinese is terrific. The best response to flattery is a smile and a humble reply, to avoid sounding arrogant. It's good to send the flattering compliments in the other direction, even though it may feel strange at first. A barrage of vehement denials will be the first reaction of many Taiwanese, followed by a beaming smile.

Another concern of visitors to Taiwan is the concept of *guānxi*. Chinese society, generally speaking, is centred on a tight network of family and friends who provide support and assistance during difficult times. To get something done, it's often been easier to go through a back door, rather than through official channels. What this means, for example, is that if someone needs help, a sister's brother-in-law's neighbour will be contacted to solve the problem. If a favour is offered, the receiver is obligated to return the favour sometime in the future. This keeps the *guānxi* system running smoothly. In order to survive in Chinese society, it's important to learn the art of giving and receiving favours.

> In order to survive in Chinese society, it's important to learn the art of giving and receiving favours.

## LIFESTYLE

Chinese culture is traditionally centred on the family, which was once considered a microcosm of society as a whole. Most families in Taiwan live in crowded urban conditions with an average of five to six people living in a three-bedroom apartment. Gone are the days when extended families lived together around a central courtyard, with four or more generations living under one roof. Still, extended family remains exceedingly important, with grandparents commonly acting as caretakers for grandchildren with adult children working and financially supporting their ageing parents.

Rapid growth in Taiwan has brought new educational and economic opportunities to a large segment of the population. The quality of life in Taiwan is much higher than in many other countries, with a life expectancy of 78 years for women and 71 years for men. Many of the younger generation are putting off marriage until they've completed university, settled into a good job and acquired enough money to purchase the essentials, principally an apartment and a car, before having a family.

The Taiwanese are stereotyped as living to work and, admittedly, this stereotype has some truth to it. When it comes to education, children are put through a rigorous educational system, with hours of homework and evening cram schools. Junior high school is probably the toughest times for students, who must prepare for brutal tests to try and get a place in the best high schools. In high school come the equally difficult university placement tests. After achieving an undergraduate degree, many students go on to graduate school. Upon graduation, students are expected to land a well-paying job, most often in business or engineering.

The stereotype of the frugal Taiwanese also has some truth to it, with many Taiwanese working long hours to save enough money for the important purchases in life and putting the rest in the bank for a rainy day. This is largely due to the lack of a social safety net in Taiwan. The government spends far less on social welfare programmes in Taiwan than it does on defence. The elderly and the disabled rely on friends and family to take care of them, rather than on the minimal social insurance provided by the government.

The most difficult social problem facing Taiwan is the strain caused by its rapid transformation from a largely agrarian society into an urban society in such a short amount of time. Some of the effects of Taiwan's rapid transformation are pollution, housing shortages and public health problems. The government lacks adequate policies to monitor food and water safety. Taiwan's farmers spray large amounts of unregulated pesticides on crops, which some believe have contributed to Taiwan's rising cancer rate. Visitors to Taiwan are warned not to drink the tap water, for fear of waterborne illnesses such as *E.coli.*

In addition is the fear that the traditional values of family and community are falling apart as the island faces a rising drug and crime rate. The government takes a no-nonsense policy towards drugs and that applies to foreigners as well. Police routinely raid nightclubs and bars searching for illegal substances. Sometimes if they can't single out a user, they'll arrest everyone in the club and haul them off to jail! To be safe, don't get involved in Taiwan's drug scene as the penalty could mean a long jail sentence or even death.

Despite these dire sounding problems, things aren't as bleak as they seem. Growing public awareness of the issues is putting pressure on the government to implement policies to improve the quality of life in Taiwan.

## POPULATION

Taiwan is second only to Bangladesh in having the highest population density in the world. Most of Taiwan's residents live in crowded urban areas, the most densely populated cities being Taipei, Kaohsiung and Taichung. The Taipei–Keelung area accounts for 42% of Taiwan's entire population.

Over 98% of Taiwan's inhabitants are Han Chinese, with the other 2% being indigenous. The earliest inhabitants came from southern China and Austronesia between 12,000 and 15,000 years ago, settling on the east coast and the alluvial plains of the west. Many of the Chinese immigrants who arrived in Taiwan in the 14th century intermarried with the aborigines and later European settlers. Increased immigration forced many aboriginal groups into the mountains, earning them the name 'mountain people' by the Chinese.

The population of Taiwan's nine main indigenous tribes is approximately 433,689. These groups live throughout Taiwan, though the majority are concentrated in the Hualien and Taitung counties, the Central Mountain Range and Nantou County. The Hualien–Taitung area is home to the Ami, Taiwan's largest indigenous group, which accounts for one-third of Taiwan's aboriginal population. The Yami, who live on Lanyu Island, number the fewest at just 9000 members.

Some of the earliest Han Chinese immigrants were from China's Fujian province. They spoke the Hoklo dialect, which some now refer to as Taiwanese. These Fujian immigrants make up roughly 70% of Taiwan's current population. The Hakka people followed the Fujianese into Taiwan in the 17th century, settling themselves into the foothills of the Central Mountain Range. Nowadays, most Hakka live in the northwestern counties of Taoyuan, Miaoli and Hsinchu, and make up between 10% and 15% of Taiwan's population. Some Hakka also live on the east coast.

The remaining 12% to 15% of Taiwan's population are immigrants or descendents of those who came over from mainland China with the Kuomintang (KMT) between 1945 and 1949. Taiwan's mainland community is quite diverse and made up of a variety of ethnic and linguistic groups, including Hakka, Cantonese and Fujianese.

www.atayal.org
One of the most comprehensive sites on Taiwan's aboriginal peoples. The site provides detailed information on the history and customs of the nine major tribes in Taiwan.

## SPORT

Since the establishment of the five-day work week, increasing numbers of Taiwanese are finding the time to pursue outdoor activities and organised sports. Because of the lack of space in Taiwan and ageing sports facilities, the government has taken initiatives to build more sports centres and parks.

**DID YOU KNOW?**

The origin of the Dragon Boat Festival goes back 2500 years.

Basketball *(lánqiú)* and baseball *(bàngqiú)* are two of the most popular organised sports in Taiwan. The teams in Taiwan's Chinese Professional Baseball League include the Brother Elephants, China Trust Whales, President Lions, Makoto Gida, Sinon Bulls and First Securities Agan. Because the teams don't have a home stadium, games rotate in various local stadiums around the island.

Basketball is popular largely because it can be played indoors and is not dependent on Taiwan's volatile weather. Amusingly, the most strident fans of basketball in Taiwan are junior high school girls, who have fan clubs devoted to their favourite stars.

Golf *(gāoěrfū)* is the oldest organised sport in Taiwan and a favourite pastime for the well-to-do. Most golf clubs are open to the public and only require a guest membership to play. The Professional Golf Association of the ROC holds annual tournaments in Taiwan and participates in international competitions.

Martial arts have always been practised in Taiwan as a way to keep fit and keep healthy by regulating ones 'vital energy', or chi *(qì)*. There are more than 20 different kinds of martial arts including the one most foreigners are familiar with, taichi *(tàijíquán)*. Taichi is graceful but powerful slow-motion shadow-boxing and is commonly practised in the early morning as the sun rises. The 2-28 Peace Park or the Sun Yat-sen Memorial in Taipei are good places to watch taichi practitioners.

Dragon boat racing, another traditional sport, takes place in June. The Taipei International Dragon Boat Race Championships attracts local and international competitors.

## RELIGION

Traditional religious beliefs are alive and flourishing in Taiwan, with little to no government interference. Religion on the island is syncretic, dominated by ancestor worship, Taoism and Buddhism. The religious views of the Taiwanese are quite eclectic and most think little of combining elements from various religions to suit their needs, not necessarily adhering to one particular religious path. This eclecticism is something that many Christian missionaries have found frustrating; many Taiwanese don't feel that a conversion to Christianity should imply giving up the myriad of folk beliefs that have long-standing meaning to their culture.

Religion is a fundamental part of Taiwanese society, despite its modern progressive appearance. Though many Taiwanese wouldn't identify themselves with an organised religion, most participate in the age-old folk customs that have dominated Chinese culture for centuries. In most Taiwanese homes is a shrine, meant as a sacred place to burn incense and place offerings for ancestors. Many Taiwanese wear amulets for good luck and the jade bracelets that adorn many women's wrists were once thought to have supernatural powers to protect the wearer from harm.

### Folk Religion

Most residents of towns and villages practise special folk customs that pertain to a historical event or person particular to that area. Folk temples are dedicated to the myriad of gods and goddesses that populate

Taiwanese folk religion. Some of these deities were actually real people who later became deified due to their earthly reputation as a hero or a healer. The warrior Guan Yu, the famous general from China's legendary Three Kingdoms, has temples dedicated to him all over Taiwan. The most popular deities in Taiwan are the God of Heaven, who personifies justice, the Earth God, who watches over the harvest, and the House God, who protects families when they move into new homes.

By far, the most popular deity in Taiwan is Matsu, Goddess of the Sea (see p276), who watches over fishermen when they go out to sea. Matsu's birthday, which falls on the 23rd of the third lunar month, is one of the most important religious festivals in Taiwan and Matsu temples around the island take part in celebrations to honour the goddess.

## Taoism

There are some 4.55 million Taoists in Taiwan who worship at over 7000 temples around the island. Taoist deities in temples sometimes share space with folk deities and the two religions are often intertwined. Some say that Taoist temples have a carnival-like atmosphere, with their bright colours and garish statues.

> By far, the most popular deity in Taiwan is Matsu, Goddess of the Sea

The philosophy of Taoism (Dàojiào) is based on the *Tao Te Ching*, a work attributed to the sage philosopher Lao-tzu, whose shadowy existence can be traced back to the 6th century BC. An amalgamation of folk beliefs and ritual, Taoism placed an emphasis on individual freedom, laissez-faire government and harmony with nature. The Tao, or way, according to Lao-tzu, is the essence of all things in the universe but ultimately cannot be defined. A central facet of Taoism is the concept of *wúwéi*, or 'non-action', meaning to live in harmony with the universe without forcing things to your will.

In time, Taoism split into two branches – religious Taoism and philosophical Taoism, each taking very different approaches to Lao-tzu's teachings. Religious Taoism, borrowing concepts from Buddhism and folk religion, became ultimately concerned with the afterlife and achieving immortality. Taoist magicians banished demons through exorcisms and won over the public with demonstrations of their supernatural powers. China lost several emperors who died after drinking elixirs given to them by Taoists promising eternal life. Philosophical Taoism remained a way of life for hermits and sages, those who withdrew from the public life.

Chuang-tzu (Zhuangzi) is one of the most interesting Taoist writers and the Chinese often quote him today. Numerous translations of his work exist and are easy to locate in bookshops around Taipei.

During the Japanese occupation of Taiwan, many Taoist temples were forced to become Buddhist. It wasn't until the KMT arrived that the Taoist temples were restored to their original status. Many of the Chinese immigrants who came after 1945 considered themselves Taoist and established Taoist organisations and fellowships in addition to schools, hospitals and publishing houses.

## Confucianism

Confucian *(Rújiā Sīxiǎng)* values and beliefs form the foundation of Chinese culture. The central theme of Confucian doctrine is the conduct of human relationships for the attainment of harmony and overall good for society. Confucius (551–479 BC), or Master Kong, lived during the upheavals of China's Warring States era, a time of disunity and fear. Master Kong took it upon himself to re-educate his fellow citizens in the words and deeds of earlier Chinese rulers, whom he believed had wisdom that could be applied to his chaotic times. His goal was to reform society through government. Society, he taught, was comprised of five relationships: ruler and subject, husband and wife, father and son, elder and younger, and friends. Other things he taught were deference to authority and devotion to family.

Over the course of his lifetime Confucius attracted a steady following of students. After his death at age 72, disciples carried on his work and thousands of books were published with sayings and advice attributed to the philosopher. The five classics of Confucianism are the *Wujing*, consisting of the *I Ching (Book of Changes)*, *Shijing (Book of Poetry)*, *Shujing (Book of History)*, *Liji (Book of Rites)* and *Chuzu (Spring and Autumn Annals)*. Confucian disciples also published other collections of his work, including the *Great Learning*, *Doctrine of the Mean* and *Classic of Filial Piety*. Perhaps the single most influential book attributed to Confucius is the *Lunyu (Analects)*, a collection of essays and dialogues between Confucius and his students. This slim little book contains the central teachings of Confucianism and is standard memorisation for Chinese children.

Over time Confucianism developed as a philosophy, with Confucius' words and teachings adopted by Chinese emperors. One of his most important followers was Meng-tze (Mencius; 372–289 BC) who continued to spread the Confucian teachings and expand on Confucian thought.

Confucianism's influence on modern Taiwan society remains strong, as it does in most Chinese communities around the globe. Family is the most important unit of society, friends come second and country comes last. The close bonds between family and friends are one of the most admirable attributes of Chinese culture, a lasting legacy of Confucian teachings.

Confucianism's influence on modern Taiwan society remains strong

## Buddhism

When Buddhism reached China in the 1st century AD it was already about four centuries old in India and split into two schools: the Hinayana and Mahayana. In the Hinayana tradition, it was believed that Siddhartha Guatama was the sole Buddha who had given humans a simple path to attain freedom from suffering. The Hinayana stressed that Buddha was not a god but a man who had attained perfection and left the cycle of suffering. In the Mahayana school, Siddhartha was believed to be the reincarnation of a series of Buddhas, stretching from the past into an indefinite future. In later Mahayana beliefs, Buddhas became gods of transcendence and listened to the prayers of followers. It was Mahayana Buddhism that entered China and eventually made its way to Taiwan and other parts of northeast Asia.

The Silk Road was the primary means by which Buddhist thought and imagery spread from India. Caravans from India transported merchants and Buddhist missionaries, along with cargoes of textiles, ivory and spices. Buddhist material culture, in the form of manuscripts, images and other portable icons, also travelled along the trade routes, carried abroad by those who needed religious objects for protection, worship or for proselytising purposes.

When Buddhism entered China, its exotic nature, with chanting, strange coloured robes, incense and foreign images, was an attraction for many Chinese disillusioned with the uptight formalism of Confucianism. Buddhism, with its elaborate explanations of karma and how to find relief from suffering, offered answers to the afterlife that neither Taoism nor Confucianism could address.

Slowly, the religion drew more followers, spreading throughout China. However, Buddhism had its share of critics and many Chinese were afraid that the foreign religion was a threat to the Chinese identity, which was firmly grounded in Confucian ideals. The growth of Buddhism was slowed by persecutions and outright abolition by various emperors. During the later years of the Tang dynasty (AD 618–907), Buddhism experienced some of its most severe persecutions and the religion never completely recovered.

Buddhism came to Taiwan in the 17th century, after the Ming loyalist Cheng Cheng-kung drove out the Dutch and relocated his troops to Taiwan. With him came a steady stream of Buddhist monks who had faced persecution in China and wanted to set up temples and monasteries on the island.

Many Japanese were devout Buddhists and supported the growth of Buddhism during their occupation. They were active supporters in the building of temples on the island and financed the construction of Buddhist schools and hospitals.

Buddhists in Taiwan largely follow the Mahayana school, believing in redemption for all mankind. In many Buddhist temples on the island, visitors will see the female bodhisattva Kuanyin, the Goddess of Mercy, who watches and protects people from harm. Translated, the name Kuanyin means 'the one who listens to complaints'.

## Temples

Taiwanese temples are where most travellers will get their first exposure to the traditional religions of Taiwan. Taiwanese temples show amazing craftsmanship, with temple architecture governed by a strict set of rules. The shape of the roof, the placement of the beams and columns and the location of deities are all carefully placed following the use of feng shui, a complex cosmological system designed to create harmonious surroundings in accordance with the natural laws of the universe. Some of the most famous temples in Taiwan include the Longshan Temple (p69) in Taipei, Chaotien Temple (p227) on Peikang and the Longshan Temple (p209) in Lugang.

The exterior of many temples in Taiwan look very similar. However, Taoist, Buddhist and Confucian temples are all fairly easy to distinguish once you know what to look for. Buddhist temples have fewer images, except for statues of the Buddha seated in the middle of the temple on an altar. Guanyin is the next most common deity you'll see, sometimes accompanied by other bodhisattvas. Well-financed Buddhist temples have monks or nuns living in residence, with space for living quarters and a communal dining hall serving vegetarian food. In many cases, it's possible to eat at Buddhist temples, though you may need to make arrangements in advance. Temple stays are also possible in various places around the island.

Taoist and folk temples are much gaudier inside, with brightly painted statues of deities and colourful murals of scenes from Chinese mythology. On the main altar is the principal deity of the temple, often flanked by some lesser-ranked gods. In front of the altar is a table loaded with bowls of fruit and goodies. There's usually an incense pot in front of the altar and another larger pot outside in front of the temple. This is where you'll see worshippers light incense and bow to the deity. Fierce-looking temple guardians are often painted on the doors to the entrance of the temple to scare away evil spirits. Large furnaces also stand in the courtyard; these are for burning 'ghost money', paper money meant to keep the ancestors

*Temple architecture is governed by feng shui*

happy in heaven. You'll often see miniature versions of these furnaces in front of stores and offices. Taoist temples are at their most vibrant during Lunar New Year, when people bang drums and set off firecrackers.

Confucian temples are the most sedate and lack the colour and noise of Taoist or Buddhist temples. Often, the temples are in a park-like setting and are very peaceful places to relax and escape from city noise.

The Taiwanese have an eclectic approach to religion and it's possible to see elements from Buddhist and Taoist temples combined together. Temple rituals vary, though the most common rituals travellers might see are exorcisms performed by mediums or people using divining blocks to tell the future. Next to the altar in most temples are oracle blocks (small blocks of wood or plastic). A devotee will take two of these blocks and drop them on the floor. If one block lands convex side up, and the other flat side up, the answer to the question is positive. If the blocks both land convex side up, the answer is negative. If both land flat side up, the answer is ambiguous and the divination process must start all over again. Another way to tell the future is to consult oracles, which are in a cylindrical container next to the altar, filled with bamboo strips marked with numbers. The devotee takes a bamboo strip and uses the divining blocks to see if the strip is the correct one to be using for the problem. If yes, then the number on the strip is matched to an oracle with the same number on which the answer is written.

**DID YOU KNOW?**

Taiwan has more temples per capita than any other country in the world.

## WOMEN IN TAIWAN

The Taiwan constitution forbids discrimination on the basis of gender, though Taiwanese women face many of the same problems other women face the world over. In traditional Chinese society, women were seen as the caretakers, secondary to their husbands and subordinate to the husband's family. Now, 45% of Taiwanese women work outside the home and are struggling to alter long-held beliefs regarding their inferior status.

Though educational opportunities are the same for both men and women, few women in Taiwan are encouraged to enter male-dominated fields such as science and technology. When women and men do hold the same jobs, statistics show that women make two-thirds less than men with fewer chances for promotion. In addition to working, women still have primary responsibility of the household and taking care of the children.

Taiwan's women's movement began in the 1970s and has made significant progress in putting pressure on the government to change legislation regarding family laws and marriage. Today, women share the same property rights as their husbands, something unheard of even 10 years ago. Progress has also been made in the areas of teenage prostitution, labour laws and health issues.

## ARTS

Taiwanese art is a diverse mix of mainland Chinese influence, Western art trends and indigenous traditions. Much of the art travellers will encounter in Taiwan has its roots in mainland China, carried over by centuries of immigration. The National Palace Museum (p79) in Taipei is a dazzling showcase of traditional Chinese arts and crafts and is one of the best places in the world to gain an understanding of Chinese art forms.

While Taiwan has preserved many traditional Chinese arts, it has also created a distinctive art tradition of its own, independent from the mainland. Over the past few decades, Taiwanese artists have tried to discover the unique characteristics that define Taiwanese art. This quest for identity is one of the most important themes in the contemporary Taiwanese art world. Taiwanese artists have pursued this question not only through traditional media such as oil painting and ceramic sculpture, but also through more modern approaches such as multimedia installation and video, performance art and film.

## Chinese Traditional Arts

### PAINTING

The origins of Chinese painting lie in the Bronze Age, beginning with representational figures of humans, animals and demons inscribed on bronze vessels. The emphasis on brushwork and line in these works was and remains the defining element of traditional Chinese painting. In fact, the character *huà*, 'to paint', represents a brush tracing the boundaries of a field. While Western art values colour, composition and texture, the quality of a Chinese painting has shown from early on the great importance placed on brush technique.

Painting flourished during the Tang dynasty. The most painted subjects were scenes of court life and animals. The Tang also saw a rise in the popularity of landscape painting. The idyllic natural worlds depicted in Tang landscapes are beautifully detailed in brilliant washes of blues and greens.

During the Northern and Southern Sung dynasties, landscape painting rose to new heights of excellence. Sung painters preferred moody, romantic landscapes with swirling mist-covered mountains and imaginary locales. One master of the Sung painting style is Fan K'uan, the creator of *Travellers Among Mountains and Streams*, seen in the National Palace Museum. Painted in the early 11th century, it depicts an enormous craggy cliff rising up behind a Buddhist temple, hidden in the trees. This painting captures the essence of China's main religions: the Confucian sense of order and harmony, the Taoist identification with nature, and the emotional transcendence of Buddhism.

With the invasion of the Mongols, Yuan dynasty painting took on a much different tone than the Sung. Yuan paintings have large empty spaces and are quite austere compared to those of the Tang and Sung. Chao Meng-fu's *Autumn Colours on the Chiao and Hua Mountains* from 1296 is a good example of Yuan attention to space and form. This painting is also on permanent display in the National Palace Museum.

The Ming dynasty saw a return to earlier styles of painting. Wen Chen-ming is famous for his paintings of gnarled old trees. *Old Trees by a Cold Waterfall*, in the National Palace collection, shows how artists during this time conveyed conventional subject matter in progressive new ways.

The Qing dynasty saw a continuation of the Ming schools but with more emphasis on patterns and bright colours. Political turmoil, especially in the 19th century, took its toll on China's artistic circles and the quality of Qing paintings suffered. One influential Qing painter was not Chinese, but Italian. Giuseppe Castiglione, or Lang Shih-ning in Chinese, was a Jesuit who brought Italian painting techniques to China. He became a popular court painter and painted many imperial portraits, attempting to synthesise Italian and Chinese styles. One work, *One Hundred Horses at Pasture*, shows his attempt to merge Western realism with Chinese landscape.

### CERAMICS

The Chinese began making pottery over 8000 years ago. The first vessels were handcrafted earthenware, primarily used for religious purposes. The invention of the pottery wheel during the late Neolithic period led to the

*The Chinese began making pottery over 8000 years ago.*

establishment of foundries and workshops and the eventual development of a ceramics industry.

Over the centuries Chinese potters perfected their craft, introducing many new exciting styles and techniques. Art thrived under the Tang dynasty and the ceramic arts were no exception. One of the most famous styles from this period is *san-ts'ai*, or 'three-coloured ware', named because of the liberal use of bright yellow, green and white glaze. Blue-green *ch'ing-tz'u*, or celadons, were another popular item and demand for them grew in countries as far away as Egypt and Persia.

The Yuan dynasty saw the first production of China's most famous type of porcelain, often referred to simply as 'blue-and-white'. Cobalt blue paint, obtained from Persia, was applied with a brush as an underglaze directly to white porcelain and then the vessel was covered with another transparent glaze and fired. This technique was perfected under the Ming dynasty and ceramics made in this style became hugely popular all over the world, eventually acquiring the name 'Chinaware', whether produced in China or not. Jingdezhen, in Jiangxi province, was established during the Yuan as the centre of the ceramics industry and still retains that importance today.

During the Qing dynasty, porcelain techniques were further refined and developed, showing superb craftsmanship and ingenuity. British and European consumers dominated the export market, having an insatiable appetite for Chinese vases and bowls decorated with flowers and landscapes. The Qing is also known for its stunning monochromatic ware, especially the ox-blood vases and enamel decorated porcelain.

## Modern Art

When the Japanese landed in Taiwan in 1895, they introduced Western styles of painting to the island. One of the most important Japanese artists to do so was Ishikawa Kinichiro, now considered the father of modern Taiwanese art. Ishikawa was a great influence on many Taiwanese painters, teaching them to paint the tropical landscapes of Taiwan in a French impressionistic style. Some of Ishikawa's students include Yang San-lang, Li Shih-chiao and Li Mei-shu, who travelled to Japan to study watercolour and oil painting at the Tokyo Fine Arts Institute. Yang San-lang became the most recognised painter of his generation for his watercolours of rural Taiwanese life.

After WWII, with the shift to mainland Chinese control, the Nationalists encouraged artists to paint traditional Chinese landscapes. Artists uprooted from the mainland taught a younger generation of artists Chinese ink painting and watercolour. Later, during the 1950s, as Americans became more involved in Taiwanese politics, the attention once again turned to Western styles of painting. In 1957 the May Art Society and the Oriental Art Society were founded, organisations that questioned the conservatism of current Taiwanese art.

In the early 1960s artists became disillusioned with traditional Chinese painting and began to imitate Western art trends, in particular abstract art. Private art groups were founded such as the Eastern Art Group and the Fifth Moon Group. An important artist of the 1960s was Liu Kuo-sung, who painted abstract designs using the traditional Chinese medium of ink and water. He was shunned by the art academies but found recognition abroad, becoming one of the most important Taiwanese painters of his generation. A well-known painting of his is *Dance of Spiritual Rhythm* (1964).

During the 1970s a strong nativist movement, sometimes referred to as 'Taiwan Consciousness', began to develop. Artists looked neither to the

**In the early 1960s artists became disillusioned with traditional Chinese painting and began to imitate Western art trends.**

West nor to mainland China for inspiration but to the island of Taiwan itself. They found inspiration in Taiwanese folk traditions and the arts and crafts of Taiwan's indigenous tribes. A significant artist who emerged at this time was Chu Ming, who, despite having no formal training as an artist, gained recognition for his imaginative paintings and sculptures, inspired by Taiwanese folk traditions. The Juming Museum (p124) in northern Taiwan has over 1000 of his works on display.

Taiwan began opening up to the international art world in the 1980s, playing host to a large number of Chinese and Western exhibits. Some Taiwanese artists who had moved abroad returned to Taiwan to participate in the new artistic developments sweeping the island. One of the most important events of the early 1980s was the opening of the Taipei Fine Arts Museum (p76). This museum was to play a crucial role in making Taiwan a valuable participant in the international art world. The ending of martial law in 1987 was another watershed in the development of Taiwanese art. For the first time, artists could actively criticise their political system without suffering the consequences.

The 1990s saw the nativist movement grow stronger as Taiwanese artists became ever more determined to construct their own art history. Artists were faced with the challenge of creating something unique out of long-standing traditions. Alternative art spaces opened, such as IT Park and Apt 2 in Taipei. In addition, Taiwan began to participate even more on the international stage and was actively bringing Taiwanese art to the rest of the world. In 1992 Taiwan artist Lee Ming-sheng was asked to join the international exhibition Documenta, held in Kassel, Germany. In 1993 Taiwanese artists were asked to exhibit in the Venice Biennale for the first time, eventually leading to Taiwan's own art pavilion at the Biennale in 1995, something that continues to this day.

Taiwan's first local biennale, titled 'Quest for Identity', was held in 1996 and artists from all over Taiwan were invited, including indigenous artists. Two years later, the Taipei Fine Arts Museum organised Taiwan's first international biennale titled 'Site of Desire'. Over 36 artists from northeast Asia participated, to international acclaim.

The 21st century has seen a continuation of the events that occurred in the 1980s and 1990s. In addition, some artists have gone to extreme lengths to express their anxiety about the Taiwanese sense of selfhood in a rapidly changing global environment. Artists such as Yuan Goang-ming and Chen Chieh-jen have drawn international attention for their depictions of contemporary Taipei and the psychological emptiness of the city landscape. Chen Chieh-jen in particular is notable for his disturbing series of photographs titled *The Twelve Karmas Under the City*. Other artists such as Kuo Chüan-ch'iu see their work as an escape from the political realities of everyday life. Kuo's paintings of quiet nocturnal landscapes, filled with magical birds and trees, depict a world far removed from the urban chaos of modern Taipei.

> Artists such as Yuan Goang-ming and Chen Chieh-jen have drawn international attention for their depictions of contemporary Taipei.

## Indigenous Arts & Crafts

The indigenous peoples of Taiwan have their own distinct art traditions, including woodcarving, weaving and basket making. The Shung Ye Museum of Formosan Aborigines (p82) is an excellent place to learn about the arts and crafts of Taiwan's aboriginals. The Ketagalan Cultural Centre (p108) in Beitou, Taipei, features aboriginal culture exhibitions, a multimedia showroom, an aboriginal theme library, research facilities, and conference and performance space. Taitung's National Museum of Prehistory (p183) also has worthy exhibits devoted to traditional arts and crafts.

### WOODCARVING

Several aboriginal tribes are famous for the high quality of their wood-carvings. The Yami of Lanyu Island (p192) are known for their handmade canoes, constructed without nails or glue. The canoes have marvellous carved relief designs embellished with human and sun motifs painted in white, red and black.

The Paiwan and Rukai also excel at woodcarving, building homes that feature elaborate carvings of humans, snakes and fantastical creatures.

### WEAVING

The indigenous peoples produce some amazing textiles. The most well known are those of the Atayal, who create striking intricate designs in contrasting colours of black, blue, white and red.

### DANCE & MUSIC

The music of Taiwan's aboriginals has become extremely popular over the past few years, due in part to the new-found awareness of aboriginal cultures by the Taiwanese. Vocal music is one way the aborigines have preserved their history and legends, passing down songs from one generation to the next. Music stores in Taiwan's larger cities carry recordings of various aboriginal singers.

Aboriginal dances are great fun to watch, though most dancing is clearly marketed for tourists. Earlier, dances were usually centred on a religious festival, accompanied by singing and musical instruments. One of the best dance troupes in Taiwan is the Formosa Aboriginal Dance Troupe, made up of performers representing several different tribes. The troupe is recognised internationally and if you get a chance to see them, by all means go.

> Aboriginal dances are great fun to watch, though most dancing is clearly marketed for tourists.

## Performing Arts

### TAIWANESE OPERA

Taiwanese opera is an offshoot of Beijing opera (jīngjù), a sophisticated art form that has been an important part of Chinese culture for over 900 years.

Most Westerners are initially turned off by the caterwauling and ear-splitting shrills of Chinese opera singers, accompanied by banging drums, gongs and wooden clappers. However, once your ears stop bleeding, it really is hard not to be entranced by the artistry of opera performances, with its dazzling costumes, make-up and amazing acrobatics. Foreign visitors are encouraged to give Chinese opera a chance, just for the experience.

Chinese opera has been formally in existence since the northern Song dynasty (960–1126), developing out of China's long balladic tradition. Performances were put on by travelling entertainers, often families, in teahouses frequented by China's working classes. Performances were drawn from popular legends and folklore, often about sexy young ghosts and the foolish young men who fell under their spell. Different operatic forms developed around China and gradually the art form became more acceptable by China's elite. Beijing opera became officially recognised in 1790, when performances were staged for the imperial family.

Chinese opera was first introduced to Taiwan in the 1600s by immigrants from Fujian and Guangdong provinces. Opera was initially performed on auspicious occasions such as weddings, birthdays and temple festivals. Later, it developed into a more public art form, drawing larger audiences. The Taiwanese opera seen today is actually a mixture of Beijing opera, Chinese southern-style opera and local folk songs, influenced by the music of Taiwan's aboriginal peoples.

Taiwanese opera is complimented by a wide range of musical instruments, including drums, gongs, flutes and two- and three-stringed mandolins. Today you may even come across a 'disco opera', with electric guitars and synthesizers.

## DANCE

Modern dance in Taiwan has its roots in the 1940s, introduced to Taiwan by the Japanese. The American dancers Alvin Ailey and Paul Taylor toured through Taiwan in the 1960s, having enormous influence on local dancers. The Taiwanese dancer Liu Feng-shueh, now considered the godmother of Taiwan modern dance, set up a studio in 1967 and created her own dance troupe. In 1976 she formed the Neoclassic Dance Company, which still gives performances to crowds today.

Cai Ruei-yue is another dancer who was influenced by American dance technique. Cai studied in Tokyo and later established the China Dance Company, whose premises burned down in 1999. One of her most famous students is Lin Hwai-min, founder of the world-renowned Cloud Gate Dance Company (see the boxed text below).

The Cloud Gate Dance Company has influenced a number of dance companies including the Taipei Dance Circle and Dance Forum Taipei, who fuse Western dance styles with traditional Chinese dance. One group that is interesting to watch for its inspiration from Chinese folk legends is the Legend Lin Dance Theatre.

In 2000 Cloud Gate Dance Company and Legend Lin were invited to perform in the 2000 French Lyon Biennial Dance Festival. Along with the dancers, the artist Chen Chieh-jen (p39) was also invited to participate.

> If a musician played in the wrong tone, it could mean the fall of a dynasty!

## Music
### TRADITIONAL CHINESE MUSIC

Traditional Chinese instrumental pieces are often based on ancient Chinese poetry, making them very symbolic in form. Unlike Western music, tone is considered more important than melody. Music to the Chinese was once believed to have cosmological significance and in early times, if a musician played in the wrong tone, it could mean the fall of a dynasty!

Some common Chinese instruments include the two-stringed mandolin (*èrhú*), three-stringed mandolin (*sānxuán*), zither (*gǔzhēng*), flute (*dízi*) and two-stringed viola (*húqín*).

---

### CLOUD GATE DANCE COMPANY

The premier dance company in Taiwan is the Cloud Gate Dance Company, founded in the early 1970s by Lin Hwai-min. Lin was a student under Martha Graham and upon his return to Taiwan in 1973 desired to combine modern dance techniques with Chinese opera.

Lin's first works were based on stories and legends from Chinese classical literature. Soon, however, Lin decided to try to explore Taiwanese identity in his work. *Legacy,* one of Lin's most important works, tells the story of the first Taiwanese settlers. Later, Lin expanded his performances to include Tibetan, Indian and Indonesian influences. *Nine Songs*, performed in 1995 at New York's Kennedy Centre, takes its inspiration from the works of the ancient poet Chu Yuan, borrowing movements from Chinese opera and dance from India and Java.

Cloud Gate performances are breathtaking in their colour and movements and an incredible experience not to be missed.

Groups in Taiwan that perform Chinese music professionally are the Taipei Municipal Chinese Classical Orchestra, the National Chinese Orchestra, the Kaohsiung Chinese Orchestra and the Chinese Orchestra of the Broadcasting Corporation of China.

## CONTEMPORARY MUSIC

www.ibiblio.org/chinese-music/html/traditional.htm
Downloads of traditional Chinese music.

For the past few decades, Taiwan's pop music world has been dominated by sentimental love ballads. Now, a growing alternative music movement has swept the island, promoted by Taiwan's booming outdoor music festivals. These festivals, held in industrial parks and beaches, are attracting scores of teenagers and college students who come to let their hair down and (literally) shake off the pressures of school life.

The first outdoor music event was the Ragged Live Festival, held in Taipei in 1994. The next year two Western expats organised a musical event called Spring Scream, held in Kenting, which was to become the largest outdoor concert of the year.

Spring Scream is held annually in April and lasts three days, featuring indie bands from around the island playing to thousands of fans. The festival has helped to launch the careers of some bands, who have found moderate success in selling their albums in Singapore and Japan.

Spring Scream has encouraged the start of other music festivals held around the island, including the Ho Hai Yan Indie Award Taiwan Rock Festival, held at Fulong Beach (p132) in northern Taiwan annually in July.

**DID YOU KNOW?**

The first Taiwanese film was made in 1925, titled *Whose Fault Is It.*

## Cinema

Taiwan produces some fine movies, though most are dismal failures at the home box office. Internationally, however, many movies are quite successful and take home international awards. Lack of support from home means that many young Taiwanese filmmakers are forced to take on second jobs to finance their work. It's not that the average Taiwanese doesn't appreciate the films made by their fellow brethren; it's just that they don't get to see them. The problems lie mainly in distribution. Locally made movies often get pushed aside for Hong Kong or American blockbusters and are only shown in smaller art houses for brief periods. To try to draw interest (and money), Taipei hosts some notable film festivals every year, including the Taipei Golden Horse Film Festival. Attending the Golden Horse is a wonderful way to support a struggling industry and see some great films that won't make it into the general theatres. The best place to see indie movies, both Taiwan-made and foreign, is at the SPOT Taipei Film House (p101).

Taiwanese cinema has a long history, going all the way back to 1901, with Japanese-made documentaries and feature films. Silent era films often used a Japanese convention called *rensageki*, a mix of film and theatre with moving images supplementing performances on stage.

When the KMT took over Taiwan, they set up their own movie industry as a way to 'educate' the Taiwanese population in all things Chinese. The movie business was short-lived, however, because there was little interest in KMT morality plays and, on top of that, only a few of the older residents of the island could speak Mandarin.

In the 1960s the government created the Central Motion Picture Corporation (CMP) and the movie industry finally took off. During the 1960s and 1970s, audiences were treated to a deluge of romantic melodramas and martial arts epics and in the late 1970s a disturbing subgenre called 'social realism', full of brutal violence and sex.

In the 1980s the Taiwanese grew tired of the repetitive films of the past two decades and film makers had to find a way to compete with foreign made films. During this time, two film makers emerged who would have a strong impact on how Taiwanese cinema was seen abroad, though most locally made movies from this point forward would only be seen in art houses. Hou Hsiao-hsien, considered the most important director of this New Wave movement, broke away from escapist movies and chose instead to make movies that depicted the gritty reality of Taiwan life. *The Sandwich Man* (1983) is one of the best examples of Taiwan's New Wave ideals, establishing it as a realistic artistic movement. The movie is an adaptation of three short stories by the Taiwanese author Huang Chun-ming (p43), which explore life in Taiwan during the 1950s and 1960s. One segment of the movie is taken from the story 'The Taste of Apples', and is about a young boy from the countryside who encounters tragedy when he moves from the countryside to Taipei.

*Wintry Night* by the Taiwanese author Li Qiao is a compelling epic about the life of a Hakka family who settle in Taiwan in the 1890s.

Another of Hou Hsiao-hsien's movies, *A Time to Live and a Time to Die* (1985), also explores childhood in rural Taiwan during the Cold War era. Probably Hou Hsiao-hsien's most successful film is *City of Sadness* (1989), which follows the lives of a Taiwanese family living through the KMT takeover of Taiwan and the 2-28 Incident. This movie was the first to break the silence surrounding the tragedy. *City of Sadness* won the Golden Lion award at the 1989 Venice Film Festival. Hou Hsiao-hsien has continued to produce some masterful work, including the brilliant *The Puppet Master* (1993), an examination of the life of 84-year-old puppeteer Li Tien-lu, who is considered a 'living treasure' of the Taiwanese. Most recently, Hou Hsiao-hsien shot *Millennium Mambo* (2001), a more conventional story about a woman torn between two men.

Edward Yang is another important director whose work goes in a very different direction than that of Hou Hsiao-hsien. Yang's films concern Taiwan urban life, often from the viewpoint of women. Yang's movies address the problems facing people living in modern-day Taipei. One of his best works is *Yi Yi* (2000), which tells the story of a middle-class family whose life falls apart when the maternal grandmother of the wife has a stroke. The old woman's illness precipitates a series of events that challenge the ties that hold the family together.

*Wild Kids* is written by Chang Tachun, one of Taiwan's most popular authors. This insightful story centres around a Taipei teenager who gets caught up in Taipei's underground crime world.

Ang Lee is Taiwan's most famous director, known for his mega-hit *Crouching Tiger, Hidden Dragon* (2000). Ang's first film was *Pushing Hands* (1992), filmed in New York with funding from the CMP. His next movie, *The Wedding Banquet* (1993), took a bold step in exploring homosexuality in Chinese culture and was quite controversial in Taiwan. After achieving international success, Ang joined Hollywood and filmed *Sense and Sensibility* (1995), *The Ice Storm* (1997), *Ride with the Devil* (1999) and most recently *Hero* and *Hulk* (2003).

## Literature

Although Taiwanese writers have produced a significant body of literature, many books have not been translated into English and remain inaccessible to most foreigners. In bookshops around Taiwan, it's easy to find English translations of the Chinese classics, such as Dream of the Red Chamber, The Three Kingdoms, Story of the Stone and Journey to the West. To find English translations of Taiwanese works, Internet bookshops are the best way to go. The works mentioned below are all available online. To learn more about Taiwanese literature check out the National Museum of Literature in Tainan.

Much of modern Taiwanese literature is about the harsh realities of Taiwan's history and present-day social issues. One of the most controversial novels, translated into English, is Pai Hsien-yung's *Crystal Boys,* a novel about Taiwan's gay scene. Much of the novel revolves around Taipei's New Park, now the 2-28 Peace Park, and the site of the first Gay Pride Festival in Taiwan.

Another book concerning homosexuality is *Notes of a Desolate Man* by Chu T'ienwen. The novel won a slew of awards, including Notable Book of the Year by the New York Times for its frank examination of AIDS and homosexuality in Taiwan.

Highly recommended for its insight into modern Taiwan history is *Wintry Night* by Li Qiao, an epic that spans half a century of colonisation from the point of view of Taiwanese settlers.

Huang Chun-ming's *A Taste of Bitter Apples* is another excellent book that the Taiwanese film director Hou Hsiao-hsien turned into the movie *Sandwich Man* (p43).

# Environment

## THE LAND

Taiwan lies 165km off the coast of mainland China, separated by the Taiwan Strait. The shape of the island has sometimes been compared to a tobacco leaf or a sweet potato. The area of the island is 36,000 sq km, roughly the size of the Netherlands. Taiwan is 394km in length and 144km wide at its widest point. The territory of the island includes 15 offshore islands; the most important are the Penghu Archipelago and the islands of Matsu and Kinmen in the Taiwan Strait and, off the east coast, Green Island and Lanyu.

Mountains are the most dominant feature on Taiwan. The island is divided in half by the Central Mountain Range, a series of jagged mountain peaks that stretch for over 170km from north to south. Taiwan's highest mountain is Yushan (Jade Mountain), rising at 3950m, making it one of the tallest mountains in northeast Asia.

Fertile plains and basins make up most of western Taiwan, crisscrossed with many small rivers that empty into the sea. The majority of Taiwanese live on the west coast, which has the most suitable land for agriculture. The east coast, with its towering seaside cliffs and rocky volcanic coastline, is the most sparsely populated. The Central Cross-Island Hwy (p153) and the South Cross-Island Hwy (p248) link the island from east to west, cutting through spectacular mountain scenery.

Taiwan's climate is subtropical, with heavy monsoon rains battering northern Taiwan between October and March and southern Taiwan between May and September. Winters are damp and wet, summers hot and humid.

Taiwan sits on the colliding Eurasian and Philippine plates which constantly grind together, causing earthquakes, mountains and a fair share of hot springs. Hualien (p165) on the east coast is very close to the subduction zone, making it more vulnerable to earthquakes. The entire island is riddled with fault lines and prone to earthquakes. The most recent devastating earthquake occurred on 21 September 1999 and measured 7.3 on the Richter scale. The earthquake caused tremendous damage, thousands died and people are still cleaning up the damage, especially around Taichung and along the Central Cross-Island Hwy.

## WILDLIFE

Taiwan's lush mountainous landscape is home to a wide range of flora and fauna, mostly found in Taiwan's undeveloped mountain peaks, far from human contact.

### Animals

Intense cultivation of land and heavy industry has put great pressure on Taiwan's wildlife population, especially along the west coast. Taiwan's mountains and east coast are the best places to spot wildlife, though this will probably be limited to birds and butterflies.

The Central Mountain Range has the largest amount of remaining forest in Taiwan and is home to a wide range of animals including the wild boar, Formosan macaque, Formosan black bear, sambar deer and pheasants.

The Formosan black bear is the largest mammal on the island and lives at altitudes above 2000m. It's highly unlikely you'll see one as they're very elusive.

**DID YOU KNOW?**

Hualien is one of the largest marble producing regions in the world.

http://tean.formosa.org The Taiwan Environmental Action Network is an organisation run by Taiwanese living overseas. Their site is very comprehensive.

Another elusive animal is the Formosan clouded leopard, which lives in the lowlands of the Central Mountain Range. Sadly, the last sighting of the leopard was in 1985 and authorities are not certain if any more of these animals remain in the wild.

**DID YOU KNOW?**

There are 174 native Taiwanese animals on the national protected list.

## Plants

More than half of Taiwan is covered with dense forest and experts claim that the island is home to over 4002 types of plants, 1000 of them found only in Taiwan. Some of these include the Chinese juniper and cowtail pine, though the most common species travellers will come across are bamboo, spruce, fir and cypress at higher altitudes. Taiwan was once covered with camphor forests but, sadly, most of these have been logged to near extinction. The largest remaining camphor forest is at Fuyuan Forest Recreational Area (p180) in the Eastern Rift Valley.

## NATIONAL PARKS

About 19.5% of Taiwan is now protected, with 18 nature reserves, 24 forest reserves, 12 coastal reserves, seven wildlife refuges and six national parks. Environmental conservation is relatively young in Taiwan but Taiwan's Department of National Parks and the Council of Agriculture hope to reverse some of the damage caused by Taiwan's poor environmental policies of the past.

**DID YOU KNOW?**

Over 58% of Taiwan is covered in forest.

In addition to national parks, designated scenic areas have been established across the island, including the East Coast National Scenic Area between Hualien and Taitung (p181), the North-East Corner National Scenic Area and the Matsu and Penghu National Scenic Areas.

## ENVIRONMENTAL ISSUES

Taiwan's 'economic miracle' has meant that the natural beauty of the island has been compromised for greater economic prosperity. Pollution, urban sprawl and industrial waste have all taken a heavy toll on the island. Vast tracts of forests have been destroyed, decimating animal habitats and causing extensive soil degradation. Poaching of illegal animals for Chinese medicine has pushed certain animals to near extinction.

| National Park | Features | Activities | Best Time to Visit | Page |
|---|---|---|---|---|
| Kenting | beach resort | swimming with tropical fish, diving in pristine coral reefs, migratory bird watching | summer | p264 |
| Yushan | tallest mountain in Taiwan, rare Formosan salamander, Formosan black bear | hiking alpine tundra and cedar forests | summer, autumn, spring | p235 |
| Yangmingshan | beautiful mountain park with varied climate, butterflies | hiking | summer, autumn, spring | p110 |
| Taroko | spectacular gorge, Formosan macaque, hot springs, pheasants | hiking | summer, autumn, spring | p173 |
| Sheiba | diverse mountain terrain, Formosan landlocked salmon | hiking | summer, autumn, spring | p145 |

In Taiwan's larger cities, the air quality is so poor people wear surgical masks to try to minimise the risks of breathing in smog and car exhaust fumes, the major source of air pollution. Piles of garbage lie on city street corners and rivers are contaminated with industrial and household waste. Over the past decade, the Taiwanese have taken their government to task for these issues and the environmental situation is slowly improving. Schools are now teaching environmental awareness from an early age and the government has started cracking down hard on factories that do not follow environmental regulations. Grassroots environmental organisations have sprung up all over Taiwan, protesting against powerful state-owned factories that continue to be the island's worst pollutants.

Unfortunately, the challenges Taiwan faces to improve its environment are formidable. With the establishment of the five-day work week, many Taiwanese use their weekends and holidays to visit national parks and recreation areas, increasing the environmental pressure on an already fragile ecosystem. As Taiwan's population increases, water shortages and dwindling energy resources are another major headache. Other difficult issues concern the dumping of nuclear waste on Lanyu Island (p192), causing possible contamination of water and land.

So far, the government hasn't come up with tenable solutions to these problems. With limited funds and lack of international support, Taiwan is left to deal with most of these issues on its own. Hopefully, with growing public pressure, things on Taiwan's environmental front will change for the better in the not so distant future.

http://tepu.yam.org.tw/intro.html Taiwan's most well-known environmental group, Taiwan Environmental Protection Union, has a good website that explains its history and mission.

# Food & Drink

Taiwan's reputation for having the best Chinese food in northeast Asia is well deserved. The island offers an enormous array of places to eat – from simple night market food stalls to fancy five-star restaurants – serving up just about every kind of Chinese cuisine available, from local delicacies to dishes from the far-flung corners of mainland China.

Taiwan's history is reflected in its culinary culture. What many consider traditional Taiwanese cuisine derives from the foods of the island's aboriginal peoples, who for centuries relied on simple dishes of wild vegetables, sweet potatoes and seafood. During the Japanese occupation, the Japanese introduced a love of miso (fermented soybean paste) to the Taiwanese, who like to use it liberally as a seasoning on grilled meats. When droves of mainland Chinese immigrants arrived in Taiwan after 1949, they brought with them the various regional dishes of their homeland.

As Taiwan's prosperity has expanded, so has the Taiwanese culinary scene. Now, not only is it easy to find traditional Chinese dishes on the island but also Western and Chinese fast-food chains, and international cuisines that range from Tex Mex to French crepes. In the past few years the Taiwanese have gone caffeine mad, and even in the smallest of towns it's possible to buzz up on cappuccino at any time of the day.

There's no question that the Taiwanese love their food. A well-quoted saying is that there's a snack shop every three steps and a restaurant every five. Eating out is a popular activity for Taiwanese of all ages, and in the evenings restaurants are crowded, lively places. The likeliest way to find the best restaurants in Taiwan is to follow the noise – the noisier the better. The more crowded the restaurant, the tastier the food. Of course, some of the best food is not found in restaurants. Gourmands know that some of the most mouth-watering treats are found in night markets in and around Taiwan's cities.

## STAPLES
### Rice

Rice is an inseparable part of virtually every Taiwanese meal. The Taiwanese don't ask 'Have you had your dinner/lunch yet?' but 'Have you eaten rice yet?' Rice comes in lots of different preparations – as a porridge (congee) served with plates of pickled vegetables at breakfast, fried with

---

**TRAVEL YOUR TASTEBUDS**

Eating in Taiwan can be an overwhelming experience, especially with so many delicious foods to try. It's important to venture beyond the more conventional dishes of fried rice (*chǎofàn*) or fried noodles (*chǎomiàn*) that seem to be available at every hole in the wall roadside stand. What about a savoury dish of wontons (*húndún*), filled with leeks and minced pork?

For a meal on the run, consider picking up an omelette stuffed with pickled radishes, spring onions and filled with hot sauce (*jiānbǐng*). If time is not an issue, sit down to a simmering pot of vegetables and meats, cooked in a spicy broth (*huǒ guō*).

For adventurous eaters, may we suggest delectable stinky tofu (*chòu dòufu* – some say it's the equivalent to European stinky cheese. Or how about fried sandworms (*chǎo shāchóng*), a speciality of Kinmen and best served hot, and – last but not least – Hakka style stir-fried ginger intestines (*jiāngsī chǎo dàcháng*)?

tiny shrimps, pork or vegetables and eaten at lunch or as a snack. Plain steamed white rice accompanies most restaurant meals, except formal banquets, where it won't be served at all.

The art of rice cultivation was first brought to Taiwan by settlers from mainland China. There are three kinds of rice grown in Taiwan: sticky rice, which is used in rice pudding, rice cakes, dumplings and sausages or served plain with gravy; Penglai rice, a short polished rice that comes from Japan; and Tsailai rice, which is most often ground and used in rice noodles.

## Noodles

Noodles are thought to have originated in northern China during the Han dynasty (206–220 BC) when the Chinese developed techniques for large-scale flour grinding. Not only were noodles nutritious, cheap and versatile, they were portable and could be stored for long periods. Legend credits Marco Polo with having introduced noodles to Italy in 1295.

Chinese like to eat noodles on birthdays and on the New Year, because their long thin shape symbolises longevity. That's why it's bad luck to break noodles before cooking them.

Taiwan has several types of noodles which are worth mentioning. Hand-pulled noodles *(lā miàn)* are created when the noodle puller repeatedly stretches a piece of wheat-flour dough, folding it over and stretching again, until a network of noodle strands materialise. Thin, translucent noodles made from rice flour are common in the city's Southeast Asian restaurants.

## Soup

Many Taiwanese will insist that a balanced meal simply must have soup. Traditionally it was the beverage component of the meal; nowadays it shares that role with other liquids. A balanced meal contributes to the balance of Yin and Yang in the body (and thus a body's health), and soup is the main vehicle for the delivery of medicinal and balance-enhancing properties of foods. It gives you heat in winter and keeps you cool in summer.

## REGIONAL CUISINES IN TAIWAN

Chinese cuisine in Taiwan can be divided into several styles of cooking, though the boundaries are often blurred. Generally, Chinese food in Taiwan falls into Taiwanese, Hakka, Cantonese, Fujianese, Sichuanese, Beijing and Shanghainese categories. See the Menu Decoder (p56) for pinyin and Taiwanese spellings of dishes described in the following sections.

## Taiwanese

It's not easy to come up with a clear definition of Taiwanese food, as it's been influenced over the past several hundred years by various groups of people who arrived on the island's shores. As a rule, Taiwanese cooking is rather rustic, with an emphasis on seafood, sweet potatoes and taro root, cooked very simply without a lot of fuss. Chicken rates second in popularity to seafood, followed by pork, beef and lamb. Little fish stir-fried with peanuts and pickled vegetables *(xiǎoyú huāshēng)* is an example of a Taiwanese favourite. Something completely unique to Taiwan is its use of a local variant of basil *(jiǔcéngtǎ)*, which frequently flavours soups and fish dishes. The Taiwanese like to cook with chilli, though dishes are never as mouth-searing as those in Sichuanese cuisine.

**DID YOU KNOW?**

There are 44 different cooking methods in Chinese cuisine.

## Hakka

Hakka cuisine is having a renaissance in Taiwan, with Hakka-style dishes being featured in restaurants across the country. The dishes of the Hakka are very rich and hearty, suitable for people who historically made their living as farmers and needed plenty of energy to work the fields. Dishes are often salty and vinegary, with strong flavours. Pork is a favourite of the Hakka, often cut up into large pieces, fried and then stewed in a marinade.

Hakka cuisine is also known for its tasty snacks. Some of these include salty flour balls made from mushrooms *(zhà shūcài bǐng),* shrimp and pork turnip cakes *(kèjiāguǒ)* and sticky rice dipped in sugar or peanut powder *(kèjiā máshǔ).*

## Cantonese

Sichuan food is known as the hottest of all China's cuisines, so take care when ordering.

This is what non-Chinese consider 'Chinese' food, largely because most émigré restaurateurs originate from Guangdong (Canton) or Hong Kong. Cantonese flavours are generally more subtle than other Chinese styles – almost sweet, with very few spicy dishes. Sweet-and-sour and oyster sauces are common. The Cantonese are almost religious about the importance of fresh ingredients, which is why so many restaurants are lined with tanks full of finned and shell-clad creatures.

Not only are the ingredients more varied than elsewhere in China, but the methods of preparation also reach their peak of sophistication in the south, where the appearance and texture of foods are prized alongside their freshness. Such refinement is a far cry from the austere cuisine of the north and the earthy fare of the west. Consequently, the southerners' gourmandise and exotic tastes – for dogs, cats, monkeys, lizards and rats – have earned them a long-established reputation around China.

Expensive dishes – some truly tasty, others that appeal more for their 'face' value – include abalone, shark's fin and bird's nest. Pigeon is a Cantonese speciality, served in various ways but most commonly roasted.

Cantonese dim sum *(diǎnxīn)* snacks are famous and can be found in restaurants around Taiwan's bigger cities. Apart from barbecued pork dumplings, you'll find spring rolls *(chūn juǎn),* flat rice noodles *(héfěn),* rice porridge *(zhōu)* and, of course, the acquired taste of chickens' feet.

## Fujianese

Fujianese cuisine is popular throughout Taiwan, and was brought to the island by the many Fujian mainlanders who immigrated in the 18th and 20th centuries. Fujian cuisine dominates on the Taiwan Strait islands of Matsu and Kinmen, which are only a stone's throw away from Fujian province. The cuisine is best known for its seafood, often cooked in red wine and simmered slowly in dark soy sauce, sugar and spices. One of Fujian's most famous dishes is 'Buddha Jumps Over the Wall', a stew of seafood, chicken, duck and pork simmered in a jar of rice wine. The dish got its name because it is believed that the smell is so delicious Buddha would climb a wall for a taste.

It is in this region that Chinese vegetarian cuisine reached its apex, partly thanks to the availability of fresh ingredients and partly because of the specialisation of generations of chefs. As might be expected, seasoning is light to allow the natural flavours of the fresh ingredients to be fully appreciated.

## Sichuanese

Sichuan food is known as the hottest of all China's cuisines, so take care when ordering. Lethal red chillies (introduced by Spanish traders in the early Qing dynasty), aniseed, peppercorns and pungent 'flower pepper' are used, and dishes are simmered to give the chilli peppers time to work into the food. Meats are often marinated, pickled or otherwise processed before cooking, which is generally by stir- or explode-frying.

Famous dishes include camphor tea duck *(zhāngchá yāzi)*, Granny Ma's tofu *(mápó dòufu)* and spicy chicken with peanuts *(gōngbǎo jīdīng)*. Sichuan is a long distance from the coast, so pork, chicken and beef – not seafood – are the staples.

## Beijing

In the north of mainland China wheat or millet, rather than rice, is traditional. Its most common incarnations are steamed dumplings and noodles, while arguably the most famous Chinese dish of all, Peking duck, is also served with typical northern ingredients: wheat pancakes, spring onions and fermented bean paste. The range of vegetables is limited in the north, so there is a heavy reliance on freshwater fish and chicken; cabbage is ubiquitous and seems to fill any available space on trains, buses and lorries in the winter.

## Shanghainese

The cuisine of Shanghai is generally sweeter and oilier than China's other cuisines, and features a lot of fish and seafood, especially cod, river eel and shrimp. The word for fish *(yú)* is a homonym for 'plenty' or 'surplus'; fish is a mandatory dish for most banquets and celebrations.

Common Shanghainese fish dishes include fish with corn and pine nuts *(sōngrén yùmǐ)*, Songjiang perch *(lúyú)*, pomfret *(chāngyú)* and yellow croaker *(huángyú)*. Fish is usually steamed but can be stir-fried, pan-fried or grilled.

Other Shanghainese dishes are cold salty chicken *(xiánjī)*, which tastes better than it sounds, and drunken chicken *(zuìjī)*, because it is marinated in Shaoxing rice wine. 'Lion's head' *(shīzitóu)* is actually steamed pork meatballs; a variation on the theme is crab meat mixed with meatballs *(xièfěn shī tóuzi)*.

> **DID YOU KNOW?**
> Peanuts are a symbol of longevity to the Chinese.

# DRINKS
## Tea & Coffee

Tea is a fundamental part of Chinese life. In fact, an old Chinese saying identifies tea as one of the seven basic necessities of life, along with fuel, oil, rice, salt, soy sauce and vinegar. The Chinese were the first to cultivate tea, and the art of brewing and drinking tea has been popular since the Tang dynasty (AD 618–907). Fujian settlers introduced tea to Taiwan over 200 years ago; a fondness for the beverage quickly took hold and tea became one of Taiwan's main exports.

Nowadays, coffee has displaced tea somewhat in popularity because of its romantic appeal. However, wherever you go in Taiwan it is common to see groups of old men gathered around tables in parks or in front of temples chatting and drinking tea from small clay teapots. These teapots can be found in teashops all over Taiwan and come in a mind-boggling array of sizes, shapes and quality. Some are truly works of art, decorated with poems and exquisitely carved. Taiwan has a fair share of teahouses, many tucked away off busy streets, that offer a tranquil escape from city life.

Taiwan produces some excellent teas. Dongding Wulong tea is the most prized in Taiwan and sells around the world. It's a green tea, and only allowed to ferment for half the length of black tea to bring out the flavour and aroma. After the leaves are picked, they go through a process called 'warm rolling', where they are bruised to aid in the fermentation process and then dried.

The Japanese introduced to Taiwan a love for coffee and it's not hard to find a decent cup of coffee on the island, though it won't be cheap. Gone are the days when all you could find was a cup of instant mud. Now, even the humblest of roadside stands usually boasts a cappuccino maker. Expect to pay NT90 to NT100 for a cup in one of Taiwan's ubiquitous cafés, more in upmarket restaurants. Starbucks has hit Taiwan in a big way and is popular with Taiwan's young and hip.

On almost every street corner are bubble-tea shops, small stands specialising in bubble tea, a mixture of tea, milk, flavouring, sugar and giant black tapioca balls. Also called pearl tea, the sweet drink is popular with students who gather at tea stands after school to socialise and relax.

Bubble tea comes in an infinite variety of flavours; passionfruit, papaya and taro are a few of the most common. The pastel coloured drinks are served in clear cups with giant straws, so that you can sip up the chewy tapioca balls that rest at the bottom. Some find the gummy texture of the tapioca balls repellent but many others find that the cold, sweet drink is a perfect refresher on a sticky summer day.

> **Bubble tea comes in an infinite variety of flavours; passionfruit, papaya and taro are a few of the most common.**

### Juices

Fresh fruit stands selling juices and smoothies are all over Taiwan, and these drinks make wonderful thirst quenchers on a hot summer day. All you have to do is point at the fruits you want and the person standing behind the counter will whip them up in a blender for you, adding water or milk. Especially good are iced papaya milkshakes with banana.

Generally, you'll find that fresh fruit juices sold on the streets are cheaper than in the West. Expect to pay around NT20 to NT30 a cup.

## WHERE TO EAT & DRINK

Taiwan offers a variety of restaurants to suit any budget. At the low end of the scale, night markets offer the most choices and the best opportunities for trying local foods. Always ask before ordering, though, as some items (like seafood) can be more expensive than they look. Night markets open in the early evenings and stay open until the wee hours of the morning.

Budget eats can also be found in the many generic-looking eateries that crowd the cities' main streets and alleys. These places usually offer good food in no-frill surroundings. Portions are filling and cheap. You should expect to pay around NT80 to NT100 for a meal. You'll know if it's a good (and hygienic) place to eat if it's full of locals. Small restaurants often open in the morning and stay open until late at night, sometimes closing for a few hours in the afternoon if business is light.

More upmarket restaurants can vary from casual to formal and food prices will be higher than the food served in roadside stands and small family-run eateries, though the quality may not differ.

The most upmarket restaurants are often located in five-star hotels and it's a good idea to book a table ahead of time if going with a group of friends. Note that formal rarely means black tie to the Chinese, it generally means dressy – avoid wearing flip-flops and shorts. Tipping is not common practice.

Larger cities in Taiwan offer a wide choice of restaurants serving Western foods. Steakhouses have become quite popular with the locals and Italian-style restaurants are fairly common. Taipei has a large international restaurant scene with restaurants serving dishes from around the globe.

Restaurants generally open at around noon for lunch, close around 2pm and reopen in the evening for dinner. Bars often keep long hours in Taiwan, opening in the afternoon and closing late at night. Most bars offer a limited menu, some offer full-course meals. Expect to pay around NT150 or more for a beer.

## Quick Eats

Eating in Taiwan's colourful night markets is an experience not to be missed. Some of the island's best treats can be sampled in the markets, making it a gourmet's paradise. Taiwan's markets are fairly hygienic, though make sure to eat only at the busiest of places to avoid getting sick.

Dumplings *(shuǐjiǎo)* are fantastic in Taiwan and a delicious, inexpensive way to fill up. They're best described as Chinese ravioli, stuffed with meat, spring onion and greens. They are sometimes served by the bowl in a soup, sometimes dry by weight (250g or half a *jīn* is normally enough). Locals mix chilli *(làjiāo)*, vinegar *(cù)* and soy sauce *(jiàngyóu)* in a bowl according to taste and dip the ravioli in. Watch out – vinegar and soy sauce look almost identical! The slippery buggers can be tricky to eat with chopsticks so don't wear white as you'll get sprayed in soy whenever you drop them in the bowl. Dumplings are often created by family minifactories – one person stretches the pastry, another makes the filling and a third spoons the filling into the pastry, finishing with a little twist.

Other street snacks include fried tofu *(zhá doùfú)*, tea eggs (soaked in soy sauce; *cháyè dàn)*, tofu soaked in soy sauce *(lǔ doùfú)* and baked sweet potatoes *(kǎo fānshǔ)*, which can be bought by weight.

Keep an eye open for Thousand Year Eggs *(pídàn)* – ducks' eggs that are covered in straw and stored underground for six months (the traditional recipe has them soaked in horses' urine before burial!). The yolk becomes green and the white becomes jelly. More interesting snacks available at markets include chickens' feet *(jī jiǎo)*, pigs' ears *(zhū ěrduo)*, pigs' trotters *(zhū jiǎo)* and even pigs' faces *(zhū tóupí)*.

## VEGETARIANS & VEGANS

The Chinese are masters at adding variety to vegetarian cooking and creating 'mock meat' dishes. Chinese vegetarian food is based on tofu or gluten to which chefs do some miraculous things. Not only is it made to taste like any food you could possibly think of, it's also made to look like it. A dish that is sculptured to look like spareribs or a chicken can be made from layered pieces of dried tofu, or fashioned from mashed taro root.

Buddhist vegetarian restaurants are easy to find. Just look for the gigantic *savastika* (an ancient Buddhist symbol that looks like a reverse swastika) hung in front of the restaurant.

> Eating in Taiwan's colourful night markets is an experience not to be missed.

---

**TAIWAN'S TOP FIVE**

- Shida Night Market, Taipei (p94)
- Mountain Legend Café, Qingan Village, Miaoli County (p145)
- Grandma's Eatery, Matsu (p277)
- Do It True, Taipei (p97)
- Zorba Garden, Shanyuan, Taitung County (p181)

## WHINING & DINING

Taiwan is a child-friendly place and children are welcome in restaurants. Budget eateries won't have special menus for children nor will they supply booster seats. Higher end restaurants should be able to offer these things. Taiwan has many restaurants that offer set meals and cater to families. Some of these places have special meals for children, usually consisting of fried chicken or fish. Fast-food restaurants are another option for their child-friendly atmosphere.

Taiwan's supermarkets sell Western baby formula and puréed baby foods, as well as infant cereals. For more information on children see p311.

**DID YOU KNOW?**

By the 14th century vegetarian cooking was already an independent school of Chinese cuisine.

## HABITS & CUSTOMS

A traditional breakfast in Taiwan usually consists of watery rice with seaweed, clay-oven rolls and steamed buns, served plain or with fillings. This is generally washed down with hot soybean milk, sweetened or plain. Nowadays, a Taiwan breakfast shows strong Western influence, with fried eggs, sandwiches and coffee being popular items for school kids and office workers to eat on the run. Most breakfast places open at about 7am and close mid-morning.

The Taiwanese generally eat lunch between 11.30am and 2pm, many taking their mid-day meal from any number of small eateries on the streets. Self-serve cafeterias *(zìzhù cān)* are a good option, and offer plenty of meat and vegetable dishes to choose from.

Dinner in Taiwan is usually eaten from 5pm to 11pm, though some restaurants and food stalls in bigger cities stay open 24 hours. Dinner choices are much the same as lunch, though night markets have many more snack foods and are the places to go to for tasty barbeque and stinky tofu, commonly sold at night. In international hotels and restaurants, dinner is a more formal affair and can include everything from sirloin steak to that Thai favourite, *phàt thai* (rice noodles stir-fried with egg, tofu and peanuts).

Eating Chinese-style is well established in the West and wouldn't faze most people these days. It's a rewarding way to eat for many reasons. First, eating together really does mean sharing food since all diners eat dishes from communal bowls, making it much more of a social event than Western-style eating (and arguably contributing to closer family bonds). On the one hand, no one wants to appear greedy by taking too much and depriving others. On the other, people can eat as much or as little as they want from each bowl, according to their own taste, without offending the host. This method of serving even allows people to select combinations of foods to eat together to suit their own taste, particularly when a variety of sauces and dips are provided as accompaniments.

Although Chinese restaurants have a reputation in the West for being noisy, tasteless and basic (Formica tables, tacky calendars and plastic chopsticks), this only shows that Westerners don't appreciate the same things when going out to eat. While most Westerners need to feel they've got value for money by the quality of the ambience and service, for most Chinese the quality of the food is paramount. Good restaurants gain a reputation solely for the quality of their food, no matter what the décor and no matter how far out of the way.

There aren't many rules of etiquette attached to Chinese restaurants. In fact, you may find that Chinese table manners are extremely relaxed. Large groups in particular often wreak carnage and desolation wherever they dine.

## BANQUETS

The banquet is the apex of the Chinese dining experience. Virtually all significant business deals in China are clinched at the banquet table.

Dishes are served in sequence, beginning with cold appetisers and continuing through 10 or more courses. Soup, usually a thin broth to aid digestion, is generally served after the main course.

The idea is to serve or order far more than everyone can eat. Empty bowls imply a stingy host. Rice is considered a cheap filler and rarely appears at a banquet – don't ask for it, as this would imply that the snacks and main courses are insufficient, causing embarrassment to the host.

It's best to wait for some signal from the host before digging in. You will most likely be invited to take the first taste. Often your host will serve it to you, placing a piece of meat, chicken or fish in your bowl. If a whole fish is served, you might be offered the head, the cheeks of which are considered to be the tastiest part. It's OK to decline; someone else will gladly devour the delicacy.

Never drink alone. Imbibing is conducted via toasts, which will usually commence with a general toast by the host, followed by the main guest reply toast and then settle down to frequent toasts to individuals. A toast is conducted by raising your glass in both hands in the direction of the person you wish to toast and crying out *gānbēi*, literally 'dry the glass'. Chinese do not clink glasses. Drain your glass in one hit. It is not unusual for everyone to end up very drunk, though at very formal banquets this is frowned upon. Raising your tea or water glass in a toast is not very respectful so unless you have deep-rooted convictions against alcohol, it's best to drink at least a mouthful.

Don't be late for a formal banquet; it's considered extremely rude. The banquet ends when the food and toasts end – the Chinese don't linger after the meal. You may find yourself being applauded when you enter a large banquet. It is polite to applaud back.

Ang Lee's *Eat Drink Man Woman* is a wonderful movie about a Taiwanese chef and his three estranged daughters. The best part about this movie are the close-ups of food!

---

### EATING DOS & DON'TS

■ Every customer gets an individual bowl of rice or a small soup bowl. It is quite acceptable to hold the bowl close to your lips and shovel the contents into your mouth using chopsticks. If the food contains bones, just put them out on the tablecloth or into a separate bowl, if one is provided. Restaurants are prepared for this – the staff change the tablecloth after each customer leaves.

■ Remember to fill your neighbours' tea cups when they are empty, as yours will be filled by them. You can thank the pourer by tapping your middle finger on the table gently. On no account serve yourself tea without serving others first. When your teapot needs a refill, signal this to the waiter by taking the lid off the pot.

■ Chinese toothpick etiquette is similar to that of neighbouring Asian countries. One hand wields the toothpick while the other shields the mouth from prying eyes.

■ Probably the most important piece of etiquette comes with the bill: although you are expected to try to pay, you shouldn't argue too hard, as the one who extended the invitation will inevitably foot the bill. Going Dutch is unheard of except among the closest of friends.

■ Never commit the terrible faux pas of sticking your chopsticks into your rice. Two chopsticks stuck vertically into a rice bowl resemble incense sticks in a bowl of ashes and is considered an omen of death.

## EAT YOUR WORDS

See also the Language chapter (p343) for more useful terms and phrases to help you enjoy eating out in Taiwan.

### Useful Phrases

| | | |
|---|---|---|
| I don't want MSG. | *Wǒ bú yào wèijīng.* | 我不要味精 |
| I'm vegetarian. | *Wǒ chī sù.* | 我吃素 |
| Not too spicy | *Bù yào tài là.* | 不要太辣 |
| menu | *càidān* | 菜單 |
| bill (check) | *mǎidān/jiézhàng* | 買單結帳 |
| set meal (no menu) | *tàocān* | 套餐 |
| Let's eat. | *Chī fàn.* | 吃飯 |
| Cheers! | *Gānbēi!* | 乾杯! |
| chopsticks | *kuàizi* | 筷子 |
| knife | *dàozi* | 刀子 |
| fork | *chāzi* | 叉子 |
| spoon | *tiáogēng/tāngchí* | 調羹/湯匙 |
| hot | *rède* | 熱的 |
| ice cold | *bīngde* | 冰的 |

### Menu Decoder

#### RICE DISHES

| | | |
|---|---|---|
| *jīròu chǎofàn* | 雞肉炒飯 | fried rice with chicken |
| *dàn chǎofàn* | 蛋炒飯 | fried rice with egg |
| *báifàn* | 白飯 | steamed white rice |
| *lǔroù fàn* | 魯肉飯 | pork mince in soy sauce with rice |
| *sān bǎo fàn* | 三寶飯 | BBQ pork, chicken & roast duck with rice |
| *shūcài chǎofàn* | 蔬菜炒飯 | fried rice with vegetables |
| *xīfàn/zhōu* | 稀飯/粥 | watery rice porridge (congee) |
| *zhà páigǔ fàn* | 炸排骨飯 | deep fried pork chop with rice |

#### NOODLE DISHES

| | | |
|---|---|---|
| *gān miàn* | 乾麵 | noodles (not soupy) |
| *húndún miàn* | 餛飩麵 | wontons & noodles |
| *jīsī chǎomiàn* | 雞絲炒麵 | fried noodles with chicken |
| *jīsī tāngmiàn* | 雞絲湯麵 | soupy noodles with chicken |
| *májiàng miàn* | 麻醬麵 | sesame paste noodles |
| *niúròu chǎomiàn* | 牛肉炒麵 | fried noodles with beef |
| *niúròu miàn* | 牛肉麵 | soupy beef noodles |
| *ròusī chǎomiàn* | 肉絲炒麵 | fried noodles with pork |
| *shūcài chǎomiàn* | 蔬菜炒麵 | fried noodles with vegetables |
| *tāngmiàn* | 湯麵 | noodles in soup |
| *xiārén chǎomiàn* | 蝦仁炒麵 | fried noodles with shrimp |
| *zhájiàng miàn* | 炸醬麵 | bean & meat noodles |

#### BREAD, BUNS & DUMPLINGS

| | | |
|---|---|---|
| *cōngyóu bǐng* | 蔥油餅 | spring onion pancakes |
| *guōtiē* | 鍋貼 | pot stickers/pan-grilled dumplings |
| *mántóu* | 饅頭 | steamed buns |
| *ròu bāozǐ* | 肉包子 | steamed meat buns |
| *shāobǐng* | 燒餅 | clay oven rolls |
| *shuǐjiǎo* | 水餃 | boiled dumplings |
| *shǔijiān bāo* | 水煎包 | pan-grilled buns |
| *sùcài bāozǐ* | 素菜包子 | steamed vegetable buns |
| *xiǎo lóng tāng bāo* | 小籠湯包 | steamed meat buns & meat sauce |

## SOUP

| | | |
|---|---|---|
| gě lì tāng | 蛤蠣湯 | clam & turnip soup |
| gòng wán tāng | 貢丸湯 | Taiwanese meatball soup |
| húndùn tāng | 餛飩湯 | wonton soup |
| ròu gēng | 肉羹湯 | meat potage |
| sān xiān tāng | 三鮮湯 | three kinds of seafood soup |
| suānlà tāng | 酸辣湯 | hot & sour soup |
| yóu yú gēng | 魷魚羹 | cuttlefish potage |

## VEGETABLE & TOFU DISHES

| | | |
|---|---|---|
| báicài xiān shuānggū | 白菜鮮雙菇 | bok choy & mushrooms |
| càifǔ dàn | 菜脯蛋 | omelette with pickled radishes |
| chòu dòufu | 臭豆腐 | stinky tofu |
| cuìpí dòufu | 脆皮豆腐 | crispy skin tofu |
| hēimù'ěr mèn dòufu | 黑木耳燜豆腐 | tofu with wood ear mushrooms |
| jiāngzhí qīngdòu | 薑汁青豆 | string beans with ginger |
| lúshuǐ dòufu | 滷水豆腐 | smoked tofu |
| shāguō dòufu | 砂鍋豆腐 | clay pot tofu |
| táng liánǒu | 糖蓮藕 | sweet & sour lotus root cakes |

## BEEF DISHES

| | | |
|---|---|---|
| háoyóu niúròu | 蠔油牛肉 | beef with oyster sauce |
| hóngshāo niúròu | 紅燒牛肉 | beef braised in soy sauce |
| niúròu fàn | 牛肉飯 | beef with rice |
| tiěbǎn niúròu | 鐵板牛肉 | beef steak platter |

## CHICKEN DISHES

| | | |
|---|---|---|
| háoyóu jīkuài | 蠔油雞塊 | diced chicken in oyster sauce |
| hóngshāo jīkuài | 紅燒雞塊 | chicken braised in soy sauce |
| jītuǐ fàn | 雞腿飯 | chicken leg with rice |
| tángcù jīdīng | 糖醋雞丁 | sweet & sour chicken |

www.sinica.edu.tw/tit
/dining/0695
For a general overview of
Taiwanese cuisine.

## PORK DISHES

| | | |
|---|---|---|
| dōng pō ròu | 東坡肉 | stewed pork with brown sauce |
| gūlǔ ròu | 咕嚕肉 | sweet & sour pork |
| háoyóu ròusī | 蠔油肉絲 | pork with oyster sauce |
| jiàngbào ròudīng | 醬爆肉丁 | diced pork with soy sauce |
| páigǔ fàn | 排骨飯 | pork chop with rice |
| ròu yuán | 肉圓 | deep-fried pork-mince buns |

## DUCK DISHES

| | | |
|---|---|---|
| yāròu fàn | 鴨肉飯 | duck with rice |
| yāxiě gāo | 鴨血糕 | frozen duck blood & rice |

## SEAFOOD DISHES

| | | |
|---|---|---|
| gélì | 蛤蠣 | clams |
| gōngbào xiārén | 宮爆蝦仁 | diced shrimp with peanuts |
| hóngshāo yú | 紅燒魚 | fish braised in soy sauce |
| kē zǎi jiān | 蚵仔煎 | oyster omelette |
| lóngxiā | 龍蝦 | lobster |
| pángxiè | 螃蟹 | crab |
| xiǎoyú huāshēng | 小魚花生 | fish stir-fried with peanuts & pickled vegetables |
| yóuyú | 魷魚 | squid |
| zhāngyú | 章魚 | octopus |

## MAINLAND CHINESE SPECIALITIES
### Hakka Dishes

| | | |
|---|---|---|
| *bǎntiáo* | 板條 | flat rice noodles |
| *chéngzhī jīliǔ* | 橙汁雞柳 | chicken & orange sauce |
| *kèjiāguǒ* | 客家粿 | shrimp & pork turnip cakes |
| *kèjiā máshǔ* | 客家麻糬 | sticky rice dipped in sugar or peanut powder |
| *kèjiā xiǎo chǎo* | 客家小炒 | stir-fried cuttlefish, leeks, tofu & pork |
| *kǔguā xiándàn* | 苦瓜鹹蛋 | salty eggs & bitter melon |
| *zhà shūcài bǐng* | 炸蔬菜餅 | salty flour balls made from mushrooms |

### Cantonese Dishes

| | | |
|---|---|---|
| *chasiu* | 叉燒酥 | barbecued pork dumplings |
| *dōngjiāng yánjú jī* | 東江盐焗雞 | salt-baked chicken |
| *héfěn* | 河粉 | flat rice noodles |
| *hóngshāo dàpái chì* | 紅燒大排翅 | stewed shark's fin with pork & chicken feet |
| *mì zhī chāshāo* | 蜜汁叉燒 | roast pork with honey |
| *tàiyé jī* | 太爺雞 | smoked chicken with tea & sugar |
| *zhōu* | 粥 | Cantonese rice porridge |

### Fujianese Dishes

| | | |
|---|---|---|
| *fó tiào qiáng* | 佛跳墙 | Buddha Jumps Over the Wall |
| *méicài gān kòuròu* | 梅菜干扣肉 | steamed pork with dried mustard |
| *qīxīng yúwán tāng* | 七星魚丸湯 | fish ball soup with eel, shrimp & pork |

### Sichuanese Dishes

| | | |
|---|---|---|
| *guàiwèi jī* | 怪味雞 | shredded chicken in a hot pepper & sesame sauce |
| *gōngbǎo jīdīng* | 宮保雞丁 | spicy chicken with peanuts |
| *huíguō ròu* | 回鍋肉 | twice-cooked pork with salty & hot sauce |
| *málà dòufu* | 麻辣豆腐 | spicy tofu |
| *mápó dòufu* | 麻婆豆腐 | Granny Ma's tofu |
| *zhāngchá yāzi* | 樟茶鴨 | camphor tea duck |

### Shanghainese Dishes

| | | |
|---|---|---|
| *dàzhá xiè* | 大閘蟹 | hairy crabs |
| *jīngdū páigǔ* | 京都排骨 | Mandarin-style pork ribs |
| *lúyú* | 鱸魚 | Songjiang perch |
| *shīzitóu* | 獅子頭 | 'lion's head' (steamed pork meatballs) |
| *sōngrén yùmǐ* | 松仁玉米 | fish with corn & pine nuts |
| *xiánshuǐjī* | 鹹水雞 | cold salty chicken |
| *xiāngsū jī* | 香酥雞 | crispy chicken |
| *xièfěn shīzitóu* | 蟹粉獅子頭 | lion's head meatballs with crab |
| *zuìjī* | 醉雞 | drunken chicken |

## DRINKS
### Alcohol

| | | |
|---|---|---|
| *bái pútáo jiǔ* | 白葡萄酒 | white wine |
| *hóng pútáo jiǔ* | 紅葡萄酒 | red wine |
| *mǐjiǔ* | 米酒 | rice wine |
| *píjiǔ* | 啤酒 | beer |

## Nonalcoholic

| | | |
|---|---|---|
| *liǔdīng zhī* | 柳丁汁 | orange juice |
| *dòujiāng* | 豆漿 | soybean milk |
| *kuàngquán shuǐ* | 礦泉水 | mineral water |
| *niúnǎi* | 牛奶 | milk |
| *qìshuǐ* | 汽水 | soft drink (soda) |
| *shuǐ* | 水 | water |
| *yézi zhī* | 椰子汁 | coconut juice |

## Tea & Coffee

| | | |
|---|---|---|
| *hóng chá* | 紅茶 | black tea |
| *júhuā chá* | 菊花茶 | chrysanthemum tea |
| *kāfēi* | 咖啡 | coffee |
| *lǜ chá* | 綠茶 | green tea |
| *luòshén chá* | 洛神茶 | hibiscus tea |
| *mài chá* | 麥茶 | wheat tea |
| *mòlìhuā chá* | 茉莉花茶 | jasmine tea |
| *wūlóng chá* | 烏龍茶 | oolong tea |
| *zhēnzhū nǎi chá* | 珍珠奶茶 | milk tea with tapioca balls |

# Taipei

CONTENTS

If you want to understand Taipei, just cross the street. The little green men on the city's 'walk' lights don't just flash; they're animated, ambling amiably as displays above them count down the seconds until the light changes back to red. As you cross, the street alongside you turns into a river of trucks, buses and cars, fearless taxis trying to turn precariously close, and scooters too numerous to count. In those last crucial seconds, the little green men go into double time.

That's Taipei in a nutshell. Taiwan's capital is frenetic, energetic and busy, busy, busy. Most of the city is barely a century old, but how it's made up for lost time!

It wasn't long ago that Taipei exemplified the ills of rampant, rapid urbanisation: stultifying traffic, ugly architecture and dense smog. Today some backstreets (and even some *front* streets) are as jumbled as ever, but the city's bustling shopping malls and department stores, art venues, theatres, cafés and clubs feel undeniably cosmopolitan. New skyscrapers, including the world's tallest building, are adding something of a skyline. The Mass Rapid Transit (MRT), Taipei's underground railway system, has helped unclog streets and reduce pollution.

And, of course, Taipei is one of the world's great food capitals. In no other city is Chinese cuisine present in such breadth and quality – from Beijing duck to Cantonese dim sum, as well as Taiwan's own indigenous foods – at budgets from ridiculously cheap to sublimely expensive.

Hurry up, the green man's leaving.

## HIGHLIGHTS

- Take in five millennia of Chinese art history at the **National Palace Museum** (p79)
- Shop, snack or just taste the atmosphere in Taipei's bustling **night markets** (p105), or the fun and fashionable **Ximending** (p70) and **Xinyi** (p77) districts
- Experience spirituality at **Longshan Temple** (p69), **Xingtian Temple** (p74), **Hsiahai City God Temple** (p76), **Confucius Temple** (p75), **Chihnan Temple** (p83) or at the **Museum of World Religions** (p84)
- Get a glimpse into the life of Taiwan's one-time dictator at **Chiang Kai-shek Memorial Hall** (p69)
- Hike, soak or do both in **Beitou** (p107) and **Yangmingshan National Park** (p110)

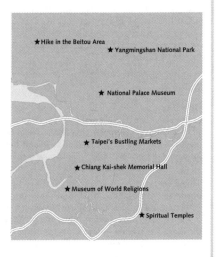

★ Hike in the Beitou Area
★ Yangmingshan National Park
★ National Palace Museum
★ Taipei's Bustling Markets
★ Chiang Kai-shek Memorial Hall
★ Museum of World Religions
★ Spiritual Temples

| ■ TELEPHONE CODE: 03 | ■ POPULATION: 2.64 MILLION |
| --- | --- |

**TAIPEI**

# HISTORY

Some four million years ago, the basin that houses Taipei was a lake surrounded by mountains.

Fast forward to the last millennium: the area was variously under control of Dutch, Spanish and Qing-dynasty forces. In 1709, settlers from China's Fujian province received permission from the Qing government to emigrate to Taiwan, and eventually founded the community of Manka (now the Wanhua District, p68) near the Danshui River. Manka, and later Dadaocheng (see Zhongshan, p74) became trading ports for tea and camphor and set the stage for more settlement from China, and economic development.

Taipei was incorporated into a prefecture in 1875, and construction of a walled city began in 1882. While the walls are long since gone (they formed a box bordered by the current Zhongshan S Rd, Aiguo W Rd, Zhonghua S Rd, Sec 1 and Zhongxiao W Rd, Sec 1), the North Gate and Little South Gate can still be seen (p70).

Under Japanese rule (1895–1945), Taipei became administrative headquarters for the island. Although the Japanese police ruled with an iron hand, Japanese engineers left a basic infrastructure, and buildings remaining from that era are among the city's most prized. After the decampment of the Nationalist forces of Chiang Kai-shek to Taipei in 1949, the city eventually grew to its present size (272 sq km) and governmental structure of 12 districts.

> **POPULATION TIMELINE**
>
> **1920** 170,000
> **1932** 600,000
> **1968** 1.56 million
> **present** 2.64 million

Today, Taipei is Taiwan's undisputed capital of politics, business and culture.

# ORIENTATION

The historic core of Taipei is just a tiny corner of the modern metropolis, in a section known as Wanhua, southwest of Taipei Main Station, near the Danshui River. The city spreads out from here, mostly to the east and north.

Central contemporary Taipei is constructed on a grid, with major streets running east-west and north-south. Taipei breaks these major streets up by direction (eg east and west) and then into sections numbered according to the distance from the central axis (Sec 1, Sec 2 etc). So, for example, the Fine Arts Museum is at 181 Zhongshan N Rd, Sec 3. Zhongshan Rd forms the central Y-axis, and a combination of Civil Blvd and Bade Rd makes the central X-axis.

Taipei also has numbered 'lanes', which generally run perpendicular to the main streets. Major sights, hotels and restaurants are located along the main streets, but for more intimate places you'll probably find yourself in the lanes. A typical address is 5 Lane 260, Guangfu S Rd. Lane 260 is where

---

**TAIPEI IN...**

**One Day**

Get an early start at Taipei's must-see, the **National Palace Museum** (p79). Make a late-afternoon stop at **Longshan Temple** (p69) and arrive in **Snake Alley** (p70) in time for its famous night market. If money is no object, dine at **Tainan Tien-tsu-mien** (p93), or head to the night market for dining *al fresco* and *à pied*. Finish with a show of Chinese opera at **Taipei Eye** (p100).

**Three Days**

In addition to the above, head to the Xinyi District to view the massive **statue of Sun Yat-sen** (p78) up close and learn about city history at the **Discovery Centre of Taipei** (p77). Head then to the excellent food court at **Taipei 101** (p78). Spend the afternoon shopping in the area or at the movies at **Warner Village Cinemas** (p104). Try a fashionable **lounge bar** (p102) at night.

For day three, get out of town. Start at the impressive gardens of the **Shilin Official Residence** (p81) of former president Chiang Kai-shek, and continue up to **Beitou** (p107) and its famous hot-spring retreats – whether you warm up, chill out or fill up, you can't go wrong.

260 would be if it were a building, and 5 indicates the building number within the lane (head here and you'll find the Italian restaurant Osteria Rialto; p97). Alleys are to lanes as lanes are to streets: the address of the Fortuna Hostel is 5 Alley 9, Lane 27, Tingzhou Rd, Sec 3, meaning that the alley is at position 9 along Lane 27, and so on. It looks complicated, but it's actually quite logical. Where the address includes a floor, we've included that too.

Many locales are an easy walk from the MRT; we've noted MRT stops where they are useful.

Taipei proper is divided into 12 districts (qū; Zhongshan, Xinyi, Beitou etc). Occasionally the names also correspond to districts of interest to visitors, but usually they're most useful as parts of postal addresses. More than likely, however, visitors will concentrate on neighbourhoods within these districts, notably Dinghao (east of the

## HANDY-DANDY STREET DECODER

One complication for visitors to Taipei is that streets go by so many names, at least in Roman letters. Until roughly the beginning of the 21st century, the city used the Wade-Giles system of Romanisation of Chinese place names, then it switched to Pinyin, the current standard in the Chinese-speaking world. But in practical terms there's no common approach to street names; spellings can be one way or the other, or even random, oddball spellings.

Add to that the fact that the city recently instituted a system of numbering its major streets. Numbered 'boulevards' run east-west, and numbered 'avenues' run north-south. The numbers of the boulevards (1st, 2nd etc) start at the southern end of the city, while the numbers of the avenues start at the western end. Theoretically, this numbering system was designed to help foreigners make sense of it all, but in practice locals have no idea which street corresponds to which number.

| Chinese | Wade-Giles | Pinyin | Number |
|---|---|---|---|
| **East-West Streets** | | | |
| 和平路 | Hoping Rd | Heping Rd | 1st Blvd |
| 信義路 | Hsinyi Rd | Xinyi Rd | 2nd Blvd |
| 仁愛路 | Jen-ai Rd | Renai Rd | 3rd Blvd |
| 忠孝路 | Chunghsiao Rd | Zhongxiao Rd | 4th Blvd |
| 市民大道 | Civil (aka Civic) Blvd | | 5th Blvd |
| 長安路/八德路 | Chang'an/Pateh Rds | Chang'an/Bade Rds | 6th Blvd |
| 南京路 | Nanking Rd | Nanjing Rd | 7th Blvd |
| 民生路 | | Minsheng Rd | 8th Blvd |
| 民權路 | Minchiuan Rd | Minquan Rd | 9th Blvd |
| 民族路 | Minchu Rd | Minzu Rd | 10th Blvd |
| **North-South Streets** | | | |
| 環河路 | Huanho Rd | Huanhe Rd | 1st Ave |
| 中華路 | Junghua Rd | Zhonghua Rd | 2nd Ave |
| 延平路 | Yenping Rd | Yanping Rd | 3rd Ave |
| 重慶路 | Chungching Rd | Chongqing Rd | 4th Ave |
| 承德路 | Chengteh Rd | Chengde Rd | 5th Ave |
| 中山路 | Chungshan Rd | Zhongshan Rd | 6th Ave |
| 林森路 | | Linsen Rd | 7th Ave |
| 新生北路/金山南路 | Hsinsheng N/Chingshan S Rds | Xinsheng N/Jinshan S Rds | 8th Ave |
| 松江路/新生南路 | Sungchiang/Hsinsheng S Rds | Songjiang/Xinsheng S Rds | 9th Ave |
| 建國路 | Chienkuo Rd | Jianguo Rd | 10th Ave |
| 復興路 | Fuhsing Rd | Fuxing Rd | 11th Ave |
| 敦化路 | Tunhwa Rd | Dunhua Rd | 12th Ave |
| 光復路 | Kongfu Rd | Guangfu Rd | 13th Ave |
| 基隆路 | Keelung Rd | | 14th Ave |

Danshui River

Ⓐ Ⓑ Ⓒ Ⓓ

**1** ①

15

• Bali

15

Danshui Ⓜ

See Danshui Map p116

2

Ⓜ Hongshulin

BEITOU

Shamaoshan (643m) ▲

Ⓜ Zhuwei

15

Fuxinggang Ⓜ

Ⓜ Xin Beitou

See Shilin & Tianmu Map p82

Ⓜ Zhongyi

Ⓜ Beitou

**2** ②

Guandu Ⓜ

▲ 3

2

Ⓜ Qiyan

Ⓜ Qilian

Ⓜ Shipai

2

Ⓜ

**3** ③

🌸

See Zhongshan Map p75

ZHONGSHAN

Ⓜ

Zhongqing N Rd

Xinsheng Rd

Jianguo Rd

3

1

DATUNG

Ⓜ

**4** ④
To Kaohsiung (320km)

1

5 Ⓜ

Taipei Main Station

ZHONGCHENG

Danshui River

Ⓜ

Ⓜ

Ⓜ

Ⓜ

Roosevelt Rd

Ⓜ Jiangzicui

WANHUA

Old Town Centre, Da'an & Shida Map p72

Ⓜ Xinpu

106

Gongguan Ⓜ

Hsintien River

Banqiao Ⓜ

5 🏛

Ⓜ Dingxi

**5** ⑤ 1

🚉 Banqiao Train Station
● 4

64

**9** ⑨

Ⓜ Yongan Market

Waniong

3

Ⓜ Jingan

Jingmei

Ⓜ Nanshijiao

Dapinglin

🌸 ③

64

Xindian City Hall

**6** ⑥

3

● Pitan

Xindian

To Hsinchu (70km)

110

0 ————— 10 km
0 ————— 6 miles

**E** **F** **G** **H**

PACIFIC OCEAN

Cisingshan (1120m)

Yangmingshan National Park

**SIGHTS & ACTIVITIES**
Chihnan Temple 木柵指南宮 .......................... **1** F5
Guandu Nature Park 關渡自然公園 .............. **2** C2
Guandu Temple 關渡宮 ................................. **3** B2
Lin Family Mansion & Garden 林家花園 ....... **4** B5
Museum Of World Religions
　　世界宗教博物館 ...................................... **5** D5
National Palace Museum 故宮博物院 ............ **6** E3
Shung Ye Museum of Formosan Aborigines
　　順益台灣原住民博物館 .......................... **7** E3
Taipei Zoo 木柵動物園 .................................. **8** E5

**EATING** 🍴 (p98)
Lian Hsin Yuan Vegetarian Restaurant
世界宗教博物館,
蓮心園素食餐廳 ........................................(see 5)

**ENTERTAINMENT** 🎭 (p100)
National Taiwan Junior College of
Performing Arts
　　國立台灣戲曲專科學校 .......................... **9** E3

SHILIN

See Yangmingshan National Park & Beitou Map pp112–13

**2**

**NEIHU**

🎭 9

Tahu Park

Keelung River

**1**

To Keelung (2km)

**3**

NGSHAN ✈

Sun Yat-sen Fwy

**5**

Keelung River

Xizhi ○

lanjing E Rd

Songshan Train Station

Nangang Train Station

Ⓜ Nangang

Ⓜ Kunyang

ll Blvd

**5** Ⓜ Houshanpi

ongxiao E Rd Ⓜ Ⓜ Ⓜ

Ⓜ Yongchun

Nankang ○ Tea Park

**4**

A'AN Keelung Rd

XINYI

Nine-Five ▲ Peak (374m)

North No.3 Fwy

**3**

NANKANG

See Songshan & Xinyi Map p80

Ⓜ Linguang

106

Ⓜ Xinhai

Wanfang Community

Ⓜ Muzha

Ⓜ Taipei Zoo

**5**

106

**5**

Ⓜ Wanfang Hospital

8 🏛

🏛 1

eizhang

WENSHAN

● Maokong

**6**

9

Pinglin ○

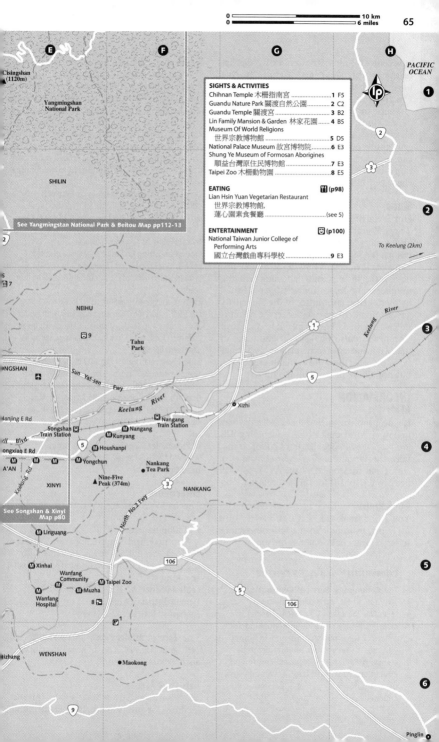

**TAIPEI**

city centre), Shida (the university district to the south), Shilin and Tianmu (to the north) and the mountain Yangmingshan, which dominates the northern city limits.

There are also several 'cities' within Taipei city limits (eg Banqiao). Taipei County also covers a wide area – this chapter covers only those portions of Taipei County that can be reached by MRT. For other locations, please consult the Northern Taiwan chapter (p119).

## Maps

Our favourite map for central Taipei is the *Taipei Visitor's Map* published by Asiamap and available free at hotels and tourist points. It's regularly updated and has street names in the current Pinyin spelling. It also depicts the all-important lanes and building numbers. The *Taipei Tourist Map* published by the tourism committee of the Taipei city government, covers a wider territory but is not as detailed. The Taipei Rapid Transit Corporation also publishes useful maps of the MRT and city, some broken up by station environs; these are available at stations, but not all are in stock all the time.

## INFORMATION
### ATMs

It's no problem to find an ATM anywhere in Taipei. Most major banks, including **ICBC** (cnr Zhongshan N & Nanjing E Rds) have ATMs. If that fails, the ubiquitous 7-Eleven convenience stores and McDonald's have ATMs as well. See Money (p318) for further information.

## Bookshops

You'll find book sellers at nearly every turn in Taipei, from hole-in-the-wall newsstands to large local chains. Not surprisingly, most

---

**COMMUNITY SERVICES CENTRE**

The **Community Services Centre** (Map p82; ☎ 2836 8134; www.community.com.tw; 25 Lane 290, Zhongshan N Rd, Sec 6, Tianmu) is a clearing house for foreigners looking for practical information on living in Taipei, whether it's newcomer orientation, understanding Chinese colleagues, continuing education, cooking classes, travel outings or – should you need it – Western-style counselling.

---

books are in Chinese, but in the larger stores you will find foreign-language books (mostly English) filed by subject with their Chinese counterparts. If you're interested in browsing smaller bookshops, around 40 shops vie for your business on Chongqing Rd, the long-standing bookshop street southwest of Taipei Main Station. Newsstands around the city (MRT stations and the like) typically carry an assortment of English-language magazines and newspapers.

**Caves Books** (Dūnhuáng Shūjú) Tianmu (Map p82; ☎ 2874 2199; 5 Lane 38, Tianyu St) Zhongshan (Map pp74-5; ☎ 2537 1666; 103 Zhongshan N Rd, Sec 2) Long-standing favourite among local expats, known for carrying books in English about learning Chinese.

**Crane Publishing Co Ltd** (Wénhè Chūbǎnshè; Map pp72-3; ☎ 2322 5437; 59 Chongqing S Rd, Sec 2) Teachers and students of ESL should head here for all their needs.

**Eslite** (Chéngpǐn; Map pp80-1; ☎ 2775 5977; 245 Dunhua S Rd) Taipei's most renowned bookshop, with locations all over town. The flagship Dunhua S Rd location is the first place most locals would look for foreign-language books, particularly on travel.

**fnac** (Fǎyǎkè; Map pp80-1; ☎ 8712 0331; Asiaworld Shopping Plaza, 337 Nanjing E Rd, Sec 3) French retailer selling everything from books to the latest hi-tech gadgets.

**GinGin's Taiwan** (Jīngjīng Shūkù Jīngpǐndiàn; Map pp72-3; ☎ 2364 2006; 7-14 Alley 8, Lane 210, Roosevelt Rd, Sec 3; MRT Guting) Gay and lesbian bookshop and café.

**Le Pigeonnier** (Xìngē Fǎguó Shūdiàn; Map pp72-3; ☎ 2517 2616; 9 Lane 97, Songjiang Rd) Specialist in French books.

## Emergency

The national emergency contact numbers are ☎ 110 for police and ☎ 119 for fire and ambulance.

You may find English speakers at police stations throughout town, but the following police stations have dedicated English-speaking staff:

**Central District** ( ☎ 2555 4275, 2556 6007)
**Tianmu District** ( ☎ 2881 3835)
**Zhongshan District** ( ☎ 2511 1395)

The **Foreign Affairs Police** (Map pp72-3; ☎ 2381 7494; 96 Yanping S Rd) can help with concerns such as visa extensions.

## Internet Access

Most hotels and even hostels have Internet facilities for guests to use. If you're bringing your own laptop, ADSL connections are common, and virtually any telephone will plug into your laptop modem – although you will need to check the access number for your particular service. However, watch the costs – they range from free to through-the-nose. See also the National Central Library (below).

## Laundry
Hostels and the YMCA have laundry machines on site, but getting your wash done at higher-end lodgings can be quite expensive. However, there are small cleaning shops in the alleys and lanes of many districts, especially around Shida, where local folk will take in your wash and have it ready for you the next day. Typical is **Shida Zizhu Xiyi** (Shīdà Zhìzhù Xǐyī; Map pp72-3; ☎ 2362 1047; 72 Longquan St).

One reputable chain of laundries (aka 'coin laundries') is **E-clean** (Měishì Zhìzù Xǐyī; Map pp72-3; ☎ 0952-763 132; 159-1 Shida Rd; ☺ 24hr), which is convenient to MRT stations; there's a **branch** (47 Zhongxiao E Rd, Sec 5) near MRT Taipei City Hall station. For the smallest machines (8kg of clothes), washers cost NT50 per load and dryers NT10 for six minutes. Packets of detergent are available for NT10. You might also try **Shabon Coin Laundry** (Map pp74-5; 122 Minquan E Rd, Sec 2; ☺ 24hr), where washers cost NT60 per load, dryer NT10 for six minutes.

## Left Luggage
Left-luggage facilities are scarce in town. However, in Taipei Main Station there are a few rows of coin lockers on the basement floor. Costs are smallest/largest NT50/100 per day (not per 24 hours – note that these lockers begin and end their days at 10pm) or NT20 and up per three-hour period in the newer, computerised lockers. In either type of locker, the longest you will be able to store your belongings is 72 hours.

At Songshan Domestic Airport, small /medium/large lockers cost NT30/50/100 per 24 hours or portion thereof.

## Library
The **National Central Library** (Guójiā Túshūguǎn; Map pp72-3; ☎ 2361 9132; 20 Zhongshan S Rd; ☺ 9am-9pm Tue-Fri, 9am-5pm Sat & Sun) has fine Chinese-language collections, current and back issues of over 650 foreign magazines, a dozen newspapers in English, rare books

and an art gallery on the 4th floor, a fine-arts collection, including many titles in English, and dozens of computers for free Internet use. If you're planning a trip to Taiwan's hinterlands, you can make photocopies of road atlases and topographic maps (2nd floor). To enter, you'll need a library card – temporary (one-day) cards can be picked up at the entrance (bring ID). For the computers, you'll need to sign up for a scheduled time, and it's best to do so well in advance.

## Media
For radio listeners, ICRT (International Community Radio Taipei; 100.7FM, 576AM) is the local English-language radio station, broadcasting a mixture of Western pop, rock and jazz, news and informational programming. See Practicalities (p308) for information on newspapers, magazines and television.

Several magazines published in English have loads of useful information. These include *Wow Taipei* (published by the city government) and *Taiwan Fun* (www.taiwanfun .com).

## Medical Services
The most foreigner-friendly hospital in Taipei is **Adventist Hospital** (Map pp80-1; ☎ 2771 8151; 424 Bade Rd, Sec 2), with English-speaking staff. **Central Clinic** (Map pp80-1; ☎ 2751 0211; 77 Zhongxiao E Rd, Sec 4) and **Mackay Hospital** (Map pp74-5; ☎ 2543 3535; 92 Zhongshan N Rd, Sec 2) are also well regarded.

The **Hospital of Traditional Chinese Medicine** (Táiběi Shìlì Zhōngyī Yīyuàn; Map pp72-3; ☎ 2388 7088; 100 Kunming St; appointment registration ☺ 8am-11.30am & 1-4.30pm Mon-Fri, 5-8.30pm Tue-Fri, 8-11.30am Sat) also houses the **STD clinic** (Táiběi Shìlì Xìngbìng Fángzhì Suǒ; ☎ 2370 3739). Other hospitals include:

**Air Force Hospital** (Kōngjūn Yīyuàn; Map pp80-1; ☎ 2764 2151; 131 Chienkang Rd)

**Cathay General Hospital** (Guótài Zōnghé Yīyuàn; Map pp80-1; ☎ 2708 2121; 280 Renai Rd, Sec 4)

**Chang Gung Hospital** (Cháng Gēng Yīyuàn; Map pp80-1; ☎ 2713 5211; 199 Dunhua N Rd)

**National Taiwan University Hospital** (Táidà Yīyuàn; Map pp72-3; ☎ 2312 3456; 1 Changde St)

**Veterans General Hospital** (Róngmín Zǒng Yīyuàn; Map pp82; ☎ Chinese 2871 2121, English 2875 7346; 201 Shipai Rd, Sec 2, Shilin)

**Yangming Hospital** (Yángmíng Yīyuàn; Map pp82; ☎ 2835 3456; 105 Yusheng St, Shilin)

## Post

Taipei's main post office, the GPO or **North Gate Post Office** (Map pp72-3; Zhongxiao W Rd), is southwest of Taipei Main Station. Come here to claim poste restante (p319). There are post offices throughout the city.

## Tourist Information

The **Tourism Bureau** (Map pp80-1; ☎ 2717 3737; 345 Zhongxiao E Rd, Sec 4; ☺ 8am-7pm) is across from the Sun Yat-sen Memorial Hall. It's got the usual assortment of maps and pamphlets plus fairly helpful staff. It also has a **business office** (Map pp80-1; ☎ 2349 1635; 9th fl, 280 Zhongxiao E Rd, Sec 4; ☺ 8am-5pm) diagonally across the street and a block or so away. It has similar information, though its location deep inside the building makes it a little hard to find.

At Taipei Main Station is an **information booth** (☺ 8am-8pm) next to the ticket counters.

## Travel Agencies

The best place to look for a travel agent is just south of Songshan Domestic Airport, around Dunhua N Rd.

Beware that some agencies will quote prices based on a group fare, which may not be available by the time you go in to ticket the reservation.

## SIGHTS

For generations of tourists, visiting Taipei meant touring the National Palace Museum and moving on. Taking nothing away from the National Palace Museum (it should be a priority on any visit), we feel sorry for those generations of visitors. There are some lively and colourful temples, sights depicting history and personages, destinations for kids, and other attractions that defy quick description. And no visit would be complete without a trip to one of Taipei's street markets – particularly the night markets – teeming with clothing, homewares, food and amusements.

### Old Town Centre      Map pp72-3

The Wanhua District, originally known as Manka, was the first part of the city to be developed. It was encircled by walls and gates (p70), and even if the historic character is gone it's still a hub of activity, both traditional (Longshan Temple) and contemporary (Ximending). We've also included the national government district and Taipei Main Station area under this heading.

### 2-28 PEACE PARK 二二八和平公園

This handsome **park** (Èrèrbā Hépíng Gōngyuán) is dedicated to the memory of the 2-28 Rebellion and those who died in it (p25). A number of red-painted pavilions with attractive carvings in their cornices provide a pleasant picnic venue, and at the centre of the park is the memorial itself, a steeled sculpture surrounded by three enormous cubes turned on their corners.

The **2-28 Memorial Museum** (Èrèrbā Jìniànguǎn; ☎ 2389 7228; 3 Ketagalan Blvd; adult/concession NT20/10; ☺ 10am-5pm, closed Mon; MRT NTU University Hospital) offers a thorough explanation of the uprising and its importance to Taiwan. English signage is said to be in the works, but in the meantime there's usually someone on hand to walk you through in English. The building itself housed the radio station from where Kuomintang (KMT; Nationalist Party) officials tried to calm the masses.

In front of the museum is a Buddhist prayer bell, access to which is via a stone path. It's said that if you walk on the path in your bare feet you'll get a foot massage. We say 'ouch'. The park is also a good place to spot early morning practitioners of taichi.

At the north end of the park is the **National Taiwan Museum** (Guólì Táiwān Bówùguǎn), with exhibits on the flora and fauna of the island, as well as special exhibits. Its lack of English signage, however, may make it less accessible to non-Chinese-speaking visitors.

### BOTANICAL GARDENS 植物園

For a nice break from the hustle and bustle of the city, this large and pleasant **park** (Zhíwùyuán; ☎ 2381 7107; 53 Nanhai Rd; admission free; ☺ 4am-10pm; MRT Xiao Nanmen) features bricked walkways, gardens themed for the Chinese zodiac and Chinese literature, and

---

**FLOWER SEASON**

Taipei prides itself on its flowers, which bloom in full force from around mid-February to mid-March. During this time the transit authority operates special bus routes from strategic stations along the MRT line. Check with tourist offices for details.

a marvellous lotus pond. It's operated by the Taiwan Forestry Research Institute.

## CHIANG KAI-SHEK MEMORIAL HALL
中正紀念堂

A massive traditional-style Chinese gate on Zhongshan Rd provides your first framed view of this imposing **hall** (Zhōngzhèng Jìniàn Táng; ☎ 2343 1100; 21 Zhongshan S Rd; admission free; ⊙ 9am-5pm; MRT Chiang Kai-shek Memorial Hall), a 70m-tall memorial to Taiwan's one-time dictator. Its white walls and blue octagonal roof are grandiose without being, well, communist, and on the ground floor you'll find a museum dedicated to Chiang's life, with an assortment of military uniforms, medals, paintings and manuscripts, along with two humungous black Cadillacs he used.

Up a flight of 89 steps (denoting Chiang's age when he died), an oversized bronze sculpture of the man himself occupies a cavernous hall and looks out towards the gate. He's flanked by two motionless guards with bayoneted rifles and, behind him, carved into the white marble walls, are Chinese characters reading 'ethics,' 'democracy' and 'science', the Three Principles of the People. The hall opened in 1980, five years after Chiang's death.

The grounds (250,000 sq metres) also include the **National Theatre** and **National Concert Hall**, and the plazas and gardens around the three buildings are Taipei's grandest and best-used. You can find everything from art exhibitions to kids practicing hip-hop dancing and in-line skating. Sometimes on weekends, marching bands and drill teams rehearse their routines accompanied only by percussion, a sight to make you go 'hmm!?!'

## LONGSHAN TEMPLE 龍山寺
If you can visit only one religious site in Taipei, make it this **temple** (Lóngshān Sì; ☎ 2302 5162; 211 Guangzhou St; admission free; ⊙ 6am-10.20pm, from 5am in 2nd & 7th months of Chinese calendar; MRT Longshan Temple). Others are larger, grander, even more intimate, but this one has it all.

The temple dates back to 1738 and is positioned on the site where, it is said, a man left an amulet of the Guanyin (goddess of mercy) hanging on a tree, where it gave off a brilliant light even after dark.

Start by the waterfall outside the main hall: the stones that line the courtyard where you're standing were originally ballast on the ships that ferried immigrants from Fujian province across the often treacherous Taiwan Straits. Once you enter the main building, the intimate courtyard is a riot of reds and golds and carved stone columns. Note the enormous bronze incense burner before the main hall. Good times to visit are around 6am, 8am and 5pm when crowds of worshippers gather and engage in hypnotic chanting.

Typical of Taiwanese temples, this one is multidenominational. Although the Guanyin is still the central deity worshipped here, the temple enshrines 165 other deities. Along the back wall are several bays containing different deities – on the right is the patron of scholarly pursuits, while on the left is the god of military pursuits and business people. The goddess Matsu (p276) is in the centre, to provide for the safe return of travellers by sea or land (air travellers pay their respects to the Guanyin) – she's flanked by two male guards: one is said to see 1000 miles, while the other can hear 1000 miles.

The lights on columns in the back of the temple each represent one person whose family made a donation in his or her honour.

An elaborate covered market was under construction across from Longshan Temple at the time of research.

## NATIONAL MUSEUM OF HISTORY
國立歷史博物館

Just outside the Botanical Gardens, Taiwan's first **museum** (Guólì Lìshǐ Bówùguǎn; ☎ 2361 0270; 49 Nanhai Rd; adult/concession NT20/10, child & senior free; ⊙ 10am-6pm, closed Mon; MRT Chiang Kai-shek Memorial Hall or Xiao Nanmen) is still an anchor of local arts and culture in an elegant Japanese-era building. 'History' is actually a misnomer – Chinese *art* history would be more accurate. Specialities include tricolour ceramic vessels and sculptures, and ancient bronzes, while the **National Gallery** (Guójiā Huàláng) on the 2nd floor has changing exhibits of works by Taiwanese artists. Special shows attract peak attendance – past shows have included Mayan art, Giacometti and the terracotta warriors of Xi'an. The tearoom on the 3rd floor has views of the Botanical Gardens' lotus pond.

A tour in English takes place at 3pm each afternoon.

A museum of human rights is due to open nearby in the next few years.

### POSTAL MUSEUM 郵政博物館

You say you can't imagine six storeys' worth of exhibits about mail and stamps? Think again. The Taiwan **postal museum** (Yóuzhèng Bówùguǎn; ☎ 2394 5185; 45 Chongqing S Rd, Sec 2; adult /student NT5/3, child & senior free; ☽ 9am-5pm, closed Mon; MRT Chiang Kai-shek Memorial Hall) showcases around 80,000 stamp specimens from over 120 countries, postal uniforms, hardware and signage from around 30 countries, and models of Taiwanese mail-delivery methods of yore (buffalo-skin raft, anyone?). Sure it's quirky, but it's so sincere that it's hard not to admire.

This museum is also one place where Taiwan's isolation from the rest of the world is starkly evident. The collections of postal artefacts from many countries stop at 1971 when Taiwan left the United Nations and many countries would no longer recognise Taiwan.

A shop on the ground floor sells stamps and souvenirs, and if you're so inspired, a number of shops in the immediate area are popular with collectors.

### PRESIDENTIAL BUILDING 總統府

Built in 1919 as the headquarters of the Japanese occupying forces, this **building** (Zǒngtǒng Fǔ; ☎ 2311 3731; www.president.gov.tw; 122 Chongqing S Rd, Sec 1; admission free, passport required; ☽ 9am-noon Mon-Fri; MRT Ximen) has housed the offices of the president since 1949. Its ornate brickwork is typical of the Japanese era, and at 85m it was the tallest building in town for decades.

---

#### CITY GATES

Two gates in the southwest corner of what's now the city centre are all that remain of the original walls that once enclosed the old city. Even if both are overshadowed by nearby highways, these unique relics are worth checking out: **Xiaonanmen** (Xiǎonánmén, Little South Gate; cnr Aiguo W & Yanping S Rds) or **Beimen** (Běimén, North Gate; cnr Zhongxiao W & Yanping S Rds), a short walk west of Taipei Main Station.

---

Exhibits include documents from Taiwanese history (both originals and copies) and artefacts of the Japanese occupation (lacquerware, statuary etc). Although most signage is in Chinese, there is usually an English speaker on hand to guide you through. At the gift shop you can pick up a presidential windbreaker (NT500).

Most of the time, visitors are permitted to see only the gardens and ground-floor exhibition halls. However, the rest of the building opens for six days each year; check the website or inquire for details.

### SNAKE ALLEY 華西街夜市

Part tourist mecca, part carnival sideshow, Taipei's most famous **night market** (Huáxijiē Yèshì; Huaxi St; ☽ 7pm-midnight; MRT Longshan Temple) needs to be seen. The name sounds a little tawdry, and indeed its heritage goes back to a time when prostitution was legal in town, but these days this arcade is well-lit, basically cheerful and lined with clothing boutiques, sweet shops, snack shops, foot-massage shops, souvenir shops, restaurants of many stripes (Tainan Tan-tsu-mien, p93, is one of the city's best regarded) and the occasional erotic toy shop.

Ah yes, the snakes. Skilled snake-handlers in storefronts use tiny microphones and a well-honed patter to lure guiltily curious eyes and when the crowd gets large enough you might see the handler play with a cobra like it's a Slinky, taunt it with a metal rod (which can elicit a lightning-quick reaction!), feed it a mouse or disembowel it before your very eyes. The meat ends up in soup or stir-fried with vegetables, while the blood is mixed with Chinese liquor, a cocktail said to be good for virility and a host of ailments. Don't worry, you won't be served snake unless you visit a restaurant that specialises in it.

The snake handling (and for some, the snakes themselves) are not for the squeamish, so in case you have different ideas of a fun night on the town there are other night-market stalls in the surrounding streets – shops on Xiyuan St for example, offer massage by the blind.

### XIMENDING 西門町

Epicentre of Taiwan's youth culture, this eight-branched intersection (Xīméndīng) dates from the Japanese era and is now

---

**TOP FIVE HISTORIC SITES**

- **City gates** (p70)
- **Dihua Market** (p76)
- **Lin Family Mansion and Gardens** (p83)
- **Beitou Hot Spring Museum** (p108)
- **Red Pavilion Theatre** (p70)

---

chock-full of shops selling fashion, fast-food, sneakers, sunglasses, scarves, Sanrio, Sony and spaghetti – in short, anything that young-and-trendies adore. The pedestrian streets northwest of the main intersection, between Chengdu Rd and Wuchang St, are the focus of the action.

While it's busy most of the time, nights and weekends are prime time, especially Friday and Saturday nights. You might catch a musical act on a temporary stage set up on the streets, and if you want to see a film Wuchang St is home to many cinemas. If you need a piercing or tattoo, try the lanes and alleys off or Xining S Rd and Emei St.

Ximending is also home to some fine examples of Japanese period architecture, notably the **Red Pavilion Theatre** (Hónglóu Jùchǎng; Map pp72-3; ☎ 2311 9380; 10 Chengdu Rd; free except during events; ⏲ 1-10pm Mon-Fri, 10am-

10pm Sat & Sun; MRT Ximen). This wooden, octagonal structure was originally a public market, then a theatre for Chinese opera and a second-run cinema. Today it's a multipurpose centre for vocal and visual arts – exhibits and performances change frequently.

## Da'an & Shida 大安區, 師大區

These districts in the southern part of the city centre are built around Shida (Taipei Normal University) and Da'an Park. Thus, Shida is studenty and funky, while Da'an is breezy and more grown up, yet without the slick modernity of Xinyi (p77). Both feature famous food streets (Shida Night Market, Yongkang St and Tonghua Night Market) and Da'an is also known for the weekend **jade and flower markets** (Map pp72-3; Jianguo S Rd).

### CHANG FOUNDATION MUSEUM
鴻禧美術館

Despite its less-than-grand entrance (beneath an apartment building), this handsome **museum** (Hóngxǐ Měishùguǎn; Map pp72-3; ☎ 2356 9575; 63 Renai Rd, Sec 2; adult/student NT100/50; ⏲ 10.30am-4.30pm, closed Mon & between exhibits) is home to one of the world's finest private collections of Chinese art, owned by the Chang family. Many visitors liken the

---

**TOP FIVE CONTEMPORARY BUILDINGS**

Although Taipei is not exactly known for its architecture, we believe in rewarding what we like. To wit, our own (admittedly subjective) list.

- **China Life Insurance Co Building** (Map pp80-1; 122 Dunhua N Rd) Architect Steven CF Chang tried to express the combination of strength and humility necessary for a corporate headquarters. The single, massive column supports the upper storeys and creates an open space; it's designed to respect both the environment and the crowd.

- **Chunghwa Television Building** (Map pp80-1; 100 Guangfu S Rd) The 1984-built headquarters of this TV network has a pyramid-like structure, meaning that the 14-storey building does not overly impose on its neighbourhood.

- **Core Pacific 'Living Mall'** (p104) The 'core' is an 11-storey sphere seemingly suspended at the centre of an L-shaped shopping extravaganza. The sphere was inspired by the 'pi' disc from earliest Chinese art, while the rest of the building is said to resemble two dragons fighting for the ball. The building opened in 2001.

- **Hang Kuo Building** (Map pp80-1; 167 Dunhua N Rd) Its cantilevered structure is meant to suggest a traditional Chinese roof. The open core allows sunlight in, while lots of garden space is meant to convey a new concept of an office.

- **Taipei 101** (p78) The world's tallest building (for now) was built to resemble a stalk of bamboo, tied with elegant ribbons at each fret. It opened in 2003.

TAIPEI

museum to a more accessible version of the National Palace Museum. Exhibits change twice a year and are themed according to motif (eg birds as used in art) or category (eg Chinese musical instruments). Pieces come from the museum's own collection (including some ceramics that are more than 2000 years old) or are borrowed from other collections. At any one time you're likely to find jade, bronzes, ceramics, paintings and Buddhist images. Excellent signage is in both English and Chinese.

### CHILDREN'S TRANSPORTATION MUSEUM
兒童交通博物館

It sounds a little underwhelming, and let's be frank, indoors it is. This **museum** (Értóng Jiāotōng Bówùguǎn; Map pp72-3; ☎ 2369 0001; 2 Tingzhou Rd, Sec 3; admission NT60; ☼ 9am-6pm) has exhibits of trains, buses and motorcycles, as well as video games that teach kids traffic rules and how to cross the street (the games are actually pretty popular). Downstairs are some rather tame rides for small children.

But the rubber meets the road out back, where amusement park–style rides are meant for kids of all ages. The highlight: children above 140cm in height can drive little gas-powered cars around a 3km race track (parents sit in the passenger seat and can cringe or brake as needed!). Smaller kids can ride coin-operated motor scooters.

Admission is by point ticket (1 point = NT1). You must purchase 100 points for

**OLD TOWN CENTRE, DA' AN & SHIDA**

MARTIN MOOS

Mass Rapid Transit (MRT; p106), Taipei

MARTIN MOOS

Neon signs, Taipei

Grand Hotel (p90), Taipei

JOHN BORTHWICK

# TAIPEI TRANSPORT

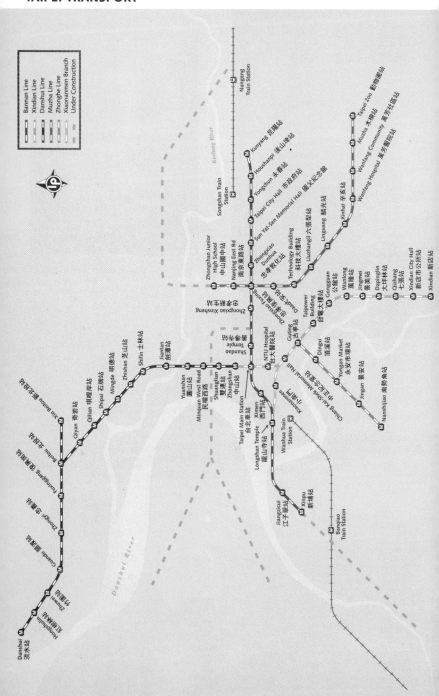

starters, and it costs NT60 to enter the museum, leaving any remaining points to be credited towards rides. Most rides cost 50 points; the cars cost NT100.

## DA'AN PARK 大安公園

Bordered by Xinyi, Jianguo, Heping and Xinsheng Rds, this large **park** (Dà'ān Gōngyuán, Map pp72-3) is a great place to see Taipei at play. There are basketball courts, a foot-massage walking path, flower beds and the usual park accoutrements. On big holidays, especially Christmas, New Year and Chinese New Year, the amphitheatre hosts free stage shows with some of Taiwan's biggest names.

## TAIPEI WATER PARK 自來水園區

One of Taipei's quirkier offerings, this **park** (Zìláishǔi Yuán Qū; Map pp72-3; ☎ 8369 5145; 1 Shuiyuan St; adult/child NT100/50; ☉ 9am-6pm, closed Mon; MRT Gongguan) is on the site of the pump house that began providing clean water in 1909. Prior to its opening, waterborne diseases were a major problem for this fast-developing city. The elegant, baroque, colonnaded former pump house is now the **Museum of Drinking Water** (Zìláishǔi Bówùguǎn) and a popular wedding-portrait backdrop. You can enter the building to see the workings. Other draws are the outdoor activities: walking trails on an adjacent hill

**TAIPEI**

---

### CONFUCIUS, IN TABLET FORM

If you're wondering why Confucius is represented by tablets and not a sculpture like other deities, you have to go back to the 14th century. The emperor Tai Tsu (1368–98) became very upset that there was no consistency in the likenesses of Confucius from temple to temple, so he decreed that the great man be represented by memorial tablets instead.

---

(check out the red baroque water-storage tank) and an assortment of fountains and pools for the whole family to play in.

Be sure to watch the movie (available in English) inside the pump house at the beginning of your visit for an introduction to the history and facilities.

### XINGTIAN TEMPLE 行天宫

This **temple** (Xíngtiān Gōng; Map pp72-3; ☎ 2502 7924; 109 Minquan E Rd, Sec 2; admission free; ☿ 3.30am-11pm) is one of the city's busiest. It's dedicated to Guangong (AD 162–219), a famous red-faced general who became deified and is worshipped as the god of war and, by extension, martial arts. Businesspeople also flock here as Guangong was said to be adept at finance.

Although it does not have the history of other temples (the present building dates from 1967), it has heft. One distinctive feature is the large shed that covers the central courtyard, where suppliants leave their

daily offerings on tables. Temple officials wear handsome royal blue robes.

Xingtian Temple is popular for fortune-telling. Within the temple grounds you'll hear, and then see, visitors dropping oracle blocks (p35). Fortune-tellers can often be found even in the pedestrian underpass outside the temple.

The temple god is celebrated on the 24th day of the sixth lunar month, and at smaller festivals during the third and ninth lunar months.

### Zhongshan 中山區

This area on the north side of the city centre features some large-scale museums and parks, and some important temples. The western part of this district, near the Danshui River, is sometimes known as Dadaocheng or Datong.

### BAO-AN TEMPLE 保安宫

From humble Qing-dynasty origins, today this Taoist **temple** (Bǎoān Gōng; Map pp74-5; ☎ 2595 1676; 61 Hami St; admission free; ☿ 7am-10pm; MRT Yuanshan) is one of the city's leading religious sites. An original, wooden structure was completed in 1760 by immigrants from Fujian province who brought their own materials with them. The current temple, dating from 1805, took 25 years to complete.

The temple deity is the emperor Baoshen, famous as a doctor and great healer. As such, the temple gets many visitors who come to pray for good health. The goddess of birth is enshrined in the bell tower,

---

flanked by 12 female aides, each of whom assist with childbirth during a particular month, so naturally it's long been popular with women coming to pray for safe childbirth, particularly of a son. Other gods commemorated here are patrons of business and good fortune.

The two open-mouthed lions (one male, the other female) are said to be an appeal for the rule of law and good government.

### CHILDREN'S RECREATION CENTRE
兒童育樂中心
Just south of the Keelung River, this large **park** (Értóng Yùlè Zhōngxīn; Map pp74-5; ☎ 2593 2211; 66 Zhongshan N Rd, Sec 3; NT30, additional for planetarium shows; ⏰ 9am-5pm, closed Mon) features a 'world

of yesterday' with historical Chinese toys and folk arts, and a 'world of tomorrow' with, among other things, a planetarium.

### CONFUCIUS TEMPLE 孔子廟
Modelled after the temple in Confucius' native town of Shandong, this **temple** (Kǒng Miào; Map pp74-5; ☎ 2592 3934; 275 Dalong St; admission free; ⏰ 8.30am-9pm Tue-Sat, 8.30am-5pm Sun; MRT Yuanshan) is based on classical Chinese temple architecture. Confucius (551–479 BC) is generally acknowledged as China's greatest educator and scholar. Whereas education had previously been exclusively for nobility, he promoted popular education.

Confucius valued simplicity, a trait seen in the temple's architecture and relatively

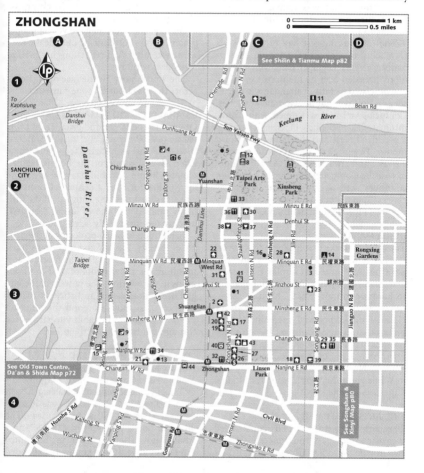

muted adornments. Inscriptions that might be found on columns, doors and windows in other temples are banned here – who would have the temerity to think his or her writing could compare with that of the great master? However, you might take note of the detailed carvings of dragons on the temple's Ling Xing Gate and the fired pottery on the Yi Gate. The central Ta Cheng hall is one of the few traditional wooden buildings in Taiwan and contains a Confucius tablet. A seven-storey pagoda in the centre of the roof is said to drive away evil spirits. A total of 186 tablets on the premises represent the Confucian disciples.

The temple at this site (13,935 sq metres) dates back to 1928, replacing the original 1879 temple that was damaged beyond repair during a rebellion under Japanese occupation.

The temple's biggest day of the year is Confucius' birthday, celebrated on 28 September. Events begin at 6am with a ceremony presided over by the mayor of Taipei and officiated by rafts of attendants, supervisors and officers, all in elaborate costumes. Confucius' spirit is welcomed with drumming, music, bowing, incense, chanting, a sacrificial feast and the burning of spirit money. Tickets go on sale about five days in advance and always sell out. At other times of year the Confucian tradition of education continues with weekly Chinese calligraphy classes (2pm to 4pm Wednesday) and poetry readings (2pm to 4pm Saturday).

### DIHUA MARKET 迪化街
The several blocks that make up this **market** (Díhuà Shìcháng; Map pp74-5) are Taipei's best-preserved examples of historic architecture. Styles range from Fujianese to Baroque to modernist. The area, sometimes called 'Grocery Street', is known for Chinese medicines and medicinal herbs, bolts of cloth and sundries. It's quite atmospheric. The best shopping is in the afternoons and in the weeks leading up to Chinese New Year.

While you're here, don't miss the Hsiahai City God Temple (right).

### FINE ARTS MUSEUM 市立美術館
This airy, four-storey, 1980s-constructed box of marble, glass and concrete specialises in contemporary art, with a particular focus on Taiwanese artists. Although the **museum's** (Shìlì Měishùguǎn; Map pp74-5; ☎ 2595 7656; 181 Zhongshan N Rd, Sec 3; adult/student/senior NT30/15/free; ⏱ 9.30am-5.30pm, closed Mon; MRT Yuanshan) exhibits change annually (some more frequently), works from the permanent collection are always on display, including pieces by Taiwanese painters and sculptors from the Japanese period to the present. Some of the bigger names are Chen Chengpo, Kuo Po-chan, Liao Chi-chun and Yang Mao-in. Some of the pieces echo the European impressionists, while others were influenced by Asian folk crafts or Japanese painting schools. With any luck you'll see a scroll painting by Chen Chi-kwan, whose signature motif is amusing monkeys. Exhibits might also include wood-block prints, photography and installation art.

On weekends you may see young people practising hip-hop dancing outside the museum, watching their reflections in the large plate glass windows.

The Taipei Story House (see opposite) is across the plaza north of the museum.

### HSIAHAI CITY GOD TEMPLE 霞海城隍廟
Others may be larger and grander, but this **temple** (Xiáhǎi Chénghuáng Miào; Map pp74-5; 61 Dihua St, Sec 1) teems with character – and characters. It's also one of the best-preserved temples in the city and has had the same appearance for over a century. Go on the city god's birthday (the 13th day of the fifth lunar month) for one of Taipei's biggest, loudest and most lively celebrations.

In addition to being protector of the people of the city, the city god also keeps track of good and evil deeds done by mortals, and monitors the movements of souls and demons in the afterlife. The powers of the city god are almost carrot-and-stick in nature: the power to motivate good thoughts on the one hand, and the ability to strike fear through punishment on the other.

### LIN ANTAI OLD HOMESTEAD 林安泰古厝
Not to be confused with the Lin Family Mansion and Garden in Banqiao (p83), this is Taipei's oldest **residential building** (Línàntài Gǔcuò; Map pp74-5; ☎ 2598 1572; Binjiang St; admission free; ⏱ 9am-9pm Tue-Sat, 9am-5pm Sun). The 30-room house was built in 1783–87, near what is now Dunhua S Rd, in the southern Fujian style. It was gradually expanded

as this wealthy merchant family grew; the home reached its present size in 1823.

However, the city also expanded and in the 1970s this historic home was to be destroyed as the road was widened. Thankfully, public outcry saved it, the building was painstakingly dismantled and, in 1983, rebuilt on this field across from Xinsheng Park on the northern reaches of the city centre. Today the house is notable for its central courtyard, swallowtail roof and period furniture. We're not sure the Lin family would have wanted their house in the shadow of an expressway (as it currently is) but we bet they'd be glad it's been preserved.

It's also under the flight path of the Songshan Domestic Airport; some people enjoy the noisy fun of lying on the grass and watching the planes skimming directly overhead.

### MUSEUM OF CONTEMPORARY ART TAIPEI 台北當代藝術館

Taiwan's first museum dedicated explicitly to contemporary art, **MOCA** (Táiběi Dāngdài Yìshùguǎn; Map pp72-3; ☎ 2552 3721; www.mocataipei.org.tw; 39 Chang'an W Rd; admission NT50; ☻ 10am-6pm, closed Mon; MRT Zhongshan) occupies an important Japanese-era building that was once Taipei's city hall. Shows are all special exhibits and fill anything from one gallery to the entire museum; they might include architecture, design, fashion, digital and video art, even comic books. Check the website or inquire for current exhibition information.

And yes, MOCA's café sells, er, mocha.

### SU HO PAPER MUSEUM 樹火紀念紙博物館

Don't blink or you might walk right past the store front housing this four-storey **museum** (Shùhuǒ Jìniàn Zhǐ Bówùguǎn; Map p72-3; ☎ 2507 5539; 68 Chang'an E Rd, Sec 2; admission NT100, NT180 with paper-making session; ☻ by appointment 9.30am-4.30pm Mon-Sat). Fulfilling the lifelong dream of Taiwanese paper-maker Mr Chen Su Ho, this museum features special exhibits of ultra-creative uses of paper (eg as sculpture or installation art). No matter when you visit, you can make your own sheet of paper in the museum's workshop and learn about the materials and process. English-language audio guide available. Exhibits change two or three times a year.

The museum shop sells handmade cards, elegant kites and other trinkets made from handmade paper. See also the Chang Chen Cotton Paper Art Centre (p105), down the block.

### TAIPEI ARTIST VILLAGE 台北國際藝術村

An important venue for Taipei's international art scene, this one-time government office **building** (Táiběi Guójì Yìshùcūn; Map pp72-3; ☎ 3393 7377; www.tav.tcg.gov.tw; 7 Beiping E Rd; admission free; ☻ 10am-6pm) is the temporary home of 10 guest artists from around the world. On the ground floor are a small gallery, café and gift shop, while upstairs are the artists' living and working spaces. You can occasionally find individual artists exhibiting their work in their own studios and there's a general open studio a few times per year (check the website for schedules).

### TAIPEI STORY HOUSE 台北故事館

Just north of the Fine Arts Museum, this **house** (Táiběi Gùshìguǎn; Map pp74-5; ☎ 2587 5565; 181-1 Zhongshan N Rd, Sec 3; adult/student NT30/20, child & senior free; ☻ 10.30am-6pm, closed Mon; MRT Yuanshan) was built in 1914 by an aristocratic tea trader. Its style was said to have been inspired by a building he saw while visiting the 1900 Paris Expo. Today the house is an exhibition space for Taipei nostalgia and history. Exhibits change frequently and might include goodies such as toys, matchboxes and comic books.

The gift shop features the work of a dozen local artists and the **tearoom** (mains NT250-650, Chinese-/English-style tea NT320/280; ☻ lunch Tue-Sun, dinner nightly) serves afternoon tea and French-style cuisine.

## Xinyi 信義區      Map pp80-1

While central Taipei is characterised by its older neighbourhoods, there's nary an old structure to be found in Xinyi, east of the city centre. Instead you'll find spiffy new high-rise office blocks and hotels, city hall and some fashionable and trendy night spots and restaurants. Oh, and there's a little edifice called Taipei 101.

### DISCOVERY CENTRE OF TAIPEI 台北探索館

Inside Taipei city hall, this **complex** (Táiběi Tànsuǒguǎn; ☎ 2725 8630; 1 Shifu Rd; admission free; ☻ 9am-5pm, closed Mon; MRT Taipei City Hall) is a good place to get your bearings on the city and its history. You can see maps and models depicting Taipei's evolution from a walled, gated city in 1882 to the bustling metropolis it is today, as well as clues to its geography, topography, commerce, famous residents and natural resources. There's a free audio guide in English.

## SUN YAT-SEN MEMORIAL HALL
國父紀念館

Occupying an entire city block, this **hall** (Guófù Jìniànguǎn; ☎ 2758 8008; 505 Renai Rd, Sec 4; admission free; ⊙ 9am-5pm; MRT Sun Yat-sen Memorial Hall) serves as a cultural centre (concerts, performances and special events), a large public park and a museum of the life of the man considered the founder of modern China. A huge statue of Dr Sun sits in a cavernous lobby facing the park to the south of the hall. It's guarded by two implacable sentries – you can watch the changing of the guards, an intricate choreography involving much spinning of bayoneted rifles and precision stepping. Morning visitors practising taichi on the grounds provide another kind of choreography.

The **Yogi House Café** (mains NT120-180) on the 2nd floor serves a changing selection of organic dishes, snacks and desserts.

## TAIPEI 101 台北國際金融中心
The world's tallest building, **Taipei International Financial Centre 101** (Táiběi Guójì Jīnróng Zhōngxīn;

---

### DR SUN YAT-SEN

Sun Yat-sen (1866–1925) was a man of many facets, and even many names.

His given name was Sun Wen but he was also known as Sun Zhongshan (from the sobriquet 'woodcutter of the central mountain'), 'father of the nation' in Taiwan and 'father of the revolution' in mainland China. 'Dr', by contrast, was an earned title. After childhood in Guangdong province and adolescence in Hawaii, he earned a medical degree in 1892 and became a practising physician. It was not long, though, before his attentions turned to the brutality and corruption he saw within the Qing dynasty (1644–1911), the shame of losing Taiwan to the Japanese and the dream of improving China's lot through modernisation.

He organised a reform movement in Hong Kong and after a failed coup in Guangzhou in 1895 he spent the next 16 years in exile, raising money for the cause in Europe, North America and Japan. During that time he proclaimed his Three Principles of the People: nationalism (mínzú), democracy (mínquán) and livelihood (mínshēng).

In 1911 a military uprising at Wuchang, Hubei province, became the catalyst for the end of five millennia of Chinese dynastic rule and the beginning of the Republic of China (ROC). Sun returned to China and was named provisional president, a provisional government was established under the Kuomintang (KMT; Nationalist Party) in Nanjing, and the next year (1912) became Year One of the calendar that is still used in Taiwan today.

However, China remained fractured. While southern provinces had declared independence from dynastic rule, many northern provinces had not, and warlords controlled various regions, making unification difficult. Sun spent the next few years out of China, but in 1917 he established a military government in Guangzhou, and his protégé Chiang Kai-shek became commandant of a new military academy for KMT soldiers. The next several years were spent trying to form alliances with communists, among others.

Sun died of liver cancer in 1925 in Beijing after travelling there to participate in an ill-fated national reconstruction conference. He never saw his dream realised, and his death set the stage for decades of both internal and international conflict. His widow, Soong Ching-ling (a generation his junior), eventually became a high official in the Chinese communist party; her sister Soong Mei-ling (1898–2003; p85) became better known to the world as Madame Chiang Kai-shek. Sun is entombed near Nanjing.

Today, both Taiwan and the mainland claim Sun as their own. The Three Principles of the People figure prominently in the political philosophy of both, yet each with its own politically appropriate interpretation. Sun's face appears on the NT100 bill, the grounds of Sun Yat-sen Memorial Hall fill an entire city block in Taipei, and Zhongshan, Minzu, Minsheng and Minquan are common street names throughout Taiwan. On May Day on the mainland, officials have abandoned pictures of Marx and Lenin for those of Sun, not least to make the case for reunification.

45 Shifu Rd; MRT Taipei City Hall) is 101 storeys, 508m tall and built to resemble a stalk of bamboo with graceful ropes tied around the bamboo's nodes. Construction began in 1997 and the exterior was completed in autumn 2003. The interior (including observation deck) was not completed at the time of writing. Until completion, visitors will have to be content with the lower floors – this shouldn't be too difficult as it contains a very ritzy shopping mall and the best Asian food court we've ever seen, with selections from across the continent served in a dizzying variety of bowls, plates, pots, sizzling trays and burners.

Taipei 101 will hold the world's tallest building title for about five years. There's a space race on, and in 2008 a new building in Dubai is slated to open at a height of about 610m. Even if that structure is not realised, the Freedom Tower on the site of New York's World Trade Centre is due to open in 2009, at 541m.

## Shilin & Tianmu 士林區、天母區

North of the city centre and adjacent to Beitou, Shilin (Shìlín) has some of the city's best-known cultural attractions (particularly the National Palace Museum), while further up Zhongshan N Rd, the newer district of Tianmu (Tiānmǔ) is home to antique shops and foreign products, foods, schools, literature and people. Nearby are the large Dayeh Takashimaya department store (p104) and Taipei's new baseball stadium.

Apart from that, there's not much of interest to tourists in Tianmu, but there is a popular hike from near the end of the bus line to the Chinese Cultural University on Yangmingshan.

### MARTYRS' SHRINE 忠烈祠

Against a backdrop of mountains across the Keelung River from the city centre, the monumental **National Revolutionary Martyrs' Shrine** (Zōngliècí; Map pp74-5; ☎ 2349 1635; 139 Beian Rd; admission free; ☽ 9am-5pm) enshrines the dead of the wars fought on behalf of the ROC. The complex covers around 5000 sq metres, and the main sanctuary was modelled after the Taiho Palace in Beijing. Plaques, paintings and friezes in the arcade surrounding the main sanctuary describe the details of various 20th-century rebellions and battles. A bell tower and drum tower are used during memorial ceremonies.

The main reason most people go here, however, is to see the hourly changing of the guards. Blue-uniformed, silver-helmeted, implacable and silent they wield and spin their bayoneted rifles with the precision of a drill team. The public is able to march along with the guards as they tread the path from the sanctuary to the main gate hundreds of metres away – notice the yellowed lines on the paving stones, marks of decades of wear under black-soled boots.

While the ceremony seems rather staid, if you look closely you'll notice a whole culture behind the guards. They have their own minders – stage managers almost – who untangle tassels and make sure each military braid is just so. We wonder if these guys go to Taipei's cushy lounge bars after work, but we suspect not.

The shrine is about 10 minutes' walk east of the Grand Hotel.

### NATIONAL PALACE MUSEUM 故宮博物院

If there's one must-see in Taipei, it is this **museum** (Gùgōng Bówùyuàn; Map pp64-5; ☎ 2881 2021; 221 Zhishan Rd, Sec 2; adult/concession/child under school age NT100/50/free; ☽ 9am-5pm), home to the world's finest collection of Chinese art (around 650,000 pieces).

Given its large collections, the museum rotates its exhibits frequently, meaning you're likely to find a new discovery each time you visit. However, some treasures are always on display, including:

**Concentric ivory balls** (gallery No 3–06) It may not look like much at first, but consider that it's 17 balls, one inside the next, carved from a single piece of ivory in the late 19th century. The chain from which the balls hang was carved from the same piece, and no glue was used.

**Pair of bronze vessels** (gallery No 3–04) The Mao-kung Ting ritual cooking vessel and San P'an ritual water vessel. Both are richly inscribed with hundreds of Chinese characters – the latter is a peace treaty.

**Qing dynasty jade screen** (gallery No 3–07) At 2m high and eight panels (2.5m) wide, this amazing folding screen is decorated in a floral and bird pattern.

**Sung dynasty ceramics** (gallery No 2–07) Including celadon works, immaculately preserved.

It's also fascinating to peruse the timeline on the museum's 1st floor comparing Chinese art history with world history – quite sobering to realise that the great works of Western art began to appear only about 80% of the way through Chinese art history.

The museum offers free guided tours in English at 10am and 3pm. Tour contents vary with each guide, but all offer a good overview. If you prefer to move about at your own pace, there's an English-language headphone guide (NT200).

Dining options at the museum include the **San Hsi Tang tearoom** (dumplings & snacks NT50-

75) on the 4th floor. Try the *san ch'ing* tea (NT120) with citron, plum blossom and pine seeds, or Taiwan's own oolong tea (NT100 – order it weak!). Plus, you get panoramic views. The museum **restaurant** (mains NT160-360), in a separate building, serves Chinese dishes cafeteria style, along with ice cream and cake.

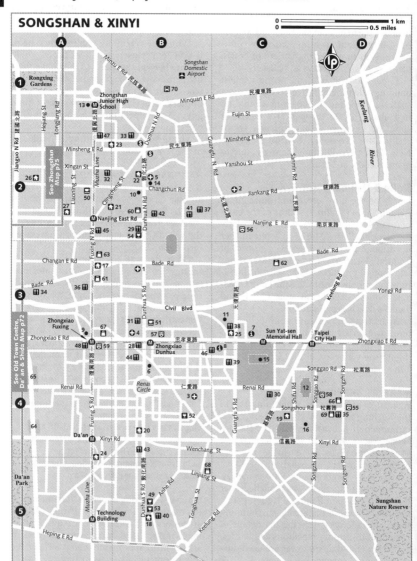

**SONGSHAN & XINYI**

Gift shops are extensive, with reproductions of ceramics and paintings, porcelain, scrolls, art books, puzzles and, er, mouse pads. A handkerchief or brass bookmark will set you back NT80, while art reproductions on scrolls can go for NT2500.

Also within the grounds is the **Chih-shan Garden** (Zhìshàn Yuán; admission NT10; ☺ 7am-7pm, closed Mon). This Garden of Protected Benevolence is a stroll garden in the literary style of the Sung and Ming dynasties; it's likened to a landscape painting that gradually reveals itself as you walk through it. You won't be the only shutterbug amid its ponds, pavilions, miniature groves of bamboo, rocks and trees. It's got covered walkways in case the weather doesn't cooperate, and if it's nice out the garden is a great place for a picnic.

To reach the museum, take the MRT to Shilin station (Red Line), exit to Zhongzheng Rd (north exit), and catch bus 304, 255,

Red 30, Minibus 18, Minibus 19 or Culture Bus 101. Some of these buses stop at the plaza at the base of the hill and you will have to climb the many flights of stairs to the museum; others go all the way to the museum entrance.

### SHILIN OFFICIAL RESIDENCE 士林官邸

What is it about dictators? From the Pharaohs to the Bourbon kings of France to the shoguns of Japan, they built pleasure domes on the backs of those they purported to govern. And yet for all this unpleasantness, the buildings remain inspiring legacies.

Chiang Kai-shek was no exception. The main features of this sprawling **estate** (Shìlín Guāndǐ; Map p82; 60 Fulin Rd; admission free; ☺ 8.30am-5pm Mon-Fri, 8am-7pm Sat & Sun; MRT Shilin), one of 15 around the country, are its fabulous gardens (Chinese-style, Western-style, a rose garden etc). There is also a horticultural exhibition hall often filled with artful displays

TAIPEI

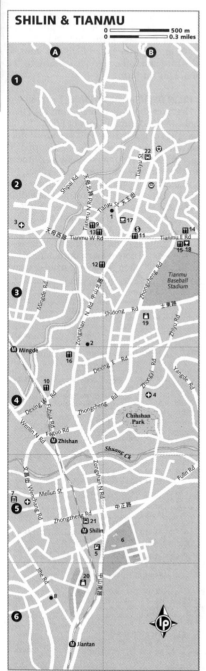

of flowers and plants. Rafts of gardeners take care of them all.

The residence was Chiang's main home until his death in 1975. The estate was closed to the public until the late 1990s, when then-mayor Chen Shuibian decided to turn it into a park. Chiang's widow, Madame Soong, who still claimed title to the property, was none too pleased, but eventually a compromise was reached and the gardens were opened to the public while the house remained closed. Even after her death, the house stayed off-limits, though at the time of writing there were rumours that it might open.

The estate is just off Zhongshan N Road, Sec 5. The main entrance is about 10 minutes' walk from the Shilin MRT stop.

## SHUNG YE MUSEUM OF FORMOSAN ABORIGINES 順益台灣原住民博物館

This **museum** (Shùnyì Táiwān Yuánzhùmín Bówùguǎn; Map pp64–5; ☎ 2841 2611; www.museum.org.tw; 282 Jishan Rd, Sec 2; adult/concession NT150/100; ⊙ 9am–

5pm, closed Mon & 20 Jan-20 Feb) gives highlights of nine Taiwanese indigenous tribes. These Austronesian peoples are related through blood or linguistic ties to people across pre-colonial Oceania, as far away as Madagascar. The tribes developed pottery, basketry, wood carvings, musical instruments and colourful costumes. You'll see fine examples displayed and video footage in English offers a worthy summary.

As Chinese culture came to hold more sway in Taiwan, the tribes' prevalence fell away, but there has been a good deal of renewed interest recently, tied in part to the wish among Taiwanese officials to establish an independent Taiwanese identity. And if you think that these tribes are somehow too obscure to have touched your life, the Song of Salvation of the native Ami people gained international prominence as one of the musical themes of the 1996 Olympics in Atlanta.

The museum is about 200m past the bus stop for the National Palace Museum, across the street.

### TAIPEI ASTRONOMICAL MUSEUM
天文科學教育館

Opened in 1997, this **museum** (Tiānwén Kēxué Jiàoyùguǎn; Map p82; ☎ 2831 4551; www.tam.gov.tw; 363 Jihe Rd; adult/concession NT40/20; ☉ 8.50am-5pm, closed Mon; MRT Shilin or Jiantan) is four floors of constellations, ancient astronomy, space science and technology, telescopes and observatories. Exhibits are attractive and thorough, although most signage is in Chinese only. Other more English-speaker-friendly attractions (at an extra charge) are an IMAX theatre, a 3-D theatre (presentations change frequently) and the 'Cosmic Adventure', an amusement park–style ride through outer space.

### TAIPEI SEA WORLD 台北海洋館

If you like your aquariums with sweep and grandeur, you'll probably be disappointed, but Taipei's **aquarium** (Táiběi Hǎiyángguǎn; Map p82; ☎ 2880 2310; 128 Jihe Rd; adult/concession/senior NT480/430/350; ☉ 9am-10pm; MRT Jiantan) is OK as a quick diversion. It's the only aquarium we've ever seen in a high-rise building and, as a result, it's as cramped inside as you'd expect, as well as a bit lacklustre (although the fish are pretty). Though there's little English signage you'll be able to learn the Chinese and Latin names of the creature you ate for dinner the night before. Downstairs are amusements for the kiddies.

## South of the City Centre    Map pp64-5
### CHIHNAN TEMPLE 木柵指南宮

If you're the type who feels that the journey is part of the experience of visiting a temple, then **Chihnan Temple** (Zhǐnán Gōng; 115 Wanshou Rd) is for you. This 1891 edifice is in the Wenshan District, about 19km southeast of central Taipei, and you have to climb 1200 steps to reach it. It's said that each step adds 20 seconds to your life – that's over six hours just for going up! There are landings at frequent intervals for you to rest.

The temple itself combines Buddhist, Confucian and Taoist worship. Once you ascend the steps, you'll reach a first hall and follow a covered pathway (up more steps!), and then you'll finally see it, like a multi-coloured, multitiered wedding cake tucked into the mountain side. The effect is quite startling and the views are incomparable.

The only people who should not visit, according to local legend, are young couples. The original temple was devoted to the worship of Liu Dung-bin, one of the eight immortals who was said to be unlucky in love and takes his revenge by breaking up blossoming relationships.

### LIN FAMILY MANSION & GARDEN
林家花園

Driving through this busy section of town, it may be difficult to believe that this was once all farmland. Yet in 1778 one Mr Lin Yang-yin migrated from Fujian province, and his family amassed a great fortune trading rice and salt with the mainland. Eventually the family (not to be confused with the Lin Antai family, p76) came to have huge farm holdings in what is now Banqiao City – and became fabulously wealthy from their holdings and the rice grown there. Their **mansion** and its 20,000-sq-metre **grounds** (Línjiā Huāyuán; ☎ 2965 3061; fax 2967 5264; 9 Ximen St, Banqiao City; admission 100NT; ☉ 9am-5pm, closed Mon) are well worth the trip.

The house was built in 1853 but opened to the public only in 2001. It is a prime example of a Qing-period mansion, with receiving halls, a library and performance stages. There are eye-popping uses of gold leaf on the doors and gates among other decorations of auspicious imagery. From the Grain Viewing Pavilion family members were able to look out over the farmers at work. It is said that the residential buildings are all tongue-and-groove construction, meaning that no nails were used. Plus it's all set amid ponds and gardens you might swear you've seen in paintings.

Admission to the estate is by tour only. There are 16 scheduled one-hour tours a day (in Chinese only); they fill up early in peak season. If you don't speak Chinese, you should have someone phone or fax at least a week in advance to schedule a tour in English.

From Taipei Main Station or Xinpu MRT station, take bus 307 or 310 to Beimen St and it's about a 100m walk to the main entrance.

### MUSEUM OF WORLD RELIGIONS
世界宗教博物館

This futuristic **venue** (Shìjiè Zōngjiào Bówùguǎn; ☎ 8231 6699; 7th fl, Pacific Department Store, 236 Zhongshan Rd, Sec 1, Yonghe City; adult/concession/student NT150/120/80; ☻ 10am-7pm, closed Mon) was founded by a Buddhist order with the idea of building harmony by showing the commonality of all religions. The same designer as the Holocaust Museum in Washington, DC, incorporated symbols, art, ritual objects and ceremonies to illuminate 10 of the world's great religions. Highlights include scale models of some of the signature buildings (Chartres Cathedral, Ise Shrine in Japan etc), which can be viewed from inside via tiny cameras, and films on various rites.

Signage in English is mostly fine and there's an English audio guide (NT80) to selected exhibits, though it does not cover the famous buildings. The museum's café is the Lian Hsin Yuan Vegetarian Restaurant (p98).

Take the MRT to Dingxi station and transfer to bus 706, 297, 51, 243 or Orange bus 6. Alternatively, it's about a 20-minute walk from the station.

### TAIPEI ZOO 木柵動物園

Celebrating its 100th anniversary in 2005, the **zoo** (Mùzhà Dòngwùyuán; ☎ 2938 2300; 30 Xingguang Rd, Sec 2; adult/concession NT60/30; ☻ 9am-5pm; MRT Muzha) attracts five million visitors each year, making it one of Taiwan's top attractions. It is sprawling (165 hectares and 1.5km across), with over 300 species (not

---

### THE NATIONAL PALACE MUSEUM: AN ART ODYSSEY

The National Palace Museum traces its origins back thousands of years. As early as the Western Han dynasty (206 BC–AD 9), emperors sent teams of servants to confiscate all manner of art, and many of these items eventually found a home in the Forbidden City in Beijing (established in the 1400s). The Forbidden City lived up to its name – unauthorised visitors could be tortured and executed – so you might say that the viewing public for these art treasures was rather limited (chiefly emperors, empresses and consorts).

The Chinese revolution of 1911 brought the KMT to power, although the Emperor Puyi did not leave the Forbidden City until 1924. Thus 1925 marked the first time that ordinary Chinese citizens could enter the Forbidden City, and the palace became China's National Palace Museum.

The Japanese invasion of Manchuria in 1931 foreshadowed war and the museum's contents were moved for safekeeping. The priceless treasures spent the war years shuttling among KMT stronghold cities in southern China (Nanjing, Emei, Chongqing etc). Despite heavy bombings and fierce battles, virtually the entire collection survived and a public exhibition was held in Nanjing in 1947.

In 1949, with the communist defeat of the KMT imminent, the collection was moved once again, to the Taiwanese port of Keelung. As the KMT retreat was supposed to be temporary, the collection stayed warehoused for over a decade, but in 1965 the National Palace Museum first opened its doors in Taipei. Miraculously, not a single piece was broken in all this transit.

Not surprisingly, the collection remains a major bone of contention with the mainland. While mainland leaders have long accused Taiwan of stealing the collection and demanded its return, the Taiwanese reply, with some justification, that many treasures would likely have fallen victim to rampaging Red Guards who were intent on destroying all vestiges of China's bourgeois past during the Cultural Revolution of the 1960s.

including humans), extensive gardens, including a tropical rainforest zone, and home to community events. The most popular animals are the koalas and penguins.

If you don't feel like walking the entire zoo, there's a minitrain (adult/senior NT5/3).

There are loads of eating opportunities inside the zoo (lunch boxes for NT70 and snacks for less), or if you feel like something more substantial there's a food court in the Zoo Mall (p93), on the other side of the MRT Muzha station.

## ACTIVITIES
### Fitness Clubs
**Alexander Health Clubs** (Map pp80-1; ☯ 6am-11pm) Zhongshan ( ☎ 2586 3850); Zhongxiao ( ☎ 2762 3866; 4th & 5th fl, Neo 19 Bldg, 12 Songshou Rd) An established national chain with over 20 locations island-wide.

---

### 'ONE LOVED POWER...'

Few figures in world politics of the 20th century were more polarising than Soong Mei-ling, better known to the world as Madame Chiang Kai-shek. One of the last WWII-era players, she died in 2003 at the age of 105, and the extraordinary span of her life went from an era of bound feet and dynastic rule, through revolution, war, military dictatorship and exile. Through it all she held forth with disarming grace that often masked brutality.

Soong was born in 1898, the youngest girl among six children. Her father had studied in America with Methodist missionaries but returned to China to make his fortune selling Bibles in Chinese and help finance Sun Yat-sen's overthrow of the Qing dynasty (p78). The three Soong sons became bankers, while one of the daughters married one of the world's wealthiest men, Soong married Chiang, and the third married Sun himself. It was said of the three daughters: 'One loved money, one loved power and one loved China'.

At the age of 10, Soong left Shanghai to study in the American state of Georgia, there acquiring a trademark Southern accent and beginning a long association with the USA. She graduated in 1917 from Wellesley, the exclusive women's college, and returned to Shanghai, but there she felt profoundly out of place and refused to marry a number of wealthy Chinese suitors.

Following Sun Yat-sen's death in 1925, a rising military member of his staff named Chiang Kai-shek sought the hand of Sun's widow, Soong's sister, but he was rebuffed. By rights, Soong should have rebuffed him too. He was Confucian, she was deeply Christian; he was married and kept concubines, she would never stand for that. But after he divorced, offered to dispatch his concubines and agreed to study the Bible, the two were married in 1927. A week later, Chiang set about planning his takeover of China.

The relationship of Soong and Chiang was unwavering. They discussed everything and although he was less than charismatic she personified charm and intellect. Throughout the following decades Soong was the voice of the KMT to the world. In 1943 she became the first Chinese woman to address a joint session of the US Congress, pleading for help against the Japanese, and her speeches across America drew crowds in the tens of thousands. By the end of her tour, America had pledged billions of dollars of support for the KMT in WWII. Despite the public persona, her stay at the White House was marked by ill temper and excessive demands on the staff. Eleanor Roosevelt remarked, 'She can talk beautifully about democracy but does not know how to live democracy'.

After WWII, Soong returned to America again to plead for funds to fight the communists, but this time she was rebuffed, not least because of allegations that money sent earlier had ended up in the hands of Nationalist officials and Soong family members. Still, through the following decades she was an important – some would say vital – link between the KMT government and the outside world.

Chiang's stature gradually diminished under the weight of martial law, corruption and, most significantly, UN recognition of China. He died in 1975 with Soong at his side, and when Chiang Ching-kuo (his son from a previous marriage) took over as Taiwanese leader, Soong moved to New York where she lived the rest of her life. Occasionally she attempted to intervene in Taiwanese politics, but Chen Shui-bian's election in 2000 ended 51 years of KMT rule, along with any effective influence she had. Taiwan's flag was not lowered after her death.

**California Fitness** (Jiāzhōu Jiànshēn Zhōngxīn; Map pp72-3; ☎ 2311 7000; 100 Zhongxiao W Rd, Sec 1; guest pass NT700 per day; ❤ 6am-midnight Mon-Sat, 8am-midnight Sun) This gym is as cutting-edge as the health clubs in its namesake home state. You'll find the latest equipment and shiny metallic locker rooms with steam and sauna. It's affiliated with California/24-Hour Fitness clubs in other countries.

## Spas & Saunas

This is a complicated topic. The spas and saunas of Beitou and Yangmingshan are pretty straightforward, but we've *heard* that others in town can be a little edgy. Particularly in the areas around Linsen N Rd, you'll find loads of places offering massage to men, with offers of extra services, so we're not recommending any of them.

If that is your interest, you should have no trouble finding one. If there are young women sitting around in the lobby looking tempting as they try to usher you inside, it's a good bet the place is what you think it is.

However, if it's a legitimate massage/spa/sauna experience that you're after, here are some wonderful options. See also spa listings under Beitou (p108) and Yangmingshan (p111).

**Eliza Lady Plaza** (Yīlìshā Shìnǚ Xiūjiān Guǎngchǎng; Map pp80-1; ☎ 2516 0191; 8 Lane 402, Fuxing N Rd; prices vary; ❤ 24hr) Its name about says it all. Women at Eliza pamper themselves with baths, saunas, beauty treatments, plus a café and shopping.

**Tianlong Sauna** (Tiānlóngsān Wēnruǎn; Map pp74-5; ☎ 2555 2277; 9th fl, 73 Chongqing N Rd, Sec 1; admission NT500) For men only, this sauna is a large facility with all kinds of options for getting warm and wet. Admission includes a private cabin for up to 12 hours. Treatments such as facials and massages start at NT2000.

## Hiking

A day hike makes for an excellent escape from the heat and pressure of the big city. *Taipei Day Trips 2* by Richard Saunders is an excellent resource, covering anywhere from close-in Yangmingshan to further-flung northern Taiwan. The original *Taipei Day Trips* was out of print at the time of writing; we hope it will be back again by the time you read this.

## Swimming

There are a few public outdoor swimming pools around town and some hotels have arrangements whereby you can use their pools for a fee – we've noted hotels with pools in the Sleeping section (p88). However, outdoor swimming is a seasonal thing in Taipei, usually reserved for warmer months. The following indoor facilities are open year round.

**My Island** (Húoshuǐ Jiànkāng Shìjiè; Map p82; ☎ 8861 4633; 31 Lane 505, Zhongshan N Rd, Sec 5; adult/student /child NT400/350/200, adult Sat & Sun NT500; ❤ 24hr) My Island is an airy, professional facility with an eight-lane 25m pool and a spa with a variety of pools. In addition to a swimsuit, you must also have a bathing cap, goggles and towel (these are available

---

### THE TEAHOUSES OF MAOKONG

For an afternoon of casual hiking or tea sipping in a quaint brick house on a scenic bluff, consider Maokong (Māokōng; Map pp64-5), the mountainous region behind Taipei Zoo: it's like Yangmingshan without the crowds. Some fans of the area include former president Lee Dung-hui who loved coming here so much he refused to allow the (mostly illegal) teahouses to be torn down.

Bus 15 from the zoo (NT15) leaves every hour on weekdays and every 30 minutes on weekends. When you get on the bus, show the driver one of the following addresses and he'll drop you off outside.

**Chenxi Teahouse** (Chénxī Cháfáng; ☎ 2936 4336; 53 Lane 34, Zhinan Rd, Sec 3; ❤ 24hr) Use this place as a reference point to get to some good hiking trails. Get off the bus, go through the arch and head up and right. Take the stairs and at the top look for a map. You'll see trails going in all directions.

**PLC Tea Tavern** (Hóngmùwū Xiūxián Cháguǎn; ☎ 2939 9706; 33 Lane 38, Zhinan Rd, Sec 3; per person NT300-400; ❤ 11.30-12.30am) This is the place where you want to drink tea in Maokong. Tables are set on the verandas of a traditional red-brick house. The view, with Chihnan Temple across a steep green valley, forms the perfect backdrop to an afternoon of *pàochá* (making tea).

for purchase). There's also a gym, but unfortunately that's open to annual members only.

**Yuquan Park Pool** (Yùquán Gōngyuán Shuǐ Yóuyǒng Chí; Map pp74-5; ☎ 2556 2539; 28 Xining N Rd; admission NT110; ☒ 5.30-7.30am, 8am-5pm & 6-10.30pm) A new (2004) facility near the centre of town. Its glass atrium features a water slide that empties into hot-water baths, and there are nearby 'massage waterfalls'. Oh yes, there's also a 25m pool.

## TAIPEI FOR CHILDREN

Beyond obvious choices such as the Taipei Zoo (p84), Children's Recreation Centre (p75), Taipei Astronomical Museum (p83), Taipei Sea World (p83), Children's Transportation Museum (p72), Taipei Water Park (p73) and the various parks around town, Taipei also offers great opportunities to expose children to Chinese culture. Perhaps, try a Chinese opera performance (p100).

Kids also seem to love marching with the guards at the Martyrs' Shrine (p79), while the Chiang Kai-shek Memorial Hall (p69) offers plenty of space for them to run around. And the night markets are alluring for kids of all ages. Just be sure to hold your child's hands – the markets can be busy!

Chinese restaurants are made for kids, especially dumpling houses – the perfect-sized food – or try the impressively messy, colourful desserts at Ice Monster (p94).

## TOURS

You won't have any trouble finding an organisation to take you on a bus tour of Taipei; the companies listed under Tours in the Transport chapter (p332) all offer them. Three-hour city tours (adult/child NT700/600) take in the Martyrs' Shrine, National Palace Museum, Chiang Kai-shek Memorial Hall, a temple visit and some shopping – although at three hours you won't get more than a taste of any one site. Other options include a Wulai aboriginal village tour (adult/child NT900/700, four hours), a Taipei-by-night tour (NT1200, 3½ hours) and a culture tour that takes in Chinese opera (NT1200, three hours).

Even if you're just transiting through Chiang Kai-shek Airport, the Taiwan tourism authorities offer a free half-day tour of Chiang Kai-shek Memorial Hall, the Presidential Building, National Palace Museum and Martyrs' Shrine. At the time of writing,

---

### FOOT MASSAGE

Imagine you're lying back in a comfy chair, your eyes closed and your legs stretched out before you while a professional massages your feet. Relaxed?

Now imagine the masseur or masseuse deliberately hitting a pressure point, causing you to 'Ooh-aah-*AAH*!' in pain. That's foot massage, one of the quintessential Taiwan experiences.

The pain – and it hurts so good – corresponds to parts of your body that ail you. Reflexology, as foot massage is also known, works from a chart showing dozens of points on your feet that correspond to the rest of your body, from your pituitary to your privates, plus joints, bones and innards. There are no secrets between you and your reflexologist – if you come in with even minor sinus congestion, he or she will know. Massaging the pressure points is said to stimulate the corresponding part of the body to heal itself.

Don't be embarrassed about howling with pain; the Taiwanese grandma in the next chair will probably out-howl you by far. And if you're ticklish, don't be surprised if you suddenly laugh.

It's hard not to stumble across a foot-massage shop in Taipei. English-speaking shops are rare but in most cases the foot chart, hand gestures and involuntary outbursts are all you'll need to communicate. Japanese is spoken at some of the better-known shops. **Giwado** (Zíhétáng; Map pp72-3; ☎ 2523 3376; 59 Xinsheng N Rd, Sec 1) and **Zaichunguan** (Zàichūnguǎn; Map pp74-5; ☎ 2595 3341; 77 Minquan E Rd, Sec 1) get Japanese tourists by the minibus-load. There's a number of smaller shops on Minquan E Rd, Sec 1, diagonally across from Xingtian Temple (p74). For foot massage in English, try **Hyatt Fitness Shop** (Kǎiyuè Nánnǚ Jiànkāng Guǎngchǎng; Map pp72-3; ☎ 2581 1616; 16 Chang'an E Rd, Sec 1).

At most shops, foot massages start at NT700 for 30 minutes, but some shops are as cheap as NT550.

tours depart the airport around 7am and return by 1.30pm, but check for the latest information at the half-day-tour counters at either terminal. You must have your ticket or boarding pass for your continuing flight, complete some paperwork and carry your belongings with you, but again we emphasise: it's *free*.

## FESTIVALS & EVENTS

In addition to national festivals (p315), interesting events include the birthdays of the city god (p76) and Confucius (p316). Christmas Eve has become a de facto holiday too; bars and restaurants throw parties.

## SLEEPING

For Taipei lodgings, price pretty well equates to quality. A modest difference in budget can mean a big difference in standards and services. While rooms at the lower end of the scale can be rather grotty and perhaps smell of mildew, at top-end lodgings you can look forward to world-class amenities and facilities: pool, spa, fitness club, sauna and fine restaurants.

For the purposes of this chapter, budget lodgings have basic rates of up to about NT1600 per room – dorm beds in hostels start at about NT250. Mid-range rates are up to about NT4000, and anything above that is considered top end. Note that when Taipei hotels list rates for a 'single' room, it often refers to a room with one queen-size bed that most travellers will find big enough for two.

---

### GAY & LESBIAN TAIPEI

Although Taipei's no San Francisco, London, West Hollywood or Amsterdam, by East Asian standards the gay scene here is fairly progressive and well developed. There's a quite decent assortment of nightlife, bookshops, shops, saunas and social options. Unlike other cities, there's no one gay district but, rather, venues are scattered throughout town. Taipei hosted one of Asia's first Gay Pride parades (in 2-28 Peace Park), which is now an annual event, and gay life here is well documented in film and literature (p43). For bars, clubs and the like, see p100. Further information is available on the web at www.utopia-asia.com.

---

The room rates listed here are the 'rack rate', the base rate charged at peak times. However, be sure to ask about discounts at mid-range and top-end hotels – 30% is not uncommon. Many hotels also throw in breakfast, though you may have to ask when you reserve. Upmarket hotels tend to charge a 10% service fee and 5% value-added tax (VAT) on top of their rates.

Budget options are scattered around town, but the highest concentration is within striking distance of Taipei Main Station (Old Town Centre and Zhongshan listings). Huaining St is particularly good for budget and mid-range options. Hostels tend to be tucked into other buildings, either residential or, in some cases, commercial, so you may need to hone your urban orienteering skills. Some hostels offer weekly or monthly rates. Note that hostels usually require you to bring your own towels, and some require linen.

Many lodgings can arrange for chauffeured private cars between the hotel and Chiang Kai-shek Airport, typically costing from NT1200 to NT1800.

If you plan on using the hotel's swimming pool, note that many pools are outdoors and may close in cooler months – be sure to check ahead.

### Old Town Centre
#### BUDGET

**Taipei YMCA International Guest House** (Táiběishì Zhōngguó Jīdūjiào Qīngniánhuì; Map pp72-3; ☎ 2311 3201; rv@ymca-taipei.org.tw; 19 Xuchang St; s/tw from NT1600/1900 incl breakfast; ☐) The Y attracts a mix of teachers, students, business people and anyone else looking for honest value. Rooms are as plain as in a monastery but well-kept and happy. Large rooms can be upgraded for (four-person) family use. There's a laundry on site for guests.

**Fortune Hotel** (Fújūn Dàfàndiàn; Map pp74-5; ☎ 2555 1121; fax 2556 6217; 5th-10th fl, 62 Chongqing N Rd, Sec 1; s/tw/tr NT1200/1400/1600) Popular with Taiwanese budget travellers, the Fortune is from the '70s and feels like it. There's an old-style attendant's counter on each floor. All rooms have private bath, phone and TV, but not all have curtains for your shower.

**Taipei Asia World Hostel** (Zhōnghuá Mínguó Guójì Qīngnián Zhījiā Xiéhuì; Map pp72-3; ☎ 2331 7272; www. yh.org.tw; 12th fl, 50 Zhongxiao W Rd, Sec 1; dm with /without Youth Hostel Card NT400/500) Although its

**THE AUTHOR'S CHOICE**

**Kodak Hotel Taipei III** (Kēdá Dàfàndiàn Táiběi Sāndiàn; Map pp72-3; ☎ 2531 9999; www .khotel.com.tw; 15 Lane 83, Zhongshan N Rd, Sec 1; r from NT3600 incl breakfast; 🖳 ) Despite its mid-range price, the K III gives more expensive hotels a run for their money. Although rooms are not enormous, they feature flat-screen TVs with DVD players, silk bedspreads and Jacuzzi bathtubs. No-smoking rooms are available. Note: although the address is a lane off Zhongshan N Rd, the hotel is actually closer to Linsen N Rd.

location in a high-rise office building across from the station is a little off-putting, you'll find 26 beds, rooms with private baths and lockers, and free laundry service.

**MID-RANGE**

**Chun Chuai Han She Hotel** (Jūnshuài Hánshè Shāngwù Lǚdiàn; Map pp72-3; ☎ 2371 8812; fax 2389 5151; 4th fl, 68 Chengdu Rd; r from NT2280 incl breakfast) Museumlit *objets d'art* in the corridors are your entrée to this small Ximending hotel's crisp, clean rooms. The catch: it's hard to find. The entrance is around the corner from Chengdu Rd. A red sign in the lobby reads 'hotel'.

**Cosmos Hotel** (Tiānchéng Dàfàndiàn; Map pp72-3; ☎ 2361 7856; cosmos@cosmos-hotel.com.tw; 43 Zhongxiao W Rd, Sec 1; d/tw from NT3000/3800; 🖳 ) Practically next to Taipei Main Station, the Cosmos may be a little dated and its décor a bit mismatched, but it's immaculately kept and there's a gym and sauna.

**Royal Castle Hotel** (Chéngdū Dàfàndiàn; Map pp72-3; ☎ 2383 1123; fax 2371 5511; 115 Chengdu Rd; r from NT2400) Another sane choice in Ximending, the Royal Castle was renovated in 2003 with marble bathrooms and dark wood trim. Rooms are not huge but contain coffee and tea service, and hot and cold drinking water spouts.

**Hotel Flowers** (Huáhuá Dàfàndiàn; Map pp72-3; ☎ 2312 3811; 19 Hankou Rd, Sec 1; r from NT2000) Serviceable and friendly business hotel at the corner of busy Huaning Rd, meaning that snacks abound just outside. Taipei Main Station is a few minutes' walk away.

**Keyman's Hotel** (Huáiníng Lǚdiàn; Map pp72-3; ☎ 2311 4811; fax 2311 5212; 1 Huaining St; r from NT2080) It's ageing and rooms are a little

small, but it's a decent deal for the convenient location.

**TOP END**

**Sheraton Taipei** (Táiběi Xǐláidēng Dàfàndiàn; Map pp72-3; ☎ 2321 5511; www.sheraton-taipei.com; 12 Zhongxiao E Rd, Sec 1; r from NT5000; 🖳 🖭 ) This massive 686-room hotel is near shopping and government offices, with some of the city's favourite restaurants (such as Momoyama, p93) and 'ladies' rooms with special amenities and services. At the time of writing it was in the midst of an expensive renovation, so it should be quite something by the time you visit. Rates may have changed too by the time you read this.

## Da'an & Shida
**BUDGET**

**Fortuna Hostel** (Map pp72-3; www.fullgass.net/fortuna hostel.htm; 3rd fl, 5 Alley 9, Lane 27, Tingzhou Rd, Sec 3) Travellers speak highly of this foreignowned hostel, with laundry and kitchen facilities and a cosy atmosphere.

**MID-RANGE**

**Friends Star Hotel** (Yǒuxīng Fàndiàn; Map pp72-3; ☎ 2394 3121; fax 2386 7791; 11 Heping Rd, Sec 1; r from NT2300 incl breakfast) Opened in 2002, immediately outside the MRT station and a close hop to the nightlife of Shida, the Friends Star is a good deal for this part of town. Small, windowless rooms cost least, but in any case you should ask for a room away from busy Heping Rd. Rates include free in-room ADSL connection with your own laptop.

**THE AUTHOR'S CHOICE**

**Taipei Fullerton Hotel** (Táiběi Fùdūn Fàndiàn; Map pp80-1; ☎ 2703 1234; www.taipeifullerton. com.tw; 41 Fuxing S Rd, Sec 2; r from NT4200 incl breakfast; 🖳 ) Renovated in 2003, its 95 rooms have a boutique feel and slick, contemporary décor that would feel at home in San Francisco or Tokyo. Rates include use of business centre, sauna and fitness centre.

## Zhongshan
**BUDGET**

**Queen Hotel** (Huánghòu Bīnguǎn; Map pp72-3; ☎ 2559 0489; 2nd fl, 226 Chang'an W Rd; s/d from NT650/700) Obviously budget but comfy, rooms have phone and some of their original (1950s) tile work. There's no English sign out front and you'll be lucky to find an English speaker inside, but it's right off a colourful market alley.

**Formosa Hostels I & II** (Map pp74–5; ☎ 2511 9625, mobile 0910-015 449) Formosa I (3rd fl, 16 Lane 20, Zhongshan N Rd, Sec 2); Formosa II (2nd fl, 5 Lane 62, Zhongshan N Rd, Sec 2; dm/tw/s NT250/260/350) These hostels are more short-term than some other local hostels. While extremely basic, both are decently kept. Formosa II is of a nicer standard, but Formosa I is nonsmoking – it's upstairs in an office building. Simple cooking and laundry facilities are available.

**Happy Family Hostels I, II & III** (Kuàilè Jiātíng; Map pp72–3; ☎ 2375 3443; www.taiwan-hostel.com; 2 Lane 56, Zhongshan N Rd, Sec 1; dm/s/d from NT260/400/500) Try to catch gregarious English-speaking owner Mr Lee; he's been in business for decades and is familiar with the needs of budget travellers. His three facilities are all located within close range of one another, but the office is at the address listed here (look for 'Happy Family' in red letters on the 2nd-floor window). Although all of the facilities are very simple, Happy Family III is the newest and nicest. Happy Family II gets a younger, more party-oriented crowd. There are shared toilets and hot-water showers on each floor, cable TV in the living rooms and free use of washing machines, although there's a seasonal charge for air conditioning.

### MID-RANGE
Note that many of these hotels offer substantial discounts.

**Friends Spring Hotel** (Yŏuchūn Fàndiàn; Map pp74–5; ☎ 2597 2588; fax 2598 6664; 55 Minquan W Rd; s/tw from NT2500/3200 incl breakfast; 🖳) This excellent deal was redecorated in 2003. Rates include English-language newspapers and free ADSL hook-up with your own laptop. It's close to the MRT Minquan W Rd stop.

**Emperor Hotel** (Guówáng Dàfàndiàn; Map pp72–3; ☎ 2581 1111; emperhtl@ms9.hinet.net; 118 Nanjing E Rd, Sec 1; r from NT3400 incl breakfast; 🖳) Its décor is a little dated, but this well-kept hotel is in an excellent location near shopping and surrounded by dining (lots of Japanese restaurants nearby).

**Hotel Delight** (Dàxīn Dàfàndiàn; Map pp74–5; ☎ 2565 2155; fax 2581 6493; 2 Lane 27, Zhongshan N Rd, Sec 2; s/d from NT1850/2120 incl breakfast) Upsides: well-priced, European style, primo location, free juice and water in in-room fridges. Downsides: rooms could use an update and there's no Internet connection on site. Some rooms have bathtubs, others have showers.

**Taipei Fortuna Hotel** (Fùdū Dàfàndiàn; Map pp74–5; ☎ 2563 1111; www.taipei-fortuna.com.tw; 122 Zhongshan N Rd, Sec 2; r from 3400; 🖳) Around the corner from the Minquan W Rd MRT station, this high-rise is often busy with tour groups. It's ageing only moderately well, but rooms are a decent size for the price. Health club with sauna on the premises.

### TOP END
**Hôtel Royal Taipei** (Lǎoyé Dàjiǔdiàn; Map pp74–5; ☎ 2542 3266; www.royal-taipei.com.tw; 37-1 Zhongshan N Rd, Sec 2; r from NT7200; 🖳 🏊) With a spiffy contemporary remodel (dark wood and white linen) by French designers, this very central hotel is quietly impressive. It's got fine attention to service, a gym, sauna, bathrobes, a safe and minibar in each of the 202 rooms, and free ADSL connections.

---

### THE AUTHOR'S CHOICE

**Grand Hotel** (Yuánshān Dàfàndiàn; Map pp74–5; ☎ 2886 8888; 1 Lane 1, Zhongshan N Rd, Sec 4; r from NT4800; 🖳 🏊) The pride and joy of the city and a tourist attraction in itself, the Grand demands to be seen even if you don't stay here. This 1970s reconstruction of the original 1952 building is a Chinese-style high-rise just across the Keelung River from the city centre. Its lobby, resplendent with red columns and painted beams, might remind you of temples you've seen around town. Rooms, too, are suitably spacious and old-style Chinese – choose from city or mountain views. Recreation includes a golf driving range, tennis, fitness centre and sauna, and there are 10 dining options.

**Grand Formosa Regent** (Jīnghuá Jiǔdiàn; Map pp74–5; ☎ 2523 8000; www.grandformosa.com.tw; 41 Zhongshan N Rd, Sec 2; r from NT8300; 🖳 🏊) Tops in every way, from the gold-leaf accents and exclusive shopping to the mountain views from the rooftop pool. It's got the largest standard rooms in Taipei with deep-soaking tubs. The super-minimalist Wellspring Spa is one of the loveliest we've seen anywhere.

**Ambassador Hotel** (Guóbīn Dàfàndiàn; Map pp74-5; ☎ 2551 1111; www.ambassadorhotel.com.tw; 63 Zhongshan N Rd, Sec 2; r from NT5900; 🖳 📧 ) Crisp, contemporary and international in style, the 430-room Ambassador is a long-time favourite of business travellers and flight crews. There is blond wood and marble throughout, and there's a spa with massage services. Executive floors (extra charge) carry extra benefits.

**Taipei International Hotel** (Táiběi Guójì Fàndiàn; Map pp72-3; ☎ 2562 7569; fax 2531 8376; 66 Nanjing E Rd, Sec 1; r from NT6600 incl breakfast; 🖳 ) Eurasian in feel and well located at the corner of Linsen N Rd, the International opened in 2003 with reasonably sized rooms with dark wood trim and cool bathroom faucets. Other amenities include a gym and daily newspaper delivery.

**Riviera Hotel** (Ōuhuá Jiǔdiàn; Map pp72-3; ☎ 2585 3258; www.rivierataipei.com; 646 Linsen N Rd; d/tw from NT6000/7000; 🖳 ) An easy walk from the Zone nightlife district and the Fine Arts Museum, the Riviera makes a point of never accepting tour groups. The result is a quiet atmosphere intended for business travellers. Rooms have an ironing board, and 'executive' rooms have separate work spaces. Plus, there's a rooftop jogging track and exercise equipment.

## Songshan & Xinyi
### BUDGET

**World Scholar House** (Map pp72-3; ☎ 2541 8113; www.worldscholarhouse.com; 8th fl, Alley 2, Lane 38, Songjiang Rd; dm/d NT300/700) Despite the high-falutin name, this hostel is pretty basic. Still, expat English teachers seem to make a cosy community for themselves here. There are laundry and ironing facilities. Weekly and monthly rates available.

**Taipei Hostel** (Map pp72-3; ☎ 2395 2950; www.taipeihostel.com; 6th fl, 11 Lane 5, Linsen N Rd; dm/s/d NT250/500/550) Rather downtrodden but busy nonetheless, this hostel is on a quiet backstreet and has a large TV/socialising room, kitchen facilities, washer/dryer, ADSL use (with your own laptop) and rooftop garden. BYO linen and towels. The website has tips and links to information on Taipei and teaching English.

### MID-RANGE

**Baguio Hotel** (Bìyáo Dàfàndiàn; Map pp80-1; ☎ 2781 3121; www.baguio-hotel.com.tw; 367 Bade Rd, Sec 2; d/tw from NT1730/1950) A bit long in the tooth but well kept and friendly, this central hotel has some Chinese art on the walls.

**Happiness Hotel** (Háoyuè Dàfàndiàn; Map pp72-3; ☎ 2517 7272; Hotel_A@hotmail.com; 18 Lane 97, Songjiang Rd; r from NT2600 incl breakfast; 🖳 ) Some visitors may find the décor a little frilly and there are no shower curtains, but otherwise this is an excellent choice on a quiet block. Washing machines available and rates are often discounted.

**First Hotel** (Dìyī Dàfàndiàn; Map pp74-5; ☎ 2551 2277; www.firsthoteltaipei.com; 63 Nanjing E Rd, Sec 2; s & tw from NT2700 incl breakfast; 🖳 ) A solid mid-range choice, the First makes the most of its four-decade-old shell and smallish rooms with renovated facilities and several restaurant options.

**Golden China Hotel** (Kānghuá Dàfàndiàn; Map pp74-5; ☎ 2521 5151; www.golden-china.com.tw; 306 Songjiang Rd; r from NT3400; 🖳 ) Rooms are large for the price, if a little plain, and some have ADSL connections. There are simple workout facilities and a rooftop putting green. Nonsmoking floors are available.

**Leofoo Hotel** (Liùfú Kèzhàn; Map pp74-5; ☎ 2507 3211; hotel@leofoo.com.tw; 168 Changchun Rd; r from NT2420 incl breakfast; 🖳 ) Décor here is contemporary

---

### THE AUTHOR'S CHOICE

**Far Eastern Plaza Hotel** (Yuǎndōng Guójì Dàfàndiàn; Map pp80-1; ☎ 2378 8888; www.shangri-la.com; 201 Dunhua S Rd, Sec 2; s/d from NT8700/9200; 🖳 📧 ) The row of fancy cars parked in front is your first indication of this hotel's luxe status, and as you ascend the hotel's 43 storeys you'll be convinced. There's a sauna, fitness centre, business centre and shopping and dining. Chinese art features throughout, and rooms have walk-in closets. Even the bathrooms have TVs and Jacuzzi tubs, but don't pass up the glorious Jacuzzi and pool on the rooftop.

**Les Suites Taipei** (Táiběi Shànglǚ; Map pp80-1; ☎ 8712 7688; www.slh.com/taiwan/taipei/hotel_tailes.html; 12 Qingcheng St; r from NT6500; 🖳 ) Intimate and hidden, yet only steps from shopping, dining and the MRT, this fashionable, 90-room boutique hotel has a super-cool contemporary look, gym, nonsmoking lounge with tea and cookies, and cigar and wine lounge. Rooms are crisp and up-to-date.

Chinese, and rooms include satellite TV and a fridge. Bonus: discounts to the movie theatre next door.

**Waikoloa Hotel** (Wéikèlè Fàndiàn; Map pp80-1; ☎ 2507 0168; www.waikoloa.com.tw; 187 Changchun Rd; r from NT2560 incl breakfast; ▢ ) The Waikoloa was given a complete makeover in 2003, with rooms decorated in Japanese, Chinese or Chinese-via-Versailles styles. There's free Internet access.

### TOP END

**Evergreen Laurel Hotel** (Táiběi Chánglóng Guìguàn Jiǔdiàn; Map pp72-3; ☎ 2501 9988; www.evergreen-hotels.com; 63 Songjiang Rd; r from NT8000; ▢ ) Opened in 2001 with 100 cool rooms, this high-rise is full of goodies such as Italian furniture, fax machines, gold-plated sinks, plasma TVs and an Olympic-quality health club. It's operated by the owners of Eva Air so there are often promotional packages.

**Grand Hyatt Hotel** (Táiběi Jūnyuè Dàfàndiàn; Map pp80-1; ☎ 2720 1234; www.taipei.grand.hyatt.com; 2 Songshou Rd; r from NT6200; ▢ ▣ ) A Xinyi icon, massive (over 850 rooms) and soaring. Rooms have three phone lines, there's a business centre, health club and the Ziga Zaga nightclub (p102) and it's close to Xinyi shopping and dining.

**Mandarina Crown Hotel** (Zhōngtài Bīnguǎn; Map pp80-1; ☎ 2721 1201; hotel@mcrown.com.tw; 166 Dunhua N Rd; r from NT7200; ▢ ) Just minutes from Songshan Domestic Airport but feels like a mini-getaway to Thailand. Its 183 rooms are sleek and cool with Southeast Asian touches and its four restaurants include Thai and Mongolian. There's a health club and sauna.

**Landis Taipei** (Yàdū Lìzhì Dàfàndiàn; Map pp74-5; ☎ 2597 1234; www.landistpe.com.tw; 41 Minquan E Rd, Sec 2; r from NT7500; ▢ ) Although this hotel dates from 1979 it feels like the 1930s, with Art Deco touches throughout. Bathrooms feature great big showerheads and frosted glass, while rooms have DVD players and European styling. Nonsmoking floors, fitness centre and outdoor Jacuzzi available. It's also known for personal service.

**Le Petit Sherwood** (Táiběi Xiǎoxīhuá Fàndiàn; Map pp80-1; ☎ 2754 1166; lps@sherwood.com.tw; 370 Dunhua S Rd, Sec 1; r from NT6200 incl breakfast; ▢ ) Boutique, sleek and unique, this newer, smaller version of Zhongshan's landmark Sherwood has 62 rooms with Italian marble and modernist furnishings.

**Sherwood Taipei** (Xīhuá Dàfàndiàn; Map pp80-1; ☎ 2718 1188; www.sherwood.com.tw; 111 Minsheng E Rd, Sec 3; r from NT8600; ▢ ▣ ) The Sherwood's king-size beds have hosted presidents and prime ministers as well as business travellers looking for easy access to the international banks nearby. There's a well-stocked gym.

**United Hotel** (Guólián Dàfàndiàn; Map pp80-1; ☎ 2772 1515; www.unitedhotel.com.tw; 200 Guangfu S Rd; s/tw from NT6000/7400; ▢ ) This high-rise looks unremarkable from the outside, but enter the lobby and you'll notice a contemporary minimalism that carries all the way through to the rooms. Glassed-in bathrooms (draw the shades if you like) feature claw-foot tubs, and there's also a fitness centre and sauna.

**Westin Taipei** (Liùfú Huánggōng; Map pp80-1; ☎ 8770 6565; www.westin.com; 133 Nanjing E Rd, Sec 3; r from NT9400; ▢ ▣ ) The high-rise Westin was built in the late 1990s and has 288 rooms, a piano bar and 12 food and beverage venues. Rooms are colourful-contemporary in style and feature separate bathtub and shower. An indoor pool means that you can swim all year – there's also a health club.

## EATING

Residents of many cities claim that their city is one of the world's great food capitals but in Taipei there's a difference: they're right, especially when it comes to Chinese food. From night-market stalls and down-and-dirty noodle and dumpling stands to luxurious eight-storey affairs with slip-covered chairs and private dining rooms, you may be overwhelmed by the choice and quality.

It comes down to history: cooks fleeing the mainland 55 years ago brought with them rich culinary traditions, and those traditions continue. No other city has such a diversity of Chinese cooking styles done so well – standouts include Beijing, Shanghai,

---

### HOW MUCH?

This book breaks down price categories for restaurants as:

▪ **Budget** meals under NT120

▪ **Mid-range** meals NT120–400

▪ **Top end** meals over NT400

**EAT STREETS**

» **Yongkang St** (Map pp72-3) The grand-daddy of them all, with dozens of choices in several intimate blocks

» **Huaning St** (Map pp72-3) Just south-west of Taipei Main Station are about a dozen tiny shops selling everything from dumplings and noodles prepared before your eyes to Chinese buffet, tiny cakes and pearl tea

» **Ximending** (Map pp72-3) Just wander; you're sure to find something

» **Linsen N Rd, Sec 1** (Map pp74-5) If you want it Japanese, you'll find it here

Cantonese and Taiwan's own cooking. We could fill an entire chapter on Taipei's food offerings so don't hesitate to ask locals for suggestions.

Don't like Chinese food? Don't fret. There are a number of fine choices from across Asia and the West. Some Western locals carp that local versions of cuisines such as French and Italian don't compare to the real thing but there are a number of Western restaurants where mother-country chefs rule the kitchen.

Vegetarians will find numerous options, although in typical Chinese places something listed on the menu as having just vegetables may well have bits of meat in it. One sure bet is to look for Buddhist restaurants, which have the Buddhist swastika on the menu.

Finally, one important note: Taipeiers eat early, at least at Chinese restaurants. Arrive much after 8pm and you're likely to close the restaurant down.

## Old Town Centre
### BUDGET
**Yitiaoleng** (Běipíng Yītiáolóng Jiǎozìguǎn; Map pp72-3; ☎ 2361 6166; 12 Emei St; dishes NT88-188; ☾ lunch & dinner) Since the 1950s this place has been serving northern-Chinese-style dumplings and hotpots. Take a Chinese-speaking friend or hone your pointing skills.

### MID-RANGE
**Red Pavilion Theatre** (Hónglóu Jùchǎng; Map pp72-3; ☎ 2311 9380; 10 Chengdu Rd; dishes NT199-299; ☾ lunch & dinner) The café in this theatre serves light meals such as spaghetti and curries in a unique, old-style setting.

### TOP END
**Momoyama** (Táoshān; Map pp72-3; ☎ 2321 5511, ext 8085; 12 Zhongxiao E Rd, Sec 1; set lunch NT500-1300, set dinner NT1300-3300, individual dishes NT100-1500; ☾ lunch & dinner) Taipei's top Japanese, downstairs at the Sheraton (p89). The stunning décor might remind you of Kyoto, especially if you book a private tatami room (extra charge). Popular with politicos.

**Tainan Tan-tsu-mien** (Huáxijiē Táinán Dànzǎimiàn; ☎ 2308 1123; 31 Huaxi St; meals NT1200-1500; ☾ lunch & dinner) Odd though it may seem to have rooms decorated like Versailles and Vienna in Snake Alley, that's what you'll find here. Select your own fish and seafood out front and the chef will suggest a preparation (grilled, steamed, fried etc). Don't forget the shop's namesake noodles (made with ground pork); NT50 for a small bowl.

## Da'an & Shida
### BUDGET
**HDC** (cnr Longquan Rd & Lane 26, Taishun St; chicken NT40) There's almost always a line at this

**FOOD COURTS WORTH NOTING**

» **Taipei 101** (p78) Hands down the best food court we've ever seen, with flavours from across Asia and plenty of other places as well

» **Jiancheng Circle** (Map pp74-5; ☾ lunch & dinner) In the middle of the traffic circle where Nanjing and Chongqing Rds meet, Taipei's 'noodle circle' is a glass cylinder with two spiralling concentric floors of dozens of food stalls. Options run from snacking and dining to hotpots and juices. Most dishes are under NT100.

» **Zoo Mall** (Map pp64-5; 30 Xingguang Rd, Sec 2; ☾ lunch & dinner) A fine option if you're headed to the zoo or Chihnan Temple

» Pretty much any department store or shopping mall

tiny stand near the north end of the Shida Night Market. People come for one dish: a half-breast of chicken that's breaded, deep fried, sprinkled with red and black pepper and served piping hot. Eat your heart out, Colonel Sanders.

**Ice Monster** (Bīngguǎn; Map pp72-3; ☎ 2394 8279; 15 Yongkang St; dishes NT80-150; 🕑 10.30am-midnight summer, 11.30am-11pm winter) It's hard to imagine anything more refreshing on a hot summer day – or after a big winter-time dinner around the corner – than shaved ice topped with chunks of strawberry, kiwi fruit or (most famously) mango and a scoop of mango sorbet.

**Shida Night Market** (Map pp72-3; 🕑 dinner) A classic place for a light meal, in the streets east of Shida Rd and south of Heping E Rd. You may well see students lined up in front of popular places; non-Chinese-speakers can just point and eat.

**Yang's Bakery** (Yángjiā Shuǐjiǎoguǎn; Map pp80-1; ☎ 2772 1190; 278 Zhongxiao E Rd, Sec 3; dumpling plates around NT50-70; 🕑 lunch & dinner) This 40-plus-year-old northern-Chinese-style place is unpretentious to the max and has no English menu, but that doesn't matter. Order yourself some *dàguōtiē* (long rolled dumplings, steamed then fried) or *yángjiāshuǐjiǎo* (pork dumplings) and you'll see what we mean. There's also very decent *niúròumiàn* (beef noodle soup) and the small plates of side dishes are fine too.

## MID-RANGE

**Daxiangyuan Chuancai** (Dàxiāngyuán Chuāncàiguǎn; Map pp72-3; ☎ 2362 9333; 21 Yunhe St; mains NT80-268; 🕑 lunch & dinner) Simple, family-style place off a leafy stretch of Shida Rd, with Sichuan-style classics such as *mapo* tofu, *kungpao* chicken, *yuxiang* eggplant and dry-fried string beans.

**Dintaifung** (Dǐngtàifēng; Map pp72-3; ☎ 2321 8927; 194 Xinyi Rd, Sec 2; dumplings NT140-290; 🕑 lunch & dinner) With Taipei's most celebrated dumplings, Dintaifung is deservedly popular for Shanghai-style treats made fresh to order. Try the classic *xiǎolóngbāo* (steamed pork dumplings). Don't be surprised to see a queue out the front day and night.

**Gao Ji** (Gāojì, Kao's Snack Collection; Map pp72-3; ☎ 2341 9984; 5 Yongkang St; dishes NT30-300; 🕑 9am-10pm Mon-Fri, 7am-10pm Sat & Sun) While Dintaifung gets bigger crowds, many locals swear that this shop around the corner is cheaper, better and less hassle. Kao's has been around since 1950, so it must be doing something right. Snack on teeny-tiny plates of prepared vegetables or feast on steamer trays full of dumplings in dozens of varieties. We love the steamed custard buns for dessert. Most dishes are under NT150.

**Gaoryo** (Gāolìbàng; Map pp80-1; ☎ 2772 8649; 40 Lane 51, Da'an Rd, Sec 1; mains NT150-280; 🕑 lunch & dinner, closed 1st & 3rd Mon of month) Lots of restaurants around town call themselves Korean, but this stucco-walled place feels like the real thing, with classics such as *bulgogi* and *galbi* (grilled meat dishes), and a lovely assortment of *banchan* (side dishes). The hard part is finding it (exit 9 from MRT Zhongxiao Dunhua station).

**Grandma Nitti's** (Zhōngxī Měishí; Map pp72-3; ☎ 2369 9751; 8 Lane 93, Shida Rd; mains NT150-400; 🕑 9am-11pm Mon-Sat, 10am-11pm Sun) Grandma serves good ol' Western comfort food – waffles, burgers, Philly cheese steaks and family-size pastas. Breakfast is served until dinner time. There's a comfy street-side terrace, or the windowed space upstairs is a great place to mull over the newspaper. Some carp that the service is a little inattentive, but at these prices…

**Huiliu** (Map pp72-3; 9 Lane 31, Yongkang St; meals NT120-350; 🕑 lunch & dinner, closed Mon) Across a pleasant little park from Taipei's favourite food street, this city-goes-*rustique* vegetarian place serves quiches, pizzas, pastas, salads and dishes of Asian persuasion.

**Lan Ji** (Lánjì Málà Huǒguō; ☎ 2322 4523; 19 Jinshan S Rd, Sec 1; ingredients NT50-400; 🕑 5.30pm-5am, closed Sun) It's a hole in the wall, but a can't-miss spot for Taiwanese hotpot. Order yours with any number of meats and/or vegetables and your desired level of spice. Special pots with dividers down the centre allow companions with different taste in spice to still share the same pot.

## SELF-CATERING

**Bee Cheng Hiang** (Měizhēnxiāng; Map pp80-1; ☎ 2731 5667; 12 Zhongxiao E Rd, Sec 4; 300g jerky NT240-290) If you're invited to a Taiwanese home, the dried barbecued meats from this popular shop make an excellent house gift. Choose from beef, pork or lamb with a variety of flavours from sweet to savoury to spicy. Pick up a pre-made package or watch the workers roast the meat before your eyes. Other locations are in Shin Kong

Mitsukoshi (p104) and Dayeh Takashimaya (p104) department stores. It's great year round, but especially at Chinese New Year.

**Mami Store** (Māmī Shāngdiàn; Map pp72-3; ☎ 2369 9868; 6 Lane 117, Shida Rd) Whether you need American-style spaghetti sauce, German canned vegetables or Thai curries, this small, eclectic store has it. You can also get kitchen supplies such as bakeware and bowls.

## Zhongshan
### BUDGET
**Joy Yuan Taiwan Buffet** (Qiáoyuán Quánzìzhùcān; Map pp72-3; ☎ 2550 0777; 171 Chang'an W Rd; dishes NT5-50; ☺ lunch & dinner) Busy and spotless, this cafeteria-style buffet restaurant has dozens of selections. There's a high turnover, so the food's always fresh. Most dishes are under NT30. Takeaway lunch boxes (*biàndāng*) cost NT60.

### MID-RANGE
**Celestial Restaurant** (Tiānchú Cāntīng; Map pp80-1; ☎ 2521 1097; 3rd fl, 1 Nanjing W Rd; mains NT165-380, Beijing duck from NT750; ☺ lunch & dinner) Lovers of Beijing-style cooking have been coming to this classic for generations. In addition to Beijing duck (expensive but meant for sharing), try the elegant, comforting 'green beans (actually peas) with shredded chicken' (NT300). Enter off Nanjing W Rd.

**G'day Café** (Qíngxī Cānfáng; Map pp80-1; ☎ 2717 5927; 180 Xingan St; mains NT120-320; ☺ 10am-10pm Mon-Sat, 10am-5pm Sun, closed last Mon of month) Popular with local expats, this informal spot serves comfort food in the American/Italian/Mexican tradition, including breakfast (steak and eggs, anyone?), soups of the day, burgers, tacos and apple pie with ice cream.

**Green Leaf** (Qīngyè Cāntīng; Map pp72-3; ☎ 2571 3859; 1 Lane 105, Zhongshan N Rd, Sec 1; mains NT128-298; ☺ lunch & dinner) This perennial favourite serves everything Taiwanese, from dumplings to full plates in vintage 1964 décor. Service is professional, fast and workmanlike, and the huge menu is well translated. Some more expensive seafood options cost up to NT1288.

**Haibawang** (Hǎibàwáng Qíjiàndiàn; Map pp74-5; ☎ 2596 3141; 59 Zhongshan N Rd, Sec 3; mains NT100-600; ☺ lunch & dinner) The speciality here is Taiwanese hotpot in an elegant setting, eight storeys adjacent to the Taipei Arts Park by the Fine Arts Museum. If you're not up for hotpot (or some lovely Taiwanese seafood plates), some floors feature Italian or buffet-style dining.

**Hatsuho** (Chūsuì Jūjiǔwū; Map pp72-3; ☎ 2522 1251; 112 Nanjing E Rd, Sec 1; dishes NT80-320; ☺ lunch & dinner) Just steps from the Emperor Hotel, you'll find this country-Japanese-style place for sashimi, grilled fishes, *yakitori* (grilled chicken skewers) and *okonomiyaki* (savoury pancakes). You can choose *hori-kotatsu* seating, with your feet in a well under the table.

**My Home Steak** (Wǒjiā Niúpái; Map pp74-5; ☎ 2504 8152; 182 Changchun Rd; mains NT130-370; ☺ lunch & dinner) No highbrow experience, but this small shop is spotlessly clean and reasonably priced. Steaks are served on sizzling-hot plates with your choice of sauce (although we avoid the overly sweet mushroom sauce), pasta and a fried egg. Prices include a modest but unlimited salad, soup and dessert bar.

**Seoul Korean Barbecue** (Hànchéng Cāntīng; Map pp72-3; ☎ 2511 2326; 4 Lane 33, Zhongshan N Rd, Sec 1; dishes NT90-150; ☺ lunch & dinner) Probably the most elegant Korean restaurant in town, Seoul's five storeys are redolent with the rich aromas of soy sauce and garlic. Décor is sumptuous hardwood.

**Shin Yeh** (Xīnyè Táicài Běndiàn; Map pp74-5; ☎ 2596 3255; 34-1 Shuangcheng St; mains NT120-485; ☺ lunch & dinner) This popular Taiwanese restaurant has multiple locations, but you can't miss with this one, adjacent to the Zone nightlife district (p100). It's known for being fast and inexpensive.

### TOP END
**Zum Fass** (Xiāngyí Déguó Liàolí; Map pp72-3; ☎ 2531 3815; 55 Lane 119, Linsen N Rd; mains NT250-650; ☺ lunch Sun, dinner nightly) This cellar restaurant serves traditional German cooking (eg sausages, *Jägerschnitzel* – pork cutlet with mushrooms) and feels positively Teutonic inside. Despite the address, it's a bit of a way from Linsen N Rd.

## Songshan
### BUDGET
**Liaochen Niuroumian** (Liaochen Niúròumiàn; Map pp80-1; 1 Alley 9, Lane 133, Nanjing E Rd, Sec 4; small /large noodle soup NT70/80; ☺ lunch & dinner, closed Sun) On a lane loaded with street food stalls, come here for famous beef noodle soup and a minimum of atmosphere.

**Little Saigon** (Map pp80-1; ☎ 2731 8037; 24 Lane 116, Guangfu S Rd; most dishes NT80-150; ☽ lunch & dinner) Near the Chunghwa Television building, this little store front serves *pho* (Vietnamese noodle soup) and rice dishes.

**New York Bagels** (Yuányùfēng; Map pp72-3; ☎ 2507 5660; 28 Yitong St; bagels NT50, sandwiches NT95-185; ☽ breakfast, lunch & dinner) Fans of the movie *Yi-Yi* will recognise this shop, and local journalists love it too. Classics from New York's famed H&H Bagels include plain, sesame and onion, alongside newfangled flavours such as blueberry and jalapeño. Top them with everything from cream cheese to smoked salmon to roast beef.

**Sihua Vegetarian Buffet** (Shífāng Sùshí Zìzhùcān; Map pp80-1; ☎ 2546 2836; 63 Nanjing E Rd, Sec 4; lunch/dinner NT40/60; ☽ lunch & dinner, closed Sun) The décor could be described as nil, but we'll be charitable and call it Buddhist simplicity. The food is simple too, but there's a nice variety of dishes prepared according to Buddhist vegetarian principles.

### MID-RANGE

**Hindustan** (Yǔdūsītǎn; Map pp80-1; ☎ 2718 5608; 43 Lane 313, Fuxing N Rd; mains NT220-350; ☽ lunch Mon-Sat, dinner nightly) Although its address is off Fuxing N Rd, it's actually closer to Dunhua N Rd. It's known especially for its tandoori dishes, but also for biryanis and seafood.

**Kiki** (Kiki Lǎomā Cāntīng; Map pp80-1; ☎ 2752 2781; 28 Fuxing S Rd, Sec 1; mains NT120-420; ☽ lunch & dinner) If you like your Chinese food spicy and served in a loud yet vibrant atmosphere, look no further. Kiki's three storeys of pan-Chinese are as busy, friendly and trendy as the young staff, and the dishes are huge and satisfying (faves include stir-fried chicken with chilli sauce, and stir-fried watercress with preserved tofu). It's open until 2am.

**Silver Spoon** (Yíngtānchí; Map pp80-1; ☎ 2716 6773; 19 Nanjing E Rd, Sec 4; lunch/dinner buffet NT380/520; ☽ lunch & dinner) Sure it's sophisticated, with nightclub lighting, black chairs, right angles, concrete floors and groovy beats, but the aromas of Thai food show that they haven't forgotten that it's about eating too.

**Taoranting** (Táorántíng; Map pp80-1; ☎ 2778 7805; 2nd fl, 86 Fuxing N Rd; mains NT120-240; ☽ lunch & dinner) An old-line Beijing-style place with bright red seat-backs. It's a good choice for Beijing duck (NT800) or a flaming pot with pickled vegetables and Chinese cabbage (NT900). Large plates are meant for sharing.

**Very Thai** (Fēichǎng Tài Gàiniàn Cāntīng; ☎ 2546 6745; 319 Fuxing N Rd; mains NT150-450; ☽ lunch & dinner) Very dark and very cool, this mod-Thai spot has black-on-black décor and lovely dishes. Most dishes cost under NT300. It's open, you guessed it, very late.

### TOP END

**Dan Ryan's Chicago Grill** (Zhījiāgē Cāntīng; Map pp80-1; ☎ 2778 8800; 8 Dunhua N Rd; mains NT220-820; ☽ lunch & dinner) Homesick Midwesterners (or New Yorkers or Californians or Irish) can feel right at home dining on steaks, chops and salads in huge quantities.

**Lawry's The Prime Rib** (Láoruìsī Niúleìpaí Cāntīng; Map pp80-1; ☎ 3762 1312; 12th fl, 'Living Mall', 134 Bade Rd, Sec 4; mains NT790-1690; ☽ lunch & dinner) This institution from Beverly Hills has now landed in Taiwan, with huge roast-beef dinners and a signature 'spinning bowl' salad prepared table-side.

**Paris 1930** (Bālítīng; Map pp74-5; ☎ 2597 1234; 41 Minquan E Rd, Sec 2; meals NT1800-3000; ☽ dinner) This restaurant in the Landis Hotel is consistently rated the best French in town, with six-plus-course dinners. There's piano music and a refined atmosphere, and the hotel's Deco setting provides a suitably sophisticated backdrop.

**Shabu-jan** (Chán; Map pp80-1; ☎ 8761 6677; 11th fl, 'Living Mall', 134 Bade Rd, Sec 4; dinners NT620-1680; ☽ lunch & dinner) Lots of places around Taipei claim to serve *shabu-shabu*, a Japanese hotpot of thinly sliced beef which you dip into sauces, but Shabu-jan (Japanese name: Shabu-zen) has the home-country pedigree to go with it.

### SELF-CATERING

**SOGO Department Store** (Tàipíngyáng Chóngguāng Bǎihuò; Map pp80-1; ☎ 2776 5555; 45 Zhongxiao E Rd, Sec 4) Has a worthwhile supermarket.

## Xinyi      Map pp80-1

### MID-RANGE

**City Star** (Jīngxīng Gǎngshì Yǐnchá; ☎ 2741 2625; 2nd fl, 216 Dunhua S Rd, Sec 1; mains NT100-360, dim sum NT50-120; ☽ 24hr) Cantonese food is good for the soul, and whether you need it in the middle of the day or the middle of the night, this comfortably contemporary restaurant is there for you. There's an enormous picture menu and with any luck you'll catch one of its frequent specials (eg five plates of dim sum for NT300 at lunch).

**Do It True** (Dùyìchù; ☎ 2729 7853; 506 Renai Rd, Sec 4; mains NT140-380; ✐ lunch & dinner) Across the street from Sun Yat-sen Memorial Hall, Do It True is operated by a veteran Beijing chef. Just about every table orders the spicy braised pork with sesame buns. Pine-smoked chicken and delicate steamed vegetable dumplings are also popular. Caveats: small plates (including the pork) can be *very* small, and service can be indifferent.

**Treasure Box Korean BBQ** (Hánzhēnguǎn; ☎ 2741 5880; 45 Lane 240, Guangfu S Rd; dishes NT120-150; ✐ lunch & dinner) Informal but clean, with grills in the tables and exhaust fans above them, this Korean owned and operated spot has been serving grills, rice dishes, hotpots and side dishes since 1955. All-you-can-eat barbecue starts at adult/child NT289/150 (more on weekends).

**Osteria Rialto** (Yáduǒ; ☎ 2778 1536; 5 Lane 260, Guangfu S Rd; mains NT260-780; ✐ lunch & dinner) Comfortable trattoria serving house-made pastas that are better than they need be at these prices and, of course, a nice Chianti. Enjoy it all in the comfortable dining room or alfresco.

**People** (Rénjiān; ☎ 2735 2288; 191 Anhe Rd, Sec 2; mains NT280-480; ✐ lunch & dinner) Head down the stairs for creative pan-Asian meals served in a very mod, spot-lit, postindustrial setting. To enter, stick your hand inside the lantern outside the main door. The chichi bar gives any lounge in town a run for its money.

**TOP END**

**Jogoya** (Shànggéwū; ☎ 8789 5678; 3rd fl, 22 Songshou Rd; buffet NT528-728; ✐ 11.30-3am) Some locals call it Japanese, but this super-contempo spot has selections from across Asia in a maze-like buffet that seems to go on forever: hotpots to sushi, desserts, prepared dishes and foods you give the chefs to cook. Inside, it's all marble, mirrors and pin-spot lighting. Prices fluctuate by time of day (mid-afternoon and late night are cheapest).

**Sung Tung Lok** (Xīntónglè Cāntīng; lunch from NT1880, dinner from NT3520; ✐ lunch & dinner) Dunhua S Rd, Sec 2 ( ☎ 2700 1818; 34 Dunhua S Rd, Sec 2); Dunhua S Rd, Sec 1 ( ☎ 2752 9797; 2 Lane 232, Dunhua S Rd, Sec 1) These two locations feature staff from Hong Kong, elegant, intimate settings and menus of famous Cantonese-style dishes,

with an emphasis on seafood. There's no English menu, but staff members can help you out.

**SELF-CATERING**

**Jason's** (1st basement fl, Taipei 101, 45 Shifu Rd) Taipei's leading purveyor of Western foods, although it's known for being a little pricey.

## Shilin & Tianmu           Map p82
**BUDGET**

**Tian Yun Wonton** (Tiānyún Biǎnshí; ☎ 2874 7448; 14 Lane 9, Tianmu N Rd; dishes NT30-110; ✐ lunch & dinner) While there's zero atmosphere in this corner shop, it's got a 50-year history and a famous Set No 3 (stewed pork with noodles). No MSG used.

**MID-RANGE**

**Fang's Restaurant** (Fāngjiā Xiǎoguǎn; ☎ 2872 8402; 7 Tianmu E Rd; mains NT160-560; ✐ lunch & dinner) You can find excellent plates of Jiangzi-style (Shanghai regional) cooking at this well-regarded, spotless local favourite. Just about every table also seems to order a tray of 'mini-mall steamed buns' – tiny soup dumplings (NT260 for a serving of 20).

**Jake's Country Kitchen** (Xiāngxiāng Měimò Xīcān; ☎ 2871 5289; 705 Zhongshan N Rd, Sec 6; dishes NT70-280; ✐ breakfast, lunch & dinner) Head here for the kind of food you must normally go to a diner – or at least a bowling alley or ski lodge – to try. There are big American-style breakfasts, fried chicken, omelettes, a number of Mexican choices and Boston cream pie.

**Café Onion** (Yángcōng; ☎ 2873 9992; 1-7 Lane 9, Tianmu N Rd; mains NT160-550; ✐ lunch & dinner) The menu is largely pastas and steaks, but you're also paying for the atmosphere, which is youthful, cosy and spread out over four windowed store fronts. Décor is country-French. Reservations recommended.

**Tianmu Seafood Restaurant** (Tiānmǔ Yúdiàn; ☎ 2874 5562; 101 Tianmu E Rd; mains NT150-380; ✐ dinner) Part beach shack, part comfy parlour and admired by locals and foreigners alike for food that recalls the Penghu Archipelago in the Taiwan Strait – clams, lobster, fish and shrimp.

**TOP END**

**Ticino Swiss Restaurant** (Ruìhuá Cāntīng; ☎ 2876 1101; 2 Lane 82, Tianmu E Rd; dishes NT420-780; ✐ lunch & dinner) You didn't know you needed fondue in Taipei? This cosy Swiss restaurant may convince you with its dark wood, white spackled walls and linen tablecloths. Meat /cheese fondues start at NT550/650.

### SELF-CATERING

**Uli's Euro Deli** (Fùlìdélì Cāntīng; ☎ 2831 2741; 17 Keqiang St; meals NT160-490; ✹ lunch & dinner) From *weisswurst* to pork knuckles, Uli (originally from the German highlands) cures and sells all his own meats. There's also a comfortable dining room where you can enjoy the customary sides and treats such as cheesecake and Warsteiner beer.

**Carrefour** (☎ 8006 7555; 47 Dexing Rd) The French hypermarket is a good (though often cramped) self-catering option.

## South of the City Centre

**Lian Hsin Yuan Vegetarian Restaurant** (Liánxīnyuán Sùshí Cāntīng; Map pp64-5; ☎ 8231 6668; 7th fl, 2 Baosheng Rd, Yonghe City; weekday/holiday buffet NT370/398, weekday/holiday tea time NT218/250; ✹ 11am-9pm) The Museum of World Religions was founded by a Buddhist order, and its restaurant serves meals from that tradition. Selections might be Japanese or Taiwanese inspired, and there are some lovely cakes and desserts.

## DRINKING
### Cafés

Considering that Taiwan makes much of the oolong tea it ships around the world, visitors are often surprised to see coffee houses on seemingly every corner. Popular chains include Barista, Mr Brown, Chicco D'Oro, Dante, Doutor, Is Coffee and, of course, Starbucks. Typical opening times are 7.30am to 10pm, and you might find folks, particularly students, camped out there for hours studying or chatting over a single cup, a pastry or light meal. McDonald's also serves the same purpose...and budget cappuccino. Other shops specialise in chocolate or ice cream.

**Chocoholic** (Qiǎokèhākè Qiáokèlì Zhuānyíndiàn; Map pp72-3; ☎ 2321 5820; 2 Lane 7, Yongkang St; drinks NT90-130; ✹ noon-11pm) If you're like us, you may find most Taipei chocolates beyond help. However, this tiny, brightly painted café comes to the rescue with cakes, chocolate drinks and a clientele of smiley young things.

**Fong Da** (Fēngdà Kāfēi; Map pp72-3; ☎ 2371 9577; 42 Chengdu Rd; ✹ 8am-10.30pm) Readers have written in praise of this coffee shop that dates from the 1950s and still uses some of the original equipment. Drip ice coffee with cookies costs NT100. We suspect that these readers rush here after they've been away for a while, because absence makes the heart grow Fong Da.

**Häagen Dazs** (single scoop NT90, set menus NT225-460) Tianmu (Map p82; 1 Alley 18, Lane 38, Tianyu St); Songshan (Map pp80-1; 173 Dunhua S Rd, Sec 1) Take your notions of ice-cream parlours from home and throw them out. Savvy Taipeiers head here for elaborate ice cream, cake and drink sets inspired by Rome, France and Japan – there's even chocolate fondue. The Tianmu location also offers a chichi setting with a lovely tree-covered garden out front. There are other Häagen Dazs locations around town but most serve just simple ice creams.

---

### BEER HOUSES

These institutions exist chiefly to help you wash down your favourite brew with spicy, salty concoctions. They're loads of fun, with large groups hanging out for hours.

**8 Immortals** (Map pp72-3; ☎ 2321 4507; 30 Xinsheng S Rd, Sec 2; dishes NT150-380; ✹ dinner) What it lacks in style it makes up for in enthusiasm. Order at the display case by the front door (seafood, meats and veggies, prepared as you like) and head upstairs to a covered (or not) roof deck overlooking Da'an Park. You can order beer by the six-pack (of 640ml bottles!), and smaller quantities are also available. If it's full, there are three similar spots down the block.

**Indian Beer House** (Yìndiàn Píjiǔwǔ; Map pp80-1; ☎ 2741 0550; 196 Bade Rd, Sec 2; meals around NT400; ✹ dinner) A Taipei institution. Dine among the dinosaurs – huge fossils all around the interior – and huge crowds of young professionals nightly.

**Jolly** (Zuólìtàishí Jiā Màijiǔ; ☎ 2632 2229; 423 Jinhu Rd; dishes NT150-450; ✹ lunch & dinner) It's way up in the Neihu District, but it's Taipei's only pub for house-brewed beer such as Weizen and Pale Ale. Beer is served with Thai food (think lettuce wraps or green curry chicken) in a tall-ceilinged, brightly painted space.

**Post Coffee** (Map pp80-1; ☎ 8771 5298; 1 Lane 260, Guangfu S Rd; ◷ noon-midnight) This shop in Xinyi offers a comfy yet contemporary escape from the chain coffee places that dominate Taipei.

## Pubs

Pubs in Taiwan have the full range of international beers and mixed drinks. Typically, beers sell for between NT100 and NT150. Hard liquor might set you back NT250. Ask around for happy hours or drink specials.

A loose affiliation of pubs has come together to promote their latest menus and events. Check out their website www .taipeipubs.com.

**45** (Map pp72-3; ☎ 2321 2140; 45 Heping Rd, Sec 1) Go up the narrow stairs and join the huge crowd (including foreigners), especially on Friday and Saturday nights. It's festooned with Americana, from licence plates to movie-star photos, and the food is American-style too.

**Carnegie's** (Map pp80-1; ☎ 2325 4433; 100 Anhe Rd, Sec 2; mains NT260-780) Carnegie's caused quite a stir when it first opened in 2001 – what with patrons dancing on the bar and all – but even if it's calmed down a notch it's still one of the liveliest nightspots in Xinyi. A great meeting place for after-work drinks. The menu includes steaks, halibut and lamb.

**DV8** (Map pp72-3; ☎ 2393 1726; 223 Jinhua St) A long-time favourite of local expats, especially English teachers. It's hard to find (across from Sound Bank Studio) but once inside it's cosy and intimate, and there are often cheap beer specials.

**Green Bar** (Map p82; ☎ 2873 3263; 84-1 Tianmu E Rd) Another icon of the foreign community, here you'll find darts, table games and the latest sports on TV.

**Jr Caffé** (Map pp72-3; ☎ 2366 1799; 80 Shida Rd) It's in the heart of the student pub zone but anyone's welcome. Glass doors mean that it doesn't get too smoky on street level, and there's foosball and pool downstairs.

**Malibu West** (Map pp74-5; ☎ 2592 8228; 9 Lane 25, Shuangcheng St) There's a pool table and dishes including burgers, pastas, pizzas and snacks. Happy hour is between 4pm and 9pm. In the heart of the Zone nightlife district (p100), it's got a tropical feel and is popular with business people and airline pilots.

**My Place** (Map pp74-5; ☎ 2591 4269; 3-1 Lane 32, Shuangcheng St) Also in the Zone, My Place bills itself as Taiwan's first pub (established 1975) and is still going strong. This Britowned establishment boasts friendly hostesses, pool and a 100-inch-screen TV for sports.

**Pig** (Map p82; ☎ 2874 0630; 78 Tianmu E Rd; dishes NT250-425) This friendly Tianmu pub certainly feels very British, and the menu includes steaks, chops, chicken and, er, enchiladas. There's no cover charge but when there's a band on (usually from 9.30pm), minimum charge for food and drink is NT400 (NT500 on Friday and Saturday).

**Roxy 99** (Map pp72-3; ☎ 2358 2813; 69 Jinshan S Rd, Sec 2) Popular with students, workers and assorted 20- and 30-somethings, Roxy 99 has a great CD collection and a food menu that includes pastas, fried rice and more adventurous fare. It's in the basement, yet manages not to feel claustrophobic.

**Saints & Sinners** (Map pp80-1; ☎ 2739 9001; 114 Anhe Rd, Sec 2; dishes NT150-550) Mix Taiwanese and foreigners, add in pool, foosball and darts, a couple of big screens to watch the game, and pepper it with music including Pearl Jam and Jason Mraz, and *voilà*: a popular new place. Menu choices include Thai, Chinese and British pub food. The house drink, the 'upside down', includes, among other things, vodka, honey, plum powder and cherry brandy.

**Shannon** (Map pp80-1; ☎ 2772 0948; 6 Dunhua N Rd) Next to Dan Ryan's Chicago Grill (p96), this cosy Irish-style pub opened in 2002 and is hugely popular with guests

---

**A NIGHT ON THE TOWN**

A typical night out for Taipei's young and fashionable might involve four venues: somewhere for dinner, a nightspot such as a club or lounge bar, another nightclub or bar and someplace to finish the night. Clubs open and close with astonishing frequency here, but locals just roll with it: it means there's always someplace new to try!

Until a few years ago, dance clubs were the rage. While there are still a number to be found, at the time of writing the trend was towards lounge bars, where drinking and looking fashionable is the name of the game.

from overseas. There's live music (think R&B) Thursday through Sunday.

**Underworld** (Map pp72-3; ☎ 2369 0103; basement, 45 Shida Rd; admission NT250) A little bit psychedelic, a little bit smoky and very friendly, this cosy, graffiti-painted basement pub pours lots of beer and Long Island iced tea. Come here after dinner at the Shida Night Market and stay for DJs spinning house music or a live band on weekends.

## Tea

Tea is an institution – and major export – in Taiwan, and Taipei has a great variety of shops that serve it, from atop serene mountains to stands in crowded markets.

Our favourite variety is 'pearl tea' *(zhēnzhū nǎichá)*, a sweetened tea with chewy black balls of tapioca at the bottom –

---

**THE ZONE**

It was once called the Combat Zone. Locals still refer to it as 'the Zone', and it's been officially smartened up as Taipei Soho (though with bars named Hollywood Baby, LAPD and Malibu West, it may remind you more of Los Angeles). Whatever you call it, this area with dozens of bars is one of the city's most storied nightlife districts. The main drag is Shuangcheng St, east of Zhongshan N Rd.

Some basics:

- in Taipei, most bartenders are female, and in the Zone traditionally most clients are male
- the Zone started out as British-style pubs, which have evolved to attract locals as well

Gone are the days when most Zone bars were barely disguised fronts for call girls. Patrons could pay a 'bar fine' and leave with a Taiwanese hostess for the night; she would expect a substantial tip.

Some clubs do still permit visitors to pay a 'bar fine' – those listed in this book do not. Whatever you do, drugs are absolutely not tolerated.

While the Zone certainly still attracts crowds (especially conventioneers and older expats), young and trendy visitors tend to go elsewhere.

---

sometimes referred to elsewhere as *boba* tea. It's served in a plastic cup with a tight seal and a thick straw. Order yours hot *(rè)* or cold *(bīng)*. Another favourite is bubble black tea *(paòmò hóngchá)*, which is frothed until it looks like beer. Both are available at tea stands and stalls citywide and should set you back around NT25.

**Remix 19** (Map pp80-1; 1st fl, 22 Songshan Rd) With its mod white-on-white décor and cool tunes, trendy Remix could pass for a lounge bar. You can sip tea (the bubble tea is recommended – it also serves some alcoholic drinks) and look fabulous while snacking on pizzas, pastas and nachos.

**Rose House** (Gǔdiǎn Méiguī Yuán; Map pp74-5; 95 Nanjing E Rd, Sec 2) Readers have written in praise of this teahouse, which, despite its normal store front, looks like it could have been decorated by Laura Ashley inside. Among its dozens of varieties are Earl Grey and Mango, sold by the cup, the set or the tin.

**Cha for Tea** (Map pp80-1; 152 Fuxing N Rd) Readers have also written to recommend this shop, which works on an interesting concept. You can drink tea here, of course, but there's a selection of foods using tea as one of the ingredients, from dumplings to mousse (most under NT100).

# ENTERTAINMENT
## Chinese Opera

While some venues around town host touring companies of Chinese opera, there are regularly scheduled performances at the following. Both of these venues project English-language subtitles so you can follow the action:

**Taipei Eye** (Táiběi Xìpéng; Map pp74-5; ☎ 2568 2677; www.taipeieye.com; 113 Zhongshan N Rd, Sec 2; tickets NT880; ☽ 8pm Thu-Sat) Situated in Zhongshan, this new venue showcases Chinese opera together with other rotating performances, including puppet theatre and aboriginal dance. Even though it's meant for tourists, audience members have the unique opportunity to watch the actors as they rehearse and put on make-up, wigs and costumes. Enter from Jinzhou St.

**National Taiwan Junior College of Performing Arts** (Guólì Táiwān Xìjù Zhuānkē Xuéxiào; Map pp64-5; ☎ 2796 2666; 177 Neihu Rd, Sec 2; adult/child NT400/200; ☽ 10am Mon & Thu) Students begin to study on this campus (also known as Fuxing Arts

## CHINESE OPERA

If you think of opera as Mozart, Puccini or the proverbial fat lady, Chinese opera will surprise you.

Sometimes called Beijing opera, Chinese opera combines with elements of Western opera, ballet and theatre, using elaborate costumes and make-up. Some visitors may find the singing nasal or even shrill, but just try to imagine a better counterpoint to the gongs, cymbals, drums and high-pitched wind and string instruments.

Sets and props are minimal. Covered, the table denotes an indoor scene. Uncovered, it might represent an outdoor bridge. If a character is carrying a riding crop, it indicates that he or she is on horseback.

Costumes and make-up, on the other hand, are wildly elaborate, used to denote stock characters – warriors and rulers, gods and demons, scholars and clowns. Each of the bold colours of the make-up, painted in an exaggerated style, carries a different meaning. For example, red in the Western world is often associated with the devil, but in Chinese opera red make-up indicates loyalty and honesty. White in Chinese opera implies cruelty and treachery. A red costume implies an emperor or high official and birds often decorate the costumes of civil officials. Elaborate headdresses, some weighing up to 500g, can be decorated with pompoms or metres-long feathers (the latter imply a high military rank).

Acrobatics also feature prominently in Chinese opera, often involving swordplay and martial arts. Audience members should applaud frequently.

While many stories derive from Chinese myths and legend, others are remarkably similar to Western operas: lovers escaping repressive parents, heroes battling foes etc. Even if the aesthetics are different, some themes are universal.

Academy) at the age of 10, and advanced students, some teachers and alumni participate in twice-weekly performances of acrobatics and Chinese opera. Admission includes a guided visit to the Beijing opera museum (which is upstairs) as well as an educational video (in English) about Chinese opera. If you arrive early, you may be lucky enough to catch students in outdoor classes.

## Cinemas

The old-time place to head for a movie is Ximending. There's a cluster of movie theatres with character along Wucheng St, with about a dozen screens among them. Leading multiplexes are at Warner Village (p104), the Core Pacific 'Living Mall' (p104) and Breeze Center (p104). The theatres at the 'Living Mall' operate 24 hours. Ticket prices hover around adult/concession/early show NT280/250/220.

**SPOT – Taipei Film House** (Táiběizhījiā Diànyǐng Zhǔtíguǎn; ☎ 2511 7786; www.spot.org.tw; 18 Zhongshan N Rd, Sec 2; nonmember/member tickets NT220/150) This is as much a cultural centre and venue for the exchange of ideas about films as it is a cinema – there's an excellent bookshop with worldwide cinema titles and the

original novels on which famous films have been based. The building, a landmark that dates back to 1925, was once the home of the US ambassador. There's also a café and wine lounge.

## Live Performances

**Gu Ling Experimental Theatre** (Gǔlíngjiē Xiǎojùcháng; Map pp72-3; ☎ 2391 9393; 2 Lane 5, Guling St) This grass-roots, community-based, avant-garde company presents music, drama, dance and children's theatre, all of it contemporary if not exactly experimental. The majority of the shows are not culturally specific, meaning that even those without Chinese-language skills will be able to follow. The building, which dates from 1906, was originally a police station and during some performances the audience can see all the way through to the former jail cells.

The **National Theatre** at Sun Yat-sen Memorial Hall (p78) and **Novel Hall for Performing Arts** (Map pp80-1; ☎ 2722 4302, ext 7999; www .novelhall.org.tw; 3 Songshou Rd) host large-scale concerts and cultural events, from dance to musicals, Chinese or Western opera and concerts of Chinese or Western classical or popular music.

## BASEBALL IN TAIWAN

If baseball is America's national pastime and Japan's national obsession, many Taiwanese consider it their national pride and glory.

Baseball arrived in Taiwan around 1895, courtesy of Japanese colonial rulers. By 1920, it was the nation's most popular sport, and in 1937 it stoked pride when a Taiwanese team won Japan's annual high-school tournament. Despite being rocked by a gambling scandal in 1997, today baseball is Taiwan's most watched sport.

The six teams of the Chinese Professional Baseball League (CPBL; p32) each play 100 games per season (early March to mid-October). The league winner is determined by the best-of-seven-game Taiwan Series. Teams are named for their corporate owners – the Brother Elephants have the largest fan base and the most championships in recent years.

Teams don't have home stadiums but rather rotate among 10 stadiums around the island; the newest was completed in 2002 in Tianmu. Instead of an American-style hot dog with mustard at the ballpark, you might try instant noodles.

A Taiwanese baseball fun fact: while Sadaharu Oh is known as Japan's home-run champ (800 homers), Taiwan claims him as its own. Oh (Wang Chen-chih in Chinese) was born in Tokyo in 1940 to a Japanese mother and Taiwanese father, yet despite his hero status in Japan, Oh still carries a Taiwanese passport. According to Richard Wang, director of international affairs for the CPBL, the fact that Oh speaks neither Mandarin nor Taiwanese doesn't lessen Taiwan's respect for him: 'Not even a bit'.

## Nightclubs

Taipei's clubs tend to open late and stay open late, some until 5am on weekends. However, they are also known to cease operating with regularity. We've recommended some long-running favourites and new ones that seem to have staying power, but to avoid disappointment it's best to check before setting out.

Many clubs have specials such as ladies' night and foreigners' night, with free or reduced admission or drink specials, often one night a week.

**2F** (Map pp72-3; ☎ 2392 2222; 15 Heping W Rd, Sec 1) This large club (capacity more than 1000) is home to both commercial and underground scenes, with everything from techno to house to trance and a selection of international DJs.

**B1** (Map pp80-1; 71 Aiguo Rd, B1; ☎ 2397 0506) If you're young, hip and dress like the latest pop or hip-hop star, you'll find loads of company here. Pay the cover charge and it's all you can drink all night.

**Brown Sugar** (Hēitáng; Map pp80-1; ☎ 8780 1110; www.brownsugar.com.tw; 101 Songren Rd; admission NT380 Sun-Thu, NT550 Fri & Sat) Taipei's iconic jazz club has recently moved to glam digs in Xinyi. The result is a swank place with lots of right angles and silk curtains. There's live jazz Monday through Saturday nights and salsa on Sunday. The food menu is classic American Southern cooking, as well as pastas, chicken and rice dishes.

**Living Room** (Map pp80-1; ☎ 8787 4154; www .livingroomtaipei.com; 3rd fl, 8 Nanjing E Rd, Sec 5; ☺ 6pm-1am) Part supper club, part music lounge, this low-key venue (just *try* to find the sign out front) is a great respite from everything huge, noisy and self-consciously trendy. Filled with sofas, curtains and wood floors, it's popular among musicians, and every night is different: jazz, jam sessions, electronica dance parties etc. The food menu is, roughly, 'tell us how much you want to spend and we'll cook for you'.

**Luxy** (Map pp80-1; ☎ 2772 1000; www.luxy-taipei .com; 5th fl, 201 Zhongxiao E Rd, Sec 4) Luxy offers something for everybody. In its several rooms you might find live international acts (think Bone Thugs & Harmony), European DJs, break-beat – and space for more than 1000 people! Check the website for the latest offerings.

**Naomi** (Map pp80-1; ☎ 2709 8295; 65 Anhe Rd, Sec 1) Metal-bead curtains, mirrored columns, red padded walls and dim lighting provide a great backdrop for this lounge bar, where well-dressed twenty- and thirty-somethings sip scotches and single malts.

**Room 18** (Map pp80-1; ☎ 2345 2778; Warner Village, 124 Songshou Rd) This dark and atmospheric basement club, with dancing, spinning, hip-hop and house, would be very much

**TAIPEI**

at home in New York or London. It gets a lot of fashionable locals and ABC (American-born Chinese) visitors. Taiwanese stars might find themselves in the VIP room. A warning: cover charges can be steep.

**Ziga Zaga** (Map pp80-1; ☎ 2720 1299, ext 3288; 2 Songshou Rd; 🕑 dancing Mon-Sat nights) This nightclub inside the Grand Hyatt is probably the slickest in town. It gets a 30-and-up crowd (including hotel guests), dancing to DJs spinning pop to hip-hop, as well as live bands. You can get Italian meals or snacks until late at night. No shorts or athletic shoes permitted.

# SHOPPING

If you're from a place where the department store is passé, you will find Taipei a breath of fresh air. Taipei's department stores are massive, multistorey affairs.

## Antiques

Taipei has little shops selling all kinds of old things all over town, including seemingly random areas where there's not much else of note. Zhongshan N Rd, Sec 6 (Map p82) in Tianmu and Jianguo S Rd (Map pp74–5), near the flower and jade markets, both have an assortment of antique shops worth checking out.

**Zaoheding** (Zǎohédǐng; Map pp72-3; 60 Yongkang St) A sort of mishmash antiques mall (aka Jīng'ān) with over a dozen small stalls. Lots of bric-a-brac and the occasional treasure – there's no phone and stalls all keep different hours.

## Chinese Handicrafts & Clothing

There's not shortage of browsing in the city's night markets, especially for clothing, but the highest concentration in one place is at the **Chinese Handicraft Mart** (Táiwān Shǒuyè Tuīguǎng Zhōngxīn; Map pp72-3; ☎ 2393 3655; 1 Suzhou Rd; 🕑 9am-5.30pm). You'll find four storeys of clothing, jade, porcelain, ceramics, tea sets, jewellery, scrolls, paintings and prints…and that's a small selection of the variety on offer here. If you missed picking up a souvenir from the National

---

**KARAOKE**

Karaoke (aka KTV in Taiwan) may have been invented in Japan, but in Taipei it's taken on a life of its own. While elsewhere you might go to sing karaoke in a bar or a karaoke box, in Taipei those 'boxes' are towers. One foreigner-friendly chain is **Party World** (Cashbox; Map pp80-1; ☎ 2521 3333; Zhongxiao E Rd). Typical is its location (capacity 2205 people!), it has 10 floors of rooms large and small that will fit your party whatever its size. Its rooms feature strobe lights and an entire menu with credible food (meals and snacks from NT70) and drink (beer from NT90). Other notable locations include Ximending (Map pp72-3). And get this, all locations are open 24 hours!

When phoning the Party World reservation line you may want to have a Chinese-speaking friend help. There they will tell you which location has facilities available for your party size and time. Hourly room-rental rates range from NT195 (smallest room, weekday morning) to NT1280 (large party room, late-night Friday and Saturday).

---

**GAY & LESBIAN NIGHTLIFE**

Taipei has no concentrated gay district. Like the rest of the city's nightlife scene, the hot club when we went to press may not even exist by the time you read this, but the establishments below have been around for a while. Visitors would do well to ask around or check www.fridae.com or www.utopia-asia.com for the latest.

Don't expect a rocking time Sunday to Thursday (it can be downright slow, though some venues become karaoke bars), but Friday and especially Saturday nights can be quite busy.

**Fresh** (Map pp72-3; ☎ 2358 7701; 2nd fl, 7 Jinshan S Rd) Taipei's gay club du jour has three floors of fun: a bar floor, a dance floor and a chill room and roof garden on top. It's friendly and international.

**Jailhouse** (☎ 2364 1623; 3 Alley 8, Lane 316, Roosevelt Rd, Sec 3) Above the Gonggang night market is this long-standing, if tiny, lesbian bar. There's a small dance floor and occasional drink specials.

**Source** (Map pp72-3; ☎ 3393 1678; 1-2 Roosevelt Rd, Sec 1) There's a small bar downstairs and a dance floor upstairs and the top floor is like a handsome Chinese salon of 100 years ago. Foreigners are not just welcome here, they're encouraged.

TAIPEI

## SHOPPING CENTRES & DISTRICTS

With all the ritzy, contemporary shopping centres in Taipei you might well wonder 'What recession?' Here are some of the most popular.

- **Breeze Center** (Wēifēng Guǎngchǎng; Map pp80-1; ☎ 6600 8888; 39 Fuxing N Rd, Sec 1) Nine floors above ground and three below, it's got worldwide brands, including Ralph Lauren, Coach, Marc Jacobs, Omega and Prada...and that's just on the ground floor. The top floors include the Ambassador movie theatres.

- **Core Pacific 'Living Mall'** (Jīnghuáchéng; Map pp80-1; ☎ 3762 1888; 138 Bade Rd, Sec 4) The central architectural concept here is the 'core', a sort of Death Star suspended among the mall's 15 storeys. Most stores are open 11am to 10.30pm (11pm Friday and Saturday), but the 13-screen Cinemark Theatre stays open 24 hours.

- The shopping district north of the **Grand Formosa Regent** (Map pp74-5) Hotel features Gucci, Louis Vuitton and Taiwan's own acclaimed Shiatzy Chen.

- **Warner Village** (Huá'nà Wēixiù Yǐngchéng; Map pp80-1; 124 Songshou Rd) The centrepiece of this market, one of several hubs in Xinyi, is the 18-screen Warner Village cinema. The centre is busy all day long (and especially on weekends), with international boutiques such as FCUK, Monique Japan, Maybelline, Boots and Aveda, and there's a popular food court. The ritzy **Shin Kong Mitsukoshi Department Store** (Xīnguāng Sānyuè Bǎihuò; Map pp80-1; ☎ 8780 1000; 11 Songshou Rd) is just to the north.

- **Ximending** (p70) Head here for anything youth oriented.

- **Dinghao District** (Map pp80-1; Zhongxiao E Rd, Sec 4) Anchored by the landmark **SOGO Department Store** (Tàipíngyáng SOGO Bǎihuò; ☎ 7713 5555; 45 Zhongxiao E Rd, Sec 4), and adjacent to the MRT (Zhongxiao Fuxing station), it's Taiwan's most famous shopping street, with shops big and small, restaurants, cafés and nightspots.

- **Dayeh Takashimaya** (Dàyè Gāodǎowū; Map p82; 55 Zhongcheng Rd, Sec 2; ☎ 2831 2345) In a sense all of ritzy Tianmu is a shopping district, but this new mall near the baseball stadium certainly brings them in.

Palace Museum, you can find a selection here. While nothing here is unique and you may do better price-wise elsewhere, you're assured of decent quality, and the displays are nice. The Handicraft Mart is an easy walk from both the government centre and Taipei Main Station.

## Clothing

Taipei is basically one big open-air shopping mall. Out the front of busy train stations and in the city's covered arcades, virtually every footpath features some kind of vendor selling clothes, some seasonal, some eternal, some of decent quality and some blatant – shall we say – 'aspirants' to famous names (our favourite: a 'Blueberry – London' logo on a Burberry-type plaid). And let's not forget the astounding variety and price competition of the night markets.

**Designers Gallery of Sunrise Department Store** (Zhōngxìng Bǎihuò; Map pp80-1; 2nd fl, 15 Fuxing N Rd,

Sec 1) This place has an excellent concentration of Taiwan's leading designers on offer. Alongside the likes of international names such as Dolce & Gabbana, Yohji Yamamoto and Kenzo, you'll find Shiatzy Chen, Isabelle Wen and Charin Yeh, just to name a few.

## Computers & Electronics

**Guanghua St** (Map pp72-3; Bade Rd, Sec 1) is to electronics what Taipei's night markets are to clothes and foods, a can't-miss cacophony of shopping opportunities: computers, electronics, components, even CDs and mobile phones. Competition is fierce and bargaining is expected.

**Nova Computer Arcade** (NOVA Zīxùn Guǎngchǎng; Map pp72-3; ☎ 2381 4833; 100 Guangjian Rd) This arcade is located in the shadow of Taipei Main Station. It has about 130 shops (although some are more like booths) dealing in computers, components, digital cameras etc.

Chinese opera performers, National Taiwan Junior College of Performing Arts (p100), Taipei

TOM COCKREM

TOM COCKREM

Local craft on display, Yingge (p152)

National Theatre (p69), Taipei

MARTIN MOOS

Face-reading stall, Snake Alley (p70), Taipei

ALAIN EVRARD

MARTIN MOOS

Lunar New Year festivities (p317),
Taipei

Ceiling of the gate at Bao-an Temple (p74), Taipei

MART

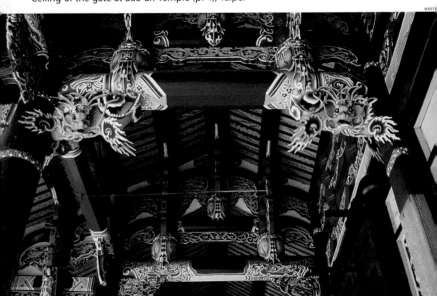

## Jade

Pretty much any shopping street around town has a shop selling jade, but on weekends you won't want to miss the **Jianguo Weekend Jade Market** (Map pp80-1) under the expressway on Jianguo S Rd, north of Renai Rd. Not recommended for folks with small children, because the market can get crowded.

## Night Markets

If you haven't visited at least one night market, you have not truly experienced Taipei. Some markets specialise in clothes, others in street foods, still others in toys, titillation and things that can't be defined. Along with Snake Alley (p70) and the Shida Night Market (p94) these are our favourites:

**Tonghua Night Market** (Map pp80-1) Lots of food, handbags, men's and women's clothing and casual accessories. The centre of the action is on Linjiang St.

**Shilin Night Market** (Map p82) Considered by many to be the king of Taipei's night markets, this sprawling indoor-outdoor place is just steps form MRT Jiantan station. It teems with stalls selling snacks, clothing, footwear and game arcades.

Also keep in mind that at the Shida Night Market (p94), you can find all sorts of basic appliances and useful things for the home, in addition to the great street foods it is famous for.

## Paper

In addition to the shop at the Su Ho Paper Museum (p77), head down the street for a huge selection of handcrafted paper at the much larger **Chang Chen Cotton Paper Art Centre** (Chángchūn Miánzhǐ Yìshù Zhōngxīn; Map pp72-3; ☎ 2507 5535; 74 Chang'an E Rd, Sec 2; ☺ 9am-7pm Mon-Fri, 9am-6pm Sat). 'Big deal', you say? Then think of it as art or sculpture. Some examples: paper that's been tie-dyed or flecked with tiny leaves or large pieces of pulp. Use it for anything from notes to wrappers to wallpaper. Much of the paper for sale here comes from Puli, the paper-making centre in central Taiwan. Most papers cost between NT15 and NT90 for a 60cm by 90cm sheet.

## Stamps

The streets around the postal museum (p70) have an assortment of shops selling stamps and collecting supplies from around the world.

## Tea & Tea Supplies

Oolong tea is one of Taiwan's most celebrated exports, and a number of shops handle it. You'll find small shops in every corner of the city, but for most you'll need to speak Chinese.

**Ten Ren Tea Company** (Tiānrén Míngchá; Map pp72-3; ☎ 2541 5660; 11 Lane 105, Zhongshan N Rd, Sec 1) Probably the nation's most reputable chain.

---

### SPECIALITY SHOPPING STREETS

Although Taipei's shopping malls and night markets sometimes seem full to overflowing with products of virtually every sort, other streets have several, sometimes dozens, of shops dedicated to a particular product. They're worth a stroll for a peek into local customs, even if you don't buy. Some examples:

- **Wedding dresses** Aiguo Rd, across from the Chiang Kai-shek Memorial Hall, and Zhongshan N Rd, near Minquan Rd (Map pp72-3)

- **Religious articles** Xiyuan Rd, west of Longshan Temple (Map pp72-3)

- **Funeral urns** Minquan E Rd, Sec 2, near Xinsheng Temple (Map pp74-5)

- **Menswear** Tacheng St, just south of the Dihua Market

- **Books** Chongqing Rd, southwest of Taipei Main Station (Map pp72-3)

- **Outdoor/backpacking gear** Zhongshan N Rd, Sec 1, just north of the intersection of Zhongxiao E Rd, west side of the street (Map pp72-3). **Taibei Shanshui** (Táiběi Shānshuǐ; ☎ 2361 9507; 12 Zhongshan N Rd, Sec 1) and **Tingshaniou** (Dēngshānyǒu; ☎ 2311 6027; 18 & 22 Zhongshan N Rd, Sec 1) are two popular options.

- **Chinese silk jackets and embroidered shoes** Yuanling St, west of Chongqing S Rd, just north of Baoqing Rd (Map pp72-3)

There are a couple of dozen locations in Taipei alone, including at the big department stores.

**Wang de Chuan** (Wángdéchuán Cházhuāng; Map pp74-5; ☎ 2561 8738; 14-1 Changchun Rd) A lovely space with red tea containers and handsome brick walls. Wang de Chuan has been in business since 1862.

## GETTING THERE & AWAY
See p329 for information.

## GETTING AROUND
The Taipei Rapid Transit Association (TRTA) operates the city's bus and underground railway systems, and there are many private bus lines that crisscross the city. You can find fares, route maps and lots of other information at www.dot.taipei.gov.tw.

### To/From the Airport
Two airports serve Taipei. The international airport is Chiang Kai-shek International Airport (airport code TPE; locally known as CKS Airport), in Taoyuan, approximately 50km west of the city centre. Songshan Airport, just north of the city centre, handles domestic traffic. This means that if you are transiting through Taipei between an international flight and a domestic flight, you must first get from one airport to the other. See p325 for details of these airports.

Taxis from CKS Airport to the city centre cost NT1200, but NT1000 going the other direction – it's more expensive from the

---

**FLOWERS, FLOWERS, FLOWERS**

The **Jianguo Weekend Flower Market** (Map pp80-1) takes place weekends and holidays beneath the freeway on Jianguo S Rd. And we're not sure what to make of **Natural Flower Materials Co** (Shādàjiě Huācūnyuàn; ☎ 2531 2799; 7 Lane 50, Zhongshan N Rd, Sec 2), although we know we love it. It feels like one part art gallery and one part plant store, and pretty much everything here is made from or covered with dried plants or plant products. They decorate screens, sculptures, clocks and more; some primitive, some sublime and some look like they belong in a museum. The drawback: you probably won't be able to take your purchases back to your home country.

---

airport to the city because of an airport surcharge. Many hotels also offer private car services at a typical mark-up of between NT200 and NT800 over a taxi; however this is usually luxury car transport such as a Mercedes Benz.

### Car & Motorcycle
We strongly recommend that visitors not drive in Taipei. Traffic can be a bear, and public transport will usually get you where you want to go on time. For information on car and motorcycles hire see p331.

### Public Transport
#### SUBWAY (MRT)
Taipei was once a transit nightmare. The city's streets were choked with cars, taxis and scooters, and the only public transport was bus.

The streets are still busy, but a subway (underground railway) system is changing all that. It's called the MRT (Mass Rapid Transit; Map pp72-3) and though its name lacks panache, the service makes up for it in convenience and efficiency. Trains are comfortable, they're usually not too crowded (OK, except at rush hour) and the routes are continually expanding to serve even more of the city. Plus, all signage and most announcements are in English as well as Chinese. Most places within the city centre are (or soon will be) within about a 20-minute walk of an MRT station.

If there's any complaint we have about the MRT, it's that we wish it would run later so it could be used into the wee hours.

MRT fares are based on distance. The base fare is NT20, and you'll pay NT65 for the longest trip. Single tickets can be purchased, using cash, from machines located in every MRT station. The fare for each destination is noted in both English and Chinese on a map by the machine. Coins and bills are accepted, and change is provided.

You *could* buy single tickets for each ride you take, but if you're going to be in town for any length of time it makes sense to invest in an Easy Card, the TRTA's stored-value card. Adult/child Easy Cards sell for NT500/300, of which NT100 is a deposit. The rest is valid for subway and bus fares and even for payments at certain car parks. It saves the hassle of queuing for tickets and fumbling for change and, the best part, the

Easy Card gives users a 20% discount on MRT fares. Additionally, if you use your Easy Card and transfer between the MRT and a bus within two hours, the bus ride is half-price. If you're taking a bus on your way to the MRT, the same discount applies – it will be calculated when you exit the MRT.

To use your Easy Card, wave it across a reader like a scanner at the grocery store. Savvy Easy Card users wave the card through their wallet or handbag. The reader will tell you how much value you have left. When the value drops below NT100, the reader will beep.

Easy Cards can be purchased from machines at many MRT stations (instructions available in English). Cash is accepted at most stations, and you can add value to your Easy Card using either cash or bank/credit cards, although foreign cards tend not to work. Some stations have both cash and card versions of the Easy Card machines.

When you're done using your Easy Card, simply take it to an MRT ticket booth and your deposit plus any stored value will be refunded.

### BUS

While not as easy to use as the MRT (not least because buses are only starting to have English signage or announcements), Taipei's buses are a time-honoured and reliable mode of transport.

There are several types of buses, run by several companies, although that won't matter to most travellers as all of them accept Easy Card. Each bus is numbered on the front and sometimes on the side, and larger buses have the start and end points of the routes in Chinese and some Romanisation. Note, however, that it's not always clear which direction the bus is headed. Most buses are full-sized, and there are also minibuses (sometimes called 'red' *hóng* buses, with the character 紅 before the route number).

MRT stations all have a map – somewhere – of bus stops in their vicinities. If you can't find the map, just ask the attendant. Once you've located the bus stop, stand by the sign for your bus and if you see it coming be sure to wave it down – there may be several routes converging at the same stop, and drivers often assume that passengers will identify themselves for pick-up.

Note that Taipei's buses may not necessarily pull all the way up to the kerb. Occasionally the bus will stop a lane away, though you usually do not have to step *through* traffic to board the bus.

Fares are NT15 on most routes within the city centre, though that can double or triple on longer routes. On larger buses, you can board at either the front or rear but must get off at the front – you pay your fare as you exit. However, not every bus operates in this way and the driver will let you know if you need to pay in some other manner.

### Taxi

Taipei's taxis – distinctively yellow – are metered and charge by distance and waiting time. Base fare is NT70 for the first 1.5km, plus NT5 for each 300m thereafter. After midnight, the base fare is NT70 for the first 1.2km, plus NT5 for each 250m thereafter. Taxis also charge NT5 for every two minutes that the car is idle (eg sitting in traffic or at a red light). This two minutes is cumulative and appears on the meter.

You won't have any trouble finding a taxi in the city centre – they're everywhere. There are taxi stands around the city, but most folks just hail one from the side of the road. If an approaching taxi is free, it will have a red light in the windscreen – or if you're looking like you need a taxi it may well honk or just stop for you.

# AROUND TAIPEI

## BEITOU 北投

It's a well-kept secret, but Taiwan is filled with hot springs. Taipei's northern suburb of Beitou (Běitóu) is the locals' easiest choice when they need a quick soak in sulphurous waters.

The hot springs *(wēnquán)* in this district have been a lure for tourism as far back as the Japanese era. Japan also has a strong hot-spring culture, so the occupiers were quick to see the value in Beitou's waters. They put up handsome bathing houses and inns with indoor and/or outdoor baths, koi ponds, tatami rooms and the like; some of these still exist today. Thanks in large part to these attractive buildings, Beitou is also known as the Hollywood of Taiwan; more than 100 Taiwanese films have been shot here.

Not too long ago, the waters themselves were the priority, and comforts such as attractive baths, meals and massages came a distant second. That's changed, big time, and Beitou offers dozens of bathing options, from simply soaking your feet in the roadside creeks (for free) to glam private baths in ritzy high-rise resorts (big bucks). The latter might include the use of several public pools, with optional massages and multicourse dinners, even karaoke. Popular day-trip packages combine a hot-spring visit with lunch or dinner.

Beitou's downside is that it can be crowded, especially in peak season.

## Orientation & Information

The resort area is a few minutes' walk from MRT Xin Beitou station (Map pp112-14). Inside the eye-shaped Beitou Park are the Beitou Hot Spring Museum and public hot springs. A number of high-rise hot-spring hotels line Guangming Rd on the park's southern side. The park is bordered to the north by Zhongshan Rd, where you'll find the Ketagalan Culture Centre and the route towards the Di-re Valley, the hot springs source for many of the resorts. Where Guangming and Zhongshan Rds converge at the far end of the park, you can continue along the mountain roads to some deluxe resorts. Most of these have shuttle buses to/from MRT Xin Beitou station.

During the Hot Spring Carnival in October, Beitou's resorts offer special packages.

## Sights & Activities
### BEITOU HOT SPRING MUSEUM
北投縕泉博物館

On the site of one of the original Japanese-era hot-spring baths, this handsome **museum** (Běitóu Wēnquán Bówùguǎn; Map pp112-14; ☎ 2893 9981; 2 Zhongshan Rd; admission free; ⊗ 9am-5pm, closed Mon) mixes a Victorian exterior with a variety of architectural styles inside. Upstairs, wooden verandas surround a large Japanese-style tatami room where bathers once took tea and relaxed after their baths. The former baths downstairs feel almost Roman in their construction, and old scrubbing brushes, buckets and other implements of Taiwanese hot-spring bathing are displayed.

Note that you have to remove your shoes at the entrance and put slippers on to enter the museum.

---

### THE COLOUR OF WATER

Beitou's hot springs can be classified by colour. Green sulphurous waters are slightly corrosive and are said to be good for muscle aches and pains. White sulphurous waters are mildly acidic and therapeutic for arthritis and gynaecological problems, while reddish (iron-oxide) waters are mildly alkaline and are used to treat rheumatic problems and nervous complaints. All are good for skin disorders.

---

### DI-RE VALLEY 地熱谷

Throughout the Japanese occupation this **geothermal valley** (Dìrè Gǔ, Hell Valley; Map pp112-14; ☎ 2883 5156; Zhongshan Rd) was considered one of the country's great scenic wonders; a visit by the Japanese crown prince sealed Beitou's reputation as *the* hot-spring destination in Taiwan. These days it's interesting to walk through, and the valley's 3500 sq metres of bubbling waters and sulphurous gases leave no question as to the origins of its name. Although the waters are not suitable for bathing – in some spots they reach 90°C – it is the source of many of the hot springs used by the resorts in town.

### KETAGALAN CULTURE CENTRE
凱達格蘭文化館

Opened in 2002, this multistorey **centre** (Kǎidágélán Wénhuàguǎn; Map pp112-14; ☎ 2898 6500; 3-1 Zhongshan Rd; admission free; ⊗ 9am-5pm, closed Mon) exploring Taiwan's aboriginal culture is worth a stop. Exhibits are mostly on the 2nd and 3rd floors, while there are performance stages and temporary exhibits on other floors. The upper floors house study centres and a library. Although signage is in Chinese, English-language leaflets explain Taiwan's tribes in detail.

### HOT SPRINGS

Practically next to the Beitou Hot Spring Museum, Beitou's **outdoor public bath** (Gōnggòng Lùtiān Wēnquán; Map pp112-14; ☎ 2893 7014; Zhongshan Rd; weekday/weekend NT20/40; ⊗ 8.30-11.15am, noon-2.45pm, 3.30-6.15pm & 7-9.45pm) is set into the hillside and offers mixed bathing for men and women (a swimsuit and your own towel required). It closes every few hours for cleaning, so be sure to allow yourself enough time to enjoy it. It is one of the least expensive options in town.

**Longnaitang** (Lóngnăitāng, dragon hot springs; Map pp112-14; ☎ 2891 2236; 244 Guangming Rd; admission NT70; ⏰ 6.30am-9pm) is one of Beitou's original bathhouses and is also one of the most popular. Its popularity is a little puzzling, as it's rather cramped and crude, and there's only indoor bathing, but thanks to its history it gets loads of visitors, especially from Japan.

You could be forgiven for mistaking **Asia Pacific Resort** (Yàtài Wēnquán Shēnghuóguǎn; Map pp112-14; ☎ 2898 2088; 21 Yinguang Lane, Wenquan Rd; weekday (4hr)/weekend (2hr) NT400/500; ⏰ 8.30-1am Mon-Fri, 8.30-2am Sat & Sun) for a hotel. In the narrow roads east of the town centre, this bathing/dining/meeting complex boasts contemporary Japanese-style minimalism with raked sand gardens and indoor and outdoor baths, including white-water mineral baths. Private rooms start at NT900, and the restaurant serves Chinese/Taiwanese food (lunch or dinner including hot-spring visit starts at NT880). There are also plans to build hotel rooms at the complex.

See p109 for bathing options inside large resorts.

**TAIWAN FOLK ARTS MUSEUM** 北投文物館
In a building that was originally a Japanese officers' club, this impressive **museum** (Běitóu Wénwùguǎn; Map pp112-14; ☎ 2891 2318; 32 Youya Rd) holds over 5000 items and features handsome exhibits on Taiwanese folk and aboriginal traditions. The costume and embroidery collections are particularly extensive. English signage is excellent. It's worth a visit for the architecture alone, said to be in the Tang-dynasty style, but inside you might well think you are in Kyoto, amid wooden walkways, tatami rooms and shoji screens. During WWII, the building was a retreat for kamikaze pilots preparing for their final flights, and after the occupation it was a guesthouse for foreign dignitaries.

Unfortunately, the museum has been closed for renovations and is not scheduled to reopen until 2006 (costing upwards of NT50 million!). However, Shann Garden (p110), the impressive teahouse next door, is to remain open during that time.

## Sleeping

Don't expect to find any budget lodgings in Beitou. Most accommodation in this resort district is geared towards travellers with money, or at least visitors who don't mind a moderate splurge for an overnight or weekend escape.

**Whispering Pine Inn** (Yíngsōnggé Lǚshè; Map pp112-14; ☎ 2895 1531; fax 2891 2037; 1st & 2nd fl, 21 Youya Rd; d NT3600) More than 80 years old, this Japanese-style inn is a registered historic

---

### HOW TO VISIT A HOT SPRING

If you're going to use a public bath (whether in a hotel or at a dedicated indoor or outdoor bathing facility), here are some rules of etiquette and good sense.

▪ Get naked. Very few facilities permit any sort of clothing to be worn in the water. Bathers are separated by gender.

▪ Rinse your body before climbing into the tub. Use soap and shampoo if available, and make sure none gets into the tub.

▪ Touch the water with your hand to make sure it's not too hot.

▪ If the temperature is OK, step in slowly. If you find the water too hot, there may be a cold-water tap. Moving around in the water will only make it seem warmer.

▪ Once you're in the tub (to quote the sign at Lengshuikeng in Yangmingshan National Park), 'Do not do anything that will make other users uncomfortable'. We assume you know what that means.

More modest visitors will be pleased to know that many resorts rent rooms with private baths. Charges typically start at NT1000 for two hours, but can easily be twice that. The rooms are cleaned after each guest leaves.

TAIPEI

landmark, with indoor stone baths and rooms in which you can sleep on either beds or tatami. It's worth a stay here just to be around the beautiful original woodwork. No phones or TVs.

**Spring City Resort** (Běitóu Chūntiān Jiǔdiàn; Map pp112-14; ☎ 2897 5555; www.springresort.com.tw; 18 Youya Rd; d/tw from NT5800/6600; ⓧ) If you like your hot-spring resorts remote and polished, this 98-room hill-side resort is the place for you. The décor of the public indoor areas is all marble and blonde wood. The resort has indoor, outdoor and in-room baths and offers various spa-treatment options. Rooms have a variety of styles (eg mountain view, Japanese). Use of the spa costs from adult/child NT600/400 for nonguests and spa meal plans are also available.

**SweetMe Hot Spring Resort** (Shuǐměi Wēnquán Hùiguǎn; Map pp112-14; ☎ 2898 3838; www.sweetme .com.tw; 224 Guangming Rd; d/tw from NT5600/6200 incl breakfast) Across from Beitou Park and an easy walk from Xin Beitou station, the SweetMe has an odd name but beautiful facilities – it opened in 2003 as the latest incarnation of an older, high-rise resort. There are indoor and outdoor baths, extensive spa and dining facilities and Japanese touches throughout. Even basic guest rooms have handsome bathtubs.

## Eating

**Shann Garden** (Cányuán Huāyuán Jǐngguān Cāntīng; Map pp112-14; ☎ 2896 5700, ext 201; 34 Youya Rd) By the Folk Arts Museum, this complex of Japanese-era buildings sits on the hill-side with indoor and outdoor dining, a teahouse and sweeping views – a great setting by any measure. It's famous for Mongolian barbecue, but at the time of writing it was due to begin a chef's-choice dinner.

## Shopping

In Beitou many shops selling sandals, but there's only one **E Sen Chiji** (E Shēnqíjì; Map pp112-14; ☎ 2897 7533), home of the 'miracle shoes' for which Mr Lin Pai-zhang won Taiwanese and German awards for new inventions. These heavy wooden sandals (from NT450) look like reverse high heels, steeply angled with the toes up high and the heels down low. It's really painful to stand on them (and for heaven's sake don't try to walk in them!), but they're said to be good for the posture, beauty and men's and women's ailments.

## Getting There & Away

Beitou is most easily reached by MRT. Take the Danshui (red) line to Beitou station and transfer to a spur train to Xin Beitou station and the resort area just beyond. Before 7am and after 9pm, services between Beitou and Xin Beitou may be by shuttle bus.

A planned cable car between Beitou and Yangmingshan has been on-again-off-again for years. As we went to press it was set to open in 2006, but locals (who worry about the views being ruined) caution that it may never be built.

# YANGMINGSHAN NATIONAL PARK
陽明山國家公園

How fortunate Taipei is to have this park (Yángmíngshān Guójiā Gōngyuán) at its doorstep, with majestic mountains, hot springs, tall grasses, forests of bamboo and broad-leaved trees, and some handsome lodgings and restaurants. Among its 1200-plus species of plants, the area is particularly known for rhododendrons, azaleas and Japanese cherry trees. It's also the location of Chiang Kai-shek's most spectacular villa. This all makes Yangmingshan an excellent escape for hiking, cycling (pedal or motor), soaking or just getting away from it all. During flower season (late February to early April) the park is awash in colour – and tourists.

Like Beitou, a major attraction of Yangmingshan is the hot-spring baths. The park is filled with sulphur steam vents (kēng) – the largest being Xiaoyoukeng in the northwestern part of the park. To the east, Lengshuikeng has hot-spring baths open to the public for free.

However, while Beitou is awash in new resorts, Yangmingshan as a national park is protected, and no new construction can take place. This can also mean that some of the lodgings are not as spiffy as in Beitou, but the trade-off is that they feel more historic.

The area just outside the park's boundaries tends to be more developed. Many well-to-do Taiwanese and expats live on the mountains' lower reaches, and there are schools and churches serving the community.

## Orientation & Information

The centrepiece of the park is Cisingshan (Qīxīngshān), northern Taiwan's tallest peak at 1120m.

Yangmingshan bus station (Map pp112-14) is near the south entrance of the park, and from here you can catch a shuttle bus around the park (p114). There are some cafés and convenience stores near the bus station – otherwise the offerings are pretty few and far between.

There are visitors centres at major tourist sights within the park, and most usually have an English speaker on hand. All the centres have simple maps of the park, including basic information and hiking trails in English. At the national park's headquarters, you can pick up a detailed map of the park for NT50.

Generally Yangmingshan is about 3°C cooler than central Taipei. The weather here is extremely changeable, and visitors should be prepared for rain, wind and cold no matter how beautiful it is in the city. The period from July to September has the most stable weather, although afternoon thunderstorms are common. Autumn brings monsoons and humidity, chilly rain and fog. Very occasionally in winter it snows on the park's peaks, bringing out hordes trying to experience this phenomenon.

## Sights

Chiang Kai-shek had 15 villas, of which **Yangming Shuwu** (Yángmíng Shūwū, Yangming Villa; Map pp112-14; ☎ 2861 1444; adult/concession NT50/30; ⊙ tours 9am & 1.30pm, closed Mon) was the last (built in 1970) and the grandest. Its valley setting makes for quite a sight, especially in March when its gardens are in full bloom. It also provides quite an insight into the life of the president and madame. Even before you reach the house, you'll see bushes pruned into five clumps (symbolising Chiang's rank as a five-star general) and the hidden guard posts where an entire military police battalion could be stationed.

Despite its boxy exterior, the main house is surprisingly interesting. Inside are several dining rooms, both Chinese and Western, a life-size portrait of Chiang with eyes that seem to follow you around the room, the salon where assistants read the Chiangs the newspapers each morning (good news only, allegedly), Madame Chiang's painting room and some glass panels etched from her works. While the furniture is mostly reproduction, most of the building itself is original and quite grand.

Tours are held in Chinese and Japanese, although English-language tours can be scheduled by phoning the **national park visitor centre** (Map pp112-14; ☎ 2861 3601) at least one week in advance.

## Activities

### HIKING

There are dozens of hiking options in the park: stop at the national park visitor centre for a simple map with trail instructions. One popular hike on **Cisingshan** starts at Xiaoyoukeng (northwest of Cisingshan) and goes to the top of the mountain. You can also hike from the national park visitor centre. It's much more challenging, but you'll pass Cising Park, with panoramic views of Taipei.

Another worthwhile route is through **Datun Nature Park** (Dàtún Guójiā Gōngyuán), on the park's western side. It's in a hollow surrounded by old-growth trees and plants, said to be untouched for 300 years. There are marshes in this area with wooden planks over them. The downside: the park shuttle bus does not go to Datun, so you must walk or arrange your own transport.

### HOT SPRINGS

The public **Lengshuikeng** (Lěngshuǐkēng; Map pp112-14; ☎ 2861 0036; admission free; ⊙ 9am-5pm, closed Mon) bath on the park's eastern side has separate men's and women's indoor baths, although free admission means there can be long queues to enter. Its name means 'cold water valley', and by comparison to other local hot springs it's chilly, at 40°C. High iron content makes its waters reddish brown. Technically, Lengshuikeng is open to 5pm, but in fact it's often open later, so phone ahead if you're considering an after-hours visit.

The **Matsao Huayi Village** (Mǎcáo Huáyìcūn; Map pp112-14; ☎ 2861 6351; 20 Lane 251, Xuzihu Rd; admission NT150; ⊙ 24hr) takes some effort to reach but it's well worth it for the region's greatest variety of outdoor baths. There are dozens of options, including large pools, volcanic mud pools, cold pools and small pools for you and your friends, as well as massage services and a huge restaurant. The water comes directly from a dormant volcano and does not need heating. Around 1000 people a day have been known to visit on busy weekends. To get here, it's best to have

# YANGMINGSHAN NATIONAL PARK & BEITOU

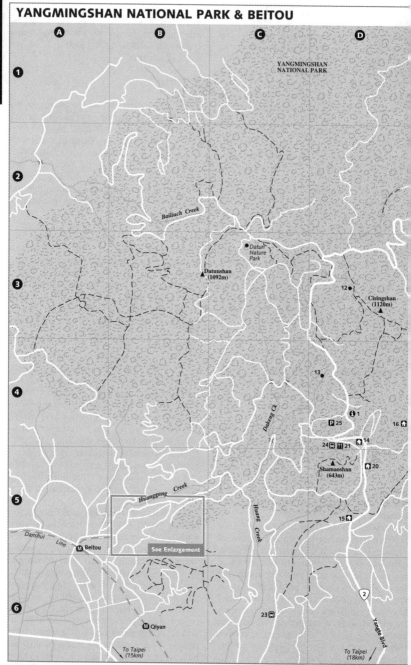

YANGMINGSHAN
NATIONAL PARK

Bailiuch Creek

Datun Nature Park

Datunshan
(1092m)

12

Cisingshan
(1120m)

13

Dakeng Ck

P 25

1

16

24   21

14

20

Shamaoshan
(643m)

Huanggang Creek

15

Huang Creek

See Enlargement

Danshui Line

Beitou

2

Qiyan

23

Yangte Blvd

To Taipei
(15km)

To Taipei
(18km)

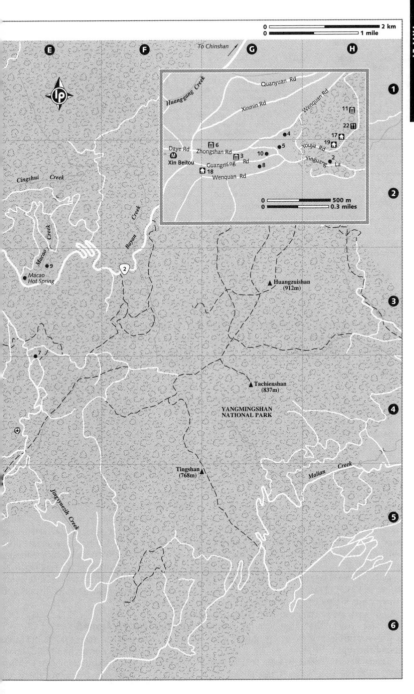

0 ————————————————— 2 km
0 ————————————————— 1 mile

To Chinshan

Huanggang Creek

Quanyuan Rd

Xinmin Rd

Wenquan Rd

11

22

17

Daye Rd

6

Zhongshan Rd

19

Xin Beitou

Youya Rd

4

5

3

10

Guangming Rd

Yinguang

2

18

8

Wenquan Rd

La

Cingshui Creek

0 ————————————————— 500 m
0 ————————————————— 0.3 miles

Macao Creek

Boyan Creek

9

2

Macao
Hot Spring

Huangzuishan
(912m)

7

Tachienshan
(837m)

YANGMINGSHAN
NATIONAL PARK

Tingshan
(768m)

Malian Creek

Jingweizih Creek

your own transport, or there are very occasional buses from the city centre (ask a Chinese-speaking friend to inquire about the latest schedules). Alternatively, you can catch the Yangmingshan shuttle bus to the turn-off for Matsao hot spring and walk about 3km.

Matsao Huayi village also has accommodation (p114).

## Sleeping

**International Hotel** (Guójì Dàlǚguǎn; Map pp112-14; ☎ 2861 7100, toll free 0800-291277; 7 Hushan Rd, Sec 1; r from NT2310 incl breakfast) Built in 1952 and maintaining its original character, the International has a rustic stone façade and rooms that make you feel that you've stepped back in time (they're a little worn). In any case, the hotel is close to the hot-spring source (baths are both public and in-room). Both Japanese and Western-style rooms available. Day use of rooms from NT990.

**Landis Resort Yangmingshan** (Yángmíngshān Zhōngguó Lìzhì Dàfàndiàn; Map pp112-14; ☎ 2861 6661; www.landisresort.com.tw; 237 Gezhi Rd; r from NT7000) With its low-slung profile, slate surfaces and lots of grainy wood and plate glass, this grand yet intimate resort feels inspired by Frank Lloyd Wright. Rooms in the 'de luxe' category and up have hot-spring baths, but any guest may use the spa and indoor pools.

**Matsao Huayi Village** (Mǎcáo Huāyìcūn; Map pp112-14; ☎ 2861 6351; 20 Lane 251, Xuzihu Rd; d weekday /weekend from NT1600/2000) One of our favourite hot-spring resorts, even if it is hard to reach (see p111), the village also has about a dozen simple rooms where guests can spend the night.

**Sakura Resort** (Yīnghuā Wēnquán Dùjiàcūn; Map pp112-14; ☎ 2862 3666; 16 Alley 71, Lane 101, Jingshan

Rd; cottages from NT8500) On the former site of a lowly camping ground, this spiffy resort opened in 2003. The cabins have private hot-spring baths and sleep six to eight people. There's also a fancy contemporary restaurant serving seasonal specialities. There are frequently substantial discounts on weekdays, and camping facilities were due to reopen as we went to press. You can also make use of the hot springs without staying at the resort. Prices start at NT1200 for two hours.

**Yangmingshan Hostel** (Liánqíng Yángmíngshān Zhāodàisuǒ; Map pp112-14; ☎ 2861 6601; yangmin.hostel@ msa.hinet.net; 12 Yangming Rd, Sec 1; d/tr/q NT1610/ 2070/2530) Despite its name, this was originally the most expensive resort in Yangmingshan. It was built in 1924 and it became an army retreat after Japanese occupation – unrenovated rooms still have all the charm of a barracks. However, it's gradually being updated to comfortable, contemporary standards – the lovely spa, including original stone walls, was renovated in 2003 (admission NT250 for day visitors).

## Eating

**Ping Shan** (Map pp112-14; ☎ 2861 4162; 11 Hushan Rd, Sec 1; meals NT260-280; ☺ breakfast, lunch & dinner) Among a number of small eateries near the bus station, this country-style café does lovely versions of Western classics (salmon, steaks, squid-ink pasta), plus a few Japanese choices and Thai curries. Many dishes are part of sets that include starters, drinks and /or desserts.

## Getting There & Around

Bus 260 comes all the way from Taipei Main Station (NT30) via Zhongshan N Rd. From MRT Shilin station you can catch red bus 5 (NT15). Buses run frequently between about 5.40am and 10.30pm. Bus 230 and minibus 9 also run into the park from Beitou, while Daohan minibus 15 heads into the park from Jiantan.

Note that if approaching from the park's main entrance on Yangte Blvd, passenger cars require permits from 8am to 3pm weekends and holidays. Only residents can obtain permits. Other forms of transport are permitted within the park without a permit, and some locals circumvent the permit requirement by approaching the park via Tianmu or Beitou.

On weekends and holidays, a shuttle bus does the circuit around Yangmingshan's main road every 15 minutes (hourly on weekdays), beginning at Yangmingshan bus station. The cost is NT15 per ride, or NT60 per day during flower-viewing season (late February to early March).

# GUANDU 關渡區
## Sight & Activities
### GUANDU NATURE PARK 關渡自然公園
Ten years in the planning, this **nature preserve** (Guāndù Zìrán Gōngyuán; Map pp64-5; ☎ 2858 7417; 55 Guandu Rd; adult/concession/children below 90cm NT50/30/free; ☻ 9am-5pm, closed 3rd Mon each month) opened in 2001 under the control of the Wild Bird Society of Taipei. Over 100 species of birds, 150 species of plants and 800 species of animals live here, on about 58 hectares of grasses, mangroves, saltwater marsh and freshwater ponds at the confluence of the Danshui and Keelung Rivers (and smaller tributaries). As it's a rather new preserve, it will take some time for all the flora and fauna to grow in (especially the mangroves), but it's a worthwhile effort. The park is known for excellent birdwatching. There are wooden paths through the park, and surveying the scene from the nature centre you can almost forget the high-rises you saw on the way in.

On weekdays, it's rather busy with school groups, and with other tourists at weekends. Monday mornings are the least crowded.

### GUANDU TEMPLE 關渡宮
Dating back to 1661 is Taiwan's oldest **temple** (Guāndù Gōng; Map pp64-5; 360 Zhixing Rd) dedicated to Matsu (goddess of the sea, p276). It does not look like much from the street, but looks can be deceiving. To the right of the main hall, enter a 100m-plus tunnel through

the mountain (lined with brightly painted deities in cases), and you'll end up on a balcony with sweeping views of the Danshui riverscape. Naturally, the balcony has a rich assortment of stone carvings; take special note of the intricately carved and painted ceiling. Around the marble façade of the back of the temple, there's a hill-side park where you can contemplate an impressive frieze.

Legend has it that three banyan trees on the site died on the same day in 1895, which locals took as an omen of impending disaster. Was it coincidence that the Japanese occupation began the same year?

## Getting There & Around
Take the MRT Danshui (red) line to Guandu station. Leave by exit 1 and cross under the overpass to reach the nature park and temple. Both are about 15 minutes' walk from the station along Zhixing Rd (where there are a number of informal restaurants for a quick lunch). To reach the nature park, turn left when you see the playground. To reach the temple, continue on to the end of Zhixing Rd. Bus 302 terminates at the temple. It's an easy walk (less than 10 minutes) between the nature park and temple.

# HONGSHULIN 紅樹林
One stop before the end of the MRT Danshui line is one of the world's largest remaining mangrove, er, groves (Hóngshùlín). Its 60 hectares are worth exploring, and there are fine views across the Danshui River to Guanyinshan (p124). If you'd like to combine it with a visit to Danshui, it's about a 30-minute walk. There's a bicycle path between them as well.

# DANSHUI 淡水
### pop 110,000
This is it: where Taipei's Danshui River meets the sea. Although Danshui (Dànshuǐ) is still in Taipei County, the journey here, past mountains and mangrove forests, feels like a trip well out of town. Central Danshui is like a miniature, more relaxed and intimate version of Taipei. There are plenty of attractive sights outside the town centre, as well as unique insights into Taiwanese history as well as hawker food to enjoy.

## History
Danshui means 'fresh water', and fittingly it was once Taiwan's largest fishing port (a

title that now belongs to Keelung). Today, fishing is only a minor industry here.

Danshui's strategic location made it an important defensive post for centuries. In 1629 the town's most famous landmark, Fort San Domingo, was established by the Spanish; it was later controlled by the Dutch, Chinese and British. Other signs of Western influence include Taiwan's oldest Western-style university. A shrine dates from the Japanese occupation, and there are some fine examples of historic Taiwanese temples and markets.

These days, Danshui is a popular day trip for Taipeiers, and the northern reaches of the area have some new tourist wharves and attractions.

Danshui is also a testament to Taiwan's written history, in that its name is probably transliterated more ways than any other location in Taipei County; common alternatives include Tamsui and Tanshui.

### Orientation

From the MRT Danshui station towards the centre of town, the river front is on your

left, while the town itself gradually slopes up the hills to the right. Across the river is the mountain Guanyinshan (p125) and the town of Bali (p124), a quick ferry ride away. Ferries also leave for Danshui's Fisherman's Wharf tourist area, near the mouth of the river. Buses from the station take you to the various sights around town, and sights within the town centre are easily reached by taxi.

### Sights

Map pp116-17

The order of these listings is structured so that you can use them as the itinerary for a day trip.

Start with a visit to the **morning market** (☼ sunrise-noon) in the town centre. Nestled in its alleys are a cacophony of shops and stalls busy selling fish, vegetables, meats, clothing and the like. You can brush elbows with local women doing their errands and join them at Danshui's colourful **Longshan Temple** (Lóngshān Sì) to make an offering.

About 100m further along Zhongcheng Rd you'll pass **Fuyou Temple** (Fúyòu Gōng), the oldest in Danshui (1796). It's dedicated to Matsu (p276), the goddess of the sea,

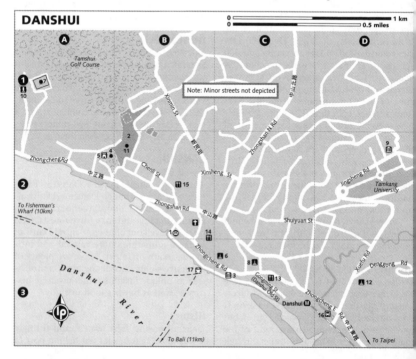

which should be no surprise given Danshui's seafaring heritage. In bygone days, wives and families would come here to pray for the safe return – or for the souls – of their menfolk.

Danshui's most famous sight is **Fort San Domingo** (Hóngmáo Chéng; ☎ 2623 1001; adult/student NT30/20; ☷ 9am-5pm, closed Mon). The hill on which it sits has been home to a fort since the Spanish occupation of northern Taiwan (1626–41). The original fort no longer exists – there are two theories on its demise: either that the Spanish destroyed it during their 1641 retreat from the Dutch, or that the Dutch razed it in order to build a stronger structure. In any case, the basic structure of the current fort dates from 1642.

The fort was under Chinese control from 1683 to 1867, and in 1724 a wall with four gates was built around it, of which only one gate still stands.

In an 1868 treaty, the British took over the fort, made it their consulate and painted it its current red (it had previously been white). Adjacent to the fort is the 1891 **consular residence**, with original tiles from Java, ceiling fans, and furnishings recreated from photographic records. The consulate was closed under Japanese occupation but reopened after WWII, and the British retained it until 1972 when diplomatic relations with Taiwan were broken off.

The fort's present-day offices and ticket booth near the entrance were once guards' and servants' quarters. Inside you can view

the jail cells they built for insubordinate sailors and businessmen. There are sweeping views from the fort itself.

In Chinese, the fort is commonly known as Hóngmáo Chéng, or 'red-body-hair fort'. There are different theories on this too – referring to the colour of the hair of the Dutch and Brits who stayed there, the colour their skin turned when sunburned etc.

The fort has been closed for renovations and is due to reopen in summer 2005.

Up the hill from the fort is **Alethia University** (Zhēnlǐ Dàxué), the first Western-style university in Taiwan. It was founded by a Canadian Presbyterian missionary, Dr George Leslie Mackay, who first came to Taiwan in 1872 and is revered in certain Taiwanese circles for introducing Western techniques of education and medicine. Thanks in no small part to Mackay's influence, Presbyterian is the most popular Christian denomination in Taiwan. The university's original building, **Oxford College** (1882), fronts a Chinese-style pond and a large, more recent, chapel.

About 1km beyond Fort San Domingo, **Huwei Fort** (Hùwěi Pàotái; adult/student NT25/15; ☷ 9am-5pm, closed Mon) is less flashy than its Dutch-built cousin, but no less interesting. This well-camouflaged fort dates from 1886. If Fort San Domingo is meant to convey authority, Huwei Fort was built for military action. It has thick walls, massive gates, four batteries and steep steps to its ramparts to deter intruders (try it and you'll see what we mean, but watch your step!). An inscription above the main entrance reads 'key to northern gate', denoting the fort's importance in the defence of the island. It was also used by the Japanese but never saw military action. In April and May, the fort's chinaberry trees are awash in purple flowers.

Nearly adjacent is Danshui's **Martyrs' Shrine** (Táiběixiàn Zhōngliècí; admission free; ☷ 9am-5pm, closed Mon), the site of which was originally a Japanese Shinto shrine in honour of Japan's emperors. In the 1970s it was rebuilt in memory of Taiwan's martyrs. It's now a popular spot for wedding photos, particularly in the gardens at the front. The shrine is much more peaceful and less militaristic than its counterpart in Taipei.

The Martyrs' Shrine is on the way to Huwei Fort. For the fort itself, head towards the Tamshui Golf Course, and turn left before the main car park.

Across town, **Yinshan Temple** (Yínshān Sì; ☎ 2625 2930; cnr Denggong & Xuefu Rds; admission free; ☼ 6am-6pm May-Oct, 6am-4.30pm Nov-Apr) is a protected national treasure and is considered Taiwan's best-preserved example of temple architecture of the Qing dynasty (AD 644–1911). Although small, it's a riot of sculpture, especially the tiny glass and ceramic figurines and flowers among the roofing tiles. This is also the city god temple for Danshui. Another unique feature is that the temple, founded 300 years ago, remains in the control of the 21 families who founded it. The current building dates to 1822, and it was most recently renovated in 1992.

Continuing up Xuefu Rd, you'll end up at the Danshui campus of Tamkang University (which has over 27,000 students), home of the **Maritime Museum** (Hǎishì Bówùguǎn; admission free; ☼ 9am-5pm, closed Mon). This four-storey museum is shaped like an ocean liner, which is appropriate as it used to be a training centre for sailors and maritime engineers. The museum's collection is anchored by dozens of large model ships from around the world – steamers, frigates, explorers' ships and aircraft carriers – as well as an aboriginal canoe from Taiwan's Lanyu Island. You can learn about the treasure ship of Taiwanese admiral Cheng Ho, said to have navigated the Red Sea, Persian Gulf and East Africa 87 years before Columbus sailed. On the 4th floor, the 'ship's bridge' offers excellent views of distant buildings and Guanyinshan.

Back in the town centre, **Chez Jean** (Sānxiéchéng Bǐngpù; ☎ 2621 2177; 81 Zhongzheng Rd; ☼ 9am-9pm) has been making traditional Chinese wedding cakes since 1935. You can sample many flavours of these dense, nutty, calorie-filled treats. On the river side of the building, the shop's **Musée des Trois Mouquetaires** exhibits implements used to make the wedding cakes; most interesting are the elaborately carved moulds used to press them out. The very enthusiastic owner doesn't speak English (try French, if you can). The shop also offers flyers for Danshui's tourist attractions.

Nearby Gongming St, one block in from the harbour, is Danshui's 'old street'. Finish your day along the river-side promenade, where there are a number of casual restaurants and snack stands facing the water. This is also where you catch the ferry to Bali and the Guanyinshan area, as well as Danshui's Fisherman's Wharf.

## Eating
Map pp116-17

**Red Castle 1899** (Dáguānlóu; ☎ 8631 1168; 6 Lane 2, Sanmin St; dishes NT180-360; ☼ lunch & dinner) A Victorian-style architectural landmark (built between 1895 and 1899), Red Castle underwent extensive renovations and opened to the public as a restaurant in 2000. Specialities include steamed tofu in lotus leaves with ground pork. From the front gate, you have to climb 106 steps to reach it!

Diners on a budget will want to hit the row of **student restaurants** (Chenli St), on the way to Alethia University.

Don't neglect the dozens of eateries on and around Danshui's harbour-front promenade and on Gongming St. In addition to the more common stinky tofu and tall ice-cream cones, you'll find local specialities such as 'iron eggs' (regular eggs that have been boiled, shelled and roasted until they turn black, leathery and the size of marbles). *A-gi*, fist-sized pouches of fried tofu filled with bean-thread noodles and served in hot broth, are also a Danshui delicacy. Flavours vary, but we like the ones at **Bengang Seafood** (Běn'gǎng Hǎixiān; 45 Gongming St; a-gi NT25), especially with finely ground pepper sprinkled on top.

## Getting There & Around

Danshui is at the end of the MRT Danshui (red) line. The journey from Taipei Main Station takes about 35 minutes and costs NT50.

If you're going to Fisherman's Wharf, take red bus 26 from Danshui MRT station (NT15, 15 minutes). A more interesting option is the 15-minute ferry trip operated by **Suen Fung Ferry Company** (☎ 8630 1845; Danshui docks; adult/child NT40/20; ☼ 9am-8pm Mon-Fri, 9am-10pm Sat & Sun).

The same ferry company also operates boats from Danshui to Bali (p124; adult/child NT18/10; ☼ 6.15am-8pm).

## Around Danshui

Fisherman's Wharf, downriver, is plainly for tourists, but it's not bad as an escape for an afternoon or to watch the sun set. The 'wharf' itself has a promenade on its upper deck, while below are shops, restaurants and amusements. Across the bridge on the mainland is a huge Chinese seafood restaurant.

# Northern Taiwan

CONTENTS

When the five-day work week first came into effect in Taiwan many people predicted it would be the downfall of the country. Not only would it ruin the economy but also it would cause social unrest. After all, what would people do for two whole days a week without work? And where would they go? The few spots set up for tourism would be so overwhelmed they would be a nightmare to visit.

This scenario, of course, never happened. Here's what did happen: people began to go out more, and new areas began to develop. One example is the mountain resort of Taian. Previously little known, even to Taiwanese, the area now has some of the best hot springs facilities on the island, and is a hub for low-altitude hiking. Other examples are the coastal waters and islands, like Keelung and Turtle Island. Where once they were forbidden territories, these wildly scenic spots are now open to leisure boats and offer some of the most rewarding day trips in Taiwan.

Old favourites remain, such as the stunningly scenic Central Cross-Island and North Cross-Island Hwys, the old town of Jiufen, with its narrow streets and quaint hillside teahouses, and the crazy rock formations along the cape at Yeliu. But even these have improved, if only because with so many other places to visit, they are less crowded than before.

In short, the north has come of age as a top spot for travel. There are also folk art centres, forest reserves, beaches (eight of them) and the must-see towns of Yingge, Sanyi and Pinglin, which are dedicated to ceramics, woodcarving and tea, respectively.

Transport in the north is convenient and cheap, and most of the places in this chapter are only one or two hours from Taipei.

## HIGHLIGHTS

- Learn tea preparation techniques and cycle through emerald tea fields in **Pinglin** (p148)
- Try your hand at pottery making and tour the 'old street' in **Yingge** (p152)
- Have a hot spring and hike historic trails in the mountains at **Taian** (p142)
- Send a sky lantern into the air, hike quiet trails and view the 'Niagara of Taiwan' along the **Pingxi Branch Rail Line** (p130)
- Admire the work of master woodcarvers and stroll through the countryside on abandoned train tracks at **Sanyi** (p146)

# NORTH COAST & GUANYINSHAN NATIONAL SCENIC AREA

☎ 02

It's odd that the north coast, which has so much to offer the foreign traveller or resident expat, is so seldom visited. Many people visit the strange rock formations at Yeliu when they first arrive in Taiwan (often taken there by Taiwanese friends), and perhaps go to a beach or eat a little seafood at Danshui, but then seldom or never return.

It's true that in years past much of the coast was blighted by hideous construction, garbage-filled beaches and stinking rivers, and this certainly did not leave one wanting to come back for more. But it's also true that in recent years much of the coast, as much of the rest of the country, is experiencing a kind of rebirth.

The establishment of the North Coast and Guanyinshan National Scenic Area Administration in 2002 has certainly been instrumental in the change. Check out its website (www.northguan-nsa.gov.tw) for more sights and activities.

## WANLI 萬里

The little town of Wanli (Wànlǐ), northwest of Keelung, is known as the best lightplane flying area (for the air conditions and scenery) in northern Taiwan. For more information contact the **Green Bay Flying Club** (☎ 2492 4458).

## GREEN BAY 翡翠灣

This is the best **beach** (Fěicuì Wān) in the Wanli area. The 1km strip features light brown sand and waves high enough for surfing.

The beach is privately run by the visibly ageing Howard Plaza Hotel. Admission (adult/child NT500/300, admission free October to May), which we feel is too high for what is offered, includes use of the beach and playground area pools, showers and changing rooms. Swimming is only permitted in summer months between 8am and 5pm.

To get to Green Bay from Taipei take a Taiwan Bus Company bus from Taipei North Station heading to Jinshan. Buses (NT85) run every 15 minutes.

## YELIU 野柳

Just a few kilometres north of Green Bay sits a limestone **cape** (Yěliǔ; adult/child NT50/25; ☺ 8am-5pm) that has long attracted people to its delightfully odd rock formations. Eons of wind and sea erosion can be observed first-hand in hundreds of pitted and moulded rocks with quaint (but accurate) names like **Queen's Head** (Nǚwáng Tóu) and **Fairy's Shoe** (Xiānnǚ Xié). It's a geologist's dreamland but also a fascinating place for the day-tripper.

The **Yeliu Visitor Centre** (Yěliǔ Lǚkè Fúwù Zhōngxīn; ☎ 2492 2016; ☺ 8am-5pm) has an informative English brochure explaining the general conditions that created the cape and also the specific forces that formed different kinds of rock shapes, such as the mushrooms rocks, marine potholes and honeycomb rocks. You could easily spend a couple of happy hours here exploring the rocks, snapping photos and walking out to the top of the promontory for a fantastic view of the East China Sea.

The park has been cleaned up and improved in recent years and the new boardwalks and English signs make getting around simple. Unfortunately the area outside the park is still an eyesore and may give you a bad impression as you drive in. Nearby restaurants, though they can often look like shanties, serve fresh and delicious seafood.

To get to the park, take a Taiwan Bus Company bus from Taipei North Station heading to Jinshan. Buses (NT85) run every 15 minutes.

**TaiPower North Visitor Centre** (核二場台電北部展示館; Héèrchǎng Táidiàn Běibù Zhǎnshì Guǎn; ☎ 2498 5112; 60 Badou, Yeliu Village; admission free; ☺ 9.30am-5.30pm Jun-Sep, 9am-4.30pm Oct-May) is an exhibition hall for the nuclear power plant. Now you may be thinking this is some diabolical plan inspired by a local Mr Burns, but the centre actually makes for a fun stopover. Children especially will be interested in the interactive displays, shows and novel video games.

The 1st floor features a scaled cut-away model of a nuclear power reactor. A five-minute show featuring a talking robot (in English or Chinese) explains the principals

NORTHERN TAIWAN

## NORTHERN TAIWAN

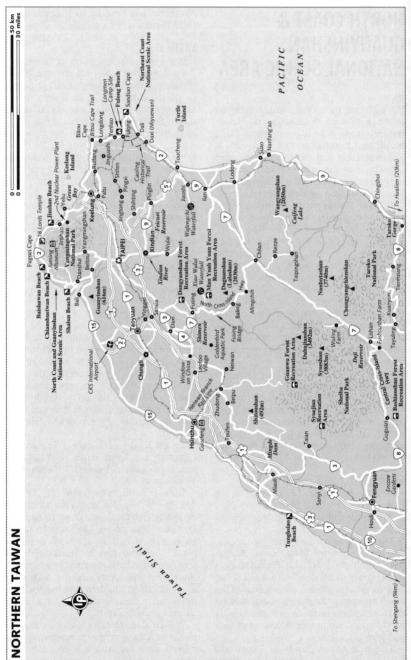

50 km
30 miles

PACIFIC OCEAN

Taiwan Strait

Northeast Coast National Scenic Area

Longmen Camp Site
Fulong Beach
Sandiao Cape
Bitou Cape Trail
Longdong
Yenliao
Daxi (Miyuewan)
Turtle Island

Bitou Cape
Rufang
Jinguashi
Shifen
Jingtong
Pingxi
Shihting
Caoling Historical Trail
Wufengchi Waterfall
Pinglin
Feicui Reservoir

2nd Nuclear Power Plant
Jinshan Beach
Yehliu
Green Bay
Keelung Island
Keelung
Patu

Jinshan Temple
18 Lords Temple
Jinshan
Yangmingshan National Park
Beitou
Yangmingshan
Danshui
TAIPEI
Xindian
Xiao Wulai Waterfall
Wulai
Xindian River

Fuguei Cape
Baishawan Beach
Chianshuei/wan Beach
Shalun Beach
Bali
Guanyinshan (616m)

North Coast and Guanyinshan National Scenic Area

Turning Museum
Toucheng
Suao
Nanfang'ao

Lodong
Ilan
Jiaoxi
Chilan
Renze
Taipingshan
Wangyangshan (2050m)
Caifeng Lake

Chingshui
To Hualien (20km)
Taroko Gorge
Taroko National Park
Tianhsiang
Chungyangchienshan
Nanhutashan (3740m)

Guanyinshan
Yingge
Sansia
Daxi
Fusing
Dongyanshan Forest Recreation Area
Man Yuah Yuan Forest Recreation Area
Daguanshan (Lalashan) (2030m)
North Cross-Island Hwy
Baling
Mingchih
Fusing Bridge
Lishan
Deji Reservoir
Kuanyun
Fushoushan Farm
Wuling Farm
Tayuling
Encore Gardens

Taoyuan
Shimen Reservoir
Goldenbird Aquatic Park
Newan

Chungli
Window on China
Leofoo Village
CKS International Airport

Hsinchu
Guyfeng
Neiwan Branch Rail Line
Zhudong
Beipu
Toufen
Shitoushan (492m)
Taian
Syuejian Recreation Area
Mingde Dam
Miaoli
Sanyi

Guanwu Forest Recreation Area
Dabajianshan (3492m)
Syueshan (3883m)
Sheba National Park
Guguan
Central Cross-Island Hwy
Bashianshan Forest Recreation Area

Tunghsiao Beach
Houli
Fengyuan
To Shengang (9km)

of nuclear fission and how it works to create energy. The script is written at a 10-year-old level but most adults will learn something too (we did!). To start this show (or any other), ask for the key at the reception desk near the front doors.

The nuclear power plant is just off Provincial Hwy 2. When you enter the plant grounds the centre is on the immediate right. There is no English sign on the building.

## JINSHAN (CHINSHAN) 金山

Jinshan (Jīnshān) is a small town hemmed in by the mountains of Yangmingshan to the west and the East China Sea to the east. Because it extends out onto a cape, the town features not one but two long sandy beaches within a kilometre walk of each other. Of the two, the beach featuring Jinshan Seaside Park is certainly the better, but at the time of writing, it looked like some work was being done to the second to bring it up to standard. For now, it offers pleasant walks only occasionally interrupted by fishing nets and rusting equipment.

In addition to beaches, Jinshan also features a number of pleasant hot springs hotels. Overall, the place makes for a fun day trip or even an overnight stay from Taipei.

## Sights & Activities
### JINSHAN YOUTH ACTIVITY CENTRE
金山青年活動中心
The **centre** (Jīnshān Qīngnián Huódòng Zhōngxīn; ☎ 2885 2151; CYCCSYAC@ms10.hinet.net; 1 Jinnian Rd, Jinshan Township) runs the park at **New Jinshan Beach** (Xīn Jīnshān Hǎishǔi Yùchǎng; adult/child NT100/60; ⏰ 8am-5pm). Facilities are well maintained and include showers and change rooms. There is no swimming after 5pm (when the lifeguards go off-duty), or from October to May, but you can stay at the beach if you wish.

The centre has **cabins** (with double bed from NT2900) decorated with clean, minimalist tile and wood interiors, and a **camp site** (tent site NT500) which features showers and a barbecue area. It is clean and well organised but can be very crowded in summer. Simple meals can be purchased at the **café** (meals NT150; ⏰ 7.30am-9.30pm).

One new feature of the centre is the **hot springs gymnasium** (adult/child NT300/150; ⏰ 7am-11pm) featuring indoor and outdoor pools and a host of other good facilities. The cen-

tre's brochure claims that this is the largest hot springs gymnasium in south Asia.

### HOT SPRINGS
One of the best hot springs hotels in Jinshan is the **San Francisco Governor Warm Spring Resort** (舊金山總督溫泉; Jiùjīnshān Zǒngdū Wēnquán; ☎ 2408 2628; 196 Minsheng Rd, Yufeng Village; unlimited use NT300; ⏰ 8am-midnight). The segregated, open-air rooftop pools have fabulous mountain and sea views.

To get to the hotel from the youth activity centre, turn right as you exit the compound. Stay right when the road splits and when it splits again, you'll see the hotel on the left. The hotel's a large grey stone building and is not much more than a kilometre from the Youth Activity Centre.

## Getting There & Away
Take a Taiwan Bus Company bus from Taipei North Station heading to Jinshan. Buses (NT95) run every 15 minutes. The last stop is right within the gates of the centre.

## 18 LORDS TEMPLE 十八王公
People sometimes refer to this **temple** (Shíbā Wánggōng) as the 'dog temple'. According to one version of the legend, 17 fishermen went missing one day. One loyal dog pined for days for the return of his master until, unable to bear the suffering any longer, leaped into the foaming sea and drowned himself. Local people were so impressed by this act of loyalty they built a temple in honour of the dog.

Years later, the KMT constructed the first nuclear power plant behind the temple. Both buildings now are just off Provincial Hwy 2.

The temple, we should warn, is not at all picturesque. In fact, you can barely see it for the ugly crowded shops and stalls. Still, the opportunity to be blessed by a dog should not be missed if you are in the area.

## BAISHAWAN 白沙灣
Probably the nicest stretch of sandy beach along the north coast is at this little bay (Báishāwān), which translates as 'white sand bay'. The **North Coast National Scenic Area Administration** ( ☎ 2363 4503; Shiayuankeng, Demao Village; ⏰ 8am-5pm) office is here and this has helped to clean up the area and keep it clean.

**NORTHERN TAIWAN**

The entrance to the beach is down a road 100m or so off Hwy 2. Swimming is permitted during summer (June to September). The hills behind the beach are a popular venue for parasailing.

As you face the ocean, **Linshan Cape** (麟山鼻; Línshānbí) is to the left. This cape, along with the beach itself, was formed by a volcanic eruption of Mt Datun in Yangmingshan Park (p110) 800,000 years ago. You can walk to the cape in about 10 minutes. At the cape follow the signs to an area of interestingly eroded rocks. While not as spectacular as those at Yeliu, they make for a nice diversion from swimming and sunbathing.

To get to the beach take the Keelung Express bus (NT43) from the **Danshui Motor Transport Company** ( ☎ 2621 3340) near the Danshui MRT station (p106). Buses run every 30 minutes between Danshui and Keelung.

## JUMING MUSEUM 朱銘美術館

Juming is an internationally recognised sculptor from Miaoli County. The **Juming Museum** (Zhūmíng Měishùguǎn; ☎ 2486 9940; www .juming.org.tw; adult/child NT250/220; ⏰ 10am-6pm Tue-Sun May-Oct, 10am-5pm Nov-Apr) is a 15-hectare park built to display the creative works of the artist, including works that have been displayed in Paris, Hong Kong and Tokyo. One thing to remember when you visit is that works are displayed both indoors and out. For Juming, the entire park is the museum!

A shuttle bus (including admission to museum NT400) runs from the Taipei Fine Arts Museum on Zhongshan Rd at 8.40am and 1.10pm, returning at noon and 5pm. For more information check out the museum's excellent website.

## BALI 八里

This **Bali** (Bālǐ) is not an island but a fishing town across the river from Danshui. The town is being revamped as part of the government's plans to develop both banks of the Danshui River. Unlike the right bank, which has been progressing for years, the left, including Bali, is changing overnight.

At the time of writing, the construction of a new waterfront recreation district near the ferry piers had reached the point where you could see that this place is going to be fabulous. There were bike paths, boardwalks, pavilions, parks, museums and a host of new cafés, restaurants and bars, many with decks and patios taking advantage of the romantic views across the river.

## Orientation & Information

Bali is at the northern end of the Danshui River where it empties into the Taiwan Strait. This is a simple place to get around as everything is built up alongside the river. Just follow the boardwalk or bike path to catch the sights.

As you get off the ferry from Danshui, you'll see a large map in English and Chinese, illustrating the area and its attractions. This map can also be found at many other locations along the walking and cycling routes.

## Sights & Activities
### CYCLING

At the time of writing a 7km **bike path** (jiǎotàchē zhuānyòng dào) had been built from the Guandu Bridge to the Shihsanhang Museum of Archaeology (see below). By the end of 2004, this path should connect with the one on the other side making it possible to cycle all the way from Bali to Fisherman's Wharf in Danshui (p118), or south to Guandu Nature Park (p115).

You can rent bikes from several shops near the ferry terminal. Rates are about NT50 an hour and shops are open till late on weekends.

### GUANHAI PIER 觀海長堤

The emerald volcano Kuanyinshan rises steeply behind the town, and across the river are the lush hills of Yangmingshan. It's an amazingly scenic location and at night when the lights of Danshui sparkle across the water, it's heaven for romantics. The place to take this all in, day or night, is the **Guanhai Pier** (Guānhǎi Chángtí) at the end of the boardwalk.

### SHIHSANHANG MUSEUM OF ARCHAEOLOGY 十三行博物館

The **museum** (Shísānháng Bówùguǎn; ☎ 2619 1313; www.sshm.tpc.gov.tw; 200 Museum Ave; adult/child NT100/70; ⏰ 9.30am-8pm Mon-Fri, 9.30am-9pm Sat & Sun Apr-Oct; 9.30am-5pm Mon-Fri, 9.30am-6pm Sat & Sun Nov-Mar) opened in April 2003 and features the culturally sophisticated remains (including ironwork) of the Shihsanhang culture. This extinct tribe of aboriginals flourished around Bali 500 to 1800 years ago.

You can reach the museum by walking or cycling from the ferry, or taking a Red 13 bus from the Guandu MRT station. Check out www.taipeitimes.com /News/feat/archives/2003/04/26/203614 and www.taipeitimes.com/News/taiwan /archives/2003/04/11/201628 for more about the Shihsanhang people and museum.

### FORMOSA FUN COAST 八仙樂園

Just past the museum and featuring 12 hectares of slides, pools and artificial rivers, is this popular **water park** (Bāxiān Lèyuán; ☎ 2610 5200; 1-6 Xiaguzi Village; adult/child NT590/490; ☺ 9am-7.30pm Mon-Fri, 8.30am-10pm Sat-Sun Jul & Aug; 10am-6pm Mon-Fri, 9.30-6pm Sat-Sun Sep) formerly known as Formosa Water Park. In addition to some super-speedy tunnels and slides, the park has a 700m long canal you can float down on inner tubes.

You can reach the park by walking or cycling from the ferry, or taking a Red 13 bus from the Guandu MRT station.

### GUANYINSHAN 觀音山
**616m**

The volcanic peak of **Guanyinshan** (Guānyīnshān) is not only a beautiful landmark for Bali, but a rewarding hike. The views from the top take in Danshui, the Taipei Basin and Taiwan Strait. Sunsets are outstanding.

To get to the start of the trails exit the ferry at Bali Wharf and walk straight up the small lane to the main road. Go left and walk 200m to the petrol station. Turn right, cross the street and head up the road. Follow the road 5km up to the start of the **Yinghan Peak Trail** (Yìnghànlǐn), a winding, 1.4km stone path. From the petrol station the way is obvious and there are English road signs.

Near the trailhead you'll find the **Guanyinshan Visitor Centre** ( ☎ 2292 8888; 130 Lingyun Rd, Sec 3; Wugu Township; ☺ 9am-5pm) and the start of other trails.

### Getting There & Away

Ferries (adult/child NT18/10) run frequently from Danshui from 6am to 10pm and later on weekends and in summer. There are two ferry routes: one from Danshui Wharf to Bali Wharf, and one from Fisherman's Wharf to Zou-an Wharf, just half a kilometre north of Bali Wharf. You can take a bike on the ferry for an additional NT20.

# NORTHEAST COAST NATIONAL SCENIC AREA

This is where the mountains meet the sea. Taiwan was formed by volcanoes and the land rises or juts from the ocean astonishingly quickly. For most of Taiwan's recent history, the best vantage point to observe this, namely the sea, was forbidden to all save fishermen and the military. In recent years, thanks to the Blue Hwy program (p133), the coastal waters have opened up to leisure craft. Dolphin and whale watching are possible, but the most popular excursions are to small offshore islands, including volcanic Turtle Island.

If you want to get right down into the water there are several good beaches, and even two ocean water pools. For history buffs there are old military forts in Keelung, and the abandoned gold, coal and copper mines in Jiufen and Jinguashi. The northeast coast even has some good hikes, including the 8km Caoling Historic Trail and the 3km path along the cliff tops at Bitou Cape.

The main visitor centre for the area is situated in Fulong. You can pick up excellent English language brochures introducing more of the area than we can cover. If you want to check things out before you go, log on to the scenic area's website at www .necoast-nsa.gov.tw.

## KEELUNG (JILONG) 基隆
☎ 02 / pop 399,000

**Keelung** (Jīlóng) is the second-largest port in Taiwan, and the busiest in terms of sheer volume of goods imported and exported. If you look carefully around the docks, you could probably find a little smuggling going on. Far safer is to examine the remnants of a colourful past that did include real smugglers and pirates, as well as a host of opportunistic invaders from the Japanese to the Dutch, Spanish and French.

Keelung is coming into its own as a tourist destination. Owing to its strategic

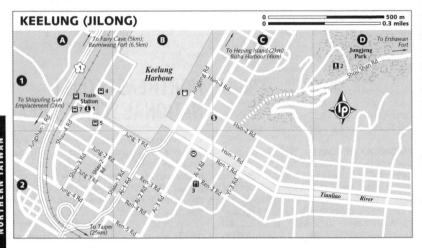

KEELUNG (JILONG)

NORTHERN TAIWAN

importance over the centuries as a military base, it has a number of well-preserved forts. Its proximity to the sea means you'll find ocean parks, scenic lookouts and, thanks to the Blue Hwy programme, the opportunity to visit Keelung Island, a small rocky islet just off the coast.

Keelung is well known for its wet, drizzly winters. When the temperature drops across the north its lowest point is usually in Keelung. Depending on your personality, these damp, mist-shrouded days can be the perfect time to visit relics. If you visit in summer, plan your trip early to avoid late-afternoon thunderstorms.

## Orientation & Information

Keelung is not a large city and you can visit most sights by bus within 30 minutes. If you think 5km is nothing to walk, you could get around on foot.

Just across from the train station is the **Keelung Tourist Service Centre** ( ☎ 2428 7664; 1 Gangsi Rd; http://tour-3.klcg.gov.tw/introduction.htm; ⏰ 8.30am-noon & 1.30-5pm). The centre stocks English-language brochures and usually there is a staff member who speaks English. A board outside the office shows bus routes to various tourist sights and if you need to stay the night there is another board with pictures and numbers of hotels in the area.

## Sights

### KEELUNG ISLAND 基隆嶼
The **island** (Jīlóng Yǔ), a mere 5km offshore,

houses a small military base. Until recent years, it was off limits to the public. It's a tiny spot of land, no more than 21 hectares in size, but with its rugged high cliffs and emerald peak, it's a natural destination for sightseers. Foreign travellers should bring their passport or Alien Resident Certificate (ARC) when they visit.

Boats to Keelung island (adult/child NT300/200) leave from **Bisha Fishing Harbour** (碧砂漁港; Bìshā Yúgǎng) 20km east of Keelung. Boats are privately operated and run when they are full, which can be every 30 minutes on a busy summer weekend, or every 1½ hours during the week. The round trip to the island takes two hours including about 40 minutes on the island itself. By the time you read this the path up to the lighthouse (182m) should be completed. The lookout from the top will undoubtedly become one of the star attractions of the trip.

To get to Bisha Fishing Harbour take bus 103 from the train station. Buses are frequent and the trip takes about 20 minutes.

### JUNGJENG PARK 中正公園
You can walk to this pleasant hillside **park** (Zhōngzhèng Gōngyuán) from the train station in about 30 minutes (you can also catch bus 101, 103 or 105). The way is easy and the 22m white **Guanyin** (Guānyīn) statue looming over the skyline is not only your guide but your destination. Inside the statue, a set of stairs leads to an impressive ocean view.

**Ershawan Fort** (二沙灣; Èrsháwān), is also known as Haiman Tienxian (Sea-gate Fort), and is a further kilometre up the road. This is a first-class historical relic and was used to defend Taiwan during the first Opium War. It's certainly a dramatic sight despite being in partial ruins. Of note are the imposing main gate and the five cannons still tucked into their battery emplacements.

### FAIRY CAVE 仙洞巖

You might think we're sending you to see just a bland temple when you first approach this sight. But just step behind the temple and you will find a deep sea-eroded **cave** (Xiāndòngyán) over 80m long. You can enter the well-lit cave and follow it to an open cavern where there are two further tunnels to explore. These tunnels are much smaller than the first, however, and may prove a bit too tight at times for larger Western folk.

The Fairy Cave is about 5km from the train station. You can reach it by bus 301.

About 1.5km past the cave is **Baimiwang Fort** (白米甕; Báimǐ Ōng), once an important Qing dynasty military base. The concrete and steel fort is in great shape and, as it faces the sea, there are stunning views of the ocean and Keelung port. The fort is a five-minute walk uphill from the last stop on the 301 bus route, so you can either visit the fort first, and then walk back to the Fairy Cave, or walk there from the Fairy Cave.

### OTHER SIGHTS

Keelung has many other sights worth visiting, including **Heping Island** (和平島; Hépíng Dǎo) and the **Shiqiuling Gun Emplacements** (獅球嶺砲台; Shīqiúlǐng Pàotái). Check at the tourist centre for more information.

## Festivals

Keelung is host to the **Keelung Ghost Festival** (Zhōngyuán Jié), one of the 12 major festivals in Taiwan. The festival lasts the entire seventh lunar month and each year a different Keelung clan is chosen to sponsor the events. Highlights include folk art performances, the opening of the gates of Hell and the release of burning water lanterns.

## Eating

The **Temple Street Night Market** (Jīlóng Miàokǒu; ☯ 5pm-2am), popularly called the Keelung Night Market, has what many consider the best snack food (predominantly seafood-based) in Taiwan. In recent years the market was reorganised and now the stalls on Ren-3rd Rd are numbered and include signs in English, Japanese and Chinese explaining what is sold. This efficiency has made the bustling, traditional atmosphere of the market even more enjoyable.

## Getting There & Around

Trains from Taipei to Keelung (NT43, 40 minutes, every 20 minutes) run till 11.30pm. Buses to local sights start at the city bus hub near the train station area and cost NT12 no matter the distance. Buses to sights along the Northeast Coast National Scenic Area and North Coast and Guanyinshan National Scenic Area start from the **Keelung Bus Company station** (☎ 2433 6111), which is also near the train station.

Ferries to Matsu Island (p273) also begin in Keelung at Pier 2.

## JIUFEN 九份

☎ 02

Nestled against the mountains and hemmed in by the sea is **Jiufen** (Jiǔfèn), one of the quaintest stops along the travel routes of Taiwan. The village was once a settlement of nine families. Then, in 1890, gold was discovered and the population swelled. By the 1930s the place was known as 'Little Shanghai'.

For decades Jiufen supplied gold to the Japanese empire. When the gold dried up Jiufen, like Lugang (p207), became a heritage backwater just waiting to be rediscovered.

The discovery happened with the shooting of the 1989 film *City of Sadness,* set in Jiufen. After seeing the movie, urban Taiwanese began to flock to the old village in search of a way of life that had been all

NORTHERN TAIWAN

but swept away in the rush to modernisation. The old town, rich in decorative old teahouses, Japanese-style homes and traditional narrow lanes gave them exactly what they were looking for.

Today, despite the tourists, Jiufen remains a highlight for many travellers. For many expats it's one of the first places they think of to take visiting family and friends.

## Orientation

The main route into Jiufen, and the only road you can drive on, is County Road 102. There are two main roads in the town itself, Chingpien Rd, an old mining cart track, and Jishan St, a narrow covered alley. Jishan St and a long set of stairs called Shuchi Rd are where you'll find most of the teahouses, craft shops, galleries and food stalls; in fact, this is where you'll find the atmosphere and charm Jiufen is famous for.

## Sights & Activities

### MOUNT JILONG 雞籠山

You can't miss this emerald colossus for the way it dominates the skyline. At only

588m, **Jilongshan** (Jīlóngshān) may read like a rather puny giant, but it rises up so fast and steep, it's dizzying to stare at it from below.

You can climb the peak in about 40 minutes on a set of stone stairs. Bring a sweater as you may want to linger at the top and it can get chilly.

### JISHAN STREET 基山街

Narrow, covered **Jishan Street** (Jīshān Jiē) often leaves lasting impressions. It's really just one long tiled lane but spending a few hours here browsing the nick-nack, curio and craft shops is a lot of fun.

One of the most popular activities on the street is snacking. Some distinctive snacks to look for include taro balls (yùyuǎn), fish balls (yúwán), herbal cakes (cǎozǐ gāo) and Xianguang cakes (Xiánguāng bǐng). Two popular stalls (you can tell by the long queues) are **Huang Mama** (黃媽媽蒟蒻專賣店; Huáng Māmā Jǔruò Zhuānmàidiàn; 75 Jinshan Rd) and **Ah Lan** (阿蘭草仔粿; Ālán Cǎozǎiguǒ; 90 Jinshan Rd). Huang Mama sells sweet jelly cakes (jǔròu) and Ah Lan herbal cakes.

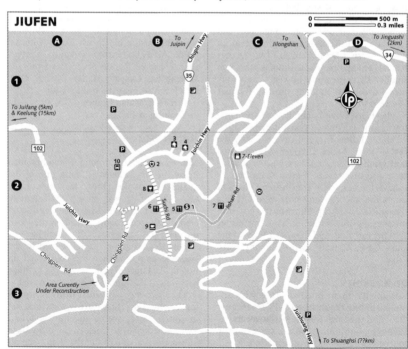

## TEAHOUSES

Apart from shopping, strolling and snacking, the main attraction in Jiufen is spending a few hours in a stylish traditional teahouse sipping fine tea. The best shops, which are mostly on the stair-street Shuchi Rd, are like folk art museums, filled with curios and antiques.

The price for making your own tea (*pào chá*) is much the same everywhere: NT400 for a packet of leaves and NT100 for your water fee. Most shops also offer food. Among the best teahouses are the following.

**Jiufen Teahouse** (Jiǔfèn Cháfáng; ☎ 2496 9056; 142 Jishan St; ◷ 10am-10pm) The owner claims his business, housed in a 90-year-old building, was the first teahouse in Jiufen. There's no view but the wood interior and outdoor garden provide all the atmosphere you need.

**City of Sadness** (Bēiqíng Chéngshì; ☎ 2496 9917; 35 Shuchi Rd; ◷ 10am-10pm) Much of the teahouse's namesake was filmed here, and for good reason; it's a photogenic location and has a quiet, nostalgic atmosphere. Downstairs there is an interesting craft gallery.

**Bafan Gold Site Teahouse** (Bāfān Cháguǎn; ☎ 2496 0692; 300 Chinpien Rd; ◷ 10am-10pm) This three-storey teahouse is well stocked with antique furnishings and sits in a quaint old building to boot. Indoor and outdoor seating is available. The views from the decks are the perfect complement to Chinese tea brewed the classical way.

## Sleeping

There are many guesthouses along Chingpien Rd, most offering substandard doubles for NT1000 a night. Much better is the accommodation at the **Jiufen Kite Museum** (Fēngzheng Bówùguǎn; ☎ 2496 7709; 20 Kungwei Lane; r NT1500-2500).

You couldn't mistake this place for one of the stylish old homes in the area, but the views are fantastic from some rooms and the whole establishment is very clean and new.

**Mark's B&B** (Mǎkè Cūnzhuāng; ☎ 2497 2889; 86 Chiche Rd; d/tw NT1600/2800) The nicest rooms here have excellent views over the cape-dotted shoreline stretching down from Jiufen. Furnishings are a little cheap looking but new and certainly clean, and the red brick walls add a touch of atmosphere.

## Getting There & Away

Take a train from Taipei to Ruifang (fast/slow train NT80/38, 40/60 minutes, every 30 minutes), then exit on the right-hand side of the station and cross the road to catch the bus heading to Jinguashi. Get off at the second bus stop in Jiufen (near the 7-Eleven). The 7-Eleven is right at the start of covered Jinshan Rd. Buses run frequently.

Much easier, however, is to pay for a taxi (NT200) from Ruifang to Jiufen.

## JINGUASHI 金瓜石

One of the exciting new developments along the northeast coast is the opening of **Jinguashi** (Jīnguāshí) to tourism. This little town, like Jiufen 2km away, features old houses on hillsides, narrow lanes and stairways and relics of a bygone era of gold mining. Unlike Jiufen, however, it is almost tourist free, at least for now.

In the summer of 2004, a **Tourist Centre** was scheduled to open in conjunction with a **gold mining museum** (jīnkuàng bówùguǎn) that will include mine cart rides, and the opening of the **Prince's Guest House** (太子賓館; Tàizǐ Bīngguǎn), an official residence for the Japanese royal family when visiting Taiwan.

At the time of writing, numerous signs in English were being placed around the area. One will lead to the **memorial** for the 1000 plus Commonwealth POWs who were interned in the area at Kinkaseki, the notorious Japanese prisoner of war camp.

On a lighter note, there is a pair of old **copper smelting refineries** (十三層; shísāncéng) as you head down to the sea that inspire such a heavy, dystopic, industrial awe they have been used as background for music videos. Nearby is the **Golden Waterfall** (黃金瀑布; Huángjīn Pùbù), so called because the water is a yellow hue from the copper and iron deposits it picks up passing through mines.

All in all, the Jiufen–Jinguashi area is developing nicely and a stop here should be on the agenda for anyone visiting the north of Taiwan.

For transport to Jinguashi see Jiufen (p129).

## PINGXI BRANCH RAIL LINE 平溪支線
☎ 02

Of the three small branch lines that have remained open for tourism, this 12km route (Píngxī Zhīxiàn) is the closest to Taipei and can be reached within 45 minutes. At the time of writing, some sights along the way were changing on a weekly basis. Things that won't change, however, and that make this area a rewarding day trip are the Shifen Waterfall (the broadest fall in Taiwan), the old Japanese-era train station at Jingtong, the excellent but little used hiking trails, and the opportunity to send a sky lantern floating into the night sky.

### Orientation & Information
The line begins in Ruifang, just off the east coast near Jiufen, and extends to Jingtong, just south of the eastern suburbs of Taipei. For the first-time traveller the most interesting stops are Shifen and Jingtong. The entire ride is about 45 minutes.

At the **Shifen Scenic Administration Office** ( ☎ 2495 8409; 136 Nanshan Village, Pingxi; ☺ 8am-5.30pm) you can pick up English-language brochures and consult the large maps on the 1st floor.

### Getting There & Around
Catch a train from Taipei to Ruifang (fast /slow train NT80/62, 40/50 minutes, every 30 minutes) and then transfer to the Pingxi Line on the same platform. All-day train passes are NT50 and give you a discount on admission to the Shifen Waterfall.

Every sight listed along the Pingxi Branch Rail Line can be reached easily on foot from the various stations. You can also rent bikes (per hour NT50) at a few shops in Shifen.

## JINGTONG 菁桐
### Sights & Activities
#### JINGTONG STATION
The coal mining industry in the Pingxi area operated for 100 years before finally closing in the mid-1980s. Jingtong station, the last station on the line, once served as a major

centre for coal shipping. Today it has one of the best-preserved traditional station houses in Taiwan. With nearby displays of old coal carts and electric train engines, a **photo museum** (admission free; ☺ 9am-6pm) and a developing 'old street', it's a good place to begin your exploration of the Pingxi line.

Across the tracks from the station is a giant concrete watering depot and above that the red brick ruins of a coal washing machine. Still higher, on a bluff overlooking the station are the remains of a mining settlement, including an open tunnel with a massive slab of coal blocking the entrance. This is a great location for photos.

For more on the history of coal mining in Taiwan check out www.taipeitimes.com /News/feat/archives/2002/09/29/170075.

#### HIKING
The excellent trails around Jingtong are never crowded, even on weekends. For a leisurely walk through clean, lush forests, follow the path from the train station to the mining settlement and then turn right onto the track. For a real hike, consider climbing to the top of pointy **Shulong Jian** (Shǔlángjiān), the highest mountain in the area at around 622m.

Walk up to the ruins of the red-brick coal washing station overlooking the tracks. Go left past the ruins and head up the small paved road until another small road crosses over. You'll see a paved path with a bamboo fence on the other side. Follow this route up five minutes until you come to an empty lot and see English signs pointing towards Shulong Jian and **Stone Bamboo Mountain** (Shísǔnjiān). Both trails are pleasant though Shulong Jian has stone steps the whole way up and a small lookout where you can see over the mountaintops to Taipei 101 ( 8).

You can hike to the top and back from Shulong Jian in under two hours from the train station. In the early morning and late afternoon you can sometimes see a troop of monkeys near the top.

For more hikes in the area pick up a copy of *Taipei Day Trips II* (p310).

#### PRINCE'S GUEST HOUSE 太子賓館
This sprawling 10-room Japanese-style wood **house** (Tàizǐ Bīnguǎn; admission NT50; ☺ 10am-5pm Sat & Sun & holidays) was built in 1939 with wood from Alishan. Today, both the interior and

exterior are in almost perfect condition, only in need of a little spit and polish (and paint) around the edges. On weekends you can tour inside the house and examine the old furniture, books and rooms.

The house sits on a little picturesque flat by the river. To reach it, exit the Jingtong train station, turn right and follow the 'old street' to the main road. Cross the street to the bridge and you'll see the house to the right in a cluster of trees. You can't miss it.

## Eating

**Palace Restaurant** (皇宮咖啡簡餐; Huánggōng Kāfēi Jiǎncān; 5 Baishijiao, Baishi Village; 11am-9pm, closed Mon; set meals NT220) This place has a pleasant atmosphere and is the best place to eat along the Pingxi Line. The restaurant is set in an old Japanese-era house and features an all-wood design. Guests can sit on the floor Japanese style or at tables.

To reach the house, cross the bridge by the Prince's Guest House and turn right. The house is 100m down the road. There are signs in Chinese.

**Moca Cafe** (紅寶精典咖啡餐坊; Hóngbǎo Jīngdiǎn Kāfēi Cānfāng; 168 Jingtong Old Street; 9am-6pm) When you exit the train station, turn right and follow the 'old street' 30m to this shop. This café only serves drinks but make sure you try the traditional and hearty sesame paste drink (miànchá; NT30); it's great on a chilly day.

## SHIFEN 十分
☎ 02

## Sights & Activities

### SHIFEN WATERFALL 十分瀑布

The upstream watersheds of the Keelung River receive more than 6000mm of rain a year, and have more waterfalls than any other river system in Taiwan. The most spectacular of these is the 40m-wide Shifen Waterfall (Shífēn Pùbù), the broadest waterfall in Taiwan.

A park has been built up around the **falls** (adult/child NT180/100; 7.30am-6pm), complete with coffee shops, lookouts and stone trails that allow you to get right beside the falls. Be sure to explore the whole grounds as the giant rock area downstream is quite fascinating.

To reach the falls, turn right as you exit the train at Shifen station. Walk about 15 minutes until you come to a split in the road. Follow the lower road another five minutes to the tourist office. The waterfall path begins behind this building and takes another 15 minutes of walking.

It is best to visit the falls after heavy rain. When the water level is too low, the falls can appear muddy from sediment picked up by the river. Also, don't mistake (as many do) the first set of falls you encounter, called the **Eyeglasses Waterfall** (眼鏡瀑布; Yǎnjìng Pùbù), for the much larger Shifen falls.

### TAIWAN COAL MINE HISTORY & CULTURE EXHIBITION HALL
台灣煤礦歷史文化陳列館

A few minutes-walk to the right of the Shifen station leads to the 40-hectare **Taiwan Coal Mine History & Culture Exhibition Hall** (Táiwān Měikuàng Lìshǐ Wénhuà Chénlièguǎn; ☎ 2495 8680; 5 Tingliao Tsu; adult/child NT200/160; 8.30-5.30pm). Everything on display is authentic mining equipment from the rotors, to the motors, to

---

**SKY LANTERNS**

A sky lantern (tiāndēng) is a paper lantern with a combustible element attached to the underside. When the element is lit hot air rises into the lantern sack and the lantern floats into the sky like a hot-air balloon.

In Pingxi people have been sending sky lanterns into the air for generations. Long ago, the remote mountainous villages were prone to attacks from bandits and marauders. Sky lanterns were used to signal to others, often women and children who were sent packing into the high hills at the first sign of trouble, when conditions were safe again.

Today, people light sky lanterns for the sublime thrill of watching glowing colourful objects float up against a dark sky. People often write special messages on the lanterns, for example wishing peace and prosperity for family and friends.

You can light lanterns any time of year (NT150) in Pingxi, Jingtong or Shifen, but the best time is at Lantern Festival when thousands of lanterns are sent into the air at the same time. This has been called one of the most divine sights in Taiwan, and we have to agree.

Check out www.gio.gov.tw/info/festival _c/glue_e/taipei1.htm for a short video.

the conveyor belts, coal washing machines, electric transport trains and mine tunnels. Some might feel things are a bit too authentic here and should be fixed up a little to make it more attractive to visitors.

For most people the 1km ride on the electric train and the chance to operate a working jigger (there's 100m of track to practise on) will be the star attractions. Those with an interest in engineering will appreciate being able to get right up and under the old mine equipment.

At the time of writing, the main mine tunnel was being repaired and drained of water to allow tourists to enter. For hikers, there is a three-hour (return) hike up to a weather station starting just to the left of the mine tunnel.

## Eating

Around the Shifen train station you can sample traditional snacks like sweet potatoes cooked in wheat sugar and steamed taro.

## BITOU CAPE 鼻頭角

One of three capes along the north coast, **Bitou Cape** (Bítóujiǎo) is of note for its stunningly beautiful sea-eroded cliffs, and **Bitou Cape Trail** (鼻頭角步道; Bítóujiǎo Bùdào). The trail, which includes a walk out to a lighthouse, joins the longer Longdong Cape Trail (see right) to the south to give you an hour or two of walking.

You couldn't ask for a more magnificent setting, nor a more geologically intriguing area. The rock formations at one part of the trail were formed six million years ago while those at another, only 3km away, were formed 60 million years ago. For fun, make a bet with your companions to see who can tell which is which.

The trail starts near the bus stop before the tunnel. There is an English map here.

To get to Bitou take the Fulong bus (one hour, every 30 minutes) from the Keelung Bus Company station in Keelung (p127).

## LONGDONG 龍洞

Just through the tunnel past Bitou Cape is **Longdong** (Lóngdòng) of which there are two sections to note: **Longdong Coast Park** (Lóngdòngwān Gōngyuán; adult/child NT100/50) in the north and **Longdong South Ocean Park** (Lóngdòng Nánkǒu Hǎiyáng Gōngyuán; adult/child NT100/50) in the south. Both places feature outdoor seawater

swimming pools, diving areas and marine exhibition rooms. Swimming is permitted from June to October between 8am and 6pm.

Behind the ocean park is an area described as having the best rock climbing in northern Taiwan. Check out www.geocities .com/Yosemite/1976 for more information.

The two sections of Longdong are connect-ed by the **Longdong Cape Trail** (Lóngdòngwānjiá Bùdào), which also connects with Bitou Cape via the Bitou Cape Trail (left). To get to Longdong take the Fulong bus (one hour, every 30 minutes) from the Keelung Bus Company station in Keelung.

## YENLIAO 鹽寮

This is Taiwan's longest **beach** (Yánliáo) and one of the best places for swimming, sandcastle building and water sports along the north coast. You have to pay (adult/child NT180/90) to enter the beach area. Facilities include a swimming pool, Southeast-Asian theme café and changing rooms.

To get to Yenliao Beach take a train to Fulong (fast/slow train NT132/85, 60/80 minutes, every 30 minutes) 5km to the south and then take a taxi or the Fulong to Keelung bus (15 minutes, every 30 minutes).

## LONGMEN RIVERSIDE CAMPING RESORT 龍門露營區

The popular northeast coast is well served by this excellent 37-hectare **campsite and recreation park** (Lóngmén Lùyín Qū; ☎ 02-2499 1791) by the Shuangshi River. Accommodation (for up to 1600 people) includes **tent sites** (4-person site incl tent from NT800) and A-frame **log cabins** (2-/4-person NT2300/3500).

The camp site is well laid out and facilities are clean and modern. Bicycles, barbecues and rowboats are available for rent. The camp site is within walking distance of Fulong Beach (see below).

## FULONG BEACH 福隆海水浴場

The most popular **beach** (Fúlóng Hǎishuǐ Yùchǎng; admission NT50) in northern Taiwan is also one of the best and easiest to get to. Fulong has a long white-sand beach and a calm sea well suited for swimming, sailing and other water sports. The headquarters for the Northeast Coast National Scenic Area is based in Fulong at the **Fulong Visitor Centre** ( ☎ 02-2499 1115; www.necoast-nsa.gov.tw/36; Singlong St, Fulong Village; ⏰ 8am-5pm). Check out the visitor centre's website for more information.

To get to the beach take a train from Taipei to Fulong (fast/slow train NT132/85, 60/80 minutes, every 30 minutes).

## CAOLING (TSAOLING) HISTORIC TRAIL
草嶺古道

In 1807 the government in Taiwan had the **Caoling Trail** (Cǎolǐng Gǔdào) built to provide transport between Danshui and Ilan. The 8.5km section that remains today, between Dali and Kungliao, is the only ancient road left in Taiwan.

The trail is in fine shape after being repaired by the tourism board. The three- or four-hour walk (one-way) takes you through wooded areas, grasslands and along hilltops. It's immensely satisfying, especially now that a new section of trail has been added at Fulong, allowing you to bypass the public road. In addition, the **Taoyuan Valley Trail** (桃園谷步道; Táoyuángǔ Bùdào), starting in Daxi (see below), now joins the Caoling trail, doubling the length of the walkable route.

Start your walk in Fulong, Kungliao or Dali. In Dali the trail starts by a temple near the **Tali Visitor Centre** ( ☎ 03-978 0727, ext 101; 11 Binhai Rd, Sec 7, Shihcheng; ☯ 8am-5pm). Maps and trail information are available at the centre.

You can get to Dali by train (fast/slow NT90/70, 90/120 minutes, every two hours) from Taipei.

## DAXI 大溪
☎ 02

Also known as Honeymoon Bay, **Daxi** (Dàxī) draws the surfing crowd with waves that can reach up to 3m. The sandy beach is also popular with the expat crowd looking to get away from the crowds at other beaches further north.

To get to Daxi, take a train (fast/slow NT104/76, 95/120 minutes, every two hours) from Taipei. When you get off at Daxi, cross the road and walk south about 600m along the seawall to reach the beach. In the other direction are the surf shops where you can rent boards (NT500) and wet suits (NT200).

One place where English is spoken is the **Spider Surf Club** (台灣蜘蛛衝浪俱樂部; Táiwān Zhīzhū Chōnglàng Jùlèbù; ☎ 2738 7860; www.spidersurfing.com; 96 Binghai Rd, Sec 5, Toucheng). The club offers surfing lessons (room and board NT3000) and accommodation (NT300) on weekends.

There are a few places to eat around the surf shops but they have irregular hours.

## BLUE HWY

This odd name refers to the government's opening up of previously forbidden coastal waters to recreational boat trips. For visitors this means the opportunity to view the stunning coastal landscape from the best vantage point: at sea.

At the time of writing, this program was still developing. Boats run from March to October and are privately operated. Getting to Keelung Island proved relatively simple – just show up and go – while Turtle Island required advanced applications. In essence this means you need a Chinese-speaking person to help you.

Call the **English Tourist Hotline** ( ☎ 02-2717 3737) or **Northeast Coast National Scenic Administration** ( ☎ 02-2499 1115) for more information.

## TURTLE ISLAND 龜山島
☎ 03

One intriguing Blue Hwy destination is this captivating **volcanic islet** (Gūishān Dǎo), 10km off the coast of Ilan. Turtle Island is less than 3km long, yet rises up to 400m and is ecologically quite rich, supporting 13 species of butterflies and 33 species of birds.

The island also has numerous quirky geological features, the so-called 'eight wonders'. These include underwater hot springs that turn the offshore water into a bubbling cauldron, volcanic fumaroles that spout steam, and a 'turtle head' that faces right or left depending on where you stand on shore.

Turtle Island is open from 1 March to 31 October (closed Monday) from 9am to 4pm. You must apply at least two weeks in advance for a special permit if you wish to land on the island. You can download a copy of the application but only from the Chinese section of the northeast coast's website. Contact the **Tali Visitor Centre** ( ☎ 978 0727, ext 101; 11 Binhai Rd, Sec 7, Shihcheng; ☯ 8am-5pm) in Dali for more information.

A trip to the island, including time on the island, costs NT800. If you wish to only see the island, and not land, you don't need a permit. Reservations are still recommended, however. The price for touring around the island is NT600.

Boats leave from the **Wushih Fishing Harbour** (Wūshígǎng) in **Toucheng** (Tóuchéng).

To get there, take a train from Taipei to Toucheng (NT189, 75 minutes, every 30 minutes) and then catch a shuttle bus to the harbour.

## WUFENGCHI WATERFALL 五峰旗大瀑布

Almost directly in line with Turtle Island on the mainland is another impressive wonder of the natural world, the **Wufengchi Waterfall** (Wǔfēngchí Pùbù). There are three layers to the falls and each one is more impressive than the last. For some excellent photos check out www.geocities.com/kenmerk /Wufengchi.html.

The falls are 3.5km west of the **Jiaoshi train station** (礁溪火車站; Jiāoxī Huǒchēzhàn). There is no public transport to the falls so you must walk or catch a taxi (NT150). Near the falls are a number of upmarket hot springs hotels with facilities ranging from communal outdoor pools to private tubs. The water in Jiaoshi is odourless and very high in minerals and has been popular since the Japanese discovered it early last century.

Trains to Jiaoshi (Chiaoshi; fast/slow train NT205/158, 85/110 minutes) leave Taipei about every half-hour.

## LODONG 羅東

☎ 03 / pop 68,000

Not far south of Jiaoshi is this small Ilan County **town** (Lódōng) that has put itself on the map with its massively popular children's festival and new centre dedicated to reviving traditional arts in Taiwan.

### Sights

#### ILAN INTERNATIONAL CHILDREN'S FOLKLORE & FOLKGAME FESTIVAL 國際童玩藝術節

Every summer for four to five weeks in July and August, Ilan County plays host to this **festival** (Guójì Tóngwàn Yìshù Jié; ☎ 950 2097; adult/ child NT350/225), one of the 12 major annual festivals in Taiwan. Top children's performers and performing troops are brought in from around the world. In addition, there are exhibits of toys and games and sales of exotic children's toys. For families this is a must-see.

The festival is held in **Chinshui Park** (親水公園; Qīnshuǐ Gōngyuán), which has facilities for rowing, wading and getting wet and wild in summer.

#### NATIONAL CENTRE OF TRADITIONAL ARTS 國立傳統藝術中心

Lovers of traditional arts and crafts will be thrilled with this recent addition to the Taiwanese cultural scene. The stated goal of the **centre** (Guólì Chuántǒng Yìshù Zhōngxīn; ☎ 960 5230, ex 164; 301 Bin Hai Rd; admission free; ⊙ 9am-9pm) is to provide a venue for research and performance of folk music, opera, dance, toy making and even acrobatics.

For visitors there is an exhibition hall, a learning centre, a temple especially built to help preserve temple-related arts and a folk-arts street where you can browse for glassware, paper-cuttings and glove puppets in a recreated traditional township atmosphere. Live performances are common and if 2003 was any indication, special non-Han related events, such as world music festivals, will also be held on occasion.

Hopefully, by the time you read this the centre's website (www.ncfta.gov.tw) will have its English section completed.

### Getting There & Around

Trains to Lodong (fast/slow train NT244/188, 110/130 minutes) leave Taipei about every half-hour. Once in Lodong, it's a short taxi ride to the arts centre or water park. During festival times shuttle buses run between the train station and both sites.

## TAIPINGSHAN NATIONAL FOREST RECREATION AREA 太平山國家森林遊樂區

Alishan (p223), Bashianshan (p155) and this 12,600-hectare **forest recreation area** (Tàipíngshān Guójiā Sēnlín Yóulè Qū; adult/child NT150/100) were the three top logging sites in Taiwan during the 20th century. Taipingshan only became a protected area in 1983 and has just started to develop into a top mountain resort. Fortunately, development here means building trails, restarting an old logging train for short passenger rides and providing basic accommodation to visitors. The park's people have made it clear that they are not about to let any resorts be built in the area. Nature is the draw here and they intend to keep it as unspoiled as possible. For more information on the park's history, resources and attractions check out the excellent website http://recreate.forest .gov.tw.

**Accommodation** ( ☎ 954 6055; fax 954 6406; tw /cottage from NT2200; ⏱ 8.10-11.30am & 1.10-5pm Mon-Fri, 8-11.30am Sat) in Taipingshan village includes breakfast and dinner. Lunch is an extra NT165. You must make room reservations in advance.

It's not that easy to get to or around Taipingshan if you don't have your own vehicle. **Taiwan Bus Company** ( ☎ 03-936 5441) runs one bus a day (NT244, 2½ hours) from Ilan but only on weekends. The bus usually leaves at 9.30am but call to confirm this. The best time to visit the park is from April to November.

# NORTH CROSS-ISLAND HWY

If you're looking for majestic scenery but want a change of pace from coastal waters and rugged shorelines, try a journey down National Hwy 7, also known as the **North Cross-Island Hwy** (Běibù Héngguàn Gōnglù).

The highway starts in the old Taoyuan County town of Daxi (not to be confused with the Ilan County town of Daxi on the northeast coast), famous for its excellent *dòugān* (firm tofu) and Qing dynasty façades on Heping St. At first the road winds through the countryside, passing flower farms and settlements, including the burial grounds of former leader Chiang Kai-shek. After passing above Shimen Reservoir, the largest body of water in northern Taiwan, the road narrows and starts to rise and wind its way along steep gorges, across precipitously high bridges and, in general, through some of the most breathtaking mountain scenery in Taiwan.

At Chilan, the highway descends suddenly and enters the flood plains of the Lanyang River. Spur routes head up to Wuling Farm (p156) and across to Lodong (p134) and Ilan.

You can drive the highway in a day, but there are many rewarding stops leading to waterfalls, caves, forest reserves and strands of ancient trees. It's best to have your own transport, but you can do most of the route by bus. Choose one or two sights carefully and make a day of it. In addition to great scenery there is good food, and if the season is right, excellent fresh fruit.

The entire highway can literally become a car park during Chinese New Year and hot summer weekends. Late autumn and winter are especially good times to go as the crowds are thin and the sights seem improved by the chill and mist in the air.

## Information

The **Cihu Service Centre** ( ☎ 03-388 3552; 3 Beiwei; ⏱ 8.30am-5pm), just off Hwy 7 at the back of a large car park, covers Taoyuan County and sights along the North Cross-Island Hwy. The centre is half a kilometre before the turn-off for the tomb of Chiang Kai-shek.

The centre's facilities and staff are excellent. Younger staff members can usually speak English while older ones know the area well and are enthusiastic to help you find the best places to go. Large photo displays and maps help orientate you and whet your appetite to get on the road.

*Taipei Day Trips II* (p310) has an informative write up about this area including a number of very interesting hikes that are too detailed for us to include.

## Getting There & Around

Catch a train to Taoyuan and then a **Taoyuan Bus Company** (桃園客運; Táoyuán Kèyùn; ☎ 03-388 2002) bus to Daxi, the start of the highway. The Taoyuan Bus Company station is straight up the road from the train station.

From Daxi you can catch a bus to most of the sights listed below but be warned that most are only served by one or two buses a day in the morning so it's best to call to confirm the schedule. Too many things in Taiwan are changing now so you don't want to rely on old schedules that can leave you stuck.

## CIHU 慈湖

**Cihu** (Cíhú; Lake Kindness) is a quiet, scenic park where the remains of Chiang Kai-shek's body are entombed. If you decide to visit, note that you will be expected to give a respectful bow to the old general.

You can get to Cihu from Daxi on a Taoyuan Bus Company bus (NT19, 20 minutes). Buses are frequent.

## SHIMEN RESERVOIR 石門水庫

The **reservoir** (Shímén Shuǐkù; adult/child NT80/40) is the largest body of fresh water in the north. Construction was completed in

1964 at a cost of NT3.2 billion and today the dam serves multiple purposes: irrigation, public water supply, power generation and recreational facility. Water from the dam serves Taoyuan, Taipei and Hsinchu Counties.

In the past, when there were few areas for outdoor leisure in Taiwan, the dam was deservedly popular for the beauty of its dark green hills and green-blue water, its numerous scenic pavilions and well laid-out parks. There's no doubting its appeal, but today it's hardly a must-see destination.

Shimen makes for a good half-day trip if you're in the area, or find yourself one of the thousands of Canadians living in Taoyuan or Chungli and looking for some fresh air. The **tourist service centre** ( 8.30am-5pm) on the far western side of the lake has English booklets about the dam and there are large maps around the dam with clear directions to parks and trails. There are also boat tours (NT150) of the lake. These leave when they are full, however, so weekday sailings are few and far between.

Buses (NT61) to the dam leave Taoyuan only once a day at 8.30am. If you're coming from Taipei, take the train two stops past Taoyuan to Chungli (中壢; Zhōnglì). Buses run about every hour from here.

All buses drop you off inside the tollgate. If you wish to climb **Shimen Mountain** (Shímánshān; elevation 551m) get off before the tollgate. The trail starts just a few metres back. It takes about an hour to reach the top.

## FUSING 復興
☎ 03

The aboriginal town of **Fusing** (Fùxīng), 18km down Hwy 7 from Daxi, makes for an excellent pit stop, or an even better base from which to explore the whole area. You can stay (or at least have a coffee) at the new Youth Activity Centre, site of a former summer villa of Chiang Kai-shek. In town, you can get solid, aboriginal-style food, such as mountain pig and chicken, rice steamed in bamboo tubes (jútǒng fàn) and a variety of noodle dishes served with the mushrooms for which Fusing is famous.

The **Youth Activity Centre** (青年活動中心; Qīngnián Huódòng Zhōngxīn; ☎ 382 2276; 1 Jungshan Rd; d/tw NT2600/1900 incl breakfast) sits in a pretty, landscaped park, on land formerly occu-

pied by one of Chiang Kai-shek's summer villas (it burned down in 1992). This should clue you in to the fact that it's incredibly scenic here. The park is on a high ridge overlooking an arm of Shimen Dam. Views from the rooms and from the patio of the **coffee shop** (coffee/tea NT100; h7am-10.30pm) are postcard perfect.

The centre has large, comfortably furnished rooms with balcony lookouts, and the pricing can be a steal for one person. If you are placed in a three-person room that normally charges NT2400 for a night you may get the room for only NT800. That's a pauper's price for a king's view! Room 404 has one of the best views in the whole building.

You can pick up an English brochure at the centre that highlights the attractions in the area.

### HSIKOU TAI DI 溪口台地
To the far right as you face the centre lies a set of stairs leading to a trail down to this **inlet** (Xīkǒu Táidì) of Shimen Dam. At the bottom of the stairs you can cross the inlet on an old suspension bridge.

Just a few metres down the trail a dirt road veers right. If you follow this for half a kilometre you'll come to **Senling Shui An** (森鄰水岸; Sēnlín Shuǐàn; ☎ 03-382 1330; 6 Hsikou Tai; coffee NT100; 9am-9pm) on a small bluff beside a tiny aboriginal settlement. The view here is even more incredible than at the centre and the coffee much better. The owner speaks good English and used to be a pub singer. If there are enough people at the café he will take out his guitar and play.

### DONGYANSHAN FOREST RECREATION AREA 東眼山森林遊樂園
About 1km past Fusing is the turn-off for this 916-hectare **forest recreation area** (Dōngyǎnshān Sēnlín Yóulèyuán). There are no buses but if you have your own vehicle it's a pretty 13km drive up a good road to the **tourist centre** (☎ 03-382 1506; http://recreate.fores.gov.tw; 8am-5pm) where you can buy simple meals and maps for the area.

The park's altitude ranges from 650m to 1200m, making it a perfect cool retreat in summer. There are many trails, some nature interpretation walks suitable for families, but many others involving two- to three-hour hikes up small mountains. The longest hike is along a 16km trail that actually connects Dongyanshan with neighbouring **Man Yueh Yuan Forest Recreation Area** (滿月圓森林遊樂區; Mǎnyuèyuán Sēnlín Yóulè Qū) near Sansia (p153). All trails start out near the tourist centre and are well marked and easy to follow.

## XIAO WULAI WATERFALL 小烏來瀑布

Of the four spectacular falls in northern Taiwan, Wufengchi (p134), Shifen (p131), Wulai (p151) and this, **Xiao Wulai** (Xiǎowūlái Pùbù), we have to say that the 40m Xiao Wulai is our favourite. Like Wufengchi and Wulai, this fall is long and cascading, but unlike the other two you can view Xiao Wulai from a ridge almost half a kilometre away. The sweeping scene of steep mountain peaks and the long waterfall bears a remarkable likeness to the famous Soong dynasty landscape *Travellers in Mountains and Streams*.

You can get right up to the falls on the trails starting from the ridge lookout. There are also a few smaller falls to explore in the area and an amazing boulder called the **Wind Moving Rock** (小烏來風動石; Xiǎoniǎolái Fēngdòngshí). This 3m-high rounded stone is balanced on such a small surface it appears ready to topple at any time.

The road up to the falls is off Hwy 7. If you are driving the sign (in Chinese) for the turn-off is just past the 20.5km mark. Two kilometres up the road you'll run into a tollbooth (NT50) charging entrance into the waterfall scenic area. The ridge lookout and the start of the trails down are just a few metres past the tollbooth.

There are only two buses (NT67) in the morning from Daxi that go directly to the falls.

## FUSING BRIDGE 復興橋

A kilometre past the turn-off for Xiao Wulai is this Hwy 7 **landmark** (Fùxīng Qiáo), a steel span bridge formerly famous for its striking violet colour now sadly a light green. Beside this bridge is the bowstring arched Loufu Bridge, built to relieve the traffic bottlenecks that often occurred on the narrow Fusing Bridge.

Today Fusing Bridge is a popular venue for bungee jumping. Contact **Bungee Jump International** (☎ 02-2758 8858) for more information. On the other side of the bridge, on the right, there is a trail leading down to the river valley.

## UPPER BALING 上巴陵

This tiny **aboriginal village** (Shàng Bālíng) off Hwy 7 is famous for its reserve of ancient cypress trees on **Daguan (Lalashan) Mountain** (達觀山; Dáguānshān). The village is about an hour's drive from Fusing and yet can be disturbingly crowded on summer weekends and holidays. This is definitely a place to keep for a quiet winter weekday.

The way to the old tree area is clearly designated from Upper Baling. A 3.7km path winds through the forest and each tree is specially marked to indicate its age, species, height and diameter. There are over 100 old trees, the oldest being a reported 2800 years old!

To get to the reserve, exit Hwy 7 onto County Road 116 at the village of (lower) **Baling** (巴陵; Bālíng). Pay your entrance fee at the tollbooth (NT150; ⏱ 7am-6pm) and then continue another 13km up a very steep road to Upper Baling and the path to the ancient trees.

The Baling area is also famous for its peaches and pears, and in summer and autumn you can pick or buy these straight from the orchards. To get to Baling and Upper Baling take a Taoyuan Bus Company bus (NT132) from Daxi. There are only a few buses a day so check the current schedule before you head out.

# TAOYUAN TO MIAOLI

Hiking fans, whether serious mountaineers or fit day-trippers, may have found their home in this small section of northwestern Taiwan. In Sheiba National Park on the border of Hsinchu and Miaoli counties, there are 50 peaks over 3000m, including Dabajianshan, sometimes called the most beautiful peak in Taiwan. In nearby Taian Hot Springs, on the other hand, all the hikes (and there are many) are under 2000m though some may still require more than one day to complete.

But it's not all wilderness here. In Sanyi, a small town about two hours south of Taipei, the attraction is woodcarving. And the Hsinchu Science Park, often called Taiwan's Silicon Valley, is as far from a natural setting

NORTHERN TAIWAN

as you can get. The park is not much of an attraction but nearby Hsinchu city has many fascinating relics, including Guqifeng, a temple complex with one of the most astonishing private collections of Chinese antiques in Taiwan.

Most of this region is well served by train and bus, except for unfortunately, Taian and Sheiba.

## HSINCHU 新竹
☎ 03 / pop 409,000

The oldest city in northern Taiwan, and long a base for traditional industries like glass-making and noodles, **Hsinchu** (Xīnzhú) sprang into the modern era in 1980 with the establishment of the science park. The park has often been described as the Silicon Val-

ley of Taiwan and is the centre of the high technology industry.

Though it's the most famous landmark of the city, the park does not offer much to the average tourist. Instead, for sights, you must turn to the city's past. It's not well known, but Hsinchu has a fair number of temples, arches, historical house and cultural museums. One museum, in a temple, has a collection of statues and antiques possibly more interesting to the average visitor than that at the National Palace Museum.

Hsinchu makes for a rewarding day trip from Taipei or Taichung. Leaving early morning, you could see all the important sights, catch a movie in a lovely old theatre from the 1930s, have a final drink near romantic Chinshui Park, and be back in Taipei

---

### THE BETEL NUT BEAUTY

It's said that in advertising sex sells, as do small cute animals and children. In Taiwan, the sexy teenage betel nut beauty, sitting in a glass booth often lined with Hello Kitty paraphernalia, has managed to conflate all three ideals into one.

Betel nut *(bīnláng)* is a US$1 billion dollar industry in this country. The nut is the seed of the betel palm – a tree that grows throughout Asia – and is usually slit down the middle, mixed with lime, and wrapped in a leaf before being chewed. The effects on the mind and body are comparable to nicotine and caffeine, and it is extremely popular with truck drivers who need to stay alert for long periods of time but don't want to have to stop to use the bathroom, as they would if they drank coffee.

However, frequent chewing may lead to oral cancer. It certainly leads to excessive salivation and the betel nut chewer is constantly forced to spit out unsightly wads of red 'juice'. The spit stains streets for months and this is but one reason many cities wish to ban the substance. On the positive side, chewing is said to reduce cavities and can be used to help remove tapeworms.

Betel nut is chewed in many countries but only Taiwan has the betel nut beauty *(bīnláng xīshī)*, named after Xi Shi, a legendary paragon of Chinese beauty. The betel nut beauty is a young, often extremely pretty girl who sits in a glass booth on the side of the road wearing as little as possible to attract customers. The phenomenon started in the 1990s and grew quickly, through competition and one-upmanship, to the point where literally nothing was being worn by the girls but see-through skirts and blouses.

At this point there was a nationwide crackdown (Taipei had been enforcing its own restrictions for some time already). A policy of three nos was promulgated: no exposure of breasts, bellies or buttocks.

This triggered a landslide of debate. For some (including most of the betel nut girls) this was a clear violation of civil rights. (Why could they not wear what other women were wearing in public?) For others, it was a sign of patriarchal meddling and an opportunity to denounce the industry as a scourge on the environment. The betel nut tree has very shallow roots and causes soil erosion wherever planted. In a country like Taiwan where typhoons are an annual event this has lead to killer landslides on many occasions.

But, as to be expected with such a profitable industry, there is no danger of it being shut down any time soon. It does seem, though, that the glory days of the betel nut beauty are behind us. Bikinis and short skirts are still common but you're unlikely to see anything too outrageous, even in the deep south.

For more information, including pictures, check out http://taiwan.8m.net/betelnut.html.

before midnight. A weekend visit could be conceived of if you included a trip to Shitoushan (p142), Guanwu Forest Recreation Area (p145) or Neiwan (p141).

## Information & Orientation

The town centre is very small and most sights can be reached on foot. Hsinchu lacks good footpath in many places, but the traffic is not bad during the day and the constant wind (this is the Windy City) keeps the air pollution down.

Hsinchu roads use Hanyu Pinyin for their Romanisation scheme. Almost all streets have Romanised signs making the city easy for English-speaking travellers to get around.

The **Hsinchu Cultural Bureau** ( ☎ 531 9756; http://hcccc.hccg.gov.tw; 1 Lane 15, Dongda Rd, Sec 2; ✆ 9am-5pm Wed-Sun) acts as the city's tourist centre. It has several excellent books and maps on the Hsinchu area in English, including one dedicated to the city's relics. There are exhibition and performance halls in the same complex. Ask at the reception area for a schedule of events.

The science park has an **administration centre** ( ☎ 577 3311; 2 Shinan Rd, Sec 2; ✆ 8am-6pm) where you can get maps and books about the park.

There are plenty of banks in the town centre area as well as ATMs in 7-Elevens and other convenience stores.

## Sights & Activities

### GUQIFENG 古奇峰

This temple complex on **Guqi mountain** (Gǔqífēng) houses one of the most impressive private collections of Chinese artefacts we have seen. A few standouts include a life-size Chinese bed made out of pure jade, two 2m-long ivory dragon boats, an almost life-size stone rearing horse, several miniature villages carved from wood and a number of stuffed animals, including an entire giraffe head from the shoulders up.

The large temple grounds descend down the slope of the mountain and display literally hundreds upon hundreds of interesting sculpted work on every knoll, nook and overhang. At the base of the grounds sits a pond landscaped with grottos and caves to look like a classical painting. It's a little wild now and could use a bit of fixing up, but it still holds the power to fascinate.

There are no public buses to Guqifeng. A taxi will cost around NT200.

At the time of writing, the 20m statue of Guangong (the war god), which used to house the artefacts, was being repaired. When work is finished the artefacts will be displayed once again, inside the statue. At this time admission will be probably charged.

### RELICS

Hsinchu was called Hsinchang by the early Chinese settlers who built a bamboo fence *(hsinchang)* around the city to protect themselves from Taiya, Saisha and Pingpu aboriginals. In 1826 a solid brick wall was constructed around the city. Only one portion of the wall remains today, the **Eastern Gate** (Dōng Dàmén), but it is in fine shape and, situated as it is in the middle of a busy intersection, a great central landmark.

The second most famous landmark is the **City God Temple** (Chénghuáng Miào). Built in 1748, it has the highest rank of all the city god temples in Taiwan. The front of the temple is now unfortunately covered with food stalls, but you can still get close to the fine artwork of the interior, much of it done by master Chinese artisans.

For more information on these and other important relics, pick up a copy of the excellent 'Hsinchu Historic Sites' at the cultural bureau.

### MUSEUMS

It is not well known, even by Taiwanese, that Hsinchu has a long history of glassmaking, nor that in recent years several local artists have gained international status. The **Municipal Glass Museum** (Bōlí Gōngyì Bówùguǎn; ☎ 562 6091; www.hcgm.gov.tw; 2 Dongda Rd, Sec 2; adult/child NT20/10; ✆ 9am-5pm Wed-Sun) was designed in part to promote and display the active glass scene. Informative English tours are available if you request them in advance (by phone or email).

The museum is situated in attractive **Hsinchu Park** (Xīnzhú Gōngyuán), which also features a **Confucius Temple** (Kǒngmiào; ✆ 8.30am-4.30pm Wed-Sun) and zoo. The zoo was being renovated at the time of writing. We don't know what the animal displays will look like, but the zoo grounds themselves were surprisingly lovely.

The **Municipal Image Museum** (Yǐnshàng Bówùguǎn; ☎ 528 5840; www.hmim.gov.tw; 65 Zhongzheng Rd;

adult/child NT20/10; 🕑 9.30am–noon, 1.30–5pm & 6.30–7pm Wed–Sun) occupies a stylish old building that was once the first air-conditioned movie theatre in Hsinchu. The museum now acts as a movie relics museum, educational centre and a public movie theatre. Movies are shown at 7.10pm Wednesday to Friday and at 10am, 2pm and 7pm on Saturday and Sunday. Admission is a low NT20.

### HSINCHU SCIENCE PARK 科學園區

The **science park** (Kēxué Yuán Qū) was established in 1980 and now features more than 350 companies. It's not a tourist attraction by any means, but for an offbeat adventure pick up the book (NT400) *High-lighting Nature at the Industrial Work Place* at the administration centre and do a tour. The book shows the parks, gardens and interesting architectural features of 150 companies that took part in an environmental aesthetics contest in 2003.

## Sleeping

Hsinchu has plenty of hotels, though most are designed for the high-end traveller doing business or work at the science park.

**Dong Cheng Hotel** ( ☎ 522 2648; 1, Lane 5, Fuhou St; d/tw NT750/1100) This nondescript budget hotel hit the jackpot when the neighbourhood around it was transformed into romantic **Chinshui Park** (Chīnshǔi Gōngyuán). It's one of the cheapest hotels in town and

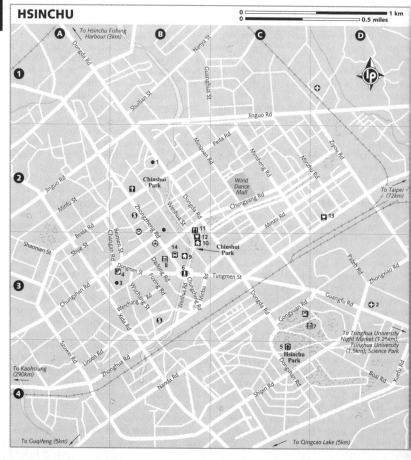

HSINCHU

it's in one of the best areas to be in for the casual visitor. Restaurants, bars and cafés abound.

**Sol Downtown Hotel** ( ☎ 533 5276; fax 533 5750; 10 Wenhua St; d/tw incl breakfast NT3800/4700) This is an upmarket business hotel, with ADSL in every room and a conference hall, but is suitable for the average visitor looking for a little luxury. The hotel is right across from Chinshui Park.

## Eating

The train station area is chock-a-block full of places to eat, both on the streets and in the shopping malls.

**Jia Ni Zhu Restaurant** (16 Wenhua St; dishes NT130; ☯ lunch & dinner) The Japanese owner and chef makes inexpensive but authentic oolong noodle and rice dishes.

For information about traditional eating, from duck noodles to 'Black Cat steamed buns', check out the webpage http://hcccc .hccg.gov.tw. Almost 50 restaurants and stalls are listed (including hours and addresses), with pictures and useful English descriptions of the dishes and establishments.

## Drinking

Hsinchu has a pretty active pub scene. The **Pig and Whistle** (102 Zhonghua Rd, Sec 2; beer from NT150; ☯ 11.30-2am) is a long-running favourite with the older business crowd. The up-

stairs dance floor ( ☯ 9am-5am) has no cover charge for foreigners. This is also a popular place for Western foods like burgers, steaks and pizzas, though we found the fare below average.

**Flying Pig** (Zhūwō Jiǔbā; 12 Wenhua St; beer/cocktails NT120/200; ☯ 7pm-4am) You'll find a younger, more casual crowd here compared to the Pig and Whistle. The bar features a DJ and dance floor and is just across the street from Chinshui Park.

## Shopping

For high-quality glass products ask at the glass museum for the numbers and addresses of Hsinchu artisans.

## Getting There & Around

Trains leave from Taipei (fast/slow train NT180/116, 60/90 minutes) and Taichung (fast/slow train NT198/128, 60/90 minutes) run from 5am to 11pm. Don't forget to stop and admire the old station in Hsinchu, built in 1913.

Taxis are rare in Hsinchu. Get your hotel to call before you head out and keep the number of the driver with you.

Public buses are NT15. Bus 15 does a loop around the city. Many department stores run their own buses from the train station.

## NEIWAN BRANCH RAIL LINE 內灣支線

The Japanese originally built this **line** (Nèi-wān Zhīxiàn) to haul timber out of the mountains around Neiwan. Like the Jiji (p211), Pingxi (p130) and Alishan (p223) lines, it has been kept open to promote tourism in the area. Compared to the other three, however, we have to say that Neiwan is not quiet ready for prime time. Certainly a lot of work was being done to the area at the time of writing, but it was uncertain where it would lead. New signs lead to imaginary destinations and old signs were smudged and faded beyond recognition.

A new tourist service centre being built at the beginning of town just off County Road 120, should make this area more accessible to travellers once it's completed. Regardless, Neiwan still offers a cool, fresh summer retreat from the pollution and heat of the cities. Pack a lunch and a bathing suit and head down to the river, a five-minute walk from the train station. You can also

NORTHERN TAIWAN

consider going in spring when the fireflies come out in numbers.

Neiwan is about 20km southeast of Hsinchu. To get there catch a train to Hsinchu (from Taipei fast/slow train NT180/116, 60/90 minutes) and then transfer (on the same platform) to the Neiwan Line (NT41, 50 minutes). There are trains about every 90 minutes.

Go to http://203.67.46.20 and click on Neiwan Line for the complete train schedule.

## SHITOUSHAN 獅頭山

☎ 03 / elevation 492m

**Shitoushan** (Shītóushān) is a foothill on the border of Miaoli and Hsinchu counties. Beautiful dense forests and rugged rock faces define the topography but if you ask anyone it is the temples tucked into caves and hugging the slopes that have given the place its fame. Shitoushan is sacred ground for the island's Buddhists and draws big crowds on the weekend to worship or simply to enjoy the beauty and tranquillity of the mountain.

**Yuanguang Temple** (元光寺; Yuánguāng Sì) was the first temple to be constructed in the area (in 1894). Many more were added over the years, including **Chuanhua Hall** (勸化堂; Quànhuà Táng), which today also serves as a guesthouse, and the **main gate**, built in 1940 by the Japanese to celebrate the 2600th anniversary of their royal court. There are 11 temples, five on the front side of the mountain, six on the back, as well as numerous smaller shrines, arches and pagodas. Shitoushan is a veritable temple wonderland and a great hit with photographers, nature lovers and temple aficionados.

Many of the temples have been built out of stone and have used the natural contours of the mountain to guide their final shape. Quaint stone trails link temple to temple. Some places to note are **Wanfo Shrine** (萬佛庵; Wànfóān; 10,000 Buddhas Shrine), **Wanya Pavilion** (望月亭; Wàngyuè Tíng; Seeing the Moon Pavilion), which is at the highest point on the trails, and the temple in **Suilien Cave** (水簾洞; Shǔilián Dòng) that features a small waterfall. Give yourself at least three hours to explore the area.

Visitors (including non-Buddhists) are allowed to stay overnight at **Chuanhua Hall** (☎ 782 2020; d/tw NT800/1100). Excellent vegetarian meals are NT60 each. The old rules forbidding talk during meals or couples sleeping together are no longer enforced. From the car park it's a five-minute walk to Chuanhua Hall. There's a large map (with some English on it) on the right side of the car park to show you the way.

It's not easy to get to Shitoushan as there are no buses from Zhudong. Those wishing to bus it must now catch a train to Miaoli and then a bus to Toufen (頭份; Tóufèn). The Miaoli bus runs from Jungjeng Rd (中正路), two blocks up from the train station. When you get to Jungjeng turn right and walk about 30m to the bus stop. Wait here for a bus heading to Toufen.

At Toufen, transfer to a bus going to Shitoushan. Get off the bus at the **Longmen Gate** (龍門口; Lóngmén Kǒu) and walk (one hour) up to the car park. Occasionally there are local people at the gate who will drive you up for NT100.

If you're walking up, ignore the sign to the **Lion's Head Mountain Visitor Centre** (☎ 580 9296; 60-8 Liouliao, Cising Village; ☉ 9am-5pm). That's another hour's walk, and in any case, the centre is for the larger Lion Head Mountain Scenic Area and has little specific English information on Shitoushan. (And its map is backwards!)

If you have a car, it is worth driving towards the visitor centre to have a meal or just a coffee at the **Rattan Restaurant** (藤坪山莊; Téngpíng Shānzhuāng; ☎ 580 0199; 2 Tungping, Qixin Village; dishes NT200; ☉ 9am-9pm Wed-Sun). This is the only building you'll see along the way so it's hard to miss. The restaurant's balcony faces onto a lush valley and offers a ringside seat for firefly viewing in spring. The area around the restaurant is a protected zone and the owner is very knowledgeable about the local plants and animals.

## TAIAN HOT SPRINGS 泰安溫泉

☎ 037

There are hot springs all over Taiwan, and beautiful mountains for hiking, too, but this little slice of **Miaoli County** (Tàiān Wēnquán) is special. For one thing, it has hot spring water so good the Japanese built an officers' club here to take advantage of it. Also, unlike many mountainous areas in Taiwan, Taian is not a one-hit wonder. There are more than a half-dozen good hikes here and local resorts offer outdoor adventure activities like

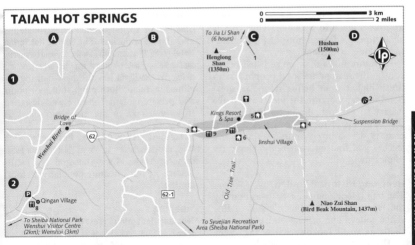

## TAIAN HOT SPRINGS

river tracing, paintball and abseiling. As for hot springing, well, the facilities come in all shapes, sizes and prices.

Taian has only recently started attracting visitors and so is, for now, blessedly free of over development. It can still get crowded, especially on weekends when the weather is cool, or during the hugely popular strawberry season in autumn. Visit from July to September, or almost any weekday, when the pace of business really slows down.

## Orientation & Information

Taian is in southeastern Miaoli County, near Sheiba National Park (p145). The area is not precisely defined on any map, but is more or less the region that County Road 62 runs through. Beginning just outside the town of Wenshui, 62 runs for 16km alongside the Wenshui River before ending in a car park just below the Japanese Police Officers' Club.

Most visitors stay within the last 3km stretch of 62, in an area of Taian known as **Jinshui Village** (Jīnshǔi Cūn). Here, almost all the area's attractions, restaurants and places to stay are accessible by foot. A tourist map, in Chinese, is available at the Tenglong Hot Spring Resort (p144).

**Sheiba National Park Wenshui Visitor Centre** ( ☎ 996 100; www.spnp.gov.tw; 100 Shuiweiping, Dahu; ◷ 9am-4.30pm, closed Mon) is just at the start of 62. It doesn't have any information on Taian, however.

## Sights & Activities

### SHUI YUN WATERFALL 水雲瀑布

The **waterfall** (Shǔiyún Pùbù) is pretty and the path to it takes you along a river, through a forest and up a canyon. Start at the car park at the end of 62 and follow the trail beside the river for 1km until you reach a suspension bridge. Cross the bridge and climb the stairs on the other side.

The trail now enters the forest and splits. Take the lower path (the upper leads to Hushan). After a few minutes you'll come to a ledge. Climb down (there are ropes) and then follow the left bank of the river up the canyon for about 30 to 40 minutes. The whole trip should take under two hours.

### HIKING

Once the Syuejian Recreation Area has opened in Sheiba National Park, it will be possible to hike from Taian all the way to the park. Taian will also become the main driving route into Syuejian. This area is about to explode as a hotspot for low altitude hiking in Taiwan.

For more hikes than we've listed below consult the map or ask local people. Try to finish higher trails before noon, as afternoon fog can obscure the views and make it easy to get lost. Be aware that due to the elevation of most hikes, this is leech country. Use a lit cigarette to remove any leeches you find on your body. Never try to pick them off!

### Henglong Historical Trail 橫龍古道

The **trail** (Hénglóng Gǔ Dào) was built by the Japanese in 1908 but it's still in fine shape today. The official end of the trail (with its small lookout across the valley to Hushan) is a strenuous 1½-hour hike through elm, maple and bamboo forests. Those with good stamina can continue for another six hours to reach Jia Li Shan (佳里山), just south of Shitoushan in the next township.

The well-marked trailhead starts at the end of a narrow 6km road that winds its way up from the Henglong Shan aboriginal village. This road is well worth walking on its own, as with a slow pace you can enjoy both persimmon groves close up and a watercolour-like canvas of mountaintops in the distance.

### Henglong Shan 橫龍山

**Henglong Shan's** (Hénglóng Shān; 1350m) not-so-well-marked trailhead starts about 20m before Henglong Historical Trail. This is an easier hike than the historical trail, as it's not as steep and has more level ground. The return trip takes around 90 minutes if you don't stop to glory in the yodel-inspiring views from the top.

### Hushan 虎山

The most difficult of Taian's hikes is up to **Hushan** (Hǔshān; 1500m), as it involves some climbing with ropes (the ropes are already in place). Start on the trail to Shui Yun Waterfall and when the path splits after the suspension bridge take the upper route.

It's easy to lose the main trail on this hike so don't attempt it alone! The return trip takes about five hours.

### HOT SPRINGS 溫泉

Taian's hot spring water is clear, tasteless and almost odourless. The **Sunrise Hot Spring Hotel** (Rìchū Wēnquán Dùjià Fàndiàn; 34 Heng Long Shan, Jinshui Village; public outdoor pool for unlimited time NT300; ☻ 8am-10pm) has the best bathing facilities in Taian. Both public outdoor pools and private taofang tubs are well designed to let you take in the mountain views as you bathe.

**Japanese Police Officers' Hot Spring Club** (Jǐngguāng Shānzhuāng; 18 Jinshui Village; indoor public pools unlimited time NT70; ☻ 8am-9pm) The facilities are old but still quite popular with local families.

## Sleeping

**Tenglong Hot Spring Resort** (Ténglóng Shānzhuāng; 5 Henglong Shan, Jinshui Village; camping NT300, with tent & sleeping bags for up to 8 people NT1000, 6-person tatami r NT3600; public pool NT200; ☻ 7am-10pm) This is probably the most central place for the budget traveller to stay. The resort is close to most hikes, activities and places to eat, and also runs a number of outdoor adventure activities. For campers, not-so-clean bathrooms with sinks and toilets are available, but you'll need to jump in the river or the resort's hot springs if you want to bathe.

There are several locally owned B&Bs in Jinshui Village. **Cai Ju B&B** (Càijú Mínsù; 83-2 YuanDun, Jinshui Village; 1-4 person r with shared/private bathroom NT2000/2500) has clean rooms and a garden to enjoy breakfast in the morning. The family will make a Western-style breakfast of home-made sausages (low-fat, delicious), eggs, coffee and toast if you ask beforehand.

**Sunrise Hot Spring Hotel** (Rìchū Wēnquán Dùjià Fàndiàn; ☎ 941 988; 34 Heng Long Shan, Jinshui Village; d/tw 4500/7000) This is the best hotel in Taian, and in fact one of the nicest hot springs hotels we have seen in Taiwan. Rooms are stylish in a funky Japanese way, coolly accessorised and feature bathrooms with large stone tubs and rose-coloured marble walls.

## Eating

Taian's not Taipei, but with local food prepared by local cooks with fresh local ingredients, you're bound to be satisfied with your meals. In addition to aboriginal dishes like wild game and mountain vegetables, try to sample traditional Hakka dishes like salty eggs and bitter melon, or rice steamed (and served) in bamboo tubes (*jútǒng fàn*).

There is, unfortunately, not a lot of choice when it comes to breakfast. You can stay at a B&B, go to an expensive resort restaurant or make your own. For the last option there are convenience stores at Tenglong Hot Spring Resort ( 7am-10pm) and Cai Ju B&B ( 10am-11pm).

For lunch and dinner, a number of inexpensive but good **food stalls** (dishes NT100; 11am-10pm) have set up shop beside the suspension bridge into Tenglong Hot Spring Resort. A plate of deer meat costs NT150.

**Riverside Restaurant** (Chuānshàng Cāntīng; 46 Yun Dun, Jinshui Village; dishes NT180; 10am-10pm) Enjoy tasty, local food and the warble of the Wenshui River on a long open-air wood patio.

**Mountain Legend Café** (Shānzhōng Chuánqí; 16 Qingan Village; set meals NT180, à la carte dishes NT150; 10am-9pm) This Qingan Village café is the newer and upper portion of a restaurant that has been in the Peng family for three generations. It's nicer to sit up on top but definitely ask for the downstairs menu, which features great fried tofu, yummy salty eggs and bitter melon, and maybe the best mountain chicken (with Hakka orange sauce) in all of Taiwan. The café sits atop the Turtle Nest (Gūi Xuè), a large rock standing in the exact location where the three Miaoli County townships intersect. The most powerful feng shui in all of Taian is right here.

## Shopping

You can buy boxes of fruit (pears, strawberries and persimmons) in season from roadside stalls throughout the area. On weekends in Qingan Village there's a small outdoor market. Look for funky aboriginal jewellery and Hakka *lei cha* (pounded tea) and snacks. Hours are 'morning to evening' as the locals will tell you.

## Getting There & Away

Fast trains run from Taipei (NT257, 1½ hours, every hour) to Miaoli from 5am to noon. In Miaoli, catch the Dahu (大湖; Dàhú) bus and get off at Wenshui (NT48, 30 minutes). These buses run roughly every 20 minutes, from 6am to 10pm, and leave from the left side of the Miaoli train station car park.

From Wenshui it's about a NT300 taxi ride into Jinshui Village.

## SHEIBA NATIONAL PARK 雪霸國家公園

Many rivers and one mountain range run through this 76,000-hectare **national park** (Xuěbà Guójiā Gōngyuán) in northern Taiwan. Sheiba National Park is home to 51 mountain peaks over 3000m and is the primary source of drinking water for northern and central Taiwan.

The park was established in 1992 and much of it remains inaccessible, in fact prohibited. The three sections you are permitted to enter are at Wuling Farm (p156), Guanwu (see below) and Syuejian, which should be open by the end of 2004.

The park's **headquarters** ( 037-996 100; www. spnp.gov.tw; 100 Shuiweiping, Dahu; 9am-4.30pm, closed Mon) are on the road to Taian Hot Springs . Here you can pick up a number of brochures and check out some interesting ecological displays. English-speaking staff are usually on hand.

The best months for hiking in the park are October to December and March to April. In winter trails are often snowed in and after April seasonal heavy rains, including monsoons, are common.

## GUANWU FOREST RECREATION AREA
觀霧森林遊樂區

This is one of the better **forest recreation areas** (Guānwù Sēnlín Yóulè Qū) if you're looking for a more rugged experience compared to the tame resort atmosphere of a place like Alishan. There are many trails to choose from, most less than three hours long and leading to mountain peaks or scenic waterfalls. All trails are well marked and easy to follow. The area's **visitor centre** ( 037-276 300; 8.30am-5pm) has English maps and brochures.

It's possible to do Guanwu as a day trip – it's only 60km from Hsinchu – but you must have your own vehicle. Buses from Hsinchu only go as far as Cingcyuan, which is still 20km from the forest recreation area. If you wish to stay overnight, accommodation and meals must be arranged in advance ( 03-521 8853). For more information about trails, accommodation and the natural features of the park, check out the excellent website http://recreate.forest.gov.tw.

NORTHERN TAIWAN

## DABAJIANSHAN 大霸尖山
elevation 3942m

The top of this **mountain** (Dàbàjiān Shān), which means 'Big Chief Pointed Mountain', has been called a 'wonder peak' and one of the most beautiful in Taiwan. Considering its company that is saying quite a lot. As with other high alpine mountains you need a Class A permit (see p311) to attempt Dabajianshan.

The hike takes about three days to complete, including two overnight stays on the mountain in **Hut 99** (Jiǔjiǔ Shāzhuāng) at 2800m. For more information and pictures check out the website on p145.

## SANYI 三義

Over 100 years ago a Japanese officer discovered that camphor grew in abundance in the nearby hills around this small Hsinchu County town (Sānyì). Camphor makes for excellent wood products: it is aromatic, extremely heavy and can resist termites and other wood-destroying insects. The officer established the first wood business and over time Sanyi became *the* woodcarving region in Taiwan. Today, nearly half the population is engaged in the business (with the other half probably wishing they were too). On the main thoroughfare (Jungjeng Rd) alone there are over 200 shops.

Like the ceramic capital Yingge, Sanyi has striven in recent years to expand on the cultural dimension of the woodcarving business by building a museum of wood sculpture and encouraging master artisans to settle in one small pedestrian-only strip near the museum. This is in marked contrast to Yingge where all the best ceramic shops are actually away from the established pedestrian-only 'old street'.

Also in contrast to Yingge, Sanyi has good Hakka food, and a couple of excellent hikes or walks, the best of which takes advantage of 12km of abandoned train tracks rolling through unspoiled countryside. Sanyi also excels in eye-candy. While not everyone enjoys looking at dainty ceramic vases and bowls (as at Yingge), who isn't impressed, awed, and appreciative of 3m cypress carvings of savage-faced folk gods?

Sanyi is not a lovely little town. Overall, it's as nondescript, even ugly, as most others in Taiwan. However, since you will spend most of your day in shops surrounded by lovely, even incredible wood products, or out strolling down the train tracks in the quaint countryside, this shouldn't matter.

### Orientation

The sights in Sanyi are spread out but you can manage them by public transport and walking. Jungjeng Rd is the main thoroughfare in town and everything you want to see is either on this road or a short distance off it. Shueimei St, where the main commercial wood shops are, is actually part of Jungjeng and begins 2.4km from the train station just past the turn-off for the museum.

### Sights & Activities
#### WOODCARVING

There are hundreds of stores in Sanyi selling and making wood products that range from 3m religious statues (our favourites), to traditional furniture, to high-end art pieces. Most stores are clustered in two areas. One is **Shueimei St** (Shǔiměi Jiē), which is actually just a few blocks of Jungjeng Rd. To get there from the train station, walk up to Jungjeng Rd (the main road) and turn left. Walk for 2.4km until you see the sign for the wood museum on the right. The next few blocks of Jungjeng are called Shueimei St. Most of the work in this area is commercial in nature though still extremely interesting visually.

The second important area is **Guangsheng Village** (Guǎngshēng Xīnchéng) up near the museum. At the government's request, a number of the island's top woodcarvers have set up shop. The work here, however, is much more experimental and may not appeal to the untutored eye the way the work on Shueimei St does.

To get to the village, turn right on Jungjeng Rd when you see the sign to the wood museum. Follow the road up and then to the right. The village (really just a couple of modern-looking streets) is above the large car park.

Most stores in both areas close around 6pm though a few stay open till 10pm or later on weekends.

#### MIAOLI WOOD SCULPTURE MUSEUM
苗栗木雕博物館

The **museum** (Miáolì Mùdiāo Bówùguǎn; ☎ 037-876 009; 88 Kuangsheng Village; adult/child NT60/50; ⊙ 9am-5pm, closed Mon & holidays) opened in 1995 with the goal of promoting wood culture. Exhibits include the origins of woodcarving in Sanyi, religious deities and introductions to the carving styles of each Chinese dynasty.

Exhibits tend to be sparse, however, offering only a few examples, and have no real English explanations save the title. If you're an average visitor, you could give this place a miss and not feel you lost out on your visit to Sanyi.

#### HIKING

Built during the Japanese era without the use of nails, the beautiful and historic **Sheng Shing Train Station** (勝興火車站; Shèngxīng Huǒchēzhàn) is now part of a popular walking route. The station used to be the highest in the area, but was closed in 1997 when a lower route was built. Walkers soon discovered that 10km of open track through mostly undeveloped countryside had also been abandoned when the station was closed.

Today, the area right around the station is crowded with cafés and food stalls, but the tracks are undisturbed and really a treat to stroll along especially when you get to pass through the long tunnels. The tunnel just past the station, in fact, is 1km long and takes 20 minutes to grope your way through. Try to remember to bring a torch (flashlight) and someone you love!

You can get to the station directly by catching the shuttle bus from the Sanyi train station or the Miaoli Wood Sculpture Museum. Or you can follow the signs on Shueimei St and turn left just before the 7-Eleven. The road will take you down to the tracks in about five minutes. Head up once you are on the tracks.

Four kilometres past the station stands the picturesque (and very photogenic) ruin of the **Long Deng Viaduct** (Lóngténg Duàn Qiáo). This curious scene is made all the more interesting when you realise that the terracotta brick arches were made with sticky rice and clam shells.

The **April Snow Trail** (四月雪步道; Sìyuè Xuě Bùdào) begins just to the right of the Wood Sculpture Museum and takes you through a beautiful forest of Yu Tung trees whose white blossoms in April and early May have given the trail its name. In winter the forest floor is littered with fallen leaves and homesick Canadians or northern Europeans would do well to visit. The trail leads, in about 30 minutes, to a massive open tea field with excellent views.

### Festivals

**Sanyi Woodcarving Festival** (三義木雕節; Sānyì Mùdiāo Jié) in May is one of the 12 major annual festivals in Taiwan. Artists from around Taiwan are invited to display their best work and to create new works, in wood and ice, right on the street. There are also opportunities to try your hand at woodcarving and to sample Hakka food.

The **Miaoli Mask Festival** (苗栗國際假面藝術節; Miáolì Guójì Jiǎ Miàn Yìshù Jié) has proven so popular it is now held every year in the **Shangri-La Theme Park** (香格里拉樂園; Xiānggélǐlā Lèyuán) in Miaoli County. The event is international in scope, with 400 masks from 40 countries participating in the 2004 festival. Quite often the performances – dance, puppet shows, folk plays – are not really mask related, but as they are professionally executed and highly entertaining no-one seems to care. The festival runs for several weeks, usually in late March and early April.

### Eating

There are a number of restaurants along Jungjeng Rd and around Guangsheng Village. Just past the KLG (a KFC rip-off featuring a plump chicken in the Colonel's suit) on Jungjeng Rd (in the Shueimei Rd area) there is **Shengxing Restaurant** (勝興客棧; Shèngxīng Kèzhàn; 72 Shengxing Village; dishes NT180; 9am-9pm) serving tasty Hakka dishes in a charming rustic atmosphere.

### Getting There & Around

There are only a few trains from Taipei each day that stop in Sanyi. If you want to spend the day the only useful trains are at 6.04am, 11.19am and 11.24am (fast/slow train NT192/139, 130/150 minutes). From the train station, walk up the lane to Jungjeng Rd and cross the street to catch the weekend tourist shuttle bus (NT70, every 10 minutes). The bus stops at the museum first and then at Sheng Shing Train Station.

# TAIPEI COUNTY

With so many different activities possible within an hour's drive of Taipei City, there's

NORTHERN TAIWAN

no reason to ever complain that there's nothing to do. In the small area covered in this section – middle Taipei County so to speak – there are speciality museums, hiking trails, cycling routes, hot springs, pristine rivers for swimming, old streets for shopping, a small town dedicated to ceramics, another to tea growing and, in a third, the most beautifully restored temple in all Taiwan.

## PINGLIN 坪林
☎ 02 / pop 7000

**Pinglin** (Pínglín), which means 'forest on level ground', is famous nationwide for its locally grown Bao Chung tea. Only an hour from Taipei by bus, it is also well loved by day-trippers for its steep emerald mountains that rise up like volcanoes, picture-perfect tea fields and clear, swimmable rivers.

In recent years the town has worked hard to improve itself for tourism. It's doing this the right way by working with the natural and cultural resources in the area. Hence you'll find bike paths, hiking trails, suspension bridges and popular 'fish-viewing paths'. You'll also find the world's largest

tea museum, where you can learn not only how tea is grown and processed, but also how to drink it.

### Information & Orientation
Pinglin is quite small and easy to navigate. You can walk from the tea museum to the end of the dikes in 40 minutes. The tea museum serves as the unofficial tourist office and there is usually someone there who can speak English.

The Taiwan Tourism Bureau publishes a useful brochure called 'Experiencing Taiwan's Tea Culture'. The brochure covers, among other things, how to brew a good cup of tea.

### Sights & Activities
**TEA MUSEUM** 茶葉博物館
The **museum** (Cháyè Bówùguǎn; ☎ 2665 6035; fax 2665-7138; 19-1 Sung Chi Keng, Shui Te Village; adult/child NT100/50; ☺ 9am-5pm) houses numerous displays to educate visitors on the history of tea production in Taiwan, the culture of tea drinking and tea-making methods and machines. Everything is in Chinese but you

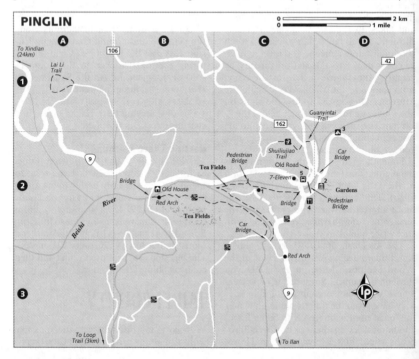

**PINGLIN**

can get an English-speaking guide if you call or fax ahead of time.

Sharing the grounds with the museum are a classical style teahouse and a pretty 5-hectare garden spread out up the mountainside behind the museum. Admission to the garden is free but the teahouse charges about NT200 per person on average for making tea. There is a leaflet (in English) available to help you learn the steps to make tea the proper way. Staff are also on hand to offer assistance.

### CYCLING

Pinglin's **bike path** (*jiǎotāchē zhuānyòng dào*) runs for almost 20km through open tea fields and undeveloped mountain valleys. Cars are permitted on much of the route, but as most roads are dead ends you'll find little traffic even on holidays.

The first few kilometres of the path can be a little steep at times, but afterwards it is a long downhill run and then a smooth ride alongside the Beishi River. The designated bike path signs are large and blue with a white outline of a cyclist in the centre. The first section of the route can be a bit tricky, but you can't get lost.

You can rent bikes at the **He Huan Campground** (Héhuān Lùyíng Dùjià Shānzhuāng; ☎ 2665 6424; 5-1 Shuide Village; per hr NT80) any time of day. From the camp ground, ride back towards town and then follow Hwy 9 for about 700m. Turn right at the big red arch and you are at the start of the bike route.

### HIKING

**Shuiliujiao Trail** 水柳腳登山步道

You can start this **trail** (Shuǐliǔjiǎo Bùdào) at either end of town but it seems less strenuous to begin at the museum. To get to the trailhead, cross the bridge near the museum, turn right, and walk about 200m. On the left you'll see the sign for the **Guanyintai Trail** (Guānyīntái Bùdào).

Take the Guanyintai trail up to the Guanyin statue and then down again. On the other side of County Road 42 and 106 you'll find the start of the Shuiliujiao Trail. This trail is steep also and leads you to the suspension bridge at the beginning of town. From here you can follow the different bike paths. One section, called the **Fish-Viewing Path** (Guānyú Bùdào), is a favourite with children as they can easily spot dozens of fish in the river. A special silver-coloured fish that 'flashes' when it turns is particularly delightful to watch.

A return trip from the museum and back can take as little as one hour.

## Festivals

Pinglin has become the default location for the April **Taiwan Tea Expo** (台灣茶藝博覽會; Táiwān Chá Yì Bólán Hùi), one of the 12 major annual festivals in Taiwan. Come to sample tea and tea products from all over the country, to learn to distinguish the varieties of tea and to observe some old dances and songs associated with tea culture.

## Eating

**He Huan Restaurant** (Héhuān Cháyàn Fēngwèi Cāntīng; 5-1 Shuide Village; dishes NT200; ☺ 10.30am-6pm Mon-Fri, to 10.30pm or when the last customer leaves Sat & Sun) The speciality here is food made with tea. Not every dish is successful in our opinion, but the deep-fried tea leaves (*cháyè xiāngsū*; NT150) are a hit with most people. The menu is in Chinese but there are pictures to aid selection.

## Shopping

On the main drag into town there are no end of stores selling tea and products made with tea. While tea jellies, popsicles and sticky rice are inexpensive, a jar of good **Bao Chung tea** (Bāozhǒng Chá), the local speciality, can cost thousands of dollars. In our opinion, though, it is one of the most delicious teas in Taiwan and easily appreciated by the untrained palate.

## Getting There & Away

In Taipei, take the MRT to the Xindian station. Turn right on the main road in front of the station and walk a few blocks to the 7-Eleven. Just past the 7-Eleven you'll see a bus stop. Hsindian Bus Company buses to Pinglin stop here every 30 minutes during morning rush hour (approximately 6am to 9am) and every 90 minutes afterwards. Buses have no numbers or English on them so look for the Pinglin characters.

The bus drops you off in the centre of Pinglin. It's a short walk from here to the museum.

# WULAI 烏來

☎ 02

The little aboriginal village of **Wulai** (Wūlái) has long been considered one of the top hot springs resorts in northern Taiwan. The name Wulai comes from the Atayal 'Kirofu-Ulai', meaning 'hot and poisonous'. It's hard to disagree with the hot label, but the odourless, potable, silky spring water (referred to

by the Japanese as a 'beauty bath') is anything but poisonous.

One reason for the success of Wulai is the breadth of activities on offer. Besides hot springing, there is a small tram ride, a gondola ride past the magnificent 80m Wulai Falls, a nearby forest reserve and an aboriginal village offering tasty food and interesting shopping.

A day in Wulai can be as rough or pampering as you like. You can spend thousands on hotel hot springs or bathe for free in the river. You can wander around amusement parks or hike through cedar forests. It's your choice.

## Orientation

The main tourist areas are Wulai Village and Wulai Falls 2km from the village. The village is just a pedestrian-only street filled with shops and hot springs hotels. To get to the falls cross the toll bridge (NT25) at the end of the village and walk or take the **cable car** (adult/child NT50/30; ☺ 8am-5pm).

## Sights & Activities
### HOT SPRINGS

There are dozens of hot spring hotels scattered around Wulai. Many are concentrated around the village or on the way to the waterfall. Others are set in the western hills but you will need a car to reach these. Most hotels display pictures outside making it simple to choose the type of spring experience you want: communal, private, wood tub, ceramic tub, mountain view, river view etc.

Most hotels also offer overnight accommodation, usually for several thousand

**WULAI**

dollars a night or more. All hotels offer discounts of 10% to 35% during the week. A few we can recommend include the following:

**Sakaenoya Spring Resort** (Róngzhījiā Wēnquán Biéguǎn; ☎ 2661 8001; 85 WenQuan St) This is one of the newer hotels in town. Tubs are ceramic but reasonably priced at NT600 to NT1500 for 90 minutes.

**Shanggu Qingliu** (Shànggǔ Qīngliú Wēnquán Huìguǎn; ☎ 2661 6700; 101 Wenquan St) You'll find the setting here very pleasant and the views as soothing as the hot springs water. Communal baths are NT450 for unlimited time.

**Full Moon Spa** (Míngyuè Wēnquán; ☎ 2661 7678; 1 Lane 85, Wulai St) This is a lovely hotel with new facilities and pretty grounds. It is also one of the few places in Wulai to have mixed communal baths (per person unlimited time NT300). Rooms are elegantly decorated using wood and marble, making this hotel a good choice if you want to rent a private tub (per hour NT1200 to NT2500).

**Spring Park Urai Spa and Resort** ( ☎ 2661 6555; 33 Yanti Wulai Shiang) This is one of the most luxurious spring hotels in Wulai. The hotel sits off the main road into Wulai and overlooks the Nanshi River. Communal pools (per hour NT1000) have high-end facilities and fabulous views. Rooms with marble tubs and wooden decks (per hour NT1200) look out over the river.

Down by the river the hot springs water bubbles up from natural rock fissures and people build small rock walls to gather it into pools in this **free bathing area**. This area doesn't look like much as you approach it but once you are down level with the water the ambience changes and it's very scenic and relaxing.

To get to the pools, cross the toll bridge and head in the direction of the waterfall. Take the path on the left down to the river.

### WULAI WATERFALL 烏來瀑布
This 80m **waterfall** (Wūlái Pùbù) is a wonder and the fact that you can float past it on a gondola is all the more reason to come to Wulai. The **gondola ride** (adult/child NT220/150) includes entrance to **Dreamland** (Yúnxiān Lèyuán), a resort and amusement park above the falls. The resort is not a bad place to walk around. The design is relatively tasteful and the scenery quite gorgeous. The rather small amusement park offers simple rides.

### NEIDONG FOREST RECREATION AREA 内洞森林遊樂區
About 4km past Wulai Waterfall is **Neidong Forest Recreation Area** (Nèidòng Sēnlín Yóulè Qū; http://recreate.forest.gov.tw; adult/child NT80/40 Mon-Fri), popularly known as Wawagu. For most, the main attractions here are the sweet-smelling cedar forests and the three-tiered **HsinHsian Waterfall** (Xīnxián Pùbù). For some, though, it's the chance to swim in one of the many natural pools formed by the Neidong Creek that's most enticing.

There are only a few trails in the park, the longest about a 90-minute walk, and all are well marked with signposts. For more information check out the excellent website listed above.

### HIKING
*Taipei Day Trips II* (p310) lists some interesting hikes in the area including one from Wulai all the way to Ilan on the east coast.

## Eating
Aboriginal cuisine is the standard fare in Wulai, which is welcome as it's almost always fresh and delicious. A few mouthwatering selections include mountain vegetables and wild pig (not really wild anymore in the Wulai area), sticky rice steamed and served in bamboo tubes (*jútǒng fàn*) and freshwater fish. Snacks and alcoholic drinks made from millet (*xiǎomǐ*) can be found at many shops and stalls in the village.

Some specific places to try include the 30-year-old **Wulai Snack Shop** (Wūlái Xiǎochīdiàn; 91 Wulai St; dishes from NT100; ⏰ 11am-10pm), the **Taiya Popo Restaurant** (Tàiyǎ Pópo Měishídiàn; 14 Wulai St; meals NT300; ⏰ 11am-10pm Sun-Thu, 11am-midnight Fri-Sat) in Wulai Village and the **Aboriginal Restaurant** (Yuánzhùmín Měishí Cāntīng; 12 Pubu Rd; meals NT300; ⏰ 9am-9pm) near the waterfall. The latter also features aboriginal theme cultural shows.

## Shopping
After a century of rule by the Chinese and Japanese, the Atayal have lost much of their culture, and the goods you see on sale today in Wulai are not exactly representative of traditional patterns and craft. Still, many products are well made and make for interesting gifts and home decorations.

## Getting There & Away

Buses to Wulai (NT32, 40 minutes, every 30 minutes) run frequently from near the Taipei Xindian MRT station (the last stop on the line). When you get off the elevators, walk to the main road in front of the station and turn right. Walk two blocks to the bus stop just past the 7-Eleven. Buses are not numbered so look for the Taipei–Xindian–Wulai characters.

## YINGGE 鶯歌
☎ 02

'C is for Ceramics. C is for – Yingge?' Well, not quite, but 'Yingge is for ceramics' is something almost any Taiwanese can chant. This little town (Yīnggē) in the very southern part of Taipei County lives by and for the production of high and low quality ceramic and pottery objects: everything from cupboard handles to Soong dynasty vases.

Pottery was introduced to Yingge in 1804, and a century later ceramics also began to be developed. Both industries flourished due to the excellent local clay and good local transport network, originally by river and later by rail.

In recent years the town made the successful leap from manufacturing base to cultural venue. The opening in 1999 of the NT6-billion-dollar Yingge Ceramics Museum and the creation of the 'Old Street' solidified this crossover, and put Yingge on the traveller's map for all lovers of traditional crafts.

Yingge makes an enjoyable, long day trip from Taipei and fits in naturally with a brief stopover at nearby Sansia for a look at the masterfully restored Tzushr Temple.

## Orientation

At the train station, English signs direct you left or right to the Old Street and ceramics museum. Ignore the signs and exit on the right side of the station no matter where you want to go. Turn right when you're outside and walk down the road until you reach a big four-way intersection.

To get to the Old Street, turn right, pass through the tunnel and then head towards the arches on the left. The Old Street begins here.

To reach the ceramics museum, turn left at the four-way and walk another five minutes. Just past the petrol station you'll see the museum on the right.

There are few footpaths in Yingge, which makes walking unpleasant. If you're travelling with children consider taking a taxi (to museum NT100). On the other hand, the walk to the museum passes all the best shops in town (the shops with the most interesting and creative works).

## Sights & Activities
### YINGGE CERAMICS MUSEUM
鶯歌陶瓷博物館

Most people think that pottery and ceramics are the same thing, but they are quite different. They use different types of clay and are fired at very different temperatures: pottery under 1250°C, ceramics above 1260°C. Humans have been making pottery for around 8000 years but only mastered the ceramic process around 3000 years ago.

If you didn't know this (and we didn't), then it's time to head to the new, stylish and terrifically informative **Yingge Ceramics Museum** (Yīnggē Táocí Bówùguǎn; ☎ 8677 2727; www.ceramics.tpc.gov.tw; 200 Wenhua Rd; adult/child NT100/70; ⏰ 9.30am-5pm Tue-Fri, 9.30am-6pm Sat & Sun). Exhibits cover everything from 'snake kilns' (p216) to the various woods used in firing, to influences on Taiwanese ceramics from China, Japan and the Netherlands. The occasional humorous exhibit, like the use of porcelain in modern-day bathroom fixtures, help keep interest high as you move around the three floors.

Adults can make their own pots on weekends (2pm and 3.40pm) while supervised children's workshops are run weekday afternoons and all day on weekends. Instructions are in Chinese only though it's common to have someone around who can speak English and help out.

### YINGGE OLD STREET 鶯歌老街

Yingge was one of the first towns to set up a touristy 'old street' (lǎojiē) and it's still an example to others. Dozens of pottery shops and stalls, large and small, compete for your business here and you could spend hours just browsing. Prices start around NT30 for a cup or saucer, but these will most certainly be mass-produced or even 'made in Japan'. Quality Yingge pieces can cost tens of thousands, though the best shops are not even on the old street but on the main road between the train station and ceramics museum.

Still, the old street is picturesque with its cobbled road, traditional street lamps, and walk-in kiln, and it's made even more charming by nightfall. No restaurants stand out in the area but there are plenty of street vendors to line your stomach with snacks.

Most shops start to close between 6pm and 7pm.

## Festivals
Yingge is host every October to the **Yingge Ceramics Festival** (Yīnggē Táocí Jiānliánhuá). While the festival is by no means bad, in past years we've felt there was nothing special enough to recommend a visit during these days over nonfestival times.

## Getting There & Away
Trains from Taipei (NT31, 30 minutes) run about every 30 minutes.

## SANSIA 三峽
☎ 02

Across National Hwy 3 from Yingge is this old town (Sānxiá), most noted for a temple that has been under reconstruction since 1947 and is still two decades away from completion! You'll also find an 'old street' here, more authentic than the one at Yingge, though perhaps not as much fun, and far better food. In short, Sansia and Yingge go hand in hand, contrasting and complementing each other like peanut butter and chocolate.

The website http://taiwan.wcn.com.tw/en/taipei/Sanshia offers an excellent, if slightly dated introduction to Sansia, including a detailed look at the Tzushr Temple.

## Sights
### TZUSHR TEMPLE 祖師廟
Originally constructed in 1769, the **temple** (Zǔshī Miào) has been rebuilt three times. The last involved the life's work of Professor Li Mei-shu, a Western-trained painter who supervised reconstruction with such fastidious care that today the temple is a showcase of traditional carving, painting and temple relief. If you plan to see only one temple in Taiwan, make it this one.

### HISTORICAL MEMORIAL MUSEUM
三峽鎮歷史博物館
Even without us pointing it out, you'd probably notice this 72-year-old **brick museum** (Lìshǐ Bówùguǎn; ☎ 8674 3994; 18 Jungshan Rd;

admission free; ⏱ 9am-4.30pm). During Japanese times it was called the most beautiful official building in Taiwan. Today the museum houses displays on the history and culture of Sansia, including a special section on the Tzushr Temple.

To get to the museum, turn right as you exit the temple, walk down the alley to Minquan Rd, turn right, and then left at the first chance. The museum is just up the road on the right.

### MINCHUAN OLD STREET 民權老街
There are over 100 buildings on this old street (lǎojiē), dating from the end of the Qing dynasty to the early years of the Japanese colonial era. While some shops sell interesting curios (like Marilyn Monroe lighters), and others focus on antiques, still others manage to do a brisk trade in the coffin business.

To reach the old street turn right as you exit the temple and walk up the alley to Minquan St. This is the beginning of the old street area.

## Eating
Sansia has much better choices when it comes to food than Yingge. One Sansia speciality to try is green bamboo shoots, and one very quaint little teahouse to sample them in is **Sanjiao Yong Restaurant** (三角湧餐飲坊; Sānjiǎoyǒng Cānyǐnfāng; 40 Jungshan Rd; dishes NT160; ⏱ 10.30am-10.30pm), just up the street from the Historical Memorial Museum. Ingredients are locally grown and prepared Hakka style.

## Getting There & Around
The only sensible way to get to Sansia is to take a taxi from Yingge (from ceramics museum NT110) to the temple. Once you are at the temple all the other sights are within walking distance.

# CENTRAL CROSS-ISLAND HWY

Hewn from the granite of the Central Mountain Range, with a peak altitude of 2565m, this 277km highway (Zhōngbù Héngguàn Gōnglù) was the work of ex-soldiers, student volunteers and convicts.

Plans for uniting the two sides of Taiwan with a highway were conceived in the early 1950s. Full-scale work began in 1956 but was delayed by typhoons and earthquakes. In 1960 the highway finally opened, and a fast, convenient route from Taichung across to Taroko National Park was a reality.

Just over 40 years later, the highway closed again after the worst earthquake in a century struck the centre of Taiwan: 1999's 6.9 magnitude earthquake (see below). Since then, reconstruction of the highway has been continuous. The final section to remain closed – a gap from Guguan to Lishan – was scheduled to reopen in the summer of 2004. Another quake or typhoon, though, could easily set this date back again.

If all goes to plan, however, travellers will again be able to see some of the most spectacular high alpine scenery anywhere in the world. Unfortunately, beyond the drama of sheer drop-offs and rocky mountains, the route doesn't offer much. There is an overdeveloped hot springs town, a forest reserve, a dam and a pretty fruit growing area that used to house one of Chiang Kai-shek's summer villas, but nothing that really stands out.

Perhaps the best way to experience the highway is as part of a trip somewhere else: down to Wuling Farm (p156) or Taroko National Park (p173), for example. A stop at Fushoushan (p156) for some fabulous scenery is fine, but you won't miss much if all you do is pass through.

## GUGUAN 谷關
☎ 04

The first stop along the highway is the hot springs village of **Guguan** (Gǔguān), which sits right on the edge of the beautiful Dajia River gorge. Unfortunately, overdevelopment and overcrowding on weekends make this place much less attractive than it could be. And with so many hotels competing for a share in a finite resource, we have to question whether the hot spring water in most places is even pure.

That said, there is a pleasant walk from town to the opposite side of the Dajia River gorge, and the local food is very good. At the time of writing, there was talk of building a gondola a few kilometres out of town to take people across the gorge and up the mountain into Nantou County.

---

**THE 921 EARTHQUAKE**

It came in the night, which was a mercy of sorts. On 21 September 1999 at 1.27am, a 6.9 magnitude quake, with a shallow epicentre almost in the exact centre of Taiwan, shook the island awake. It was the worst earthquake in modern Taiwanese history, and would eventually lay claim to over 2000 lives.

The hardest hit area was around Puli (p220) in Nantou County. While much of the island suffered the loss of electricity and drinking water for 48 hours, some people here were still living in tents a year later.

Almost everywhere there was destruction. Some of this was inevitable, owing to the scale of the quake, but much was the result of shoddy construction and the habitual abuse of building codes. Supporting walls, to list one particularly egregious example, were found in some places to have been made of empty cooking oilcans and wadded newspaper.

The public demanded justice but few have ever been prosecuted.

Mainland China used the quake as an opportunity to promote its One China policy and insisted UN relief organisations seek approval from Beijing before they launch rescue efforts. But for every shameful misuse of the tragedy, there were more examples of generosity, decency, bravery and goodwill. Donations of money, food and supplies flooded in both from Taiwan and around the world. Reports of vandalism or looting were unheard of. The various Buddhist organisations in Taiwan, in particular Tzu Chi, received accolades for their relief efforts. In many cases, they were on the scene faster than the government.

Today, there are few obvious signs of what happened. When the Central Cross-Island Hwy finally reopens the last major reconstruction of an earthquake-damaged zone would have been completed.

If you wish to learn more about this catastrophe there is a **921 Earthquake Museum** ( ☎ 04-2339 0906; 42 Fushing Rd, Sec 1, Wufeng; admission free; ⓨ 9am-4.30pm Tue-Sun) in Taichung County.

## Orientation & Information

The town is small and hemmed in by the highway on the right and the Dajia River gorge on the left. You can walk from one end to the other in about 30 minutes.

**Guguan Visitor Centre** ( ☎ 2595 1496; 192-3 Dongguan Rd, Sec 1; ✆ 8.30am-5pm Mon-Sat, 8.30am-4pm Sun) is just on the left when you first enter town. The staff can speak a little English and are extremely friendly. You can pick up brochures and maps as well as hotel and hot springs information. The map of the town is in Chinese but it's simple to read and the tourist office staff can point out the different sights.

## Activities

### HIKING

There's only one hike in the area, and it takes you across the gorge and into the hills. Start at the park a kilometre into town on the left. Cross the suspension bridge at the back and follow the well-marked trail on the other side. The way is scenic and after walking for about an hour you'll reach the far end of town near the Four Seasons Hotel.

You will see there is a pay suspension bridge when you first enter town. This belongs to the Dragon Valley Hotel and formerly led to a beautiful waterfall. The falls, however, were destroyed in the 921 earthquake.

### HOT SPRINGS

If you do decide to stop for a soak you'll have no end of choices. Following are a couple of places we can recommend.

**Yi Do Hot Spring Resort** (伊豆溫泉; Yìdòu Wēnquán; ☎ 2595 0315; 5 Fenshao Lane; unlimited time in public pool NT250; ✆ 24hr) The outdoor pools have a good mountain view as long as your back is to the car park. Private rooms (per hour from NT800) feature quaint stone tubs set in a small, private, fenced-in garden. Try to get the cabin rooms otherwise you'll be able to hear your neighbours just over the thin bamboo fence. The hotel has an excellent restaurant (meals NT300) serving Japanese, Shanghainese and aboriginal food.

To get to the hotel look for the sign (in Chinese) on the right about half a kilometre into town. Follow the lane up and then left 200m to the hotel.

**Dragon Valley Hotel & Paradise** (龍谷觀光大飯店; Lónggǔ Guānguāng Dàfàndiàn; ☎ 2591 1396; 138 Dongguan Rd, Sec 1; unlimited time public pool NT300; ✆ 7am-noon & 2-11pm) The hotel is right on the edge of the gorge. The nude pools, set in a bamboo hut atmosphere, have the best views. The hotel is the large complex on the left when you first enter town.

## Eating

There are rows of stalls and small open restaurants on the main drag serving fish, wild pig, mountain chicken and mountain vegetables. Most of these places sell meals by the table, however. A single traveller should probably eat at one of the hotels or just buy simple dishes like beef noodles (NT100).

**Mucha Cafe** (94 Guguan Rd, Sec 1; drinks NT120; ✆ noon-midnight). The owner of the café speaks English and is a good source of information about the area.

## Getting There & Away

There are 10 buses a day (NT158, two hours) from Taichung to Guguan leaving from the Fengyuan Bus Company station. If you are coming from Taipei by train, stop at Fengyuan (Fāngyuán; fast/slow train NT343/265, 120/150 minutes, every 30 minutes) and catch the bus (NT121, one hour) from there. The bus drops you off at the far (eastern) end of town across from the Mucha Cafe.

## BASHIANSHAN FOREST RECREATION AREA 八仙山森林遊樂區

The turn-off for this old logging site, now a **forest reserve** (Bāxiānshān Sēnlín Yóulè Qū; http://recreate.forest.gov.tw; adult/child NT150/75), is just before Guguan. There are a number of enjoyable hikes in the reserve – from two to six hours in walking time – all starting from the **service centre** ( ☎ 04-2595 1214; ✆ 8.30am-5pm) at the end of the road.

All trails are clearly marked with English signs. There are even English interpretation signs explaining sites along the paths that were once part of the logging industry.

There is no camping in the reserve but there are two- and four-person **cabins** (d/tw from NT1840/2580). Meals are available but cost extra. Check the reserve's website for more details.

NORTHERN TAIWAN

## LISHAN 梨山
**elevation 1900m**

This small community (Líshān) at the end of the Central Cross-Island Hwy's main route is famous for its mountain-grown apples and pears. At the daily open market, Taiwanese from all over come to buy fruit straight from the source. The market sits in front of the **Lishan Guest House** (梨山賓館; Líshān Bīnguǎn), a Qing-dynasty style building on the way out of town as you head towards Wuling Farm (see right).

Fruit in Lishan is much cheaper than in the cities but be careful when buying it in packages: the fruit on the bottom may not be fresh. If a vendor gets angry (as does happen) when you try to examine all the fruit before purchasing it, leave and go to the another stall.

Lishan is about a four-hour drive from Taichung and is a transit point for buses going north to Wuling Farm (right) and Ilan, east to Taroko National Park (p173) and south to nearby Fushoushan (below). When the highway opens between Lishan and Guguan, buses will once more run from Taichung and Fengyuan. Call the **Fengyuan Bus Company** ( ☎ 04 -2222 3454) for more information.

## FUSHOUSHAN FARM 福壽山農場
☎ 04

During the 1950s and '60s the government of Taiwan sent retired soldiers to turn a number of mountainous areas into model farms. Six kilometres south of Lishan over 800 acres were developed at a place called **Fushoushan** (Fúshòushān). At an altitude of 1800m to 2500m, the farm was perfect for the cultivation of northern produce like apple, pears, peaches, tea and flowers. Tea especially proved to be of such high quality that today Fushoushan Evergreen Tea is served at all presidential banquets.

Tourists have long called on the farm, impressed by the dramatic high alpine scenes, and by the sights of the orchards in full blossom in spring and ripe with fruit in summer and autumn. Today, however, the farm is reinventing itself to attract more visitors to come and stay.

If you want to stop somewhere along the highway to savour the sweeping panoramas and maybe walk around a little, or even stay the night, Fushoushan is your best choice.

### Orientation & Information

The **visitor centre** ( ☎ 2598 9205; www.fushoushan .com.tw; 29 Fushou Rd; ⏰ 7am-9.30pm) is a large complex and includes a restaurant, conference rooms, tourist centre and rooms for rent. You can pick up a useful English brochure with map here.

### Sights

The major sight in Fushoushan is **Tienchi** (天池; Tiānchí; Heaven's Pond; elevation 2590m), yet another of Chiang Kai-shek's summer villas. Tienchi sits on a small plateau about 6km from Fushoushan. The pond in 'Heaven's Pond' refers to a tiny body of still water near the villa that supposedly never dries up. The sight of this may not impress you much but the views from the edges of the plateau should, as long as they are not obscured by afternoon fog.

A walking trail now connects the visitor centre with Tienchi. Be warned though that the air is a little thin up there. Take your time and use the beauty all around you as an excuse to stop often.

### Sleeping

The visitor centre runs a number of places to sleep, most for around NT2000 a night. Book or make inquiries at the tourist office. A new 300-person **camp site** (per site NT300) was recently built near Tienchi. The site does not have much shade but it does have great views. A restaurant, barbecue area and bathrooms with showers are available.

If you're looking for something special try the rooms at **Sunglu Villa** (d from NT5500). This used to be the guesthouse of former president Chiang Ching-guo.

### Getting There & Away

Buses to Fushoushan run from Lishan daily. Check with the **Fengyuan Bus Company** ( ☎ 2222 3454) for the schedule.

## WULING FARM 武陵農場
☎ 04

Here's yet another farm built in the high mountains by retired soldiers. **Wuling Farm** (Wǔlíng Nóngchǎng; admission NT160) sometimes called Wuling Forest Leisure Park, was established in 1963 as a fruit growing area and became part of Sheiba National Park in 1992. Farming is being phased out these

NORTHERN TAIWAN

days or minimised, as hiking, camping and nature preservation take precedence.

For most travellers, a trip to Wuling makes sense as part of a longer journey filled with other interesting stops, but it is not a must-see on its own unless you're an avid climber and want to tackle Syuejian, Taiwan's second-highest mountain. For long-term expat residents, Wuling makes for a nice romantic weekend getaway, or a cool break from the heat in summer.

## Orientation & Information

There is only one main road through the park, with an offshoot to the camping ground and Wuling National Hostel. At the time of writing walking and cycling paths were being built alongside the road.

The new **Travel Service Centre** ( ☎ 2590 1350; 9am-4.30pm) should be open by the time you read this. It is just to the west of the bus station. Fans of Oscar Wilde will be sure to treasure the Bunbury Map available at the entrance gate of the centre.

Check out the forest recreation area website (http://recreate.forest.gov.tw) for more information.

## Sights & Activities
### HIKING

Many hikers come to Wuling to tackle **Syuejian** (雪山主峰; Xuěshān; elevation 3884m), the second-highest peak in Taiwan. The 30km trail, which takes two days to complete, is well established and features huts for climbers to stay at near the top. A Class A mountain permit (see p311) is needed, however, to climb Syuejian, making it off-limits unless you go with a hiking club.

For the average hiker the park offers short walks down by the **Riverside Park** (Xībīn Gōngyuán) or strolls along newly built paths alongside the main road. The only challenging hike is to **Taoshan Waterfall** (桃山瀑布; Táoshān Pùbù; elevation 2500m), 4.5km from the end of the road near the Wuling Mountain Hostel. The falls are 50m high and well worth the 90-minute hike.

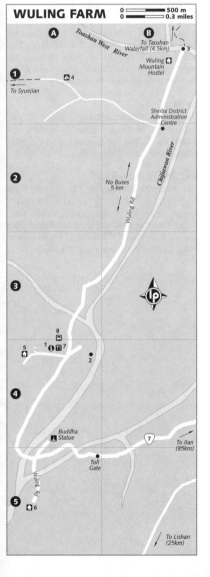

### WULING FARM

| 0 | 500 m |
| 0 | 0.3 miles |

NORTHERN TAIWAN

**SALMON**

Wuling Farm is well known for its efforts to preserve the unique **Formosan landlocked Salmon** (櫻花鉤吻鮭; Yīnghuā Gōuwěn Guī). Unlike other salmon, these never leave the cool freshwater rivers they were born in. The best place to see the salmon is below the **Wuling Suspension Bridge** (武陵吊橋; Wǔlíng Diàoqiáo).

## Sleeping

**Camping ground** (Lùyíng guǎnlǐ zhōngxīn; ☎ 2590 1265; sites from NT400) The camping ground is near the trailhead to Syuejian and so makes for an obvious choice for mountain-climbing groups. For the average visitor the grounds offer clean, modern facilities (including showers and a convenience store), raised camping platforms and sites with parking included.

**Wuling National Hostel** (Wǔlíng Bīnguǎn; ☎ 2590 1259; 3-1 Wuling Rd; 2-/4-person cabins NT2420/3190) The cabins are nothing special but compared to the rooms at the Wuling Mountain Hostel (at the other end of the park and also government run) they are at least worth the price. Food is available for guests and nonguests at the hostel's **restaurant** (meals NT200; ☺ breakfast, lunch & dinner). Note that breakfast hours are from 7am to 9am.

**Hola Resort Hotel** (Wǔlíng Fùyě Dùjiàcūn; ☎ 2590 1399; 3-16 Wuling Rd; d/tw NT5800/8800) This is by far the best accommodation in Wuling and an excellent hotel by any standard. Rooms are spacious and modern. Delicious Western and Chinese breakfast and dinner buffets (guests only) are included in the room price. English is spoken by some staff members.

Some of the excellent hotel amenities include an indoor spa, free tea-making area (where an on-duty master can show you how to brew a perfect cup) and evening concerts by rotating guest musicians. The sun sets early in Taiwan, even in summer, so you'll appreciate having after-dark activities such as these at a mountain resort.

## Eating

There's a **convenience store** (☺ 9am-5pm) near the visitor centre for instant noodles and snack foods, but for proper meals the only places to eat are the hotels.

## Getting There & Away

The **Fengyuan Bus Company** ( ☎ 2523 4175) runs buses from Taichung to Wuling Farm (with a transfer in Lishan) but at the time of writing the new schedule (to begin after the completion of the Central Cross-Island Hwy in 2004) had not been released.

# East Coast

EAST COAST

Isolated from the west coast and northern Taiwan by the Central Mountain Range, eastern Taiwan is unsurpassed in rugged, natural beauty. The Taiwanese call this part of the island 'Pure Land', alluding to a Buddhist vision of paradise. From Suao in the north to Taitung in the south, the eastern coastline traverses some spectacular terrain. Towering seaside cliffs, fine-sand beaches and deep-cut gorges gradually give way to rice paddies, mango groves and occasional sightings of water buffalo. The varied landscape is the result of the collision of the Eurasian and Philippine plates, causing a proliferation of valleys, rifts and hot springs. The constant friction between the two plates makes eastern Taiwan prone to earthquakes, most minor, some severe.

Eastern Taiwan has the highest concentration of indigenous peoples in Taiwan. The tribes retain their own distinct languages and cultural traditions, despite living in such close proximity to one another. To this day, many tribal members still practise their traditional lifestyles, even in the face of rapid commercial development. Visiting a tribal village or attending one of the many festivals held throughout the year along the east coast offers travellers an opportunity to participate in a way of life far removed from the frenetic pace of Taiwan's big cities.

The best way to experience eastern Taiwan is to drive along the coastal highway, taking time to stop and explore some of the magnificent scenic attractions along the way. For outdoor enthusiasts, opportunities exist for hiking, white-water rafting, swimming, diving and cycling.

## HIGHLIGHTS

- Take a drive down the exhilarating **Suao–Hualien Hwy** (p165), a white-knuckle ride with stunning views of the eastern coastline
- Hike in magnificent **Taroko Gorge** (p173), Taiwan's premier tourist attraction
- Ride the rapids of the **Hsiukuluan River** (p179), the longest river in eastern Taiwan
- Snorkel off the coast of **Green Island** (p189), with opportunities to see pristine coral reefs
- Visit an active archaeological site at **Peinan Cultural Park** (p184)

★ Suao-Hualien
★ Taroko Gorge
★ Hsiukuluan River
★ Peinan Cultural Park
★ Green Island

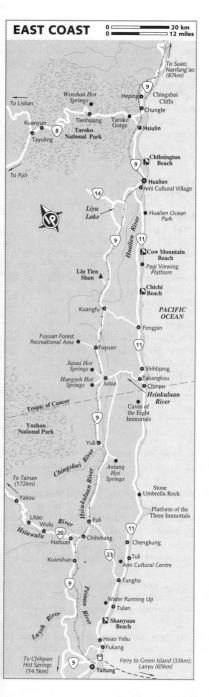

**EAST COAST**

0 ——— 20 km
0 ——— 12 miles

To Suao;
Nanfang'ao (87km)

Wenshan Hot Springs
To Lishan
Heping
Chingshui Cliffs
Chungte
Kuanyun
Tiehsiang
Taroko Gorge
Taroko National Park
Hsiulin
Tayuling
To Puli
Chihsingtan Beach
Hualien
Ami Cultural Village
Liyu Lake
Hualien Ocean Park
Hualien River
Cow Mountain Beach
Paqi Viewing Platform
Lin Tien Shan
Chichi Beach
Kuangfu
PACIFIC OCEAN
Fuyuan Forest Recreational Area
Fengpin
Fuyuan
Juisui Hot Springs
Shihtiping
Hungyeh Hot Springs
Juisui
Takangkou
Chinpu
Hsiukuluan River
Tropic of Cancer
Caves of the Eight Immortals
Yushan National Park
Chingshui River
Yuli
Antung Hot Springs
Stone Umbrella Rock
To Tainan (172km)
Yakou
Platform of the Three Immortals
Litao
Wulu
River
Fuli
Hsinwulu
Haituan
Chihshang
Chengkung
Kuanshan
Tuli
Ami Cultural Centre
Tungho
Peinan River
Water Running Up
Tulan
Shanyuan Beach
Luyeh River
Hsiao Yeliu
Fukang
To Chihpen Hot Springs (14.5km)
Ferry to Green Island (33km); Lanyu (65km)
Taitung

## Culture & History

Hualien and Taitung Counties are the principal counties of the east coast, and home to the Ami, Atayal, Kavalan, Puyuma and Yami peoples. The Ami, who make their homes in fishing villages along the east coast, number about 140,000. The Yami, with a population of 9000, have the fewest numbers and live on tiny Lanyu Island, southeast of Taitung.

Along the east coast there is little industry except fishing and the only crops are rice and fruit. Tourism is slowly growing as an industry, with most of the attractions being natural.

Because of the geographical isolation of the east coast, the area was very slow to develop and there were few settlers along the east coast before the 20th century except for the indigenous tribes. Things began to change after the Japanese cessation, when the land was cultivated and permanent settlements were established. Hualien was the first to attract Han immigrants, but Taitung soon became popular with migrants too. The Japanese used Taitung as a base for expansion into the Pacific, opening it up to the outside world by building the Eastern Railway Line in 1926 and establishing light-industry factories such as wood mills and sugar processing plants. These factories drew a large number of workers from other parts of Taiwan, especially the Hakka, who were to become the largest ethnic group in Taitung. With the completion of the Central Cross-Island Hwy in 1961 and the South Cross-Island Hwy in 1972, the isolation of the east coast ended for good.

Today, the east coast is home to a diverse mix of ethnic groups and their cultural traditions can be seen in towns scattered across the region. The indigenous people still have a strong influence over the area, reflected in the large numbers of annual festivals held throughout the year and the food visitors will encounter when travelling through the region.

Off the east coast are the two small volcanic islands of Lanyu (p192) and Green Island (p189). Green Island is a scuba-diving paradise and Lanyu offers a chance to understand the culture of the Yami people, many of whom still retain their traditional way of life.

**EAST COAST**

## Climate

Travelling from north to south along the east coast brings subtle variations in temperature. Things get warmer and more tropical the further south you go and the vegetation becomes more lush. Hualien is always slightly cooler than Taitung, and Taroko Gorge can be chilly even in summer, so bring a jacket. Of course, if you're visiting Taroko Gorge in winter, warm clothes are a must.

Mid-August to October is typhoon season and the east coast is frequently battered with severe thunderstorms. Winters are chilly and the pervasive dampness can make it seem much colder than the actual temperature. Out on Green Island and Lanyu, winters are cold and windy, with rain falling endlessly. Summers are hot and the sun is fierce.

There's no perfect time for travelling to the east coast. However, if you're heading out to Lanyu or Green Island, summer is ideal for water activities and there are few hitches in transport. During winter, ferry services are erratic and flights only leave when there are clear skies; a rarity between November and March.

## Getting Around

Having your own transport is the most convenient way to see eastern Taiwan because it gives you the freedom to explore regions that are inaccessible to bus and train passengers. However, there are some drawbacks to consider. Driving the Suao–Hualien Hwy can be a frightening experience, even for very confident drivers. Hairpin bends, blind curves, narrow roads and insane drivers make for some perilous driving conditions. On the other hand, driving the coastal road between Hualien and Taitung is a breeze, with light traffic on weekdays and plenty of places to pull off the road and explore.

# ILAN COUNTY

## SUAO 蘇澳

☎ 03 / pop 47,000

Suao is a grubby little port town without a lot of notable attractions and it's no more than a stopping point before heading down the scenic east coast. The town isn't entirely devoid of charm, however, and is worth a look if time allows.

### Sights

A visit to the **Suao Cold Springs** (Sūaò Lěng Quán; admission NT70; ☼ 8am-10pm) should be the first destination for anyone suffering in Taiwan's steaming summer heat. The carbonated cold springs were discovered by the Japanese in 1928 and are the only one of their kind in

---

**ABORIGINAL FESTIVALS ON THE EAST COAST**

▪ **Ami Harvest Festival** This festival is the largest in Taiwan and takes place every July or August in various towns around Hualien and Taitung Counties. Tribal chiefs choose the exact date in June.

▪ **Bunun Ear Shooting Festival, Millet Harvest Festival** The Ear Shooting Festival takes place around the end of April and is meant to honour the legendary hunting heroes of the tribe and to teach young boys how to use bows and arrows. The Millet Harvest Festival is held after the April millet harvest. Both festivals take place in towns throughout the East Rift Valley.

▪ **Paiwan Bamboo Pole Festival** The Paiwan tribe holds this festival every five years in November to honour their ancestors and to pray for a good harvest. The festival takes place in Dajen Township, Taitung.

▪ **Puyuma Monkey Festival** This festival is a coming-of-age ceremony for the young men of the Puyuma tribe who go through special rituals to become warriors. Ceremonial dances are held, imitating monkey movements. The festival is celebrated by tribal members in Peinan township, near Taitung.

▪ **Yami Flying Fish Festival** The Yami hold this festival every year prior to the flying-fish season (spring). Like the Puyuma Monkey Festival, the festival celebrates a young man's passage into adulthood.

Taiwan. The water doesn't have the sulphurous smell of hot springs and is completely odourless. Locals use the fizzy stuff for making Suao's famous goat-meat soup.

Suao has a number of temples scattered around town, all within walking distance of the old train station. These include the **Hsienkung Temple** (Xiāngōng Miào), **Hsiangkuang Temple** (Xiánguāng Sì) and the **Tienchun Temple** (Tiānjūn Miào).

## Sleeping

**Jinhua Hotel** (Jīnhuá Dà Lǔshè; ☎ 996 2526; 1 Lengchuan Rd; d NT1000, q from NT1200) One of the best deals in Suao. The hotel is right next to the cold springs and across from the train station. Rooms are spotless and bathrooms feature piped-in hot springs.

**Suao Hotel** (Sūaò Fàndiàn; ☎ 996 5181; 7 Sutung Chung Rd; r from NT1500) Comfortable rooms, though a little overpriced. This place caters to tour groups, which stop here before heading down to Hualien and Taroko Gorge.

## Eating

Locals like to gather at the **Luwang Cafeteria** (Lùwáng Zìzhù Cān; meals NT70; ☺ lunch & dinner), across from the post office. Food is hardly gourmet but it is cheap and filling.

## Getting There & Around
### BUS

There are hourly buses travelling between Taipei and Suao daily. From Taipei, buses leave from the Taipei North Station. The first bus leaves at 6.30am and the last is at 8.30pm. The direct bus travels through the mountains and is much faster than taking the coastal bus, which travels to Keelung and requires a transfer to Suao.

Another option is the Airbus, which travels the Hualien–Ilan–Taipei route daily. This is more comfortable than the regular bus. Buses leave every two hours from Taipei and Hualien. Buses drop passengers off at the New Suao train station (Xīn Sūaò), about 4km out of town.

### TRAIN

There are two train stations in Suao: the Old Train Station (Jiù Zhàn) in central Suao and the New Suao station. Most trains from Taipei and Hualien stop at the new station, though a few local trains stop at the old station. If you get dropped off at the new station, about 4km out of town, a shuttle bus can take you to town.

**EAST COAST**

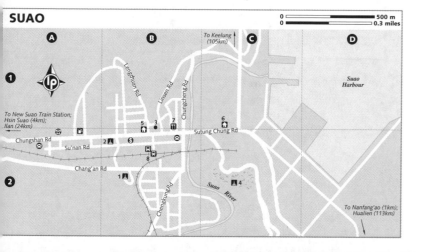

EAST COAST

### TAXI

Drivers wait outside the bus and train stations. They're willing to use their meters but be aware that it's an additional NT50 on top of the metered fare. If a taxi is too much, the town is small enough to explore on foot.

## NANFANG'AO 南方澳

Nanfang'ao (Nánfāng'aò) has a much more pleasant atmosphere than Suao. The harbour area is lively, with small shops and vendors giving it a holiday feel.

The Japanese dredged Nanfang'ao Harbour in 1922 and it became Taiwan's third-largest port after Keelung and Kaohsiung. The 1940s and 1950s were Nanfang'ao's heyday, with the fish and shipping trades booming. The prosperity didn't last, though, as the fishing industry began to decline in the 1960s and residents started moving away. Today, most people working on the docks are from out of town or overseas.

### Sights

**Nantien Temple** (Nántiān Gōng), on the harbour, is always crowded with worshippers.

A lovely statue of Matsu, Goddess of the Sea (p276), presides over all the activities.

One of Nanfang'ao's smelliest attractions is the **Fish Market** (Yúshì), at the end of the harbour. The best time to come is in the morning, when you'll see freshly caught yellowfin tuna, octopus and hammerhead sharks flopping around on the pier. The smell and the gore are certainly not for the faint-hearted, but at least you'll have an idea of what to order for dinner.

### Eating

Nanfang'ao is full of excellent little seafood restaurants. A good place to look is around Nantien Temple.

### Getting There & Around

To get to Nanfang'ao from Suao by taxi will cost you NT120 plus the surcharge. The town is small enough to explore on foot.

To get to Nanfang'ao from Suao on foot, you must walk along the Suao–Hualien Hwy (Sūhuā Gōnglù) that leads south off of Sutung Chung Rd. The highway is full of speeding maniacs so be careful.

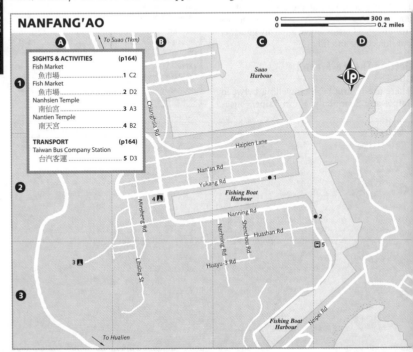

**NANFANG'AO**

| SIGHTS & ACTIVITIES | (p164) |
| Fish Market | |
| 魚市場...............................**1** C2 |
| Fish Market | |
| 魚市場...............................**2** D2 |
| Nanhsien Temple | |
| 南仙宮...............................**3** A3 |
| Nantien Temple | |
| 南天宮...............................**4** B2 |
| | |
| **TRANSPORT** | **(p164)** |
| Taiwan Bus Company Station | |
| 台汽客運 ...........................**5** D3 |

To Suao (1km)

Suao Harbour

Changhsia Rd

Haipien Lane

Nan'an Rd

Yukang Rd

Fishing Boat Harbour

Minsheng Rd

Nanning Rd

Nanheng Rd

Shenchou Rd

Huashan Rd

Lhsing St

Huayu-3 Rd

Neipei Rd

Fishing Boat Harbour

To Hualien

# HUALIEN COUNTY

## SUAO TO HUALIEN

The Suao–Hualien Hwy stretches for 118km along the Suao-Hualien coastline. Carved into sheer cliff walls that at times soar 1000m above the Pacific Ocean, the road is a heart-stopper, offering bird's-eye views of the rocky seashore below.

The beginnings of the road go back to 1874, when China's Qing government ordered a road to be built along the east coast, hoping to alleviate some of the isolation of the region. The Japanese widened the road in 1920, battling with landslides and earthquakes, and the road didn't officially open for public use until 1932. When the narrow road was first built, vehicles could only move in one direction at a time. Control stations were set up to monitor traffic and give waiting vehicles the all clear to move forward once the highway was empty of oncoming traffic. The road has since widened to allow two-way traffic, but not so wide that buses don't have to literally scrape past each other to get by. A plan to expand the highway even further into a 'super highway', something that critics claim would inflict heavy environmental damage on the area, has been put on hold.

The most breathtaking section of the highway is the 20km stretch between the towns of Chungte and Heping, where the Chingshui cliffs loom over 1000m above the ocean. The highway twists its way precariously around these towering walls of marble and granite, defying gravity and giving thrill-seekers the ride of their life.

## HUALIEN 花蓮

☎ 03 / pop 110,000

Hualien (Huālián) is eastern Taiwan's largest city and a base for tourists visiting Taroko Gorge, Taiwan's most famous scenic spot. Hualien doesn't have many attractions but there are still enough things to do to keep visitors occupied for a day or two.

The city sits on a narrow plain, nestled between the Central Mountain Range and the Pacific Ocean. Hualien was largely isolated from the rest of Taiwan until the 20th century. In 1959, the perilous Central Cross-Island Hwy was completed. It wasn't until the 1960s that Hualien's population began to grow and the city developed.

The main export of Hualien is marble, on display everywhere in hotels, footpaths and public buildings. The northern road into the city is lined with marble shops and factories that process the stone and fashion it into various items for public use. The mining of marble is causing enormous environmental damage in the surrounding mountains and it's wise to steer clear of this purchase.

Despite a steady influx of tourists, Hualien remains a laid-back place, with a relaxed attitude that sets it apart from other Taiwanese cities. Traffic is light and life moves along at a leisurely pace.

### Orientation

Hualien isn't a large place and it's easy to get around on foot. The city can be divided into three areas. The train station is where most travellers arrive and is surrounded by budget and mid-range hotels. It's also where the bus stations are located for those wishing to go to Taitung or Taroko Gorge. The city centre is the most developed part of town, with department stores, fancy boutiques and a range of hotels. It's also where the foreign exchange banks are and Hualien's other bus station. The third part of town is the harbour area, where the five-star hotels and fancy restaurants are to be found.

The oldest part of the city is near the Meilun River on Mingli Rd. Here you'll find some old Japanese style-buildings that haven't yet been torn down.

### Information

#### BOOKSHOPS

**Caves Books** (319 Linsen Rd; ⏾ 9am-6pm Mon-Fri & 10am-8pm Sat & Sun) A wide selection of English teaching materials but little else in the way of English books and magazines.

#### MEDICAL SERVICES

**Hualien Hospital** (Huālián Yīyuàn; ☎ 835 1825; 600 Chungcheng Rd) In central Hualien.

**Tzu-chi Buddhist Hospital** (Cíjì Yīyuàn; ☎ 856 1825; 8 Hsinsheng Rd) A hospital known for its excellent facilities.

#### MONEY

**Bank of Taiwan** ( ☎ 832 2151; 3 Kungyuan Rd) Directly across the street from ICBC. ATMs also take international debit and credit cards.

**ICBC** ( ☎ 835 0191; 26 Kungyuan Rd) Changes foreign currency, including travellers cheques. ATM takes international debit and credit cards.

**EAST COAST**

# HUALIEN

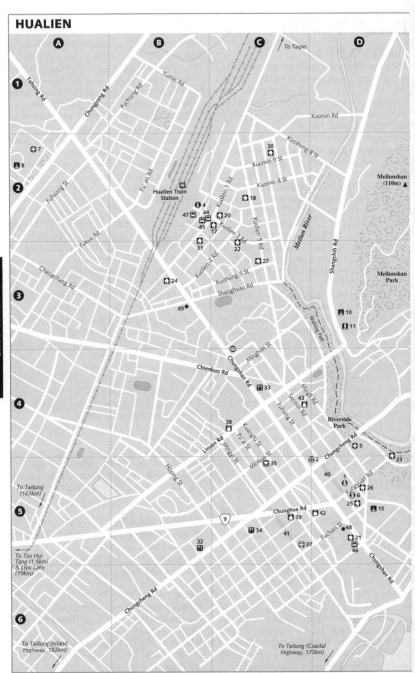

To Taipei

Kuomin Rd

Meilunshan
(110m) ▲

Meilunshan
Park

Tehsing Rd

Chungyang Rd

Fuchiang Rd

Yumin Rd

Kuoshing-8 St

Kuomin-9 St

Kuomin-8 St

Fuhsiang St

Fukuo Rd

Fu'an Rd

Hualien Train
Station

Kuolien-1 Rd

Kuolien-3 Rd

Kuolien-5 Rd

Meilun River

Shangchih Rd

Chiengchang Rd

Kuolien-2 Rd

Kuohsing-5 St

Shanghsiao Rd

Walking Path

Minghin St

Chungshan Rd

Chienkuo Rd

Minglu Rd

Sanmin Rd

Fuhsing St

Riverside
Park

Linsen Rd

Kuangfu St

Po'ai St

Mingli St

Minkuo St

Chungcheng Rd

Kungyuan Rd

Hoping St

To Taitung
(163km)

Chunghua Rd

Fuchien St

To Tzu Hui
Tang (1.5km)
& Liyu Lake
(19km)

Chungcheng Rd

To Taitung (Inland
Highway, 182km)

To Taitung (Coastal
Highway, 170km)

Chungshan Rd

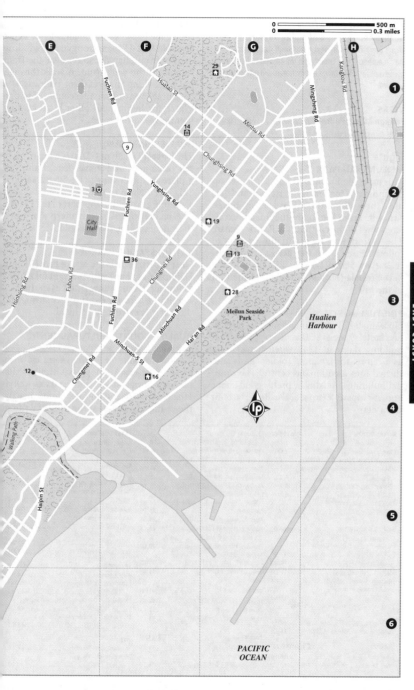

## TOURIST INFORMATION
**Hualien County Information Centre** (Huālián Xiāng Lǚyóu Fúwù Zhōngxīn) Next to the train station but few staff members speak English and the office is of limited use except for a few brochures on hotels and restaurants in town.

## VISAS
**Foreign Affairs Police** ( ☎ 822 4023; 21 Fuchien Rd) Takes care of visa extensions.

# Sights

## MEILUNSHAN PARK 美崙山公園
This **park** (Měilúnshān Gōngyuán) rises up behind the Hualien train station and has pleasant walking trails that lead up to the summit. From the top of the hill are excellent views of the city and the Pacific Ocean. The easiest way to get to the park is to follow Linsen Rd north across the bridge. A **Martyrs' Shrine** (Zhōng Liè Cí) and the **Hukuo Temple** (Hùguó Gōng) sit at the foot of the hill.

## PINETUM HOSTEL 松園別館
Up a small hill off Chungmei Rd is the **Pinetum hostel** (Sōngyuán Bié Guǎn; 26 Shuiyuan Rd). This building dates to 1943 when it was built as a retreat for Japanese soldiers and later turned into a command centre. The original buildings are still in pretty good shape and it's possible to see Hualien Harbour from here.

## RIVERSIDE PARK 溪畔公園
Along the banks of the Meilun River is the **Riverside Park** (Xīpàn Gōngyuán), winding its way from Shanghsiao St, near the train station, to the waterfront. A walk through the park along the well-kept pathway is a pleasurable way to spend a couple of hours. Watch for herons and other birds cooling themselves in the river.

## HUALIEN HARBOUR 花蓮港
The **harbour** (Huālián Gǎng) is a dusty place full of cement and gravel trucks and not a place to linger long. The **fish market** (Yú Shì) is the place to see the varieties of fish swimming around in this part of the Pacific. The market opens in the afternoon, when the catches of the day are sold.

## MEILUN SEASIDE PARK 美崙海濱公園
Near the harbour is the **seaside park** (Měilún Hǎibīn Gōngyuán) with pleasant bike paths following the coastline. Don't even think of swimming here – the surf is very strong and the water is extremely polluted.

## HUALIEN COUNTY CULTURAL CENTRE 花蓮鄉文化局
The **cultural centre** (Huālián Xiāng Wénhuà Jú; 6 Wenchien Rd; ⏰ 9am-noon & 1.30-5pm) has exhibits displaying aboriginal arts and crafts as well as Hualien history and culture. Unfortunately, the centre was closed at the time of writing.

MARTIN MOOS

Taroko Gorge (p173), Hualien County

Pagoda, Tienhsiang (p177)

MARTIN MOOS

JOHN BORTHWICK

Aboriginal girl in traditional dress

MARTIN MOOS

Caterpillar-like green tea leaves

Platform of the Three Immortals (p181), Taitung County

Breadfruit and other local produce for sale

Brightly coloured pillar at a Taoist temple

Traditional Ami cuisine

In the same complex is the **Hualien Stone Carving Museum** (Huālián Xiāng Shí Diāo Bówùguǎn; 8 Wenfu Rd; 🕙 9am-5pm, closed Mon) with displays of traditional and contemporary stone carvings, a traditional art of Hualien. The museum will probably only appeal to those who have an interest in this art form.

### TSAI PINGYANG ABORIGINAL WOODCARVING MUSEUM
蔡平陽山地木雕藝術館
This is another **museum** (Cài Píngyáng Shāndì Mùdiāo Yìshù Guǎn; 180 Chunghsing Rd) devoted to traditional arts, with woodcarvings from various aboriginal tribes on display.

### TUNGCHINGCHAN TEMPLE 東淨禪寺
This **temple** (Dōngjìngchán Sì) is an active place of worship in central Hualien, tucked away off Huakang Rd. Chanting can sometimes be heard coming from the temple in the evenings. One notable thing about this temple is the extensive use of local marble on the floors and pillars.

### CHINGSZU TEMPLE 靜思佛堂
The **Chingszu Temple** (Jìngsī Fó Táng; Chungyang Rd) is an important Buddhist temple between the Tzu-chi Buddhist Hospital and university. The 10-storey temple took 14 years to construct and its simple white and grey exterior is very impressive. The temple roof is in the style of the Tang dynasty, decorated with carvings of *fētiān* (flying goddesses). There is also a large exhibition hall with excellent displays showcasing the organisation's activities around the world. Exhibits are in English and Chinese.

### TZU HUI TANG 慈惠堂
The **Tzu Hui Tang** (Cí Huì Táng), or 'Temple of Motherly Love', is an elaborately decorated Taoist temple on the outskirts of the city. Behind the temple is a four-storey hall dedicated to the Jade Emperor (Yù Huáng Dà Dì Tiān), which can house over 2000 pilgrims. The temple is most lively during the Lunar New Year festivities when people come from all over Taiwan to celebrate.

## Tours
**Hualien Travel Service** (Huālián Lǚxíngshè; ☎ 833 8146; 137 Chungshan Rd) A good, long-standing reputation for its English-language tours to Ami Cultural Village and other tourist spots.

**Merry Travel Services** (Mínglì Lǚxíngshè; ☎ 835 5447; 549-2 Chungshan Rd) Merry has inexpensive tours to Taroko and the Hualien vicinity. Tours are Chinese-language but can get you to places that are difficult to reach by bus or train.

## Festivals & Events
One of the long-standing traditions of Hualien is stone carving, not surprising considering the city's main export is marble. The **Hualien International Stone Sculpture Festival**, established in 1997, showcases the work of local artists and promotes Hualien to the international art world. During the 2003 festival, Hualien sculptors teamed up with a group of Italian artists from Seravezza, famous for its stonework, to arrange various exhibitions and demonstrations of the art. The festival lasted for over a month and received international acclaim. The festival takes place annually in towns around Hualien County.

Every August, the **Ami Harvest Festival** (Fēngnián Jì) is held in various towns around the county. The festival is celebrated with dancing, singing and traditional foods. The harvest festival is considered the most important festival of the year by the Ami and towns compete to throw the best party.

## Sleeping
### BUDGET
**Chan Tai Hotel** (Qiántái Dà Fàndiàn; ☎ 833 0121; 83-1 Kuolien-1 Rd; d/tr NT800/1200) The Chan Tai is conveniently located opposite the train station and has clean, reasonably priced rooms and courteous management.

**Yongqi Hotel** (Yǒngqí Dà Fàndiàn; ☎ 835 6111; 139 Kuolien-1 Rd; d/tr NT800/1200) This hotel is another good budget option and a popular place for travellers. The accommodation is simple but comfortable.

**Hualien Hero House** (Guó Jūn Yīngxióng Guǎn; ☎ 832 4161; 60-1 Chunghsiao St; d NT1080, bed in 4 person r NT300) The best thing about the Hero House is that it's centrally located and offers substantial discounts during winter.

**Dashin Hotel** (Dàxìn Dà Lǚshè; ☎ 832 2125; 101 Chungshan Rd; d NT600) The Dashin looks shabby on the outside but is surprisingly spiffy inside. Rooms are a great deal, making this a well-liked place by the backpacker crowd.

**Lux Hotel** (Tiānrén Dà Fàndiàn; ☎ 832 3173; 20 Fuhsing St; r from NT400) This cheap hotel is not

**EAST COAST**

as nice as the Dashin and rooms are a bit depressing. However, it's in a good location and not bad considering the price.

**Sande Hotel** (Sāndé Fàndiàn; ☎ 836 2136; 77 Kuomin-9 St; d/tr NT700/800) This hotel appears to have fallen on hard times. Rooms are in disrepair and dirty. Only consider it if everywhere else is full.

### MID-RANGE
**Charming City Hotel** (Xiāng Chéng Dà Fàndiàn; ☎ 835 3355; 19 Kuohsing-2 St; tw NT1800) This hotel has smart-looking rooms and is a short walk from the train station. Management isn't willing to give discounts, even in the off-season, unlike many of the other hotels in the area.

**Naluwan Hotel** (Nǎlǔwān Fàndiàn; ☎ 836 0103; 7-3 Kuolien-5 Rd; tw NT2700) This is a fancy-looking place with aboriginal décor. The rooms are spacious, with comfortable beds and attractive furnishings.

**Hohuan Hotel** (Héhuān Dà Fàndiàn; ☎ 835 0171; 105 Kuolien-3 Rd; d/tr NT2000/2800) The Hohuan is another excellent hotel in the train station area with plush rococo-style decorated rooms and windows in the bathrooms. This place offers sizable discounts in winter.

**Ching Yeh Hotel** (Qīng Yè Dà Fàndiàn; ☎ 833 0186; 83 Kuolien-1 Rd; d from NT1300) The Ching Yeh is one of the best options by the train station. Rooms are small but tastefully furnished and very clean. Some rooms have views of the mountains.

**Lihsing Hotel** (Lìxīng Dà Fàndiàn; ☎ 834 7411; 589 Chungshan Rd; d NT1400) A popular place with tour groups, this hotel is often fully booked weeks in advance. Rooms are a good size and fairly clean.

### TOP END
**Marshal Hotel** (Tǒngshuài Dà Fàndiàn; ☎ 832 6123; 36 Kungyuan Rd; d/tw NT2800/2940) The Marshal is one of the 'luxury' hotels in central Hualien. Rooms are OK value but prices are high for what you get. Very loud tinny music blares from speakers in the lobby – try to get a room on the upper floor to avoid all the noise.

**Astar Hotel** (Yàshìdū Dà Fàndiàn; ☎ 832 6111; 6-1 Minchuan Rd; tw NT2000) Painted pink, white and turquoise, this hotel looks like it belongs in 1960s California. The location across from Hualien Harbour means guests have good views of the water but also of the dust and noise of ongoing construction. Rooms on the upper floors are less prone to the sounds and fumes of dump trucks as they go rumbling by.

**Chinatrust Hotel** (Zhōngxīn Dà Fàndiàn; ☎ 822 1171; 2 Yunghsing Rd; d/tr NT4500/5100) This five-star hotel has superb facilities and is one of the best places in town for a splurge. The hotel has a swimming pool, coffee shops and a Chinese and Western restaurant.

**Ola Hotel** (Huí Lán Kè Zhàn; ☎ 822 7188; 11 Hai'an Rd; d/tw NT3200/3600) Whimsical décor sets this place apart from Hualien's other hotels in this price range. Rooms are bright and comfortable and management is very friendly.

**Parkview Hotel** (Měilún Dà Fàndiàn; ☎ 822 2111; 1-1 Linyuan Rd; d/tw NT4800/5800) This hotel is the

---

### EAST COAST EATING

Hualien and Taitung Counties have a diverse mix of aboriginals, Hakka, Taiwanese and former mainland Chinese, all contributing to the unique culinary traditions of the area. One of the most influential cuisines in Hualien is the food cooked by the Ami people, who are known for their simple dishes of fruits, flowers, taro and wild vegetables, cooked to emphasise their natural flavours without a lot of seasoning or additives. Dishes from betel-nut flowers, sorghum and rattan are common and can be seen in night markets and restaurants around Hualien.

Fruit grown in eastern Taiwan is tastier and fresher than fruit grown in other parts of Taiwan and of much higher quality. Pineapples, mangoes and watermelons can be seen growing along the sides of the roads and some orchards allow you to pick your own fruit and pay by the weight. City markets have tables heaped with a colourful assortment of common and exotic fruits, including star fruit, pomelos, coconuts, durian, papaya and lychees, all offered at prices much cheaper than you'd pay on the west coast.

Other delicacies to try include the dumplings in Hualien, the dried fish of Chengkung and the sticky rice of Taitung. Seafood is a speciality all along the coast and the best places to find it are in Chengkung, Shihtiping and Fukang Harbour, north of Taitung.

top-rated place in Hualien and attracts a large number of well-heeled clients. Amenities include a golf course, tennis courts, gourmet restaurant, swimming pool and everything else you can imagine.

## Eating

Hualien cuisine is a mixture of typical Taiwanese cuisine (soups and noodles) and the food of the aboriginal tribes who for centuries have sustained themselves on fishing and wild vegetables and flowers. The most enjoyable way to try the local food is to head to one of the many markets and sample what's on display. Central Hualien, along Fuhsing St, is a good place to start, as well as the markets around Chungcheng and Chungshan Rds. Some things to sample include stewed spareribs (dūn páigú), bitter gourd (kǔguā) and fried sunflowers (chǎo kuí).

**Hualien Pian Shi** (Huālián Piǎn Shí; 307 Chungcheng Rd; mains NT30; ☺ breakfast, lunch & dinner) This is a tiny place with an excellent reputation among locals for its delicious meat-filled dumplings and wontons.

**Ye Hsiang Shi Dian** (Yè Xiāng Shí Diàn; 42 Hsinyi St; mains NT40; ☺ breakfast, lunch & dinner) This tiny place is a favourite of locals for its steaming bowls of pork and seafood dumplings. The restaurant has been around for over 70 years and is known all over Taiwan.

**Shan Ting Tong Ren** (Shān Dǐng Dòngrén; 330 Chungshan Rd; meals from NT80; ☺ lunch & dinner) Vegetarians will really appreciate this place for its wide selection of vegetarian dishes served cafeteria style or from the menu. The spicy 'beef' noodles (made from gluten) are especially good. Also worth trying is the iced fruit tea with pineapple juice.

For seafood, go to **Gouzaiwei night market** (Gōuzǎiwěi Yèshì), the oldest market in town and sometimes nicknamed 'seafood street'. Here you'll find squid-on-a-stick, grilled clams and even smoked shark. The market is near the intersection of Nanching and Poai Sts.

## Drinking

Hualien has many trendy cafés and teahouses along its main streets.

**Chi Chi Ho Ho** (Chī Chī Hē Hē; 170 Po'ai Rd; coffee from NT90; ☺ lunch & dinner) This café/restaurant has a warm, cosy ambience and friendly staff.

**Venus Gallery and Café** (Wéinàsī Yì Lángjí Shēnghuó Shūdiàn; 126-1 Fuchien Rd; coffee NT100; ☺ 10am-9pm Mon-Sat, 10am-6pm Sun) A two-storey art gallery/café/bookshop close to the cultural centre. The gallery sells postcards and prints of artwork by local artists, as well as recordings of local musicians. Though it's a bit far from Hualien central, it's worth the trouble to visit if you're interested in the Taiwanese art scene. The owner, Ms Lin, is the director of the Hualien International Driftwood Symposium, an arts festival dedicated to aboriginal woodcarvings.

## Entertainment

Hualien is a quiet city and the nightlife is next to nonexistent. For late-night carousing, your best bets are around the intersections of Chunghua and Chungshan Rds or along Chungcheng Rd.

The **Hsinmeichi Cinema** (Xīn Měiqī Dà Xì Yuàn; 396 Chungcheng Rd) shows English movies from time to time.

## Shopping

Hualien's main export, marble, is all over the city. Numerous souvenir shops sell pieces of the expensive rock carved up into all sorts of shapes and sizes. Be aware that the mining of marble is having a devastating effect on the local environment so please think twice before purchasing a piece of the local landscape.

More portable than marble, and with less dire consequences, are Hualien's delicious cakes and cookies, available at bakeries and gift shops around town. The **Hui Pi Hsu Cake Shop** (Huì Bǐ Xū; 65 Chunghua Rd) has been in business since 1899 and is well known for its delicious peanut and sesame cookies. Goodies are sold in bulk or in attractive wrappings and tins and make good souvenirs.

To find something with more lasting value, head to the **Ya Chi Hsiao Fang** (Yǎ Jí Xiǎo Fáng; 84 Sanmin St), a government-certified antique shop. Jade appears to be the speciality here but there are also ceramics and some beautiful statues of Kuanyin, Goddess of Mercy. What you buy here is genuinely old and of high quality.

## Getting There & Away

### AIR

Hualien is a major tourist destination for travellers heading to Taroko Gorge. There are frequent flights between Hualien and Taipei, Taichung, Tainan and Kaohsiung. The

EAST COAST

following airlines have reservation counters in Hualien airport.

**Far Eastern Air Transport** ( ☎ 826 5702)
**Mandarin Airlines** ( ☎ 826 8785)
**Transasia Airways** ( ☎ 826 1365)
**Uni Air** ( ☎ 826 7601)

### BICYCLE

Travelling down the east coast by bicycle offers plenty of opportunities to see the countryside up close, not through the window of a train or bus. The Suao–Hualien Hwy has been given the thumbs down by many cyclists for being too dangerous with the chance of being mowed down by a speeding truck too high.

Cycling between Hualien and Taitung is a worthwhile experience, with minimal weekday traffic and helpful locals along the way. It's possible to cycle down the east coast and then take the train back up the inland route.

### BUS

The Airbus runs between Taipei and Hualien (NT360, five hours, every two hours), travelling via Ilan and Keelung. The early morning bus leaves Hualien at 5am, the next at 7am etc.

Hualien has three main bus stations. The Hualien Bus Company (Huālián Kèyùn Zhàn) operates two stations, one in the city centre and the other next to the train station.

Both the Hualien Bus Company and the **Dingdong Bus Company** (Dīngdòng Kèyùn Hǎi'ān Zhàn; 138-6 Kuolien-1 Rd) run buses between Taitung and Hualien. The Dingdong buses travel along the coast, while all Hualien buses except the 10.20am bus travel inland through the East Rift Valley. Dingdong coastal buses to Taitung leave from Hualien at 11.45am, 2.10pm and 4.35pm. Hualien Bus Company buses run hourly.

Between Hualien and Taitung, it's possible to get off the bus at certain spots, do some exploring and hop on the next bus when it comes by. This is a slow way to travel, but possible. However, verify with bus drivers when the next bus is supposed to come by to avoid being stranded.

The Hualien Bus Company has buses running to Tienhsiang and the National Park Headquarters in Taroko Gorge. See p178 for more details.

### TRAIN

Taking a train through eastern Taiwan is more convenient and comfortable than taking the bus but nowhere near as scenic. The train passes through many tunnels and you won't get to see much scenery. Trains running between Taipei, Hualien and Taitung are frequent but often crowded, so make sure to buy tickets ahead of time to reserve a seat. The Hwa-Tung line runs five trains daily between Hualien and Taitung. Consider taking the bus down the coast and then a train back up through the East Rift Valley to get the best of both options.

## Getting Around

### TO/FROM THE AIRPORT

The Hualien Bus Company runs buses to the Hualien airport (NT25, every 30 minutes).

### BUS

It's much easier to get around Hualien on foot or by taxi rather than taking a bus. Bus 105 (NT10) circles the city, travelling between the train station and the city centre.

### CAR/MOTORCYCLE/SCOOTER

Vehicles are available for rent around the train station. For a scooter or motorcycle, rates are NT400 to NT500 a day and for a car NT1500 to NT2000 a day, excluding petrol. Some travellers have reported being refused a vehicle because they did not have a Taiwan licence, though they were holders of an international licence. There appears to be some truth to this but attitudes seem to vary among rental agents. If you are refused, try your luck with another agency.

### TAXI

Hualien taxi drivers congregate around the train and bus stations, hustling passengers for tours around the city and to Taroko Gorge. If you are interested, a Taroko tour will cost up to NT3000 a day, depending on the time involved.

Around town, insist that your driver use the meter, which will be cheaper than a flat fare.

## Around Hualien

**Chihsingtan Beach** (Qīxīng Tān) is about 3km north of Hualien, at the foot of a series of high cliffs. The water is too rough for wimming but this doesn't stop the crowds from flocking here on the weekends. To avoid the chaos, go north a few kilometres to find more secluded stretches of coastline. A bike path links Hualien's Seaside Park to Chihsingtan.

**Ami Cultural Village** (Āměi Wénhuà Cūn; admission NT300; 🕙 5am-8.30pm) provides visitors with an introduction to the history and culture of the Ami people. There are displays of Ami traditional arts, souvenir shops and song and dance shows put on for tourists. The 'village' is pretty tacky – to see aboriginal handicrafts and artefacts, the National Museum of Prehistory in Taitung (p183) is far superior. The village is 15 minutes south of Hualien, off Hwy 11.

**Liyu Lake** (Lǐyú Tán) sits in the foothills of the Central Mountain Range about 19km southwest of Hualien. Liyu, or Carp Lake (called this because of its fishy shape), is the largest natural inland lake in Taiwan. It's a popular place for day-trippers who want to escape the city. There are pedal and row boats for rent, camping facilities and well-marked hiking trails. For a really fun experience, check out the dragon boat races held here every June. Paragliding is also a possibility.

**Lin Tien Shan** (Lín Tián Shān) is another pleasant excursion spot about 40km from Hualien. The forested area was once a Japanese logging camp but now sits empty except for a few snack shops. At one time, over 2000 loggers lived here. Some of the old buildings remain, as well as a small museum of photographs and a locomotive. Unfortunately, a fire in 2001 destroyed much of the area and there are ongoing efforts to restore what was burned.

## TAROKO GORGE 太魯閣

Just 15km north of Hualien is Taroko National Park containing Taroko Gorge (Tàilǔgé), Taiwan's top tourist destination. With its marble-walled canyons, lush vegetation and cliffs so giant-sized they block out the sky, Taroko is Taiwan at its wildest and most pristine. The park covers over 120,000 hectares with mountain peaks rising to 3700m. The Liwu River cuts through the centre of the gorge for 20km before emptying into the sea, forging many deep valleys, ravines and waterfalls in its course. Throughout the park are the remains of old trails and hiking paths that lead visitors to hidden shrines, temples, hot springs and panoramic vistas of the mountains and the sea.

The development of the gorge began over four million years ago, when the Eurasian and Philippine plates collided, forming the massive Central Mountain Range. Marble deposits were forced upwards as the plates crashed together and over centuries of wind and water erosion, the gorge was created. The elevation gain in the gorge rises from sea level to 3740m, fostering a range of ecological zones, from tropical to alpine.

Within the park are a variety of animals and plants, and park officials boast that Taroko contains almost half of all animal species in Taiwan, including the Formosan black bear and wild boar. It's unlikely travellers will come across these animals but you may spot a Taiwan macaque or two. Unfortunately, many of the plant species in the park face near extinction so care should be taken to remain on recognised hiking paths and to not disturb the local flora.

The original inhabitants of the park area were the Atayal people, known for their fine weaving skills, facial tattoos and headhunting. Most of the Atayal have now moved out of the park and only a few families remain, supporting themselves by selling weaving to tourists. Some of the trails in the gorge were once Atayal paths used for hundreds of years as they crisscrossed the gorge to hunt, farm or fight with neighbouring tribes. Many of these have now been widened into roads or are used now as hiking trails by tourists.

The old Hohuan Trail (Héhuān Yuèlǐng Gǔdào), the precursor of the Central Cross-Island Hwy, was one of the most important trails used by the Atayal for crossing the island until the beginning of the 20th century. In 1914 the Japanese entered the gorge hoping to gain access to the forestry and mineral resources in the area. The local aboriginals resisted the intrusion but the Japanese quelled the resistors with brutal military force and began to cut roads and widen existing trails. A road was built as far as Tienhsiang, and Taroko became a popular hiking spot for Japanese tourists in the 1930s. The defeat of the Japanese in WWII meant that the goal of building a complete cross-island highway was never completed.

EAST COAST

When the Kuomintang (KMT) started the Central Cross-Island Hwy in 1956, much of it followed the old Hohuan Trail, most of it within 50m of the road used today.

The building of the Central Cross-Island Hwy was a tragic affair and 450 workers, mostly retired servicemen from mainland China, lost their lives. The project took four years, with some parts of the highway hacked out of solid rock by hand. A shrine is set up in memory of these workmen at the Eternal Spring Shrine, near the entrance of the gorge.

## Orientation & Information

The **National Park Headquarters** (Guójiā Gōngyuán Guǎnlǐ Qū; ⏱ 8.30am-4.45pm, closed 2nd Mon of month), at the entrance of the gorge, provides useful information on the status of trails and road conditions. It also has free maps and brochures of hiking trails and a bulletin board with bus schedules and notices to travellers. Also in the headquarters are a café and a souvenir shop with books for sale.

Tienhsiang (Tiānxiáng) is a tiny resort area at the other end of the gorge from the National Park Headquarters where all three of Taroko's hotels are located, along with a post office, visitors centre and a few small cafeterias next to the bus station.

## Sights & Activities

Taroko has a variety of hikes, from those that can be done in an hour to those that require an overnight stay in a camping ground. For longer treks, confirm trail conditions with staff at the National Park Headquarters before setting out.

### WENSHAN HOT SPRINGS 文山溫泉

About 3km above Tienhsiang are the lovely, secluded **Wenshan Hot Springs** (Wén Shān Wēnquán). Situated next to the Taisha River (Tàishā Xī), the springs are enclosed in an open basin of solid marble and surrounded by dense greenery. A long soak in the warm bubbling water is the perfect way to ease the aches and strains after a long day of hiking.

To get to the hot springs, take the main road from Tienhsiang up to the mouth of the first tunnel. Follow the steps down to the Liwu River and a suspension bridge. Cross the bridge and walk along the cliff-side path to reach the springs. There's a small changing room here, but no other facilities.

### MYSTERIOUS VALLEY TRAIL 神秘古步道

The **Mysterious Valley Trail** (Shénmìgǔ Bùdào) is an easy 4.4km hike along the crystal-clear Shakatang River (Shākǎdāng Xī). Coming from the direction of the National Park Headquarters, the trailhead is to the right after emerging from the first tunnel. Follow the stairs down to the river to access the path. The ice-cold river is a great place to refresh tired feet and there are many benches set up along the path to take a rest.

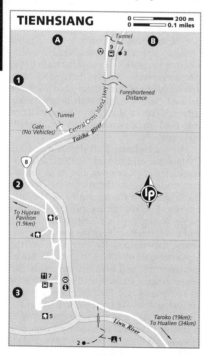

**TIENHSIANG**

0 _____ 200 m
0 _____ 0.1 miles

At the end of the Mysterious Valley Trail is another path that connects to the challenging Tali-Tatung Trail (Dàlǐ-Dàtóng), leading to Tali and Tatung, two isolated Atayal villages. The residents of these villages do not like to be disturbed and have been known to mislead hikers and give them wrong directions. At the moment, it's best to respect their privacy and avoid this hike.

### ETERNAL SPRING SHRINE TRAIL 長春祠
This **trail** (Cháng Chūn Cí) is about 3km from the National Park Headquarters. The shrine sits on a steep cliff overlooking the Liwu River above a rushing waterfall and is dedicated to the 450 workers who lost their lives building the highway. The original shrine was buried under a landslide and this is a re-creation of the first. To reach the shrine, cross the suspension bridge and hike up the steps.

### TUNNELS OF NINE TURNS 九曲洞
This section of **tunnels** (Jiǔ Qū Dòng) is one of the most scenic parts of the main highway

and the best place to see marble deposits in the gorge. It's about 5km past the Eternal Spring Shrine, between Swallow Grotto (Yànzǐ Kǒu) and the Cimu Bridge (Címǔ Qiáo). A twisting road of tunnels has been blasted through sheer marble cliffs, truly a marvel of engineering. Sadly, many workers fell to their deaths here as they attempted to carve out this perilous section of road.

### PULOWAN 布洛灣
Meaning 'echo' in Atayal, **Pulowan** (Bùluòwān; ⊙ 8.30am-4.30pm, closed 1st & 3rd Mon of month) is a

EAST COAST

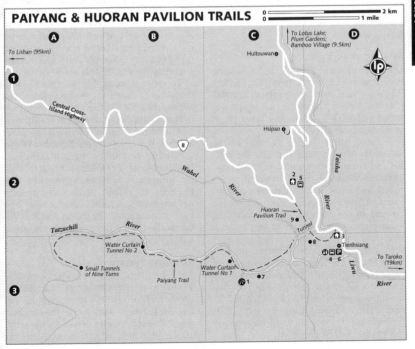

PAIYANG & HUORAN PAVILION TRAILS

small Atayal village once inhabited by the Atayal people, most of whom have left the area. Now the village has been set up for tourists, with aboriginal arts and crafts on display as well as song and dance shows. The few remaining Atayal make their living weaving and selling their wares in the Taroko gift shops. The village also has a multimedia centre featuring shows about the Atayal way of life. Behind the village are walking trails with beautiful wild flowers.

Pulowan is between the Eternal Spring Shrine and Swallow Grotto, about 8km north of the park entrance. To get to the village, look for a sign on the main road that indicates the turn-off.

The village is currently undergoing renovation so check at the National Park Headquarters to see if it's open.

### LUSHUI-HOLIU TRAIL 綠水-合流步道
Once part of the Hehuan Trail, this **trail** (Lǜshuǐ-Hèliú Bùdào) runs for 2km above the highway along a cliff, with fantastic views of the Liwu River. The trailhead is behind the Lushui Information Centre.

There are free camping facilities in Holiu with wooden platforms and bathrooms. Lushui has a small restaurant and a shop selling snacks and drinks.

### PAIYANG TRAIL 白楊步道
Up the road about 500m from Tienhsiang is the trailhead to the **Paiyang Trail** (Báiyáng Bùdào), which leads to the **Paiyang Waterfall** (Báiyáng Pùbù). The entire trek to the waterfall and back is 3.6km and takes about two hours to complete.

A 380m tunnel begins the trail to the waterfall. After passing through the tunnel and crossing over a bridge, you'll soon come to the three-tiered waterfall, at its fullest and most spectacular after a rainstorm. There's a viewing platform on the far end of the Paiyang Bridge, providing great photo opportunities of the gushing river and waterfall. Beyond the trail past the waterfall are two 'water curtain tunnels' (Dìyī Shuǐlián Dòng), so called because of the streams of water that pour down the interior walls of the tunnels. The park authorities closed off the tunnels after the 921 earthquake, deeming them too dangerous for visitors. There's no word on whether the tunnels will be reopened.

### HUORAN PAVILION TRAIL 豁然亭天祥步道
The **Huoran trail** (Huōrán Tíng Bùdào) is short and steep, gaining 400m in elevation in 1.9km. The trail leads to **Huoran Pavilion** at the top, which has fantastic views of the Liwu River and Tienhsiang. Ropes have been set up in places to help hikers, though the climb will still leave you breathless. The trail turns into a slippery mess when it rains and is best avoided. Landslides occasionally close the area so check with National Park Headquarters before starting out.

### BAMBOO VILLAGE & LOTUS POND TRAILS 竹村步道-華連湖步道
About 6km up the main road from Tienhsiang is the Huitouwan (Huítóuwān) trailhead, on a switchback at the right side of the road behind the bus stop. The **trail** (Zhúcūn Bùdào, Liánhuā Chí Bùdào) starts out following the Taisha River and is quite scary in parts, especially where it's been chiselled into the walls of a cliff. The trail divides at the Chinghsi and Chiumei suspension bridges. The main trail follows the river, going on to Plum Garden (Méi Yuán) and further up to Bamboo Village while the other trail continues on over the bridge for another 4.3km to **Lotus Pond**. At Lotus Pond is a small hostel run by former workmen on the Central Cross-Island Hwy. Lotus Pond is too swampy to be very pretty but the surrounding bamboo forests are beautiful.

To get to Bamboo Village, take the trail from the Chiumei suspension bridge that follows the river. First you'll reach the village of **Plum Garden**, about 6km from the Huitouwan trailhead. Continue walking for about another 4km until you reach **Bamboo Village**, situated on the southeastern side of the Jiming Mountains. The village is beautiful during spring and summer, surrounded with flowers and bamboo. Peaches and mulberries are local specialities here, coming into harvest in autumn. The trek to Bamboo Village is about 9.2km from Huitouwan, about a three-hour walk one-way.

### HSIANGTE TEMPLE 祥德廟
Just before Tienhsiang is a suspension bridge leading to the **Hsiangte Temple** (Xiángdé Sì), sitting high on a cliff overlooking the valley. The temple is named after the Buddhist monk Kuangchin, who prayed for the safety of the workmen who were building the

Central Cross-Island Hwy. Surrounding the temple are plum trees and a gleaming white statue of Kuanyin, the Goddess of Mercy.

## Sleeping

### HSIULIN 秀林

Hsiulin (Xiùlín) is the small town right outside of the Taroko park entrance. There are a couple of hotels here in case the park is closed when you arrive.

**Taroko Hotel** (Tàilǔgé Fàndiàn; ☎ 861 1558; r from NT1300) This place has pretty good rooms that are reasonably priced for a resort area.

**Li Wu Guesthouse** (Lì Wù Kè Zhàn; ☎ 861 0769; dm NT500, d NT2000) The only other option in town is this place, with rooms and dorms for both budget and mid-range travellers.

### TIENHSIANG

**Catholic Hostel** (Tiānzhǔ Táng; ☎ 869 1203; dm NT250, r from NT300) The Catholic Hostel has been the principal budget hotel in Tienhsiang for years. The place is getting a bit shabby but it still offers decent rooms and dorms at no-nonsense prices. Some rooms have balconies with terrific views of the gorge.

**Tienhsiang Youth Activity Centre** (Tiānxiáng Qīngnián Huódòng Zhōngxīn; ☎ 869 1111; dm NT300, r from NT1400) Up the hill from the Catholic Hostel is the Youth Activity Centre, which is the only other budget option in the gorge. Rooms are quite nice and many travellers consider the dorms here better value than those in the Catholic Hostel.

**Grand Formosa Hotel** (Jīnghuá Dùjià Jiǔdiàn; ☎ 869 1155; tr from NT5800) This is the first building you'll see upon entering Tienhsiang. The five-star hotel is fairly generic, both inside and out. Rooms are comfortable and spacious, with fancy marble bathrooms. The hotel boasts a lounge, two restaurants, a café and a gift shop.

### CAMPING

It's possible to camp at Taroko at designated camping sites. Staff at the National Park Headquarters can advise as to which sites are open and what facilities to expect. It's wise to bring your own gear and plenty of warm clothes, just in case the weather turns bad.

## Eating

**Tienhsiang Youth Activity Centre** (☎ 869 1111; breakfast NT65, lunch & dinner NT150) Meals are available to guests and nonguests. Breakfast is served between 7am and 8.30am, lunch, noon to 2pm, and dinner, 6pm to 8pm. There's no need to buy a ticket but you should notify the hotel a few hours in advance so kitchen staff can prepare enough food. For breakfast, let the centre know before 9pm the night before.

**Grand Formosa Hotel** (lunch/dinner buffet NT600/650) The breakfast buffet is free for guests but NT400 for everyone else. The food in the Western restaurant is mediocre. The food in the Chinese restaurant is much better.

The cafeterias around the bus station sell barely edible food at very high prices. Try to get the food while it's hot, before the grease has a chance to congeal.

EAST COAST

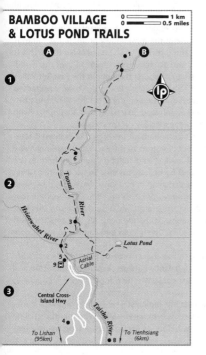

## BAMBOO VILLAGE & LOTUS POND TRAILS

0 — 1 km
0 — 0.5 miles

| SIGHTS & ACTIVITIES | (p176) |
| --- | --- |
| Bamboo Village 竹村 | **1** B1 |
| Chinghsi Suspension Bridge 清溪吊橋 | **2** A3 |
| Chiumei Suspension Bridge 九梅吊橋 | **3** A2 |
| Hsipao 西寶 | **4** A3 |
| Huitouwan 迴頭灣 | **5** A3 |
| Plum Garden 梅園 | **6** A2 |
| Taosai Suspension Bridge 陶塞吊橋 | **7** B1 |
| Wenshan 文山 | **8** B3 |

| TRANSPORT | (p178) |
| --- | --- |
| Bus Stop 公車站 | **9** A3 |

## Getting There & Away

### BUS
The Hualien Bus Company has frequent bus services to Taroko Gorge. From Hualien to Tienhsiang (NT107), buses run at 8.30am, 10.40am, 12.30pm and 1.30pm. There are eight buses daily from Hualien to the National Park Headquarters (NT58). The earliest bus leaves from Hualien at 8am and the last bus at 8.30pm.

### CAR/MOTORCYCLE/SCOOTER
Taking your own transport through Taroko Gorge gives you the opportunity to explore the park at your leisure. Unless you have excellent defensive driving skills, however, navigating around the sharp twists and turns of the highway can be an unnerving experience. If driving, avoid holidays and weekends at all costs, when tour buses take over the narrow road.

### TAXI
Taxi tours to the gorge are easy enough to arrange – cabbies will come looking for you, not the other way around. A return trip through the gorge by taxi will cost around NT2000 from Hualien. Another option is to have your driver take you through the gorge and drop you off at Tienhsiang, which

---

### TAIWAN'S EAST COAST – A NATURAL WONDERLAND

Ever since the Democratic Progressive Party (DPP) came to power in Taiwan, it's been actively promoting tourism across the island, in the hope of stimulating the economy and increasing a sense of nationalistic pride in the Taiwanese. The policy of 'natural resort areas in every prefecture' applies especially to the east coast, which is seen by many as an underdeveloped wonderland waiting to be explored. Over the past few years, tourist farms have been set up in agricultural areas to give urban-bound tourists a chance to experience rural farm life. Luxury resorts have been built in forests and along the coast; they fill to capacity on weekends and during holidays when the Taiwanese leave the cities in droves for much-needed vacations and family time. With all of the development going on, or in the planning stage, the isolation of the east coast is bound to come to an end in the not-too-distant future.

Many of the promoted activities on the east coast are designed to take advantage of the natural marvels that abound along scenic Hwys 9 and 11. One of the most widely promoted activities is the much-touted (and deservedly so) white-water rafting trip down the Hsiukuluan River. This is a breathtaking ride through some amazing scenery and attracts visitors from all over the world. Hot springs are another popular attraction, with a string of resorts throughout the East Rift Valley and the well-known Chihpen Hot Springs, south of Taitung. Cycling is another heavily promoted activity. Cycling routes are being built along the coast and through the East Rift Valley. The town of Kuanshan, about 50km north of Taitung, has well-maintained bike paths that are popular with families. Diving and snorkelling are also top activities, especially off Green Island.

All of this development has environmentalists concerned about the effects of increased tourism on an already fragile ecosystem. With the number of visitors to the east coast growing every year, water supplies are slowly being depleted and Hualien and Taitung County authorities are concerned about the amount of garbage left behind by holiday-makers. Some activities being promoted as 'ecotours' by tourist authorities, whale watching in particular, have raised the eyebrows of critics who want to see more regulations set in place to monitor unscrupulous tour operators. Many are afraid that some whale-watching operators are actually chasing dolphins and whales, causing disruptions to the migratory habits. At the moment, it's best to steer clear of the whale-watching tours advertised around Hualien, Chengkung and Taitung to avoid contributing to the problem.

Government and tourist authorities are listening to the concerns being raised by Taiwan's environmentalists and have vowed to try to maintain a balance between expansion and ecological preservation to protect the unique beauty of the east coast. Whether or not they will be able to uphold their promises is another story.

Despite growing development along the east coast, the region still lacks the commercial frenzy of other parts of Taiwan and manages to retain its sleepy, backwater status. With things certain to change, the best time to visit the east coast is now, before its idyllic allure disappears forever.

will cost about NT1500. Drivers will charge more if they have to wait while you hike or do any extracurricular exploring. In that case, it's probably better to take public transport.

### TOUR BUS

All travel agencies in Hualien and Taipei can arrange full- or half-day tours of the gorge. For an English-language tour, contact Hualien Travel Service (p169), which has full-day tours that include lunch.

Taking a tour is a convenient way to see Taroko but it doesn't leave enough time for exploring. Many tours hustle visitors through the gorge and then spend most of their time in souvenir shops and marble factories.

### TRAIN

The Hsincheng (Xín Chéng) train station is quite close to the park entrance and preferred by travellers who don't want to go to Hualien.

### WALKING

Quite a few visitors take a bus to Tienhsiang and walk the 19km back down to the National Park Headquarters. While this is a great way to take in all of the scenery, increased traffic in the gorge has spoiled a once-enjoyable walk. If you do walk, wear reflective clothing and bring a torch (flashlight) for the tunnels. Try leaving as early in the morning as possible to avoid traffic.

## HUALIEN TO KUANSHAN

There are two ways of reaching Taitung from Hualien. Hwy 9 cuts through the verdant East Rift Valley (Huādōng Zòng Gǔ), while Hwy 11 travels down the east coast, skirting some stunning coastal scenery. The East Rift Valley is a long, narrow region of hot springs, forest and rivers between the Central Mountain Range and the Coastal Mountain Range (Hǎi'àn Shānmò). Special activities in the region include opportunities for stays in mountain retreats and white-water rafting down the Hsiukuluan River. In contrast, the coastal route provides chances for visiting small aboriginal fishing villages, beaches and Lanyu and Green Islands. Much of the territory along the highway falls under the East Coast National Scenic Area (Dōnghǎi'àn Guójiā

Fēngjǐng Qū), established in 1988 and managed by the Taiwan Tourism Bureau.

**Hualien Ocean Park** (Huālián Hǎiyáng Gōngyuán; 89 Yanliao Village; admission adult NT790, child & student NT690, senior NT590; ◷ 9am-5pm) is a large aquarium/amusement park south of Hualien off Hwy 11. The facilities here are first-class and attractions include dolphin shows, sea lion exhibits and a water fun park. Kids will love this place. Overlooking the park on top of a cliff is the **Bellevista Hotel** (Yuǎn Lái Dà Fàndiàn; ☎ 812 3999; r NT5040), with magnificent views of the mountains and sea.

**Cow Mountain Beach** (Niú Shān) is an untouristed strip of sand several kilometres south of Hualien Ocean Park. It's a nice place to enjoy the surf and escape the crowds of the more developed beaches on the east coast. There are few facilities here so bring plenty of food, water and sunscreen.

**Paqi Viewing Platform** (Bāqí Tiào Wàngtái) is between Cow Mountain Beach and Chichi Seaside Resort. There are great views of the coastline from the platform and some high-powered binoculars to spy on fishermen down on the rocks below.

**Chichi Seaside Resort** (Jīqí Hǎishuǐ Yùchǎng) is one of the more 'official' beaches along the east coast, complete with lifeguards, change rooms, toilets and showers. It's even possible to camp and wooden platforms are provided for tents. Parasailing, boating and swimming are some of the main activities in this area.

**Shihtiping** (Shítīpíng) is a small fishing village halfway between Hualien and Taitung, 30km south of Chichi Seaside Resort. Shihtiping means 'stone steps', referring to the volcanic rock along the coastline here that has slowly eroded to form natural stone steps.

The small town of **Juisui** (Ruìsuì) in the East Rift Valley is used as a base for whitewater rafting trips down the **Hsiukuluan River** (Xiùgūluán Xī). It's also the site of the **Juisui Hot Springs** (Ruìsuì Wēnquán), about 4km out of town. To get there, it's possible to rent a bicycle in town or take a taxi. Juisui is conveniently located on the Hualien–Taitung train line. About 2km from the Juisui train station, near the Tropic of Cancer monument, are two large **megaliths** that stand upright next to the highway. Some say these stones are the transformed bodies of twins who married, much to the anger of their tribe, and were changed in to stone. Scientists believe that the megaliths are actually relics of the ancient Peinan people, who lived in the region over 5000 years ago.

The Juisui Hot Springs are the only carbonated hot springs in Taiwan and were first opened as a resort by the Japanese in 1919. The water has been piped into the **Juisui Hot Springs Hotel** (Ruìsuì Wēnquán Shān Zhuāng; ☎ 887 2170; r NT1800) but you don't need to be a guest to use the springs and can pay less than the hotel price, depending on how long you want to soak.

A **raft trip** down the Hsiukuluan River is the main reason many people come here. The river originates from the Hsiukuluan Mountain Range, flows north through the Huatung Valley and eventually empties into the sea at the aboriginal town of Takangkou. The portion of the river from Juisui to Takangkou is 24km long, twisting and turning its way through gorges and steep cliffs.

Rafting trips can be arranged in Juisui or through travel agents in Taipei and Hualien. Trips generally cost between NT750 and NT900, depending on whether or not you have your own transport. The river is the site of the International White-Water Rafting Race, held annually in June, attracting competitors from all over the world.

The **Hungyeh Hot Springs** (Hóngyè Wēnquán) are 2km south of Juisui. The water is piped into private bathhouses in the **Hungyeh Hotsprings Hotel** (Hóngyè Wēnquán Lūshè; ☎ 887 2176; r from NT1300). Like the Juisui Hotel, it's not necessary to stay here to use the springs. For non-guests it costs NT70 for a 30-minute soak.

The **Antung Hot Springs** (Āntōng Wēnquán) are about 8km south of the town of Yuli on the Hualien–Taitung train line. The springs are piped into the **Antung Hot Springs Hotel** (Āntōng Wēnquán Fàndiàn; ☎ 888 6108; r NT2000) or you can try them free of charge in the river below the hotel where the hot water seeps through the rocks.

Cycling is one of the most enjoyable ways to explore the Eastern Rift Valley. One good route is to cycle from Juisui to the **Fuyuan Forest Recreational Area** (Fùyuán Sēnlín Yóulè Qū), about 20km north. You can spend the night in the forest and cycle back to Juisui the next day. Fuyuan Forest is a peaceful 235-hectare camphor forest with many good

walking trails and waterfalls. There's a valley famous for its butterflies, which swarm here from March to August. Cabins rent for NT1400 a night and food is provided though you might want to bring your own in case you don't like what's on offer.

Another cycling spot is at the former logging town of **Kuanshan** (Guān Shān) 50km north of Taitung, at the end of the East Rift Valley on Hwy 9. The main reason to come here is to take advantage of the bicycle paths set up in the city's large **riverside park** (entry NT50, bike rental NT150-500) which pleasantly wind their way through colourful rice paddies and fields of colza and sugar cane. Another path leading from the park follows a river and is a great place for bird-watching, with viewing platforms set up at various points to allow visitors to bird-watch unseen. Buses stop in Kuanshan on their way to and from Tienchih on the South Cross-Island Hwy.

# TAITUNG COUNTY

Taitung County is in southeastern Taiwan wedged between the Coastal Mountain Range and the Pacific Ocean. The county does not bring in the tourists like its neighbouring county to the north, which has Taroko Gorge as its huge drawcard. Taitung County remains one of the most undeveloped regions in Taiwan and a great place for visitors looking to escape from the big cities. The rocky volcanic coastline contains its fair share of scenic attractions and there are a number of beaches and recreation areas along the way where you can stop and enjoy a bit of surf.

## NORTH OF TAITUNG

The **Caves of the Eight Immortals** (Bā Xiān Dòng, ⏳ 8.30am-noon & 1.30-5pm) are about a 1½-hour drive south of Hualien and a mandatory stop for all tour buses going up and down the east coast. The series of caves is directly off of Hwy 9, hidden under a tall cliff. They are a prime archaeological site and relics gathered from the caves have proven that they have been inhabited since prehistoric times. The caves have now been turned into temples and decorated with colourful religious icons. The main cave contains a shrine facing the ocean, with a smaller adjacent cave containing images of Buddha. The trail leads up to the 'thundering sea cave', and further up to another cave with a shrine. From the top of the cliff, there are great views of the coastline below. The mist that perpetually shrouds the caves gives the place an eerie feel.

The **Platform of the Three Immortals** (Sān Xiān Tái; 8.30am-noon & 1.30-5pm) is another stop for tourist buses. Here, a series of arched bridges span the shallow water off the coastline, leading to a small island with some pretty rock pools. The site is a pleasant enough spot for a visit, though very crowded on weekends and during holidays.

To the south of the Platform of the Three Immortals is the fishing village of **Chengkung** (Chénggōng), the largest town between Hualien and Taitung. The town has a lively fish market and is a good place to sample local seafood. Every afternoon between 3pm and 4pm, the daily catch is unloaded and goes on auction. All the noise and excitement makes the auction entertaining to watch. Around the harbour are plenty of small seafood restaurants worth checking out. Dried fish slices are a speciality of Chengkung, which make a very good, though smelly, snack. If you happen to pass by Chengkung around lunch or dinner time, you're in for a real treat.

About 11km south of Chengkung is the **Ami Cultural Centre** (Āměi Zú Mínsú Zhōngxīn; 9am-noon & 1.30-4pm), which is highly recommended for its exhibits of Ami handicrafts and traditional architecture. Buses running up and down the east coast can get you to the centre. Make sure to tell your driver you want to get off at the Tung Kuan Chu bus stop (Dōng Guǎn Chǔ Zhàn). The centre is outside of the aboriginal town of Tuli (Dūlì), also on the east-coast highway.

Around 30km south of Chengkung is the odd geological wonder **Water Running Up** (Shuǐ Wǎng Shàng Liú), outside the small town of Tulan (Dūlán). Look for a road-side sign that leads to a large ditch west off the highway. The water in the ditch appears to be flowing upwards, obviously a trick of the eye.

**Hsiao Yeliu** (Xiǎo Yě Liǔ) is known for its bizarre rock and coral formations, formed over thousands of years by wind and water erosion. The coastal landscape is truly unearthly here, with rocks curving and twisting into all manner of fantastic shapes. Hsiao

Yeliu is named after the larger Yeliu on the north coast (p121).

**Shanyuan Beach** (Shānyuán Hǎishuǐ Yùchǎng; admission NT60) is the closest beach to Taitung. With its soft yellow sand and strong surf, the beach attracts droves of visitors on weekends who come to swim, parasail and snorkel in the amazingly blue water. Camping is permitted here and there are clean showers with changing facilities. Overlooking the beach is the terrific **Zorba Garden Restaurant** (129 Fusan Rd; meals NT300; lunch & dinner, closed Wed), which specialises in authentic Italian cuisine. The lasagne is probably the best you'll find in Taiwan.

## TAITUNG 台東
☎ 089 / pop 117,000

Taitung (Táidōng) is a small city on the southeastern coast and a gateway for visits to Chihpen, the famous hot springs resort to the south, and Lanyu and Green Islands. Taitung is not a top tourist destination in itself but that doesn't mean it's not a good place to linger for a day or two. The city possesses an excellent museum on aboriginal culture and is home to one of the most important archaeological sites in Taiwan. In addition, the cooling ocean breezes that roll in make Taitung feel cooler than some of Taiwan's larger inland cities, making it a refreshing place to be during the hot, sticky summer.

Some feel that Taitung's backwater status is not going to last very long. The county government is pushing tourism hard, using the county's strong aboriginal presence as a way to bring in tourists and money. Plans for more five-star hotels and fancy golf courses are already in the works. At the moment, Taitung remains the quiet, relaxed place it has always been but who knows how long this will last.

### Information
**Bank of Taiwan** ( ☎ 324 210; 313 Chungshan Rd) Will exchange foreign currency and has an ATM that takes international debit cards.
**Foreign Affairs Police** ( ☎ 334 756; 268 Chungshan Rd) Takes care of all visa issues.

### Sights
#### LIYU SHAN 鯉魚山
Also known as Carp Hill, **Liyu Shan** (Lǐyú Shān) is on the western side of Taitung, near the old train station. This park is the largest

EAST COAST

EAST COAST

# TAITUNG

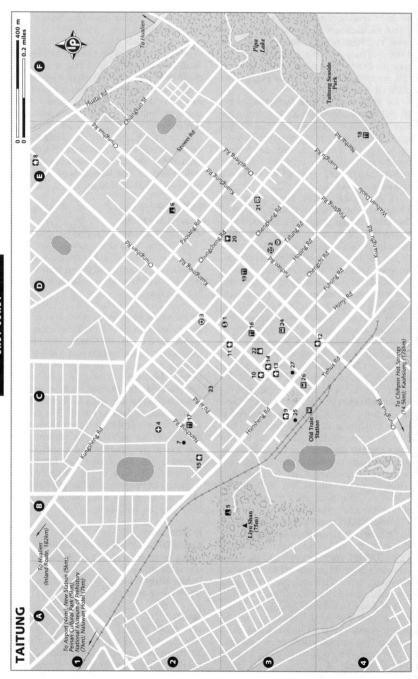

To Hualien
(Inland Route, 182km)

To Airport (4km); New Station (5km);
Peinan Cultural Park (5km);
National Museum of Prehistory
(7km); Naliuwan Hotel (7km)

To Hualien

Pipa
Lake

Taitung Seaside
Park

Old Train
Station

Lisu Shan
(75m)

To Chihpen Hot Springs
(14.5km); Kaohsiung (178km)

400 m
0.2 miles

in Taitung and boasts plenty of greenery and walking trails. The mountain stands only 75m high but still offers good views of the city and ocean from the top. The four-storey **Dragon Phoenix Temple** (Lóng Fèng Fógōng) sits at the foot of the mountain, ornately decorated with tiny statues of the goddess Kuanyin. Visitors are allowed inside the temple and in the large pagoda next to it. In the mornings and on weekends, the courtyard in front of the temple is full of retirees playing mah-jongg and practising martial arts.

### MATSU TEMPLE 天后宮

On the northern side of town, the **Matsu Temple** (Mǎzǔ Tiānhòu Gōng) is dedicated to Matsu, Goddess of the Sea. The temple was built in 1889 and has an elaborately carved roof and beams, decorated with scenes from Chinese mythology. The temple is especially lively during Matsu's birthday when locals congregate here to pay their respects to the goddess.

### TAITUNG SEASIDE PARK 台東海濱公園

This **park** (Táidōng Hǎibīn Gōngyuán) along the water has some nice views of the coast, walking paths and tables and benches for picnicking. Though there's a beach, it's not recommended that you swim here. Strong undercurrents and very deep water make the conditions dangerous.

### TAITUNG COUNTY CULTURAL CENTRE 台東縣文化局

The **cultural centre** (Táidōng Xiàn Wénhuà Jú; 25 Nanching Rd; 9-11.50am & 1.30-5pm, closed Mon) occa-

sionally hosts live music and theatre events from local and international artists. There are plenty of free brochures to take if you can read Chinese. Staff are not very helpful and don't seem to know what to do with foreigners. There's a library next door with a limited selection of magazines in English as well as lockers and a copy machine. Behind the library is a public swimming pool, closed for repairs at the time of research.

### FRUIT STREET 水果市場

Few people would argue that Taitung has some of the freshest and most delicious fruit in Taiwan. In central Taitung, between Po'ai and Chungshan Rds, there's a lively **fruit street** (shuǐguǒ jiē), selling a colourful assortment of fruit, including pineapples, coconuts, bananas, mangoes, dragon fruit and papayas. Taitung's most famous fruit is the delicious custard apple, nicknamed 'Buddha's fruit' (shìjiā) because its shape resembles the head of the curly haired Shakyamuni.

### NATIONAL MUSEUM OF PREHISTORY 國立史前博物館

This is the best **museum** (Guólì Shǐqián Bówùguǎn; 1 Museum Rd, 950 Fengtien Li; admission NT80; 9am-5pm, closed Mon) on the east coast devoted to early aboriginal cultures. The museum features excellent bilingual exhibits on the history of Taiwan's indigenous people in addition to exhibits on the natural history and ecological development of the country. The museum bookshop has a fine selection of English books on Taiwanese history and indigenous tribes.

EAST COAST

Getting to the museum is problematic as it's inconveniently located outside Taitung's city limits in the middle of nowhere. The Dingdong Bus Company will theoretically drop you off near to the museum on its way up to Hualien, but no-one, including the staff at the bus company, can confirm this. The most straightforward way to reach the museum is to take the train to Kanglo station (Kānglè Zhàn) and then walk about 10 minutes to the museum. This means getting to the new train station by bus or taxi from Taitung and catching the train to the museum.

Another option for getting to the museum is to just take a taxi. This will cost about NT200 from the old train station in Taitung. Get your driver to wait for you or to come back at a certain time, otherwise you could get stranded.

### PEINAN CULTURAL PARK 卑南文化公園

This is an active **archaeological site** (Bēinán Wénhuà Gōngyuán; 200 Cultural Park Rd, 950 Nanwang Li; ☾ 8.30am-noon & 1-5pm, closed Mon) on the original dwelling grounds of the Puyuma tribe, who lived here almost 5000 years ago. The site contains the largest prehistoric settlement found in Taiwan and thought to originally cover almost 300,000 hectares. The park was discovered in 1980 when construction workers were building the new railway station. Workers were shocked to unearth an ancient graveyard containing several thousand stone coffins. Soon after, archaeologists were called in to investigate and a museum was built on the site. Other items were later found, including buildings and various household implements.

Visitors are welcome to walk around the park and witness the ongoing excavations. There is a small museum that charges a nominal fee for entry. The park is about a 10-minute walk from the new train station.

### Tours

The **Lanyu Travel Agency** (Lányŭ Lǚxíng Shè; 130 Hsinsheng Rd) is close to the old train station and is the best-known place in the city to book tours around Taitung and to Green and Lanyu Islands. Staff speak limited English so it's a good idea to have what you need written down before you approach them.

### Festivals & Events

The **Festival of Austronesian Cultures** is held annually at the National Museum of Prehistory. The festival is a great opportunity to see traditional aboriginal handicrafts, musical instruments and woodcarvings as well as to try a smorgasbord of local foods. The festival not only includes the participation of Taiwan's aboriginals but also aboriginal groups from several South Pacific nations who are believed to share a common ancestry with Taiwan's indigenous people.

The **Ami Harvest Festival** is another large festival in the region and takes place in July or August every year in towns around Taitung County. It's a boisterous event, with plenty of singing and dancing.

### Sleeping

#### BUDGET

**Gringo Hostel** ( ☎ 355 565; 52 Hsinsheng Rd; dm NT200, r from NT400; ☐ ) This well-liked backpacker hostel near the old train station has a good reputation. Rooms are basic but clean and the owners are very friendly. A small restaurant is on the ground floor. All guests get a free pass to the nearby Amigo Pub.

**Eastern Hotel** (Dōng Zhǐ Xiàng Dà Fàndiàn; ☎ 310 171; 374 Chungshan Rd; d NT1000) This is one of the best budget options near the old train station. Rooms are small but immaculate and come with cable TV.

**Teachers and Public Workers Hostel** (Gōngjiào Huìguǎn; ☎ 310 142; 19 Nanching Rd; d/tw NT900/1050) Next door to the cultural centre, this hotel has large, attractive rooms and offers substantial discounts to teachers, students and public workers.

**Fuyuan Hotel** (Fúyuán Dà Fàndiàn; ☎ 331 1369; 72 Wenhua St; d/tr NT600/900, q NT1200) This pleasant hotel is centrally located in a busy market area in the middle of everything. Rooms are amazingly quiet, in spite of the noise and bustle outside.

**Hotel Hsin Fu Chih** (Xīnfúzhì Dà Lǚshè; ☎ 331 101; 417 Chungshan Rd; d NT800) The rooms in the Hsin Fu Chih are old but decent, though the bathrooms and furnishings could use some updating.

**Chung Tai Hotel** (Zhōngtái Bīnguǎn; ☎ 325 167; 414 Chungshan Rd; d NT500) Conveniently located next to the Hualien Bus Company Station, this hotel is one of the cheapest places to stay in town. Unfortunately, the rooms are dirty and full of bugs. It's not recommended that you stay here unless everywhere else in town is full.

**MID-RANGE & TOP END**
**San Po Hotel** (Sān Bó Dà Fàndiàn; ☎ 324 696; 393 Chungshan Rd; d NT2600) This hotel has fairly nice rooms, but they are a little overpriced. In fact, the quality of this hotel doesn't really differ from the cheaper options in the same neighbourhood.

**Aboriginal Cultural Centre** (Yuán Zúmín Wénhuà Huìguǎn; ☎ 340 605; 10 Chungshan Rd; d/tr NT1200/1450) The cultural centre has clean, spacious rooms with balconies. Unfortunately, it's about 1km out of town and a fair distance from everything unless you have your own transport.

**Naluwan Hotel** (Nàlùwān Dà Jiǔdiàn; ☎ 239 777; 66 Lienhang Rd; d NT5900; 🏊) This international-standard hotel has beautifully furnished rooms, decorated with aboriginal textiles. Amenities include restaurants and a shopping arcade.

## Eating
Eating in Taitung can be a lot of fun, especially in the night markets and along Nanching Rd. Some local favourites are sticky rice *(tóngzī mǐ gāo)* and meat dumplings. If you're brave, you can try some pork blood soup *(zhū xiè tāng)*, a Puyuma delicacy.

**Chi Li Hsiang Shui Chien Pao** (Qī Lǐ Xiāng Shuǐ Jiānbāo; 385 Lane 7, Chengchi Rd; dumplings NT20-30; 🕒 3.30pm-2am) This is a tiny place on the corner of Nanching and Chengchi Rds that sells very tasty fried dumplings. The restaurant is a little hard to find and there's no English sign – look for the large picture of Donald Duck out front.

**Beikang Xiao Chi Pu** (Běigǎng Xiǎo Chībù; 212 Kuangming Rd; sticky rice NT25-40; 🕒 breakfast, lunch & dinner) The Beikang is another unassuming little place that has been around for over 20 years. The sticky rice here is some of the best in town. Try it with some thick meat soup *(roù gēng).*

**Only Have Eyes For** (372 Chunghua Rd; meals NT100; 🕒 lunch & dinner) If you're looking for a more comfortable place, this restaurant will do. Only Have Eyes For has set meals that include a main course, soup and dessert. The curry chicken meal is pretty good, as is the vegetarian option, which is some sort of vegetable gravy served over rice. Portions are large and filling.

**Céleste Café** (Hǎibīn Kāfēi Guǎn; 18 Lane 4, Datong Rd; meals NT150; 🕒 lunch & dinner) For Western dishes, this café/restaurant, across from the Taitung Seaside Park, is a good choice. You can eat your sandwich, spaghetti or lasagne alfresco on the patio while watching the waves.

## Drinking
Taitung doesn't have much of a pub scene. One of the few places in town with music and drinks is the **Amigo Pub** (249 Chungcheng Rd; drinks NT150; 🕒 7pm-4am), which is free to guests at the Gringo Hostel.

## Entertainment
People-watching in Taitung Seaside Park is probably the most entertaining thing to do in town.

The **Tatung Cinema** (Dàtóng Xìyuàn; 129 Chungcheng Rd) occasionally shows English-language movies.

## Shopping
Taitung's specialities are mainly the edible kind, with fruit and dried fish at the top of the list. Another speciality is the high-quality tea grown in the neighbouring region of Lu Yeh (Lù Yě). The tea is sold in shops around town and makes a good gift for Taiwanese friends.

Aboriginal arts and crafts are on sale at the gift shops at the National Museum of Prehistory and the Peinan Cultural Park. The Szuwei Rd Sunday night market and the city market in the centre of town are good places to try out local foods.

## Getting There & Away
### AIR
Taitung is connected by air to Taipei, Taichung, Kaohsiung and Lanyu and Green Islands. The following airlines have booking counters at the airport.
**Far Eastern Transport** ( ☎ 390 388)
**Mandarin Airlines** ( ☎ 326 677)
**Uni Air** ( ☎ 362 626)

### BUS
Taitung has four bus stations and finding which bus goes to where can be confusing. The Dingdong Bus Station, across from the old train station, runs daily buses up to Hualien (four hours, depart 6.10am, 8.30am and 1.40pm) along the east coast. From

Hualien to Taitung, buses leave at 11.45am, 2.10pm and 4.35pm.

If you want to skip the east coast and travel through the Eastern Rift Valley, the Hualien Bus Company has services for the inland route. The Hualien Bus Company is next door to the Dingdong Bus Company.

The Taiwan Bus Company Station (Táiqì Kèyùnzhàn) runs buses to Kaohsiung (4½ hours) frequently. There are no direct buses to Kenting. It's necessary to get on a bus headed for Kaohsiung and switch buses at Fengkang.

Buses that head across the mountains via the South Cross-Island Hwy also depart from the Taiwan Bus Company Station. Most people who want to do this trip come from the direction of Tainan so they can hike the downhill portion that leads into Taitung. If you're not planning on doing much hiking, then either direction is fine. The only bus to Tienchih, the termination point for Taitung buses going along the highway, leaves at the unsightly hour of 6.40am. The bus will arrive in Tienchih before noon, where you can switch to an ongoing bus to travel the rest of the highway.

The Dingdong Inland Bus Station (Dǐngdōng Kèyùn Shānxiànzòng Zhàn) has 11 daily buses to Chihpen Hot Springs. There are also buses to the new train station.

### TRAIN

There are two train stations in Taitung: the old station (Jiù Zhàn) in town and a new station (Xīn Zhàn) several kilometres out of town. Be aware that the old station is defunct and trains no longer stop there. It is mainly used as a drop-off point for taxis and buses. When taking a taxi to the train station, be clear with your driver which one you mean. A taxi to the train station from Taitung will cost around NT200.

There is a frequent train service between Hualien and Taitung (see p172 for more details). The train follows the inland route through the Eastern Rift Valley, an interesting route with opportunities for visiting hot springs and experiencing white-water rafting.

## Getting Around
### TO/FROM THE AIRPORT

A taxi to or from the airport will cost a flat fare of NT250. Bus service to the airport is inconsistent so it's advisable not to rely on it.

### CAR/ MOTORCYCLE/SCOOTER

Getting around by car or motorcycle is a great way to see the city and visit surrounding areas. Traffic is light in Taitung and the roads are well maintained. Rentals are available around the old train station and typically cost NT400 a day for a motorcycle and NT1500 a day for a small car, not including petrol. Some rental agencies are refusing customers who don't have a Taiwanese licence. Attitudes vary so try your luck at more than one agency.

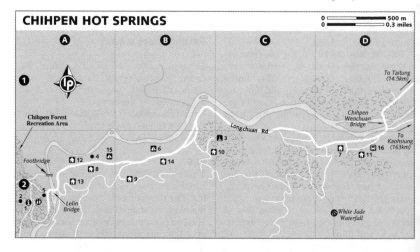

**TAXI**

Drivers congregate around the new and old train stations hustling passengers. The only time a taxi should charge a flat fare is to the airport or new train station. If your driver refuses to use the meter for anywhere else, get another driver.

## CHIHPEN HOT SPRINGS 知本溫泉

☎ 089

The Chihpen Hot Springs (Zhīběn Wēnquán) are about 15km southwest of Taitung, in a canyon at the foot of a mountain range. Chihpen is one of Taiwan's oldest and most famous hot-spring resorts. It was first built in the early 20th century by the Japanese, who discovered the therapeutic effects of the hot springs when they saw how the local aborigines would soak in the water to relieve joint pain and muscle strains. The Japanese dubbed the area 'Chihpen', or 'source of wisdom'.

Nowadays, the resort is a top-rated tourist attraction, with five-star hotels, KTV and streams of traffic clogging the highway into the canyon. Luckily, getting away from all the noise and bustle isn't difficult. At the far end of the canyon, beyond the cluster of hotels that dominate the first and middle section of the roads, is a lovely forest with walking paths and botanical gardens. Also hidden off the main road is a waterfall and a magnificent Buddhist temple.

### Sights & Activities

Sadly, most of the hot springs are diverted into the hotels for private use. You don't need to be a guest at most hotels to use their pools, but you will need to pay a fee.

**Dongtair Hotel** (Dōngtái Dà Fàndiàn; admission adult/child NT300/200) has an outdoor pool that is open to the public and is across the road from the hotel.

The **Hotel Rainbow** (Hóng Quán Dà Fàndiàn; admission NT150) also lets you soak in its pools, even if you're not staying there.

**Hotel Royal Chihpen** (Lǎoyè Dà Jiǔdiàn; admission adult/child NT350/200) is the finest hotel in Chihpen and has the swankiest pools.

There are other hotels in Chihpen that also allow nonguests to use their pools. These are listed in the Sleeping section.

For those who prefer their hot springs in a more natural environment, the **Yunshanyuan** (Yúnshānyuán Lùyíng Qū; admission NT100) and **Awayang** (Āyāwàng Lùyíng Qū; admission NT150) camping grounds have attractive outdoor pools that can be used by nonguests.

Besides hot springs, Chihpen also has some other notable attractions. Along the main road, several hundred metres into the canyon, is a small road on the left leading to the **White Jade Waterfall** (Báiyù Pùbù). Follow the road about 1km uphill to see the waterfall, most impressive after heavy rains.

The **Chingchueh Temple** (Qīngjué Sì) sits incongruously next to the Hotel Royal Chihpen. This elegant Buddhist temple is home to a beautiful white-jade Buddha from Myanmar and a bronze Buddha from Thailand. The temple is undergoing major renovation but will hopefully reopen by the time this book goes to press.

At the far end of the canyon is the **Chihpen Forest Recreation Area** (Zhīběn Sēnlín Yóulè Qū; admission NT100; ☯ 7am-5pm), a lovely forested area with hiking trails, rivers and waterfalls. In some parts of the forest you can hear Taiwan macaques crashing around in the trees overhead. Tourists are not permitted to camp in the park.

The further up the canyon you travel, the prettier the scenery gets. It's worth exploring the region around the forest recreation area more thoroughly, if you have the time.

### Sleeping

**BUDGET**

**Mingchuan Hotel** (Míngquán Lǚyóu Shānzhuāng; ☎ 513 996; 267 Lane 2, Longchuan Rd; d NT800, cabins NT1200-1500) This hotel is adjacent to the forest recreation area and has quiet motel-style rooms and private cabins for rent. Some rooms have excellent views of the canyon.

**Longchuan Hotel** (Lóngquán Shānzhuāng; ☎ 513 930; 216 Longchuan Rd; d NT800-1200, tr NT1800-2800) Some rooms here are quite large and feature piped-in hot springs. However, the sheets are none too clean and the place needs a good scrub.

**Songquan Hotel** (Sōngquán Shānzhuāng; ☎ 510 073; 136 Lane 6, Longchuan Rd; tw NT1200) This place has very spiffy rooms and is a good budget option.

**Yunshanyuan Camping Area** ( ☎ 510 769; 2 people with tent NT350, 6 people with tent NT600, without tent NT1000) The Yunshanyuan is close to the forest recreation centre and provides a clean, quiet place to camp.

**Awayang Camping Area** ( ☎ 515 827; 2 people with tent NT350, without tent NT1000) This is another good camping ground with facilities similar to the Yunshanyuan.

**MID-RANGE & TOP END**

**Hotel Rainbow** ( ☎ 513 181; 139 Lane 11, Longchuan Rd; r NT2800) Sitting above the main road, overlooking the canyon, the Hotel Rainbow offers airy rooms with great views. Rooms come with breakfast and free use of the hotel hot springs.

**Dongtair Hotel** ( ☎ 512 290; 147 Longchuan Rd; tw NT4600) This is one the most popular hotels in Chihpen, with clean, comfortable rooms and excellent hot-springs facilities. The hotel offers a breakfast buffet for NT150.

**Hoya Hot Springs Resort** (Zhìběn Fùyě Dùjià Cūn; ☎ 515 005; 30 Longchuan Rd; d NT4900) The Hoya is a five-star hotel and has all the usual facilities. Rooms have large windows and are tastefully furnished. In the off season, rates here drop 40%, making the place quite a bargain.

**Chihpen Hotel** (Zhìběn Dà Fàndiàn; ☎ 512 220; 35 Longchuan Rd; r NT3200) This is one of the older hotels in Chihpen, boasting some of the largest hot springs in the area. Rooms are a little dated, but still in good shape for an old-timer.

**Hotel Royal Chihpen** ( ☎ 510 666; 113 Lane 23, Longchuan Rd; r NT6600) The Hotel Royal Chihpen sits high on a hill, off the main road, surrounded by mountains covered in dense tropical foliage. The facilities are the best in the resort and you'll feel like a dignitary if you stay here.

## Eating

Longchuan Rd has several small restaurants and noodle stands selling food at exorbitant prices. Most visitors staying in the canyon eat at the restaurants in their hotel. At the entrance to the resort, there's a convenience store and a small grocery shop.

## Getting There & Away

**BUS**

The Dingdong Inland Bus Station in Taitung has frequent services to Chihpen. Some buses do not go all the way into Chihpen but stop at the entrance. Others will

---

**TAIWAN'S WHITE TERROR**

One of the blackest times in Taiwan's martial-law period was during the White Terror, when the government started a large-scale campaign to purge the island of political activists during the 1950s. Many who had spoken out against government policies were arrested, charged with attempting to overthrow the government and sentenced to death or life imprisonment. Some who were arrested were indeed political spies but most, it's believed, were unjustly accused. Over 90,000 people were arrested and at least half that number was executed. Taiwanese were not the only targets; a large number of mainland Chinese were arrested and killed as well.

The Green Island Lodge, or 'Oasis Villa' as it's sometimes called in English, stands empty now and many feel it's a symbol of a new period of human rights for the Taiwanese. The monument that was erected in front of the prison in 1999 is meant to not only remember the victims but also to educate Taiwanese too young to recall the period. The government has also taken measures to financially compensate former prisoners and their families and to establish the Human Rights Commission to promote human-rights education. Many human-rights advocates feel that Taiwan has a long way to go, particularly in regard to women's issues and aboriginal rights. However, most acknowledge that the government is moving in the right direction and certain tragic elements of Taiwan's past can be valuable lessons for the future.

take you all the way to the forest recreation area. Make sure when you buy your ticket you know where you'll be dropped off. To the entrance of the resort it costs NT42, to the Chingchueh Temple bus stop it's NT49 and to the forest recreation area it's NT51.

The schedule of buses to Chihpen from Taitung fluctuates so you'll need to check at the bus station for current times. At the time of writing, the first bus to Chihpen left Taitung at 6.20am.

In Chihpen, buses pick up passengers from all the major hotels, at the forest recreation centre or at the grocery shop at the entrance to the canyon. The bus schedule is posted on the windows of the grocery shop.

**TAXI**

A taxi to Chihpen from Taitung will cost about NT400.

## GREEN ISLAND 綠島

☎ 089 / pop 3000

Green Island (Lǜdǎo), a tiny volcanic island 30km east of Taitung, attracts a fair share of Taiwan's tourist market these days. The island, with its heavily eroded coastline, is making its mark as a haven for snorkelling and diving, due to its pristine coral reefs and gorgeous tropical fish. The island also boasts unique saltwater hot springs, glass-bottom boats, a camping area and a beach.

Green Island was not always thought of as a tourist destination. Instead, it was once a symbol of Taiwan's White Terror, when political prisoners were sent to languish in the island's two notorious prisons. Now, the prisons are closed and a human-rights memorial has been erected to commemorate those who suffered there.

Green Island is a tiny place and a drive around the 17km road that circles the island takes only about 30 minutes. However, most people fly in to Green Island in the morning, spend the day swimming and exploring, and fly back to Taitung in the evening.

The island is packed with tourists in summer but in winter things come to a standstill and many restaurants and tourist facilities shut down.

## Information

**Green Island Tourist Information Centre** (Lǜdǎo Yóukè Zhōngxīn; ☎ 672 027; 298 Chungliao Village;

(Y) 8am-5pm) Near the airport, the centre can help with maps and information about the island. Staff can also arrange diving trips and make reservations for the camp site in the south of the island. During summer there are daily multimedia presentations about the island.

## Sights

The 33m high **Green Island Lighthouse** (Lǜdǎo Dēngtǎ) stands in the northwestern corner of the island. It was built in 1937 under the Japanese after the American ship President Hoover struck a reef off the coast of Green Island and sunk. The KMT refurbished the lighthouse and changed the original gas lantern to an electric light.

There are three prisons on Green Island, evidence of its earlier history as a place to incarcerate political prisoners. The **Green Island Prison** (Lǜdǎo Jianyù) once housed some of Taiwan's most dangerous criminals, many thought too dangerous to keep on mainland Taiwan. The **Occupational Skills Training Centre** (Jìnnéng Xùnliàn Suǒ) was a rehabilitation centre for criminals trying to make the adjustment back into society.

The prison with the most notorious history is the **Green Island Lodge** (Lǜdǎo Shānzhuāng), now empty of prisoners. During the period of martial law many dissidents were sent here to wait out their time – some waiting more than 30 years to be released. The prison isn't exactly a tourist attraction, though many tourists are morbidly fascinated with the place and try to get glimpses of its interior through the windows. In front of the prison is a park containing the **Human Rights Memorial Monument** (Rén Chuán Jìniàn Yuán Qū), built to commemorate those who suffered here. The monument reads: 'During those times, how many mothers were crying overnight for their children imprisoned on Green Island?' Six hundred names have been carved on the monument but some former prisoners believe another 20,000 names should be added to remember all the prisoners.

Further down the coast is the **Kuanyin Cave** (Guānyīn Dòng), an underground cavern with a stalagmite in a red cape. Legend has it that during the Qing dynasty, a fisherman became lost at sea and a fiery red light came down from the sky and led him to safety in the cave. The fishermen believed the light to be the goddess Kuanyin and the stalagmite in the cape to resemble the form of the goddess. The cave was designated a sacred spot on the island and people come here from all over Taiwan to pay their respects.

Close to Kuanyin Cave is the **Yutzu Lake Ancient Dwellings** (Yòuzǐ Hú). This was the site of the first village on the island and some old stone houses still remain. Nearby is a sea-eroded cave that is worth a look inside.

Green Island has some intriguing volcanic-rock formations scattered around the coast, leading some Taiwanese to give the rocks curious names. The **Sleeping Beauty rock** (Shuì Měi Rén), off the east coast of the island, is supposed to resemble the figure of a sleeping woman. You may need to use your imagination for this one. Near Sleeping Beauty is the

**Hsiao Changcheng** (Xiǎo Chángchéng), a rock that some believe resembles the Great Wall in China, only not so great.

**Tapaisha Beach** (Dàbáishā) has fine white coral sand and is known for its stunning coral reefs, making it a good spot for snorkelling. Tourist authorities report that Green Island has over 176 types of coral and over 602 types of fish swimming around the coast. Up the road from the beach are the **Pahsien** (Bā Xiān Dòng) and **Lunghsia Caves** (Lóngxiā Dòng), both interesting to explore.

## Activities

The **Chaojih Hot Springs** (Cháorì Wēnquán; admission NT150; ☉ 5am-11pm) are a highlight of Green Island. These springs are one of only three

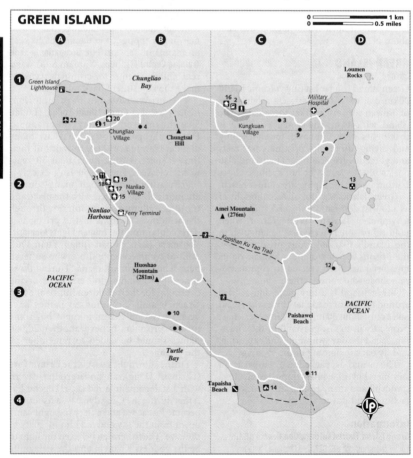

saltwater hot springs in the world; the others are on Mt Vesuvius in Italy and in Hokkaido in Japan. The three circular pools here are on the beach and the best time to come is in the early morning, to soak in the pool and watch the sunrise. On weekends, the hot springs turn into a party zone, a time best avoided.

**Huoshao Mountain** (Huǒshāoshān), translated as 'fire mountain' and actually an extinct volcano, stands a towering 281m. There are hiking trails around the mountain but you won't be able to climb all the way to the summit as it's a sensitive military area.

Another hiking trail is the **Kuoshan Ku Tao** (Guòshān Gǔ Dào), a 1.8km path that stretches from behind Nanliao Village to the east coast of the island. The walk along the path is very secluded and tranquil, a nice escape from the tourist bustle of Nanliao.

Diving and snorkelling are the most popular activities on Green Island. It seems as if every hotel on the island arranges snorkelling and diving trips. Equipment can be rented at shops in Nanliao Village and around the harbour. Rates depend on how many people you have in your group and the type of equipment you'll need to rent.

One reputable place is the **Chufu Diving Centre** (Jǔfú Qiánshuǐ; ☎ 672 238; 78-3 Kungkuan Village), near Green Island Lodge.

Don't be too frugal when renting equipment. Even if the wetsuits look miserable on a hot summer day, they do a good job of protecting you from the sun and tenacious Green Island jellyfish. If you do get stung by a jellyfish the local remedy is to use vinegar to erase the sting.

In summer, **glass-bottomed boats** (NT200) take tourists through the waters and coral reefs around Green Island, giving good glimpses of the marine life below. Boats depart from Nanliao Harbour.

## Tours

Most hotels on Green Island run daily tours around the island during summer. Prices vary according to the number of activities included on the tour. A quick tour of the sights, without a stop for a swim or a snorkelling lesson, should cost around NT250. If meals are included, prepare to spend more.

## Sleeping

Accommodation on Green Island is centred in Nanliao Village, close to the harbour. Green Island is a popular place in summer for Taiwanese tourists, which means that most hotels will be booked solid on weekends. If you're arriving over a summer weekend, it's advisable to call and reserve a room ahead of time.

**Lijing Hostel** (Lìjǐng Shānzhuāng; ☎ 672 000; 47 Kungkuan Village; dm NT500, d/tr NT2500/4500) This is the only place on the island that offers dorm accommodation, in addition to more expensive rooms.

**Seashell Hotel** (Nánbèi Fàndiàn; ☎ 672 399; 242 Chungliao Village; d NT2200-3200) This homey place is very close to the tourist information centre. Rooms are basic but cosy. The friendly owner can arrange tours around the island for guests. In the backyard are covered picnic tables to eat outside in the sunshine.

**Par Far Hotel** (Shuāng Fā Píngjià; ☎ 672 552; 146 Nanliao Village; r NT1200) The Par Far is a true bargain and highly recommended. Rooms are immaculate and very spacious. In addition, the woman who runs the hotel is willing to negotiate room prices during the off season.

**Sea Home Hotel** (Hǎi Yáng Zhī Jiā; ☎ 672 566; 42 Nanliao Village; d NT1900-3200) The Sea Home was once known as the Song Rong, and many locals still refer to it by that name. New

EAST COAST

management have given the place a make-over. Rooms are very airy and sunny, some with views of the ocean.

**Lushan Hotel** (Lúshān Fàndiàn; ☎ 672 243; 102 Nanliao Village; r NT1200-1900) The Lushan has also recently changed management. Rooms here are not up to the standards of the Par Far or Sea Home but are still comfortable and a good option if the other hotels are full.

**Kaihsin Hotel** (Kǎixīn Fàndiàn; ☎ 672 033; 102 Nanliao Village; d NT2500-4200) The Kaihsin is the largest hotel on the island with over 60 rooms and gives discounts during the off season. During summer this place buzzes with tour groups so make sure to book ahead if you want to stay here. The hotel restaurant serves up decent food.

**Camping Ground** (Lùyíng Qū; camping on grass NT200, camping on wooden platform NT300) This camping site is in the south of the island near Tapaisha Beach. The tourist information centre takes all reservations for the camp sites and rents out equipment.

## Eating

Nanliao Village has quite a few seafood restaurants. Local dishes include sea mushrooms (hǎi xiānggū) and garlic octopus (suàn xiāng zhāngyú).

**Chi Tang You Yu** (Chí Táng Yǒu Yú; 150 Nanliao Village; mains NT100; ☺ lunch & dinner) A congenial atmosphere and wonderful outdoor patio makes this a great place to have a beer and relax after a long day of diving. The garlic octopus is especially delectable.

## Getting There & Away

### AIR

**Mandarin Airlines** (☎ 672 585) has three flights a day between Taitung and Green Island (NT1028, 15 minutes) on small 19-seat prop planes. The flight takes 15 minutes and the current fare is NT1028. During winter, flights are often cancelled due to bad weather. In summer it's hard to get on a flight unless you've booked your seat several weeks ahead. Mandarin Airlines has a reservation counter in the Green Island airport.

### BOAT

During summer, boats travel frequently between Taitung and Green Island (one-way/return NT420/800). Boats travel from Fukang Harbour, north of Taitung, to Nanliao Harbour. The boat schedule fluctuates so

check with a travel agent or at one of the harbours for the exact times of departure. You can buy your ticket as you board the boat. It's not necessary to buy it in advance.

During winter, boats run infrequently, if at all, due to choppy water. If you dare to take a boat during winter, prepare your stomach in advance and brace yourself for a very rough ride.

## Getting Around

### BUS

There is a bus that circuits the island several times daily. The schedule doesn't appear to be consistent so you may be better off taking a taxi if you're in a hurry.

### CAR/MOTORCYCLE/SCOOTER

Scooters are the most enjoyable way to get around Green Island. You'll find plenty of people willing to rent you a vehicle at the harbour and the airport. Rates are generally NT400 to NT500 a day, plus petrol.

### TAXI

Taking a taxi around the island costs around NT600 for a quick trip, more if you want to stop and do some exploring.

### WALKING

Walking around the island is a viable option if you have the time. The summer sun can be fierce so bring plenty of water and sunscreen.

## LANYU ISLAND 蘭嶼

☎ 089 / pop 3000

Lanyu (Lányǔ), or Orchid Island, a volcanic island 65km south of Taitung, is the home of the Yami, an aboriginal tribe of Polynesian descent who speak their own distinct tribal tongue. The Yami call their island 'Pongso No Tao', or 'Island of the People', and over the centuries have lived primarily off the sea, supplementing their diet with taro, millet and sweet potatoes. Mountains rise out of the centre of the island with heights up to 500m, covered with a carpet of tropical rainforest. Coral reefs surround the rocky coastline, home to an abundant assortment of fish.

## History

For centuries the Yami lived peacefully on their island and it wasn't until the latter half of last century that their way of life was disturbed. With the opening of the island to tourism in the 1960s and controversial government policies, the Yami are struggling to retain their culture and identity despite increasing outside influence.

During the Japanese occupation, the island remained largely untouched. The Japanese were fascinated by the local customs of the Yami and did little to interfere with their way of life. Things changed drastically after the KMT came to power and attempted to introduce the Yami to Chinese language and culture. Boatloads of mainland Chinese were shipped to the island in the hope that interracial marriages would Sinicise the Yami population. The Yami resisted this encroachment and years of fighting with the mainlanders ensued. In the late 1960s the government ordered that the traditional underground homes of the Yami be torn down and new cement structures built in their place. The houses were poorly made and couldn't hold up to the typhoons that whip through the island every year. At about the same time the housing law was passed, the island was opened to

tourism and Taiwanese tourists began to arrive in droves. Christian missionaries also arrived, converting a large percentage of the population.

The relationship between the Yami and the Taiwanese government remained tenuous throughout the 1970s but almost came to a head when the government began using the island as a dumping ground for 100,000 barrels of nuclear waste in 1982. This sparked furious outcry from the island's residents, who demanded that the barrels be removed. The protests still continue to this day and there is evidence that 20,000 barrels

| SIGHTS & ACTIVITIES | (p194) |
| --- | --- |
| Si Kang Chai Art Studio 市岡菜 | .....1 C2 |
| Three Sisters 三姐妹 | .....2 C2 |
| Weather Station 氣象站 | .....3 C2 |
| **SLEEPING** | **(p194)** |
| Hai Yang Kuo Chi Hotel 海洋國際飯店 | .....4 B2 |
| Ku Lu Homestay 古魯民宿 | .....5 C2 |
| Lanyu Hotel 蘭嶼別館 | .....6 C2 |
| **EATING** | **(pp194-5)** |
| Jiu Bar 雅美咖啡 | .....7 C2 |
| **TRANSPORT** | **(p195)** |
| Airport 機場 | .....8 B2 |

EAST COAST

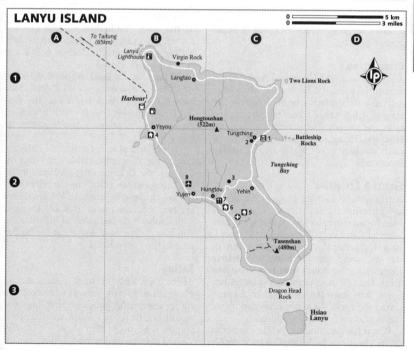

**LANYU ISLAND**

0 — 5 km
0 — 3 miles

To Taitung (65km)

Lanyu Lighthouse

Virgin Rock

Langtao

Two Lions Rock

Harbour

Hongtoushan (522m)

Yeyou

Tungching

Battleship Rocks

Tungching Bay

Hungtou

Yehin

Yujen

Tasenshan (480m)

Dragon Head Rock

Hsiao Lanyu

containing the nuclear waste are beginning to leak and the concrete trenches they are buried in are cracking. Some believe the fish are starting to die off, sparking even more outcry. The protests have caused a worldwide stir and the environmental organisation Greenpeace has jumped to defend the cause. Despite promises that the government will remove the dump, the problem remains.

In the face of this, the Yami manage to survive, even in the face of mounting social issues. Alcoholism is a serious problem on the island and many people are leaving to find greater economic prosperity on mainland Taiwan. Even so, Yami traditions on Lanyu remain alive. One of the most important cultural traditions is the building of elaborately carved wooden canoes, made from 27 individual pieces of wood, ingeniously held together without nails.

The Yami don't appear to mind visitors to their island, as long as they are treated with respect. Be mindful of taking photos, as many resent this intrusion and may demand money to be photographed. Many Yami are quite friendly when asked to explain some of their local customs and most of the younger generation can speak Mandarin Chinese.

## Orientation

A 50km road circles Lanyu and can be driven around in about 1½ hours. Six villages are located on the island's brim, a narrow flat strip of land wedged between the mountains and the sea. The principal villages are Hungtou (Hóngtóu Cūn) and Yeyou (Yēyóu Cūn), where most of the commercial activity is centred.

## Sights & Activities

A trip around Lanyu's rugged coastline is an otherworldly experience. The narrow island road winds its way past craggy cliffs, waterfalls and deep caves. Jagged volcanic-rock formations jut dramatically out of the sea, some sporting fairly imaginative names such as **Dragon Head Rock** (Lóngtóu Yán), **Kiss** and even **Virgin Rock** (Yùnǔ Yán). Some Yami insist that they are not the ones giving the rocks the silly names and blame the Taiwanese for the foolishness.

If you have an interest in Yami arts and crafts, check out the **Si Kang Chai Art Studio** (Shì

Gāng Cài; 38 Tungching Village), which has an eclectic assortment of sculptures and paintings on display. Close by is the **Three Sisters** (Sān Jiě Mèi; 23 Tungching Village), which sells woven bracelets, woodcarvings and paintings.

## Festivals

The **Flying Fish Festival** occurs every spring before the start of the flying fish season. This is traditionally a coming-of-age for young men whose societal standing was based on how many fish they could catch. During the festival, the Yami men don loincloths, silver helmets and breastplates. The blood of a freshly killed chicken is smeared on the rocks and the men chant 'return flying fish' in unison before heading out to sea in their canoes. Be aware that, according to custom, women are not allowed to participate.

## Sleeping

The hotels in Lanyu are largely run by Taiwanese.

**Lanyu Hotel** (Lányǔ Biéguǎn; ☎ 732 111; 7 Hungtou Village; dm NT500, d NT1200-1800) Located right on the waterfront, the dormitory rooms consist of an empty room with some dirty blankets on the floor. The bathrooms and showers are equally grim. The private rooms with bathrooms are much cleaner and some even have ocean views.

**Hai Yang Kuo Chi Hotel** (Hǎiyáng Guójì Fàndiàn; ☎ 732 1666; 22 Yeyou Village; d/tw NT1500/1800) Once named Orchid Island Hotel and the sign out front still says this. It's within walking distance of the harbour if you're coming or going by boat.

To meet some locals, consider a homestay. One of the most comfortable homestays on Lanyu is the **Ku Lu Homestay** (Gǔlǔ Mínsù; ☎ 732 584; 135 Hungtou Village; r NT400), up the hill behind the health clinic in Hungtou Village. There are two spacious rooms available for rent, with double beds and a shared bathroom. If you want to stay here, inquire at the Jiu Bar next to the Lanyu Hotel.

## Eating

There are plenty of small restaurants in Hungtou and Yeyou Villages where you can fill up cheaply on noodles, dumplings and rice dishes. In Yeyou Village, near the petrol station, is a grocery shop where you can buy instant noodles and peanut butter.

**Jiu Bar** (Yǎměi Kāfēi; 48 Hungtou Village; mains NT100; 11am-2.30pm & 6.30-11.30pm) A friendly place with excellent food and an inviting atmosphere. The owner, Giselle, can provide all sorts of information on what to see and do around Lanyu. She can also help arrange homestays and provide information about diving and motorcycle rentals.

## Getting There & Away

### AIR
**Mandarin Airlines** ( 732 035) has a counter in the Lanyu airport and flies small propeller-driven aircraft between Taitung and Lanyu (NT1345, 50 minutes) daily. During summer, the 19 seats on the plane fill up quickly so remember to book as far ahead as possible. During the rainy winter months, flights in and out of Lanyu are erratic due to the volatile weather conditions. If you fly into Lanyu during winter and it starts to rain, be prepared to stay on the island until the storm clears up. This could be days so carry enough cash and clean clothes with you to wait out the storm.

### BOAT
Several boat companies operate small vessels from Fukang Harbour, outside of Taitung, to Lanyu (three hours). Schedules depend on the weather and the number of passengers so verify with a travel agent or at the harbour what boats are running and when. The water is often so rough that even the sea-hardy Yami balk at the idea of taking the boat to Taitung. If you have a weak stomach, the trip will be quite an ordeal.

## Getting Around

### TO/FROM THE AIRPORT
Hotels will provide transport to and from the airport if they're notified in advance. From the airport it's about a 20-minute walk to Hungtou Village if a ride is not available.

### BUS
A bus circles the island four times a day, stopping at various points. If you see the bus, flag it down, otherwise it might not stop. This way of getting around the island is very slow and it might be easier to just rent a scooter or even walk.

### CAR/MOTORCYCLE/SCOOTER
There's a vehicle rental shop next to the Lanyu Hotel. Motorcycles cost NT500 a day and cars NT1500 a day, plus petrol. In winter, renting a car might be safer and more comfortable than a motorcycle because of the slippery road conditions.

### WALKING
Walking around the island is a wonderful way to see Lanyu up close and meet some of the village residents. The drawback is that Lanyu is large and you'll probably need more than a day to make it around the island. During winter, waterproof gear is a necessity and it's a good idea to bring plenty of water and snacks.

**EAST COAST**

# Western Taiwan

CONTENTS

WESTERN TAIWAN

Here's your opportunity to really get into the heart – and heat – of the country: a land of thriving traditions and beaches where you can swim all year round.

The route from Taichung City down to Kenting is a simple one to travel, yet has often been overlooked for the big-ticket scenic wonders along the east coast. And yet there are wonders here too: dramatic ones such as Yushan, the highest mountain in northeast Asia; and quirky ones such as the fire spring in Guanziling. The west has some of Taiwan's most varied terrain, with the greatest contrasts from region to region. Around Alishan, for example, you can go from tropical to alpine zones in just three hours.

Some of the best places to visit are so new even your Taiwanese friends may not know about them. These include the stops along the Jiji Small Rail Line, where you can cycle and hike through some of the sweetest countryside, and Dapeng Bay, a lagoon the size of Sun Moon Lake that is being developed for swimming, windsurfing and boating.

In the west there's also opportunity to explore old Taiwan. This can mean temple- and relic-hopping in the ancient capital of Tainan, witnessing heartfelt displays of folk faith in a Matsu Temple, or shopping for paper umbrellas and fans and snacking on dragon eyes and ox-tongue cookies in traditional villages such as Meinong and Lugang.

WESTERN TAIWAN

## HIGHLIGHTS

- Cycle through rural Taiwan at stops along the **Jiji Small Rail Line** (p211)
- Surf, swim, sail and visit ecologically protected zones in **Kenting National Park** (p264)
- Marvel at Taiwan's temple heritage and sample local foods in the old capital of **Tainan** (p239)
- Wander the old streets and admire the traditional architecture in **Lugang** (p207)
- Explore the winter resting grounds of the purple butterfly in the **Purple Butterfly Valley** (p259) in Maolin
- Climb the highest mountain in northeast Asia at **Yushan National Park** (p235)

- Lugang
- Jiji
- Yushan National Park
- Tainan
- Maolin
- Kenting National Park

# TAICHUNG TO SUN MOON LAKE

The trip from Taichung to Sun Moon Lake takes you from the third-largest city in Taiwan into the grain belt and then up into the foothills of the Central Mountain Range around the romantically named Sun Moon Lake. It's an immensely rewarding journey whether your interests are photogenic landscapes, temples and historical sites, shopping for local specialities or just having fun such as cycling down quaint rural lanes.

Give yourself five days to a week to explore this area – it's worth knowing well.

## TAICHUNG 台中市

☎ 04 / pop 1,023,000

The third-largest city in Taiwan, Taichung (Táizhōng) is often considered the most livable. It has the mildest weather, the least air pollution and probably the best laid out city centre (you can thank the Japanese for the latter).

There's not much you can do here that you can't do in Taipei but in Taichung it's possible to enjoy yourself at a slower pace and with more space.

Though Taipei and Taichung have very similar average temperatures, both around 22.5°C, Taichung is much drier, receiving around 1700mm of rain a year compared with Taipei's 2170mm.

### Orientation

Taichung is about two hours south of Taipei on the train and very accessible as a weekend getaway. The area around the train station is called Central Taichung but, in reality,

the focus of the city is shifting westward all the time.

Unfortunately, most of the cheap accommodation is near the train station, though Taichung is not that big and most taxi fares will cost less than NT150.

Zhongshan Rd (which turns later into Taizhonggang Rd and then Hwy 12) runs northwest through the heart of the city.

### Information

#### INTERNET ACCESS

**Internet café** (per hr NT40; 8th floor, Taichung Central Mall) Open 24 hours.

#### INTERNET RESOURCES

The city government's website (www.tccg .gov.tw/eng/index.htm) and the county's website (www.taichung.gov.tw) are useful and list some obscure sights and activities.

#### MONEY

There are plenty of banks and 7-Elevens with ATMs on Taizhonggang Rd. The **Bank of Taiwan** ( ☎ 2222 4001; Sec 1, 140 Zuyou Rd) offers moneychanging facilities in addition to an ATM.

#### TOURIST INFORMATION

The locally produced *Compass Magazine* (www.taiwanfun.com) is available free at the tourist office and many restaurants and shops around town. It's an excellent source of information about the city and you can download the latest copy of the magazine from the website.

**Tourist Information Centre** ( ☎ 2254 0809; 1F, 95 Gangheng St; ⏰ 9am-5pm Mon-Fri) The centre has useful English-language brochures on Taichung and other regions of Taiwan.

### Sights

#### CHINGMING 1ST STREET 精明一街

This one block stretch of cobbled **road** (Jīngmíng Yijiē) was Taichung's first attempt at a pedestrian-only commercial zone. While the street is popular and has a few nice cafés and restaurants, it has been eclipsed by the new tea street beside Fengle Sculpture Park.

#### FENGLE SCULPTURE PARK & LAKESIDE TEA & SHOPPING STREET
豐樂雕塑公園, 湖水岸藝術街

With its numerous stone and metal sculptures, artificial waterfall, small lake and

WESTERN TAIWAN

---

**TYPHOON MINDULLE**

On 1 July 2004, the worst typhoon to hit Taiwan in some 25 years, typhoon Mindulle, swept across central and southern Taiwan. The damage was particularly severe in Taichung and Nantou Counties, and in Alishan. Some roads and properties in these areas were researched prior to the typhoon, and may have been damaged or destroyed since, so be sure to check ahead before you go.

# WESTERN TAIWAN

0 ——————— 20 km
0 ——————— 12 miles

Taiwan Strait

To Taipei
To Taipei
To Ilan

Syueshan (3883m)
Wuling Farm
Sheiba National Park
Techi Reservoir
Taroko National Park
Houli
Fengyuan
Encore Gardens
Guguan
Lishan
Kuanyun
Tienhsiang
Taroko Gorge
Changhua
Hohuanshan (3416m)
Tsuifeng
Tayuling
Chilaishan (3607m)
Hsiulin
TAICHUNG
Huisun Forest Reserve
Wushe
Chingching Farm
Tunyuan
Chihsingtan Beach
Lugang
Taiwan Folk Village
Chung Tai Chan Temple
Puli
Aowanta Forest
Tienchih
Hualien
Caotun
Chunghsing Village
Yuchih
Formosan Aboriginal Cultural Village
Nengkaoshan (3349m)
Liyu Lake
Huatien River
Mailiao
Jiji
Shuili
Checheng
Sun Moon Lake
Sun Moon Lake National Scenic Area
Ershui
Luku
Fenghuang Valley
Chichi Beach
Touliu
Chushan
Sitou
Shanlinhsi
Beigang
Minhsiung
Meishan
Ruili
Tsaoling
Fengshan
Dongpu
Fengpin
Alishan National Scenic Area
Alishan
Yushan (3952m)
Juisui Hot Springs
Juisui
Shihtiping
Chiayi
159
Fenqihu
Shihcho
Tatachia
Hungyeh Hot Springs
Tropic of Cancer
Putai
Shanmei
Yushan National Park
Eight Fairy Cave
Yenshui
Baihe Reservoir
Guanziling
Tienchih
Yuli
Hsiukuluan River
Nankunshen
Sinying
Tsengwen Reservoir
Chiayi Farm
Meishan
Tienchih Yakou
Antung Hot Springs
Matou
Wushantou Reservoir
Kuanshan (3666m)
Litao
Wulu
Fuli
Yuching
Chiahsien
Paolai
Haituan
Chengkung
Tsochen
Nanhua
Laonong
Kuanshan
River
Sinhua
Mt Tsao Moon World
Liugui
Shanping Forest
Tungho
TAINAN
Luigui Tunnels
Tengchih Forest Recreation Area
Kuanmiao
Meinong
Dona
Pacific Ocean
Chishan
Maolin
Maolin National Scenic Area
Pehan
Shanyuan Beach
Kaoshu
Saichia
Wutai
Taitung
Chengching Lake
22
Ali
Chihpen
KAOHSIUNG
Sandimen
Chihpen Hot Springs
Green Island (Lutao)
Fengshan
10
Pingdong
Haocha
Linyuan
27
Donggang
Fangliao
Little Liuchiu Island
Dapeng Bay
Tawu
Taiwan Strait
Shiuhai Grasslands
Fengkang
Shuangliou Forest Recreation Area
199
26
26
Sichongshi
Lanyu (Orchid Island)
Hengchun
Kenting National Park
Kenting
Eluanbi

WESTERN TAIWAN

# CENTRAL TAICHUNG

To Freeway (20km);
Taichung Harbour (20km)

Qinghai Rd

Wenxin Rd

Hankou Rd

Xitun Rd

Taizhonggang Rd

Shizheng Rd

Zhongming Rd

Wenxin 1st Rd

Gancheng Rd

Jingcheng Rd

Huamei W St

Daye Rd

Little Europe

Canal District

Meicun Rd

Liming Rd

Huiwen Rd

Gongyi Rd

Dadun Rd

Dongxing Rd

Huamei St

Xiangshang Rd

Zhongming S Rd

Chungmei St

Meicun Rd

People's Park

Wuquan W Rd

Wu Quan Parkway

Wanhe Rd

Nantun Rd

Wuquan 5th St

Xiangxin S Rd

Wenxin S 5th St

Fengle Sculpture Park

**WESTERN TAIWAN**

Hiker descends the trail at Mt Yushan (p235)

MARTIN MOOS

MARTIN MOOS

Dona Hot Springs (p260)

Sunrise, Central Cross-Island Hwy (p153)

MARTIN MOOS

MARTI

Festive paper dolls, Tainan (p239)

MARTIN MOOS

Man on a bicycle

Ghost money, Matsu Temple (p242), Tainan

MARTI

Lanterns on the Love River (p254), Kaohsiung

JOHN BORTHWICK

0 — 2 km
0 — 1 mile

**E** **F** **G** **H**

To Taichung Folklore
Park (1km)

**1**

Taiyuan Rd

Chungming Rd

Jinhua N Rd

Daya Rd

Dehua St

Minchuan Rd

Jianxing St

Chungteh Rd

Beitun Rd

**12**

**2**

● 8

Chungcheng
Park

**11**

Yingcai Rd

Guanqian Rd

Sanmin Rd

Wuquan Rd

**3**

Sports
Stadium

Gongyuan Rd

Lane 229

**29**

Minquan Rd

Sanmin Rd

Shuangshih Rd

Baseball
Stadium

Yingcai Rd

Zhongshan Rd

Taiping Rd

Mintsu Rd

Chingwu Rd

**4**

Minquan Rd

Gongyuan Rd

Taichung
Park

Wuquan Rd

Zhonghua Rd

Kuang'fu Rd

Chenpkung Rd

Zhongshan Rd

**21**

Zuyou Rd

Fuxing Rd

Liuchuan E Rd

**6**

Mintsheng Rd

**1**

Shuangshih Rd

Nanking Rd

**5**

To Taipei

**3**
**5**

**40**

Liuchuan W Rd

Linsen Rd

Sanmin Rd

Kangle St

Shihfu Rd

**2**

Zuyou Rd

Liuchuan St

**18**

**41**

**36**

**35** **39**

Train
Station

Lide St

**1**

Fuxing Rd

Taichung Rd

**6**

To Kaohsiung (190km)

Zhongxiao Rd

Jiancheng Rd

**3**

**23**

WESTERN TAIWAN

nicely landscaped environment, the **sculpture park** (Fēnglè Diāosù Gōngyuán), is pleasant enough on its own. Add in the adjacent **tea street** (*chá jiē*), far superior to Chingming 1st St, and you've got one of the nicest neighbourhoods in Taichung to while away an afternoon or evening.

The tea street, which is actually two streets not one, is not on the lake but across the road from the park. One street faces Xiangxin South Rd, while the other lies inside a community square. The inner square is more interesting as it is embellished with fish ponds, benches, street lamps and a small corner store constucted in the likeness of an old-fashioned Taiwanese neighbourhood shop. The atmosphere of the street is decidedly upmarket, however, and you'll find many classy restaurants and cafés that open around noon and close about 10pm (all are closed on Mondays).

### TAIWAN MUSEUM OF ART 美術館

The **museum** (Táiwān Měishùguǎn; ☎ 2372 3552; 2 Wuquan W Rd; ◷ 9am-5pm, closed Mon) was still in the process of reconstruction at the time of writing. It should be ready by the summer of 2004. If it's not, small exhibitions of local and international artists will still be held in finished rooms. When the museum is completely up and running, a nominal entrance fee will be charged.

### TAICHUNG MUNICIPAL CULTURAL CENTRE 台中市文化中心

The **centre** (Táizhōngshì Wénhuà Zhōngxīn; ☎ 2372 7311; 600 Yincai Rd; admission free; ◷ 9am-5pm) is just east of the art museum on the same grounds. The centre has a library and several small exhibition rooms with interesting folk-art displays. An English brochure explains the centre's various functions.

### NATIONAL MUSEUM OF NATURAL SCIENCE 自然科學博物館

This was Taiwan's first **museum of science** (Zìrán Kēxué Bówùguǎn; ☎ 2322 6940; www.nmns.edu.tw; 1 Guanqian Rd; ◷ 9am-5pm, closed Mon; admission exhibition hall adult/child NT100/50, botanic garden adult/child NT20/10, space centre adult/child NT100/50, IMAX 3D theatre adult/child NT 70/30) and though lacking English explanations (except for display titles) it's still worth visiting for the visually interesting dioramas, models and exhibitions. The museum is divided into various buildings, or centres, most of which have their own entrance charges. The Byzantine fee structure is explained in English at the ticket window. To get to the museum take Taichung Bus Company bus 71.

### PAOCHUEH TEMPLE 寶覺寺

This **Buddhist temple** (Bǎojué Sì; 140 Jianxing St; admission free; ◷ 8am-5pm) features one of the largest and fattest Milefo (laughing) Buddhas in all of Taiwan. The 30m-high statue sits against a backdrop of old apartments. It has recently been given a new coat of yellow paint and is very photogenic.

## WANHE & WENCHANG TEMPLES
萬和宮, 文昌公廟
These two temples are in an old section of the newly bustling Nantun District. **Wanhe Temple** (Wànhé Gōng), a third-rank historical site, is dedicated to Matsu. The flat, grey marble outside wall and the refurbished ceiling are particularly beautiful.

The much younger **Wenchang Temple** (Wénchāng Gōng) is a branch of the original Wenchang Temple (completed in 1871) near the folklore park. Students come to these temples to ask the god Wenchang Tichun to assist them in passing exams. Near the altar you will often see a box filled with photocopies of students' test applications.

## TAICHUNG FOLKLORE PARK 台中民俗公園
The **park** (Mínsú Gōngyuán; ☎ 2245 1310; 73 Lu Shun Rd, Sec 2; adult/child NT50/20; ◷ 9am-5pm Tue-Fri, 9am-7pm Sat & Sun) is divided into several sections: there's a house built to display the trappings of a typical middle-class family with southern Fukien roots, a folk-art gallery with a tea ceremony house, and a plaza where special cultural events (such as traditional-dance and acrobatic displays) are staged during holidays. Note that when special holiday shows are scheduled the price of admission goes up (adult/child NT200/150). To get to the park take Renyou bus 105.

## ART STREET 藝術街
Here's another **road** (Yìshù Jiē) chock-a-block with cafés, restaurants and shops – this one with the atmosphere of an alternative city-centre neighbourhood. One interesting place to visit is the square on your right as you head up the road from the 7-Eleven. Here you'll find a number of artist shops, including a custom-made eyeglasses shop and sand-painting studio on the 2nd floor. Canadian leather craftsman and mask maker Roman, also on the 2nd floor, can help if you are interested in classes with any of the artists, including himself.

To get to Art St, take Renyou bus 35 or Taichung 22 and get off at Tunghai University. Spend a little time walking around the nicely landscaped campus and then walk up the hill a few blocks until you come to a big

intersection with an overpass. Turn right and walk a few more blocks until you see a 7-Eleven. Turn left and you are on Art St.

## Sleeping
### BUDGET
**Taichung Hostel** (Liánqín Táizhōng Zhāodàisuǒ; ☎ 2372 1935; 400 Meicun Rd, Sec 1; d/tw NT1800/2400) This is not a true hostel but a government-run hotel. It is the best budget accommodation deal in Taichung. Rooms are large, spotlessly clean and discounted 40% on weekends and 50% on weekdays. The hostel is on a busy road but it's just blocks from the art gallery, Wu Quan Parkway and Little Europe.

**Fuh Chun Hotel** ( ☎ 2228 3181; 1 Zhongshan Rd; r from NT500) This hotel has long been popular with foreign travellers and Taiwanese students. It is just across from the train station, on the left as you exit. The women who run the place are exceptionally nice and make a point of offering fresh fruit to their guests every day. All rooms are fine; the price seems to depend more on size than quality.

### MID-RANGE
**Park Hotel** (Jìnghuá Dàfàdiàn; ☎ 2220 5181; 17 Gung-yuan Rd; d/tw with breakfast NT1900/3360) The best feature of this hotel is that it is just across from pretty, 100-year-old Taichung Park (Táizhōng Gōngyuán). Rooms are basic and clean, though clearly ageing. Discounts of 50% are normal.

**Ful Won Hotel** (Fùwáng Dàfàdiàn; ☎ 2326 5436; 636 Wenxin Rd; s/d/tw with breakfast NT2350/2900/3200) This bright, professionally run hotel sits directly across from the big Jade Market. There is a 20% discount on rooms on weekdays, which makes staying here a good deal if you are looking for a little more luxury.

### TOP END
**Landis Taichung** (Yǒngfēngzhàn Lìzhì Jiǔdiàn; ☎ 2326 8008; 9 Taizhonggang Rd, Sec 2; d/tw/ste NT6000/6800/8800; ▣ ) The Landis is close to the city's commercial district and about 10km from Taichung's airport, making it a convenient location for the business traveller. Rooms feature high-speed Internet access and high-end comfort rather than great luxury. The hotel has a health club.

**Evergreen Laurel Hotel** (Chángróng Guìguān Jiǔdiàn; ☎ 2313 9988; 6 Taizhonggang Rd, Sec 2; d/tw/ste NT3800/5600/9400; ▣ ) Also close to the business district and airport, the Evergreen Laurel has a more spacious and relaxed atmosphere than the Landis. Facilities are still top-notch and include a business centre with English-speaking staff, a number of excellent restaurants and cafés and a health club with squash courts.

## Eating

### BUDGET

There are dozens of cheap noodle, Japanese fast-food and pizza places clustered around the train-station area. The **Chunghsiao Night Market** (Zhōngxiào Yèshì; 5pm-2am), behind the train station, is well known for its good, traditional and cheap food.

**Shantung Dumplings & Beef Noodles** (Shāndōng Jiǎoziguǎn Niúròu Miànguǎn; 96 Gongyi Rd; beef noodles NT80; 11am-9pm) At this completely ordinary-looking shop, tasty traditional home cooking with a Shantung province flavour is served in a pleasant atmosphere of jazz and blues. The beef noodles are a must-try, or you might like to taste the beef rolls (*niǔròu juǎnbǐng*; one roll NT70), a standard Shantung province dish that is not often seen in other dumpling shops.

**Finga's Base Camp** (Fēnggé Cāntīng; 2327 7750; 61 Zhongming S Rd; 7am-10pm) A deli, restaurant, butchery and bakery all in one.

### MID-RANGE

**Da Da Teahouse** ( 2221 7939; 11F 186 Fushing Rd; meals from NT300; 7am-10pm) This classy establishment strives for an authentic Cantonese atmosphere with traditional pushcarts and delicious dim sum dishes. The restaurant is in the Taichung Central Mall behind the train station.

**Pumpkin House** (Nánguāwū Niǔ'àoliáng Yìdàlì Cāntīng; 2372 8456; 108 Wu Quan 4th St; meals from NT350; 11am-midnight) The area a few blocks south of the Taichung art gallery, known as Wu Quan Parkway, has developed into a solid strip of highly individual restaurants. One of the most popular is the Pumpkin House, set in a quaint two-storey red-brick house, serving a mostly Italian menu. This is a place to linger and enjoy your food.

**Feng Chuan 1999 Restaurant** (Fēngzàn Yìjiǔjiǔjiǔ Cāntīng; 2473 5880; 712-2 Xiangxian S Rd; mains from NT260; lunch & dinner) Here's a real snazzy-looking place in which to enjoy a variety of tasty Chinese dishes. The restaurant is on the Lakeside Tea and Shopping St, across from Fengle Park.

### TOP END

**Smooth Bar & Grill** ( 2329 3468; 5-7 Lane 50, Jingcheng Rd; mains from NT300; 3pm-1am) This classic-looking bar and grill comes highly recommended. The international menu offers curries, steaks, pastas, goulash and more. The bar is well stocked and has a big-screen TV for watching sports.

**Fatty's Family Style Italian Restaurant** (Pàngzǎi Yìdàlì Cāntīng; 2319 4898; www.fattys.com.tw/index.htm; 1 Lane 50, Jingcheng Rd; mains NT250; 11.30am-10pm) Fatty's is right beside Smooth, its casual sister restaurant.

**Sono (Yuan) Japanese Restaurant** (Yuán Rìběn Liàolǐ Cāntīng; 2302 2024; 19 Lane 229, Minquan Rd; meals from NT800; lunch & dinner) In an area populated with numerous Japanese restaurants sits the oldest of them all. For over 17 years Sono has been serving Japanese food tasty enough to attract the past two presidents to dine there.

## Drinking

For tea or coffee head to one of the 'tea streets'. There are a dozen or more places to sit and relax (some with outdoor seating) in both locations. If you're looking for beer or cocktails head to Little Europe or the Canal District.

**Chun Shui Tang** (春水堂; Chūnshuǐtáng; pearl milk tea NT55) This popular place, where people say pearl milk tea (*jēnjū nǎichá*) was invented, has locations on both streets.

**Chubby's** (Yuángǔngǔn Měishífāng; 11 Jing Ming Rd; beer NT120) A come-as-you-are expat hang-out.

**La Bodega** (3 Jingcheng 2nd St; beer NT120) This is an intimate, if slightly cramped, Spanish theme bar.

**Londoner** (168 Gongyi Rd; beer NT120) Try this one with its cool blue-lit lounge zone and a casual open bar area where you can watch sports on TV.

**Smooth Bar & Grill** ( 2329 3468; 5-7 Lane 50, Jingcheng Rd; drinks from NT150; 3pm-1am) Older travellers will probably enjoy a drink here.

**Wu Wei Tsao Tang Teahouse** (Wúwéicǎotáng; 2329 6707; 106 Gongyi Rd; 10am-1pm) This delightful old-style teahouse invites guests to relax and drink tea the old-fashioned way. Soft Chinese music, thick willow trees and the swish of water from the traditional carp pool keep the outside traffic noise to a minimum. A package of tea leaves costs NT400 and the 'water fee' is NT120 per person. Snacks and set meals are also available.

## Entertainment
### CINEMAS
**Warner Village Cinema** (Huá'nà Wēixiù Yǐngchéng) Tiger City Mall (4-6F, 120-1 Henan Rd, Sec 3) Taichung Central Mall (4F, 186 Fushing Rd, Sec 4) You can book tickets in advance on the Warner Village website (www. warnervillage.com.tw).

**8½ Classic Theatre** (Bāyòu Erfēnzhīyī Fēiguāndiàn Jùchǎng; 592 Hueiwen St; ☾ 6pm-midnight, closed Tue) Movie fans will be thrilled with this little café-cum-art-house theatre/video store. Owned and run by film lover Mr Huang, 8½ offers large-screen viewings of classic and new art-house films. For long-term residents, Mr Huang sells memberships allowing you to rent from his extensive collection of films (50 rentals NT3000).

## Shopping
Lakeside Tea and Shopping St, across from Fengle Park, is a great spot for upmarket crafts and antiques.

**Ceramic Art** (Héxuān Táoyì Gōngfáng; 321-12 Wenxin S 5th Rd; ☾ noon-11pm) This place is run by well-known ceramicist Hong Chi-shuen and offers small bowls for a few hundred NT and large vases with a special cracked petal design for tens of thousands. Recommended are the Tang dynasty-style tea sets. The sets (NT6000) come wrapped in a blue cloth bag that folds up to resemble a persimmon.

**Wenxin Jade Market** (Wénxīn Yù Shìchǎng; 651 Wenxin Rd, Sec 2; ☾ Sat & Sun) Just across from the Ful Won Hotel, you can't miss the sign that reads 'Big Jade Market' in English.

## Getting There & Away
### AIR
**UNI** ( ☎ 02-2513 5533) and **Far Eastern Air Transport** ( ☎ 02-3393 5388) have daily flights between Taichung and Taipei for around NT1300.

### BUS
**Fengyuan Bus Company** ( ☎ 2222 3454), to the left of the train station in front of the Golden Plaza Department Store, runs frequent buses from Taichung to Puli (NT100, one hour). In Puli you can catch a Fengrong bus (NT45, 30 minutes, every hour) to Sun Moon Lake. To get to Sun Moon Lake directly, catch a Renyou Bus Company bus (NT181, 8am and 2.20pm). The **ticket office** ( ☎ 2225 5166; 110 Linchuan St) for intercity travel is just east of Jungjeng St.

### TRAIN
From Taipei (NT375, two hours) and Kaohsiung (fast/slow train NT470/363, 2½/three hours) there are frequent trains to Taichung from early morning until almost midnight.

## Getting Around
### TO/FROM THE AIRPORT
Taichung's Shuinan airport is in the Hsitun District, about 12km from the city centre. If you want to bus it, catch Taichung bus 105 or 115 from Luchuan St. Buses leave every 15 to 40 minutes.

### PUBLIC TRANSPORT
The bus system in Taichung is not great, but you can get to most of the major attractions and neighbourhoods. Renyou Bus Company runs the green buses and **Taichung Bus Company** ( ☎ 2225 5563) the red. Both charge NT18 for a single journey within the city.

Taichung Bus Company runs its buses from a station directly across from the train station and also from Luchuan St, a block northwest of the train station. Renyou buses also run from Luchuan St.

### SCOOTER
You can rent scooters at various shops (NT600 a day) to the right of the train station behind the bus station.

## CHANGHUA (ZHANGHUA) 彰化縣
☎ 04 / pop 231,000
Changhua City (Zhānghuà), the county capital and political heart of the area, makes an ideal base from which to explore the county and even has some treats of its own.

## Orientation & Information
Changhua is not a compact city, but you needn't wander too far from the train station during your stay. Even the Great Buddha Statue is only a couple of kilometres to the east. You can change money at **Bank of Taiwan** ( ☎ 722 5191; 130 Chunghua Rd) or **ICBC** ( ☎ 723 2111; 39 Kuangfu Rd).

The Changhua **tourist office** ( ☎ 723 7650; 3F, 39 Kuangfu Rd) has English brochures and at the time of writing was reportedly training English-speaking staff and guides.

A valuable source of travel information is the county's English website (http://tourism.chcg.gov.tw) and the city's website (www.changhua.gov.tw).

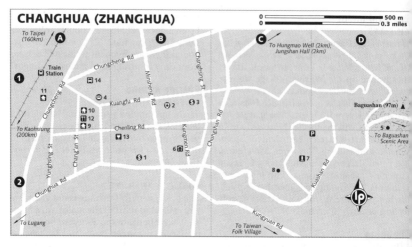

**CHANGHUA (ZHANGHUA)**

## Sights

### HONGMAO WELL 紅毛井

This 300-year-old **well** (Hóngmáo Jǐng; 542-1 l Jungshan Rd, Sec 2) is the last of the original Dutch-built wells (hence the name Hongmao, meaning 'red hair') in central Taiwan. Incredibly, the well still produces excellent-quality water and is used today by the families who live in the shanties behind **Jungshan Hall** (Zhōngshān Táng), a heritage building that was receiving a much-needed facelift at the time of writing.

The well is an odd sight these days with its crumbling stone base, sheet-metal lid and modern pumps and valves, all set under a tin roof that also holds a small earth god shrine (tǔdì gōng) and washing pool where old women still wash clothes by hand. Add to this the anomaly of being just off a very busy street, in an otherwise modern neighbourhood, and you've really got something to tell the folks about back home. To get to the well you are advised to take a taxi.

### CONFUCIUS TEMPLE 孔廟

One of the oldest **Confucius temples** (Kǒng Miào; 6 Kungmen Rd) in Taiwan, this beauty was built in 1726 and ranks as a first-class historical relic. The main attractions are the carvings, the inscribed plaque in the ancestral hall donated by Qing-dynasty emperor Chien Long and the dawn ceremony that takes place on Confucius' birthday every year (28 September).

## Sleeping

**Ing Shan Hotel** (Yīngshān Dàfàndiàn; ☎ 722 9211; 12╡ Chang'an St; d/tw NT700/1200) This hotel offers slightly musty, but otherwise clean, basic rooms.

**Rich Royal Hotel** (Fùhuáng Dàfàndiàn; ☎ 723 7117 97 Chang'an St; r from NT1000) This place feels like a love hotel when you walk down the long garage (where you can park if you are driving) to the check-in counter but it is, in fact, popular with families. Rooms are slightly frilly in design.

**Taiwan Hotel** (Táiwān Dàfàndiàn; ☎ 722 4681 48 Chungcheng Rd, Sec 2; s&d NT1200, tw NT3500) One

WESTERN TAIWAN

of the nicer hotels in Changhua and often used by resident expats to accommodate their visiting friends and family. The hotel is just to the right of the train station as you exit.

## Eating & Drinking

Changhua is famous for its meatballs (ròu yuán) and you'll find many places to try them out on Chenling St. The shop at No 203 is reported to have the tastiest and healthiest meatballs in Changhua. For more local foods check out the informative website www.changhua.gov.tw/web_e/information /infor_03.asp.

**Cat Mouse Noodle** (Māoshǔmiàn; 126 Chang'an St; noodles NT50; ⏰ 9am-8.30pm) The Changhua tourist website claims this shop's special noodle dish is one of the three culinary treasures of the city. The shop's odd name arose because the owner's nickname sounds like 'cat mouse' in Taiwanese and not because of anything you'll find in the food.

**New York Pub** (Niǔyuè Yìnyuè; 135 Chenling St; beer/ cocktails NT120/200; ⏰ 8pm-3am) Those in need of a drink will find one here and a friendly atmosphere to boot.

## Getting There & Away

From Taipei (fast/slow train NT416/332, 2½/three hours) and Kaohsiung (fast/slow train NT432/333, two/three hours) there are frequent trains from morning till late at night.

Buses to Lugang (NT38, 30 minutes) leave about every 10 minutes from the bus station near the train station. There are five special tourist buses (NT35, 40 minutes) a day to the Taiwan Folk Village. The earliest bus leaves at 9.30am.

## TAIWAN FOLK VILLAGE 台灣民俗村

Set deep in the hilly countryside off County Hwy 1, the **Taiwan Folk Village** (Táiwān Mínsú Cūn; ☎ 04-786 0815; adult/child NT350/300; ⏰ 9am-5pm) preserves the traditional architecture, arts and food of days gone by. Here you'll find accurate reproductions not only of grand structures such as temples and halls, but also of simple farmhouses made of bamboo and thatch. This is an excellent place to take photos.

There are five special tourist buses (NT35, 40 minutes) a day from Changhua. The earliest bus leaves at 9.30am.

## LUGANG (LUKANG) 鹿港

☎ 04 / pop 87,000
Ninety percent of Lugang (Lùgǎng) is as nondescript as most small towns in Taiwan. But then there is that other 10%. Comprising some of the oldest and most gorgeous temples in the country, and featuring curiously curved streets, art museums in heritage buildings and dusty old shops where equally dusty old masters create colourful fans, lanterns and tin pieces, it is this small part of Lugang that justifiably brings in the crowds.

WESTERN TAIWAN

---

### THE VIEW FROM BAGUASHAN

Changhua is best known, in fact famous, for the 22m-high **Great Buddha Statue** (Dà Fó Xiàng) that sits atop Baguashan (八卦山) looking down over the city. The statue, and its surrounding grounds, are noted for a harmonious and tranquil atmosphere. But it wasn't always so.

Bagua mountaintop has a unique tilt, which allows one to see not only over the whole city, but far out to sea as well. Not surprisingly, for centuries it was a very important military lookout post. After the Sino–Japanese War gave ownership of Taiwan to Japan, a great battle was fought on these grounds by Taiwanese patriots against the colonising Japanese. That battle put a permanent end to the military post on Baguashan.

In 1962 the Great Buddha was completed after almost 10 years of work. Visitors are permitted to walk in and up the statue, though they can no longer go to the top floor and look out of Buddha's eyes and ears. Shabby dioramas at each level depict major events in the Buddha's life.

Other notable sights in the area include the two giant **stone lions** that guard Lord Buddha, the **Nine Dragons Pond** (Jiǔlóng Chí), the park on top of Baguashan featuring **Chungling Pagoda** (Zhōnglíng Tǎ) and **lookouts** over the city. At the time of writing the park was being spruced up with new wooden walkways, pavilions, an aquarium and playground areas for children and many areas were closed off to public access.

You can easily walk up to Baguashan from the train station area or take a 10-minute taxi ride.

People call Lugang a 'living museum' and this is true as much for buildings and streets as it is for the food. Traditional dishes are cheap and readily available near all of the major sights. Look for the enticingly named phoenix eye cake, dragon whiskers and shrimp monkeys, among many other dishes.

On the central coast and just half an hour from Changhua by bus, Lugang is easily reached from anywhere on the west coast.

### History

Lugang translates as 'deer harbour', and once large herds of deer gathered here in the lush meadows adjacent to one of the best natural harbours on the west coast.

In the 17th century the Dutch came to hunt and trade pelts (which they sold to the Japanese to make samurai armour) and venison. Trade continued into the 18th century and Lugang became one of the most thriving commercial cities and ports in Taiwan. Over the years settlers from different provinces and ethnic groups in China made their home here and, almost as a gift to the future, left a fabulous legacy of temples and buildings constructed in various regional styles.

In the 19th century silt deposits began to block the harbour and in 1895 the Japanese closed it to all large ships. The city began to decline. To make matters worse, conservative elements in Lugang refused

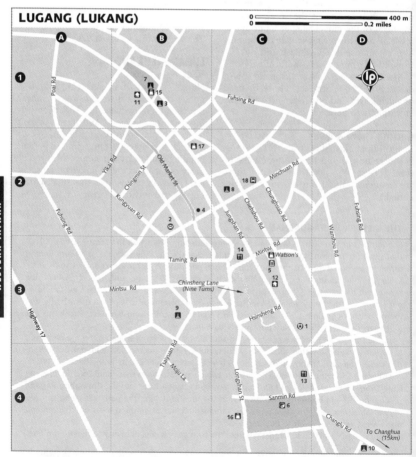

LUGANG (LUKANG)

in the early 20th century to allow trains and modern highways to be built near their city. Lugang became a backwater, only to be reborn decades later when modern Taiwanese began to search for a living connection with the past.

## Orientation & Information

You can cover the town on foot in one long day, but two are advised if you want to take your time and enjoy more than a few moments at each site.

Look out for the excellent English brochure about Lugang available at tourism offices around the country. The brochure is especially interesting for the detailed layout of Longshan Temple.

Lugang City has its own website (www .lukang.gov.tw). It's an informative introduction to the history and sites.

## Sights

### LONGSHAN TEMPLE 龍山寺

Though originally a rather small temple, the present-day **Longshan Temple** (Lóngshān Sì) covers an area of more than 100 sq metres. It's considered the best-preserved Qing-dynasty temple in Taiwan and really is a glorious architectural wonder to behold. Unfortunately, at the time of writing only the main 'Mountain Gate' and the entrance to the front court could be seen as repairs were

carried out behind. If you visit before they are finished (and you still should), check out the dragon pillars beside the doors to the front court. One dragon reaches up to the sky, while the other points to the ground.

### MATSU TEMPLE 天后宮

Another large and really splendid structure, this **temple** (Tiānhòu Gōng) was renovated in 1936 and is completely accessible today. It is said that the Matsu statue in this temple was brought to Taiwan by a Qing-dynasty general. The statue is now called 'The Black-Faced Matsu', as decades of incense smoke have discoloured her original complexion. The back of the temple holds a display of old weapons.

The area around the Matsu Temple is pedestrian-only and great crowds gather here on weekends. Vendors and the surrounding stores sell a variety of traditional snacks, sweets and drinks. The atmosphere is festive and feels authentic rather than touristy.

### FOLK ARTS MUSEUM 民俗文物館

You'll want to visit the **Folk Arts Museum** (Mínsú Wénwùguǎn; ☎ 777 2019; 152 Jungshan Rd; adult/child NT130/70; ☷ 9am-5pm, no entry after 4.30pm, closed Mon), as much for the beauty of the building and its rooms as for what it contains inside. Built in the Japanese era and originally the residence of a wealthy local family, the museum now houses a large collection of daily-life folk artefacts.

The museum is behind Jungshan Rd and is a little tricky to get to. It's best to approach it from Mintsu Rd, where you will see signs (in English) leading you down a narrow alley just before the Watson's drugstore.

### NINE-TURNS LANE 九曲巷

Here's something for the kid in you: a long, narrow **lane** (Jiǔqū Xiàng) with sharp zig-zagging turns that prevent you from seeing more than 10m in a straight line. Originally built to prevent the entry of bandits and the cold 'September Winds', the Nine-Turns Lane (actually named after the ninth month, September, and not the number of turns) is now a favourite spot for enjoying the old time atmosphere that pervades much of Lugang. (It's also the perfect place for hiding from your friends!)

WESTERN TAIWAN

## OLD MARKET STREET 古市街

The merchant streets of old Lugang are well represented (if you skip the vendors selling coffee) by the shops lining both sides of the curved, red-tiled lanes of what is now called the **Old Market Street** (Gǔshì Jiē). Many shop fronts have been restored and interiors decorated with antiques. You can shop for traditional items here or just enjoy a stroll through history.

The street makes for some interesting photos, especially where half a well sticks out from a wall. This well, appropriately named **Half-sided Well** (Bàntiān Jǐn), was built to share: the rich family inside the complex used the interior half, while the poor and passers-by were permitted to use the outside half.

## Tours

The **Lugang Cultural Foundation** ( ☎ 778 0096; tours NT2000) runs three-hour English tours on weekends. You must book at least one week in advance.

## Festivals & Events

Every year, Lugang hosts a four-day **folk-arts festival** that begins three days before the Dragon Boat Festival. This is a crowded but rewarding time to come. Matsu's birthday, the 23rd day of the third lunar month (usually in April), is also cause for an intense celebration at the Matsu Temple.

---

### ANNUAL ROCK FIGHT IN LUGANG

Surely one of the most unusual customs of old Taiwan had to be the rock fight held in Lugang every spring. During the fight, men from one particular family name would line up and throw rocks at men from another name. The atmosphere was not one of aggression and hostility but of festivity. Children and women stood on the sides and cheered, and snacks were sold by vendors who seem to have been as ubiquitous back then as they are today.

The festival died out a few years before WWII. When participants were asked why they joined in such bloody sport, some explained that it was 'tradition', while others noted that if blood was not spilled in the spring, disaster could not be averted in the coming year.

---

## Sleeping

**Lugang Matsu Temple Pilgrims' Building** (Lùgǎng Tiānhòugōng Xiāngkè Dàlóu; ☎ 775 2508; 475 Jungshan Rd; s&d/tw NT800/1500) You don't have to be a pilgrim to stay here, and the location across from the Matsu Temple, in the pedestrian-only zone, puts you right in the heart of the action and food. Rooms have an almost hospital-room bareness but are spotlessly clean. The entire hotel may be booked out months in advance of Matsu's birthday and other important festivals.

**Quanzhong Hotel** (Quánzhōng Lǚshè; ☎ 777 2640; 104 Jungshan Rd; d/tw NT650/850) This hotel has clean, basic rooms and is on the main street close to all the attractions.

## Eating

Since the pedestrian-only zone was opened around Matsu Temple, the area has become a lively market of food stalls and small restaurants. Some famous local dishes to try are shrimp monkeys (xī xià), oyster omelettes (é ā jiān), meatballs (ròu yuán) and sweet treats such as cow-tongue crackers (níushé bǐng), dragon whiskers (lóngshū táng) and malt biscuits (maìyá mǐxiāng).

**A Chen Steamed Buns** (Āzhèn Ròubāo; 71 Jungshan Rd; box of 10 NT150; 9am-7pm) The buns (baòzi), stuffed with juicy pork fillings, are mouth-watering. Go around 3pm when the buns come out of the oven fresh but be prepared to line up.

**Yu Chen Chai** (Yùzhēnzhāi Shípǐn Yǒuxiàn Gōngsī; 168 Minsu Rd; 8am-11pm) Operating for five generations, this shop sells pastries based on Qing-dynasty recipes. Try the phoenix eye cake (fèngyǎn gāo) or the green bean cake (lùdòu gāo).

## Shopping

Lugang offers great shopping (or just browsing) if you're in the market for original crafts. On Jungshan Rd you'll find the following three shops where the owners have received 'Living Heritage' awards and are considered natural treasures for their skill and dedication in preserving old crafts. At these shops, and at others along Jungshan Rd, you can watch the masters at work.

**Wan Neng Tinware** (Wànnéng Xǐpù; 84 Jungshan Rd) The master here is a fourth-generation tinsmith. Items such as elaborate dragon boats and expressive masks are expensive but worth the price for their beauty and the skill involved in creating them.

**Mr Chen's Fan Shop** (Chéncháozōng Shǒugōngshàn; 400 Jungshan Rd) The shop is just on the right before you enter the pedestrian-only area near Matsu Temple. Fans go from a few hundred dollars for the small touristy ones, to thousands of dollars for the larger and more artistic creations. Mr Chen has been making fans since he was 16.

**Wu Tun-Hou Lantern Shop** (Wúdūnhòu Dēnglóngpù; 312 Jungshan Rd) Lanterns start at a few hundred dollars and continue up to many thousands for the most gorgeous items. Mr Wu has been making lanterns for 65 years.

## Getting There & Around
Buses to Changhua (NT38, 30 minutes) leave about every 10 minutes from the station on Minquan Rd.

## JIJI SMALL RAIL LINE 集集小火車線
The **Jiji Small Rail Line** (Jíjí Xiǎo Huǒchē) begins south of Changhua in the town of Ershui. Like the Pingxi, Alishan and Neiwan lines, this 19km narrow-gauge branch has been preserved to boost local tourism. The train ride is about 45 minutes long and begins in the wide, fertile plains of Ershui, Changhua County, proceeds into the forested hills around Jiji and ends at Checheng, a vehicle yard in Nantou County surrounded by high mountains.

There are six stations along the way, the most important of which are Ershui, Jiji and Shuili, a transit point to the Sun Moon Lake Scenic Area and Dongpu, and where you'll find the main headquarters for Yushan National Park.

While the train ride is short, the list of things to see and do in this area is long: you can cycle, hike, bird- and monkey-watch, as well as visit temples, museums and historic buildings. The famous Green Tunnel of Nantou is here, as is Songbo Ridge, a sacred spot for Taiwan's Taoists. You can visit any time of year, but give yourself two days to take everything in. Summer weekends can be very crowded but on weekdays and winter weekends you can have this sweet little getaway practically to yourself.

You can get to Ershui from anywhere along the West Coast Line, but note that not every train stops there. From Changhua (NT47) it's about a 30-minute journey. At Ershui station, alight and transfer to the Jiji Small Rail Line (there are signs in English telling you where to stand on the platform). You can buy your ticket on the train. It's NT44 from Ershui to Checheng and you are allowed to alight and reboard once along the way without buying another ticket. There are nine trains a day in either direction. You can pick up a schedule at any station or go to the Taiwan Railway website (http://203.67.46.20; note that Jiji is spelt Chii-Chii).

## Ershui 二水站
Ershui (Èrshuǐ) is the first station on the line. There's an ATM at the 7-Eleven a few blocks south of the train station down the main road.

### SIGHTS & ACTIVITIES
### Cycling
The Ershui **bike path** (jiǎotāchē zhuānyòng dào) is laid out to take you right through lush fields. The cycling-only path stretches for about 7km (at the time of writing it was being extended), though country roads intersect and you can certainly ride on these too if something in the distance takes your eye. The countryside is picturesque, with temples, shrines, traditional brick villas and pagodas popping up in unexpected places. Just to the north stands Songbo Ridge, with its thick forests and crumbling cliff faces, to break up the flat landscape.

To reach the path, turn right when you exit the train station. Go 100m and then turn right to cross the train tracks. You will see the bike path on your right. Give yourself at least three hours to explore.

If it is open, you can rent bikes (per hour/day NT30/100) and get simple noodle dishes and tea drinks at the **Life Teahouse** (☎ 04-879 2123), which is just to your right as you exit the train station. The owners lived in Canada for many years and speak English. Every bike has a map attached to it and you can ask the owners to circle some of the sites that are off the bike path, but easy to reach, such as **Mr Lin's Temple** (林先生廟; Lín Xiānshēng Miào) and the **Monkey Protection Area** (二水台灣獼猴保護區; Èrshuǐ Táiwān Míhóu Bǎohù Qū).

If the teahouse is closed, there might be other shops in the square renting bikes. If not, go on to Jiji.

WESTERN TAIWAN

## Shoutian Temple 受天宮

The **temple** (Shòutiān Gōng), built in 1745, sits on the highest point on **Songbo Ridge** (松柏嶺; Sōngbó Lǐng). The temple is about 3km from Ershui and the journey there takes you across the border into Nantou County.

The interior of the temple was heavily damaged by fire several years ago and has not been fully repaired to date. The exterior, though, is still intact and covered with high relief (check out the ornate 2m-wide dragon discs on either side of the entrance). The temple grounds also offer splendid views across the valley.

Even if you aren't a temple lover it is worth walking there as the path takes you through a forest so tranquil and lovely you half expect to see Winnie the Pooh come strolling down the lane. The forest is also a prime bird-watching (and listening) area.

It takes about an hour to reach the temple from the train station. The way is gently sloped until the end, where you must climb about 100 stairs. To begin, turn right as you leave the station and walk 100m to the train crossing. Turn right (the bike path is now to your right), cross the tracks and walk straight towards the ridge. When the road splits go left, and when it splits again go right. At a T-junction you'll see a small temple in front of you. Go left, and about 200m later when you see a sign (in Chinese) for the Shoutian Temple, turn right up a narrow road and continue until you reach a large car park. There is a map in the car park with English on it but you won't need it at this point. The path up to the temple begins on the far side of the car park.

You can return the same way you went up, or, after consulting the map at the temple, take a longer alternative route down.

### EATING

There is nothing more than simple dishes at the places around the train station. Bring your own food, or pick up sandwiches and snacks at the 7-Eleven.

## Jiji (Chi Chi) 集集

☎ 049

The fifth stop down the line, **Jiji** (Jíjí) offers the most tourist facilities. Maps (in Chinese only) can be purchased for NT10 at the train station. The map is called 'Jiji Passport' and shows the bike route (in orange)

and pictures of the local attractions and their locations.

### SIGHTS & ACTIVITIES

#### Jiji Station

The original Jiji Station was levelled in the 921 earthquake (p154). As part of a plan to boost tourism in the area the **station** was rebuilt to the standards of the simple Japanese-era original and has since become very popular with Taiwanese tourists looking for a photo op on the weekend.

#### Cycling

Jiji's 10km **bike path** (jiǎotàchē zhuānyòng dào) may be even better than Ershui's. The path is very easy to follow (except near the end), with stone distance markers and clear turning signs. Signs for sights were all in Chinese at the time of writing.

The path begins just to the right of the train station. Within the first kilometre you'll see a park with old military equipment in it, the **Mingxin Academy** (明新書院; Míngxīn Shūyuàn; ☎ 276 2374; 4 Dungchang Lane; admission free; ◷ 24hr) and the **Endemic Species Research Institute** (特有生物保育中心; Tèyǒu Shēngwù Bǎoyù Zhōngxīn; ☎ 276 1331; www.tesri.gov.tw; 1 Minsheng East Rd; adult/child NT50/30; ◷ 9am-4.30pm).

The academy, founded in 1882, was once a centre for Confucian studies but is now an historical site with model traditional farmhouses sprucing up the grounds. The Endemic Species Research Institute functions as a research centre and natural-history museum for plant and animal species endemic to Taiwan. Exhibits are all in Chinese.

Some attractions on the rest of the trail include **Wuchang Temple** (see opposite), the **Jiji Waterfall** (集集瀑布; Jíjí Pùbù), the **big tree** (大樟樹; dà zhāng shù) and the **sunflower gardens** (向日葵花園; xiàngrìkuí huāyuán).

You can rent bikes (per day/electric bikes per hour NT100) at numerous locations around the train station.

#### Green Tunnel of Nantou 綠色隧道

West of Jiji, along Hwy 152, is the famous **Green Tunnel of Nantou** (Lùsè Suìdào). This is not a true tunnel but a canopy formed over the road by the high branches of hundreds of camphor trees. The tunnel runs for 4.5km and is lit at night with thousands of

Christmas lights. You can cycle out to the tunnel but it's a bit of a hard slog up the hill outside Jiji and there can be a lot of trucks along the highway. It's better to take the train to Longquan (龍泉; Lóngquán) and walk to the tunnel area.

### Great Jiji Mountain 集集大山

Hiking up the **mountain** (Jíjí Dàshān; elevation 1390m) is the most strenuous activity in the area and can take either 90 minutes or three to four hours return depending where you start.

Most people begin about 15km west of Jiji on Hwy 16. Note that along the way there are signs (in Chinese) directing you towards the mountain, but none to tell you where to turn off Hwy 16 to get to the trailhead.

A short distance past the 14.5km mark look for a small road on the left with a fire-hazard sign on a fence beside it. You can begin your hike here or continue up the winding road for another 3km until you come to the real trailhead for Great Jiji Mountain (where once again you will see a sign in Chinese). The trail is a real mountain path, not a road, and takes about 90 minutes to hike up and down. The views from the top are outstanding.

### Wuchang Temple 武昌宮

This is one of the oddest sites billed as an attraction you're likely to come across in Taiwan. Previously unknown to outsiders, the **temple** (Wǔchāng Gōng) made its name after the 921 earthquake collapsed its lower floors leaving the roof to lie in ruins on the ground. Spectacular (and very photogenic) in its state of disrepair, the temple is now one of the first things people rush to see when they come to Jiji.

To get to the temple turn right as you leave the train station and walk about 10 minutes to Ba Zhang St (八張街). Turn left and walk another 10 minutes or so. The temple is on your left. You can also reach the temple on the bike path.

### SLEEPING

**Jiji Vacation Village** (集集渡假村; Jíjí Dùjiàcūn; ☎ 276 2988; 成功路205號; s&d/tw NT2200/3000; 🖳) This is the best, if not the only, accommodation in Jiji. Room are bright, immaculately clean and have wooden floors and large comfy beds. A buffet breakfast (7am to 9.30am) and use of the swimming pool

(fed with mountain water), steam room and spa are included.

To reach the hotel, go north from the train station to Cheng Gong Rd and turn right. The peach-coloured hotel, which looks like an apartment building, is on the right.

### EATING

**Plato** (251 Minquan Rd; set meals from NT180; ☯ 10am-9pm Mon-Fri, 9am-9pm Sat & Sun) Just right of the train station as you exit, Plato, inside a giant white windmill, has OK food and a soft, Mediterranean feel. Young children and couples will enjoy the swinging wooden benches that are used instead of chairs on the 1st floor. Outside, the restaurant has arranged its patio, rather oddly, in a strand of betel nut trees. This may be the first place in Taiwan to use betel nut trees for atmosphere but it works. And with the carp ponds and flowing water that make each table its own little island, this is a pleasant spot to enjoy a meal.

**Train Head Original Food Restaurant** (火車頭集集原味廚房; Huǒchētóu Jíjí Yuánwèi Chúfáng; 301 Minquan Rd; mains NT200; ☯ 11am-3pm Mon, Tue, Thu & Fri, 11am-8.30pm Sat & Sun) This popular Chinese-style restaurant has a motto: 'locally grown foods cooked in the traditional way'. Downstairs, the restaurant runs a shop that sells various local agricultural speciality items. There's whiskey (which tastes like a decent rum), fruit wine and assorted honey products, all at reasonable prices in creatively designed packages. They make nice gifts. The restaurant and shop are across the road from the station and to the right.

### Shuili 水里

☎ 049

The penultimate stop on the Jiji Line (the last stop is at the quaint station at **Checheng**) is Shuili (Shuǐlǐ), a bland little town set among stunning mountain scenery. The town's only tourist site is the **Snake Kiln** (p216), which is 3km up Hwy 16 and actually now part of the Sun Moon Lake Scenic Area. There is an ATM at the 7-Eleven to the left as you exit the train station.

**Yushan National Park Headquarters** (☎ 277 3121; www.ysnp.gov.tw; 300, Sec 1, Jungshan Rd; ☯ 9.30am-4.30pm) is in Shuili. Here you can find English brochures and films about the park, as well as the latest road and trail information. To reach the headquarters from Shuili train station, walk straight down Minsheng Rd about

1km until you reach the river. Turn right and walk another 1km to where the road connects with Hwy 16. Turn left and cross the bridge. The park headquarters is in the white building on the right. Usually someone working can speak passable English.

### SLEEPING

There are many cheap hotels clustered around the train station.

**Huantai Hotel** ( ☎ 277 2137; 83 Minquan Rd; r NT500-600) This is the best of the lot (which is not saying much). As you exit the train station turn right when you reach the road and walk for a few minutes. The hotel is on the south side of the road.

**Ya Chou Hotel** ( ☎ 277 2151; 264 Minquan Rd; s&d/tw NT800/1200) This place is a little further down, on the opposite side of the road from the Huantai. The rooms will do for an overnight stay but not much else.

**Long Jiang Hotel** ( ☎ 277 2164; 174 Minsheng Rd; r from NT700) Some rooms here have mountain views. To get to the hotel, go straight ahead as you leave the train station and walk one minute down Minsheng Rd.

### EATING

Locally grown fruit (bananas, lychees, grapes, guavas, plums) is available and can be purchased dried, pickled or fresh.

As at Ershui, there is nothing more than simple dishes at the places around the train station. Bring your own food, or pick up sandwiches and snacks at the 7-Eleven.

### GETTING THERE & AWAY
**Bus**

From Shuili you can catch buses to Snake Kiln (NT19, 10 minutes, every hour), Sun Moon Lake (NT42, 30 minutes, hourly), Puli (NT87, one hour, every hour) and Dongpu (NT97, one hour 20 minutes, every hour). There are two bus stations in Shuili, **Yuanlin Bus Company** (員林客運; ☎ 277 0041), which runs buses to Dongpu, and **Fengrong Bus Company** (豐榮客運; ☎ 277 4609), which runs buses to the Snake Kiln, Sun Moon Lake and Puli.

To reach the Yuanlin Bus Company, exit the train station and turn left on Minquan Rd. The station is on the opposite side of the road from the 7-Eleven and just past the food stalls. The Fengrong Bus Company is further down the road on the same side.

## SUN MOON LAKE 日月潭
☎ 049

This **lake** (Rìyuè Tán) was hard hit by the 921 earthquake. Hotels were levelled, forests devastated, temples toppled, trails destroyed and roads made impassable. And yet, as some argue, it was the best thing that could have happened.

As with many sights in Taiwan before the earthquake, hotels here were ageing and facilities shabby. The earthquake forced reconstruction and improvement. Government money poured in and new nature paths, bike routes, walkways, docks, scenic areas and one super-high-end luxury resort were established. To the surprise of everyone, more tourists than ever poured into the area, setting the stage for even more improvements.

Sun Moon Lake is the largest body of fresh water in Taiwan and has one of the island's most spectacular natural landscapes. In his blue period, Picasso would have had no end of inspiration. At an altitude of 762m, the lake is encompassed by a background of high, forested mountains and boasts good weather year round. Boating is popular on the lake, both touring in large craft or in DIY rowboats. There are a number of hiking trails, some that take many hours to complete, others that are just short strolls along the waterfront.

### Orientation & Information

Sun Moon Lake is part of the 9000-hectare Sun Moon Lake National Scenic Area under the control of the Nantou County government. The scenic area stretches north to include the Formosan Aboriginal Cultural Village, south to the Snake Kiln in Shuili and the old train station at Checheng, west to Great Jiji Mountain, and east to Mount Shuishe. You can get to all these places from the lake by public transport.

Accommodation is more than plentiful, with the majority of hotels centred in Shuishe Village, on the northwestern corner of the lake. First-time visitors should this consider this the default location, especially if they are travelling without their own vehicle. From the village you can catch a bus or boat to other spots around the lake.

There was much work being carried out at the time of writing to improve the lake for tourism. One exciting development to watch out for is a boardwalk around the lake, some sections of which are already in place. For more information ask at the tourism office.

### INTERNET RESOURCES
**Sun Moon Lake National Scenic Area** (www .sunmoonlake.gov.tw)

### MONEY
There is an ATM in the village but it only accepts Taiwanese bankcards.

### TOURIST INFORMATION
**Tourist Information Office** ( ☎ 285 5668; 🕙 8.30am-5pm) Situated in Shuishe Village, across the street from the pier. English-speaking staff are on hand to help with bus and boat tour information.

## Sights & Activities
### SHUISHE VILLAGE 水社村
People refer to **Shuishe Village** (Shuǐshè Cūn) as Sun Moon Lake Village. The cobbled main road, Minsheng Rd, is pedestrian-only. The area by the new **Shuishe Pier** (Shuǐshè Mǎtóu)

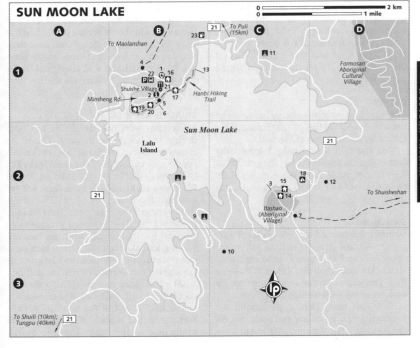

**SUN MOON LAKE**

0 ———— 2 km
0 ———— 1 mile

To Puli (15km)

To Maolanshan

Shuishe Village

Minsheng Rd

Hanbi Hiking Trail

Formosan Aboriginal Cultural Village

*Sun Moon Lake*

Lalu Island

To Shuisheshan

Itashao (Aboriginal Village)

To Shuili (10km); Tungpu (40km)

**WESTERN TAIWAN**

is particularly attractive and a great place to hang out day and night. The lookouts from **Meihe Garden** (Méihé Gōngyuán), up the hill towards the Lalu, are heavenly. At night, you can see the lights of Wenwu Temple, Itashao and Tsen Pagoda. When lit up, Wenwu Temple looks like a giant spider with red, slicked-back hair.

### ITASHAO 伊達邵碼頭

Across the lake from Shuishe is the unattractive village of **Itashao** (Yīdáshào). Note that the old name for Itashao was Dehuashe and this name still appears on the sign on the outskirts of the village. The road to the left as you enter the village leads to a block of traditional aboriginal houses. The road to the right leads down to the **Itashao Pier** (Yīdáshào Mǎtǒu), where you can catch a boat back to Shuishe.

There are two excellent hotels in Itashao and at the time of writing a new wooden pier and lakefront area were being built.

### BOATING

A popular option for sightseeing and fishing (for which you don't need a licence) is boating. You can hire private boats at Shuishe and Itashao Piers. A trip to Lalu Island costs around NT300 per person. You can also rent small rowboats for hour NT150 per hour and take yourself out on the water. See p219 for information on the public ferry.

### CYCLING

There are bike-only paths being built around the lake. Inquire at the Tourist Information Office for the location of the paths.

You can rent bikes at the **Youth Activity Centre** (Rìyuètán Qīngnián Huódòng Zhōngxīn; ☎ 285 0037; 101 Jungjeng Rd, Ru-Uei Village; per day NT250) but you'll need to drive or to take the bus there.

### SWIMMING

Swimming is banned in the lake except during the Annual Across the Lake Swim (see opposite), and in a small, protected pool about 1km east of Shuishe Village at Zhaowu Pier. You can reach the swimming area by walking along the Hanbi Hiking Trail.

Note that many people get around the swimming ban by taking rowboats out on the lake and then slipping overboard.

### HIKING

There are eight hiking trails around the lake. The trails to **Maolanshan** (Māolánshān; two hours return) and **Shuisheshan** (Shǔishèshān; seven to eight hours return) are the longest. English signs mark the trailheads for both. The trail (which is really a road) to Maolanshan begins near Shuishe Village, while the one to Shuisheshan begins at the far end of Itashao to the right of an arch in a dirt lot. The beginning of this trail is tricky to find so be sure to ask if you're on the right path.

From Shuishe Village you can walk in either direction for about 1km along the lakefront boardwalk **Hanbi Hiking Trail** (Hánbìló Zìrán Bùdào). This is a very pleasant walk at any time of day.

Other walks are listed in the tourist brochures.

### FORMOSAN ABORIGINAL CULTURAL VILLAGE 九族文化村

It's an unlikely business model, a cultural showpiece combined with an amusement park but the **village** (Jiǔzú Wénhuà Cūn; ☎ 289 5361; www.nine.com.tw; adult/child NT650/350; ☉ 8am-5.30pm) comes highly recommended. Houses and villages in the style of each of the main native Taiwanese tribes have been reproduced and there are a number of venues presenting live shows. The adventure theme areas have rides and displays and there are restaurants serving Western, Eastern and aboriginal foods. You can get to the village on the free Sun Moon Lake tourist bus.

### SHUILI SNAKE KILN 水里 蛇窯

Snake kilns were first developed in China during the late Ming dynasty. The name comes from the long, narrow, snake-like appearance of the kiln. The **Shuili Snake Kiln** (Shuǐlǐ Shéyáo; ☎ 277 0967; 41 Ting Kan Lane, Ting Kan Village; adult/child NT120/60; ☉ 8am-5.30pm), for example, is more than 30m high. The kiln is run by the grandson of the founder and the modern enterprise has been promoted as a model for traditional industries that are looking to make the switch from factory to cultural attraction. Within the kiln grounds are a gallery, museum, exhibition hall and a 921 earthquake memorial. Also worth a visit is the lovely old-fashioned teahouse.

The kiln is part of the Sun Moon Lake Scenic Area but is about a 30-minute drive south of the lake itself. The free tourist buses around Sun Moon Lake go to the kiln, as do all Fengrong buses heading to Shuili. You can catch a Fengrong bus in front of the police station.

### OTHER SIGHTS

The **Wenwu Temple** (Wénwǔ Miào), **Syuentzang Temple** (Xuánzhuàng Sì) and **Syuenguang Temple** (Xuánguāng Sì) are all interesting sights. Syuenguang Temple is said to hold the remains of the monk immortalised in the novel *Journey to the West*.

Stately **Tsen Pagoda** (Cíēn Tǎ), built by Chiang Kai-shek in honour of his mother, is also worth visiting if you have the time.

## Festivals & Events

The **Annual Across the Lake Swim**, a mass swim held every September, promotes the lake and physical fitness. This is the only time swimming is permitted.

The **Thao Tribe Annual Harvest Festival** is held every summer (the eighth month of the lunar calendar). Visitors can watch all aspects of the festival, which include fortune-telling, mortar pounding to summon the people and the sacrifice of wild animals. Festivities last for several days and take place in Itashao Village.

Other festivals that have been held over the past few years and may continue (consult the tourist office) include an **international fireworks show** and a **cherry blossom festival**.

## Sleeping

Shuishe Village is drowning in hotels and more are on the way. Other places around the lake are quieter and less developed but this also means there is less to do, particularly at night. All hotels at the lake offer discounts during the week and often on the weekend, too. These can be up to 50%. Rooms that face the lake are always the most expensive.

### BUDGET

**Homestays** (d NT1000-1200) can be arranged at the tourist office. A single person can bargain for a lower price.

**Sun Moon Bay Campsite** (Rìyuèwān Lùyíng Nóng-chǎng; ☎ 285 6622; per person NT150) The camping ground is set beside the lake and has clean grounds with some trees for shade. Showers and bathrooms are on site. To reach the camping ground, turn right onto a small road just past the Youth Activity Centre.

**Min Ren Hotel** (Míngrén Fàndiàn; ☎ 855 338, ext 9; 138 Jungshan Rd; r from NT1500) Plains rooms in a plain hotel on the busy main road near other similarly priced hotels.

### MID-RANGE

**Teachers Hostel** (Jiàoshī Huìguǎn; ☎ 285 5991; 136 Zhongxing Rd; d/tw NT2500/3200) This is a hotel, not a hostel, though as the name suggests you will find many teachers here and a slightly institutional feeling. Large, comfortable rooms have private balconies from which to enjoy the corner lake view. Trails behind the hotel lead directly down to the water and the Hanbi Hiking Trail.

The hotel is a 10-minute walk up the hill from the village. Single female travellers without transport should be aware that parts of the walk are isolated and dark at night.

**Apollo Hotel** (Hóngbīn Dàfàndiàn; ☎ 285 5382; 3 Minsheng St; d/tw NT2500/3200) Situated on the pedestrian-only street, this hotel offers small but cosy rooms, some with balconies overlooking the lake. Staff speak limited English.

**Harbour Resort Hotel** (Mǎtóu Xiūxián Dàfàndiàn; ☎ 285 5143; 11 Minsheng Rd; d/tw NT2400/4500) This modern-looking building is the last hotel on Minsheng before the dock. Lakeside rooms are bright and airy and have excellent views from the balconies. There is a simple spa in the basement for guests.

**Full House Resort Hotel** (Fùháoqún Dùjià Mínsù; ☎ 285 0307; www.fhsml.idv.tw; 8 Shuishe St; d/tw NT2800/4500) The hotel, really a B&B, is set in a two-storey wood house behind a small garden in Itashao Village. The lobby and restaurant are filled with quirky *objets d'art* that reflect the individualistic taste of the owner. Rooms are large, with slick wood interiors and nice bathrooms. Travellers bored with the same-old same-old of Taiwanese hotels would do well to stay here. The hotel also runs a 24-hour café.

### TOP END

**Spa Home** (☎ 285 5166; fax 285 5577; 95 Jungshan Rd; r NT5800, weekdays NT4600) Rooms are all doubles with an extra sofa for lounging, and include two breakfasts, night tea on the café balcony, and a 1½-hour massage for one person.

**Lingo's Wood International Resort** (Zhéyuán Mínglì Huìguǎn; ☎ 285 0055; fax 285 0077; 31 Shuishe St; d/tw with breakfast NT5900/12,000, weekday discount 20%) It's hard to pin this place down, as it's lovely and luxurious, and yet it's a compete mish-mash of styles: think upscale wood lodge meets high-end KTV lobby. The location, however, right on the water's edge, couldn't be better. Rooms are bright and spacious and their warm, all-wood interiors feel just right when you're looking out across the lake. The hotel offers free bikes for guests.

Lingo's is on the Itashao side of the lake. If you take a boat across, it's on the left.

## Eating & Drinking

Sun Moon Lake is not a budget destination unless you plan to camp and cook for yourself. Still, you needn't spend a fortune. There is a 7-Eleven in town for noodles and sandwiches, and cheap stir-fries are available from the nearby restaurants.

**Min Hu Old Restaurant** (Mínghú Lǎocāntīng; 15 Minsheng Rd; dishes NT150; 9am-9pm) The pedestrian-only street in Shuishe Village has many bland-looking Chinese restaurants on it. While this restaurant is no more stylish than the others, most people agree that it's the best place for tasty Chinese dishes.

**Harbour Resort Cafe & Restaurant** (Mǎtóu Xiūxián Dàfàndiàn Cāntīng; 11 Minsheng Rd; coffee NT100, meals NT150; café 9am-9.30pm, restaurant lunch &

dinner) The open, sunny café is below street level next to the pier. The coffee is lousy but the ambiance is great. You can order set meals or Chinese dishes at the restaurant above.

**Spa Home Restaurant** (95 Jungshan Rd; meals NT400; 7.30am-10pm) The restaurant features a large balcony with excellent day and night views over the lake. The Western-style menu includes lamb, fish, lasagne and chicken. Dishes are tasty but nothing special. An egg, bacon and toast breakfast (7.30am to 9.30am) is available for NT200. Even if you don't eat here, the balcony makes for a pleasant afternoon or evening tea break.

**Lingo's Resort Restaurant** (Zhéyuán Mínglíú Huìguǎn Húpàn Cāntīng; 31 Shuishe St; meals NT300; 7am-11pm) A fabulous evening in Sun Moon Lake might entail taking the last boat across the lake to Itashao in the early evening and then enjoying the scrumptious fare at Lingo's. All dishes are made with local ingredients, including lake fish and mountain vegetables. The restaurant overlooks the lake and even has a small open-air café on the lake where coffee, tea and alcoholic drinks are served till 11pm. (Note that you'd have to take a taxi back to Shuishe Village in the end.)

---

### THE LALU (涵碧樓), SUN MOON LAKE

The top resort on Sun Moon Lake is the **Lalu** (Hánbì Lóu; ☎ 049-285 5311; 142 Jungsing Rd; 1-bedroom ste NT12,300, villa NT16,800; 🏊 ). Australian Kerry Hill, the architect of the complex, had a clear mind for the natural when he set out to design it – the natural elements of Sun Moon Lake, that is.

In many ways, it was the right choice. When you have a backdrop as impressive as Sun Moon Lake, you should not compete with it. Kerry's design makes liberal use of teak, stone, glass and water, clean lines and flat surfaces, which allow the hotel to blend in, even fade away, and let the beauty of Sun Moon Lake take centre stage. There is elegance, space and comfort here without the slightest hint of ostentation.

One thing that sets the Lalu apart from most luxury hotels in Taiwan is the staff. They are professional, but more importantly friendly, genial even, and softly spoken.

Some of the amazing features of the resort are a swimming pool, the edges of which appear to recede into the lake waters (not an original design but impressive nonetheless), a teahouse that exudes classic gracefulness and an outdoor bar with its own fireplace to keep guests warm at night. During the day, the views from the bar are unparalleled. It's no wonder the land the hotel sits on was once one of Chiang Kai-shek's private retreats.

Nonguests are not permitted to walk around the hotel and, in any case, they would have little to see. The halls are mostly unadorned and suites are accessible only by entrance through locked doors.

Villas have their own 12m-long private swimming pool and outdoor dining pavilions.

Just to the right as you approach the hotel is the small **Chiang Kai-shek Museum** (紀念館; Jìniànguǎn; admission free; 7am-7pm Sat & Sun). The museum is worth a visit for the old photographs of Sun Moon Lake, especially those that show the original pyramid shape of Lalu Island, the resort's namesake.

**Restaurants at the Lalu** (Hánbìlóu; ☎ 285 5311; 142 Jhongsing Rd) The Lalu has three restaurants open to nonguests, including the Oriental Brasserie and Japanese Restaurant.

**Oriental Brasserie** (🕑 7am-9pm Mon-Thu, 7am-11pm Fri-Sun) The brasserie is on level seven and is divided into two sections: one serving contemporary Western cuisine and the other, Eastern. Lake-view balcony tables are very popular at lunch time.

**Japanese Restaurant** (🕑 dinner) Also on level seven, this restaurant has a stylish setting and excellent dishes but is enclosed and so offers no view. To reach both restaurants, take the stairs to the left just as you approach the reception area but before you actually enter the building.

## Getting There & Away
From Taichung, you can catch a Renyou bus to Sun Moon Lake (NT181, two hours, 8am and 2.20pm daily). Buses stop at the aboriginal cultural village before continuing on to the lake. Buses end their journey in the large car park behind the village.

From Taichung, you can also catch one of the frequent Fengyuan buses to Puli (NT100, one hour) and then transfer to a Fengrong bus to Sun Moon Lake (NT45, 30 minutes, every hour).

From Shuili, Fengrong buses run to Sun Moon Lake (NT42, 30 minutes, every hour). Buses from Puli or Shuili stop across the street from the police station.

## Getting Around
At the time of writing, visitors could get an all-day boat pass (NT150) good for travel between the three piers. There was also a free bus that went round the lake and further afield to the aboriginal cultural village and the snake kiln. Whether either of these would continue was not certain. Inquire at the tourist office.

## DONGPU (TUNGPU) 東埔
**elevation 1200m**
Directly south of Sun Moon Lake, and just over the northern tip of Yushan National Park, sits the hot-spring village of Dongpu (Dōngpǔ). The village is a popular destination for hikers looking for a good workout, good weather, remarkable scenery and the chance to soak in a nice tub at the end of it all.

Dongpu suffered damage in the 921 earthquake and for years the trails were unstable. Most are repaired and, while there are no English signs, the trail system is well marked. Always ask about conditions, however, before you head out.

The longest and most famous hike is the three-day trek to Yushan, but you will need a Class A mountain permit (see p311), which means you need to go with a group. If you travel by yourself there are shorter hikes that still take you through some truly spectacular scenery. Some famous destinations include the **Cloud Dragon Waterfall** (Yúnlóng Pùbù) and **One Girl Waterfall** (Yī Nǚ Pùbù). The furthest you can go without a permit is to **Patungkuan Meadow** (Bātōng Guān), which, at 3000m, is no mere day trip. Make sure you are well prepared for all hikes to the higher elevations.

There are plenty of hotels in Dongpu. If you wish to book ahead of time you can call the **English Tourist Hotline** (☎ 02-2717 3737) for numbers. For an inexpensive option, try the **Youth Activity Centre** (青年活動中心; qīngnián huódòng zhōngxīn; ☎ 049-270 1515; 64 Dongpu Village; r from NT700) at the high end of town. Ten-person dorm rooms are available for NT1000 but this price is fixed, meaning a single traveller would pay the same for the room as 10.

A large-scale English map of Yushan National Park (including Dongpu) is available at the Yushan National Park Headquarters in Shuili (p213). You can also inquire here about the latest road and trail conditions. The Youth Activity Centre in Dongpu has Chinese maps of the area.

To get to Dongpu from Shuili take a Yuanlin bus (NT97, one hour 20 minutes, every hour) between 6am and 5pm.

## SITOU (HSITOU) 溪頭
**elevation 1150m**
This old **forest reserve** (Xītóu), southwest of Sun Moon Lake, feels more like a holiday resort than wilderness. Trails through fir and bamboo forests are short, paved and well marked.

Accommodation in the park is limited to hotels. One place you can try is the **Youth Activity Centre** (青年活動中心; Qīngnián Huódòng Zhōngxīn; ☎ 049-261 2160; d/tw NT2000/2600), 1km from the main gate.

Buses to Sitou from Shuili (NT65, every two hours) run from the **Yuanlin bus station**

( ☎ 049-277 0041). Just south of Sitou is another forest-resort area called **Shanlinhsi** (杉林溪; Shānlínxī). This area is less developed than Sitou and offers longer hikes. Again, trails are well developed with clearly marked signs.

All buses to Sitou continue to Shanlinhsi.

## PULI 埔里
☎ 049 / pop 92,000

This town (Pǔlǐ) was hit harder than any other by the 921 earthquake (p154). It has cleaned and rebuilt itself since then and now there is little evidence that it was once the epicentre of a massive 6.9 magnitude quake.

Puli tourist brochures (and the occasional local) still like to stress the somewhat politically incorrect assertion that the town is famous for its four Ws: wine, weather, water and women. Fortunately, there are also a host of other things, none of which start with 'w', to get excited about.

### Orientation

Central Puli is small enough to walk around. Some sites, however, are a way out of town and will require a taxi ride. Taxis are not that common in Puli so it's best to have your hotel call one before you head out.

---

#### CHUNG TAI CHAN TEMPLE 中台禪寺

Completed in 2001, the massive **Chung Tai Chan Temple** (Zhōng Tái Chánsì; www.chungtai.org; ctworld @ms16.hinet.net) is more than just another modern temple – it is an international centre of Buddhist academic research, culture and the arts.

The temple is 150m tall and sits on a 60-acre lotus hill outside Puli. It took 10 years and the donations of countless members of the Chung Tai Chan Buddhist community to complete. Chung Tai Chan is an international branch of Buddhism founded by the Venerable Master Wei Chueh – the Master who is said to have revived the Zen tradition in Taiwan.

From the start, the Master was determined to build something grand, something that would appeal to the modern eye as much as the soul. To achieve this, modern technology was embraced rather than shunned. In one massive chamber, for instance, fibre optics are used to make Buddhist donation plaques glow. A giant LCD screen running Windows can even help to locate one plaque out of the thousands that line the walls, should a donor wish to see exactly where his or her plaque is located.

The temple has deservedly won numerous awards for its lighting and design. Only top-quality materials and artists, both Taiwanese and foreign, were used during construction. One master craftsman is said to have spent 10 years collecting coloured jade for the delightful 18 Lohan reliefs. Another struggled (successfully) to adapt Taiwanese folk-art colours and techniques to traditional ceiling design. Marble from 15 different countries was imported and pure teak used for the seven-storey indoor pagoda. Interestingly, the pagoda was built the old way without metal nails or screws.

Beyond the skilled artwork and engineering, however, the temple exists for those who have an interest, curiosity or passion for Buddhism. Several Westerners live in the temple and teach English to the nuns and monks. It is the responsibility of several of these nuns to give guided tours to any and all visitors.

Unlike some temples, where the emphasis of the tour is on teaching you purely about the religious and ritual aspects of Buddhism, at Chung Tai Chan you can take an historical or cultural tour if that is your interest. In other words, the nuns will help you to understand the statues, motifs and iconography as well as the art and engineering feats of the temple, as if you were in a museum. They will explain the 22 physical markings of the Buddha, why one holds a medicine ball in his hand while another holds a lotus, and why one sits on a white elephant with six tusks and another is so fat.

There is no accommodation at the temple but there are weekly meditation classes in English, and week-long retreats during Chinese New Year and summer. Other retreats, lasting three days, are held irregularly. During retreats, guests do stay at the temple.

To get to the temple, drive north on Jungjeng Rd out of Puli and then follow the signs. The temple is about 6km north of Renai Park. A taxi should cost around NT300.

For information about tours or to prearrange one, email the monastery.

---

# PULI

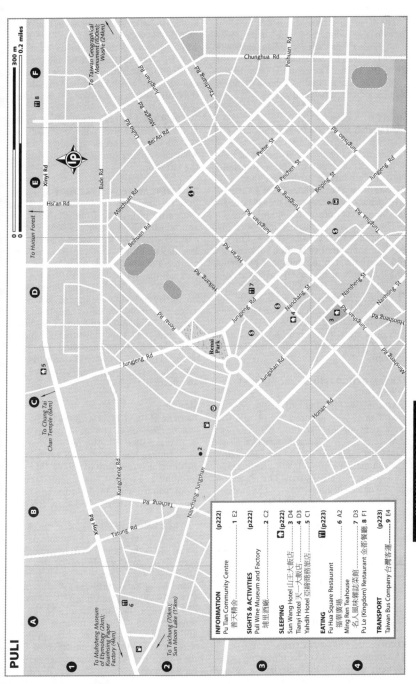

To Taiwan Geographical Monument (800m); Wushe (24km)

Chunghua Rd

To Huisun Forest

Hsi'an Rd

To Chung Tai Chan Temple (6km)

To Muhsheng Museum of Etymology (2km); Kuanhsing Paper Factory (4km)

To Taichung (70km); Sun Moon Lake (95km)

Renai Park

WESTERN TAIWAN

| INFORMATION | (p222) |
| --- | --- |
| Pu Tian Community Centre 普天精舍 | 1 E2 |
| **SIGHTS & ACTIVITIES** | **(p222)** |
| Puli Wine Museum and Factory 埔里酒廠 | 2 C2 |
| **SLEEPING** 🛏 | **(p222)** |
| Sun Wang Hotel 山王大飯店 | 3 D4 |
| Tianyi Hotel 天一大飯店 | 4 D3 |
| Yahdih Hotel 亞締商務旅店 | 5 C1 |
| **EATING** 🍴 | **(p223)** |
| Fu Hua Square Restaurant 富華廣場 | 6 A2 |
| Ming Ren Teahouse 名人風味雞坊茶館 | 7 D3 |
| Pu Le (Kingdom) Restaurant 金都餐廳 | 8 F1 |
| **TRANSPORT** | **(p223)** |
| Taiwan Bus Company 台灣客運 | 9 E4 |

The tallest and most distinctive building in town is not what it seems, ie a department store. Rather it is the new **Pu Tian Community Centre** (Pǔ Tiān Jīn Shè) built by the Jung Tai Chan Buddhists. The centre is open to the public and has a children's library, movie room, meditation hall and gallery.

## Sights

### MUHSHENG MUSEUM OF ENTOMOLOGY
木生昆蟲博物館

Taiwan has more than 400 species of butterflies, 350 of which can be seen around Puli. It's no surprise then that there is a **museum** (Mùshēng Kūnchóng Bówùguǎn; ☎ 291 3311; 622 Nan Cun Rd; adult/child NT120/100; ☉ 8am-5.30pm) dedicated to insects (mostly the butterfly) here.

The museum features a live butterfly compound and a display centre. On the 1st floor there are live beetles, stick insects and scorpions. On the 2nd floor hundreds and hundreds of preserved specimens are presented behind glass. Check out the Thai 'face' butterfly, the 'owl faced' butterfly and the very odd hermaphrodite butterfly (the male half is dark, the female light).

Guides are available but they speak only Chinese. It is easiest to take a taxi to the museum.

### TAIWAN GEOGRAPHICAL MONUMENT
台灣地理中心

If you follow Jungshan Rd to the edge of town (where it turns into Hwy 14) you will see a giant menhir-like stone with Chinese characters reading **Taiwan Geographical Monument** (台灣地理中心; Táiwān Dìlí Zhōngxīn). Though many people get their picture taken here, this is just a park sign. The plaque on the top of **Mt Hutoushan** (虎頭山; Hǔtóushān) officially marks the geographical centre of Taiwan. To reach the plaque, walk up the stairs 50m or so to the right of the menhir and follow the trail up.

Past the plaque, the trail continues to **Carp Lake** (鯉魚潭; Lǐyú Tán), a pretty, willow-lined pond with attractive pavilions and cafés overlooking the water. It's about two hours return to walk to Carp Lake. You can also drive there by taking the turn-off about 3km west of town on Hwy 14.

### KUANHSING PAPER FACTORY 廣興紙寮

The traditional craft of handmaking paper is well preserved in Puli thanks to the

**Kuanhsing Paper Factory** (Guǎnxīng Zhǐ Liáo; ☎ 291 3037; 310 Tiehshan Rd; admission free; ☉ 8am-5.30pm), which is more cottage industry than factory. Be aware that Kuanhsing is a popular destination for school field trips, as guests can not only watch paper being made but they can also try to make a sheet themselves.

You'll need to take a taxi to get to the factory. Drivers will ask for NT200 but NT150 is fair. Excellent-quality (if somewhat cute) paper products are available at the gift shop.

### PULI WINE MUSEUM & FACTORY 埔里酒廠

Puli is famous for its Shaohsing Wine (Shàoxīng Jiǔ), made from glutinous rice and wheat. The **museum** (Pǔlǐ Jiǔchǎng; ☎ 298 4006; 219 Jungshan Rd, Sec 3; admission free; ☉ 8am-5pm) has a number of old instruments and photographs on display but is for the most part not that interesting.

Across the street from the museum are the **factory** and wine-tasting area. There are a dozen or more 'wines' to sample, including some delicious fruit liqueurs. You'll also find tasty wine-flavoured ice blocks and cakes. A jug of Shaohsing wine costs about NT800. Even if you don't like the taste, the ceramic jugs make attractive gifts and decorations.

## Sleeping

**Tianyi Hotel** (Tiānyī Dàfàndiàn; ☎ 998 100, ext 2; 299 Hsian Rd; r from NT800) The lobby of this hotel displays wall-sized photos of what the place looked like after the 921 earthquake. In short, it was a heap of rubble. The new building is in good shape and has spacious rooms with tiled floors and great views unfortunately out of tiny, screened windows.

**Yahdih Hotel** (Yàdì Shāngwù Lǚdiàn; ☎ 298 5777; 701 Xinyi Rd; d/tw NT1280/2000) This hotel was only a year old at the time of writing and offered very clean, comfortable rooms that were good value for the price.

**Sun Wang Hotel** (Shānwáng Dàfàndiàn; ☎ 290 0111; 399 Jungshan Rd, Sec 2; d/tw NT2300/3500) Locals consider the Sun Wang to be the best hotel in town. Other than the fancy lobby and restaurant, most travellers probably wouldn't feel it's so much different from the others to justify spending twice as much for a room here.

## Eating & Drinking

There are plenty of noodle stands, and simple fried-rice joints around Puli.

**Ming Ren Teahouse** (Míngrén Fēngwèi Zázhì Càiguǎn; 448 Jungjeng Rd; meals NT120;  9.30am-8pm) For a cleaner, more modern atmosphere try this teahouse, which is well patronised for simple breakfast and lunch meals.

**Fu Hua Square Restaurant** (Fúhuá Guǎngchǎng; 1099 Xinyi Rd; meals NT200;  lunch & dinner) The vegetarian dim sum here is a favourite with the monks and nuns from Chung Tai Chan Temple, and for good reason. It's not often you get Cantonese vegetarian-style cooking in Taiwan (especially with a real Cantonese chef). The restaurant is just off Xinyi Rd in a small square with an arched entrance.

**Pu Le (Kingdom) Restaurant** (Jìndū Cāntíng;  299 5096; 236 Xinyi Rd; per person NT300;  lunch & dinner) Nantou County (of which Puli is part) is the biggest flower-growing region in Taiwan. Reflecting this in its cuisine is the famous Pu Le Restaurant. Gorgeous-looking and tasting dishes decorated and even cooked with fresh flowers are the specialities here. Recommended are the rose-petal salads and tempura wild-ginger flowers. This place is extremely popular and weddings are often hosted in the main dining areas. It's best to come with as many people as possible so you can try a number of dishes.

## Getting There & Away

A visit to Puli could be part of an extended visit to the Sun Moon Lake region or a weekend getaway from Taichung. From Taichung, buses to Puli (NT100, one hour) leave frequently from the Fengyuan bus station. From Sun Moon Lake, you can catch a Fengrong Company bus (NT45, 30 minutes, every hour) across from the police station.

## HUISUN FOREST RESERVE 惠蓀林場

This combination **forest research station** (Hùisūn Línchǎng; adult/child NT120/80;  7am-10pm) and recreation zone is an hour north of Puli. There are a number of trails in the reserve, from two to six hours in walking time. All are well marked with English signs. Accommodation is limited to hotels in a small village within the reserve.

Buses to Huisun (NT93, one hour) leave Puli at 8.50am and 2.15pm.

For more information about the park see http://huisun.nchu.edu.tw.

# ALISHAN NATIONAL SCENIC AREA

The Alishan National Scenic Area covers a region of over 37,000 hectares. From a starting altitude of 300m in the west at Chukou, the land quickly rises to heights of more than 2600m. As a result, the variety of plant and animal life is nothing short of amazing. One of the best ways to appreciate this variety is on the narrow-gauge Alishan forest train, which, in the space of 3½ hours (71km), takes you through tropical, subtropical, temperate and alpine zones.

Don't confuse the National Scenic Area with the popular Alishan Forest Recreation Area, which is where the small train takes you. The forest recreation area is but one part of the national scenic area. Other areas include tea-growing communities such as Ruili, the old maintenance station (and now popular hiking base) of Fenqihu and the village of Shanmei, where much of traditional Zhou aboriginal life, and much of the natural environment, is still proudly preserved.

A visit to this area is rewarding on any level. The forest recreation area offers a cool, relaxing, well-developed mountain retreat, while smaller towns offer homestays and extended hikes into pristine and often rugged terrain. Alishan can be as safe or as challenging as you want it to be. You can sip tea at a Japanese-era hotel or ford rivers. Your meals can come from a kitchen or a rough barbecue pit.

The area is well represented on its official website (www.ali.org.tw). Here, you can find information on accommodation, eating, transport and activities, as well as the history and culture of almost every village and town.

## CHIAYI 嘉義
 05

While Chiayi (Jiāyì) is not part of the Alshan National Scenic Area, almost every traveller will have to pass through here on the way in. The narrow-gauge train to Alishan (p233) leaves from Chiayi train station, as do buses and taxis. Chiayi is also the portal for onward travel to Beigang, probably the oldest and most important Matsu temple in Taiwan. There are a few sights to recommend in

WESTERN TAIWAN

# CHIAYI

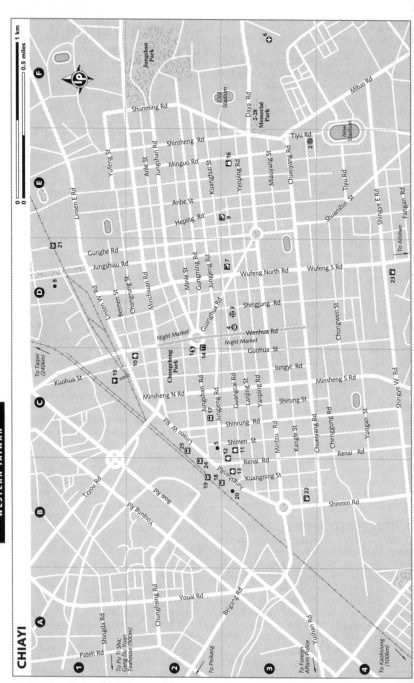

To Pu Ti Sha;
Geng Du Yuan
Teahouse (500m)

To Taipei
(240km)

To Peikang

To Foreign
Affairs Police

To Kaohsiung
(100km)

To Alishan

Pateh Rd

Shingda Rd

Chunghsing Rd

Youai Rd

Beikang Rd

Yushan Rd

Tzou Rd

Boai Rd

Youjung Rd

Kuohua St

Minsheng N Rd

Linsen W Rd

Linsen E Rd

Shunming Rd

Jungshan
Park

Old
Stadium

New
Stadium

Dava Rd

Mituo Rd

Tiyu Rd

2-28
Memorial
Park

Miauyang St

Chueiyang Rd

Shuanshin
St

Tiyu Rd

Shingye E Rd

Fangan Rd

Shinsheng Rd

Shinsheng Rd

Minguo Rd

Anhe St

Jungshan Rd

Yufeng St

Kuangtsai St

Yenping Rd

Anhe St

Heping Rd

Gunghe Rd

Jungshiau Rd

Beimen St

Changrung St

Minchuan Rd

Minle St

Gungming Rd

Jungfeng Rd

Guanghua Rd

Wufeng North Rd

Wufeng S Rd

Shingjung Rd

Chongwen St

Shuanshin St

Wenhua Rd

Guohua St

Jungyi Rd

Minsheng S Rd

Shingye W Rd

Night Market

Night Market

Chungcheng
Park

Jungshan Rd

Jungfeng Rd

Guangcai Rd

Lanjing St

Yanping Rd

Shirung St

Chueiyang Rd

Chenggung Rd

Renai Rd

Yungan St

Shinrung Rd

Shimen St

Mintzu Rd

Kangle St

Shingye W Rd

Renai Rd

Jungshung Rd

Kuangning St

Shinmin Rd

1 km
0.5 miles

Chiayi but, in general, your time here will comprise the beginning and end of your journey somewhere else.

## Orientation

Chiayi lies directly on the Tropic of Cancer. Central Chiayi is small enough to walk across in 30 minutes, though air pollution makes it unpleasant to do so. Taxis are plentiful except in the area west of the train tracks.

## Information

For information about the restaurant and entertainment scene, pick up a copy of the excellent monthly *FYI South Magazine*, which includes a pull-out map that is updated regularly. Copies are available at many bars and restaurants in town or you can download the content at the website www.taiwanfun.com.

### INTERNET ACCESS

There is a 24-hour **Internet café** (65 Tiyu Rd; per 10 min NT10) near the stadium.

### INTERNET RESOURCES

**Chiayi Expat** (www.geocities.com/allhou/chiayiscene.htm) Good information from a Chiayi expat.

**Chiayi City Government** (www.chiayi.gov.tw/newweb/index_english.htm) Good for general information about the city, including sites and activities for tourists.

### LAUNDRY

**Laundromat** (701 Jungjeng Rd; 🕒 24hr) Just northeast of the Jiaxin Hotel.

### MONEY

ATMs and currency exchange are available at the **Bank of Taiwan** ( ☎ 222 4471; 306 Jungshan Rd). There are also numerous banks and ATMs on Renai Rd near the train station.

## Sights

### COCHIN CERAMIC MUSEUM 交趾陶館

Cochin artists have been working in the Chiayi area since the Qing dynasty and have won praise from as far afield as Japan and France. The **museum** (Zhōuzhítáo Guǎn; ☎ 278 8225; 275 Jungshiau Rd; admission free; 🕒 9am-noon & 1.30-5pm Wed-Sun) is in the basement of the Chiayi Cultural Centre (Jiāyìshì Wén-Huà Zhōngxīn), across from the Beimen train station, and features several exhibits ranging from the work of master artist Yeh (1826–91) to that of small children.

Cochin (*zhāo zhǐ tǎo*) is a low-fired, brightly coloured, glaze style of ceramic and is often used to make figurines and wall decorations. You'll probably see cheap work in tourist shops around the island. The work here is outstanding and can be appreciated without any background or technical knowledge of the craft.

### TEMPLES

Chiayi has a number of beautiful temples scattered around the city. **Chenghuang Temple** (Chénghuáng Miào), also known as City God Temple, is particularly fascinating for the array of elaborately carved and dressed statues of demons and guards.

## Sleeping

There are many cheap hotels scattered around the train-station area.

**White House Hotel** (Báigōng Dàfàndiàn; ☎ 227 8046; 621 Jungshan Rd; r from NT500) This hotel offers clean, simply furnished rooms directly across from the station. The cheapest rooms have no TV.

**WESTERN TAIWAN**

**Jiaxin Hotel** (Jiāxīn Dàfàndiàn; ☎ 222 2280; 687 Jungjeng Rd; d/tw from NT500/1000) Rooms are much nicer than the low price would suggest.

**Hotel Country** ( ☎ 223 6336; 678 Guangcai Rd; d/tw with breakfast NT880/1600) This place is slightly more expensive than the others but offers a car park in the basement.

**Chinatrust Hotel** (Zhōngxìn Dàfàndiàn; ☎ 229 2233; 257 Wenhua Rd; d/tw/ste NT3400/3800/7700; 🖳 ) This is considered the top hotel in town and offers a 30% discount on weekdays. Facilities include a business centre, fitness room and VIP lounge. English service is available.

### Eating

There are many inexpensive generic restaurants and cafés on Jungshan and Renai Rds and around Chungcheng Park. The **night market** (Wenhua St; ☯ 5pm-2am), between Minchiun and Chuei Yang Rds, is also a good for cheap food.

**Pen Shui Turkey Rice** (Pēnshuǐ Huǒjīfàn; 325 Jungshan Rd; bowl NT40; ☯ 8.30am-10pm) Everyone in Taiwan knows that Chiayi is famous for its turkey rice dish (huǒ jīròu fàn). This is the place that started it all 60 years ago. The dish is simplicity itself: turkey and gravy poured over a bowl of steaming rice. Before you guffaw at the thought of getting excited over such plain fare, consider some Western favourites that are little more than mush: mashed potatoes and gravy or poutine (gravy and cheese poured over French fries).

**Pu Ti Shu** ( ☎ 234 2489; 229 Si Wei Rd; all-you-can-eat NT99; ☯ lunch & dinner) Take a taxi to get to this popular vegetarian buffet.

### Drinking

**Calgary Pub** (Kǎjiālì; ☎ 227 1626; 19 Lane 351, Guohua St; meals NT180, beer NT150; ☯ 6pm-2am) This Western-style pub is busy most nights with a mix of expats and locals. Western-style dishes such as hamburgers and pizza are available. Even though the address says Guohua St, approach from Linsen W Rd (coming from the train-station area) and turn left down the alley just before Guohua St.

**Geng Du Yuan Tea House** (Gēngdúyuán; 303-305 Siwei Rd; ☯ 10am-2am) This classical Chinese-style wood teahouse, featuring curtained booths and carp-poolside tables, is part of a chain across Taiwan. English menus illustrate the different flavours and textures of the various teas grown in the country. An average packet of tea costs NT400 but lasts for hours. There is a per-person charge of NT130 for water when making tea and snacks, and set meals are also available.

### Shopping

**Original En Dian Cookie Shop** (Ēndiānsū Chuàngshidiàn; 123 Minguo Rd; ☯ 9am-8pm) Chiayi is famous for square cookies (ēndiān sū) and this is the store that invented them. The cookies taste a lot like Graham Crackers and cost only NT45 for a box.

### Getting There & Away

Chiayi is the gateway to the Alishan National Scenic Area. You can take a train or a bus.

#### TRAIN

If you are taking the small train to Alishan, note that you can board at the Beimen station, northeast of the main station. This station is less crowded and has a few sights nearby, such as the Cochin Memorial Museum and a Japanese-era station just across the tracks, to help you pass the time while waiting for the train. At the time of writing a new park was being constructed along the tracks west of the station.

There are two trains a day to Alishan (NT399, 3½ hours, 9am and 1.30pm). The earlier train is recommended as afternoon fog in the mountains can obscure views. If you catch the train at Beimen station the schedule is slightly later. During Chinese New Year there are more scheduled trains each day.

Trains to Chiayi from Taipei (fast/slow train NT416/268, two/three hours) and Kaohsiung (fast/slow train NT432/333, two/three hours) run from morning till late at night.

#### BUS

Buses to Alishan (NT156, 2½ hours) usually leave every two hours from 7.10am until 3.10pm. Buses leave from the **Chiayi County Bus Company station** ( ☎ 224 3140; 503 Jungshan Rd), which is to the right of the train station as you exit.

Please note that at the time of writing the Chiayi County Bus Company had just purchased a fleet of new buses and was planning big changes to its schedules.

WESTERN TAIWAN

## Getting Around

You can rent scooters (per day NT200) from several shops across from the train station. Travelling on a scooter up to the Alishan National Scenic Area is highly recommended. Take the old narrow Hwy 159 for a pure mountain experience.

## Around Chiayi

### ZIYUN TEMPLE 紫雲寺

If you take Hwy 159 up from Chiayi, the first point of interest you will come across is this **temple** (Zǐyún Sì; Purple Cloud Temple) at Bantianyan (半天岩; Bàntiānyán). Ziyun dates to 1682, though it has been built and rebuilt numerous times since. The temple bell and drum are particularly beautiful and the crowds of worshippers are interesting to observe for their devotion. At times you may even see exorcisms performed here.

To the right of the temple, at the back of the car park, a 23m gold-plated Guanyin statue stands watch over Chiayi in the distance. To the right of the goddess, a road and a set of stairs both lead to a series of trails that take you up into the **Sanbao Mountains** (Sānbǎo Shān). Just below the temple are two attractive cafés, one built to take in the mountain view, and the other the scene over the valley.

### BEIGANG (PEIKANG) CHAOTIEN TEMPLE 北港

This **temple** (Cháotiān Gōng) is in the town of Beigang (Běigǎng) a short bus ride to Chiayi's northeast. Locals are likely to know the temple as the Matsu Temple (Māzǔ Miào), as it was built to worship the Goddess of the Sea.

The temple has great historical and cultural value to the people of Taiwan. It is probably the oldest Matsu temple in the country and it makes a great read (www .sinica.edu.tw/tit/festivals/0596_Peikang. html) to discover how the place went from humble beginnings to the palatial structure it is today. On Matsu's birthday (the 23rd day of the third lunar month), the goddess' statue is taken on inspection tours of the city and thousands of devotees come from all over the island to pay homage. If possible, come at this time to see Taiwanese folk culture at its best. Otherwise, Sundays are best, though if you want to examine the temple architecture a weekday might be better as the crowds are smaller.

At the time of writing, the front of the temple was being repaired and wide-angle views of the whole temple were not possible.

Buses to Beigang (NT54, 45 minutes, every 15 to 30 minutes) leave from the Chiayi Bus Company station. From the Beigang station turn right as you exit and then take the first left. Walk about three blocks and you will see the temple on the corner.

## FENQIHU 奮起湖

☎ 05 / elevation 1405m

Fenqihu (Fènqǐhú) is the halfway point on the narrow-gauge Alishan railway. This place feels like an outpost. And, indeed, in days gone by, when Alishan was a centre for logging, Fenqihu existed solely as a repair and maintenance station.

Today, the town survives mainly on tourism. There are small hotels and simple restaurants but the outpost outlook remains. And this seems just what the people want. On a crowded weekend you can't help but get caught in the festive atmosphere as people jostle on Old St, eat snacks and fruit they may never have seen before, take photos in front of the old engines and return exhilarated from hikes through the thick forests.

An afternoon stopover in Fenqihu would add a slightly rugged dimension to any trip to Alishan, while a full day or two would make for a cool, healthy weekend getaway during the hot summer months.

## Orientation & Information

Fenqihu town is tiny and you'll find your bearings quickly. As for the surrounding wilderness, the 921 earthquake destroyed many natural attractions. At the time of writing an entirely new network of trails (including a boarded circuit route) was being built while many older routes were growing over. Our map, then, by necessity, is incomplete.

The Alishan National Scenic Area tourism board has assured us that clear signs would be in place in 2004 and a tourist map (in English) made to illustrate the new developments. You should be able to pick up the map at the train station.

Fenqihu is cool year round with an average temperature of 19°C in summer and

12°C in winter. Bring along a sweater no matter what time of year and be prepared if you head out for a long hike.

## Sights & Activities

### TRAIN STATION

The **train station** platform is an obvious place to begin your exploration of Fenqihu, especially the two old engines. Across the tracks and up a small set of stairs to the left is a fenced-in strand of **square bamboo** (四方竹; *sìfāng zhú*). The stems of this species of bamboo are not curved but angled like a square.

### HIKING

Hiking is popular in this area and a new trail network is being constructed. Much of this will be boarded, with wooden steps in steep areas. National park staff said that this route (a few kilometres are already in place and pass through a lovely cedar forest) will form a 10km circuit around Fenqihu and lead to all the major natural attractions. This is welcome as points south of Fenqihu, such as the **Bat Shrine** (Biǎnfú Xíng Gōng) and **Tiger Spots Cliff** (Hǔ Bān Qiào), were al-

most impossible to find as the old markers had faded beyond recognition.

### DATONGSHAN 大涷山

Like Chushan at Alishan, this **mountain** (Dàdòngshān; 1976m) is a popular sunrise viewing spot. The sunrise here can last for over three minutes in good weather, much longer than at Alishan.

The trailhead begins almost 4km from Fenqihu and is unmistakable with its large trail map and small rest area. Note that there are two trails starting from the rest area. The right-hand trail goes to the **18 Arahats Cave** (Shíbā Lóhàn Dòng) while the left leads to Datongshan. It takes about one hour to hike to the top. If you start your hike in Fenqihu give yourself around four hours. On weekends, hotels run shuttle buses to the trailhead.

### OLD STREET 老街

This **street** (Lǎo Jiē) has no impressive or even really old architecture but instead that authentic Fenqihu frontier atmosphere. The street is narrow, crowded, small, covered

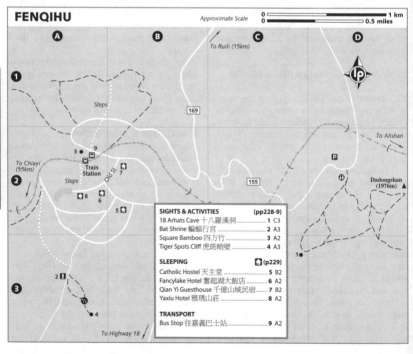

**FENQIHU**

Approximate Scale

0 — 1 km
0 — 0.5 miles

To Ruili (15km)

To Alishan

To Chiayi (55km)

Steps

Train Station

Steps

Dadongshan (1976m) ▲

To Highway 18

WESTERN TAIWAN

and quite entertaining. You'll find products such as a traditional Taiwanese facial cream or handmade jelly drinks (ai yù) that are rarely seen these days. It's good to come here between meals.

## Sleeping

**Catholic Hostel** (Tiānzhǔtáng; ☎ 256 1035; dm/s/d with shared bath NT250/500/800) Run by a sweet Swiss sister (who speaks good English), the hostel is as clean as a whistle. Advanced bookings are advisable on the weekend. The hostel is a few minutes walk from the station.

**Qian Yi Guesthouse** (Qiānyì Shānchéng Mínsù; ☎ 256 1933; r from NT1200, weekdays NT800) The price of a room here depends on the number of people using it. Rooms are tiled, clean and simply decorated. The owners will allow foreign travellers to use the washing machine on the rooftop balcony.

**Yaxiu Hotel** (Yǎxiù Shānzhuāng; ☎ 256 1336; d/tw NT1200/1600, no weekday discounts) This is the newest hotel in town and features large rooms, a comfy setting and the feel of a typical city hotel. To reach it, follow the stairs to the left off Old St. There is an English sign to guide you.

**Fancylake Hotel** (Fènqíhú Dàfàndiàn ☎ 256 1888; r from NT2000) This is the best hotel in town and with its all-wood interior and cabin-style rooms, it suits the Fenqihu spirit perfectly.

## Eating

There aren't many restaurants in Fenqihu but what there are serve surprisingly tasty food. A meal for two of mountain vegetables and game costs NT600 but simple noodle dishes are much less. Several convenience stores in town sell instant noodles, and barbecue stalls set up on the streets outside town offering delicious sausages and wild pig.

Restaurant hours are not fixed but expect places to close early (or not open at all) on weekdays and around 9pm on weekends.

### LOCAL SPECIALITIES

Fenqihu's railway lunchbox (鐵路便當; tiělù biàndāng; NT80) is very popular and can be bought at the Fancylake Hotel or at the station when the Alishan train makes its stop. Train cakes (火車餅; huǒchē bǐng), a type of square mooncake with a train stamped on the surface, are also popular and can be picked up on Old St.

Outside the Qian Yi Guesthouse you can often pick up fresh jars of high quality Alishan wasabi. In the same place is the musttry tomato/passionfruit. You won't see this anywhere else in Taiwan. The fruit is small and oval shaped and looks a bit like a passionfruit. The flavour though is a delicious mix of sweet and sour, exactly as if you'd mixed tomatoes and passionfruit together. To eat, cut off the top of the fruit and suck out the inside.

## Getting There & Away

The drive up old Hwy 159 to Fenqihu is wonderfully scenic, but then so is the train ride. Trains (NT241) depart Chiayi everyday at 9am and 1.30pm (there are more trains during holidays) and arrive in Fenqihu just over two hours later.

## RUILI (JUILI) 瑞里

☎ 05 / pop 970 / elevation 1000m

It takes a bit of planning to get to Ruili (Ruìlǐ) but the rewards, especially midweek, are worth it. You'll have panoramic mountain scenes, bamboo forests, caves, waterfalls and ancient walking trails practically to yourself. Ruili is a small, quiet mountain community that thrives on tourism and tea growing. The locals have been working to preserve the environment for a long time and, as a result, they can now boast that it's one of the best places in the country for watching fireflies. From March to June the mountainsides literally sparkle as countless fireflies turn on throughout the night.

You can visit any time of year, though winter nights are chilly and hotel rooms aren't heated.

Like so many other places in Taiwan, new pavilions, paths and sights were being built or opened up in Ruili at the time of writing.

## Information

**Ruitai Tourist Centre** ( ☎ 250 1070; 1-1 Ruili Village; ☯ 8.30am-5pm) Offers useful maps, brochures (hopefully in English by the time you arrive) and a very knowledgeable, friendly staff of locals. These people really love their land and want to share its treasures with you. The centre covers not only Ruili but nearby (and even more remote) Taihe (太和, Tàihé) and Ruifong (瑞峰, Ruìfēng). The centre has Internet access (for checking email).

WESTERN TAIWAN

WESTERN TAIWAN

## Sights & Activities

### WATERFALLS

Ruili has two impressive falls. The **Cloud Pool Waterfall** (Yúntán Pùbù) is reached by a series of steep stairs. The return walk from the car park, which is just past the 22km mark on County Rd 122, takes about 45 minutes.

It takes about two hours to hike to the **Twin River Waterfall** (Shuāngxī Pùbù) if you start across the street from the Meihua Hotel, or 30 minutes from the Rey Lee Hotel. Signs are clear at both starting points.

### RUITAI OLD TRAIL 瑞太古道

This **hiking trail** (Ruìtài Gúdào) was once the route for agricultural products (and school children) to travel between Ruili and Taihe. Now it's a very enjoyable two- or three-hour journey through bamboo forests. Scenic spots along the way include **Wangyou Forest** (Wàngyōu Lín) and **Hero Hill** (Yīnxióng Pō). The trail starts about 150m east of the Chingye Hotel and is well marked.

Fifty metres before the trailhead are a set of stairs leading up to the **Green Tunnel** (Lùsè Suìdào), a length of road sealed off from the sky by tall, overhanging bamboo.

### SWALLOW CLIFF 燕子崖

The **cliff** (Yànzǐyái) is a large rock overhang pitted with the work of countless swallows building nests in the soft stone. The hike is for the Stairmaster crowd (there are 1600 stone steps) and takes one hour return. Along the way you pass 1000-year-old **Bat Cave** (Biānfú Dòng). If you continue for another hour you'll reach the **Twin River Waterfall**.

The steps to Swallow Cliff begin across from the Meihua Hotel. The trailhead is well marked.

## Sleeping

The tourist centre can help with homestays and hotel bookings.

**Roulan Lodge** ( ☎ 250 1210; fax 250 1555; 10 Ruili Village; d/tw/cabins NT1600/2200/3200, weekday discount 20%) This is by far the best place to stay in Ruili and not just for the comfortable wooden cabins and rooms. Every night the owners (who have often appeared on Taiwanese TV for their efforts to preserve the

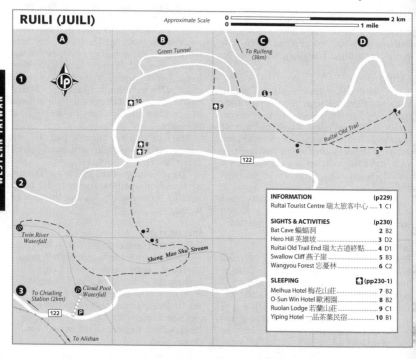

**RUILI (JUILI)**

Approximate Scale

0 — 2 km
0 — 1 mile

natural heritage of Ruili) show a film (in Chinese) to introduce fireflies and the local history. They then invite guests to make tea and traditional snacks in a quaint old room filled with tools and curios from the past. During firefly season, nightly tours to prime watching areas are arranged.

**Meihua Hotel** (Méihuā Shānzhuāng; ☎ 250 1668; 103-1 Ruili Village; d/tw NT1500/2000, weekday discounts 40%) Tiled-floor rooms are spotlessly clean but nondescript, save the excellent mountains views from the 2nd floor. Characterless cabins for three to five people (from NT1700) are also available.

**O-Sun Win Hotel** (Ōuxiàngyuán; ☎ 250 1222; fax 250 1808; 103 Ruili Village; d/tw NT2000/3500, weekday discount 40%) This relatively new hotel is just behind and up from the Meihua Hotel and so boasts even better views, especially from the 3rd floor.

**Yiping Hotel** (Yīpíncháyè Mínsù; ☎ 250 1559; epintea@ms62.hinet.net; 102-2 Ruili Village; d/tw NT1800/2400) The owners of this hotel are also tea growers and on the ground floor guests are invited to help themselves to tea. All rooms feature wood interiors, with each floor offering a slightly different style. Tea-factory tours can be arranged.

## Eating

Most restaurants are in the hotels. An average set meal will cost NT200. You can buy lunchboxes from the Meihua Hotel restaurant.

## Getting There & Around

The Ruili bus schedule was up in the air at the time of writing due to the purchase of new buses by the **Chiayi County Bus Company** (☎ 224 3140). The company station is to the right of the train station as you exit.

You can take the Alishan train to Chiaoliping (交力坪; Jiāolìpíng; NT174) and then call a hotel in Ruili to pick you up. If there are enough of you, the hotel probably won't charge anything. Otherwise, the pick-up fee will be around NT300.

It's best to have your own transport when in Ruili, as the sights are spread out and there is no public transport.

## ALISHAN FOREST RECREATION AREA

阿里山

☎ 05

Nearly every Taiwanese person you meet will recommend that you go to Alishan

(Ālǐshān), even if they have never been there themselves. They will speak in excited tones of a small mountain train, pristine alpine forests, cherry blossoms, sacred trees and the chance to see a perfect sunrise and 'sea of clouds'.

Is it worth the hype? Most think so, though a few leave unimpressed. If you're looking for challenging hikes in rugged nature you'll definitely be disappointed. Most trails are smooth, scenic walks around strands of old trees, shrines, ponds and gardens. Alishan is like a romantic retreat filled with natural, historical, artificial and spiritual attractions, rather than a national park as many Westerners use the term.

You can visit Alishan at any time of year. In spring the cherry trees are in bloom, while in autumn and winter the sunrises and sunsets are said to be the best. Summer is busy with city folk looking for a cool retreat.

The climate is cool even in summer (at least compared to lower altitudes). In spring and summer late-afternoon thunderstorms are common. During winter the mountain tops may get a light dusting of snow. Summer temperatures average from 13°C to 24°C, while those in winter are 5°C to 16°C. You should bring a coat or sweater and an umbrella or raincoat, no matter what time of year you visit.

## History

The Zhou people were the earliest inhabitants of the Alishan region and legend has it that the name Alishan comes from their famed chief and hunter Ali (or Abali). Modern development began with the Japanese in the 19th century, when they came to exploit the abundant stands of cypress. In 1906 the first railway into the mountain was established and by 1913 the tracks had reached Alishan.

When Taiwan was returned to China in 1945 most of the cypress was gone, though the Japanese had replanted other species in the area, including the cherry blossom trees that now bring in so many tourists in spring. The first steps towards creating a forest park were taken in 1975. Since then the protected area has grown to 1400 hectares from an initial 175. The park (adult/child NT150/100, holidays NT200/100) is open every day of the year.

WESTERN TAIWAN

# ALISHAN FOREST RECREATION AREA

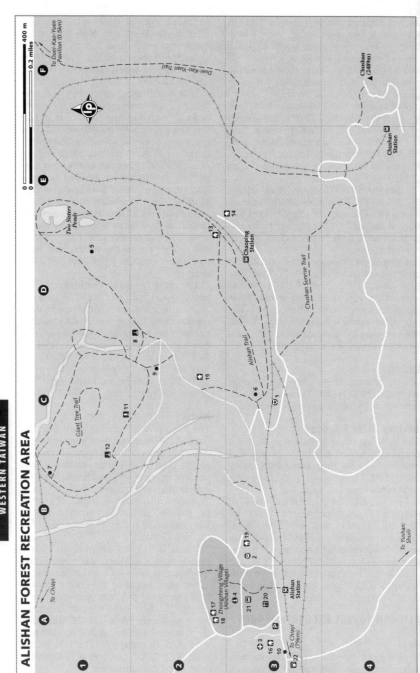

## Orientation

Despite its size, it's simple to get your bearings in Alishan. Most people stay in what is technically Zhongzheng Village, though most just refer to it as Alishan Village. The village comprises a car park, post office, bus station, visitor centre and most of the hotels and restaurants.

Paths around the park are broad and attractions are marked with English signs. Traffic is not permitted in the park so you can walk on roads as well as trails without concern. With a basic map of the area you will have no trouble finding your way around.

## Information

### INTERNET RESOURCES

For information about train and bus schedules, hotels, attractions and weather, try the official website (www.aliorg.tw).

### MEDICAL SERVICES

**Public health clinic** ( ☎ 267 9806; ☼ 8am-5pm) Doctors are in Friday and Saturday afternoons. Nurses are available at other times. Just down the road from the Catholic Hostel, near the entrance gate.

### MONEY

There's an ATM in the post office in the village. It accepts only Taiwan-issued cards.

### TOURIST INFORMATION

Try to get hold of an English version of *Handbook for Foreign Travel to Taiwan's Alishan Forest Recreation Area*, as it is one of the best short guides to the park.

**Visitor Centre** ( ☎ 267 9917; ☼ 8am-5pm) English maps and brochures are available, though you can find the same ones in visitor centres in Taipei, Taichung and Kaohsiung.

## Sights & Activities

### ALISHAN FOREST TRAIN

For many people, taking the train up to Alishan is the peak experience of their entire trip. For this is no ordinary train and certainly no ordinary ride. The Alishan Forest Train runs on narrow-gauge track (762mm) and is one of only three remaining steep-grade alpine trains in the world. The track begins at 30m and ascends to above 2200m in 3½ hours. The total length of track is 71km and includes 49 tunnels and 77 bridges.

For those who understand exactly what this implies, the train ride is probably a must. For others, suffice to say the ride is a very pleasant trip on a small train up a steep mountain.

People have called the train ride a rolling 'botanical museum'. The first section is through a subtropical zone and rolls through banana, bamboo and longan plantations. At 800m the environment turns temperate and camphor, cedar and tea abound. At 1800m (past the Pingcherna station) the train enters alpine country and cypress, fir, pine and hemlock become the dominant plants.

As you ride up it may feel like the train is going backwards. It is! The train employs a unique system of switchbacks (much like hiking trails on a steep mountainside) that allow it to traverse slopes ordinarily too steep for trains.

Those with a passion for trains, or whose curiosity has been whetted by the ride up, should visit the old **steam yarder** (*jíchǎi jī*) near Chaoping station that was used until 1951 to haul logs up onto the rail cars.

### SUNRISE

Almost everyone who visits Alishan partakes in the ritual sunrise viewing, whether

**WESTERN TAIWAN**

for the chi, the breathtaking scenery, the festivity or simply because it is the 'thing to do'. When you check into a hotel you will inevitably hear the question, 'Yàobúyào kàn rìchū?', which means, 'Do you want to see the sunrise?'.

There are two main viewing venues: the summit of **Chushan** (Zhùshān; 2489m) and **Tatajia** (Tǎtǎjiā), a mountain pass 2610m above sea level in nearby Yushan National Park. To reach Chushan you can either take the train from Chaoping station (one-way/round-trip NT100/150, departure varies according to the season), or hike up along the **Chushan Sunrise Trail** (Zhùshān Guānrìchū Bùdào). The train takes about 25 minutes while hiking can take up to 1½ hours if you start in the village.

If you wish to see the sunrise at Tatajia, pay for a seat on one of the sunrise-tour minibuses (NT300, three hours). This is quite simple and every hotel can arrange it for you. Buses come directly to your hotel and most days there will be other guests also taking the bus or train so you can just follow their lead.

The minibus has several advantages over the train in that it stops at numerous scenic locations, such as the monkey-viewing area and the site of a few ancient trees on the way back from the sunrise viewing.

It's worth considering whether you are a 'morning person' before agreeing to get up at 4am. By the time you get back to your hotel you may be so exhausted that you can do nothing else but sleep for the rest of the afternoon.

### HIKING

For the Chushan Sunrise Trail, see above.

The 2km **Alishan Trail** (阿里山遊覽步道; Ālǐshān Yóulǎn Bùdào) begins at the **Plum Tree Garden** (Méiyuán), goes past Chaoping station, rounds the **Two Sister Ponds** (Jiěmèitán), goes through the **Magnolia Garden** (Mùlányuán) and then heads down to **Shouchen Temple** (Shòuzhèn Gōng).

You can head back to the village from here or continue to the old-tree area. If you keep going you'll find stands of ancient cypress, the remains of the 3000-year-old **Sacred Tree** (Ālǐshān Shénmù), the **Tree Spirit Monument** (Shùlíng Tǎ) ·commemorating a stand of ancient trees felled in 1936 and **Tzuyan Temple** (Cíyún Sì). The temple houses

a bronze Sakyamuni Buddha sent by the king of Thailand to the Japanese emperor. Rumour has it that the inside of the statue is filled with gold dust!

Give yourself three hours to complete both trails.

The **Duei-Kao-Yueh Trail** (對高岳步道; Dùigāoyuè Bùdào) takes around three hours return if you start from Chaoping station. Combine it, as many do, with a walk (or train ride up) to Chushan first, and you can stretch that into a good four-hour workout up and down many steep sections of trail. Make sure you bring a jacket and rain gear as the temperature becomes noticeably cooler at the top.

### Festivals

The **Cherry Blossom Festival** runs in March or April for two weeks while the trees are in bloom. This is an extremely busy time for the park.

### Sleeping

Alishan has more than a dozen hotels, but on weekends or during the Cherry Blossom Festival, when more than 10,000 people a day visit the park, you could find yourself without a room if you didn't book in advance. The majority of hotels are in the village behind and down from the car park. This is a convenient place to stay as there are a dozen or more places to eat, but it does feel as if you are staying in a big car park.

Most hotels offer weekday and low-season discounts, which can be up to 50%. Room prices can also vary in winter depending on whether there is central heating.

**Catholic Hostel** (Tiānzhǔtáng; ☎ 267 9602; dm/d/tw NT250/1000/2000) The hostel is not always open (especially on weekdays) so call Brother Fan before you go.

**Alishan House** (Ālǐshān Bīnguǎn; ☎ 267 9811, ext 6; d/tw/ste NT2300/3600/7000) This lovely Japanese-era building is Alishan's top hotel for service, comfort, style and feng shui. Like much of Alishan, this charm of this place is subtle and may strike you after you've left. Rooms are smoke free and there is a large public balcony for guests to enjoy the sunsets.

In 2006 the hotel plans to open a new five-star resort around the current hotel. Planned features include a ballroom, indoor amphitheatre, spa and gym. The hotel is up a distance from the village but when

WESTERN TAIWAN

the new resort is finished it will feature something unique in Alishan: nightlife.

**Alishan Gou Hotel** (Ālīshān'gé Dàfàndiàn; ☎ 267 9711; d/tw NT2200/3200) Part of the Alishan House group, this hotel features simple rooms with pleasant mountain views. The hotel **restaurant** (dishes from NT80; ☽ breakfast, lunch & dinner) has outdoor seating.

**Alishan House Annex** (Ālīshān Bīnguǎn Biéshù; ☎ 267 9811; 5-/8-person cabins NT4000/6000) Also part of the Alishan House group are these charming, almost dainty cabins set back among flower gardens and trees. A stay here would be alpine life at its sweetest.

## Eating

Most of the restaurants in Alishan are clustered around the car park and serve similar fare at similar prices: hotpots, stir-fries and local vegetables and meat dishes for around NT100 to NT200. Most are open for breakfast, lunch and dinner, though occasionally places close for one shift. English menus are not available.

There is a 24-hour grocery shop in the car-park area. Instant noodles and hot and cold drinks are available. The shop has a microwave for heating up food.

**Alishan House Restaurant** (Ālīshān Bīnguǎn Cāntīng; ☎ 267 9811, ext 6; dishes NT200; ☽ breakfast, lunch & dinner) This quietly charming restaurant serves some of the best food in Alishan and has an English menu. Chinese-style dishes include local fish and game. The views from window tables are excellent. Breakfast hours are 7am to 8.30am.

## Shopping

Around the car park, a half-dozen open-air shops sell dried goods such as Alishan High Mountain Tea (Ālīshān gāoshān chá), plums, cherries and wet items such as fruit liqueurs. Sticky rice *(moji)* in almost every conceivable flavour is also sold, as are aboriginal crafts displaying varying degrees of skill and price. The hardwood bowls with decorative weave are very durable and make nice gifts.

## Getting There & Away

### BUS

Buses to Alishan (NT156, 2½ hours, every two hours) from Chiayi leave from 7.10am until 3.10pm (at the time of writing the schedule was under revision, so call ahead) from the Chiayi County Bus Company station.

### TRAIN

There are three train stations in Alishan: the main Alishan station in Zhongzheng Village (this station was being rebuilt at the time of writing); Chaoping station, a few minutes up the track; and Chushan station, 25 minutes away where the train drops off passengers in the morning to watch the sunrise.

The Alishan Forest Railway leaves Chiayi station (NT399, 3½ hours) daily at 9am and 1.30pm. During Chinese New Year extra trains are scheduled.

## DANAYIGU ECOLOGICAL PARK
那伊谷自然生態保育公園

If you have your own vehicle, plan on a side trip to Shanmei to see this astonishing **park** (Dánàyīgǔ Zìrán Shēngtài Bǎoyù Gōngyuán; ☎ 05-258 6994; adult/child NT100/60, weekday NT80/40, parking car/scooter NT50/20; ☽ 8am-5pm).

From 1989 to 1999 the Zhou people closed off the dying 18km **Danayigu Creek** (達娜伊谷溪; Dánàyī Gǔxī) to all outsiders. The plan was to clean up the river and protect and restock the dwindling fish population. The success of the project amazed everyone. Today, in certain natural river pools, literally hundreds of fish squirm and wiggle in as little as one shallow square metre of water. It's a sight more akin to a healthy coral reef than a mountain stream.

The surrounding parkland is a model of ecological diversity. Zhou tribesmen give tours of the park and while they speak only Mandarin, it can still be worthwhile to join in if only because you will be forced to stop every few feet to discover yet another species of plant life.

Food is available at several rustic shops. The barbecued wild boar and sausages are lean and delicious.

To reach the park, take Hwy 18 east of Chiayi towards Alishan. At Lungmei (龍美; Lóngměi) you will see a sign directing you to Shanmei and Danayigu (Tanayiko) Ecological Park via County Rd 129 south. The trip from Chiayi takes about an hour by car. There is no public transport.

## YUSHAN NATIONAL PARK 玉山國家公園

The **Yushan National Park** (Yùshān Guójiā Gōngyuán) is not part of the Alishan National Scenic Area but they are such close neighbours that a trip to one often entails a visit to the other. Yushan covers over

WESTERN TAIWAN

100,000 hectares, or 3% of the landmass of Taiwan. It's the largest and most pristine of all the parks in Taiwan. It is also the most grand. There are 30 peaks over 3000m and six vegetative zones harbouring 50% of the endemic plant species in the country. The landscape of the park is strikingly rugged, with deep valleys and high mountains. In general the park tends to be wet in summer and dry in winter.

The park is well set up for the serious mountaineer. There are huts, cabins and camping grounds established all over the park. Most of these are in restricted areas, which means you need a Class A mountain permit (see p311) and a qualified guide.

Day-tripping from Alishan to Tatajia for a short hike or two is possible for those with a vehicle.

## Orientation

Yushan National Park covers areas in Chiayi, Nantou, Kaohsiung and Hualien Counties. A 20km drive west will take you to the Alishan Forest Recreation Area, while a drive from Kaohsiung to Taitung on Hwy 20 (Southern Cross Hwy) runs through the southern portion of the park.

## Information

Other than in Meishankou in the south, and Dongpu just outside the park boundaries in the north, there is no accommodation for the casual hiker.

### INTERNET RESOURCES

For detailed information on hiking routes (including how to obtain a Class A mountain permit), current trail, road and weather conditions, as well as articles on plant and animal life in the park try www.ysnp.gov.tw.

### TOURIST INFORMATION

There are four visitor centres for the park. All can provide maps in English, brochures and information on current trail conditions.

**Meishan** ( ☎ 07-686 6181; 44-5, Meishan, Kaohsiung County; ☯ 9am-4.30pm, closed Mon following 2nd & 4th Sun of every month. If these are national holidays, closed Tue)

**Nanan** ( ☎ 03-888 7560; 83-3, Choching, Hualien County; ☯ 9am-4.30pm, closed 2nd Tue of every month. If a national holiday, closed Wed)

**Shuili** ( ☎ 049-277 3121; 300 Jungshan Rd, Sec 1; Shuili, Nantou County; ☯ 9.30am-4.30pm) This is the park headquarters. Note that it's in Shuili an hour north of the actual park.

**Tatajia** ( ☎ 049-270 2200; 118 Taiping Rd, Tungfu, Nantou County; ☯ 9am-4.30pm, closed 2nd & 4th Tue of every month. If these are national holidays, closed Wed)

## Activities

### HIKING

Geologically speaking, Taiwan is a pretty active place. The Central Mountain Range is the result of the pushing and shoving of two major tectonic plates. The crowning glory of this mountain range is Yushan. At 3952m, it is the highest mountain in northeast Asia, higher than Mt Fuji in Japan.

Not surprisingly, the mountain attracts climbing enthusiasts from all over the world. In recent years a limit of 100 climbers a day has been imposed to minimise environmental damage. All climbers must obtain a Class A mountain permit and an accompanying guide before they can begin their climb. For foreigners this means you will need to go with a local hiking club. The club should make all the arrangements for permits and accommodation and advise you what to bring.

The first night, climbers stay in the dorm rooms at **Tungpu Lodge** (Dōngpǔ Shānzhuāng) in Tatajia (Tǎtǎjiā). Tatajia is a mountain pass where people often go to watch the sunrise. The next day, hikers make their way to **Paiyun Hut** (Páiyún Shānzhuāng), not far from the peak of Yushan, and spend the night. Early the following morning, climbers make the ascent on Yushan, watch the sunrise, rest at the top and then hike back to Tatajia. Any reasonably fit person can handle this itinerary provided he or she does not suffer from altitude sickness.

It is also possible to climb Yushan starting in Dongpu in the north. This is a longer route and usually takes three days to complete.

Consult the park's website for more trail information.

## Getting There & Away

There is no public transport into any area of Yushan National Park except Meishankou in the south.

# GUANZILING TO TAINAN

This route takes you through Tainan County to where the beginning of Taiwanese history can be traced. It's here where the Dutch first colonised the island and where the Ming loyalist Koxinga established his government and began the development of Taiwan. Tainan County was the first area to be brought under cultivation by the Chinese. Today, there are over 90,000 acres of arable land producing mostly rice, sugar cane and grains.

Lovers of history and temples cannot miss a visit to Tainan City, the old capital of Taiwan. It's said that there are over 200 temples in the city (many of which are centuries old and fabulous works of art and architecture). Don't expect these to be static relics, however, waiting quietly to be photographed and cooed over. In Tainan, even more than most places in Taiwan, temples are an integral part of community life and examples of fervent worship can be seen every day. Around holiday times, the ritual demonstrations at places such as the Nankunshen Temple rival the intensity of Santeria.

If history is not your interest, the fire spring at the hot-spring village of Guanziling and the badlands of Mt Tsao Moon World make for pretty rewarding side trips on your way down to points further south.

Tainan County has its own tourism website (http://english.tnhg.gov.tw). It's worth checking out.

## GUANZILING 關子嶺

This small **hot-spring village** (Guānzǐlǐng) in northern Tainan County is famous for its old temples (unfortunately being repaired at the time of writing), Red Leaf Park and two geological oddities. The first concerns the hot-spring water itself, which is a light grey 'mud' colour owing to the heavy mineral content. The second is a cave where natural-gas flames burn continuously on top of a small pool of spring water. Either is a good reason to plan a day trip from Tainan or Chiayi.

### Orientation & Information

The village is divided into lower and upper sections joined by a series of stone steps. The lower village is the older part of town. It's not that pleasant through here as many of the buildings are shabby and the hot-spring owners send people out onto the street to entice you into their establishment.

There's an ATM in the 7-Eleven in the lower village.

### Sights & Activities

#### WATER FIRE CAVE 水火洞

The **cave** (Shǔihuǒ Dòng; ⏱ 24hr), which is really more of a grotto, is a wonder. In a small pool of spring water, natural gas from far

WESTERN TAIWAN

---

### YENSHUI FIREWORKS FESTIVAL 鹽水蜂炮

There may be nothing stranger in this land than the annual **Yenshui Fireworks Festival** (Yénshǔi Fēngpà) – or battle, or blow-out – in which thousands of people place themselves willingly in the melee of exploding fireworks. It is like a massive, unruly game of paintball but with real explosives.

The festival has been going on for 100 years. It began as a countermeasure to a severe cholera epidemic, which explains the sense of mortal danger that still lingers in the air at festival time. (Or could it be those rocket hives pointed at the crowd?)

Some people travel from overseas every year to be part of the excitement. Tens of thousands more come in from all parts of Taiwan. Accidents, burns and lost eyes are all common, though most try to mitigate damage by wearing protective clothing. A motorcycle helmet is considered mandatory, though you will see men proving their machismo by going bare faced.

Yenshui is in the north of Tainan County. You can reach the town by taking an express train to nearby Sinying and then a taxi. Be prepared to be out all night if you go and take care of your valuables. The festival happens every year on Lantern Festival, two weeks after Chinese New Year.

For more information check out the article at www.taipeitimes.com/News/archives/2002/02/22/0000124935.

underground seeps up and ignites as it hits the surface air. The result is a surreal dance of flames atop pure water. The cave is in a small park. If possible, try to visit the area at night.

If you don't have a vehicle you could hike to the cave (6km) on the main road in 1½ hours from the park in the upper village (where the bus drops you off). It's a very pleasant hike on a weekday when traffic is light, as you are surrounded by forested mountains the whole time.

### RED LEAF PARK 紅葉公園
The Japanese built this **park** (Hóngyè Gōng-yuán) and, as usual, they knew what they were doing. The feng shui here is fantastic but more importantly so are the clear, all-natural views. Though the park is not very high, you feel as if you are in big country. It's quite unlike any other mountain experience in Taiwan.

To reach the park from the upper village, take the stairs down behind the new park, across from all the barbecue shops. At the bottom of the stairs, follow the road down for 100m as it bends and you'll see on the right a sign 'Horng Yeh Park' pointing to a wooden arch and a set of stairs. The stairs lead directly to the park. From the first park it should take about 30 minutes of walking.

### HOT SPRINGS
Guanziling's mud hot springs have always been considered therapeutic. In recent years several new hotels have opened, offering improved facilities and a variety of bathing options.

**Maple Hot Spring Cottage** (紅葉溫泉度假山莊; Hóngyè Wēnquán Dùjià Shānzhuāng; ☎ 06-682 2821; 關嶺路65-9號; unlimited use of public pools adult/child NT350/200; ☽ 10am-10pm) has a nice outdoor public pool set in a valley off the main road. To get to the pool, walk up from the new park about 1km. On the right you will see a café perched on the side of the hill. You can buy tickets here for the pools below.

## Getting There & Around
Guanziling is essentially one long dip off Hwy 172. It's best to take your own transport here but if you can't, take a bus (NT67, one hour, every hour) from the Chiayi Bus Company station in Chiayi. Buses stop at the 7-Eleven in the lower village and then continue another 1km to the new park in the upper village. It's better to get off at this stop. Red Leaf Park is close and the better hot-spring resorts are in this area.

## TSOCHEN 左鎮
This Tainan County **township** (Zuǒzhèn) is rich in fossil remains and was the site of the earliest human settlement in Taiwan, the so-called Tsochen man. The area is also blessed, or cursed, with chalky, saline, alkaline soil, the worst of which forms a grimly picturesque, barren section of badlands known as the Moon World. A visit to Tsochen makes a nice day trip from Tainan.

## Sights
### TSAI LIAO FOSSIL MUSEUM 菜寮化石館
The Tsochen area is prime fossil-hunting ground. Most of the fossils come from the Pleistocene era (1.8 million to 10,000 years ago), when Tsochen was repeatedly covered by water. The first fossils were discovered by a Japanese professor in the 1930s. After that the region became famous and many elderly Tsochen people can remember looking for fossils as children to sell to collectors.

The **museum** (Càiliáo Huàshíguǎn; ☎ 06-573 1174; 61-1 Junghe Village; admission free; ☽ 8.30am-noon & 1.30-5pm, closed Mon) began as the amateur collections of teachers and students. There are almost 1000 fossils on display; some of the more impressive include two perfect, 40cm-long mesosauri, the skull of an ancient rhino and numerous starfish and other marine animals embedded in rock. Some tiny fragments of human bones inspire the imagination more than please the eye.

### MT TSAO MOON WORLD 草山月世界
There are places in Taiwan that feel remote, but few that feel as desolate as this 200-hectare section of chalky badlands. **Mt Tsao Moon World** (Cǎoshān Yuè Shìjiè) is not completely, or even mostly, barren (owing to a species of tenacious bamboo) but there are large eerie-looking patches of bare terrain and chalky hills completely eroded on one or the other side.

To reach the Moon World, drive north of the museum on Hwy 20. Just past the 27km mark, you'll see a sign for the turn-off to Nanhua. Turn right here and proceed about 1km. When you see a sign in Chinese to Moon World, follow it right. Drive 5km down this road until you see a set of signs that indicate Erliao Pavilion (二寮觀日亭; Èrliáo Guānrìtíng) is straight ahead and Hill 308 (308高地瞭望台; Sānlíngbā Gāodì Liàowàngtái) is left. The exact boundaries of the Moon World are hard to define but this junction (with its statue of a boy flautist sitting on the moon) certainly feels like the start.

It's 9km to **Hill 308** from this turn and along the way you'll pass a number of pavilions, lookouts and suspension bridges. The views from these places are good, but those at the top of Hill 308 are outstanding and will impress upon you why the area is called Moon World. If you want to take photos, go in the morning when the light from the east shines directly on the chalk faces.

# TAINAN CITY 台南市
☎ 06 / pop 725,000

No visit to Taiwan should overlook Tainan (Táinán), the oldest city in the country. Tainan is where Taiwan's modern history began and where much of its traditional culture continues to thrive. In this former capital you can see a Dutch-built fort, some of the first streets in Taiwan and the earliest Matsu temples. In fact, Tainan maintains a wealth of traditional temples, relics, rituals and ceremonies, as well as traditional foods unmatched by any other city in Taiwan. It's a feast for the eye, the stomach and the historical imagination.

Tainan is not like Lugang, however, a small town that thrives mostly on its heritage. Tainan is the fourth-largest city of Taiwan and has all the amenities and facilities of any other region. There are shopping malls, luxury hotels, sharp-looking cafés and trendy bars. Tainan has industries producing metals, textiles and machinery, as well as a new science park that promises to bring the city into the avant-garde of Taiwan's hi-tech revolution.

You can visit Tainan any time of year, though local festival days are particularly rewarding. Give yourself at least a couple of days to see the sights and observe the local culture.

## History
The area around modern Tainan City was settled by the Chinese in 1590 and soon after used by the colonising Dutch as a base for their trade with Japan and China. The Dutch ruled from 1624 until 1662, the year they were expelled by the Ming loyalist Koxinga.

Koxinga established his central government in Tainan and worked to build up the city. In 1683, when the Qing dynasty regained control of Taiwan and turned it into an official province, Tainan was chosen as the capital. Tainan remained the political, cultural and economic centre of the island until 1885, when the capital moved to Taipei.

## Orientation
Almost all the sights in Tainan are concentrated around the city centre and the Anping District. Both areas are compact enough to get around on foot, though you will need a taxi to get from one to the other.

## Information
Tainan has a unique and very intelligent system of providing tourist information on the back of receipts. When you pay to enter the Chikan Towers, for example, you are given a large receipt with a history and map of the tower on the back. The Confucius Temple receipt is the best, as it lists the hours and prices of admission to all the other sights.

In general, Tainan is a friendly town for the English-speaking traveller. Major sights such as the Confucius Temple not only have English interpretation signs, but also large brown signs in English throughout the city pointing the way.

### CULTURAL CENTRE
**Tainan Cultural Centre** ( ☎ 269 2864; 332 Junghua Rd, Sec 3; ☯ 9am-5pm)

### INTERNET RESOURCES
The Tainan City government website (www.tncg.gov.tw/eng.htm) has good background information about some major sites and temples.

Part of the official tourism website for Taiwan, http://taiwan.net.tw describes in detail 20 temples and historical sites in Tainan. Go to the English section and click 'site map', then Tainan City.

A good personal site by a Tainan expat is www.geocities.com/allhou/tainanscene.htm.

WESTERN TAIWAN

# CENTRAL TAINAN

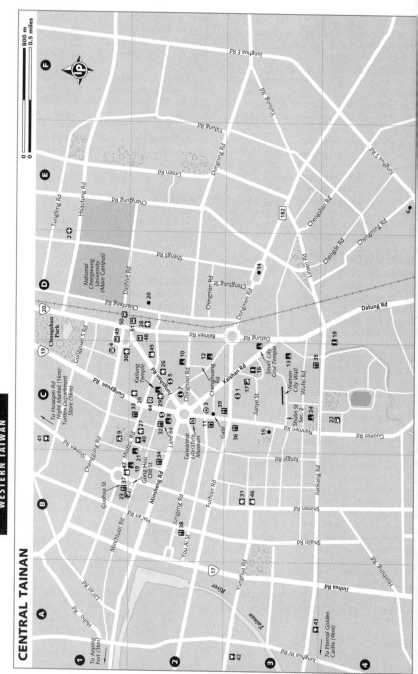

0        800 m
0        0.5 miles

#### MONEY

There are ATMs in most 7-Elevens (which are everywhere) in Tainan. You can use the ATMs or change money at **ICBC** (☎ 223 1231; 90 Jungshan Rd) or **Bank of Taiwan** (☎ 222 6181; 155 Fuchian Rd, Sec 1).

#### TOURIST INFORMATION

The *FYI South Magazine* (www.taiwanfun.com) is a free monthly entertainment magazine in English focusing on the south of Taiwan. You can pick up a copy at the tourist centre or many restaurants and entertainment venues across town. You can also download it at the website.

**Travel Information Centre** (☎ 226 5681; 10F, 243 Minchiuan Rd, Sec 1; ⏰ 8.30am-5pm Mon-Fri) This centre has numerous excellent English brochures about the sights around Tainan City. Staff speak some English and try to be as helpful as possible.

## Sights

#### CHIKAN TOWERS 赤崁樓

These impressive **towers** (Chìkǎn Lóu; 212 Mintzu Rd; adult/child NT50/25; ⏰ 8.30am-9pm) have gone through many masters (Ming, Qing, Japanese and the KMT) since their foundation was first laid by the Dutch in 1653. At the time of construction, the tide reached right up to the fort's outer walls. Much has been added, reconstructed and even carried away over the years, but the towers are in fine shape and are a grade-one historical site.

The nine stone turtles with tablets on their backs hail from the Qing dynasty. For fun, check out the backs of the tablets. You can see how the carver made a mistake in his work on one tablet and, rather than starting over with a fresh slab, simply turned the stone around and redid everything on the other side.

There are English explanations around the site as well as a brochure you can pick up when you enter.

#### OFFICIAL GOD OF WAR TEMPLE 祀典武廟

This **temple** (Sì Diǎn Wǔ Miào; 229 Yungfu Rd, Sec 2; admission free; ⏰ 9am-5pm) masterpiece is the oldest War God (Guan Di or Guan Gong) temple in Taiwan and was once a centre of official sacrificial rites. The building's overall size and structure were established in 1690, though much splendid artwork and many historically valuable objects have been added over the years.

Some interesting features to note are the deep rose-coloured outer wall, the beggar seats built into the doorframe and bamboo-shaped poem on a scroll at the back, which is said to have been written by Guan Gong himself.

The Guanyin shrine, also at the back of the temple, is said to hold the most beautiful Guanyin in Tainan. The nearby plum tree was planted (according to legend) by Koxinga's grandson over 300 years ago.

| INFORMATION | (pp239-41) | |
|---|---|---|
| Bank of Taiwan 台灣銀行 | **1** | C3 |
| Chengkung University Hospital 成大醫院 | **2** | D1 |
| Foreign Affairs Police (Visa Extensions) 警察外事課 | **3** | C2 |
| GPO IF 總局 | **4** | C1 |
| ICBC 中國國際商業銀行 | **5** | C2 |
| Tainan Cultural Centre 文化中心 | **6** | E4 |
| Travel Information Centre 旅遊中心 | **7** | C2 |
| **SIGHTS & ACTIVITIES** | **(pp241-4)** | |
| Altar of Heaven 天壇 | **8** | C2 |
| Chikan Towers 赤崁樓 | **9** | C1 |
| City God Temple 城隍廟 | **10** | C2 |
| Confucius Temple 孔子廟 | **11** | C2 |
| Dongyue Temple 東嶽殿 | **12** | C2 |
| Fahua Temple 法華寺 | **13** | C3 |
| Great East Gate 大東門 | **14** | D3 |
| Great South Gate 大南門城 | **15** | C3 |
| Koxinga's Shrine 延平郡王祠 | **16** | C3 |
| Lady LinShui's Temple 臨水夫人媽廟 | **17** | C3 |
| Martyr's Shrine 烈祠祠 | **18** | D4 |
| Matsu Temple 大天后宮 | **19** | B2 |
| Motorbike Rentals 機車出租 | **20** | D2 |
| Official God of War Temple 祀典武廟 | **21** | B2 |
| Swimming Pool 游泳池 | **22** | C4 |
| Water Fair Temple 水仙宮 | **23** | B1 |
| Wufei Temple 五妃廟 | **24** | C3 |
| **SLEEPING** | **(p246)** | |
| Akira Top Hotel 立人大飯店 | **25** | C2 |
| Asia Hotel 東亞樓大飯店 | **26** | C2 |
| Cambridge Hotel 劍橋大飯店 | **27** | C2 |
| Cheng Kuang Hotel 成光別館 | **28** | D2 |
| Hann Gong Hotel 漢宮大飯店 | **29** | C2 |
| Hotel Tainan 台南大飯店 | **30** | C1 |
| Taiyih Landis 大億麗緻酒店 | **31** | B3 |
| **EATING** | **(pp246-7)** | |
| A Xia Restaurant 阿霞飯店 | **32** | C2 |
| Chi Kin Dandanman 赤崁擔擔麵 | **33** | C2 |
| Fish Noodles 魚麵 | **34** | B2 |
| Glory Earth 地球咖啡烘焙美食 | **35** | C3 |
| Lily Fruit Shop 莉莉水果店 | **36** | C3 |
| Old Vegetarian Restaurant 素食餐廳 | **37** | B1 |
| Rong-Sheng Mi-kao 榮盛米糕 | **38** | B2 |
| The Green House 府前路一段196巷 21號3樓 | **39** | C2 |
| **DRINKING** | **(p247)** | |
| A Chuan Melon Drink 阿川冬瓜茶 | **40** | C2 |
| Armory Pub 公園南路82號 | **41** | C1 |
| Geng Du Yuan Tea House 耕讀園 | **42** | A3 |
| Willie's Second Base Bar & Grill 葳笠二壘酒吧 | **43** | A3 |
| **ENTERTAINMENT** | **(p247)** | |
| Warner Village Cinemas 華納威秀影城 | **44** | C2 |
| **SHOPPING** | **(pp247-8)** | |
| Shin Kong Mitsukoshi Department Store 台南中山新光三越百貨 | **45** | C2 |
| Shin Kong Mitsukoshi Department Store 台南新天地新光三越 | **46** | B3 |
| Shuang Chun Chang Shoes 雙全昌鞋行 | **47** | B1 |
| **TRANSPORT** | **(p248)** | |
| Hsingnan Bus Company 興南客運站 | **48** | D2 |
| Local Bus Station 市內公車站 | **49** | D1 |
| Tainan Train Station 台南火車站 | **50** | D1 |
| Taiwan Bus Company Station 台汽客運站 | **51** | D2 |

## MATSU TEMPLE 大天后宮

This **temple** (Dà Tiānhòu Gōng; 18 Lane 227, Yungfu Rd, Sec 2; admission free; ⏰ 9am-5pm) is just what you'd expect from a Taiwanese temple: old, gorgeous, complex, quirky and lively. The temple was once the palace of Ning-Jin, the last king of the Ming dynasty. If you wish to confirm visually that a king's status is lower than an emperor's, count the steps to the shrine: there are only seven; an emperor would get nine.

Some features to note (besides the elaborate carvings and paintings) include the 300-year-old Matsu statue and the shrine in the back to Matsu's parents that used to be King Ning-Jin's bedroom. If you look up you'll see the roof beam where the king's concubines hanged themselves (see Wufei Temple, opposite).

For fun, check out the eyes and feet of the door guards. You'll notice they point or stare at you from every angle you face them.

## ALTAR OF HEAVEN 天壇

Have you had a run of bad luck lately? Then visit this **temple** (Tiāntán; 16 Lane 84, Jungyi Rd, Sec 2; admission free; ⏰ 9am-5pm) and pray to the supreme Taoist entity, the Jade Emperor (or Lord of Heaven), to help you out. Tainan families have been doing this for generations on the 1st and 15th of every month.

The temple is noteworthy for two things. First, it has no statue of the god – the original temple was established as a temporary measure and, though it has lasted for 300 years, no statue has ever been added. The other feature of note is the famous Yī (One) inscription over the altar, which signifies that for heaven and earth there is only one true way: humanity and righteousness.

## CONFUCIUS TEMPLE 孔廟

You expect a **Confucius Temple** (Kǒng Miào; 2 Nan-men Rd; adult/child NT50/25; ⏰ 8.30am-9pm) to exude the calm, grace and dignified beauty of traditional Chinese culture, and this, the first Confucian temple in Taiwan, doesn't disappoint.

You must pay to enter the palace area but your receipt comes with an excellent short brochure and map of the temple. One thing to look for that is not on the brochure is the stone tablet on the right as you enter the Edification Hall. The words on the tablet explain the school rules (the site was once a centre for Confucian studies), such as prohibitions against gambling, drinking and cheating.

Across the street from the temple entrance is an old **stone arch**, built in 1777.

## GREAT SOUTH GATE 大南門城

The garrison commander in you will love the martial feel of this old **city gate** (Dà Nánmén Chéng; Lane 34, Nanmen Rd; admission free; ⏰ 8.30am-5.30pm), the only one in Tainan that still has much of its defensive wall intact. The inner grounds feature several cannons and a section of the old wall marvellously overgrown with thick roots.

WESTERN TAIWAN

---

### ENGLISH IN, ENGLISH OUT

You're walking down the road one evening in Tainan when suddenly you hear a loud voice call out, 'Tea or coffee?' The answer soon rings back, 'Tea, please'. The message and answer are then repeated several times, first in English, then Mandarin and then Taiwanese.

What is going on here? Did you just pass a cram school? Or some multilingual café? No, you have just been witness to the daily English lesson brought each day to the city by, no, not the education board, but the sanitation department. That is, you've just heard one of the infamous English-language-learning garbage trucks of Tainan.

It was a creative idea, to be sure: raise the level of English among Tainan residents by exposing them to simple conversational lessons that are changed every week. The brainchild of the mayor's wife, the lessons have perhaps not inculcated the average citizen so much as repulsed them. Locals say they have learned to drop their garbage off and then leave as quickly as possible.

Still, there are some who have benefited from the experiment. When asked by a TV crew to repeat one of the lessons he had heard for the past week, one sanitation worker was able to say, 'Good morning, and how are you today?' with very little accent. The mayor was quick to point out that, 'Obviously we're aware that it's impossible to learn English properly this way and still recommend going to school to study'.

You can climb to the top of the walls and even, rather oddly, enjoy a coffee on them in the evenings.

## KOXINGA'S SHRINE 延平郡王祠

Koxinga (Cheng Cheng-kung) was born of a pirate/merchant father and Japanese aristocratic mother. When the Manchus ended the Ming dynasty, Koxinga, King of Yenping, led his army to Taiwan (in 1661). His plan was to build a base from which he could launch an attack on the Manchus to restore the Ming. The Dutch were already in Taiwan, having established the island as a colony in 1624, but after nine months battling against the military genius of Koxinga, the European colonialists surrendered.

Koxinga did much to improve conditions in Taiwan. He established schools, proper government and trained the people in weaponry and warfare. But, like the KMT of modern times, he did not live to see the mainland retaken. He died after only a year in Taiwan and his grandson surrendered to the Manchus in 1683.

The **Koxinga Shrine** (Yánpíng Jùnwáng Cí; 152 Kaishan Rd; adult/child NT50/25; 8.30am-9pm) is the only such shrine to have been granted official status. You can see the box that held the original imperial edict from 1874 (and the request for official status) hanging in the shrine room.

The **museum** beside the shrine features displays of traditional puppets and clothing, as well as models and paintings of Fort Zeelandia. There are English explanations of most things here and at the shrine.

## WUFEI TEMPLE 五妃廟

When Koxinga's grandson surrendered to the Manchus in 1683, all hope ended of restoring the Ming dynasty. King Ning Jin, the last contender for the Ming throne, was living in Taiwan at the time but knew his time was up. Before he committed suicide he urged his concubines to 'get thee to a nunnery'. The concubines refused and decided to end their lives too. They hanged themselves on a roof beam in the bedroom of the king's palace, now the shrine to Matsu's parents at the Matsu Temple.

A dainty **temple** (Wǔfēi Miào; admission free; 8.30am-9pm), off Wufei Rd, was constructed in the concubines' honour and now sits in a half-acre garden park. The real tombs of the

ladies are behind the shrine and are covered with cement. There are some English explanations at the site.

## LADY LINSHUI'S TEMPLE 臨水夫人媽廟

Just behind Koxinga's Shrine is a **temple** (Línshǔi Fūrén Mā Miào; 1 Jianye St; admission free; 9am-5pm), the elaborate design and excessive ornamentation of which should, according to tradition, clue you in to the fact that it honours a woman. At Lady Linshui's Temple, or Chen Ching Gu Temple, women come to ask for protection of their children. This is demanding work and the goddess employs 36 assistants (three for each month), whose statuettes can be seen in little glass vaults around the inside walls of the temple.

In addition to offerings of incense, you'll often see flowers, face powder and make-up left at the temple.

## DONGYUE TEMPLE 東嶽殿

This is the **temple** (Dōngyuè Diàn; 110 Minchiuan; admission free; 9am-5pm) of Eastern Mountain and holds the shrines of several gods. In the first is the city god, Chenghuang, in the second, Zizang Wang, the Buddhist king of the underworld, and in the last, a number of demon gods who rule the underworld. To the left of this area is a small shrine dedicated to Guanyin.

People often come to this temple to communicate with the dead through spiritual mediums. It's a fascinating place, and the grim murals depicting life in hell, as graphic as anything by Hieronymus Bosch, only add to the impression that the supernatural is alive and well.

## CITY GOD TEMPLE 城隍廟

The City God tallies our good and bad deeds in this life after we die. Hence it is not unusual that his image appears in the Dongyue Temple, dedicated to the underworld god, nor that these two temples are very close to each other.

When you enter the **City God Temple** (Chénghuáng Miào; 28 Guosheng Rd; admission free; 9am-5pm) you'll probably notice two things. First, there are two large abacuses. These are used by the god to calculate if you have done more good than bad in life to allow you to proceed to heaven. Second, there is large sign overhead with a gold inscription. This

WESTERN TAIWAN

inscription translates roughly as 'You've come at last', which implies that like everyone else, you will die and face your day of reckoning.

The pink slips of paper you often see on the altar are from students asking for help to pass an exam.

### ANPING 安平區
Besides central Tainan, the western Anping (Ānpíng) District has the most interesting concentration of relics and temples. While our map does not extend as far as this area, you can pick up a brochure at the tourist office that shows the location of all the sights below.

### Anping Fort (Fort Zeelandia) 安平古堡
In 1624 the Dutch seized the area known as Anping to establish a military and commercial base in Taiwan. **Fort Zeelandia** (Ānpíng Gǔbǎo; adult/child NT50/25; ☼ 8.30am-5.30pm) was finished in 1634 and was a stronghold of Dutch power until captured by Koxinga in 1661. The present day fort was reconstructed by the Japanese and is well worth a visit. There is still a marvellous old section of the original wall remaining and a well-stocked folk museum. Several archaeological digs have also been taking place on the grounds in recent years, so you never know what will have been found by the time you arrive.

### Medicine God Temple 妙壽宮
There are a number of beautiful old temples around Anping. This small **temple** (Miào Shòu Gōng; admission free; ☼ 9am-5pm) is not one of them but it features two small lion statues out front that have an interesting story.

A young scholar in the Qing dynasty prayed to the Medicine God to help him pass an imperial exam. He promised that if he passed he would reward the god by paying to have two lion statues made for the temple. Well, the scholar did pass the exam. Unfortunately, poor man that he was, he could only afford the two diminutive felines you see today.

### Anping Matsu Temple 安平天后宮
The **Matsu Temple** (Ānpíng Tiānhòu Gōng; admission free; ☼ 9am-5pm) in Anping was the first Matsu temple in Taiwan. (The city-centre one was the first *official* Matsu temple.) The Anping temple features what is probably the oldest Matsu statue in all of Taiwan. It's not the one you think (the biggest one in the back shrine), but rather the middle one on the second row of Matsu statues.

Near the altar you can pick up a little packet of 'safe rice' to take home. The packets are designed to keep you and your family safe.

### Anping Old Streets 安平老街
Anping has some of the oldest streets in Taiwan, including **Shiaujung St** (效忠街; Xiào zhōngjiē), and **Yenping St** (延平街; Yánpíngjiē) both of which are to the right of Fort Zeelandia as you face the entrance. At the end of the block along Shiaujung St and just around the corner is the entrance to the historic **Ha Shan Hall** (海山館; Hǎishānguǎn). At the time of writing you could not enter the building, which is unfortunate as it is a veritable museum of charms, pendants, implements, spells, lotions and potions to ward off evil.

Yenping St has been turned into something like the Old Market St in Lugang (p210), with old shops spiffed up to attract tourists. Both streets feature several traditional restaurants well worth a visit if you wish to sample traditional Tainan foods (p247).

### Eternal Golden Castle 億載金城
Like many famous sights around Tainan, this **fort** (Yìzǎi Jīn Chéng; 16 Nanwen Rd; adult/child NT50/25 ☼ 8.30am-5pm) goes by different names – Erkunshen Cannon Fort, Anping Big Cannon Fort and Eternal Golden Castle. The fortress was built in 1876 to shore up Taiwan's defences against the Japanese threat.

Not much remains of the original fortress, though, oddly, the arched front gate which is intact, was built with bricks pilfered from Fort Zeelandia. The reconstructed fort is still an impressive site and the cannons make for good photo ops. If you have time you can challenge yourself and any companions to find the one real cannon among all the reproductions.

The castle is a few kilometres from the other sites at Anping so you may want to take a taxi there to save time.

## Walking Tour
The following walking tour covers all of the major temples and sights in central Tainan. You'll have plenty of opportunity to sample

local snacks and drinks along the way so it's best to go on a light or empty stomach.

The walk begins at the peaceful **Confucius Temple** (1; p242) on Nanmen Rd. A few blocks south on Nanmen you'll find the grand **Great South Gate** (2; p242) and just east on Shulin a large section of the **old wall** (3; p242) that used to connect with the gate. On Shulin St, take the first right and head down a quiet lane filled with quaint cafés and teahouses. When you reach Wufei Rd, check out the dainty **Wufei Temple** (4; p243), built to honour the concubines of the last contender to the Ming throne.

Now look for building No 76 on the left as you head east down Wufei Rd. When you see the number, turn left onto a small lane. Fifty metres on the left you'll see the grounds of the 300-year-old **Fahua Temple** (5). When the temple was first built, the ocean reached the edge of the outer wall.

Continue up the alley until you reach a large intersection. Head north up Kaishan Rd until you see **Koxinga's Shrine** (6; p243) on the left. When you leave the compound, take the back right gate to visit **Lady Linshui's**

Temple (7; p243). You'll mostly see women at this elaborate temple, asking for protection for their children from Lady Lin and her 36 helpers.

Now get back on Kaishan Rd and turn right at the intersection. Head east down Fuchian Rd and then turn left at the big intersection onto Minchiuan. At the **Dongyue Temple** (8; p243) check out the terrifying visions of hell painted on the walls.

Continue up Minchiuan to Chenghuang Rd and turn right. At the end of this short street you'll see the **City God Temple** (9; p243) across the road. The god has been waiting for you!

Now head west down Chingnian and then turn right up Minchiuan. Cross Gungyuan and turn left. You'll see a bank and then a small alley. Turn right into the alley to get to the **Altar of Heaven** (10; p242). If you're hungry, consider the seafood at **A Xia Restaurant** (11; p247).

When you leave the alley, it's a quick left and then a right onto Minsheng. A block later, turn right up Yungfu St. Two blocks ahead you'll see the beautiful deep rose-coloured walls of the **Official God of War Temple** (12; p241) on the left and **A Chuan Melon Drink** (13; p247) on the right. Both are worth a stop.

Now continue to the end of Yungfu St to the **Chikan Towers** (14; p241). Legend has it that the old well here leads all the way to Fort Zeelandia in Anping!

On the opposite side of the street, a tiny alley leads to the **Matsu Temple** (15; p242). Don't forget to check out the door guards and the roof beam!

When you leave the temple, walk straight ahead to Shimen Rd. Turn left, and at a tiny alley called Gong Hou Jie, turn right. Proceed down the alley until you reach Guohua St. Cross the street and enter the market. About 30m in, look to the right for the **Water Fair Temple** (16), an old command post and one of the few temples in Tainan to face east.

Your Tainan walking tour has now ended and rather appropriately, we think, beside an old temple in an old market.

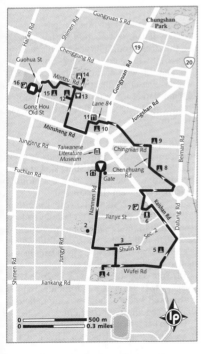

## Tours

**Taoyuan Culture Tourism Association** ( ☎ 235 3341; oriform@ms4.hinet.net; 374 Yuping-9th Rd; half-day/full-day tours NT2000/3000) This historical society

WESTERN TAIWAN

offers half-day or full-day tours in English around Tainan. Members are steeped in local history and culture, passionate about their city and can literally open doors to show you what's behind. However, the society building is hard to find. It's best to call and arrange a guide to meet you at your hotel.

## Festivals

Traditional Chinese holidays such as the **Dragon Boat Festival** (Duānwǔjié) and the **Lunar New Year** (Chūnjié) are celebrated in a big way in Tainan. In addition, the birthdays of the various temple deities (Matsu, Confucius, Lady Linshui) usually feature colourful and lively events at the respective temples.

## Sleeping

### BUDGET

**Asia Hotel** (Dōngyàlóu Dàfàndiàn; ☎ 222 6171; 100 Jungshan Rd; d/tw NT1000/1400) The hotel is getting old but it's well maintained and very popular with students and others looking for budget accommodation, especially during holidays. Rooms are quite large for the price.

**Cheng Kuang Hotel** (Chéngguāng Biéguǎn; ☎ 222 1188; 294 Beimen Rd; s/d NT600/1000) This hotel is conveniently close to the train station. Rooms are small, simply furnished but well maintained.

**Hann Gong Hotel** ( ☎ 226 9115; 199 Jungshan Rd; r from NT700) Rooms are pretty basic here but the owners are a sweet old couple who will make you feel welcome.

### MID-RANGE

**Akira Top Hotel** (Lìrén Dàfàndiàn; ☎ 226 5261; 88 Gungyuan Rd; d/tw incl breakfast NT980/1680) This place is popular with families and features rather small but comfortably furnished rooms. The hotel is in a good location, close to restaurants, bars, cafés and Jungshan Park.

**Cambridge Hotel** (Jiànqiáo Dàfàndiàn; ☎ 221 9966; 269 Mintzu Rd, Sec 2; d/tw NT2200/2600; 🖳 ) This hotel is well positioned in the business district and also just a stone's throw from the Chikan Towers. Facilities include underground parking, a business centre, ADSL in every room and direct service to the Tainan Science Park. Rooms are nicely furnished and have passed all the latest fire-safety regulations. This is an obvious choice for a business traveller but also those looking for a bit more comfort.

### TOP END

**Hotel Tainan** (Táinán Dàfàndiàn; ☎ 228 9101; www.hotel-tainan.com.tw;1 Chenggung Rd; d/tw/ste NT3200/3600/5000; 🖳 ) Many consider this one of Tainan's top hotels and certainly the service is top notch. Rooms are furnished comfortably in a modern style with a few Chinese touches. The hotel includes a business centre and health club. The buffet meals at the **Jade Room Restaurant** (meals NT270-600; ☺ breakfast, lunch & dinner) come highly recommended.

**Taiyih Landis** (Dàyìlìzhì Jiǔdiàn; ☎ 213 5555; www.tayihlandis.com.tw; 600 Shimen Rd, Sec 1; d/tw/ste incl buffet breakfast NT5600/5000/8000) This hotel opened just a few years ago in the central business district and is the only five-star place in town. Elegantly designed rooms come with their own workstation and feature flatscreen TVs and lovely marble bathrooms. The hotel is close to the new upmarket Shin Kong Mitsukoshi Department Store, as well as a number of cultural attractions.

## Eating

For simple cafés and inexpensive noodle, rice and Japanese fast-food outlets, check out the area around Warner Village. For bars, nightclubs and fancier cafés, visit Jiankang Rd, west of the Martyrs' Shrine.

Locals will often direct you to the **Hsiaopei Rd Night Market** for traditional foods, however the places listed in this section are far superior.

### CENTRAL TAINAN

For seafood and shrimp meatballs (xiārén ròuyuán) try the **Guo Hua Street Market** near the Matsu Temple. There is also a famous **vegetarian restaurant** (157 Guo Hua St).

Just west of Chikan Towers, on either side of 242 Mintzu Rd, are a famous **seafood congee stall** (hǎixiān zhōu) and the original **danzi mian stall** (dànzǐ miàn). A little south is an old **shop** (15 Minsheng St, Sec 2) famous for its fish noodles (yú miàn).

**Lily Fruit Shop** (199 Fuchian Rd, Sec 2; ☺ 11am-11pm) Across from the Confucius Temple is this well-known shop, serving delicious shaved iced and fruit (bào bīng).

**Chi Kin Dandanman** (Chìkàn Dāndānmiàn; 180 Minzu St, Sec 2; bowl NT40; ☺ 11am-3am) This is a fun place to try traditional *dànzǐ miàn* as the restaurant is set in a Japanese-era merchant's house. Dànzǐ means two baskets and a stick and refers to the baskets used to carry the noodles around for sale. The dish is a simple, refreshing mix of noodles with a tangy meat sauce.

**Rong-Sheng Mi-kao** (Róngshèng Mǐgāo; 106 Kangle Market, Jungjeng Rd; rice cakes NT30; ☺ 10am-8pm) This 67-year-old shop is said to sell the best rice cakes in Tainan. Kangle Market is off Jungjeng Rd and looks like a small ground-level mall.

**A Xia Restaurant** (Āxiá Fàndiàn; ☎ 221 9873; 7, Lane 84, Jungyi Rd, Sec 2; meals NT500-700) This famous Tainan restaurant is quite expensive but locals will tell you the seafood is worth the price. It is a popular venue for weddings and other celebrations.

### ANPING

The Anping area close to Fort Zeelandia is home to several well-known old eating establishments and a few newer ones catering to the renewed interest in traditional foods.

**An-Ping Gui Ji Local Cuisine Cultural Restaurant** (安平貴記美食文化館; Anpíng Guìjì Měishí Wénhuàguǎn; ☎ 222 9794; 延平街93號; meals NT50; ☺ 11am-10pm) This place is exactly what it sounds like. The shop is set in the Yang family's ancestral home on Yenping St and offers a host of traditional Tainan snacks at low prices. The shop features a big photo display of traditional foods (*dànzǐ miàn*, coffin cakes) and a multilanguage brochure to help visitors.

**Uncle Tiancong's Fish Ball Soup** (天從伯魚丸湯; Tiāncóngbó Yúwántāng; 延平街130號; fish ball soup NT30; ☺ 10am-7pm) At the end of the block-long Shiaujung St is this 100-year-old shop serving delicious fish ball soup.

**Jou Family Shrimp Rolls** (周氏蝦捲; Zhōushì Xiājuǎn; 安平路125號; 2 rolls NT40; ☺ 7am-7.30pm) This place on Anping Rd, heading back towards Tainan City (two blocks from the Matsu Temple), is famous for shrimp rolls, which are deep-fried but not oily.

### OTHER DISTRICTS

**Green House** (3F, 21, Lane 196, Fuchian Rd, Sec 1; dishes from NT150; ☺ breakfast, lunch & dinner) This long-running, casual Western restaurant is a popular expat hang-out. Dishes include pasta, hamburgers and Mexican.

**Glory Earth** (Dìqiú Kāfēi Hōngbèi Měishí; 102 Jiankang Rd, Sec 1; sandwiches NT90; ☺ 8am-midnight) Jiankang Rd, heading west from the Martyrs' Shrine, features block after block of sharp-looking modern cafés, restaurants and bars. Glory Earth has a stylish but relaxed atmosphere, a mostly youthful clientele, and decent drinks and sandwiches.

## Drinking

**A Chuan Melon Drink** (Āchuān Dōngguāchá; 212 Yungfu Rd, Sec 2; drinks from NT15; ☺ 9am-10pm) This well-known melon drink stand is just across from the God of War Temple and often has people lining up for a beverage.

**Geng Du Yuan Tea House** (Gēngdúyuán; 23-25 Yunghua Rd, Sec 2; ☺ 11am-2am) On a street with several modern, upscale restaurants is this decidedly classical Chinese-style wood teahouse. An average package of tea leaves costs NT400, not including a per-person water fee of NT130. English menus explain the different flavours and textures of the various teas on sale.

**Armory Pub** (☎ 226 5800; 82 Gungyuan Rd; drinks from NT120; ☺ 8pm-3am) This smoky pub is busy most nights with a good mix of laid-back locals and expats.

**Willie's Second Base Bar & Grill** (Wēilì Èrlěi Jiǔbā; ☎ 291 1050; 321 Jiankang Rd, Sec 3; drinks from NT120; ☺ 7pm-3am) Slightly upmarket sports bar run by ex-LA Dodgers pitcher Steve Wilson. Good grill-style foods such as baby back ribs (NT500) and steaks (NT350) are available.

## Entertainment

### CINEMAS

**Warner Village Cinemas** (Huánà Wēixiù Yǐngchéng; ☎ 221 5110; http://web.warnervillage.com.tw/; 60 Gungyuan Rd; adult/child NT230/210) This theatre is recommended by local mothers as the only safe one in town. You can book tickets online in English.

### NIGHTCLUBS

Dance clubs tend to come and go rather too frequently in Tainan. Ask around or check out *FYI South Magazine* for the latest hot spots.

## Shopping

**Shin Kong Mitsukoshi Department Store** (Táinán Xīntiāndì Xīnguāng Sānyuè; 658 Shimen Rd, Sec 1). Most older locals remember the days when this

WESTERN TAIWAN

location housed a prison and execution room, and not his new upscale store.

**Shuang Chun Chang Shoes** (Shuāngquánchāng Xiéháng; 316 Shimen Rd, Sec 2; ☉ 9am-10.30pm) For something traditional, check out the cute wood slippers (*mùjī*) at this 51-year-old shop near the Matsu Temple.

## Getting There & Away
### AIR
**TransAsia Airways** ( ☎ 222 7111) has daily flights between Tainan and Taipei (for around NT1700).

### TRAIN
Tainan is a major stop on the Western Line. Trains from Taipei (fast/slow train NT741/346, 3½/seven hours) and Kaohsiung (fast/slow train NT107/50, 30 minutes/one hour) run every half hour from 5am to midnight.

## Getting Around
### TO/FROM THE AIRPORT
Until the bus system gets straightened out, we can only suggest that you take a taxi.

### BUS
Tainan's public bus system had collapsed at the time of writing and was being taken over by Kaohsiung Bus Company. There was no word on which routes would remain nor how much rides would cost in the future.

### SCOOTER
You can rent scooters from several shops in front of the train station for NT200 a day.

## BAIHE TOWNSHIP
In northern Tainan County, not far west of Guanziling, Baihe Township (Báihé Zhèng) is nicknamed 'Lotus Land', not because of any left-leaning tendencies in its population but because they grow a lot of lotus here: over 300 hectares. Since 1995 the township has been hosting an annual **Lotus Festival** (白河蓮花季; Báihé Liánhuā Jì), which includes about two months of cycling tours of lotus fields, seed-shucking contests and photographic competitions. This is your chance to see what a country fair is like, Taiwanese style. The festival is held during July and August.

The place to stay is **Ama's Scenic Guesthouse** (阿嬤的家; ☎ 06-687 6899; 2-6 Liantan Borough, Baihe

Township; r NT2400) but you better book early if you want a room. The guesthouse is set in the middle of lotus fields and every morning visitors are taken out on bikes to watch the lotus blossoms unfold.

## NANKUNSHEN 南鯤身代天府
The majority of people in Tainan County worship Wang Yeh. The **temple** (Nánkūnshēn Dàitiān Fǔ) in Nankunshen is the oldest (established 1662) and most important Wang Yeh temple in the county. It's also a beautiful structure and larger than anything you'll find in Tainan City.

On most Sundays the temple atmosphere explodes with exuberant displays of ritual devotion, including fireworks, parades, chanting and occasionally, self-mutilation. If possible, try to visit during the **Welcoming Festival for Wang Yeh** (20 April, lunar calendar) or the **Birthday of Wu-tzu-yeh** (10 September, lunar calendar).

Buses to Nankunshen (NT102, 40 minutes, every hour) leave Tainan City from the **Hsingnan bus station** ( ☎ 06-211 2211; 182 Jungshan Rd). The bus station in Nankunshen is a block south of the temple, on the same road.

# SOUTH CROSS-ISLAND HWY

The **South Cross-Island Hwy** (南部橫貫公路; Nánbù Héngguàn Gōnglù) bisects southern Taiwan, running from Tainan in the west to Taitung in the east. The road passes through the southern part of the Central Mountain Range, skirting the southern side of Yushan National Park. Some people find this highway to be the most exhilarating but frightening highway in Taiwan. Parts of the high, narrow road are frequently washed away during landslides and falling rocks are all too common. The safest time to cross the highway is in winter, when the rains are lightest.

Along the highway are hot springs, aboriginal towns and plenty of hiking trails. Hiking along parts of the highway is a popular activity, especially between the mountain stations of Tienchih (Tiānchì) and Yakou (Yǎkǒu). Some people use the highway as a base for more challenging hikes up Kuanshan. Cycling across the highway is also becoming more common, though with increasing traffic this can be dangerous. Reflective clothing is a must, as well as a quality bike.

Most people start the trip across the highway from Tainan if they're hiking or cycling. The east coast drops down sharply, a difficult ascent if starting from that side.

## TAINAN–PAOLAI–MEISHANKOU

Travelling from Tainan, you'll pass through the small towns of Yuching (Yùjǐng) and Chiahsien (Jiǎxiān), neither of which have much to entice travellers. The town of Paolai (Bǎolái), considered the gateway to the South Cross-Island Hwy, has a little more to offer, being the site of the **Paolai Hot Springs** (Bǎolái Wēnquán), which are pumped into Paolai's resort hotels for private use.

The nicest place to enjoy the hot-spring baths is at the **New Paolai Hot Springs Resort** (Xīn Bǎolái Wēnquán Dùjià Cūn; ☎ 06-688 1700; d NT1500). This hotel has great views of the valley and professional management. Other hotels in town don't really measure up.

Be aware that if you are taking the 7.20am bus from Tainan and get off at Paolai, the only other buses that cross the highway terminate at Meishankou (Méishānkǒu), about two hours up the road. The buses stop in Paolai at 11.30am and 3.15pm. The bus to Tienchih swings through Paolai at around 9.30am.

The next stop on the road is the tiny town of Meishankou, home of the Bunun aboriginal tribe. Meishankou has many pleasant hiking trails and a large **botanical garden**. Across from the botanical garden is the **Bunun Aboriginal Cultural Centre** (Bùnóng Wénhuà Zhǎnxíng Zhōngxīn; ☺ 9am-4.30pm, closed Tue), which is currently closed for renovation. The Bunun hold dances here during the Lunar New Year holidays, which attract visitors from all over Taiwan.

The **Meishankou Youth Activity Centre** (Méishān Qīngnián Huódòng Zhōngxīn; ☎ 07-686 6166; d NT2000, 4-person tatami r NT2400) is the only hotel in town. It's a very quiet, relaxing place, with rooms overlooking a Japanese-style rock garden and fish pond in the inner courtyard. If the hotel is not full, you can stay in one of the tatami rooms for a discount. Breakfast is included with rooms; lunch and dinner are extra.

The 7.20am bus from Tainan stops briefly in Meishankou at 10.30am and then continues on to Tienchih, 25km down the road. There is only one bus a day to Tienchih from Meishankou. If you miss it, you may have to hitch.

## TIENCHIH–YAKOU

Tienchih (elevation 2280m) is where the Taitung and Tainan buses terminate and head back to their respective stations, and it's necessary to transfer buses to continue the journey over the mountains. Buses generally leave around 1.30pm.

Tienchih lies within **Yushan National Park** and there are trails here with opportunities for short hikes. There's also a shrine dedicated to the workers who died while building the highway. The only place to stay in Tienchih is at the minimalist **Tienchih Hostel** (Tiānchí Zhāodàisǔo; ☎ 07-678 0006; d NT300). There is nothing to eat here so bring some food with you.

Instead of taking the bus, many prefer to walk the 14km to Yakou (elevation 2728m). Increased traffic has taken some of the enjoyment out of the walk, but the scenery along the way still makes it worth it. About 6km down the highway from Tienchih is **Cypress Valley** (Kuìgě), a beautiful forest with secluded walking trails and picnic areas.

Right before Yakou is the 600m **Dakuanshan Tunnel** (Dàguānshān) on the eastern edge of Yushan National Park. At 2700m, this is the dividing line between Taitung and Kaohsiung Counties. The tunnel is dark and creepy, feeling much longer than it actually is.

Yakou is at the other end of the tunnel and the starting point for hikes up to Kuanshan (3666m). This hike should be planned in advance and requires a Class A mountain permit (see p311). At Yakou, travellers can stay in the **Yakou Hostel** (Yǎkǒu Shānzhuāng; dm NT500, tatami r NT1600). Rooms must be booked through the **Meishan Youth Activity Centre** (☎ 07-686 6166).

Food is extremely limited up here except for cookies and instant noodles. If this won't do, stock up in Tainan, Paolai or Meishankou.

## YAKOU–WULU

From Yakou it's possible to walk down to Wulu (Wùlù), passing **Litao** (Lìdào), a small

Bunun town, along the way. Litao is 30km from Yakou, about a six- or seven-hour walk. Alternatively, you can hop on the bus coming from Tienchih, which passes through Yakou at approximately 2pm.

Litao is a very relaxing place and there's not much to do here but admire the scenery and unwind. The **Litao Hostel** (Lìdào Shānzhuāng; ☎ 089-938 089; dm NT400, t NT1600) is the only hotel in town. To book a room, you must call the **Meishan Youth Activity Centre** ( ☎ 07-686 6166). The hostel has breakfast available for NT50 and lunch and dinner for NT120; these must be booked in advance.

There are two buses daily from Litao to Wulu and onwards to Taitung. The first bus leaves Litao at 8am, the second at 2.30pm. Alternatively, it's a two-hour walk to Wulu, passing through the dramatic **Wulu Canyon** (Wùlù Xiá Gǔ).

Wulu is known for its **hot springs**, something to be grateful if you're sore from walking all this time. The most luxurious place to enjoy the hot springs is the **Chief Spa Hotel** (Tiānlóng Fàndiàn; ☎ 089-935 075; r NT3000). Hot springs are piped into the hotel and only available to hotel guests. Rooms are discounted by 30% on weekdays. Behind the hotel is the **Heavenly Dragon Bridge** (Tiānlóng Diào Qiáo), a swaying suspension bridge that spans the gorge; definitely not for those afraid of heights.

In Wulu is an excellent little **Sichuan restaurant** (Sìchuān Fàndiàn; meals NT60; ☺ breakfast, lunch & dinner), where you can fill up on fried noodles and tofu with chilli at any time of the day.

The bus stops in Wulu at around 8.20am daily and continues on to Taitung, making a brief stop in the town of Kuanshan along the way.

# KAOHSIUNG CITY TO MAOLIN NATIONAL SCENIC AREA

A journey from Kaohsiung to Maolin could make for an interesting study, not only in contrasts, but also in Taiwanese history. In Kaohsiung you have the modern era (or possibly the just-passing era) of heavy industrialisation and urban pollution. Further east, in Meinong, much of premodern life still stares back at you in the form of rice and tobacco fields, three-sided Fujian-style houses and traditional craft shops.

Still further east, in Maolin, you can find the aboriginal heritage, the most ancient of all. You can also find a natural environment that has hardly been touched by humans except as they seek now to preserve it.

This whole region is massively appealing to travellers and yet is only just being discovered, even by the Taiwanese. You can visit any time of year but it's best if you bring your own vehicle. Roads are quiet on weekdays so driving is not much different from in Western countries.

## KAOHSIUNG CITY 高雄市
☎ 07 / pop 1,509,131

If you were ever asked to define 'bustling harbour city', you could always point to the southern city of Kaohsiung (Gāoxióng). This is Taiwan's largest port (the fourth- or fifth-largest in the world), the second-largest city and the centre of the heavy and petrochemical industries. As befitting its economic clout and status, Kaohsiung, like Taipei, is a 'special municipality' directly under the administration of the Executive Yuan.

Kaohsiung has a lot going for it, such as a well-developed infrastructure, two beaches within the city area, a newly rejuvenated Love River and 1000 hectares of almost-pristine forest right on its doorstep.

| INFORMATION | | |
|---|---|---|
| Chang Gung Hospital 長庚醫院 | ...... | 1 C2 |
| **SIGHTS & ACTIVITIES** | | **(pp253-4)** |
| Confucius Temple 孔廟 | ...... | 2 B1 |
| Dragon & Tiger Pagodas 龍虎塔 | ...... | 3 B1 |
| Jade Market 玉市場 | ...... | 4 B2 |
| Kaohsiung Golf Course 高秣的鬲術y場 | ...... | 5 C2 |
| Kaohsiung Museum of Fine Arts 美術館 | ...... | 6 B2 |
| National Science and Technology Museum 科學工藝博物館 | ...... | 7 B2 |
| Spring Autumn Temple 春秋閣 | ...... | 8 B1 |
| Temple of Enlightenment 天府宮 | ...... | 9 B1 |
| Xuan Tian Shang-di 玄天上帝 | ...... | 10 B1 |
| **EATING** | | 🍴 **(p255)** |
| Bagel-Bagel Foreign Sandwich Shop 貝果貝果之東西廚房左營區光興街161號 | ...... | 11 B2 |
| **DRINKING** | | 🍸 **(p256)** |
| Lighthouse Bar & Grill 燈塔美式酒館 | | 12 B2 |
| **TRANSPORT** | | **(p256)** |
| Hsiaogang Airport 高秣簽睤徽 | ...... | 13 C4 |
| Tsoying Train Station 左營火車站 | ...... | 14 B1 |

WESTERN TAIWAN

Kaohsiung today is being transformed from grim industrial warrens to a modern city of shiny cafés, riverside parks, mass public transit and cultural venues. The city's economic base is also shifting towards high technology, automation and other capital-intensive industries. Kaohsiung has all the potential to become, as its mayor desires, an international harbour city and 'the Hawaii of Taiwan'.

But it's not there yet. At the present time, we have to say that Kaohsiung is a city to keep your eye on, rather than a must see.

## Orientation

The Love River, a stink hole for years, is lovely once more and becoming a focal point for leisure, especially in the section between Jianguo and Wufu-3rd Rd. Neighbouring Yencheng District (a popular nightlife area) to the west, however, appears to be getting rundown. The Tzouying District, north of the train station, on the other hand, seems to be attracting a lot of new development and many trendy restaurants and bars are opening there.

The train-station area is a bit of a mess as building continues for the KMRT system (a mass transit system similar to the MRT in Taipei). If you wish to cross the tracks behind the station, use the tunnel starting in the train station. The fee is NT6 and you can purchase tickets in the train station.

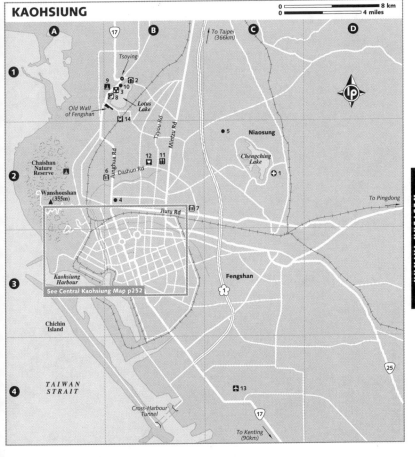

KAOHSIUNG

WESTERN TAIWAN

WESTERN TAIWAN

# CENTRAL KAOHSIUNG

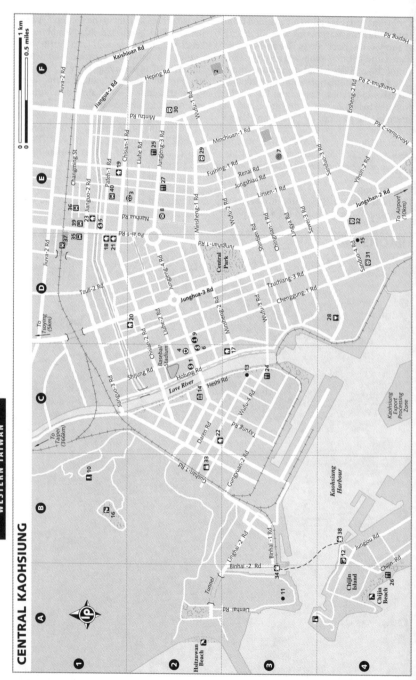

## Information

### CULTURAL CENTRE

**Chiang Kai-shek Cultural Centre** (Zhōngzhèng Wénhuà Zhōngxīn; Map opposite; ☎ 222 5136, ext 237; 67 Wufu 1 Rd; ☽ 9am-5pm, closed Mon) The centre has lecture and concert halls, galleries and a library. There are over 1000 performances a year. To get there, catch the 50 or 51 bus.

### INTERNET ACCESS

**Overtime Sports Lounge** (Map opposite; ☎ 536 8547; 308-17 Renai 3 Rd; ☽ noon-3pm & 7pm-1am Mon-Thu, noon-1am Fri & Sat ) If you buy something to eat or drink, you can use the computer free of charge.

### INTERNET RESOURCES

The best city tourism website in Taiwan is www.kaohsiung.gov.tw.

### MONEY

Kaohsiung is a large city and there are banks and ATMs everywhere, including most 7-Elevens. You can change money at **ICBC** ( ☎ 235 3001; 308 Jungshan-1st Rd) or the **Bank of Taiwan** ( ☎ 251 5131; 264 Jungjeng-4th Rd).

### TOURIST INFORMATION

The free monthly *FYI South Magazine* (www.taiwanfun.com), in English, focuses on the south of Taiwan. You can pick it up at the tourist centres or at many restaurants and entertainment venues across town. You can also download it at the website.

**Airport Tourist Centre** ( ☎ 805 7888; ☽ 9am-midnight) Open every day and the staff speak better English than their city counterparts.

**English Tourist Hotline** ( ☎ 0800 011 765)

**Tourist Office** (Map opposite; ☎ 281 1513; 5F, 235 Jungjeng-4th Rd; ☽ 9am-5pm Mon-Fri) Offers the most complete set of English-language brochures of any region in Taiwan. Look for the 'The Maps of Modern Life in Kaohsiung'.

## Sights & Activities

### LOTUS LAKE 蓮池潭

The **lake** (Liánchí Tán; Map pp250-1) has been a popular destination since the Qing dynasty and is well known for the 20 or so temples dotting the shore and nearby area.

Starting from the southern end and heading clockwise around the lake, you'll first encounter the slightly tacky **Dragon and Tiger Pagodas** (Lónghǔ Tǎ; Map pp250-1). Enter the dragon and exit the tiger for good luck. Next are the **Spring and Autumn Pavilions** (Chūnqiū Gé; Map pp250-1) dedicated to Kuan Kung, the God of War, and featuring Kuanyin riding a dragon. The pavilions extend onto the lake and make for good photos.

Across the road is the **Temple of Enlightenment** (Tiānfǔ Gōng; Map pp250-1), the largest temple in the area and worth a visit to see the two lions that lie on giant stone balls.

Next is the imposing statue of **Xuan Tian Shang-di** (Xúantiān Shàngdì; Map pp250-1), the Supreme Emperor of the Dark Heaven, and guardian of the north. Another temple of note is the **Confucian Temple** (Kǒngzǐ Miào; Map pp250-1) on the lake's northern end.

To get to the lake, take the train to **Tsoying station** (Zuǒyíng; Map pp250-1). Exit the station and walk straight ahead two blocks up Shengli Rd. The lake is unmistakable on the right.

WESTERN TAIWAN

If you continue walking past the lake on Shengli Rd you will see, on the left, the impressive **Old Wall of Fengshan** (Fēngshān Jiùchéng; Map pp250-1), built in 1825.

### HIKING

Within Kaohsiung City there is good hiking in the 1000-hectare **Chaishan Nature Reserve** (Cháishān Zìrán Gōngyuán; Map pp250-1). There's a decent brochure and map of the area at the tourist office. On weekends you can take the 56 bus to the reserve from the train station. On weekdays a taxi is best.

There are numerous trails around the uninteresting **Wanshoushan Zoo** (Wànshòushān Dòng Yuán) but we found this area lacking in good roads and trail signs.

For information on the activities of **Blue Skies Adventures** (rochem@ksts.seed.net.tw), a local nonprofit hiking club, email Mark Rochel and ask to be placed on the mailing list.

### CHIJIN (QIJIN) ISLAND 旗津

Kaohsiung City has big plans for this **island** (Qíjīn; Map pp252-3). For now, the island offers a pleasant escape from the city. Attractions include the **Seafood Street** (Hǎichǎn Jiē; Map pp252-3), **Matsu Temple** (Tiānhòu Gōng; Map pp252-3), **lighthouse** (Qíjīn Dēngtǎ; Map pp252-3; admission free; ⊗ 9am-4.30pm) and a long sandy beach where you can swim.

To reach the island, take the 1 or 31 bus to the ferry terminal. The ferry (NT10, five minutes) runs every five minutes. Pick up the 'Kaohsiung City Chichin Guide Map' at the tourist office for more details.

### HISTORIC SIGHTS

Kaohsiung has a large number of well-preserved relics scattered around the city. One of the most interesting is the **British Consulate at Takao** (Dǎgǒu Yīngguó Lǐngshì Guǎn; Map pp252-3; ☎ 531 2560; 18 Lenhai Rd; admission free; ⊗ 9am-5pm) part of Sun Yat-sen University, which also features an exhibition room of historic artefacts.

For a complete rundown of all the sites around town pick up the brochure 'The Map of Relics in Kaohsiung'.

### MUSEUMS

As befitting a city trying to modernise itself, Kaohsiung has more museums than ever. One of the most impressive (especially in terms of design) is the **Kaohsiung Museum of Fine Arts** (Gāoxióng Měishùguǎn; Map pp250-1; ☎ 555

0331; http://163.29.104.5; 20 Meishuguan Rd; adult/child NT100/80; ⊗ 9am-5pm, closed Mon). You can get to the museum on the 5 or 205 bus.

The **National Science and Technology Museum** (Kēxué Gōngyì Bówùguǎn; Map pp250-1; ☎ 316 0331; www.nstm.gov.tw; 720 Jiuru Rd; adult/child NT100/70, IMAX adult/child NT150/100; ⊗ 9am-5pm, closed Mon & Chinese New Year) features an hourly IMAX show and hands-on displays designed for children. IMAX and displays are in Chinese only.

### LOVE RIVER 愛河

The banks of the now-clean **river** (Ài Hé) have been turned into a strip of lovely parkland featuring walkways, benches, shady trees, outdoor cafés and stages. In early 2004, rainbow-coloured boats began to offer river tours.

Just back from the river is the fabulous new **Municipal Film Archives** (Diànyǐng Túshūguǎn; Map pp252-3; ☎ 551 1211; 10 Heshi Rd; admission free; ⊗ 1.30-9.30pm, closed Mon), where you can enjoy on-site private and public (in a 200-seat theatre) viewings of the archives' films.

A few blocks north of the archives is the gorgeous **Museum of History** (Lìshǐ Bówùguǎn; Map pp252-3; ☎ 531 2560; http://w4.kcg.gov.tw/~khchsmus /english/index.htm; 272 Jungjeng-4th Rd; admission free; ⊗ 9am-5pm, closed Mon), formerly the city government building during Japanese times. Inside are a number of photographic exhibits, furniture displays and special seasonal exhibits.

## Festivals

Teams from all over the world compete in the **International Flag & Drum Festival** (Guójì Qígǔjié) on the first day of the Lunar New Year. As befitting a port city, there is also the quirky **International Container Arts Festival** (Guójì Huògùi Yìshù Jié), where containers are used as art material. Past themes included 'post-civilisation' and 'containers as mode of transportation for cargo, contraband, or human smuggling'.

Many people have said good things about the shows during **Chinese New Year** at the Chiang Kai-shek Cultural Centre.

## Sleeping

### BUDGET

**International Youth Hostel IYH** (Map pp252-3; ☎ 201 2477; fax 215 6322; 120 Wenwu-1st St; dm NT300) A friendly hostel. The owner, Mrs Chen, will pick you up from the train station if you let her know you are coming.

**Hotel Skoal** (Shìguó Dàfàndiàn; Map pp252-3; ☎ 287 6151; fax 288 6020; 64 Min Zhu Heng Rd; d/tw with breakfast NT1450/2500, weekday discounts 45%) Rooms are small and a little dark, but they are kept almost fanatically clean by the maids. There's a car park across from the hotel.

**Union Hotel** (Guótǒng Dàfàndiàn; Map pp252-3; ☎ 235 0101; fax 235 1287; 295 Jianguo-2nd Rd; s&d NT880, tw NT1380) Very close to the train station, in an area with many other budget hotels, is this ageing but still respectable establishment. Rooms are styleless but the hotel is conveniently located near the train station and many cheap restaurants.

**MID-RANGE**

**Kind (Business) Hotel** (Kǎidélái Dàfàndiàn; Map pp252-3; ☎ 288 9131, ext 8; fax 288 9139; 257 Jungshan-1st Rd; d/tw with breakfast NT1200/1600) Rooms are blandly comfortable. The hotel is just up the road from the train station.

**Kingship Hotel** (Hànwáng Dàfàndiàn; Map pp252-3; ☎ 531 3131, ext 60; fax 531 3140; 98 Chishian-3rd Rd; d/tw NT2000/3200, weekday discount 10%) Those looking for a bit of flowery luxury will find it here. Rooms are bright and fresh, if slightly tacky. The hotel is very close to the Love River and the bars on Wufu-4th Rd.

**TOP END**

**Howard Plaza Hotel** (Fúhuá Dàfàndiàn; Map pp252-3; ☎ 236 2323; fax 235 8383; d/tw/ste from NT5100/5400/11,000; 🖳 ) The plaza rises up like a tower and is a popular business stay as it's centrally located and only a short drive to the airport (15 minutes) or train station (five minutes). Rooms are large and offer an atmosphere of high-end comfort. Hotel amenities include nine food and beverage outlets. Facilities include a gym and private business centre.

**Ambassador Hotel** (Guóbīn Fàndiàn; Map pp252-3; ☎ 211 5211; fax 281 1115; 202 Mingsheng-2nd Rd; s/d/tw/ ste NT4500/6600/5800/11,000; 🖳 🖳 ) This is considered one of Kaohsiung's top hotels. With its lookout over the Love River, the hotel is as good a romantic getaway as business centre. Rooms are softly lit and warmly decorated and have ADSL for those who need it. Hotel facilities include a business centre and a health club. There are three restaurants and two lounges, including the Sky Lounge on the 20th floor, which catches the sunset.

## Eating

The train-station area, especially as you head up Jungshan Rd, is filled with inexpensive cafés and restaurants. Nearby **Liuhe Night Market** (Liùhé Yèshì; Map pp252-3; 🕙 6pm-2am) is famous island-wide for its 138-plus food stalls. You can eat well here for NT150 to NT200. The 'Kaohsiung Liuhe Night Market' brochure (available at the tourist office) has pictures and English explanations of local specialities for sale at the market.

For fresh seafood head over to Chijin Island's seafood street. For pub food head to one of the joints along Wufu-4th Rd.

**Brass Rail Tavern** (Gāngguáxī Xīcān Bīsà; Map pp252-3; ☎ 533 5747; 21 Wufu-4th Rd; dishes from NT150; 🕙 5pm-1am) This friendly bar serves good Western food. Pizzas start at just over NT300, while a good steak can cost more than NT600.

**Bagel-Bagel Foreign Sandwich Shop** (Bèiguǒ Bèiguǒ Zhī Dōngxi Chúfáng; Map pp250-1; ☎ 558 8455; 161 Kuang Hsing St, Tsoying; meals NT200; 🕙 10am-11pm) The shop is well-loved by the expat community and serves bagel sandwiches (with a good selection of fillings), as well as pastas and soups. It's a long way for most travellers to go for a good sandwich but the information board and opportunity to network are invaluable for the long-term resident.

**Shou-Yu Vegetarian Buffet** (Xiùyǔ Sùshí; Map pp252-3; 274 Jungshiau-1st Rd; meals NT120; 🕙 lunch & dinner) Shou-Yu has branches in most major Taiwanese cities and is popular for the light, fresh taste of its food. The place is starting to look a bit old but the food is what brings people here.

**Ka Ra Bour Thai Food** (Kǎlābāo Tàishì Cāntíng; Map pp252-3; 54 Jungjeng-3rd Rd; dishes NT200; 🕙 lunch & dinner) Not far from Shou-Yu Vegetarian Buffet, in an area with many other mid-price dining establishments, is this long-running Thai restaurant. Flavours are light but authentic.

## Drinking

The area around Jungshan Park houses an assortment of modern cafés, and there is a well-landscaped outdoor **café** (drinks NT180; 🕙 1pm-2am) in the park itself that is especially popular on warm nights. Along the Love River, there are also many small outdoor cafés that are open into the late evening.

Yencheng District, along Wufu-4th Rd, is full of pubs and very popular but it is starting to look a bit run-down.

**WESTERN TAIWAN**

**Pig & Whistle** (Líshě Cāntīng; Map pp252-3; ☎ 330 1006; 199 Szwei-4th Rd; beer from NT150; ◷ 7pm-3am Sun-Thu, 7pm-5am Fri & Sat) This is a popular British-style pub and features satellite TV, ADSL hook-ups for laptops and pub food such as fish and chips (NT280).

**Lighthouse Bar & Grill** (Dēngtǎ Měishì Jiǔguǎn; Map pp250-1; ☎ 559 2614; 239 Fuguo-1st Rd; beer NT120; ◷ 6pm-2am) A popular new expat hang-out in Tsoying District. It's not far from the art museum and has a useful information board.

## Entertainment
### CINEMAS
**Warner Village Cinemas** (Huánà Wēixiù Yǐngchéng; Map pp252-3; ☎ 337 1234; http://web.warnervillage.com.tw; 13-14F, 21 Sanduo-4th Rd; adult NT200) Just down the street from the Sanduo Cinema Complex in the FE21' Mega Department Store. You can book tickets online in English.

### NIGHTCLUBS
**DNA Disco** (Map pp252-3; ☎ 227 2129; 4F 77 Minsheng-1st Rd; NT250 weekdays, NT500 Fri & Sat; ◷ 9.30pm-3am Sun-Thu, 9.30pm-4am Fri & Sat) Many foreigners have recommended this long-running club for a great time. It's also a good place to get the scoop on the rest of the city's nightlife.

### THEATRE
**Mindful Phoenix Arts** (Zhěnzhīfèng Yìshù Biǎoyǎn Gōngzuò; Map pp252-3; ☎ 223 0581; www.mindfulphoenix .com; 2F, 165 Jungjeng-2nd Rd; membership per month/year NT1000/10,000) A special mention should go to this government-approved nonprofit arts group for striving to not just better the arts scene in Kaohsiung, but to bring the foreign and Taiwanese community together. Training, in English and Chinese, is offered in theatre, dance, exercise and the martial arts for children and adults. Theatre and dance training result in public performance. There's a healthy mix of locals and foreigners among the staff and members, making this one of the best places for newcomers to Kaohsiung to get involved with the larger community. Sore-throated English teachers should check out the voice-training classes.

## Shopping
**Bamboo Street** (Lǎozhújiē; Map pp252-3) At the end of Wufu-4th Rd is this street where you'll find wares from the past, including traditional hats, raincoats and household articles made from bamboo.

**Jade Market** (Yù Shìchǎng; Map pp250-1; ◷ 10.30am-2.30pm Wed, Thu & Sun) The market is at the intersection of Shihchuan and Tzuli.

## Getting There & Away
### AIR
Kaohsiung's **Hsiaogang international airport** (www.kia.gov.tw) serves international and domestic carriers.

**UNI** (☎ 791 1000) and **TransAsia Airways** (☎ 335 9355) have daily flights between Taipei and Kaohsiung (around NT1900).

From Kaohsiung, you can catch flights to the Taiwan Strait islands.

### BOAT
Boats from Kaohsiung sail to the Penghu Islands.

### BUS
Buses to Foguangshan (NT63, 30 minutes, every 40 minutes), Kenting (NT250, 2 hours, every hour) and Meinung (NT168, one hour, every hour) leave from the **Kaohsiung Ke Yuan station** (Map pp252-3; ☎ 237 1230; Nanhua St). The station is to the left as you exit the train station about 100 metres along. Don't confuse this with the very busy **Taiwan Bus Company station** (Map pp252-3; Jianguo Rd). Buses 150 and 151 go to Foguangshan. The Free Go and CN bus companies, across from Kaohsiung Ke Yuan station, also run frequent buses to Kenting (NT290).

### TRAIN
Kaohsiung is the terminus for most west-coast trains. Trains to and from Taipei (fast/slow NT845/395, 4½/six hours) run frequently from early morning till almost midnight. To Taichung (fast/slow NT470/280, 2½/three hours) trains run about every two hours.

## Getting Around
The city bus hub is directly in front of the train station. The fare for a one-zone trip is NT12. If you're after a taxi, they are plentiful in Kaohsiung.

### TO/FROM THE AIRPORT
Buses to the airport (NT12, every 12 minutes) leave from the bus hub in front of the train station. There is a big aeroplane on the side of the bus. Taxis to the airport should cost less than NT200 from the city centre.

WESTERN TAIWAN

## CAR
For car rentals call **IWS** ( ☎ 0800 009 414) or **Hertz** ( ☎ 806 7288). Both have English-speaking staff and do pick-ups.

## FOGUANGSHAN 佛光山
☎ 07
The Light of Buddha Mountain, or Foguangshan (Fóguāngshān) as it is translated, is a 52-acre temple complex about a 30-minute drive from Kaohsiung. The complex serves as monastery, university and meditation centre. It is considered *the* centre of Buddhism in southern Taiwan.

The most famous feature at Foguangshan is the **Great Buddha Land** (大佛城; Dàfóchéng), where a 40m Amitabha Buddha stands over a garden of 480 smaller Buddha statues. Other notable features include the **Great Hero Hall** (如來殿; Rúlái Diàn) and an **exhibition** tracing the life of the Venerable Master Shingyun.

For several years the temple was closed, but it's been opened again and tours in English of up to a half-day can be arranged with the nuns at reception (信徒中心; xìntú zhōngxīn). Temple tours stress the ceremonial aspects of Buddhism and you will be requested to bow, kowtow and otherwise observe all forms of respect and devotion. In return, you will be instructed in Buddhist thought, history and iconography and may receive some sound advice and blessed trinkets.

The **Pilgrim's Lodge** (Jiǎushān Hùiguǎn; ☎ 656 1921; fax 656 5195; d NT2000) invites devotees and tourists to spend the night. The accommodation is surprisingly good. The meditation centres host frequent retreats for beginners and experienced practitioners. Arrangements for meditation classes or an overnight temple stay can be made in advance.

To get to the temple, take the 150 or 151 bus (NT63, 30 minutes, every 40 minutes) from the Kaohsiung Ke Yuan station.

## MEINONG 美濃
☎ 07 / pop 50,000
Hakka people (Kèjiā rén) make up about 10% to 15% of the population of Taiwan. In rural Meinong (Měinóng), settled over 200 years ago by today's ancestors, that percentage goes up to 95%. It's understandable, then, why Meinong has been one of the centres of Hakka pride in recent years.

For fans of folk art this place is a must visit. Excellent-quality paper umbrellas can be picked up here for less than NT1000 and there are several kilns producing good-quality rustic pottery. The cuisine is interesting, too, especially *léi chá* (pounded tea) and the various sticky-rice snacks.

Those with little interest in history or crafts will still find this place enjoyable. The surrounding countryside is clean and lush and cycling through the fields on quiet rural lanes is a treat.

A visit to Meinong can be a day trip from Kaohsiung or Tainan, or part of a journey into the interior towards Maolin or the South Cross-Island Hwy. At the time of writing the only accommodation in the area was a love hotel, though this will certainly change as the area continues to develop for tourism.

### Information
For more history on the Hakka people and the town of Meinong check out the website http://en.ihakka.net.

### Sights & Activities
#### CYCLING
One of the most pleasant things to do in Meinong is to get into the countryside on a bike. The town of Meinong, like most in Taiwan, is ugly, but the countryside is lush and dotted with well-preserved tobacco barns and three-sided, Fujian-style houses.

Some of the best cycling is off the main road towards the ridge. Another enjoyable route is to ride out of town on County Rd 184 east towards Liugui and then head left into the fields.

You can rent bikes on weekends just to the right of the **Meei-nong The Hakkas Museum** (美濃客家文物館; Méinóng Kèjiā Wénwùguǎn). The museum is just off Jungshan Rd, a few kilometres past the folk village, or 1km past the turn-off into town. There are signs in Chinese pointing the way.

#### MEINONG FOLK VILLAGE 美濃民俗村
The **village** (Měinóng Mínsú Cūn; ☎ 681 0072; admission free; ⏰ 8am-6pm) is an artificial recreation of an old-fashioned neighbourhood. It is definitely touristy but well worth visiting nonetheless, as you can watch traditional crafts being made as well as sample authentic Hakka *léi chá*, an assortment of sticky-rice snacks and tasty *ban tiao* (traditional flat noodles).

**WESTERN TAIWAN**

Village stores sell well-made paper umbrellas, fans and bamboo baskets. Just outside the shop, at the very back, are two metal pots filled with water. Dip your hands in the water and rub the handles of the pots. The sound is like a hundred wine glasses being rubbed at one time.

The village is just off Jungshan Rd, a few kilometres before the town centre.

### Eating
You can pick up a simple but adequate map (and a good meal) at the **Meinong Traditional Hakka Restaurant** (美濃古老客家菜; Guǎngdéxīng Zhǐsǎn; 中山路1段362-5號), about 1km after the folk village and before the actual town centre.

### Shopping
Craftsmen have been making umbrellas in Meinong for 80 years, ever since a local businessman bought up a Chinese master's shop and forced him to move to Meinong. The umbrellas are made of paper and bamboo, hand-painted and lacquered to make them durable and waterproof.

If you're looking to buy, one of the best places is **Guan De Xin Paper Umbrella Shop** (廣德興紙傘; Guǎngdéxīng Zhǐsǎn; 中山路1段361號), across the road from the Meinong Traditional Hakka Restaurant. An umbrella here costs between NT600 and NT1200.

### Getting There & Around
You can catch a bus directly into Meinong from the Kaohsiung Ke Yuan station but for orientation purposes it's better to catch a bus heading towards Liugui (NT182, one hour, every hour) and get off at the folk village.

Meinong is quite small but the surrounding countryside is expansive and you'll need a vehicle or bicycle (which you can rent) to get around.

### MEINONG TO MAOLIN
The Central Cross-Island Hwy gets all the glory but for sheer diversity of landscape and activity don't miss this stretch of road through the interior of Kaohsiung County.

The drive begins outside Meinong on County Rd 184. The first attractions of note are the **Liugui Tunnels** (六龜隧道; Liùgūi Sùidào), a series of seven long mountain tunnels opened recently for people to walk through.

Just past the tunnels, the **18 Lohan Mountains** (十八羅漢山; Shíbā Lóhànshān) begin to appear. The exotic beauty of these crags, jutting up like the rows of armour on a dinosaur's back, had us jumping out of our car every five minutes for a photo.

In the same area, you'll drive under the **wedding arch** (our name), so called because the trees on either side of the road form an arch over the top. In winter, when the trees bloom with purple flowers, the 2km stretch of road looks just like one long wedding arch.

Next you'll reach the town of **Liugui** (六龜; Liùgūi), famous for bellfruit and mangoes. If you're interested in **river rafting** continue up 184 to **Laonong** (荖濃; Lǎonóng). Inquire at the Kaohsiung tourist office for the numbers of licensed rafting companies. They change every year so be sure to get the current numbers.

Within a few kilometres of Liugui are two forest reserves: **Shanping** (扇平森林生態科學園區; Shànpíng Sēnlín Shēngtài Kēxué Yuánqū) and **Tengchih** (藤枝森林遊樂區; Téngzhǐ Sēnlín Yóulèqū; http://recreate.forest.gov.tw). Tengchih is said to be one of the best-preserved natural forests in Taiwan, while little-visited Shanping offers peaceful trails and excellent bird-watching.

The last stretch of the trip takes you down Hwy 27 to Maolin. Interestingly, the landscape looks completely different on this side even though you are just retracing your route down on the opposite bank of the river.

### MAOLIN RECREATION AREA
茂林遊憩區

☎ 07

The **recreation area** (Màolín Yǒuqì Qū), part of the much larger Maolin National Scenic Area, covers a protected region from Maolin Village to Dona. Here you'll find pristine mountain landscapes, vertiginously high suspension bridges, waterfalls, natural swimming pools and even free outdoor hot springs. Rukai aboriginal culture is strong in this part of the country, as are conservation measures to protect the winter home of the purple butterfly.

Many attractions in Maolin have been developed but, fortunately, in the way of a national park, meaning they feature well-marked trails and simple facilities that do

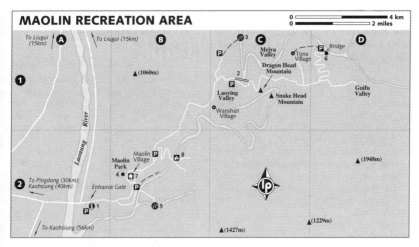

not mar the natural environment. A few days in Edenic Maolin marks the perfect end of a journey of contrasts that began in Kaohsiung, the industrial heartland of Taiwan.

## Orientation & Information

It is very simply to get around the scenic area. There is only one main road, County Rd 132, connecting the two villages.

The **Maolin National Scenic Area Administration Office** (Màolín Guójiā Fēngjǐng Qū Guǎnlǐ Chù; ☎ 680 1488; http://202.39.225.133/NSA2002/en/maulin/index.htm; 12-5 Maolin Village; ☼ 9am-5pm) is just past the **tollgate** (admission NT70; ☼ 6am-10pm) to the scenic area. Though the staff speak no English, they can offer an English map and brochure and help with homestays.

### INTERNET RESOURCES

For information about the Rukai people see www.sinica.edu.tw/tit/scenery/0296_Maolin.html, a page on the website of one of Taiwan's top research universities.

## Sights & Activities

### PURPLE BUTTERFLY VALLEY 紫蝶幽谷

Just to the left of Maolin Village is **Maolin Park** (Màolín Gōngyuán), a few hectares of butterfly protection area. Every winter (November to March), countless purple butterflies migrate from Taiwan's much-colder north to settle here. The park maintains a small display shelter but it's more fascinating to see the butterflies on the trails around the park.

The best time to watch the butterflies is between 9am and 10am, when the sun first comes over the mountains and rouses the insects from sleep. For the really spectacular show, follow the park trail up to where it connects with a small road and follow the road down into a valley.

### WATERFALLS

You can drive right up to the first of the five levels of the **Qingren Valley Waterfall** (Qíngrén Gǔ Pùbù). It's then a 10-minute walk to the second level.

From the car park it's about a 15-minute walk on a smooth stone path to the picturesque **Meiyagu Waterfall** (Měiyǎgǔ Pùbù). The pool looks perfect for swimming, though there is a sign prohibiting this activity.

### ROAD TO DONA

County Rd 132 from Maolin Village to Dona features a number of superb roadside

WESTERN TAIWAN

attractions, including the **Dona High Suspension Bridge** (Dōnà Gāudiàoqiáo), and the **Snake Head** (Shétóushān) and **Dragon Head** (Lóngtóushān) mountains, which are actually odd-shaped mounds in the middle of the river valley.

**Dona** (Dōnà) is a stronghold for Rukai aboriginal culture and stonework, including traditional shale houses, which are visible everywhere (though there is quite a bit of ugly modern development as well).

At the free outdoor **Dona Hot Springs** (Dōnà Wēnquán) visitors can bathe right beside the river in simple tubs built into the rocks. A gorgeous natural river pool, big enough for laps, lies right beside the bathing area.

You can reach the springs by a hiking trail that begins at the end of Dona Village, or by driving on County Rd 132 past the village a few kilometres.

## Sleeping

Homestays for around NT800 a night (some including breakfast) can be arranged at the administration office.

**Fungshan Agricultural Activity Centre** (Fèngshānshì Nónghuì Màolín Huìyuán Huódòng Zhōngxīn; ☎ 680 1115; 16 Maolin Village; d/tw NT1500/3200) This is the only real hotel in the area and it's beside Maolin Park. Rooms are large, spotlessly clean but very Spartan. There's a restaurant in the hotel but it's for groups only.

**Maolin Valley Taiwan Cafe Leisure Square** (Màolíngǔ Táiwān Kāfēi Xiūxián Guǎngchǎng; ☎ 680 1289; 118 Maolin Village; camp site NT300-400) This camp site by the river has showers, a small barbecue area and a convenience store.

## Eating

Your options are very limited. Little stalls are set up on the main road but be aware that these places close early (by 6pm or 7pm) on weekdays. Don't wait to eat!

On weekends, large barbecue pits are set up in Dona, but these are not suitable for a single person unless you can eat a whole chicken. Just before the tollgate there are a few other shops, including a fruit shake stand.

## Getting There & Away

There are buses from Pingdong but Maolin is just too big to be worthwhile without your own vehicle. Consider renting a scooter in Tainan (per day NT200) and riding there.

# PINGDONG CITY TO KENTING

You've reached the end of Taiwan here in Pingdong County and it's as hot as Hades in the summer. This is tropical country, but you'd guess that on your own once you saw all the sugar cane, tobacco, bananas and pineapples growing on the alluvial coastal plains.

Every year, millions of people head south for the beaches, where you can swim even in the dead of winter. Kenting National Park, which occupies the southern tip of Taiwan, has long been the country's most popular ocean playground. It's about to get

---

**LIYUSHAN MUD VOLCANO**
鯉魚山泥火山

Just south of Pingdong City is Taiwan's only active **mud volcano** (Lǐyúshān Níhuǒshān). The volcano is underground and the only evidence of its existence is a quarter-acre plot of flat muddy land that occasionally erupts in flames and bubbling mud. The period of action can last four to eight hours. During the dormant period, strange patterns form as the mud dries in the hot southern sun. Go to www.pthg.gov.tw/chinese/tour /scenic/pt14/p015.asp for a picture of this amazing oddity.

To reach the volcano, take Hwy 27 south from Pingdong. After the town of Wandan (萬丹; Wàndān), about 9km from Pingdong, be on the lookout for the sign to Liyushan (鯉魚山; Lǐyúshān), about 1km further on Hwy 17. Turn right at the sign and drive 500m until the road ends at a T-junction. Turn right and drive another 500m. Turn left and proceed about 100m. You should see a pagoda on the left. Turn right and go another 100m. You should find yourself at a small river or canal. Turn left, follow the canal for 500m and then turn right again. Not far to the left you should be able to see a yellow/orange-coloured building. That is your destination. Drive across the bridge over the canal and proceed another 70m or so. Turn left and then left again quickly into the car park of the yellow/orange building (actually a temple). The mud volcano is behind the temple.

a run for its money, though, from Dapeng Bay, a beautiful, giant inland lagoon that is finally being developed after 30 years of false starts.

In the interior, the focus is on aboriginal culture and at Sandmen, an indigenous people's theme park has been built in the mountains. Further inland, in remote villages such as Wutai, aboriginal culture thrives with the renewed pride among the people in their heritage. If you have any interest in the original inhabitants of Taiwan this is a great place to begin your explorations.

## PINGDONG 屏東

☎ 08 / pop 215,000

Though Pingdong (Píngdōng) is actually not a bad-looking little town, there is nothing for the traveller here except to begin a journey somewhere else.

### Information

There is a **tourist office** ( ☎ 732 0415; 527 Tzyou Rd/自由路527號; ☯ 9am-5pm Mon-Fri) and ATM at the 7-Eleven near the Pingdong Bus Company station. For tourist information about Pingdong County check out the website www.pthg.gov.tw.

### Sleeping

Here are a couple of places near the train station in case you need to spend the night.

**Minzu Hotel** ( ☎ 732 5121/3; 134 Minzu Rd/民族路134號; d/tw NT850/1000) Rooms are clean and simply furnished and while they could use a new paint job the place is fine for a night in transit. The hotel is a few blocks to the left of the train station; Minzu Rd is one street up from the train station. There are cafés, restaurants and even a bar near the hotel.

**Feima Hotel** ( ☎ 732 6111; 60 Guang Fu Rd/光復路60號; d/tw NT840/1400) Rooms are very clean here, though the place looks like an old love hotel with cheap nude paintings, mirrored ceilings and round beds. To reach the hotel, turn right as you exit the train station. The hotel is 30m up the road.

### Getting There & Away

Trains from Kaohsiung to Pingdong (NT31, 30 minutes) run about every 15 minutes.

The **bus station** ( ☎ 732 4103) is a block left of the train station as you exit. You can't miss

it. On weekdays, to get to the Indigenous People's Cultural Park (p261), take the bus to Shuimen (NT51, every 20 minutes) and walk or take a taxi to the park. On weekends there are buses directly to the park (NT51, one hour, every 20 minutes).

Buses to Donggang (NT63, 40 minutes) run every hour.

## SANDIMEN 三地門

☎ 08

This small aboriginal community (Sāndìmén), an hour east of Pingdong, is famous for the **Indigenous People's Cultural Park** (台灣山地文化園區; Táiwān Shāndì Wénhuà Yuánqū; ☎ 799 1219; www.tacp.gov.tw; 104 Fongjin, Peiyei Village, Majia; adult/child NT120/60; ☯ 8.30am-5pm, closed Mon). The park, set in forested mountains, covers a large area and is an excellent introduction to aboriginal culture in Taiwan.

Separate areas have been established to highlight the nine indigenous tribes. Each area features authentic, life-size displays of traditional houses and communal structures. Amazingly, displays all come with detailed English explanations. You can walk around each area if you give yourself several hours or you can ride the free shuttle buses that cruise the park every 10 minutes or so.

The park houses several interesting exhibitions and there are daily performances of aboriginal dancing. A useful English-language brochure (with map and events schedule) can be picked up at the reception area. The park's website is worth a look before you go.

From Pingdong, buses to the park (NT51, one hour, every 20 minutes) run only on weekends. On weekdays take a bus to Shuimen (水門; Shuǐmén), a small community just before Sandimen, and then walk the 2km to the park or take a taxi.

From the park it is possible to get further into the mountains to very remote aboriginal villages such as **Wutai** (霧台; Wùtái) but you'll need a Class A mountain permit (see p311) and a Taiwanese local to accompany you.

From Sandimen a 13km bike route connects with **Saichia Aero Sports Park** (賽嘉游遊樂區; Sàijiāyóu Yóulèqū; ☎ 799 2221; www.wingstaiwan.com; 20 Saichia Village), one of the premier locations in Taiwan for aviation sports such as paragliding.

## DAPENG BAY NATIONAL SCENIC AREA
大鵬灣國家風景區

At the time of writing, very few Taiwanese, let alone foreign travellers, had ever heard of Dapeng Bay (Dàpéngwān), even though this gorgeous new scenic area was only months away from its opening in June 2004. Chances are, by the time you read this the place will be well on its way to becoming the next Kenting.

Dapeng Bay is actually a lagoon and in former days hosted an army base and countless oyster farms. In 1997 the national scenic area was formed and plans drawn up to transform the lagoon into an international water resort. The area was rightly assessed to have fantastic potential. The lagoon, being inland and sheltered, does not have dangerous rip tides, or even waves for that matter, making it ideal for sea kayaking, swimming and sailing. The sun shines 300 days a year on average and northeastern monsoons do not affect the area. In addition, the land is almost all public, making overdevelopment (the bane of so many resort areas in Taiwan) easier to control.

Dapeng Bay is still years away from full development (which will include a marina, a five-star hotel complex, golf course and a small village) but in the meantime visitors can swim, sail, canoe and camp, as well as enjoy the scenic charm of the bay and the surrounding countryside.

The national scenic area covers not only Dapeng Bay but also Little Liuchiu Island (right). The island has been a popular tourist spot for years and is easily reached by a 40-minute ferry ride from the harbour at Donggang. As for getting to Dapeng Bay, buses from Kaohsiung to Kenting will stop at the entrance, just off Hwy 17 (and only about 1km to the water).

Information is available at the **National Scenic Area Tourism Bureau Office** ( ☎ 08-833 8100; www.tbnsa.gov.tw; 254 Chuang-Tou Rd), just south of Donggang on Hwy 17, or at the lovely new **Dapeng Bay Visitor Centre** (housed in a Japanese-colonial-era building).

## DONGGANG (TUNGKANG) 東港
**pop 50,000**

This fishing town (Dōnggǎng) is one of the most important in southern Taiwan and well worth visiting during the times of two festivals.

### Festivals

Bluefin tuna (hēi wěiyú) is one of the three aquatic treasures of Donggang, and is a fish so scrumptious it has been called the 'Porsche of the deep ocean' and 'the Rolls Royce of fish meat'. Years ago, the Japanese used to purchase almost all the tuna (or toro as they call it). With the weakening of the Japanese economy in the 1990s, the tuna became available to the local market. It became an instant success and soon companies were actually offering bus tours to Donggang just to sample the fish. The **Pingtung Bluefin Tuna Cultural Festival** (黑鮪魚文化季; Hēiwěiyú Wénhuàjì) has become a regular event, running May through June.

Donggang's **Boat Burning Festival** (王船祭 Wángchuánjì) takes place at the resplendent Donglong Temple (Dōnglóng Gòng once every three years. During the festival, which runs its course over eight days a boat is filled with models of a modern house, clothing, cars, horses and electrical appliances, as well as sacrificial offerings of meat. The entire model is then burnt as an offering to Wen Wang-yeh, a Tang-dynasty scholar who is said to watch over the waters of southern China. The next boat burning is scheduled for autumn 2006.

### Getting There & Away

Donggang can be reached by bus (NT63 40 minutes, every hour) from Pingdong. A Donggang harbour, ferries to Little Liuchiu Island (return NT410, 40 minutes) leave every hour in the morning and every 1½ hours in the afternoon.

## LITTLE LIUCHIU ISLAND 小琉球

This pretty coral island (Xiǎo Liúqiú Yǔ no more than 5km long, offers more than enough sea vistas, convoluted caves, sand beaches and odd rock formations to keep you happy for a long, long day. Best of all it's simple to get to and around.

The island was recently brought under the auspices of the Dapeng Bay National Scenic Area (left). This is welcome as it means the area will be protected and developed sensibly for tourism. Already you can see progress A surprisingly cool-looking camp site has been built right by the water, wood and stone boardwalks and viewing platforms have been added to scenic routes and the island in general is kept very clean.

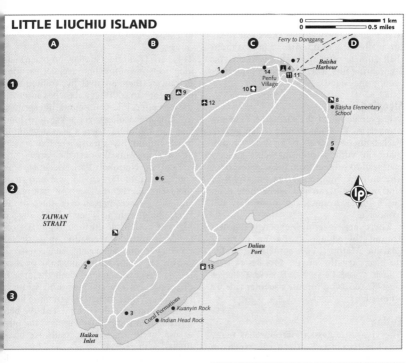

# LITTLE LIUCHIU ISLAND

Ferry to Donggang

Baisha Harbour

Penfu Village

Baisha Elementary School

TAIWAN STRAIT

Daliau Port

Coral Formations

Kuanyin Rock

Indian Head Rock

Haikou Inlet

With the new ocean-side camp site, Little Liuchiu makes for a fun overnight trip. Winter is a great time to visit as the weather is still in the mid-20°C range but the place is practically deserted. For more information check out www.tbnsa.gov.tw.

## Sights & Activities

You can ride around the island on a scooter in about 30 minutes but give yourself at least a few hours. This island was made for exploring.

Some attractions to look out for are **Vase Rock** (Huāpíng Shí), a giant eroded coral with a thin base and large head, **Black Ghost Cave** (Wūguǐ Dòng) and **Beauty Cave** (Měirén Dòng). For the bloody stories behind these names check out www.sinica.edu.tw/tit/scenery/0496_Hsiao.html.

Other must-sees include the narrow, twisting, root-strangled coral passageways at **Mountain Pig Ditch** (Shānzhū Gōu). **Lingshan Temple** (Língshān Sì), just up from the pier, offers, like several other temples on the island, fine clear views across Taiwan Strait.

| SIGHTS & ACTIVITIES | (pp263-4) |
| --- | --- |
| Beauty Cave 美人洞 | 1 C1 |
| Black Ghost Cave 烏鬼洞 | 2 A3 |
| Cliffs 斷崖 | 3 B3 |
| Lingshan Temple 靈山寺 | 4 C1 |
| Lobster Cave 龍蝦 | 5 D2 |
| Mountain Pig Ditch 山豬溝 | 6 B2 |
| Vase Rock 花瓶岩 | 7 C1 |
| Zhong An Beach 中澳海灘 | 8 D1 |

| SLEEPING | (p264) |
| --- | --- |
| Camp Site 露營區 | 9 B1 |
| Coco Resort 椰林度假村 | 10 C1 |

| EATING | (p264) |
| --- | --- |
| 7-Eleven | 11 C1 |

| TRANSPORT | (pp264) |
| --- | --- |
| Aircraft Landing Strip 機場 | 12 C1 |
| Petrol Station 加油站 | 13 C3 |
| Tollgate 知本森林遊樂區史站 | 14 C1 |

## BEACHES

The best place for a swim is at **Zhong Ao Beach** (Zhōng Ào Hǎitān). The beach at **Vase Rock** is ideal for wading as you search for sea life, while the picturesque stretch of shell-sand beach before Black Ghost Cave makes for a sweet picnic spot. You can go for a dip here as well, but only up to your knees.

Be sure to wear something on your feet if you go in the water as the coral rocks can really cut you up. Also, don't go more than 20m to 30m from shore unless you are wearing fins. There is a nasty undertow around the island.

### Sleeping

Whoever designed the knockout **camp site** (lùyíng qù; tent site NT425) should get an award. Each tent site consists of a raised wooden platform with a sloping wood canopy overhead to protect from the sun and rain. The entire campground sits on a plot of land near the ocean and, while there is no beach for swimming, the location is still wonderful.

There are several inexpensive hotels around the village at Baisha Harbour (Báishā Mǎtóu). For something a little nicer, try the quaint **Coco Resort** (Yēlín Dùjiàcūn; ☎ 08-861 4368; 20-38 Minzu Rd; 2-/4-person cabins NT2200/3200), a minute's scooter ride up a quiet lane.

### Eating

The village at Baisha Harbour has many small restaurants. You can eat expensive fresh seafood or simple stir-fries for less than NT100. There is also a 7-Eleven in the village where you can buy sandwiches and drinks.

### Getting There & Away

From Pingdong, catch a bus to Donggang (NT63, 40 minutes, every hour). The bus will first stop in town and then proceed to the harbour ferry terminals. There are two ferry terminals on the right and both offer trips to Little Liuchiu Island. The first terminal is the one we recommend. Boats to Little Liuchiu Island (return NT410, 30 minutes) leave every hour in the morning and every 1½ hours in the afternoon. The last boat back to Donggang leaves from Little Liuchui Island at 6pm.

### Getting Around

The island is only 9km around so you could easily walk it in a day. Scooters (half-day/full-day NT150/300) can be rented as soon as you get off the ferry or even before you get on the boat at Donggang from the local touts. Don't worry, they are legitimate.

## KENTING NATIONAL PARK
墾丁國家公園
☎ 08
This park (Kěndīng Guójiā Gōngyuán) has long been one of the top travel destinations in Taiwan (there are over five million visitors a year). In addition to beaches and surf, the area offers hikes, museums, hot springs, a bit of archaeology, good Western food and fun nightlife. There's also a genuine beach-community atmosphere that's been developed organically over the years.

Kenting National Park occupies the southern tip of Taiwan, an area known as the Henchun Peninsula. Low mountains and hilly terraces prevail over much of the land, along with, in a few places, rugged high cliffs. All in all, the topography is spectacularly suited for recreation, in particular cruising around sightseeing on a scooter.

You can visit Kenting any time of year, but at weekends and holidays the area is often packed, especially around Chinese New Year. While the streets are more lively at these times, traffic is congested, the better restaurants are booked up and the otherwise lovely beaches and trails are often littered with garbage.

Kenting is tropical, which means it's always warm and you can visit any time of year. The average January temperature is 21°C while in July it can get to a scorching 38°C.

### Orientation

The national park covers a large area (18,000 hectares) but as there are few major roads it is easy to get around with a simple map in hand. The majority of people stay in Kenting town, which is almost at the very southern tip of Taiwan. There are literally dozens of hotels here as well as scores of restaurants, bars and assorted shops.

Those looking for a quieter time should consider staying further down the peninsula at Sail Rock or Eluanbi. Surfers and beach bums will probably like Nanwan north of Kenting. With its single strip of shops set directly across from the bay, Nanwan looks and feels just like the archetypal beach town.

### Information

#### INTERNET RESOURCES
The official website for Kenting (www.ktnp

.gov.tw) is more than thorough in its introduction to the park.

The website www.taipeitimes.com/News/archives/2002/04/14/0000131862 has a good article about the development of Kenting from fishing village to overdeveloped tourist destination.

## MONEY

There are ATMs in the 7-Elevens in Kenting town.

## TOURIST INFORMATION

**National Park Headquarters** (Map below; ☎ 886 1321; 946 No 596, Kenting Rd; ☻ 8.30am-5pm) Here you'll find English-speaking staff and several useful English brochures and maps. The centre is a few kilometres north

| INFORMATION | (opposite) |
|---|---|
| National Park Headquarters 國家公園管理處 | 1 B3 |
| | |
| **SIGHTS & ACTIVITIES** | (pp266-7) |
| Chennan Temple 鎮南宮 | 2 B3 |
| Chikung Waterfall 七孔瀑布 | 3 C2 |
| Chiupeng Dunes 九棚沙丘 | 4 D1 |
| Chuhuo 出火 | 5 B2 |
| Dashan Hot Spring Spa | |
| 大山溫泉農場 溫泉村大梅路60-1號 | (see 11) |
| East Gate 東門 | 6 B2 |
| Fu Dog Surf & Dive | (see 13) |
| Haikou Sand Dunes 海口沙丘 | 7 A1 |
| National Museum of Marine Biology | |
| 國立海洋 生物博物館 | 8 A1 |
| Nuclear Power Plant 核能發電廠 | 9 B3 |
| Shihmen Historical Battlefield 石門古戰場 | 10 B1 |
| Sichongshi Hot Spring 四重溪溫泉 | 11 B1 |
| | |
| **SLEEPING** | (pp267-8) |
| Beach House 海邊 | (see 13) |
| Yuan Shi Ling Campground 原始林露營區 | 12 C4 |
| | |
| **EATING** | (p268) |
| Bossa Nova Café 巴沙諾瓦 | 13 B3 |

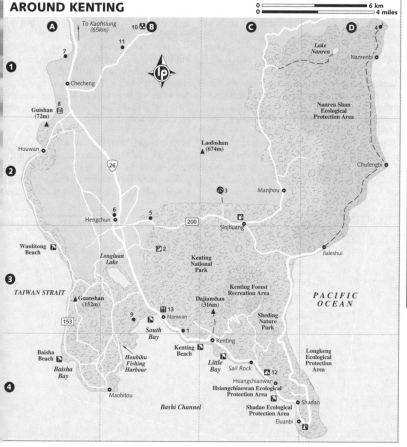

AROUND KENTING

WESTERN TAIWAN

of Kenting so you'll probably need to check into your hotel and rent a scooter before visiting.

## Dangers & Annoyances

A few years ago the national park granted control of the entire Dawan (or Kenting) Beach to the Chateau Beach Resort. While the park's people will tell you that you can simply pay a small fee to use the beach, the hotel will claim that you must stay there or at least eat a full meal to have access. We encourage you to complain at the visitor centre if you cannot gain access to the beach.

## Sights

Must-sees include the 435-hectare **Kenting Forest Recreation Area** (Kěndìng Sēnlín Yóulèqū; Map p265; admission NT100; ⏰ 8am-5pm), filled with limestone caves and botanical gardens, and **Jialeshui**, a 2.5km-long stretch of coral coastline with rocks eroded into the shapes of animals.

### NATIONAL MUSEUM OF MARINE BIOLOGY
國立海洋 生物博物館

Almost everyone will enjoy a visit to the **National Museum of Marine Biology** (Guólì Hǎiyáng Shēngwù Bówùguǎn; Map p265; 2 Houwan Rd, Checheng; adult/child under 110cm NT300/free; ⏰ 9am-6pm Mon-Fri, 8am-6pm Sat & Sun, 8am-8pm Jul & Aug). The live displays of colourful and exotic sea life are professionally and imaginatively designed. The clear tunnel that takes you into the undersea world around a sunken boat is enchanting.

### CHUHUO (TZUHUO) 出火

Kenting abounds in oddities of nature, in both inanimate formations such as the animal shapes in the eroded coral coastlines along Jialeshui and **Maobitou** (Cat's Nose; Māobítóu; Map p265) and in living matter such as the glow-in-the-dark mushrooms that come out in summer in **Sheding Nature Park** (Shèdǐng Gōngyuán; Map p265; admission free; ⏰ 8am-5pm). It only seemed appropriate then that the gas fires at **Chuhuo** (Chúhuǒ; Map p265) would eventually find their way into the park boundaries.

The fires are caused by natural gas leaking to the surface from far underground and igniting upon contact with oxygen. In the past, locals sometimes used the fires for cooking or even to heat bath water. Nowadays they bake potatoes and sell them to astonished tourists. The fires are a few minutes east of Hengchun on County Rd 200 and are best viewed at night.

Route 200 is also notable as it passes the impressive old **East Gate** (Dōngmén; Map p265) of Hengchun. In the Qing dynasty, Hengchun was a walled city. The four original gates still remain and are remarkably intact. The East Gate also still retains a long section of wall.

### ECOLOGICAL PROTECTION AREAS

The park maintains strict access controls to ecologically sensitive regions, such as the area around **Lake Nanren** (Nánrén Hú; Map p265) and the incredibly fine shell beach at

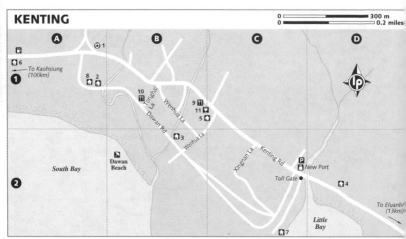

KENTING

Shadao (Shādǎo; Map p265). You can apply for permits to enter these areas ahead of time on the park's website.

## Activities

### SWIMMING

Taiwan is a volcanic island, which means the land rises steeply from the sea and the ocean begins to drop not far offshore. As a result, the waters just offshore have treacherous currents and undertows. Some sound advice from a long-term expat is not to go out much further than you can stand.

If you ignore **Kenting Beach** (Map p265), controlled by the Chateau Beach Resort, **Nanwan** (Nánwān; Map p265) and **Little Bay** (Xiǎowān; Map p265) offer the most accessible beaches for swimming and organised water sports such as surfing. The sweet little crescent beach at **Baisha Bay** (Báishā Wān; Map p265), a little further afield, is worth taking the extra time to visit. On weekday mornings it can be yours alone.

In recent years, jumping off the chin (and other protuberances) of **Sail Rock** (Chuánfán Shí; Map p265), aka Nixon Rock, has become quite popular.

### SURFING & DIVING

The waters around **Jialeshui** (Jiālèshuǐ; Map p265; admission NT80; ☼ 8am-5pm) and the nuclear power plant (Map p265) at **Nanwan** have the best surfing waves. For diving, check out the coral formations near **Sail Rock**.

For lessons in either sport (in Chinese or English), or just a little local information, there is **Fu Dog Surf & Dive** (Map p265; ☎ 0925-092 036; Nanwan Rd; ☼ 9am-9pm). Run by a certified Texan, Fu Dog has been offering openwater dives (NT1500) and PADI/NAUI certification (NT10,000) as well as surf lessons (three hours NT1000) for the past seven years. The owner lives upstairs, so the shop is technically 'open' all day.

### HIKING

The steep slab peak of **Dajianshan** (Dàjiānshān; Map p265; 316m), also called Taichienshan and just inside Kenting Forest Recreation Area, can be seen from all over. The hike to the top takes less than an hour and offers fine views of the surrounding land and sea. An early morning climb will grant you a view of the sunrise.

The seven levels of **Chikung Waterfall** (Qīkǒng Pùbù; Map p265) make for a strenuous few hours of uphill hiking. Pools between the fifth and sixth falls are big and deep enough to jump into and cool down. The turn-off to the falls is on the left as you drive along County Rd 200 from Hengchun. There is a sign but it's only in Chinese. If you reach the tiny settlement of Sinjhuang (新莊; Xīnzhuāng; Map p265), you've gone too far.

### SAILING

**Bud** (☎ 0933-011 081; three hrs per person NT500) can take up to six people out on his boat.

### BIRD-WATCHING

Kenting is prime bird-watching country and the tourist office has a special brochure highlighting the best areas, the birds themselves and tips on equipment.

## Festivals

Every April for the past 10 years bands, fans, artists (and law-enforcement officers) from around Taiwan and the world have 'followed the cows' to the site of the **Spring Scream** (www.springscream.com). As the website proclaims: 'Spring Scream is a music fest grown from simple roots with the sole purpose of bringing people together outside the city to create music and art, to be heard and to have a blast!'

## Sleeping

Bookings are advisable if there's a particular hotel you wish to stay at. Otherwise, it's possible, even during Chinese New Year, to just show up and find accommodation.

WESTERN TAIWAN

Kenting Rd and Dawan Rd are filled with budget and mid-range accommodation. Discounts of up to 50% are common on weekdays.

There are other areas to stay in the national park besides Kenting town. At Sail Rock you'll find a number of small, nondescript hotels and a few restaurants across the street from the water. This is a nice area to stay and you have the bonus of the jumping ledges on Sail Rock right at your doorstep. Prices are similar to Kenting town.

### BUDGET

Many Kenting residents can offer you private guesthouses. When you get off the bus you will probably be asked if you are interested. Prices average NT600 to NT800 on weekdays and NT1500 on weekends.

**Catholic Hostel** (Tiānzhǔjiào Huódòng Zhōngxīn; Map pp266-7; ☎ 886 1540; fax 886 1352; 2 Wenhua Lane; dm NT300, r from NT1200) The hostel is immaculately clean and a close walk to the swimming beach at Little Bay. Young student groups often stay here so don't check in if your plans are to drink and party all night.

**Yuan Shi Ling Campground** (Yuánshǐlín Lùyíngqū; Map p265; ☎ 885 1072; 238-2 Chuan Fan Rd; per person NT100) You'll find this camping ground just past Sail Rock, towards Eluanbi on the left. If you don't have your own tent you can rent one and a sleeping bag (NT300/50). Bathrooms with showers are available on site.

### MID-RANGE

**Beach House** (Hǎibiān; Map p265; ☎ 888 0440; 230 Nanwan Rd, Nanwan; dm/d/tw NT300/1500/2500) A B&B run by Taiwanese surfers. Rooms are small but bright. Almost next door to the B&B is the expat-run Fu Dog Surf & Dive.

**Cactus Café** (Xiānrénzhǎng Kāfēi; Map pp266-7; ☎ 886 2747; 126 Dawan Rd; r NT1500-2500) Our readers let us in on this one and we agree it's one of the nicest places to stay in Kenting for this price range. Simple wood and brick rooms are flooded with sunlight and feature open showers with great ocean views and large beds with crisp white linen. This is a place for the laid-back, of any age, who appreciate clean comfort and a bit of character in their lodgings.

**Kenting Youth Activity Centre** (Qīngnián Huódòng Zhōngxīn; Map pp266-7; ☎ 886 1221; 17 Xingnan Lane; d/tw NT2500/3000) This place is touted as much as an attraction as a place to lodge. The centre occupies 25 hectares of land and features a complete traditional Fujian-style village for guests to sleep in. The centre will appeal to families, not only for the historical and rather fun design (kids just love playing around the old-style buildings) but also for the fact it's on its own secluded road. The famous landmark Frog Rock (Qīngwā Shí) is just a few minutes' walk away, though the 'Frog' has eroded away and now it's just 'Rock'.

### TOP END

**Caesar Park Hotel** (Kǎisà Dàdì; Map pp266-7; ☎ 886 1888; fax 886 1818; 6 Kenting Rd; d/tw/ste NT6100/7300/14,000) For modern high-end comfort that still lets you feel you are in tropical Kenting there is the Caesar. Hotel features include a spa, business centre and children's play area. The hotel's restaurants are open to nonguests and the Western breakfast buffet is particularly popular.

**Chateau Beach Resort** (Xiàdù Shātān Jiǔdiàn; Map pp266-7; ☎ 886 2345; 451 Kenting Rd; d/tw NT4600/5400; 🖳 ) Though many people resent the chateau for monopolising the entire 5km stretch of Dawan beach (and, more egregiously, for not following its agreement with the park to keep it clean and grant easy access to nonguests), it is a splendid place to stay. Rooms and facilities are top-notch and include a beachside pool with an open-air bar.

## Eating

Kenting is a tourist town and there is no shortage of food and drink. Western dishes (and Western favourites such as curries) tend to be done well here.

**Warung Didi Restaurant** (Dídí Xiǎochī; Map pp266-7; ☎ 886 1835; 176 Dawan Rd; dishes NT240; ⏰ 5.30pm-1am, closed Tue) We should warn that this popular Kenting establishment has moved to Dawan Rd. The restaurant at the old location (called Warung Teddy) was opened by the landlords after they refused to extend the Didi owners' lease. Head to the real Didi's for the Thai curries, music, beer and beach-hut atmosphere that has made it famous. Reservations are recommended on weekends.

**Cactus Café** (Xiānrénzhǎng Kāfēi; Map pp266-7; ☎ 886 6247; 126 Dawan Rd; dishes NT150-200; ⏰ 9.30am-late) The breakfast menu (NT120 to NT160) is the best and delivers a wide selection of Western favourites such as buttermilk pancakes, scrambled eggs and yoghurt smoothies. The

WESTERN TAIWAN

restaurant also makes excellent burritos and hamburgers.

**Amy's Cucina Restaurant** (Nánxíng Dàfàndiàn; Map pp266-7; ☎ 197 7131, ext 1; 131-1 Kenting Rd; dishes NT200; ✆ 10am-midnight Oct-May, 10am-2am Jun-Sep) This was the first place in Kenting to serve pizza and it's still got some of the best Italian food in the park. The attractive red-brick design makes it suitable for hanging out and enjoying a nice dinner.

**Bossa Nova Café** (Bāshānuòwǎ; Map p265; ☎ 889 7137; 100 Nanwan Rd; meals NT200; ✆ 11am-11pm) While the dishes (Chinese and Thai with a few Western staples such as burritos and sandwiches) are tasty, the greater pleasure here is sitting on the breezy patio enjoying the views across South Bay.

## Drinking

Many restaurants, such as the Cactus Café, Warung Didi and Amy's Cucina, also serve as bars (drinks from NT100), with good music played loud in the evenings. Caesar Park Hotel has an outdoor beer garden and barbecue (per person NT750) in the evenings.

**Ocean Blue** (Hǎilán Cāntīng; Map pp266-7; ☎ 886 2600; 111 Kenting Rd; drinks from NT100; ✆ 11am-11pm weekdays, 11am-2am weekends) For dancing, check out the small but lively dance floor at this restaurant/bar.

## Getting There & Away

### AIR

Many people fly to Kaohsiung and then catch a bus to Kenting. Buses run every 20 minutes (NT250, 2½ hours) and stop right at the airport.

A domestic airport opened in Hengchun in January 2004. While Hengchun is much closer to Kenting than Kaohsiung, you will still need to catch a bus or rent your own transport to complete your journey. **Trans-Asia Airways** ( ☎ 02-2972 4599) has daily flights between Taipei and Hengchun (NT2100).

### BUS

The easiest way to get to Kenting from Kaohsiung is to catch the 'Kenting Express' (NT250, two hours, every hour) from the Kaohsiung Ke Yuan station. Nearby Free Go and CN bus companies also run buses to Kenting (NT290).

Don't try to save time by taking the train down to Pingdong as there are only two buses a day from here.

## Getting Around

The only way to get around Kenting is with your own transport. There are no buses of any kind except those coming in from Kaohsiung and Hengchun. Any hotel can arrange car, jeep or scooter rental. Most travellers use scooters and as you enter town there are scooter-rental shops (per day NT400 to NT500) to the right. You can rent bikes (per hour NT100) at the Youth Activity Centre.

## SICHONGSHI HOT SPRINGS 四重溪溫泉
☎ 08

One of the pleasures of a trip to Kenting is the sheer variety of things to see and do. Outside the park boundaries, but still accessible by car or scooter, is the hot-spring village of Sichongshi (Sìchóngxī). While you may not want to visit hot springs during the summer months, a soak in an outdoor pool with a clear starry sky above on a cool winter evening is a real treat. There are numerous hotels, many recently refurbished with up-to-date facilities, including different temperature pools, spa jets and showers. You can stay overnight but most people just come for a few hours.

Recommended by Kenting locals is **Dashan Hot Spring Spa** (Dàshān Wēnquán Nóngchǎng; Map p265; ☎ 882 5725; 60-1 Tamei Rd, Wenquan Village; unlimited time NT150; ✆ 6am-11pm). The hotel has a small animal farm with ostriches, ducks, chickens and donkeys, and a good restaurant serving mountain chicken and vegetables. The spa is at the far end of the village. Drive until you are almost out of town and turn left at the sign to Tamei Village (大梅村; Dàméicūn). Follow the road about 1km and then turn onto a dirt road marked with a sign in Chinese for the hotel. The hotel is 90m up this road.

To get to Sichongshi, follow Hwy 26 almost as far as Checheng (車城; Chēchéng) and turn right onto County Rd 199. Sichongshi is a few kilometres down the highway and is the first real settlement you pass through. It's about 32km to Sichongshi from Kenting.

## SHUANGLIOU FOREST RECREATION AREA 雙流森林遊樂區

It's well worth continuing down County Rd 199 east of Sichongshi. Along the way, you will pass the **Shihmen Historical Battlefield**

(Shímén Gǔzhànchǎng, Map p265) and be rewarded with a varying landscape of ponds, aboriginal villages, mountains and open fields.

Just before the coast, you have the choice of taking spur route 199 to the photogenic **grasslands** around Shiuhai (Xùhǎi), or continuing up 199 to Hwy 9, turning left to reach **Shuangliou Forest Recreation Area** (Shuāngliù Sēnlíng Yóulè Qū; http://recreate.forest.gov.tw; admission NT100; ☺ 8am-5pm).

The park is one of the most recently developed forest recreation areas in Taiwan. Just past the tollgate sits a spiffy new visitor centre with English brochures and maps. There are two main walking trails, one to **Shuangliuo Waterfall** (雙流瀑布; Shuāngliú Pùbù; two hours return) and the other to 630m **Mautzu Mountain** (帽子山; Màuzi Shān; three hours return). Both trails begin near the visitor centre and are well marked with English signs.

# Taiwan Strait Islands

CONTENTS

Remote and beautiful, the archipelagos of Matsu, Kinmen and Penghu in the Taiwan Strait have remained out of the travellers' spotlight until very recently. Situated between mainland China and Taiwan, these islands have been a source of tension, war and fierce political debate for more than half a century. But because of their location and history, they offer a superb window onto Taiwan's turbulent military past and rich cultural heritage.

Matsu and Kinmen are politically significant as once being front-line locations for the Republic of China (ROC) defence when the Nationalists retreated to Taiwan in 1949. With the end of martial law and the opening up of the islands in 1992, formerly off-limit military sites such as forts and battlegrounds were opened to the public and a fledgling tourist industry began.

Isolated from Taiwan for over 40 years, Matsu and Kinmen have retained their distinct cultures, much different from those of Taiwan, while slowly moving into the realities of the 21st century. Matsu's picturesque fishing villages and pristine coastline make it an excellent choice for those looking to escape the hectic pace of Taiwan's big cities. Kinmen's museums and wetlands reserve deserve top marks, as do its fiery Kaoliang liquor and exquisite ceramics.

Penghu, the most visited of the Strait Islands, is a popular resort destination that attracts beachgoers – both local and foreign – who flock here in summer for the fine sand beaches and water sports.

Tourism remains relatively undeveloped, though things are changing rapidly as the Strait Islands become more accessible to visitors. Many travellers find that a trip to the Strait Islands turns out to be the highlight of their Taiwan experience.

## HIGHLIGHTS

- Sleep in a traditional Fujian-style home on **Matsu** (opposite)

- Sample the powerful **Kaoliang liquor** (p289) of Matsu and Kinmen

- Visit Kinmen's **Kuningtou War Museum** (p292), site of the tragic 1949 battle between the communist mainlanders and Taiwanese defenders

- Bird-watch at **Shuangli Wetlands Area Centre** (p292), Kinmen

- Windsurf at **Chipei Island** (p303), Penghu

CHINA

★ Matsu
Traditional
Fujian-style Home

★ ★ Kuningtou War Museum
Shuangli Wetlands
Kinmen

Windsurfing, Chipei Island ★

Penghu

TAIWAN

## Climate

On Matsu, spring and summer are warm and wet, with the occasional typhoon. Monsoon rains begin in mid-autumn and last throughout winter. Winters are dreary and cold, with deserted beaches and empty hotels. Blustery winds and rain make travelling at this time of year difficult. Penghu, in particular, is noted for its strong winter winds, making it a favourite for windsurfers.

The islands are often very foggy, especially in the spring, and the airports can shut down for days at a time. The best time to visit is in late May, June or late August and early September to avoid the summer crowds and bad weather.

## Getting There & Away

In summer, travelling to the islands from Taiwan's major cities is no problem. Flights leave daily and there are regular ferry services leaving Keelung and Kaohsiung. Unfortunately, it's not possible to island hop from one island region to another. If you want to travel from Matsu to Kinmen, for example, it's necessary to head back to Taiwan and take another plane (or boat) to Kinmen.

In winter, travel to the islands becomes difficult. Ferry services are cut back considerably and flights may be cancelled without notice because of fog and wind conditions. See the appropriate island sections for information on prices and services.

## Getting Around

Bus service on the islands is limited and getting around this way can be frustrating. The most convenient form of transport is car or motorbike. Most rental agencies charge NT400 to NT500 a day for a motorbike, including petrol, and NT1500 and up for a car, though this can be bargained down depending on how long you want to use the vehicle. Some rental agencies require an international Drivers Licence or a Taiwan Licence, others don't ask. If renting your own transport is out of the question, hiring a taxi for the day may be your only option. It's also possible to hop on a Chinese tour bus, which often leave from central bus stations. To get to neighbouring islands, ferry services are cheap and fun, though service is dependent on the weather. For details of transport options for individual islands, check under the appropriate island section.

# MATSU

☎ 0836 / pop 9,000

The Matsu Islands are directly off the coast of mainland China's Fujian province, near the mouth of the Min River. Matsu are the principal islands in Lienchiang County and are made up of 18 islands with four townships: Nankan, Peikan, Chukuang and Tungyin. The name Matsu (馬祖; Mǎzǔ) is commonly used to refer to the entire island group. Nankan is the administrative and cultural centre as well as Matsu's largest landmass, although it's only 12.1 sq km in area.

## History

The development of Matsu began in the 1400s with the arrival of Fujianese mainlanders escaping political turmoil in their homeland. The migrant waves of the 1600s from mainland China to Taiwan saw an increase in Matsu's population as boatloads of Fujianese fisherman arrived on its shores. They brought with them the language, food, architecture and religious beliefs of their ancestors, still seen in Matsu today.

Throughout the 1700s and 1800s piracy plagued the islands, causing residents at various times to temporarily abandon their homes and find shelter elsewhere. Matsu was largely politically insignificant until the Nationalists fled to Taiwan in 1949 and established Matsu, along with Kinmen, as a front line defence against the communists. Matsu

MATSU — CHINA — Taiwan Strait
Hsiyin Township
Tungyin Township
Peikan Township
Nankan Township
Chukuang Township
0 — 30 km / 0 — 20 miles

residents saw their quiet islands transformed into battlefields and had to adjust to the constant threat of war. The mainland bombed Matsu intermittently for years until the deployment in 1958 of the US 7th Fleet prevented any further escalation.

With the ending of martial law in Matsu in 1992 and gradual demilitarisation of the islands, Matsu residents have gained a newfound sense of hope for the future. Tourism is thought to be one of the best ways to revitalise the economy and there is significant effort to restore old Fujian-style villages and promote the island as a top spot for ecotourism. In January 2001, Matsu and Kinmen made world headlines when the 'Three Small Links' (p288) permitted the islands to have limited direct travel and trade with mainland China. With the Three Small Links and tourism, Matsu is slowly opening up to the world, maintaining a delicate balance between history and progress.

## NANKAN TOWNSHIP 南竿鄉
### Orientation
Nankan Township (Nángān Xiāng) is divided into nine villages: Chiehshou (Shanlong), Chinsha, Chingshui, Chuluo, Fuhsing (Niuchao), Fu'ao (Chingtse), Jenai (Tieban), Matsu (Magang) and Ssuwei (Hsiwei). The older names for the villages in parentheses are still used sometimes. Chiehshou Village (Jièshòu Cūn) is the commercial hub of Nankan, and Nankan's newly built airport is in the northeast of the island, very close to Chiehshou. Ferries to outlying islands leave from Fu'ao Harbour (Fúaò Gǎng) in Fu'ao Village (Fúaò Cūn). The central bus station is in Chiehshou Village, at the end of the main road leading to the harbour. Tour buses and public buses depart from here.

## Information
There is a good English map of Matsu in the park in front of Chiehshou's public vegetable garden.

**Bank of Taiwan** ( ☎ 25400; 257 Chiehshou Village) The only place in Matsu to change money.

**Matsu National Scenic Area Office** (Mǎzǔ Guójiā Fēngjǐng Qū; ☎ 25630; 256 Chiehshou Village) Free brochures and maps available in English.

**Military Post Office** (Jūn Yóujú; ☎ 22050; 258 Chiehshou Village)

## Sights & Activities
### DISTILLERY TOURS
Close to Fuhsing Village (Fùxīng Cūn) is the **Matsu Distillery** (Mǎzǔ Jiǔchǎng; ☎ 22820; 208 Fuhsing Village; admission free; ☯ 8.30-11.30am & 2-5pm Mon-Fri, holidays 3-5pm), the place to try Matsu's well-known spirits: Kaoliang (Gāoliǎng jiǔ), made from sorghum, and làojiǔ medicinal rice wine. These brews are famous throughout Taiwan and popular with Taiwanese tourists. Làojiǔ, literally translated as 'old wine', is a common ingredient in Fujian-influenced Matsu dishes such as red-marinated eel and snails. It's possible to tag along with a Chinese-language tour and partake of the samples that are given out liberally at the end of each session.

### FORMER MILITARY INSTALLATIONS
Built into the foot of Niuchao (Rhino Horn) mountain, the 264m **Tunnel 88** (Bābā Kēngdào; 208 Fuhsing Village) was originally an air-raid shelter. In 1988, it was converted into a storage facility for làojiǔ and Kaoliang. Chinese-language tours take groups through the

ank, booze-smelling tunnel and let them visit the fermentation rooms. If you come without a tour group and want to look inside you'll need to register with the security guards outside. The tunnel is easy to find – look for decorative earthenware jars lined up at the entrance. It's a four-minute walk from the Matsu Distillery.

**Fushan Illuminated Wall** (Fúshān Zhàobì), is on a hilltop facing mainland China. The bright-red characters state 'sleep with one's weapons ready,' warning the communist mainlanders of Chiang Kai-shek's intentions to invade and reunify China.

The 700m **Peihai Tunnel** (Běihǎi Kēngdào; 9am-5pm Mon-Fri) was carved by soldiers out of a sheer rock face using only simple hand tools. Begun in 1968, the project took over three years and many young men lost their lives. The tunnel was used as a hiding place for military boats and is supposedly large enough to hide 120 small vessels inside its cavernous interior in case of attack.

The **Iron Fort** (Tiě Bǎo) is located on a rocky strip of granite jutting out over the sea and was once the base for Matsu's amphibious forces. It's possible to go inside the fort and take a look at the sniper slots, kitchen and sleeping quarters. Gruesome stories are told by Matsu residents of how mainland Chinese frogmen would sneak inside the fort at night, slit the throats of the Taiwanese guards on duty and carry back an ear to show their comrades.

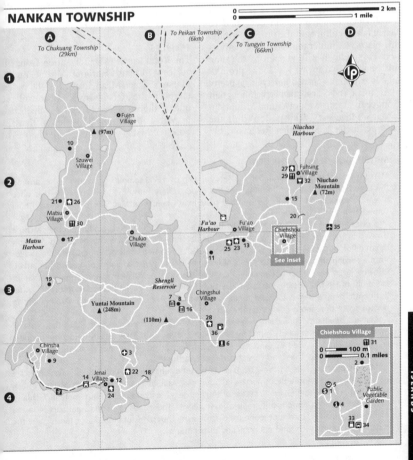

## MUSEUMS & PARKS

The **Fishery Centre** (Yúyè Zhǎnxíng Guǎn; 24 Ssuwei Village; ☺ 9am-5pm Mon-Fri) is a bizarre little place devoted to the fishing industry in Matsu. It's not that interesting but it'll give you an idea of what sea creatures are swimming out there. There are tanks with live fish and a rather creepy display of pickled fish in bottles.

Within **Chiehshou Park** (Jièshòu Gōngyuán) is the **Chiang Chingkuo Memorial** (Jīngguó Jìniàn Guǎn), a two-storey building with a bronze statue of Chiang Kai-shek's son and former president Chiang Chingkuo on the 1st floor and a photographic display of his life upstairs. Also in the park is the **Matsu Folk Culture Museum** (Mǎzǔ Mínsú Wénwù Guǎn), which was once the Matsu History Museum (and still referred to by that name in local literature) but is now being transformed into a museum dedicated to Matsu island culture. At the time of writing, this place was undergoing massive renovation. Hopefully, it will be open by the time this book goes to print – it looks promising. It overlooks **Shengli Reservoir**, a pretty place for a walk. **Shengtien Park** (Shèngtiān Gōngyuán), to the west of Yuntai Mountain, is Matsu's loveliest seaside park. Within the park perimeter is Shengtien Reservoir, the

most important source for water in Matsu and the **Shengtien Pavilion** (Shèngtiān Tíng) built in Tang-dynasty style. **Chinsha Scenic Area** (Jīnshā Fēngjǐng Qū), in the southwest corner of the island, is worth exploring. **Chinsha Village** provides an excellent opportunity to see restored Fujian-style houses. For a pleasant walk along the coastline, follow the footpath leading from Chinsha Harbour to Jenai Village.

At 248m, **Yuntai Mountain** (Yúntái Shān) is Nankan's highest peak. The scenery from the platform at the top is impressive, with a panoramic view of mainland China and nearby islets. There's also a **military museum** up here that's normally closed to the public but if you're friendly to the guards they might let you in. Inside, there's a display of maps, dry-looking documents and model of boats made by stationed soldiers.

## TEMPLES

The **Matsu Temple** (Mǎzǔ Tiānhòu Gōng) is adjacent to Matsu Harbour (Mǎzǔ Gǎng) in Matsu Village (Mǎzǔ Cūn). It's the oldest temple in the Matsu Islands and considered one of the most sacred temples dedicated to Matsu in Taiwan. It's believed that the bones of Matsu were once stored here. The

### MATSU, GODDESS OF THE SEA

Matsu is the most popular folk deity in Taiwan, with over 500 temples dedicated to her around the island. Legends about the origins of the goddess vary but most agree that she was once a real person named Lin Mo, born into a fisherman's family on Meizhou Island, Fujian, China sometime in the 10th century.

Stories are told about how Lin Mo loved the sea and was often seen standing on the seashore dressed in red, guiding ships to harbour during storms. Circumstances of the young woman's death differ, but some say that on a stormy night she drowned while attempting to save a sailor from a sinking ship. Another story tells of how Lin Mo drowned while trying to find her father, lost in a storm at sea. Her body washed up onto the shores of Nankan Island. Some say that on the night of Lin Mo's death, her spirit was seen flying up to heaven dressed in red robes. After her death, people began to build temples in memory of the brave young woman, praying to her for protection and guidance on the sea.

Matsu's popularity spread after her death and temples were soon built along the coast of mainland China, Taiwan and eventually Singapore and Japan. Statues usually depict the goddess with black skin, a beaded veil and a red cape. Sitting next to her are her loyal attendants, Eyes that See a Thousand Miles and Ears that Hear upon the Wind.

Matsu's birthday falls on the 23rd day of the third lunar month and religious festivities are held in her honour throughout north and Southeast Asia. In Taiwan, the largest Matsu Festival is the Tachia Matsu Pilgrimage. A statue of the goddess is escorted from her temple in Tachia to the Hsinkang Taoist temple, a journey of over 280km. Thousands of pilgrims participate in the march, accompanied by drums, gongs and acrobatics. Thousands of enthusiastic locals greet the travelling goddess with food offerings and prostrations.

emple becomes festive with worshippers
on Matsu's birthday. On the beach directly
in front of the temple are tanks and ar-
moured equipment, a potent reminder of
Matsu's recent military history.

The **Huakuang Tati Temple** (Huáguāng Dàdì
Miào) in Fu'ao Village is named after the
God of Fire. Legend has it that during the
Ming dynasty a Fu'ao villager dreamt that
the God of Fire came to him and told him
about an incense burner made of sandal-
wood that was buried somewhere in Fu'ao.
The man woke up, searched for the burner
and discovered it where the god had said
it would be. Later the villagers built this
temple in the god's honour. The **White Horse
God Temple** (Bái Mǎ Wén Wǔ Tiān Wáng
Miào) is a small temple devoted to the worship of a deified general who once defended
Fujian. The story is told that during the
Qing dynasty two bodies once washed up
onto Matsu's shores and the locals buried
them. Supposedly, the spirit of the general
spoke through a spirit medium, telling the
villagers to build a temple in his name,
which they did. Now, whenever a storm
approaches, locals say a light can be seen
moving across the water, guiding ships to
the harbour.

## Sleeping

### BUDGET
**Lianjiang Hotel** (Liánjiāng Shānzhuāng; ☎ 25705; 103
Matsu Village; r NT800-1200) A short walk from
Matsu Village, this quiet establishment offers a peaceful location with ocean views.
The drawback is that it looks like it hasn't
seen guests for years. Rooms are dingy,
dusty and full of cobwebs. Management
appears genuinely surprised to see guests
come through the door.

**Fuhua Hotel** (Fúhúa Lǚdiàn; ☎ 22990; 110 Fu'ao
Village; r NT1000) A friendly, family-run hotel
with simple, airy rooms very conveniently
located near Fu'ao Harbour. It's a good
place to stay if you need to catch an early
morning ferry. Try to get a room in the
back to avoid street noise.

**Kaixiang Hotel** (Kǎixiáng Kèzhàn; ☎ 22652; 108
Fu'ao Village; r NT1000) Close to the Fuhua Hotel,
this place is not as nice as its neighbour,
but still offers reasonably priced accommodation in a central location. Rooms are
adequate, though rather gloomy, and the
bathrooms could be cleaner.

### MID-RANGE
**Hailanghua Hotel** (Háilànghúa Kèzhàn; ☎ 22569; 64
Jenai Village; r from NT1200) A new hotel offering excellent value for money with spotless,
modern rooms and very friendly management. The ocean views from the coffee-shop
patio are superb – a great place to relax on
a summer evening and watch the sunset.
Make sure to book ahead as the hotel is
popular with tour groups and fills up fast.

**Night on the Bay Homestay** (Yèsù Háijiǎo;
☎ 26333; 159 Fuhsing Village; s/d/q NT1000/1200/from
NT2000) Recently restored, this waterfront
home has been opened as a guesthouse for
tourists. The granite walls and tiled roof are
typical of eastern Fujian-style architecture.
The house has one private double room, a
large central room with TV, shared bathroom with hot water and loft-style sleeping quarters for four. The house is very
draughty and cold in winter so bring warm
clothes, and possibly a sleeping bag, if you
plan to stay here at this time. The homestay
is run by the same amicable woman who
owns Grandma's Eatery (p277) – you'll
need to inquire there if you want a room.

### TOP END
**Coast Hotel** (Rìguāng Hǎi'àn Háijìng Lǚguǎn; ☎ 26666;
fax 25638; 1-1 Jenai Village; r NT2400, 3-person tatami r from
NT4000) Considered one of Nankan's lovели-
est places to stay, this small hotel boasts fabulous ocean views and an excellent restaurant
and coffee shop. There are only 10 rooms,
all tastefully furnished, most with Japanese
soaker tubs. Well recommended!

**Shennung Hostel** (Shénnóng Shānzhuāng; ☎ 26333;
84-2 Chingshui Village; r from NT3000, q from NT4000)
With Yuntai Mountain on one side and the
ocean on the other, this five-storey hotel
offers some very nice views of the surrounding areas. The building itself is an unattractive box but, inside, the rooms are large and
pleasant, with everything you'd expect from
a hotel in this price range. Management are
very helpful in arranging tours around the
island.

## Eating
**Grandma's Eatery** (Yīmā de Diàn; 143 Fuhsing
Village; mains from NT150; ◯ 10am-2pm & 5-10pm)
For traditional cuisine in a great atmosphere, this is the place to go. Nankan locals
con-gregate here in the evening to eat,
drink and swap stories. It's a lively place,

especially on weekends. The seafood is excellent – specialities include red-cooked seafood with peanuts (*hóngzāo liàolǐ*), *jiguang* cakes and fishball soup (*yúwán tāng*). Wash it all down with a bottle of home brewed *làojiǔ*.

**Mintung Chih Chu** (Mǐndōng Zhīzhū; 22 Matsu Village; mains from NT120; 11am-10.30pm) This restaurant specialises in the cuisine of eastern Fujian, where the emphasis is on fresh, delicate flavours, soups and lots of seafood. Try the delicious red-cooked 'Buddha's hand' clams (*hóngzāo fóshǒu*). Vegetarians can order the peanut-filled yam dumplings (*dìguā jiǎo*). Head upstairs for the balcony and photo gallery.

**Tiekuo** (Tiěguō; 47-2 Chiehshou Village; hotpots from NT200; lunch & dinner) On a cold, windy day in Matsu, eating hotpot is a great way to warm up. Meat, seafood and vegetarian hotpots are available here as well as dumplings and noodle dishes. This restaurant caters to tour groups but solo travellers are still welcome.

## Drinking

**Fisherman's Hut Coffee and Pub** (Yúliáo Shūzhài; 110-1 Fuhsing Village; coffee from NT90; 11.30am-11pm, summer & holidays 10am-11pm) Across the road from Grandma's Eatery, this pleasant little café is a nice place to stop and unwind after a long day.

## Shopping

In Chiehshou Village you'll find **Chiehshou Market** (Jièshòu Shìzǐ Shìchǎng; 6-9am), where you can purchase a variety of locally made goodies such as Matsu hibiscus cakes, sweets, tea, oyster pancakes and fish noodles.

## Getting There & Away

Uni Air has eight flights daily from Taipei (NT1816, 55 minutes) to Nankan airport (Nángān Jīchǎng). You must show your passport before boarding. Be prepared for last-minute cancellations and delays because of Matsu's volatile weather, especially in spring and winter.

The **Taima Boat Company** (Keelung 02-2424 6868, 2422 8267; Nankan 22395, 26655) has a ferry service that runs between Keelung and Matsu (seat NT350, dorm bed NT550-650, 2nd/3rd class NT800/1200, seven to eight hours). The boat leaves Keelung at 10pm

and travels via Tungyin Island (Dōngyǐn) to Nankan. You must book your ticket two days in advance prior to actually purchasing it. During winter, the boat schedule is unreliable and trips are cancelled frequently.

During spring and summer boats run between Nankan and the outlying islands of Matsu; schedules are cut back in autumn and winter because of bad weather. Between Nankan and Peikan, boats leave hourly from Fu'ao Harbour (round-trip NT140,10 minutes). From Nankan to Tungyin (two hours), there is one boat a day. Boats to Chukuang Township (one hour) run two or three times a day. You'll need to check at Fu'ao Harbour for current schedules and ticket prices as these seem to fluctuate with the seasons.

**Daily Air** ( 23500) runs a chartered helicopter service between Nankan, Tungyin and Chukuang (NT2200).

## Getting Around
### TO/FROM THE AIRPORT

Nankan's small size means that the airport is close to many of the main sights. Taxi and motorcycle touts hang around outside and are more than happy to offer their services. If you're travelling light, it's only a 10-minute walk to Chiehshou or Fuhsing Villages.

### CAR/MOTORCYCLE/SCOOTER

Having your own vehicle is the most convenient (and the most fun) way to see Nankan but it's not the cheapest. Motorcycle can be rented for NT500 a day but you can probably bargain the price down. If you want to get around the island in style, cars are available for NT1500 to NT2000 per day. If you're travelling with a group of people, you can rent a microbus with driver for NT4500. The information counter at the airport can help you book vehicle rentals.

### PUBLIC TRANSPORT

Buses run hourly around the island (NT15) but travelling this way will probably test your patience. Also, the bus schedules are posted in Chinese so unless you can recognise the characters of your destination you'll have a hard time getting around. If in doubt, ask one of the soldiers at the tation for help as they can usually speak little English.

During summer, tour buses leave frequently from the central bus station. Most of the time it's possible to buy a ticket as you board. The tours will be conducted in

Chinese but it's still a good way see the island. Prices vary, but average roughly NT100.

### TAXI

The flat on-call taxi rate to anywhere in Nankan is NT100. Drivers will rarely use the meter. Taxis in line-ups are usually NT200. Your taxi driver might offer to take you on a tour around the island. For this service expect to pay NT500 to NT600 an hour.

## PEIKAN TOWNSHIP 北竿

Relaxed and leisurely, Peikan Township (北竿鄉; Běigān Xiāng) makes Nankan seem boisterous in comparison. Though the island lags behind its neighbour in commercial development, it makes up for this in its coastal scenery, fine beaches and some of the best-preserved Fujian architecture on Matsu. The mountainous island makes cultivation of crops near impossible and residents are dependent on the sea for their livelihood. Many villages are almost deserted because the stagnant economy

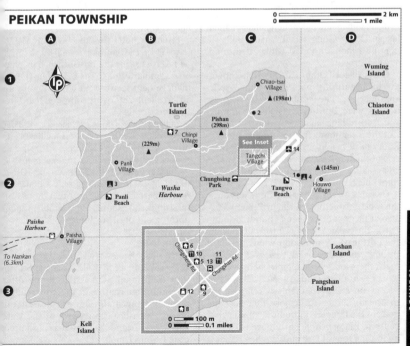

## PEIKAN TOWNSHIP

forced long-time residents to move away. But tourism has meant increased prosperity for Peikan and some former villagers have moved back to take advantage of the new economy.

Peikan Township includes the islands of Peikan (北竿; Běigān), Kaoteng, Ta-ch'iu and Hsiao-ch'iu. Peikan, the largest of the group, is the only island currently open to travellers. With the building of the new airport in Nankan, many people prefer to fly directly into Nankan and visit Peikan as a day trip. Peikan's airport, hotels and restaurants are all in Tangchi (Tángqí Cūn), the island's largest village.

## Sights

**Tangwo Beach** (Tángwò Shātān) is a thin strip of sand, divided by a road, which connects the villages of Tangchi and Houwo (Hòuwò Cūn). Before the road was built, locals had to wade through water during high tide to travel between the two villages.

**53 Houwo Village** is an old Fujian-style house that has been renovated and opened to visitors. The woman who lives there seems eager to show guests around and give them the history of the building. Also within Houwo Village is the **Yangkung Pashih Temple** (Yáng Gōng Bāshí Miào), built to honour a man who died while attempting to kill a dragon.

**Chinpi Village** (Qínbì Cūn) is well known for its beautifully preserved Fujian-style architecture. The traditional two-storey houses were built from slabs of granite and feature high, narrow windows to protect the inhabitants from wind and pirates. Roofs have bright-red or black tiles. Several of the houses are open for display. The village also has a café and homestay (see right) here.

**Chiao-tsai Village** (Qiáo Zǎi Cūn) was once the most prosperous village in Peikan. Situated at the foot of Leishan (Thunder Mountain), the village enjoys protection from the northeasterly monsoon winds that tear through the island every year. Not surprisingly, there are several temples here devoted to the Thunder God. In fact, Chiao-tsai boasts more temples than any other village in Matsu. Locals like to joke that now the gods in the temples outnumber villagers because so many people have moved away. A good time to visit is at sunset when remain-

ing villagers gather in the temples and burn incense to the gods.

**Pishan** (Pìshān) is Matsu's highest mountain at 298m and offers great views of the water and villages below. From the viewing platform at the summit, it's possible to see Tangchi, Houwo and, on a clear day, mainland China. Pishan was a key defence point against mainland soldiers and pillboxes remain scattered across the mountain top. It's possible to hike or drive to the summit but because the road is so steep, some choose to take a taxi and then hike down.

**Panli Beach** (Bǎnlǐ Hǎitān) is unusually flat for a Matsu beach. Nearby are a military base and the eye-catching pink and yellow **Matsu Temple** (Māzǔ Tiānhòu Gōng).

## Sleeping

### BUDGET

**Beihai'an Hotel** (Běihǎi'ān Lǚguǎn; ☎ 55034; Tangchi Village, 240 Chungcheng Rd; s & d NT800; ☐ ) This welcoming hotel seems to grab most of the tourist traffic in Peikan. The rooms are homely but clean, and they come with computers and free broadband Internet access. The hotel lobby is also the local barber shop.

**Biyuntian Hotel** (Bìyúntiān Lǚshè; ☎ 55461/2 Tangchi Village, 255 Chungcheng Rd; dm NT400, s & d NT800 ☐ ) Across from the post office, this place offers similar value to the Beihai'an, though management seems a bit aloof. Rooms are an excellent deal, with computers and free Internet access.

**Taijiang Hotel** (Táijiāng Dà Fàndiàn; ☎ 55250 Tangchi Village, 200 Chungcheng Rd; s & d NT800) Another good budget choice with decent rooms and conscientious management.

**Hongrui Hotel** (Hóngruì Dà Fàndiàn; ☎ 56316-20 Tangchi Village, 146 Chungcheng Rd; s & d NT800) A fourth-best choice if the other hotels are full (unlikely). Rooms are tolerable, though nothing out of the ordinary.

### MID-RANGE

**Chinpi Village Homestay** (Qínbì Mínsù Cūn; ☎ 55456 49 Chinpi Village; d/q NT1500/800 a person) Staying in a traditional Matsu-style home offers a pleasant alternative to the concrete-box hotels of Tangchi. Rooms are pleasant and breezy, with beautiful views of the water and Turtle Island. To stay here, inquire at Cafe Chinpi (opposite).

## Eating
**Hong Xing Ping Seafood Restaurant** (Hóng Xīng Píng Hǎixiān Lóu; Tangchi Village, 242 Chungcheng Rd; mains from NT120; 🕒 10am-2pm & 5-8pm) This is a good place to meet the locals and try some of Peikan's seafood. The fish noodles and sweet-and-sour yellow croaker (*tángcù huángyú*) are terrific.

**Meihua Fanyin** (Méihuā Fànyǐn; Tangchi Village, 272 Chungshan Rd; mains from NT60; 🕒 9-1.30am) There's nothing exceptional about the food here but it's a good cheap place to fill up on fried noodles and rice dishes. Servings are ample and the owner will accommodate vegetarians.

**Cafe Chinpi** (Qínbì Rénwén Kāfēi Guǎn; 49 Chinpi Village; coffee from NT100, snacks from NT50, mains from NT120; 🕒 10am-9pm) With a terrace and a view of Turtle Island, on a sunny day this is the perfect place to linger for an hour or two over coffee and Matsu pastry.

## Shopping
**A-Poh's Fish Noodles** (Ā'pó Yúmiàn; Tangchi Village, 168 Chungshan Rd; 🕒 9am-5pm Mon-Fri) This is one of the few places in Matsu that still produces fish noodles by hand, not by machine. Mrs Li, the owner, has been making these noodles for over 30 years and her shop has become a local landmark. She welcomes visitors and sometimes gives demonstrations of the noodle-making process. She sells bags of dried fish noodles for NT80.

## Getting There & Away
Since the building of the Nankan airport in 2003, most travellers fly into Nankan, where Matsu's main tourist sites are located. The smaller Peikan airport is now used mainly by soldiers. If you do fly to Peikan, remember to bring your passport.

There's an hourly boat service between Peikan and Nankan (round-trip NT140, 10 minutes) leaving from Paisha Harbour (Báishā Gǎng).

## Getting Around
### TO/FROM THE AIRPORT
Peikan airport is a short walk from any of the Tangchi hotels listed here.

### CAR/MOTORCYCLE/SCOOTER
Motorcycles and scooters are available for rent in Tangchi Village. The daily rate is NT500 but this can be bargained down.

The hotels can also arrange transport, if necessary.

### PUBLIC TRANSPORT
The bus station is very close to the airport. However, relying on buses to get around is next to impossible as they don't seem to follow the posted schedules. Don't worry about searching out bus stops – when you see a bus and need a ride, flag it down. Fares are NT10.

### TAXI
It's a flat NT100 to anywhere on the island. Drivers can give you a tour of Peikan for NT500 to NT600 an hour or NT2000 for a day.

## TUNGYIN TOWNSHIP 東引
Few people make it as far as Tungyin Township (東引鄉; Dōngyǐn Xiāng), the northernmost of the Matsu townships, but it is thought by many to be the most beautiful section of the archipelago, with its steep cliffs, grassy hills and wave-eroded coastline. The township is composed of the islands of Hsiyin (Xīyǐn) and Tungyin (Dōngyǐn), which are connected by a causeway. Hotels, restaurants and sights are on Tungyin, the larger and more tourist-oriented island.

There remains a strong military presence here and its best to ask before taking photographs.

## Information
**Tungyin Tourist Information Centre** (Dōngyǐn Yóukè Fúwù Zhōngxīn; ☎ 77266; 160-1 Lehua Village; 🕒 9am-noon &1.30-5pm) Supplies information on Tungyin history, environment and culture.

## Sights
One of Tungyin's most famous landmarks is the **Tungyung Lighthouse** (Dōngyǒng Dēngtǎ), built by the British in 1904. The simple white structure stands on a grassy hill overlooking the ocean. The lighthouse remains an important part of Taiwan's coastal defence system – taking pictures here is prohibited.

Two former military sites are now open to the public. The **Antung Tunnel** (Āndōng Kēngdào), carved through two mountains, was once a base of operations for Taiwanese soldiers. The 700m tunnel leads to a lookout tower with fantastic views of the water. The entire walk takes about one hour and is well worth it. Take care on the slippery tunnel floor and bring a warm jacket. The **Peihai Tunnel** (Běihǎi Kēngdào), like the same-named tunnel in Nankan, was once used as a hidden port to store small ships in case of attack by the communist mainlanders. Inside are bronze statues built to honour the soldiers who risked their lives building the tunnel.

Tungyin's wind- and sea-eroded coastline abounds with unusual-looking rock formations. One that has caught the imagination of residents is the **Line of Sky** (Yí Xiàn Tiān), a wind-chiselled crevice between two rocky cliffs that allows for views of the sky.

Close by the lighthouse and Line of Sky is the **Martyred Righteous Woman's Hollow** (Liè Nǚ Yìkēng), dedicated to a Qing dynasty woman who jumped into the sea to protect herself from pirates.

The **Tungyin Distillery** (Dōngyǐn Jiǔchǎng; ☎ 77142; 161 Lehua Village) has been brewing Kaoliang and Tachi liquor for over 40 years. Visits must be arranged in advance as the distillery is not an official tourist attraction.

## Sleeping

**Yingbin Hotel** (Yíngbīn Xiūxián Lǚguǎn; ☎ 76336; 78 Lehua Village; s & d NT1000) This tiny, well-managed hotel has spotless rooms and very helpful management. The hotel will arrange car and motorcycle rentals as well as tours around the island.

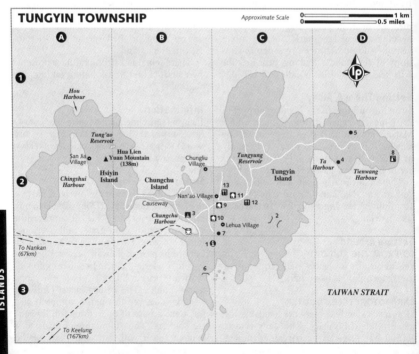

TUNGYIN TOWNSHIP

**Hsin Hua Hotel** (Xīnhuá Fàndiàn; ☎ 77600; 46 Lehua Village; s & d NT1000, q from NT2000; ☐ ) This is Tungyin's newest hotel, conveniently located near Chungchu Harbour. The hotel features a billiards room, Internet bar and restaurant.

**Binhui Hotel** (Bīnhuì Lǚshè; ☎ 77168; 29 Lehua Village; dm NT350, s & d NT800) Even smaller than the Yingbin, the Binhui has warm, cosy rooms with refrigerators and DVD players. The eight-bed dormitory is good value for those on a budget.

**Tungyin Homestay** (Dōngyǐn Mínsù; ☎ 77122; 132 Lehua Village; dm NT450) The 10-bed dormitory isn't as comfortable as Binhui's but it's a good place to go if the Binhui is full.

## Eating

**Chen Shan Mei** (Zhēn Shàn Měi; 93 Lehua Village; mains from NT120; ⏲ 2-9pm) The owner of this restaurant trained as a chef in Beijing before moving to Taiwan. The dishes range from simple stir-fries to more elaborate (and more expensive) seafood delicacies.

**Shantung Hsiao Kuan** (Shāndōng Xiǎoguǎn; 38 Chungliu Village; steamed buns from NT15; ⏲ 6am-3pm) This restaurant has been cooking up steamed buns, onion pancakes and other snacks for over 20 years. The freshly made soya milk is especially good.

## Getting There & Away

The easiest way to get to Tungyin is to catch the boat that travels between Keelung and Nankan (see p278), stopping at Tungyin en route. A round-trip ticket from Tungyin to Nankan costs NT285 for the two-hour journey. The sea can be rough so bring medicine if you're prone to seasickness.

Daily Air flies chartered helicopters from Nankan to Tungyin's heliport (NT2200).

## Getting Around

There's no public bus service on Tungyin so it's necessary to rent a motorcycle or take a taxi. Motorcycle rentals are available at Chungchu Harbour or Nan'ao Village for NT400 to NT500 a day. Taxis cost NT100 per trip.

## TUNGCHU ISLAND 東莒

Tungchu (Dōngjǔ) and Hsichu Islands make up Chukuang Township (Jǔguāng Xiāng; 莒光) and are the most southerly of the Matsu Islands. Once called the Eastern Dog and

Western Dog Islands, they were renamed after Chiang Kai-shek made his famous quote, 'Forget not that you're in Chu', a reference to an early Chinese story about a king preparing to take back territory from a rival state, and an obvious analogy to Chiang's desire to eventually take back mainland China.

If you need to escape to a remote, scarcely inhabited island, Tungchu would be a good choice. The island has little in the way of tourist sights but it does have very friendly locals, pretty scenery and excellent food. The commercial centre of Tungchu is Taping Village (Dàpíng Cūn).

## Information

**Chukuang Tourist Information Centre** (Jǔguāng Yóukè Fúwù Zhōngxīn; ☎ 89388; 1 Fu Cheng Village; ⏲ 8am-noon & 1-5.30pm) Here you'll find some good maps and photos of Tungchu and Hsichu. Most of the information is in Chinese, but there are some rather dated brochures in English if you ask.

## Sights

The **Tungchu Lighthouse** (Dōngquǎn Dēngtǎ) sits high on a hill at the northeast tip of the island. Built by the British in 1872, the white granite building aided the navigation of merchant ships during the Opium Wars.

The other main attraction of the island is the **Tapu Stone Engraving** (Dàpú Shíkè), on the south side of Tungchu. The memorial is dedicated to a general in the Ming dynasty who successfully drove pirates off the island without losing a single one of his soldiers.

## Sleeping

Within Taping Village are several homestays of similar price and quality. The best of the bunch is the newish **Remember Homestay** (Remember Mínsù; ☎ 88030; 52 Taping Village; s & d NT1000). The three-storey building has bright, clean rooms and is managed by the owner of Remember Coffee and Chao Bu Tao Ke Chan.

**Chuanlao Homestay** (Chuánlǎo Dà Mínsù; ☎ 88075; 55-1 Taping Village; s & d NT1000) This hotel was built more than five years ago and is one of the older tourist hotels on Tungchu. Rooms are basic but decent and the owner is keen to teach visitors about the island.

**Ku Hsiang Homestay** (Gùxiāng Mínsù; ☎ 88080; 79 Taping Village; s & d NT800) An unusual-looking hotel because it is so tall and narrow compared to other buildings on the island.

TAIWAN STRAIT ISLANDS

There are only a few rooms on each floor. Rooms are airy, comfy and quiet.

## Eating

**Remember Coffee** (Remember Kāfēi; 21 Taping Village; ☼ 10am-9pm; coffee from NT100, mains from NT120) This is Tungchu's friendly neighbourhood café, popular with locals and visitors. The menu features an eclectic assortment of items, from seafood to spaghetti to toast with peanut butter.

**Chao Bu Tao Ke Chan** (Zhǎo Bù Dào Kèzhàn; 68 Taping Village; ☼ lunch & dinner; mains from NT200) The name of this restaurant can literally be translated as 'Can't Find the Inn' and it offers tasty dishes such as red-cooked tofu (*hōngshāo dòufu*) or fragrant crispy fish (*xiāng sū xiān yú*). If you're so inclined, try a plate of Tungchu snails (*luó ròu*).

## Getting There & Away

There are three boats a day between Nankan and Chukuang (one hour). Boats do not travel when the sea is rough so be prepared for last-minute cancellations.

There are frequent boats between Tungchu and Hsichu (NT20). Tickets can be purchased at Meng'ao Harbour in Tungchu.

Daily Air has a helicopter service to Tungchu and Hsichu (NT2200) leaving from Nankan airport.

## Getting Around

Tungchu is small enough to explore on foot. You could walk around the island in

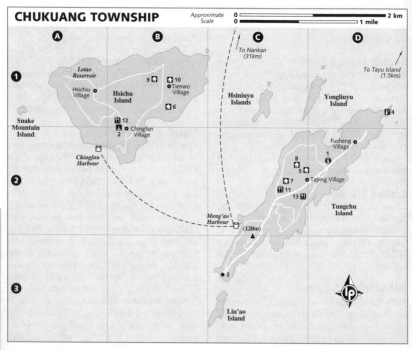

CHUKUANG TOWNSHIP

few hours. If you wish, motorcycles or scooters can be rented from Taiping Village for NT300 to NT500 a day.

## HSICHU ISLAND 西莒

Hsichu (Xījǔ) is rowdier than its sister island of Tungchu but not by much. This small island was once a busy seaport, though there's little evidence of that now. During the Korean War, American companies set themselves up in the village of Chingfan (Qīngfán Cūn) and nicknamed it 'Little Hong Kong'. Nowadays, Chingfan is still the centre of activity on the island, though most of the hotels are in the nearby village of Tienwo (Tiánwò Cūn).

### Sights

There aren't any designated tourist sites on Hsichu and there's little to do but admire the scenery. The best-known attraction is the **Chen Jiangjun Temple** (Chén Jiāngjūn Miào) near Chingfan Village. It's said that during the Qing dynasty a hero from Fujian province by the name of Chen Jiangjun drowned and his corpse floated to Hsichu. Chingfan villagers buried his body and built a temple in his name. Locals believe that when difficulties arise, the spirit of Chen will materialise, sometimes in the shape of a frog, to offer his assistance.

### Sleeping

**Haijing Hotel** (Hǎijǐng Dùjià Cūn; ☎ 88125; 68-3 Tianwo Village; s & d NT800, q NT1200) This hotel has no-frill rooms conveniently near the harbour. On the first floor are an Internet café and a karaoke club that can get very noisy at night with yodelling fishermen.

**Youyi Hostel** (Yóuyì Shān Zhuāng; ☎ 88204; 67 Tianwo Village; s & d NT800) This is one of the better hotels on Hsichu, with pleasant rooms and a relaxing atmosphere.

**Xiangcun Homestay** (Xiāngcūn Mínsù; ☎ 88116; 55 Tianwo Village; s & d NT800) The rooms here offer nothing fancy but they will do in a pinch.

### Eating

**Kuan Hai Lou** (Guān Hǎi Lóu; 40 Chingfan Village; ⏰ 9am-10pm; mains from NT70) This is considered to be the best restaurant on the island. Specialties include fresh-caught perch (lúyú), rice noodle soup (mǐfěn tāng) and 'Buddha's hand' clams. Servings are large and prices are reasonable.

### Getting There & Away

There are three boats a day between Nankan and Chukuang (one hour). In Hsichu, tickets can be bought at Chingfan Harbour (Qīngfán Gǎng). Boats do not travel when the sea is rough so be prepared for last-minute cancellations.

There are frequent boats between Tungchu and Hsichu (NT20). Tickets can also be purchased at Chingfan Harbour.

Daily Air has a helicopter service to Tungchu and Hsichu (NT2200) leaving from Nankan airport.

### Getting Around

Hsichu is small enough to explore on foot. You could walk around the island in a few hours. Alternatively, if you are foot-sore, motorcycles or scooters can be rented from Chingfan Village for NT300 to NT500 a day.

# KINMEN

☎ 082 / pop 45,000

Kinmen (金門; Jīnmén; formerly known as Quemoy), with its peaceful tree-lined streets, lakes and forest reserves, lives up to its reputation as 'a garden built upon a fortress'. Lying only 2km off the coast of mainland China's Fujian province, the island has spent more than 50 years in a political tug-of-war between the mainland and Taiwan.

Now that the shelling has stopped and martial law has ended, authorities have opened up former military bunkers and battlefields to tourism. Many military sites remain unseen, hidden in the hills and underground. Locals joke that Kinmen is hollow inside – beneath all the grass and pretty flowers are mazes of bomb shelters, tunnels and military storage units.

Kinmen is reasonably developed, despite being isolated for so many years. Kincheng has its share of Internet cafés and ATMs, and Shanwai even boasts an Italian-style restaurant. Kinmen is a visitor-friendly place and travellers can visit the sights without difficulty. However, it's necessary to take caution around restricted military areas and to pay heed to the numerous land-mine warning signs surrounding the beaches and coastal areas.

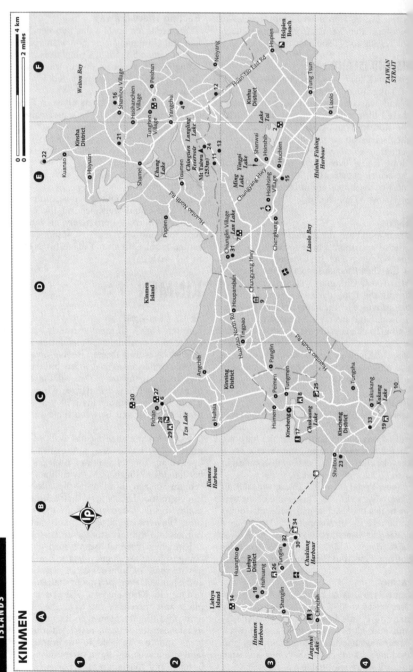

TAIWAN STRAIT ISLANDS

KINMEN

## History

Settlers began arriving on Kinmen as early as the Tang dynasty, changing the original name of the islands from Wuzhou to Kinmen, literally meaning 'Golden Gate', after the hopefully impenetrable gates that were put up to defend themselves from pirate attacks. During the Ming and Qing dynasties, increasing numbers of Chinese migrants settled on Kinmen's shores. The Ming loyalist, Koxinga, also known as Cheng Chengkung, used Kinmen as a base to liberate Kinmen and Penghu from the Dutch. In the process, he chopped down all of Kinmen's trees for his navy, something the residents still grumble about: Koxinga's massive deforestation project made Kinmen vulnerable to the winds that commonly sweep across the Strait, causing devastating soil erosion.

Kinmen was a fairly peaceful place until 1949, when Chiang Kai-shek transformed the island into a front-line defence position against the communists. His original plan was to have his soldiers recuperate on the island for a short period of time and then launch a full-fledged attack on Mao Zedong's armies, but this never happened. Instead, martial law was declared on Kinmen and the island was subject to incessant bombing from the mainland throughout the 1950s and '60s, causing international concern. Over the years, tensions have decreased gradually, but not without the occasional flare-up.

Martial law was lifted in 1993 and Kinmen residents are now allowed to travel freely to and from Taiwan. The Three Small Links (see p288) established with the mainland also allow limited trade, thus opening up the islands further to the outside world.

Established as Taiwan's sixth national park in 1995, authorities have poured a lot of money into Kinmen, hoping to turn it into a tourist destination. Soldiers have been put to good use planting trees, maintaining roads and restoring the island's old houses, many built during the Ming and Qing dynasties. With all of its natural beauty and history, Kinmen is well worth the visit.

### Orientation

Kinmen consists of 15 islands and islets at the junction of the mouth of the Chiulung River and Xiamen of mainland China. The largest islands are Kinmen and Liehyu (sometimes called 'Little Kinmen'), the only islands open to tourism. Three islets are controlled by mainland China, the other 12 by Taiwan. Kinmen is divided into five districts: Kincheng, Kinhu, Kinning, Kinsha and Liehyu. Kincheng is the largest city on Kinmen.

### KINCHENG 金城

The Kincheng District (金城鎮; Jīnchéng Zhèn) is in the southwest region of Kinmen Island, where most of the hotels are. It's the most convenient place to stay on the island. Kincheng (Jīnchéng) is the busiest town and has its share of sights and excellent little eateries.

## Information

### CULTURAL CENTRES

**Kinmen County Cultural Centre** (Jīnmén Xiàn Lì Wénhuà Zhōngxīn; ☎ 325 643; Kincheng, 66 Huandao North Rd, 8am–noon & 1.30-5pm) On the outskirts of Kincheng, the cultural centre occasionally hosts recitals and dance performances put on by local organisations. It's worth checking out.

### VISA EXTENSIONS

Visas can be extended by the **Foreign Affairs Police** ( ☎ 325 653) in Kincheng.

## Sights

With its many winding alleys and market streets, Kincheng is a fun place to explore on foot. **Mofan St** (Mófàn Jiē) is only a five-minute walk from the Kincheng Bus Station. Built in 1924, the buildings on this charming little street have brick exteriors and arched door fronts, modelled after Japanese and Western architecture. Lately, the street has been developing into a popular café district.

A short walk from Mofan St leads to the **Memorial Arch to Qiu Liang-Kung's Mother** (Qiū Liánggōng Mǔ Jiéxiào Fāng). This arch stands in the middle of a very busy market area and is a good example of Han Chinese-influenced filial devotion. Qiu Liang-Kung, a native of Kinmen who became governor of China's Zhejiang province, had the arch built in 1812 to honour his mother who refused to remarry after her husband died and lived as a widow for 28 years.

The two-storey **Kuei Pavilion** (Kuí Gé) was built in 1836 to worship the God of Litera-ture. Aspiring scholars would come here t• pray for success in the civil-service exami nations.

The **Chutzu Shrine** (Zhūzǐ Cí) sits withi• the walls of the **Wu River Academy** (Wú Jiān Shūyuàn), constructed in 1780. The shrin• honours the Neo-Confucian scholar Ch• Hsi, who sought a revival of Confucian val ues during the Sung dynasty (960–1279).

## Sleeping

### BUDGET

**Shang Bin Hotel** (Shàngbīn Fàndiàn; ☎ 321 528; 3• Minchuan Rd; s/d NT800/1000) This hotel is one o• the cheaper options in Kincheng and ha• good-value rooms, though the location is bit inconvenient.

**Kinmen Hotel** (Jīnmén Lǚguǎn; ☎ 321 567; Kin• cheng, 169 Mintsu Rd; s & d from NT1000) This hote• is in a better location than the Shang Bin• though a bit on the noisy side. It's a shor• walk from the hotel to Mofan St and th• market areas. Rooms are clean, with cabl• TV, and free ADSL is available.

**Six Brother Hotel** (Liù Guì Fàndiàn; ☎ 324 311• Kincheng, 164 Chukuang Rd; s/d/tr/q NT1000/1200/1500• 1800) Down a side street off Minchuan Rd• this is a small, quiet place with very friendl• management.

### MID-RANGE

**Ta Chen Hotel** (Dà Chéng Dà Fàndiàn; ☎ 324 85• Kincheng, 16 Mingsheng Rd; s & d from NT1200) Thi• hotel is right in the thick of things, jus• down the road from the Kincheng bus sta• tion. Rooms are shabby but clean and th• décor is a bit on the eccentric side. Watc•

---

### THREE SMALL LINKS

In 2000, Chen Shuibian's government approved the lifting of the ban on travel and trade between the mainland and the Strait Islands in a policy called the Three Small Links. Taiwan believed that by loosening restrictions, Beijing could be appeased through economic concessions rather than political ones. On 3 January 2001, the ban on cross-Strait trade was officially lifted and a boatload of Kinmen officials sailed to Xiamen in Fujian province in the first legal voyage for 52 years.

After the links were established, there was fear in Taiwan that liberalised trade with China would weaken Taiwan and make the island dependent on the mainland economy. Regardless, President Chen went so far as to allow banks in Taiwan and China to transfer funds and lifted the US$50 million limit on Taiwanese investment in projects on the mainland.

Despite these changes, the Three Small Links seem to have had little direct impact on Kinmen and Matsu residents. Small-scale trading has occurred, but because Kinmen and especially Matsu have limited economic resources, investment and development projects have been slow. Many residents are hopeful, however, believing that the Three Small Links should be considered a long-term solution to the Taiwan Strait economy, rather than an overnight overhaul.

out for weekends when boisterous tour groups overtake the place. The couple who run the hotel can arrange vehicle rentals or tours around the island.

**Hongfu Hotel** (Hóngfú Dà Fàndiàn; ☎ 326 768; Kincheng, 169 Mintsu Rd; s/d NT1200/1400) The Hongfu has noisy rooms in the middle of a bustling commercial area.

**Haifu Grand Hotel** (Hǎifú Dà Fàndiàn; ☎ 322 538; Kincheng, 85 Minchuan Rd; d/tr NT1580/2180 incl breakfast) This is one of the best hotels in this price range. The rooms are spotless. If notified in advance, someone from the hotel can pick you up at the airport.

**King Ring Hotel** (Jīnruì Dà Fàndiàn; ☎ 323 777; Kincheng, 166 Minchuan Rd; d/tr/q NT1680/1995/from NT2310) The largest hotel in Kincheng, the King Ring has a very good reputation. It's popular with tour groups so book ahead if you want to stay here.

**Kinmen Youth Activity Centre** (Jīnmén Qīngnián Huódòng Zhōngxīn; ☎ 325 722; 1 Huandao N Rd; d/tr/q NT1400/1600/from NT1800) This centre is on the outskirts of town, a fair distance away if you plan to see the town on foot. Rooms are very peaceful, but unless you have your own transport getting around is difficult.

## Eating

Central Kincheng, with its busy market streets and winding alleys, is a foodie's paradise. The area around Mofan St is chock-a-block with small stands and restaurants selling a variety of Kincheng snacks and sweets. Some of Kinmen's specialties include hard candy (gòng táng), sticky rice-noodles (miàn xiàn), fried cakes and fried sandworms (chǎo shāchóng). Come to the markets in the early morning or evening to get the best of what's on offer.

**Shou Ji Kuangtung Zhou** (Shòují Guǎngdōng Zhōu; Kincheng, 50-1 Chukuang Rd, Sec 1; mains from NT30; 6.30am-12.30pm) This restaurant, over 80 years old, dishes up steaming bowls of Cantonese-style congee. Locals favour the pig-stomach congee (zhū dù) but there are other varieties available.

**Mei Chi Su Shi Kuan** (Měizhì Sùshí Guǎn; Kincheng, 53 Chukuang Rd, Sec 1; mains from NT60; breakfast, lunch & dinner) This Buddhist restaurant is opposite the Memorial Arch to Qiu Liang-Kung's Mother. Vegetable dishes are available cafeteria-style or ordered from the wall menu.

**Wen Ji Mian** (Wénjí Miàn Xiàn Hú; Kincheng, 37 Chunghsing Shihchang; mains from NT30; 5am-noon) Here you can find Kinmen's famous sticky rice-noodle soup, served with fresh oysters. The noodles are a popular dish for breakfast, though they can be found around town at other times of the day, too.

**Lao Liu Hsiao Kuan** (Lǎo Liù Xiǎo Guǎn; 65 Minchuan Rd; mains from NT100; lunch & dinner) This restaurant is more upscale than the ones previously mentioned and is very close to the Haifu Grand Hotel. Seafood is the speciality of the house.

**Pasda Pasda Spaghetti** (Juéshì Yìdàlì; Shanwai, 17 Fuhsing Rd; mains from NT150; lunch & dinner) If you need a Western-food fix, try this Italian-style spaghetti house in Shanwai. The pasta doesn't taste as good as what you'd get from home but it's edible.

## Drinking

**Pa Sa** (Bāsà Shāokǎo Diàn; Kincheng, 13 Mofan St; coffee from NT100, alcohol NT120, mains from NT100; 11am-11pm) The Pa Sa is a chic bar/café selling a range of rice and noodle dishes as well as fruity drinks and coffees.

**Hung Lou** (Hóng Lóu; Kincheng, 24 Mofan St; coffee from NT150, alcohol NT120; 10am-11pm) A rival to the Pa Sa, this is another popular café selling a similar range of coffees, noodle dishes and alcoholic drinks.

## Shopping

Kinmen is most famous for its Kaoliang liquor, sold in fancy ceramic bottles all over Kincheng. The alcohol, made from sorghum, is a mind-numbing 58 proof. Another popular item is Kinmen's tasty hard candy, called kung (gòng) or 'tribute' candy because it was once used to pay tribute when visiting the imperial court. The candy comes in a variety of flavours, with peanut being the most common. You'll see it being sold in barrels along the streets or in boxes in more upscale gift shops. If you have a sweet tooth, the candy is a must-buy item.

More unusual souvenir items include knives made from melted-down artillery shells left over from the mainland bombardments. The knives are available all over Kinmen and come in a variety of shapes and sizes. Prices usually start at around NT800. Don't forget to pack your knives (or meat cleavers, swords or axes) in your checked baggage before trying to board the plane.

A wonderful little curio shop in central Kincheng is the **Kinmen Minsu Wenwu Chih Jia**

TAIWAN STRAIT ISLANDS

(Jīnmén Mínsú Wénwù Zhī Jiā; 124 Fuhsing Rd, Lane 1), where you can find all sorts of ceramic nick-nacks, dishes and one-of-a-kind items to take home.

## Getting There & Away

### AIR

**Uni Air** ( ☎ 324 881), **Transasia Airways** ( ☎ 321 501) and **Far Eastern Air Transport** ( ☎ 327 339) all have offices at Kinmen airport and fly directly to Kinmen from Taipei, Chiayi, Taichung, Tainan and Kaohsiung. Round-trip tickets cost between NT3200 and NT3500. In spring, Kinmen is often fogged in and flights have a tendency to cancel at the last minute. Make sure you bring your passport to show security when boarding the plane.

### BOAT

There is an infrequent ferry service between Kaohsiung and Kinmen (from NT900, 10 hours). For details call the **Harbour Bureau** (Kaohsiung ☎ 07-521 6206; Kinmen ☎ 329 988).

## Getting Around

### TO/FROM THE AIRPORT

Bus 3 travels hourly between Kincheng, Shanwai and the airport. From the airport to Kincheng or Shanwai, taxi drivers charge a flat NT250. Coming from the opposite direction, the fare should be around NT200.

### CAR/MOTORCYCLE/SCOOTER

Cars, motorbikes or scooters can easily be rented in Kincheng. Scooter rental is gen-

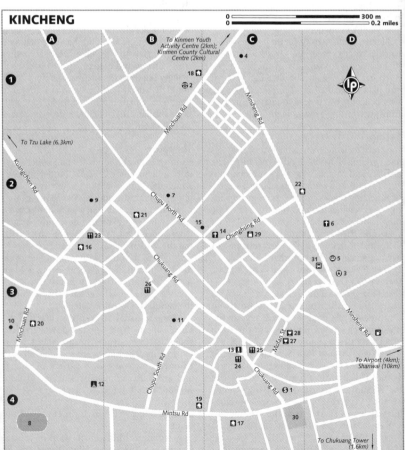

erally NT300 to NT500 a day, depending on the number of days rented. Cars can be rented for about NT1300 a day, excluding petrol. Kinmen has very little traffic and driving is the easiest way to see the island.

## PUBLIC TRANSPORT
Kinmen has bus stations in Kincheng, Shanwai and Shamei. Getting around by bus is very slow and it will take several days on public transport to see all the sites listed here. Buses run every one or two hours between 6am and 5pm, with a few buses offering services into the evenings. Bus schedules are posted in the bus stations in Chinese, but people are pretty willing to help if you know where you're going.

The following buses run from the Kincheng Bus Station: 1, 2, 3, 5, 6, 7, 10, 11 and 12. Buses 1 and 2 travel between Kincheng and Shanwai. Shanwai buses include 1, 2, 3, 18, 19, 20, 21, 22, 23, 25 and 27. Shamei buses are 5, 18, 31, 32 and 33.

Liehyu has an hourly bus service travelling north and south around the island. As it's such a tiny place, it's probably faster to walk than wait for a bus.

## TAXI
Most taxi drivers in Kinmen prefer to ask for a flat fare rather than use the meter. If you think your trip will be cheaper with the meter on (probably so), then by all means insist on this method. Flat fare is used for rides to and from the airport and for taxis waiting in taxi stands.

Taxi tours will cost around NT2000 to NT2500 a day and it's unlikely your driver will speak English. If you happen to stay at the Ta Chen Hotel, it can arrange discounted tours.

## BOAT
There is a frequent ferry service between Shuitou Harbour in Kinmen and Chiukang Harbour (NT20, around 15 minutes) on Liehyu Island. During winter, the ferry service can be suspended if the water is too choppy.

## Around Kincheng
South of Kincheng lies **Chukuang Tower** (Jǔguāng Lóu; ☯ 8am-noon & 2-5pm, closed Mon), built in 1952 as a memorial to the fallen soldiers of Kinmen. The three-storey tower is constructed in the style of a classical Chinese palace and offers a good view of Chukuang Lake and the surrounding countryside. There's an excellent museum inside with bilingual exhibits that give a good introduction to the history and culture of the region. Buses 3 and 6 go here.

The **Koxinga Shrine** (Yánpíng Jùnwáng Cí) was built in memory of the Ming general Koxinga, or Cheng Chengkung, who fought against the Dutch occupation (see p287). The shrine seems to be most popular with Taiwanese tourists – locals haven't quite forgiven him for cutting down all their trees. Bus 7 stops close by.

The **Mumahou Temple** (Mùmǎ Hòu Cí), originally thought to be built in the Tang dynasty, is a popular Taoist temple and crowded with worshippers during lunar holidays.

Shuitou Village (Shuǐtóu Cūn) is a fishing community in Kinmen's southwest corner. Most of the Fujian-style houses here once belonged to a wealthy merchant family named Huang. The **Youtang Villa** (Yǒu Táng Biéyè) was built during the Qing dynasty as a private study and later used as a publishing house. The 11m **Moon Grasping Tower** (Déyuè Lóu) was built in 1931 and served as an important building for military defence. Underground tunnels lead from the tower to the Western-style buildings nearby.

The 14th-century **Wentai Pagoda** (Wéntái Bǎotǎ) is one of the oldest constructions in Taiwan. The five-level hexagonal pagoda was originally built for the Ming emperor Hungwu as a place to honour the stars and celestial deities. There were once three pagodas here but this is the only one that remains. Within the pagoda is the **Hsuchianghsiao Ancient Inscription** (Xūjiāng Xiào Wò Jié), carved by the Ming general Hsuchiang and also known as Yu Tayou. Supposedly, the general was fond of climbing the cliffs to rest by the pagoda and look at the sea. The inscription literally reads 'Hsuchiang is shouting and lying here'. There's a stand next to the pagoda that sells eggs fermented in Kaoliang liquor, if you need a pick-me-up.

**Kukang Lake** (Gǔgāng Hú) is southeast of Wentai Pagoda and is Kinmen's largest natural lake. In warm weather it's a great place for a picnic as it's quiet and peaceful. The modern **Kukang Tower** (Gǔgāng Lóu) sits at one end of the lake. Bus 6 stops here.

The **Dishan Tunnels** (Díshān Kēngdào; 8.30am-5pm) were blasted out of solid granite in the early 1960s by soldiers and stretch 357m. Connected to the ocean, they were designed to hold up to 42 small boats in case of attack by communists. The tunnels haven't been used for 30 years because of dropping water levels and were opened to tourism in 1997. Tourists are allowed to walk through the spooky interior or follow a bridge over the entrance that leads to the piers and some forlorn-looking pillboxes.

## KINNING DISTRICT 金寧鄉

Kinning (Jīnníng Xiāng) is in the northwest of Kinmen and was the site of some ferocious battles between the communist Chinese and Taiwan. The **Kuningtou War Museum** (Gǔníngtóu Zhànshǐ Guǎn; 8.30am-5pm) sits on the site of the **Kuningtou battlefield** and provides an excellent look into one of Kinmen's most fateful battles. In the early hours of 25 October 1949, an invasion force of 10,000 mainland troops landed on Kinmen's northwest coast. After 25 hours of fierce fighting, the communists were eventually pushed into the area of Kuningtou by the ROC navy and air force. However,

mainland reinforcements arrived and joined their fellow soldiers in Kuningtou. The fighting lasted for over 56 hours but at last the communists surrendered on 27 October 1949. Over 15,000 soldiers, both mainland and ROC, were slaughtered. The museum was opened in 1984 to commemorate the battle and serve as a reminder of the tragedies of the war. Bus 10, 11 and 26 stop at the museum.

The **Peishan Old Building** (Běishān Gǔyáng Lóu) is very close to the museum and also a part of the Kuningtou battlefield. This two-storey Western-style house served as a command post for the communists during the Kuningtou conflict until it was seized back by the ROC forces. The residence is in ruins, with blasted-out windows and walls peppered with bullet holes.

The **Chenwei Residence** (Zhènwēi Dì) was built during the late 1700s and was the home of Li Kuang-hsien, farmer turned high-ranking military officer. Li died penniless at age 63, but his funeral and estate were managed by a wealthy Kuangtung businessman.

**Tzu Lake** (Cí Hú) is one of the most scenic spots on Kinmen and is a well-known habitat for migratory-birds. The saltwater lake opens to the ocean and is a great place to watch the sunset. Ducks, kingfishers, herons, mynahs and geese make their homes on the lake year round. Cormorants are known to nest here in winter. Altogether, the lake attracts more than 200 species of bird.

The **Shuangli Wetlands Area Centre** (Shuānglí Shīdì Zìrán Zhōngxīn; 8.30am-5pm) is a research facility devoted to wetlands preservation. The centre provides (in Chinese) information about the different birds in Kinmen and has many colourful photographs on display. On the 1st floor are a multimedia room, café and bird-viewing area. Bus 9, 10 and 11 stop here.

**Shuiwei Tower** (Shuǐwěi Tǎ) was originally built as a place for Kuningtou residents to pray and ask the gods for protection against the constant flooding of their crops during the rise and fall of tides. With the building of the Tzu Lake Causeway, the flooding has stopped but locals still consider the tower a place of worship.

The **Chungshan Memorial Forest** (Zhōngshān Jìniàn Lín), part of Kinmen National Forest, shows the government's dedication to re-

TAIWAN STRAIT ISLANDS

versing the environmental damage brought on by deforestation. Within the forest are the Kinmen National Park Headquarters and the **Chiang Chingkuo Memorial Hall** (Jiǎng Jīngguó Xiānshēng Jìniàn Guǎn). Bus 1 travels to the memorial hall.

## KINHU DISTRICT 金湖鎮

Kinhu District (Jīnhú Zhèn), in the southeastern part of Kinmen, is notable for its scenery, in particular Mt Taiwu and Lake Tai. Shanwai is the largest town here.

## Information

### BOOKSHOPS

**Yuan Cheng Bookstore** (源成書店; Yuán Chéng Shūdiàn; Shanwai, 20 Fuhsing Rd) Has a small selection of English books and magazines.

### MONEY

**Bank of Taiwan** (台灣銀行; ☎ 333 711; Shanwai, 4 Fuhsing Rd) The only place to change US dollars or travellers cheques on Kinmen. Some of the clerks in the bank are chatty and speak good English. They're a good source of information about what to see and do around town.

## Around Shanwai 山外

**Lake Tai** (Tài Hú) is to the south of Shanwai and about a five-minute walk from the centre of town. This 5m-deep lake was dug entirely by hand (!) in the 1960s. It's a popular picnic spot for locals and also a feeding ground for cormorants and ospreys, best seen in the early morning.

The **August 23rd Artillery War Museum** (Bā Èr Sān Zhànshǐ Jìniàn Guǎn; ☺ 8.30am-5pm) is in **Chungcheng Park** (Zhōngzhēng Gōngyuán), near the shores of Lake Tai. The museum documents the horrific battle that occurred on 23 August 1958, when the communists launched an artillery attack against Kinmen that lasted for 44 days and pummelled the island with over 474,000 shells. Outside are fighter planes, tanks and cannons used during the siege.

Adjacent to the museum is the **Mr Yu Tawei Museum** (Yú Dàwéi Xiānshēng Jìniàn Guǎn), dedicated to the ROC's first minister of defence. There are photographs on display as well as some realistic-looking (and a little creepy) wax statues of Minister Yu in uniform.

The **Banyan Garden** (Róng Yuán) next to the museum has some splendid giant banyan trees as well as **Weilu** (Wèilú), an old house that has been opened to the public. The garden sits within the perimeters of the **Chiang Kai-shek Memorial Forest** (Zhōngzhēng Gōngyuán).

At 253m, **Mt Taiwu** (Tàiwǔ Shān) is the tallest mountain on Kinmen. On the west side of Mt Taiwu is the **Mt Taiwu Cemetery** (Tàiwǔ Shān Gōng Mù), built in 1952 to honour the ROC soldiers who'd died in battle. Within the cemetery grounds are a martyrs' shrine, flower gardens and various monuments. The soldiers on duty seem very sensitive to tourists walking through the cemetery grounds so it's best to avoid taking photos. Much of the cemetery was under reconstruction at the time of writing.

On the north side of the cemetery is the Mt Taiwu footpath leading to **Don't Forget the Days in Chu** (Wú Wàng Zài Jǔ Lèshí), an inscription on a rock of Chiang Kai-shek's famous one-liner. The path leads onwards and upwards to the tranquil 800-year-old **Haiyin Temple** (Hǎiyìn Sì) and **Stone Gate Pass** (Shímén Guān). The walk takes about one hour.

**Chiu Liang-kung's Tomb** (Qiū Liánggōng Mùyuán) is the resting place of the man who built the memorial arch for his mother in central Kincheng. Chiu was so famous for his bravery in killing pirates that he was once granted an audience with the Qing emperor. Unfortunately, he died on his way home from the imperial palace. The court held a memorial and built this tomb in his honour.

**Chiunglin Village** (Qiónglín Cūn) was once the most famous village on Kinmen. The name 'Chiunglin' was given to the town by the Ming emperor Sheng Zung, who thought the original name of Pinglin was too common. Former residences of the village were all part of the Tsai clan, who were famous for their scholarly achievements. The village possesses more shrines than any other village on Kinmen. The most famous is the **Tsai Family Shrine** (Cài Shì Cí), which sits in the centre of the village and is an excellent example of Fujian architecture. The characters on the main wall read 'loyalty and filial piety' and 'honesty and thriftiness'.

The **Chiunglin Tunnel** (Qiónglín Kēngdào) is actually an entire underground village that was built in 1976 as a refuge in case of war. There are 12 entrances and exits in the village but only one is currently open to tour groups.

The **Kinmen Ceramics Factory** (Jīnmén Táocí Chǎng; 8am-noon & 1-5pm) was established in 1962 and produces some of the finest ceramics in Taiwan. One of the reasons the pottery is so famous is that it's made from the highly prized *gaoling* clay, found in abundance all over the island. The factory showroom has various wares, including fancy Kaoliang bottles, for purchase, most in the NT800 to NT3000 range. If you're looking for something less expensive and more portable, you can pick up small ceramic statues of Kinmen wind lions for around NT150.

The **Granite Hospital** (Huāgāng Yán Yīyuàn) is a three-storey underground medical facility that was built in 1980 and is composed entirely of solid granite. The hospital has over 2000 beds and treats both civilians and soldiers.

## KINSHA DISTRICT 金沙鎮

Kinsha District (Jīnshā Zhèn) is in the northeast of Kinmen. It possesses some interesting architecture from the Ming and Qing dynasties, and some up-close views of mainland China from the coast.

The **Mashan Observatory** (Mǎshān Guàn Cè) is a fortified observation station on the northeastern tip of Kinmen, only 2km from the mainland. Armed guards and dogs at the entrance are a sign that ROC forces are still keeping a close eye on their neighbour across the water. A dark, winding tunnel leads to a pillbox where you can peer through high-powered binoculars at the Fujian villagers staring back at you. To enter the observation area, you must leave your passport with the guards at the entrance.

The **Kinmen Folk Cultural Village** (Jīnmén Mínsú Wénhuà Cūn; adult/child NT50/20) in Shanhou Village (Shānhòu Cūn) is a grouping of 18 Fujian-style houses built in 1900 by overseas Kinmen merchants. The houses are all interconnected, with narrow alleys and bricked walls. The roofs sport the 'horseback ridges' and 'swallow tails' common to southern Fujian architecture. Within the village is a bookshop and several snack stands. Buses 25 and 31 service the area.

In Hsishanchien Village (Xīshānqián Cūn) stands the 18-room **Li Residence** (Lǐ Zhái), an exquisitely carved wooden house that was built in the late 19th century by the Li family, which became wealthy from doing business in Singapore.

The **Chen Chien Ancient Tomb** (Chén Jiàn Gǔ Mù) commemorates an important official of the Ming dynasty who served various posts

---

### THE AUGUST 23RD ARTILLERY WAR

In August 1955, Sino-US talks about the status of Taiwan had left mainland China feeling bitter and angry. The United States insisted that Beijing renounce the use of force against Taiwan in response to Beijing's claims that it had the right to use force on its own territory if necessary to liberate the island from Chiang Kai-shek. Upon hearing Beijing's aggressive military threats, Taiwan declared a state of emergency and prepared for the full force of a Chinese attack. On the morning of 23 August 1958, Beijing launched a ferocious bombardment on Kinmen. In just two hours the island was hit with over 42,000 shells. Alarmed, the US acted quickly to defend Kinmen, realising that if it fell, the security of Taiwan would be in severe jeopardy. The US sent a shipment of jet fighters and anti-aircraft missiles to Taiwan, along with six aircraft carriers.

The communists created a tight blockade around Kinmen's beaches and airstrip, preventing any military supplies from reaching the Taiwan military. To break through the blockade, the US knew that it would have to send military supplies to Taiwan by sea. On September 7, the US sent several warships into the Taiwan Strait to escort a convoy of Taiwan military-supply ships to the blockade. The convoy got within 5km of the blockade and was surprised that the communists refused to fire.

Instead, Beijing offered to Taiwan a very odd ceasefire – it would only fire on Kinmen on odd-numbered days. On even-numbered days the island would be left alone. Taiwan agreed to this reluctantly. The Chinese held to the ceasefire and continued to bomb Kinmen throughout September and October on odd-numbered days. By November, tensions had decreased and the bombing stopped. Tragically, almost 500,000 shells had struck Kinmen, killing over 3000 civilians. More than 1000 soldiers on the island had been killed or wounded.

TAIWAN STRAIT ISLANDS

across mainland China. He is buried with his wife on the mainland. The tomb here contains only his hat and gown. The **Chen Chen Memorial Arch** (Chén Zhēn Ēnróng Fáng), dedicated to his father, a Jinsha native, is nearby. This arch was built by order of the Ming imperial court for (father) Chen's contribution to civil service. It's one of the best-preserved Ming arches in Taiwan.

The **Forestry Administration Office** (Línwù Suǒ; ⏰ 8am-6pm) takes the credit for maintaining Kinmen's superb forest reserves. The log-cabin-like buildings sit in a wooded park surrounded by greenhouses, a pond and a playground for children.

## LIEHYU DISTRICT 列嶼鄉

Liehyu Island (Lièyǔ Xiāng) or 'Little Kinmen' (Xiǎo Jīnmén), comprises Liehyu District. The entire island is a little less than 2 sq km in area, making all sights within easy walking distance of Chiukung Harbour.

The **Victory Gate** (Shènglì Mén) is one of the first things visitors see upon arrival to Liehyu. It stands to the west of the harbour.

More interesting is the **Pata Memorial** (Bādá Loúzi), a replica of the tower that stands on the Great Wall on the mainland. The Liehyu tower was built in 1963 by the Kinmen-stationed 'Great Wall' troops to commemorate the seven soldiers who died in the 1933 battle against the Japanese in Gubeikou.

The **Chaste Maiden Temple** (Liè Nǚ Miào) is dedicated to a woman, Wang Yulan, who fought against and was killed by some communist soldiers who tried to rape her. Her body was dumped into the sea and floated up onto the shores of Liehyu, where she was buried and a temple built in her honour.

**Koxinga's Well** (Guóxìng Jǐng) is where the controversial figure (see p287) supposedly took a drink of water.

The **Huchingtou War Museum** (Hújǐngtóu Zhànshǐ Guǎn) is on the northwestern tip of Liehyu. In addition to war memorabilia, it also contains an observation room with binoculars and a broadcasting station which assaults mainland ears with Taiwanese political messages and music.

The **Siwei Tunnel** (Sìwéi Kēngdào; ⏰ 8.30am-5pm), on southeastern Liehyu, is an underground tunnel blasted through a granite reef. It's 790m in length, twice as large as the Dishan Tunnel on Kinmen.

# PENGHU ISLANDS

☎ 06 / pop 90,000

There are 64 islands in the Penghu Archipelago but only 20 are inhabited; the entire area comprises about 126 sq km. Penghu is the largest island, but 'Penghu' also refers to Makung, Huhsi, Paisha and Hsi Townships. Makung is the only city, and the only place with accommodation and banking services.

Penghu is a flat, dry place, covered with bush and grasslands, unique compared to Taiwan's mountainous subtropical environment. The wind- and water-eroded coastlines of the islands feature stunning basalt cliffs, reefs and, without question, some of the finest beaches in Taiwan.

During the very hot summer months, the islands are an excellent place for water sports, including boating, snorkelling and swimming. Fierce winter winds make Penghu a popular place for windsurfing, drawing enthusiasts from all over the world.

## History

The Penghu Islands (澎湖; Pénghú) are in the south of the Taiwan Strait, midway between mainland China and Taiwan. Over the centuries, they've served as a valuable connection point between Taiwan, mainland China, Japan and Southeast Asia. Because of its strategic position, Penghu has often fallen under the control of Asian and European colonisers, who saw the islands as prime territory for political gain.

The Dutch were the first to grab the islands in 1622, but moved to the Taiwanese mainland when they learned that the Ming imperial court had plans to remove them from Penghu by force. In 1662 the Ming loyalist Koxinga was sent to oust the Dutch from Taiwan for good. Penghu was a convenient place to station his troops as he drew up his battle plans. Some troops stayed in Penghu after the Dutch were gone and set up their own regime, which was short-lived, however, because the Qing court threw them out in 1683. The French were the next to arrive in 1884, followed in 1895 by the Japanese, who settled down and stayed for the next 50 years, only to be replaced by the Nationalists in 1945.

Penghu is rich with historical relics, evidence of its long colonial history. Martial law

TAIWAN STRAIT ISLANDS

lifted from the islands in 1979 and mainland Taiwanese were able to visit the island for the first time. Wanting to capitalise on Penghu's history and boost a drooping economy, the islands were transformed into a beach mecca for local and foreign visitors. The Penghu Archipelago has been designated a national scenic area and the islands have been given a makeover for the visitors that crowd Penghu's shores each summer.

## MAKUNG 馬公

Makung (Mǎgōng) is a pleasant town with a history that stretches back to the 14th century. Some remnants of early architecture remain, especially in central Makung around the harbour area. The Japanese have also left their mark in Makung with a number of Japanese-style administrative buildings around town. It's worth spending a day or two exploring the city before heading out to the neighbouring islands.

During summer, Makung sees a fair amount of tourist traffic and hotel prices are sky-high. In winter, the town is much

**PENGHU ISLANDS**

ore subdued and many residents close up
op and head elsewhere.

## formation

### ONEY

nk of Taiwan ( ☎ 927 9935; 24 Jenai Rd) The only
ace to change foreign currency.

### OURIST INFORMATION

enghu Tourist Service Centre (Pénghú Yóukè Fúwù
ōngxīn; ☎ 921 6445; 171 Kuanghua Lane; ☯ 8am-
m) The centre has many useful pamphlets in English on
nghu as well as a multimedia room with documentary
ns. The centre is inconveniently located outside Makung,
sting about NT200 by taxi.

uth Seas Tourist Service Centre (Nánhǎi Yóukè
wù Zhōngxīn; ☎ 926 4738; Makung Harbour Third Fish-
Dock; ☯ 8am-5pm) This centre provides information
out Chimei, Wang'an and Tongpan Islands. Boat tickets
n also be purchased here.

### SA EXTENSIONS

he Foreign Affairs Police ( ☎ 927 9935; 36 Chihping
) can take care of visa needs.

## ghts

akung is best explored on foot as many of
s most interesting sights are tucked away
narrow alleys. A good place to start
ur exploration is at the Matsu Temple (Māzǔ
nhòu Gōng; Hui-an Rd; ☯ 5am-8.30pm) near the
rbour. This temple was constructed in
e late 16th century, making it the oldest
mple in Taiwan. Sailors have been com-
g here for centuries to pray to the god-
ss Matsu (see p276) for a safe voyage.
he temple was originally built without
ing a single nail and though it has been
furbished several times over the years,
e craftsmanship remains superb.

Along Jinlung Rd is Shuncheng Gate
hùnchéng Mén) and a section of the Makung
Wall (Māgōng Gǔ Chéng). City walls were
nstructed around Makung as a defensive
easure after the occupying French left the
y in 1885. The walls were completed in
89, but the Japanese knocked down most
them, leaving only this section intact.

In a lane near the Matsu Temple is the
ihkung Ancestral Shrine (Shīgōng Cí) and
ll of a Thousand Soldiers (Wàn Jūn Jǐng).

1682, a general of the Qing dynasty,
i Lang, amassed his troops in Fujian
ovince, preparing to invade Taiwan and
nghu. Legend states that the general

prayed to Matsu for strength and in return
the goddess gave this well, with an ever-
lasting supply of water, to his soldiers. In
1843 the ancestral shrine was erected in the
general's honour.

Another historical relic is the Four Eyes
Well (Sì Yǎn Jǐng; Chungyang St). No-one can be
certain when the wells were dug but some
speculate that it might have been as long
ago as the 15th century. The area surrounding the wells is the oldest in the city, now
full of artists' boutiques, pubs and cafés.

Nearby is the Chienyi Tang Chinese Traditional Medicine Store (Qiányì Táng Zhōngyào Xíng;
42 Chungyang St; ☯ 7am-9.30pm) This one-of-a-
kind, 80-year-old building is an eclectic mix
of Western and Fujian architecture.

On Makung's western shoreline is the
Kuanyin Pavilion (Guànyīn Tíng; ☯ 5am-8pm), dedicated to Kuanyin, Goddess of Mercy. The
temple was constructed over 300 years ago
and is one of the most important places for
Buddhist worship on Penghu. The most important artefact in the temple is the old bell,
which dates back to 1696. In front of the
temple is a large waterfront park, the site of
international windsurfing competitions.

The Penghu Reclamation Hall (Pénghú Kāi Tà Guǎn;
30 Chihping Rd; admission NT30; ☯ 10am-10pm, closed Mon
& last day of each month) was once the prefectural
mansion of Penghu County. Built in 1935 by
the Japanese, the architecture is an elegant
mix of Japanese and Western styles. Inside
are displays about Penghu culture and history as well as a small library (in Chinese).

The Penghu County Cultural Area (Pénghú Xiàn
Wénhuà Yuánqū; 230 Chunghua Rd), on the edge of
Makung, has several museums and an art
gallery worth visiting. On the grounds is
the cultural bureau, a library, Penghu Marine
Exhibition Hall (Pénghú Hǎiyáng Zīyuán Guǎn; NT20;
☯ 9am-noon & 2-5pm Wed-Sun) and the Penghu
County Science Hall (Pénghú Xiàn Kèxuéguǎn; ☯ 9am-
noon & 2-5pm Wed-Sun). Both the marine hall and
the science hall have changing exhibitions
devoted to Penghu ecology and natural
resources. Most of the information is in
Chinese but the displays are interesting
enough to make a visit worthwhile. Kids,
in particular, will enjoy the dinosaur fossils
in the science hall.

Nearby is the Chao Ertai Art Museum (Zhào
Èrdài Yìguǎn; 240 Chunghua Rd; ☯ 9am-noon & 2-5pm
Wed-Sun), a gallery displaying the works of the
mainland Chinese artist Chao Ertai. After

retiring from a career as a bureaucrat, Chao moved to Penghu. He devoted the last years of his life to pottery, painting, sculpture and calligraphy and, with the help of the Penghu County government, built this gallery, which opened in 1990.

In eastern Makung you'll find the **Martyrs' Shrine** (Zhōngliè Cí) and the **Confucius Temple** (Kǒng Miào). The temple was formerly the Wenshi College, built in 1766 and an important centre of learning during the Qing dynasty. The name of the college was changed to the Confucius Temple during the Japanese occupation to take advantage of the Japanese respect for Confucius, in the hope that the college wouldn't be torn down.

## Festivals

The **Penghu Sailboard Cobia Festival** takes place at the Kuanyin Pavilion every November. The event attracts enthusiasts from all over the world. For more information check out the Penghu County website (www.penghu-nsa.gov.tw).

## Sleeping

During summer, hotel prices in Makung rise dramatically and there is a shortage of accommodation on weekends and holidays. It's important to book ahead if you're travelling during the high season. The prices listed here are summer rates; in winter (October to March) sizable discounts can be had at even the most expensive of hotels.

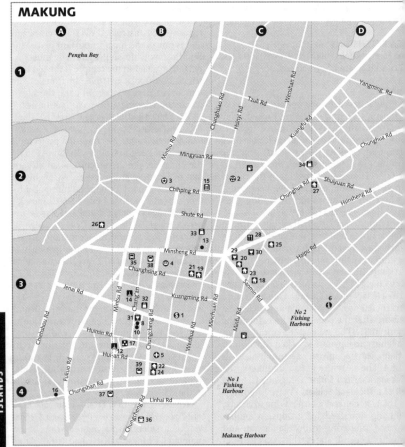

MAKUNG

## JDGET

**unghsin Hotel** (Zhōngxīn Dà Lǔshè; ☎ 927 2151; 22 unghsing Rd; r from NT700) A good budget choice. 's in a convenient location, walking dis-nce to all the Makung sights and shop-ng. The 21 rooms here fill up quickly in mmer so book ahead.

**Fulushou Hotel** (Fú Lù Shòu Fàndiàn; ☎ 927 1290; Chunghsing Rd; t/d NT1000, q from NT1600) The Fu-shou is a gem with its grassy backyard, ammock and pond. Rooms are a bit dim ut still worth the price. The owner, Mr ang, knows all the hidden treasure spots Penghu and can help with travel plans.

**Donghai Hotel** (Dōnghái Lǔshè; ☎ 927 2367; 38 San-n Rd; r from NT500) Near the fish market, this ace is cheap but run-down and dingy, and

should only be considered if all the other hotels are full.

**Chungching Hotel** (Zhōngqìng Dà Lǔshè; ☎ 927-3832; 16 Sanmin Rd; r from NT600) Cheap, reasonably clean rooms, though they are a little noisy.

### MID-RANGE & TOP-END

**Hwa Shin Palace Hotel** (Huáxīn Dà Fàndiàn; ☎ 926 4911; 40 Sanmin Rd; r NT1400-3200) The rooms here

are well-managed and comfortable, and the hotel is in a central part of town, providing a free shuttle to and from the harbour and airport. Try to get a room on an upper floor to avoid the karaoke noise at night.

**Sheng Kuo Hotel** (Shèngguó Dà Fàndiàn; ☎ 927 3891; 6 Shuiyuan Rd; d/tr NT1400/1500) The Sheng Kuo has 118 rooms, which makes it the largest hotel in Makung. Rooms are spacious, with wood floors and large windows. The hotel provides a free shuttle to the airport.

**Penghu Royal Hotel** (Ruìfù Dà Fàndiàn; ☎ 926 1182; Lane 64-33 Hsinsheng Rd; r NT2400-3800) This place has fancily decorated rooms and is one of the more popular hotels for tour groups. The best time to stay is on weekdays or during winter to take advantage of season discounts.

**Jih Lih Hotel** (Rìlì Dà Fàndiàn; ☎ 926 5898; 25 Huimin 1st Rd; d NT2200-8800) The Jih Lih has large, very pleasant rooms with deep discounts in winter. The hotel is a one-minute walk to Chungcheng Rd, the main shopping street of Makung, and close to the Peichen Temple (Běichén Gōng).

**Hotel Ever Spring** (Chángchūn Dà Fàndiàn; ☎ 927 4881; 6 Chungcheng Rd; r NT1800-3800) This is a nice place located very close to Makung Harbour, with free Internet access and breakfast. Some rooms have ocean views and there's even a 'Captain's Suite'.

**Pao Hua Hotel** (Bǎohuá Dà Fàndiàn; ☎ 927 4881; 2 Chungcheng Rd; d/t NT1800/3800) Adjacent to Makung Harbour, the Pao Hua offers spotless rooms, some with ocean views. The coffee shop on the main floor serves palatable sandwiches and snacks.

**Penghu Youth Activity Centre** (Pénghú Qíngnián Huódòng Zhōngxīn; ☎ 927 1124; 11 Chiehshou Rd; r from NT1400) The centre is more for tour groups than for individual travellers. Though the rooms are expensive in summer, there are discounts of up to 50% on winter weekdays, making the place not such a bad deal. The waterfront location is superb.

## Eating

Makung is a great place for snacks. The best place to try local foods is around the temples and market areas at night. Some things to try are the tasty pumpkin rice-noodles (jīnguā mǐfěn), salty biscuits (xián bǐng), grilled meat with rice (shāo ròu fàn) and steamed brown-sugar sponge cakes (hēi táng gāo). Of course, seafood is what Penghu is most famous for. Raw lobster (lóng xiā) and fried 'five-flavour'

balloonfish (wǔ xiāng cìhétún) are favou ites. One must-try drink is the delicious fe gru tea (fēngrú chá), served chilled or hot.

**Yung Ta Vegetarian Restaurant** (Yǒngdá Sù: Guǎn; 27 Hsinsheng Rd; mains NT60; ☺ lunch & dinn This is a tidy cafeteria-style restaurant ser ing a variety of cheap Buddhist dishes.

## Drinking

**Sunny Colony Bar** (Yángguāng Zhí Míndì; Lane 3 Chungcheng Rd; ☺ 6pm-2am; drinks NT150-180) Th bar is a trendy place to spend the evenin Speciality drinks include Penghu cactu juice (xiánrénzhǎng zhī) mixed with alcо hol. Pub grub (chips etc) is also available.

**Freud Pub** (Fúluòyídé Pub; 2-I Hsinsheng Rd; ☺ 1 2am; drinks NT90) This is a small sports bar wit a homey atmosphere. The house special the potent cocktail 'absolutely drunk', ma with six kinds of alcohol.

**Sha Ai Chuang** (Shǎ Ài Zhuāng; 14 Hsinsheng F ☺ 10am-midnight; cocktails from NT150) Loose translated as 'foolish love pub', this place w once the home of Penghu's first county chi It has been transformed into a colourful b with great ambience. The fruit-juice coc tails are especially good on a warm night.

## Shopping

Makung is full of shops selling all kinds Penghu speciality items such as pink ar black coral, shells and veined stones. Buyin these items, especially black coral, is not re ommended. The sale of coral has led to t destruction of coral reefs and the decline the marine creatures that live within them

For antiques and locally made arts a crafts, head to the 100-year-old **Chu Sheng W Wu Ji Nian Kuan** (Zhū Shèng Wen Jìniàn Guǎn; 36 Je Rd; admission NT100; ☺ 10am-9pm). This two-stor antique market has a wonderful assortme of objects for sale, the majority from the Qí dynasty. Even if you're not in the mood buy, it's still a fun place to browse.

You can buy just about anything at t bustling **Peichen Market** (Běichén Shìchán in central Makung. Come at night for son serious snack hunting.

## Getting There & Away
### AIR

Makung is well connected to Taiwan's maj cities, and flights leave daily from Taip Taichung, Tainan, Kaohsiung and Chia Travel agencies around Chungcheng R

:an help arrange tickets. The following air-
ines have offices in Makung airport.

**:ar Eastern Air Transport** ( ☎ 924 9388)
**uhsing Airlines** ( ☎ 921 8500)
**Mandarin Airlines** ( ☎ 921 6966)
**Jni Air** ( ☎ 921 6350)

### BOAT
The **Taiwan Hangye Company** (www.taiwanline.com
tw/table.htm; Kaohsiung ☎ 07-561 3866; 5 Chiehhsing-1st
t; Makung ☎ 926 4087; Makung Harbour Terminal Build-
ng) operates *Taiwanline*, a boat that travels
between Kaohsiung and Makung (NT600
o NT1300) from May through August. The
schedule changes every three months and
boats are limited in winter. Schedules are
posted online (Chinese only).

The *Tomorrow Star* runs between Putai
near Chiayi) and Makung (NT650, one
hour 10 minutes). To inquire call **Makung
Tomorrow Star** ( ☎ 926 0666; Makung Harbour Terminal
Building).

## Getting Around
### TO/FROM THE AIRPORT
An airport shuttle bus makes hourly rounds
o Makung between 7.20am and 6.50pm. A
axi to the airport costs NT300.

### CAR/MOTORCYCLE/SCOOTER
Cars, motorcycles and scooters are available for rent all over Makung and offer the
easiest way to see the island. Rates for motorbikes and scooters are generally NT350
to NT400 a day, excluding petrol. Small
cars can be rented for NT1300 a day. Most
rental agencies require an international licence or a Taiwan licence.

### PUBLIC TRANSPORT
It's next to impossible to get around Penghu
by bus. There are two bus lines that traverse
the islands and run about once an hour.
Trying to get around this way will result in
a lot of frustration.

### TAXI
Taxi drivers prefer flat rates to using the
meter. A trip to just about anywhere on
Penghu will cost NT200 to NT300. Taxi
tours can be had for about NT2500 to
NT3000 a day.

## Around Makung
The area around Makung has some unique
historical relics as well as some excellent beaches and scenery. The crumbling

---

### THE TURTLES OF PENGHU

On 15 January, the evening of the Lantern Festival, Penghu residents crowd into temples around
the islands and offer sacrificial images of turtles to the deities. They pray for prosperity and give
thanks for the good things that happened to them the previous year. The sea-turtles that migrate
through the coastal waters off Penghu have a special meaning to the islanders, who believe that
they represent longevity and fortune. Rice cakes and dough are formed into the shapes of turtles
and offered to temple deities. Sacrificial turtles are also made from gold coins, noodles, sponge
cakes and sometimes offered live. Turtles can be offered to any of the gods or goddesses, though
Matsu seems to be the local favourite. During the festivities, parades are held, with men carrying
giant palanquins down the streets bearing local gods and goddesses, accompanied by singing,
dancing and plenty of fireworks.

Some of the beliefs about turtles come from ancient Chinese myths about turtles being special
conduits between heaven and earth and capable of divining the future through the marks on
their shells. To Chinese, the turtle is considered one of the four spiritual beasts of the world,
along with dragons, chimeras and the phoenix, and in ancient times were thought to have
magical powers.

Unfortunately, there are more rice-cake turtles in Penghu now than the real thing, as Penghu's
turtle population is slowly dying out. Once, sea-turtles nested throughout Taiwan's coastal regions, including Kinmen, Lanyu and Penghu. Now, only a few nesting sites are found on Penghu's
Wang'an Island and Lanyu. Conservation efforts are ongoing in Penghu to protect the sacred
turtles from extinction. On Wang'an, the green turtles mate from March to April and nest in
July and August. Tracking programmes have been set up by Taiwanese conservation agencies
to monitor the number of turtles moving about in the waters surrounding Penghu and nesting
on the beaches.

remains of the **Tsai Tinglan Residence** (Cài Tínglán Jìn Shì Dì) still possess some charm. Tsao Tinglan was a child prodigy who grew up to be an acclaimed scholar and official. He built this Fujian-style mansion in 1846 at the height of his career.

The **Sokang Pagodas** (Soǔ Gǎng Zǐwǔ Bǎotǎ), south of Sokang Village (Suǒgǎng Cūn), are two north- and south-facing stone towers that serve a special religious purpose. The stone tablets on the towers, called *shihkantang* (*shígǎndāng*), have been blessed by a Taoist priest and contain supernatural powers to ward off evil and protect residents from natural disasters.

Not too far from the pagodas is the **Peichi Temple** (Běijí Diàn), which is known for its large gold turtle, a symbol of longevity. This temple becomes very active during the Lantern Festival (see the boxed text p301).

**Shanshui Beach** (Shānshuǐ Shātān), outside of Shanshui Village (Shānshuǐ Cūn), has smooth white sand, breaking waves and is a great place to relax. Long-net fishing, a Penghu custom, is a popular activity here – nets hundreds of feet long are dragged through the water and pulled ashore by groups of sweaty tourists, anxious to share in the catch-of-the-day. It's an amusing sight.

**Chihli Beach** (Zhìlǐ Shātān) is another beautiful spot to spend the day. The shell-sand beach stretches for over 1km and is popular with beach-sport enthusiasts and sunbathers.

In addition to beaches, Penghu also has some striking coastal scenery. The bizarre rock formations that punctuate the coastline were formed by cooling basalt magma thousands of years ago. Sea erosion has created many unusual gullies and crevices that have taken the imagination of Penghu residents and tourists. **Fengkuei Cave** (Fēngguī Dòng), on Penghu's south shore, is a sea-eroded gully that reportedly makes a peculiar sound when the wind rushes through it during high tide.

Nearby are the ruins of the **Dutch Fort** (Fēngguī Wèi Hóngmáo Chéng Wèi Zhǐ), abandoned by the Dutch when they were driven out of Penghu by the Ming army in 1624.

## TONGPAN ISLAND 桶盤嶼

This small, inhabited island, called Tongpan (Tǒngpán Yǔ) because it's supposedly shaped like a big plate, lies southwest of Makung Harbour. Walls of basalt columns surround the island, giving it a unique appearance, and the southwest of the island is a sea-eroded plain. The **Fuhai Temple** (Fúhǎi Gōng) is considered an important centre of worship and pilgrims come from Penghu and mainland Taiwan to pay their respects. The **Tongpan Artist Village** is also here, with local artists making a variety of traditional arts and crafts.

Boats leave for Tongpan (20 minutes) from the South Seas Tourist Service Centre in Makung.

## HUCHING ISLAND 虎井嶼

South of Tongpan, Huching Island (Hǔjǐng Yǔ) is a flat island with basalt columns flanking the eastern and western coastlines. The name 'Huching', literally translated as 'tiger well', comes from a legend about a tiger that once roamed the island. **Hsishan Park** (Xīshān Gōngyuán), on the western side of the island, has the remains of trenches that were dug by the Japanese army during WWII. It's rumoured that this part of the island was used as a command centre for Admiral Yamamoto's attack on Pearl Harbour. To get to the island, you'll need to charter a boat.

## HUHSI TOWNSHIP 湖西鄉
**pop 13,000**

Huhsi Township (Húxī Xiāng) is in Penghu's northeast, bordering Makung on the west and connected to Paisha Township in the northwest by the Trans-Ocean Bridge. Makung airport is located in Huhsi, about a 20-minute drive from Makung. Accommodation is limited in Huhsi and most people choose to stay in Makung.

The green expanse of pines in **Lintou Park** (Líntóu Gōngyuán; NT30) is a rare sight in dry, windswept Penghu. The one-hectare forest borders a white-sand beach, a superb spot for a picnic. To the west is the **Military Public Cemetery** (Jūnrén Gōngmù), where the body of General Chi Hsingwen is buried. The general died in the August 23rd Artillery War in 1958 (p294).

**Aimen Beach** (Ài Mén Shātān) is a favourite among locals for all kinds of water sports and beach activities. It's possible to camp out here, though in summer it can be quite crowded.

# CHISHAN & TINGKOU ISLANDS
雞善嶼, 錠鉤嶼

Chishan Island (Jīshàn Yǔ) and Tingkou Island (Dìnggōu Yǔ), along with Hsiao Paisha Island, form the Basalt Rock Conservation Area, dedicated to preserving the basalt formations seen throughout the Penghu Archipelago. Tingkou, southeast of Chishan, is sometimes called 'Little Guilin', referring to Guilin in mainland China, also known for its strange pillars of rock.

The islands play host to large numbers of migrating birds every year and are a popular spot for bird-watchers in autumn and late spring. Tingkou, in particular, is home to large colonies of terns.

The islands can only be reached by chartered boat.

# PAISHA TOWNSHIP 白沙鄉
pop 9000

Paisha Township (Báishā Xiāng) is linked in the southeast to Huhsi Township and Makung. To the west, the **Trans-Ocean Bridge** (Kuà Hǎi Dà Qiáo) connects Paisha to Hsi Township. Twenty seven islands fall under the jurisdiction of Paisha Township. Boats to these outlying islands leave from the North Seas Tourist Service Centre in Chihkan.

The **Penghu Aquarium** (Pénghú Shuǐzú Guǎn; 58 Chicou Village; admission NT200; 9am-5pm Mon-Wed & Frisun) is a two-storey marine exhibition centre that provides information on all the aquatic creatures swimming around Penghu. The highlight of the aquarium is the 14m glass tunnel, allowing visitors a fish-eye view of the sea. At the time of writing, the aquarium was closed for repairs.

Another place worth a stop is the enormous 300-year-old **Tungliang Banyan Tree** (Tōngliáng Gǔróng) in Tungliang Village. It's said that during the Qing dynasty, a ship sunk off the coast of Penghu and a small seedling floated to shore. Locals planted the seedling which grew into this magnificent tree.

# CHIPEI ISLAND 吉貝嶼

Chipei Island (Jíbèi Yǔ) is the biggest island in the northern Penghu Archipelago and boasts some very nice shell-sand beaches. The island buzzes in summer with tourists but shuts down almost completely in winter. If you come here during the off season, pack your own food and be ready for limited choices in accommodation.

**Chipei Sand Beach** (Jíbèi Shātān) is the most popular beach on the island. This long strip of golden sand juts out into the water, its size changing with the coming and going of the tides. During summer, windsurfing, boating and even parasailing are popular activities here. Equipment is available for rent in the resort or in the small shops around the beach. During winter, you'll have the whole place to yourself.

## Sleeping

The most popular place to stay on Chipei is the **Chipei Sea Paradise Resort** (Jíbèi Hǎishàng Lèyuán; 991 1311; 187 Chipei Village; cabins from NT1500), which offers tin-box 'cabins' right on the beach. Camping is possible within the resort as long as you bring your own equipment. The resort offers a wide variety of water toys for rent.

Another choice in pre-fab cabins is at the **Mingyang Hostel** (Míngyáng Shān Zhuāng; 991 1079; 182 Chipei Village; cabins from NT800), which is closer to town than the Chipei Sea Paradise but not as nice.

Chipei Village has an assortment of homestays and small hotels, but quality varies widely so be sure to look at your room before agreeing to stay anywhere.

## Eating

On Chipei are some hole-in-the-wall restaurants selling seafood and snacks. A good place next to the harbour is the **Hongmao Harbour Snack Stand** (Hóngmáo Gǎng Xiǎochī Bù; seafood from NT100), which offers seafood dishes at reasonable prices. Resorts offer fancier food but it's expensive. During winter, most eateries shut down and you might end up digging for your own clams if you're not prepared.

## Getting There & Away

Boats leave for Chipei (NT250, 15 minutes) from the North Sea Tourist Service Centre (Běi Hǎi Yóukè Fúwù Zhōngxīn) in Chihkan, in northeast Paisha, daily. Other boats also head to Chipei, but make stops at Tiechen, Hsienchiao or Kupo Islands. The schedule changes daily and boats can be cancelled at the last minute due to rough water.

# KUPO ISLAND 姑婆嶼

Kupo Island (Gūpó Yǔ) is Penghu's largest uninhabited island. What grows here in abundance is *laver*, a type of edible purple seaweed. The north side of the island is devoted to the production of *laver* and the east side to fish processing. People don't usually come to Kupo for the seaweed but for the large numbers of birds that congregate here in winter. The North Seas Tourist Service Centre has boats that travel to Kupo, depending on demand.

## HSIENCHIAO ISLAND 險礁嶼
Situated south of Chipei, this tiny island (Xiǎnjiāo Yǔ) is known for its **coral reefs** and as a good place to go scuba diving or snorkelling. The white-sand beaches are reputed to be the most beautiful in the Penghu Archipelago. To get here you'll need to arranging a chartered boat or board a boat headed in the direction of Chipei.

## TIECHEN ISLAND 鐵砧嶼
Some say this island (Tiézhēn Yǔ) looks like a chopping block, though this may be a stretch of the imagination. On the north side of the island is a small **cave**, about 10m wide, well liked by nesting birds. Small boats can take visitors into the cave to look around.

## PENG PENG BEACH 彭彭灘
This ghostly strip of sand (Péngpéng Tān) changes shape with the tides. It's the newest addition to the Penghu beach scene and an up-and-coming spot for water sports. The only drawback about getting here is that there's no harbour. That means that boats get as close to the beach as they can and then it's a wade through the water to get to shore. It's a 30-minute chartered boat ride from the North Seas Tourist Service Centre in Chihkan.

## TATSANG ISLAND 大倉嶼
Tatsang Island (Dà Cāng Yǔ) is in the middle of Penghu, Paisha and Hsi Islands, making it an intriguing intertidal zone and a good place for locals to gather shellfish. Some visitors like to 'reef walk' from Chengch'ien Village (Chéngqián Cūn) on Paisha Island to Tatsang, meaning that when the tide is out, they walk from one island to the other on the exposed sand. Needless to say, this is dangerous and not recommended. Tatsang Island has good facilities for boating, snorkelling and parasailing.

## YUANPEI ISLAND 員貝嶼
Yuanpei Island (Yuànbèi Yǔ) is situated east of Paisha Island and literally translated means 'round shell', which it somewhat resembles. Like Tatsang Island, Yuanpei can be reached on foot during low tide from Shakang (Shāgǎng) in Huhsi Township. The walk takes about three hours but it seems a foolish thing to do unless you time it very carefully (or are an exceedingly good swimmer). Yuanpei is a well-touristed place during summer. Rooms are available at the **Yuanpei Holiday Village** (Yuánbèi Shēng Tàidù Jiǎ Cūn; ☎ 993 3065; 1-1 Yuanpei Village; r NT1400).

## HSIAO PAISHA ISLAND 小白沙嶼
Tiny Hsiao Paisha (Xiǎo Báishā Yǔ) is really just a speck in the sea. Swimming and snorkelling are the main activities here.

## NIAO ISLAND 鳥嶼
Niao or 'Bird' Island (Niǎo Yǔ) lies east of Paisha and is supposedly, at the right time of year, full of birds. Authorities say that 130 species of bird have been reported here, though the numbers may be diminishing.

## MUTOU ISLAND 目斗嶼
Mutou Island (Mùdǒu Yǔ) is the northernmost of the Penghu Islands. The shallow waters around the coast are a wonderful place to see tropical fish swimming in and out of coral reefs. The **lighthouse** on Mutou was built in 1899 and its black and white stripes contrast nicely with the azure blue water.

## HSI TOWNSHIP 西鄉
Hsi Township (Xī Xiāng; West Township) is located to the west of Makung and connected to Paisha by the Trans-Ocean Bridge. The coastline is dramatic, full of steep cliffs and gullies.

**Hsiaomen Island** (Xiǎomén Yǔ) is a small island linked to the main island by a small bridge. On Hsiaomen is **Whale Cave** (Jīngyú Dòng), a hole in a rock that is supposed to resemble a whale. The story is that the hole was created when a gigantic whale crashed into the rock, leaving an imprint of his body.

Also on Hsiaomen is the **Hsiaomen Geology Museum** (Xiǎomén Dìzhì Bówùguǎn; 11-12 Xiaomen Village; ☼ 8am-5pm), with exhibits explaining the natural history of the Penghu Archipelago.

TAIWAN STRAIT ISLANDS

The 200-year-old **Ta-yi Temple** (Dàyì Gōng) is dedicated to Kuanyu, the God of War. Some say that when the French tried to attack Penghu, mysterious forces kept them away from the temple.

The **West Fortress** (Xī Tái; admission NT30; 7.30am-6.30pm summer & 8am-5.30pm winter) was built in 1887, following the Sino-French War, and 5000 soldiers were once stationed in this fortress. Interestingly, it's constructed with mud and sticky-rice pulp. It's possible to go inside and wander around.

The **Erkan Old Residences** (Èrkàn Gǔ Cuò; admission NT30; 8am-7pm) are a group of five houses that were built almost 100 years ago. The architecture is a mix of southern Fujian, Western and Japanese styles. Note the elaborately carved beams and columns.

## WANG'AN ISLAND 望安嶼

Wang'an Township (望安鄉; Wàng'ān Xiāng; population 4000) is made up of 18 islands but only Wang'an, Chiangchun, Tungchi and Tungyuping are inhabited. To get to these islands, boats leave from the South Seas Tourist Service Centre in Makung (1½ hours).

Wang'an Island doesn't have the stellar beaches or scenery of some of the other islands but it does have its own charms.

For those interested in aquatic wildlife, Wang'an has one of the few remaining sea-turtle nesting grounds left in Taiwan. Close to the harbour is the **Green Mossback Turtle Sightseeing and Preservation Centre** (Lǜ Xīguī Guānguāng Bǎo Yù Zhōngxīn; 9am-5pm). Inside are bilingual exhibits about the state of sea-turtles in Taiwan and around the world. There's also information on wildlife preservation efforts in the Strait Islands and in Taiwan proper. If you want to see the turtles, you can talk to the friendly staff here.

The **Chungshe Old Dwellings** (Zhōngshè Gǔ Cuò) are a group of abandoned but well-preserved houses in Chungshe Village (Zhōngshè Cūn). Locals say that the only reason these old houses are still standing is because there is no one left in the area to tear them down.

The highest point on the island is **Tientai Mountain** (Tiāntái Shān), actually a grassy hill with some cows. The footprint of Li Tungbin, one of China's Eight Immortals, is impressed on a rock here. His other footprint is on Hua Island (right).

## Sleeping

**Yanchuan Vacation Centre** (Yánchuān Dùjià Xiūxián Zhōngxīn; 999 1440/1; 60-2 Chungshe Village; d NT1200) A nice place, with small bungalows for rent, some of which are built on a dock right over the water. Prices are negotiable during winter. Set meals are available for NT150, which include five simple dishes and a soup.

**Wang'an Vacation Centre** (Wàng'ān Dùjià Zhōngxīn; 999 1200; 73-9 Tung'an Village; d/tr NT800/1400) This place lacks the pleasant surroundings of the Yanchuan Vacation Centre but is very close to the harbour.

## Eating

In Tung'an Village are several small homestyle restaurants that serve up noodle and rice dishes. In winter, pickings are slim and its best to bring food with you.

## Getting There & Away

**Mandarin Airlines** (Kaohsiung 07-802 6868; Makung 921 6966) flies between Kaohsiung and Wang'an. Mandarin also fly between Makung and Wang'an (NT600, 10 minutes).

Boats to Wang'an (NT170, 1½ hours) run from the South Seas Tourist Service Centre in Makung along the Wang'an–Chimei route. It's a rough ride, especially in winter, so bring something to help your stomach if you're prone to seasickness.

## Getting Around

Motorcycles are available for rent at the harbour for NT300 to NT400 a day. Alternatively, you can get around on foot, though that can be tiring.

## CHIANGCHUN ISLAND 將軍澳嶼

Chiangchun Island (Jiāngjūn'ao Yǔ) lies east of Wang'an and is clearly visible from Wang'an's harbour. The island's **coral reefs** are quite well known, making it a good destination for snorkelling and scuba diving. Chiangchun has several old temples, including the Ming-dynasty **Yong'an Temple** (Yǒng'ān Gōng). A coral-reef footpath goes around the island – an easy walk as the entire island is only 1.5km across.

Boats travel between Wang'an and Chiangchun when they have enough passengers.

## HUA ISLAND 花嶼

Hua Island (Huā Yǔ; Flower Island) is Penghu's most westerly point. What makes

TAIWAN STRAIT ISLANDS

Hua Island unique is that it's made of granite, unlike the other islands in the archipelago, which are comprised of basalt. On the island is one of Li Tungbin's **footprints** (the other is on Wang'an Island, p305) as well as a **lighthouse**.

## MAO ISLAND 貓嶼

Southwest of Wang'an, Mao Island (Māo Yǔ; Cat Island) is actually two islands – 'Big Cat' and 'Small Cat'. They got their names because they look like cats getting ready to pounce. The islands offer shelter to the many birds that stop here for winter. It's been said that over 16 species make their homes among the island's rocky cliffs. To visit the island, it's necessary to charter a boat.

## TUNGYUPING & HSIYUPING ISLANDS
東嶼坪嶼, 西嶼坪嶼

These two islands are situated south of Wang'an Island. A few tiny fishing communities are on Tungyuping (Dōng Yǔpíng Yǔ) but Hsiyuping (Xī Yǔpíng Yǔ) is uninhabited.

## TUNGCHI & HSICHI ISLANDS
東吉嶼, 西吉嶼

Tungchi Island (Dōngjí Yǔ) and Hsichi Island (Xijí Yǔ) are southeast of Wang'an Island. Tungchi has a **lighthouse** that was built by the Japanese in 1911 but little else to entice tourists. Hsichi's population has all moved away and it's just a lonely rock in the sea now.

## CHIMEI ISLAND 七美嶼
pop 3000

Chimei Island (Qīmĕi Yǔ) is the only island in Chimei Township (七美鄉; Qīmĕi Xiāng) and is located on the southern tip of the Penghu Archipelago. Because of its relative isolation, it has its own unique customs.

The name 'Chimei' translates as 'Seven Beauties' and refers to a legend about seven women during the Ming dynasty who threw themselves into a well to protect their chastity from Japanese pirates. The well was filled up and covered, and a tomb was placed on top. Mysteriously, seven trees sprung up around the tomb. This **Tomb of the Seven Virtuous Beauties** (Qīmĕi

Rén Zhǒng; adult/child NT30/15) is the most visited spot on Chimei Island.

The **Two Hearts Stone Weir** (Shuāng Xīn Shí Hù) is another 'tourist destination'. The heart-shaped fishing trap is made of stacked stones. Openings in the traps allow fish to enter during high tide but during low tide the openings in the trap are blocked.

**Cow Plateau** (Niú Mǔ Píng) is a flat expanse of grassland that offers possibilities for camping but you must bring your own tent.

### Sleeping

Several homestays are available on Chimei as well as a few hotels.

**Chimei Luhsing Jia Homestay** (Chīmĕi Lǚxìng Jiā Mínsù; ☎ 997 1265; 38 Nankang Village; d NT1200) Small but tidy rooms near the harbour.

**Wan Xing Shui Chi Homestay** (Wàn Xìng Shuǐ Zhí Mínsù; ☎ 997 2186; 65 Pinghe Village; r from NT1800). Pinghe Village is an abalone processing centre and this homestay is right in the middle of all the action. Three rooms and a living room are available to guests who wish to stay the night.

**Shuntien Inn** (Shùntiān Dà Lǚshè; ☎ 997 1024; 18 Nankang Village; d/tr NT400/1200) OK rooms that aren't too expensive.

**Fupeng Inn** (Fúpéng Lǚshè; ☎ 997 1043; 10 Nankang Village; r NT700-1200) Offers similar-value rooms as the Shuntien.

### Eating

There are small seafood restaurants around the harbour area and in Nankang Village.

### Getting There & Away

**Mandarin Airlines** (Kaohsiung ☎ 07-802 6868; Makung ☎ 921 6966) has flights between Kaohsiung and Chimei (NT1358, 35 minutes) and Chimei and Makung (NT701, 15 minutes).

Boats to Chimei (NT267, three hours) leave from the South Sea Tourism Centre in Makung along the Wang'an-Chimei route.

### Getting Around

Getting around Chimei is easiest on rented motorcycle, available at the harbour for NT300 to NT400 a day. Walking is another possibility, if you have the time and energy.

# Directory

## CONTENTS

## ACCOMMODATION

Taiwan provides the full range of lodgings, from basic and dingy hostels to world-class hotels and resorts. While there are few hidden bargains, generally speaking you get what you pay for.

Unlike in many other countries, accommodation is generally priced per room (or number of beds per room) and not per guest. What's called a 'single' room in other countries (one single bed) is rare; a 'single' in Taiwanese hotel lingo usually means a room with one queen-sized bed, which most couples find spacious enough. 'Double' generally means a double bed, while 'twin' denotes two beds per room. The lesson here: couples travel cheaper per person.

Especially in the off season or during poor weather (eg typhoons), it's pretty easy to find discounts off the hotel rack rate (30% is typical). If you're heading to a resort, the most common time to find discounts is on weekdays, while business hotels most often have weekend discounts. Sometimes you must ask, while at other times the discounts are given automatically.

If you're arriving at Chiang Kai-shek Airport, the tourist information booths at both terminals will be able to make reservations for you, as will the office in Kaohsiung's Hsiaogang International Airport. Some hotels have their own representatives at airports, but they will make reservations for their own hotels only.

Please see the glossary (p354) for a list of hotel terms.

### Camping

Camping is becoming a viable option, especially for travellers with cars.

Occasionally, camping grounds are free, but for the most part you'll have to pay. There are grass camp sites (starting around NT200 per night) and camp sites with wooden platforms on which to pitch your tent (from NT300). Camp sites already pitched with large (eight-person) tents typically go for NT800, although that may be negotiable if there are just a couple of you. Many small towns, particularly in the west, have built camping grounds recently. Most camping grounds offer showers. Camping grounds are not generally found in Taiwanese national parks and forest reserves, although cabins often are.

Remember to prepare for the elements. Higher elevations can get chilly at night and below freezing in winter, but it's important to monitor the weather carefully whatever time of year. See p312 for general weather conditions. And remember to bring bug repellent if you're going to stay by the beach.

The Tourism Bureau (p322) in Taipei has a booklet listing all the private camping grounds in Taiwan by county. It's in Chinese but still useful.

## PRACTICALITIES

### Newspapers

The first three of these daily English-language papers have substantial weekend entertainment listings and can be purchased at bookshops, hotels, convenience stores and kiosks.

- *Taipei Times* (www.taipeitimes.com)
- *China Post* (www.chinapost.com.tw)
- *Taiwan News* (www.etaiwannews.com)
- *International Herald Tribune* (www.iht.com) has worldwide circulation, available at hotels and news dealers.

### Magazines

- *Sinorama* (www.sinorama.com.tw) is an intelligent look at Taiwanese language and culture, sports, finance, history, travel and more, all presented in English and available in Chinese-English versions.
- *Travel in Taiwan* (www.sinica.edu.tw/tit) is an excellent resource for all things cultural and touristy, with calendars of events and colourful coverage.

Also look for regionally published magazines in English or bilingually, for local listings. These include *Taiwan Fun*, *Wow! Taipei* and *Taiwan Lifestyle Magazine*.

### Radio & TV

- International Community Radio Taipei (ICRT) broadcasts in English 24 hours a day at 576MHz (AM) and 100MHz (FM), with a mix of music, news and information. It broadcasts nationwide, but you don't get good reception in many areas.
- Taiwan has three broadcast networks: CTS, CTV and TTV, with shows in Chinese, including dubbed foreign shows. Cable TV is available throughout Taiwan, with the usual options on the international circuit – movie channels, news channels and the like. Some of these are available in English. The exact selection changes from venue to venue.

### Video Systems

- Taiwan uses the NTSC standard for video, the same as in Canada, Japan, Korea, Latin America and the USA. You'll find rental outlets from Blockbuster to mom'n'pop shops. Note that your TV or video player from home might not work in Taiwan.

### Electricity

- Taiwan uses the same electrical standard as the USA and Canada: 110V, 60Hz AC. Electrical sockets have two vertical slots. If you bring appliances from Europe, Australia or Southeast Asia, you'll need an adaptor or transformer. Some buildings have outlets for 220V plugs; however, these are intended for air conditioners.

### Weights & Measures

- Taiwan uses the metric system (see the conversion chart on the inside front cover) alongside ancient Chinese weights and measures. When Taiwanese measure floor space, for example, the unit of measure is the *ping* (approximately 1.82 sq metres). Fruit and vegetables are likely to be sold by the catty (*jīn*, 600g), while teas and herbal medicines are sold by the tael (*liǎng*, 37.5g).

## Homestays

On an informal basis, local people have been known to rent rooms (*mínsù*) in their homes, but you'll probably have to ask around. It's most likely that you'll find such accommodation in resort areas (where hotels tend to book up) or in aboriginal villages.

## Hostels

The only real bargain accommodation is a youth hostel dormitory (*tuán tǐ fáng*). The most basic dorm bed will cost approximately NT250 per night. Private rooms, when available, are usually tiny but can be had for about NT500. At hostels and other budget options you can often arrange for weekly or monthly rates.

While some Taiwanese hostels are affiliated with Hostelling International (and offer discounts accordingly for cardholders), many are not. Of these others, you may not be able to find any signage out front – some are technically illegal.

Hostels generally have laundry and simple cooking facilities (although the latter have been scaled back in recent years thanks to careless use by some residents), and usually there is a television, occasionally a computer hook-up and a room for socialising. The disadvantage is that hostels can be drab and smelly, and they are often crowded.

## Hotels

There's a great range of options among hotels (*fàndiàn* or *dàfàndiàn*). Starting at about NT550 per night, you can have a private room in a very basic budget hotel. For that price you're likely to find threadbare accommodation and occasional mouldy odours, but private bath, TV and phone are generally included. A shower curtain may or may not be part of the deal. Don't count on being able to make yourself understood in English. Since most Taiwanese bathe at night rather than in the morning, you may find the hot water turned on at night only at budget lodgings.

At mid-range hotels (NT1000 to NT4000 per night), you're likely to find one or more restaurants on site, Internet hook-ups (in room or shared use, in Taipei, at least), and a pitcher of hot water and some tea. Private bathrooms include shower (or bathtub with shower) and shower curtain. Décor can range from a little dated to very up-to-date. Unless you're looking for a luxury experience, most travellers will feel comfortable here. In the big cities usually at least one or two staff members speak some English, but don't expect it elsewhere. Bed and breakfasts are also gaining popularity in the countryside.

The big cities, especially Taipei, abound with international-standard top-end hotels. Typical amenities include business centres, English-speaking staff, concierge services, spa and/or fitness centre, massage services and a sense of style. In this book, 'top end' starts at NT4000 per night, though rack rates at big-city hotels can easily be double that.

Hot-spring hotels can be a special treat. These resorts commonly have both public and private baths (some quite fancy) with hot-spring water pumped in from some nearby source. It's not uncommon to have other services, such as massage, restaurants or spa treatments. Also, you needn't just be an overnight guest. Many hot-spring hotels rent rooms for up to two hours; they're cleaned after each use.

Note that if you're phoning someone at a hotel and do not speak Chinese, you may run into trouble at all but the high-end hotels as staff may not recognise the guest's name. Hint: speak clearly, and if the last name does not work, try the first name (or even nickname). If you have the room number, all the better.

## Rental Accommodation

If you're going to be in Taiwan for an extended period, getting your own place makes sense. Your employer may be able to help you set something up.

English-language newspapers carry rental listings, though these are usually luxury accommodation catering to expats on expense accounts. If you're looking for an upscale or even good mid-range apartment, it's useful to hire an agent. Look in the papers for numbers. Usually the agent charges a fee of half a month's rent.

For less-expensive accommodation, check out websites catering to the foreign community (see p11), especially if you're looking for an English-speaking landlord or roommates, or enlist the help of a Chinese-speaking friend to peruse the Chinese-language papers. You might also just choose an area where you'd like to live and look for signs tacked up (eg on telephone poles). The website www.tmm.org .tw is in Chinese but provides great listings of mid- to low-range accommodation by area and price in Taipei.

Studio apartments in Taipei generally range from NT5000 to NT10,000 per month, while a small three-bedroom might go for NT20,000. In an upper-crust neighbourhood such as Tianmu, rents can easily be double that. Outside of Taipei, a rental flat might start at NT3000. Thanks to a glut of apartments from years of overbuilding, negotiation is usually possible. One good approach is to say that you really like the place but can only afford (however much) right now.

A word of caution: some landlords assume that foreigners are irresponsible, loud and made of money. It's best to convince the landlord that you are none of the above – perhaps a Chinese-speaking friend can help with this too.

## Temple Stays

While a number of temples offer temple stays, information is not easy to come by (even for Chinese people). Two temples that offer stays are Shitoushan (p142) and Foguangshan (p257); Foguangshan has English-speaking staff. The accommodation at the temples is surprisingly good and the vegetarian meals delicious. Chung Tai Chan Temple (p220) in Puli offers stays during meditation retreats and is probably the best place in Taiwan to get a primer on Buddhist thought, history and art in English. The temple is eager to receive visitors.

## ACTIVITIES

Although Taiwan ranks among the world's most densely populated areas, opportunities for outdoor activities abound. For starters, 40% of the land is mountainous; there are dozens of peaks topping 3000m. Along the coastline are diving, surfing, snorkelling and sailing opportunities.

The tourist office's *Fun of Nature* brochure highlights all the outdoor activities the island offers and about 30 clubs (with address and phone numbers) for the various activities. Also check out **Taiwan Outdoor Adventure Sports** (www.toasports.com/index.php).

## Diving & Snorkelling

See Kenting National Park (p264), Green Island (p189), Penghu (p295) and Little Liuchiu Island (p262) for diving and snorkelling possibilities. A good website is www .homestead.com/expatdivers.

## Golf

Golf driving ranges are everywhere, even in small towns, and all major cities have golf courses, though they are often in the suburbs as land is expensive. A lot of golf courses are illegally built and controversial due to runoff from pesticides and fertilizers. The official Republic of China (ROC) golf site (www.rocgolf.com.tw/index.php) includes listings of golf courses with addresses and phone numbers.

## Hiking

Taiwan is developing into a haven for hikers of all levels. The tallest peak in northeast Asia is here (Yushan, 3952m), and there are plenty of other hills for you to wander. All three major cities – Taipei, Kaohsiung and Taichung – have mountains and trails either within the city limits or just outside.

High alpine trails are already well developed, with mountain huts along major routes. The low-altitude (under 2000m) **National Trail System** (http://trail.forest.gov.tw/index .asp) was in progress as we went to press, with billions of NT going towards development of new trails. Themes include historic, coastal and countryside trails. The forest reserve website (http://recreate.forest.gov .tw) lists about 17 forest reserves around the island, each with details of flora and fauna, park history, trails and facilities.

You can pick up *A Hiking Guide to Taiwan* by long-time Taiwan resident Lyndon Punt. If you're planning to stay around Taipei only, pick up either volume of *Taipei Day Trips* by Richard Saunders.

See also p313 for important safety notes.

## Hot Springs

The diversity of Taiwan's hot springs is amazing. You need not even leave Taipei County, with springs a short ride from the city centre in Beitou (p107), Wulai (p150) and Yangmingshan (p110). Chihpen Hot Springs (p187) in Taitung are arguably Taiwan's most famous, while Chaojih (p190) on Green Island offers one-of-a-kind salt-water springs. Taian Hot Springs (p142) are also well-regarded. Don't forget the *cold* springs in Suao (p162). But these are just an overview – there are hundreds of bathing opportunities.

## Mountaineering

Permits are required if you want to hike in certain remote mountain areas. The permit requirements are the same for foreigners as for Taiwanese nationals. Class A mountain permits are required for restricted high-mountain areas, which must be obtained before setting out at, for example, the **Taiwan Provincial Police** (Map pp72-3; ☎ 02-2321 9011; 7 Zhongxiao E Rd, Sec 1, Taipei) or the **Yushan National Park headquarters** ( ☎ 049-277 3121; 300 Zhongshan Rd, Sec 1, Shiuli, Nantou County). Climbing groups are supposed to consist of at least three people, and must also include a certified guide.

A class B permit is required for less restricted areas; pick these up at local police stations.

Usually people travel with a club, and the club handles permits for you.

## Surfing

Dude, like, we bet you had no idea that you could surf Taiwan. But the bodacious – uh, we mean 'beautiful' – isle has some bitchin' surfing beaches in the north and west, and Taipei's surfers consider Kenting (p264) totally rad.

Surfing is possible on the Penghu Islands – especially windsurfing in winter. Makung (p296) holds international windsurfing competitions in November.

## Whale-Watching

We hesitate to recommend whale-watching tours as many operators have reputations as being less than scrupulous about respecting wildlife. Contact the **North East Coast Scenic Area Administration** ( ☎ 02-2499 1115) or the **Tali Visitor Centre** ( ☎ 03-978 0727) for more information about tours.

## White-Water Rafting

See p179 for information about rafting along the Hsiukuluan River; 24km of twists and turns near Hualien, or inquire in Kaohsiung for rafting operators in nearby Laonong (p258).

## BUSINESS HOURS

Standard hours are as follows:
**Banks** ( 🕑 9.30am-3.30pm Mon-Fri)
**Convenience stores** ( 🕑 24hr)
**Department stores** ( 🕑 11am-9.30pm)
**Government offices** ( 🕑 8.30am-noon & 1.30-5.30pm)
**Museums** ( 🕑 9am-5pm, closed Monday)
**Night markets** ( 🕑 6-10.30pm)
**Offices** ( 🕑 9am-5pm Mon-Fri)
**Post Offices** ( 🕑 8am-5pm Mon-Fri)
**Restaurants** ( 🕑 11.30am-2pm & 5-9pm)
**Shops** ( 🕑 10am-9pm)
**Supermarkets** ( 🕑 To at least 8pm, sometimes 24hr)

## CHILDREN

The Taiwanese are very welcoming, and doubly so when it comes to children. If you're travelling with kids, they will probably attract a lot of positive attention (assuming they're well behaved, of course!).

The website www.parentpages.net has all kinds of forums on children in Taiwan, from birthing and midwifery to raising kids to keeping them amused.

Lonely Planet's *Travel with Children* is a useful book that prepares you for the joys and pitfalls of travelling with the little ones.

### Practicalities

You're not likely to find high chairs or booster seats for kids at lower-end restaurants, but you may well find them at more expensive places. On the other hand, stands and outdoor markets tend to be very informal. Upper-end restaurants may have set menus for families, or even kids' menus. You can generally find Western baby formula and baby foods at supermarkets.

If you're travelling by car, note that under a law enacted in 2004 children under four years of age and weighing less than 18kg must be in car safety seats. Parents who ignore the law can be fined NT500. This law does not apply to taxis, and don't expect taxis to have child safety seats.

If you need a nanny, you can go through the informal network to find one. Typically, the nanny will be from the Philippines, and costs will run from NT20,000 per month to NT35,000, the latter for an upscale location such as Tianmu in Taipei.

If you find that Taiwanese get too touchy-feely with your baby for your comfort, a good solution is to use a baby sling.

See also p54 for information on dining out with children in Taiwan.

## Sights & Activities

In general Taiwan is a great place for active families.

The cities offer courses from martial arts to painting to yo-yoing, opera and dance. The renowned Cloud Gate Dance Theatre (p41) runs children's dance programmes in the north.

Here are some suggestions for sights around the island that children will enjoy.

**Pinglin** (p148) – cycling, swimming, camping and nature observation.

**Kenting** (p264) – beach activities, aquatic museum and forest parks.

**Jiji Small Rail Line** (p211) – cycling and light walking.

**Northeast Coast National Scenic Area** (p125) – saltwater swimming pools, sea-life displays and sandy beaches perfect for kids.

**Pingxi Branch Rail Line** (p125) – little kids can sit right up front of the train and play with real trains and self-propelled trolleys at the stations.

**Sanyi** (p146) – walk along abandoned rail tracks and go through 1km-long tunnels.

## CLIMATE CHARTS

For such a small place, Taiwan has a great variety of climates. Plus, as the island sits at the confluence of various trade winds, weather is known to change frequently, especially in late autumn and winter.

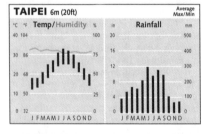

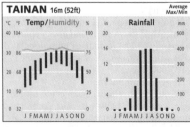

The island can be divided into essentially three climate zones: the north and east coasts (including Taipei), the central mountains and the southwest coast.

Daily temperatures in Taipei can be about 35°C in summer but rarely go below 12°C in winter. Very cold weather and snow are a function of elevation: temperatures can drop precipitously as you move from sea level to 2000m, and above 3000m you're likely to find snow.

Taiwan's most agreeable weather is in autumn, specifically October and November – it's the best time of year in Taipei. Winter in the north and on the east coast tends to be overcast and occasionally chilly with frequent drizzle – although more rain actually falls in the summer, it may not feel like it! Spring is warm and mild, but it is known for frequent rain (the locals poetically call it 'plum rain'). Spring is also notorious for the sand storms that blow in from China. These foul the air and people are advised to stay indoors.

Summers are hot and humid with frequent afternoon thunderstorms, while winter is dry and pleasantly cool. The mountains are the island's rainiest region, particularly in summer when rains fall in short thundershowers, especially in the mid-afternoon. In winter, the west side of the mountains tends to be drier than the east side.

If you're travelling to Kinmen or Matsu in winter, be prepared for cold, and don't be surprised if your flight or ferry is cancelled because of inclement weather. Winter winds in the Penghu Islands can be severe. See p9 for information on the best times to travel.

## COURSES

In addition to the following, contact the **Community Services Centre** (Map p82; ☎ 02-2836 8134; www.community.com.tw) in Taipei for updates on various courses available for visitors and expats.

### Calligraphy

Chinese-language schools (private and university) often have courses on calligraphy, painting and other Chinese arts. Inquire at the school or check one of the foreigner chat sites (www.forumosa.com or www.tealit.com) for recommendations.

You can also post ads on these websites if you are looking for a private teacher.

## Meditation

There are four main Buddhist associations in Taiwan: Tzu Chi, Fo Guang Shan, Dharma Drum and Chung Tai Chan. **Dharma Drum** (www.dharmadrum.org/ddmevent/chan_meditation/index .htm) has a branch in Taipei, offering meditation classes in English. **Chung Tai Chan** (ctworld@ms16.hinet.net) offers weekly meditation classes in Puli (p220) in English. Both groups offer weekend and week-long retreats at various times.

## Taichi

There are many schools in the cities offering courses on taichi. Again, it is best to go to one of the foreign websites or Chinese schools and ask for recommendations.

## CUSTOMS

Customs laws permit the duty-free importation of 200 cigarettes, 25 cigars or 450g of tobacco, one bottle of liquor (up to one litre), a 'reasonable' quantity of perfume and goods valued at up to NT20,000 (NT10,000 for passengers under 20 years of age).

And to quote a sign at Chiang Kai-shek Airport: 'Drug trafficking is punishable by death in the ROC'.

## DANGERS & ANNOYANCES
### Dodgy Dealings

Some troubles have been reported with illegal 'barber shops', which can be fronts for prostitution and worse. If it looks less than legit, you'd be advised to stay away.

### Food & Drink

Travellers are advised not to drink water poured directly from the tap (though it's fine to brush your teeth with). In most places you will be served water that has been boiled, which is fine to drink, and tea and bottled drinks, including water, are widely available. In general, look for plastic seal wraps, as water can sometimes be contaminated in shipping.

Avoid cafeteria-style restaurants after the lunch or dinner rush. Food can go bad if it's been sitting for a while.

While Taiwanese authorities have been shutting down polluted agricultural fields, agricultural products from mainland China, such as dried fruit and vegetables, and seafood are reputed to contain dangerous levels of pollutants, including antibiotics. Also stay away from brightly coloured local snacks (including dried fruit) as they are often bleached and full of preservatives. Speciality stores and many supermarkets in major cities sell organic produce.

### Health

If there's a SARS scare on (the last was winter 2003–04), you will be screened upon entry to virtually any public facility by means of an infrared thermometer. Some of the machines are large enough to walk through, while others are palm-sized gadgets that, for example, a hotel doorman will hold up to your forehead. If your temperature is above 38.3°C, you won't be allowed into the establishment.

### Natural Dangers

It can be extremely dangerous to hike in the mountains. Afternoon fogs are common, as are thundershowers, which can leave you soaked and chilled. There are numerous species of poisonous snake around the island, leeches and poisonous plants are problems around 1500m to 2000m, and in summer wasps sometimes attack. Although the island is small, it is easy to get lost. The forest is extremely thick in places, and trails are quickly overgrown. Never leave the trail and don't hike trails you don't know unless they are wide and clear. Prepare rain gear if you are going to be out for a few hours, and carry lots of water.

Many foreigners at first dismiss concerns about swimming too far from shore. There is no continental shelf here, meaning that the deep blue sea is just offshore, and dangerous undercurrents and riptides flow around the island. General advice: do not go out farther than you can stand on your tiptoes.

### Nightlife

Men should be careful when out at clubs. Taiwanese men can be very protective of any female in their group, even if there's

---

**ONLY-IN-TAIWAN ANNOYANCE**

Scooters must park on the footpath and tend to block pedestrian ways.

> **MIND THE DOORS!**
>
> If you're used to sliding doors that open when you're 1m or more away, note that it's different here, particularly in Taipei. Often you have to stand directly in front of the door before it will open.

no boyfriend-girlfriend relationship. Be careful about approaching a woman who is with a guy (or accepting her advances). Gangsters hang out at clubs and can be especially vicious. Also, note that Taiwanese don't fight alone.

Police have been known to raid clubs, looking for illegal drugs. Often they simply haul everyone down to the station and ask for urine samples. The police are not supposed to do this without a warrant and probable cause, but that may not stop zealous police chiefs.

Foreign victims of crime are not likely to get much help from the police.

### Street Crime & Theft

In terms of street crime, Taiwan is one of the safer places in Asia, although residential burglaries do happen. If you're staying in a youth hostel or campground, be sure to lock up your belongings securely as most of these facilities are open to the public. Sadly, your fellow travellers may pose more of a threat than any Taiwanese.

Most mid-range and top-end hotels have safes or other facilities to guard your valuables. And if you're concerned about theft, use travellers cheques.

See also p323 for more advice to women travellers.

## DISABLED TRAVELLERS

While Taipei is slowly modernising its facilities for the disabled (new buildings must now meet a building code), disabled travellers may be dismayed that the city was not built with them in mind. Footpaths are uneven, often requiring pedestrians to step up or down stairs in the middle of a block. Additionally, some kerbs are very steep, meaning that it may be a longer way up and down than you're used to. Other cities in Taiwan are not much different, and public transport is not well equipped with wheelchair access.

On the other hand, disabled parking is usually available and respected.

## DISCOUNT CARDS

Student cards are widely used for public transport as well as museums, (some) movie tickets and performances at public theatres. However, foreign student cards are not likely to be accepted. Foreigners studying Chinese can get student cards from their school, and these will be accepted.

Children's discounts usually go by height rather than age (eg discounts for children under 110cm).

## EMBASSIES & CONSULATES

Because of the 'One China Policy' adopted by the mainland, only about 20 countries and the Holy See have full diplomatic relations with Taiwan. If you're from Burkina Faso, the Dominican Republic, the Solomon Islands or the like, you're represented by a proper embassy in Taipei. Otherwise, you're likely to be represented by an office calling itself something to do with trade and/or culture. 'Institute' figures in the name of many of these offices.

Overseas, Taiwan is represented by consular, information and trade offices. Both Taiwanese legations abroad and foreign legations in Taiwan serve the same functions as embassies or consulates would elsewhere: services to their own nationals, visa processing, trade promotion and cultural programmes.

For a complete list of embassies and trade offices (both Taiwanese overseas and foreign offices in Taiwan), visit the Ministry of Foreign Affairs website (www.mofa.gov.tw).

### Taiwanese Foreign Legations

Owing to China's objections, many countries do not permit even the word 'Taiwan' to be used in the names of Taiwan's overseas legations, but you can try under 'Taipei'. A typical name is 'TECO' (Taipei Economic and Cultural Offices).

**Australia** (Taipei Economic & Cultural Office; www.teco.org.au) Canberra ( ☎ 02-6273 3344; unit 8, Tourism House, 40 Blackall St, Barton, ACT 2600) Melbourne ( ☎ 03-9650 8611; level 46, 80 Collins St, Melbourne, VIC 3000) Sydney ( ☎ 02-9223 3233; ste 1902, MLC Centre, King St, Sydney, NSW 2000)

**Canada** Ottawa ( ☎ 613-231 5080; 45 O'Connor St, ste 1960, Ottawa) Toronto ( ☎ 416-369 9030; 151 Yonge St,

ste 1202, Toronto, Ontario M5C 2W7) Vancouver ( ☎ 604-689 4111; 2008, Cathedral Pl, 925 West Georgia St, Vancouver, BC V6C 3L2)
**France** Paris (Bureau de Representation de Taipei en France; ☎ 01 44 39 88 30; 78 rue de l'Université, 75007 Paris)
**Germany** Berlin (Taipeh Vertretung in der Bundesrepublik Deutschland; ☎ 030-203 610; Markgrafenstrasse 35, 10117 Berlin)
**Hong Kong** (Chung Hwa Travel Service; ☎ 852-2525 8315; 40th fl, Tower 1, Lippo Centre, 89 Queensway)
**India** Delhi (Taipei Economic & Cultural Centre; ☎ 011-5166 2700; 12 Paschimi Marg, Vasant Vihar, New Delhi 110057)
**Ireland** Dublin (Taipei Representative Office; ☎ 01-678 5413; 8 Lower Hatch St, Dublin 2)
**Japan** Tokyo (Taipei Economic & Cultural Representative Office; ☎ 03-3280 7811; 20-2, Shirokanedai 5-chome, Minato-ku, Tokyo 108-0071)
**Netherlands** The Hague (Taipei Representative Office; ☎ 070-346 9438; Van Stolkweg 23, 2585 JM, Den Haag)
**New Zealand** Wellington (Taipei Economic & Cultural Office; ☎ 04-473 6474; Information Division, level 21, 105-109 The Terrace, Wellington)
**South Africa** Pretoria (Taipei Liaison Office; ☎ 012-430 6071; 1147 Schoeman St, Hatfield, Pretoria)
**South Korea** Seoul (Taipei Mission; ☎ 02-399 2767; 6th fl, Kwang Hwa Moon Bldg, 211 Sejong-ro, Chongro-ku, Seoul 110-050)
**Thailand** Bangkok (Taipei Economic & Cultural Office; ☎ 02-670 0200; 20th fl, Empire Tower, 195 South Sathorn Rd, Yannawa, Bangkok 10120)
**UK** London (Taipei Representative Office; ☎ 020-7881 2650; 50 Grosvenor Gardens, London SWIW OEB)
**USA** (Taipei Economic & Cultural Representative Office; www.teco-us.org) Washington ( ☎ 202-895 1800; www.tecro.org; 4201 Wisconsin Av, NW, Washington, DC 20016) Chicago ( ☎ 312-616 0100; 180 N Stetson Ave, 57th & 58th fl, Chicago, IL 60601) Los Angeles ( ☎ 213-389 1215; 3731 Wilshire Blvd, ste 700, Los Angeles, CA 90010) New York ( ☎ 212-317 7300; 885 2nd Ave, 47th fl, New York, NY 10017) San Francisco ( ☎ 415-362 7680; 555 Montgomery St, ste 501, San Francisco, CA 94111)

## Foreign Legations in Taiwan

All addresses are in Taipei unless otherwise indicated.
**Australia** (Australia Commerce & Industry Office; ☎ 02-8725 4100; www.australia.org.tw; ste 2612, International Trade Building, 333 Keelung Rd, Sec 1)
**Canada** (Canadian Trade Office in Taipei; ☎ 02-2544 3000; www.canada.org.tw; 13th fl, 365 Fuxing N Rd)
**France** (French Institute; Institut Français de Taipei; ☎ 02-2545 6061; www.fi-taipei.org; 10th fl & 14th fl, 205 Dunhua N Rd)

**Germany** (German Institute; Deutsches Institut; ☎ 02-2501 6188; 4th fl, 2 Minsheng E Rd, Sec 3)
**India** (India-Taipei Association; ☎ 02-2757 6112; 20F, 333 Keelung Rd, Sec 1)
**Ireland** (Irish Institute; ☎ 02-2725 1691; 7B-09, Taiwan World Trade Centre Building, 5 Xinyi Rd, Sec 5)
**Japan** (Interchange Association; ☎ 02-2713 8000; www.japan-taipei.org.tw; 28 Ching Cheng St)
**Netherlands** (Netherlands Trade & Investment Office; ☎ 02-2713 5760; www.ntio.org.tw; 5th fl, 133 Minsheng E Rd, Sec 3)
**New Zealand** (New Zealand Commerce & Industry Office; ☎ 02-2757 6725; 25th fl, 333 Keelung Rd, Sec 1)
**South Africa** (South Africa Liaison Office; ☎ 02-2715 3251; 13th fl, 205 Dunhua N Rd)
**South Korea** (South Korea Mission; ☎ 02-2758 8320; Room 1506, International Trade Bldg, 333 Keelung Rd, Sec 1)
**Thailand** (Thailand Trade & Economic Office; ☎ 02-2712 1882; 7th fl, 150 Fuxing N Rd)
**United Kingdom** (British Trade & Cultural Office; ☎ 02-2322 4242; 9th fl, 99 Renai Rd, Sec 2)
**USA** (American Institute in Taiwan; www.ait.org.tw; Taipei ☎ 02-2709 2000; 7 Lane 134, Xinyi Rd, Sec 3; Kaohsiung ☎ 07-238 7744; 5th fl, 2 Chungcheng Rd, Sec 3)

## FESTIVALS & EVENTS

Dates vary, so we've listed them here by month.
### FEBRUARY
**Lantern Festival** (p317)

### APRIL
**Taiwan Tea Expo** (p148) Held in Pinglin, Taipei County, it celebrates tea, tea drinking, and all the cultural displays, such as pottery, song and dance, that have developed over the years. A good time to sample teas and tea products from all over Taiwan.

### MAY
**Sanyi Woodcarving Festival** (p147) In Taiwan's woodcarving capital, this festival celebrates the craft that employs over half the town. Highlights include on-the-spot carving contests, Hakka food tasting and ice-sculpting.

### JUNE
**Dragon Boat Festival** (p317)

### JULY–AUGUST
**Ilan International Children's Folklore & Folkgame Festival** (p134) Top children's performers and performing troupes are brought in to Lodong from around the world. In addition, there are exhibits of toys and games, and sales of handmade toys.

## AUGUST

**Festival of Austronesian Cultures** (p181) In Taitung County, a stronghold for aboriginal culture in Taiwan. Good for purchasing native handicrafts.

**Keelung Ghost Festival** (p125) Each year a different Keelung clan is chosen to sponsor the events. Highlights include folk-art performances, the opening of the gates of hell and the release of burning water lanterns. Lasts the entire seventh lunar month.

## OCTOBER

**Hualien International Stone Sculpture Festival** (p165) Features the stonework of local and international artists, and folk performances.

**Yingge Ceramics Festival** (p152) Yingge is an interesting place to visit, though some visitors carp that there's nothing special to recommend a festival visit over nonfestival times.

## FOOD

This book classifies budget meals as under NT120, mid-range NT120 to NT400 and top end NT400 and up. See the Food & Drink chapter (p48) and local listings for more on Taiwan's excellent local food and eating scene.

## GAY & LESBIAN TRAVELLERS

In Taiwan's patriarchal, family-oriented society there is still a stigma attached to homosexuality, though Taiwanese gays and lesbians have made great strides towards openness and equality, particularly since the end of martial law. The island's big cities have some of the best gay life in the Chinese-speaking world. In 1997 Taipei held Taiwan's first gay-pride festival in no less a venue than the 2-28 Peace Park, and the gay community has never looked back. The Chinese-speaking world's first gay-pride parade was held in Taipei in 2003, although many marchers wore masks.

Unlike in other east Asian countries, gay and lesbian visitors will likely find their Taiwanese hosts friendly and welcoming. Taipei in particular has a number of bars and clubs, as well as shopping, salons, saunas and other gay-friendly venues. You'll find similar venues, though in far smaller numbers, in other cities as well. One good website with updated information is www .utopia-asia.com/tipstaiw.htm.

For books and films about gay life in Taiwan, see p43; see also the Gay & Lesbian Taipei boxed text (p88).

## Legal Issues

Taiwan's official stance towards gays and lesbians may be considered among the most progressive in east Asia. There is no sodomy law to penalise homosexuality, in 2002 the military lifted its ban on homosexuals and in 2003 the ROC government announced plans to legalise same-sex marriage. While this would make Taiwan the first place in east Asia to do so, the realisation may be a long time away.

However, the relationship between Taiwan's homosexual community and its police forces has been one of simmering tension over the years.

## HOLIDAYS

Taiwanese holidays are set according to either the Western calendar or the Chinese lunar calendar. Holidays in the lunar calendar fall at different times each year in the Western calendar, although the range is usually within a month. Bad times to travel are Chinese New Year, winter holidays for students (three weeks around Chinese New Year), Tomb Sweep Day, Dragon Boat Festival, summer weekends and summer holidays (July to August) and Moon Festival.

### Western Calendar Holidays

## JANUARY

**Founding Day** (Yuándàn; 1 Jan) Commemorates the founding of the ROC back in 1911. Businesses and schools close, and many remain closed on 2 January.

## FEBRUARY

**2-28** (Èrèrbā; 28 Feb) This holiday recollects events of 28 February 1947, when political dissent led to the massacre of thousands of Taiwanese. Instituted in 1997 at the behest of the DPP, but without universal public support.

## APRIL

**Tomb Sweep Day** (Qīng Míng Jié; 5 Apr or 4 Apr on leap years) Families return to the graves of their ancestors to clean them as a gesture of respect. Expect to see lots of ghost money being burned around the island. Bank holiday.

## SEPTEMBER

**Teachers' Day** (Jiàoshī Jié; 28 Sep) Originally the birthday of Confucius, now the holiday honours all teachers. Confucian temples stage ceremonies all day – a good example is Taipei's Confucius Temple (p75) – and, although people don't get the day off, the elaborate ceremonies are not to be missed. Purchase your tickets well in advance.

### OCTOBER

**National Day** (Shuāngshí Jié; 10 Oct) Sometimes called 'Double 10th Day' after its date, this day is marked by military parades, fireworks and beach parties. Bank holiday.

### DECEMBER

**Constitution Day** (Guāngfù Jié; 25 Dec) Although it was a holiday in Taiwan long before Christmas was a significant presence here, you can guess which holiday has taken over the national psyche. Although it's not a national day off, the night of the 24th can be party time.

## Lunar Year Holidays

### JANUARY–FEBRUARY

**Chinese (Lunar) New Year** (lunar date: first day of the first month) The year's most important festival is marked by special banquets and family gatherings, red envelopes of money are given as gifts and it's common for people to wear new clothes. While it's colourful, particularly during reparation season, visitors might consider staying away since many businesses and sights close for extended periods.

### FEBRUARY

**Lantern Festival** (lunar date: 15th day of the first month) Festivities vary around the country from fireworks to paper lanterns launched into the sky, but all draw large crowds. In Taipei and Kaohsiung, the festival lasts three to five days and has a different theme each year. Thousands of paper lanterns are handed out to the public, and there are dragon and lion dances, art shows, ceremonial activities and a general combining of tradition and technology. One highlight in the north is the release of thousands of sky lanterns into the air around Pingxi (p130).

### APRIL–MAY

**Birth of Matsu** (lunar date: 23rd day of third month) The birth of the Goddess of the Sea and protector of seafarers and fishermen (p276) is commemorated at several hundred temples island-wide. It's a time of (week-long) pilgrimages, puppetry, parades and dragon and lion dances. This festival is becoming more and more important every year.

### JUNE

**Dragon Boat Festival** (lunar date: fifth day of fifth month) One of the most important Chinese holidays, photogenic and colourful. The highlight is races in which long, sleek boats, decorated like dragons compete in remembrance of the suicide drowning of the poet Chu Yuan. Some of the best places to see them include Lugang (p207; where Dragon Boat Festival is part of a four-day folk festival), Keelung (p125) and Jiaoshi (p134). *Jungzi*, sticky-rice dumplings wrapped in leaves, are a culinary treat not to miss. A national holiday.

### SEPTEMBER–OCTOBER

**Moon Festival** (lunar date: 15th day of eight month) Taiwanese fill large parks (eg Taipei's Chiang Kai-shek Memorial Hall and Sun Yat-sen Memorial Hall) to celebrate the moon that is considered the year's brightest and fullest. A good time to sample tasty moon cakes. A national holiday.

## INSURANCE

A travel-insurance policy to cover theft, loss and medical problems is a good idea. There is a wide variety of policies available, so check the small print. Some things to watch out for:

Some policies specifically exclude 'dangerous activities', which can include scuba diving, motorcycling and even trekking.

A locally acquired motorcycle licence is not valid under some policies.

Some policies pay doctors or hospitals directly rather than you having to pay on the spot and claim later. If you have to claim later, make sure you keep all documentation.

Some policies ask you to call (reverse charges) a centre in your home country where an immediate assessment of your problem is made.

Check whether the policy covers ambulances or an emergency flight home.

For health insurance advice, see p335. For details on car insurance, see p332.

## INTERNET ACCESS

Taiwan is quite cyber-savvy, and if you are carrying your own laptop youll be able to connect your computer modem to the telephone line in virtually any hotel room. Check with your Internet service provider (ISP) for the local access number(s).

Many mid-range and top-end hotels, especially in the big cities, offer ADSL high-speed

---

**TAIWANESE YEARS**

While Taiwanese are familiar with the worldwide system and Chinese systems for numbering the years, Taiwan also has a unique system beginning with the year that the ROC was founded. That was 1911 in the Western calendar, or Year 0 for Taiwan. Thus 2005 will be Year 94 of the ROC. Under the Taiwanese system, 30 June 2005 would be written 94/06/30.

Internet connections for laptops. Some of these carry hefty charges (up to NT300 per day), while others include ADSL service in the room rate. Even some hostels have been known to offer an ADSL connection, although you'll need to share it.

If you're not carrying a computer with you, a number of hotels offer computers for guest use, either free of charge or in a business centre, though the latter are typically steep in price. This book denotes hotels with this type of service with the icon ▣.

There are a few cybercafés (though not as many as in some countries), and libraries are excellent places to access the Internet; access is free of charge and for a specific block of time, but you'll want to sign up early in the day or be prepared to wait in case the scheduled user does not show up. Tourist offices will sometimes let you use their computers.

For information about Taiwan on the web, see p11.

## LEGAL MATTERS

Don't even think of messing with illegal drugs in Taiwan; this includes marijuana. Smuggling can carry the death penalty and even possession can get you busted.

A common problem for foreigners is working illegally. For most Westerners, this means a fine or, at worst, a visa suspension and an order to leave the country.

Under Taiwanese law, knowingly transmitting HIV to another person is punishable by up to seven years in prison. This law also allows for mandatory testing of members of high-risk groups, namely sexual partners of HIV carriers and intravenous drug users, as well as foreigners who come to work (required for an Alien Resident Certificate; ARC).

---

**LEGAL AGE**

▨ Voting: 20

▨ Driving: 18

▨ Military conscription: 18, but most do it after their university studies

▨ Consumption of alcohol: 18

▨ Consensual sex (heterosexual or homosexual): 16

---

If you're detained by the police, you should get in touch with your country's legation in Taiwan. Even if it can't provide any direct aid, it can at least offer legal advice and notify your family.

If you are arrested, you have the right to remain silent and to request an attorney, although authorities are under no obligation to provide an attorney. You also have the right to refuse to sign any document. In most cases, a suspect cannot be detained for more than 24 hours without a warrant from a judge – notable exceptions are those with visa violations.

## MAPS

The best road map (in Chinese) is *Formosa Complete Road Atlas* by Sunriver (two volumes, about NT2000 each). However, a simple fold-out map (in English) will suffice for most purposes. City and county maps are available at tourist offices, although there are no great maps of outlying islands such as Kinmen.

Any Caves or Eslite bookshop should have English maps of Taiwan and the major cities. Often these maps include cultural and culinary highlights.

See local listings for useful local maps.

Many forest reserves and parks have maps and brochures (in English), available either at the gate or at the tourist office inside. The **Department of Land Administration** (www .land.moi.gov.tw) has downloadable 1:25,000 topographic maps.

A compass can be useful if you're going to be travelling on country roads; sometimes you may not see a road sign for kilometres.

## MONEY

Taiwan's currency is the New Taiwanese Dollar (NT). Bills come in denominations of NT50, NT100, NT500 and NT1000, while coins come in units of NT1, NT5, NT10, NT20 and NT50. One Taiwanese dollar is divided into 100 cents, but in practicality cents are not used. If someone's quoting a price to you, it will sound like '120NT'.

See the inside cover for exchange rates with key currencies.

Unlike some other countries in Asia, Taiwan uses the local currency exclusively.

Foreigners can open Taiwanese bank accounts even without an ARC. See p10 for information on costs.

## ATMs

ATMs are the easiest way to withdraw cash from your home account. Many ATMs at banks around the country carry the logos for international systems such as Accel, Cirrus, Interlink, Plus and Star. Keep in mind that there may be limits on the amount of cash that can be withdrawn per transaction or per day, and that your home financial institution may charge a fee on withdrawals from other banks.

ATMs with international facilities are easiest to find in the big cities, including at 7-Eleven convenience stores (with English-language option) and McDonald's. Banks island-wide charge a NT7 fee per withdrawal for all but their own customers.

## Cash

Nothing beats cash for convenience – or for risk if it's lost or stolen. For peace of mind, keep any extra cash in the safe deposit box at your hotel. If you're carrying foreign cash to exchange, the most widely accepted currency is US dollars.

## Credit Cards

Credit cards are widely accepted now compared to a few years ago. Most hotels (even many budget hotels) take credit cards. Small stalls or food joints never take credit cards. Most mid-range to top-end restaurants do, but always check before you decide to eat.

## Moneychangers

Private moneychangers do not proliferate in Taiwan like they do elsewhere. Hotels will change money for their guests, but banks are the most common option.

## Tipping

Tipping is not customary in restaurants or taxis (but is still appreciated). However, if a porter carries your bag in a hotel or airport, a tip of NT50 is considered courteous, and often a service charge is added to the bill at top-end hotels and mid-range restaurants.

## Travellers Cheques

As with cash, it's best if your travellers cheques are in US dollars. You get a slightly better rate on exchange, but that can be cancelled out by commissions so check carefully before you change money.

## POST

Taiwan's postal system is efficient and fast. Domestic letters generally arrive within two days, and about seven days to destinations in North America and Europe; fewer to Hong Kong or Japan. Stamps can be purchased at post offices and convenience stores.

Main post offices in the big cities have poste restante services (see city listings). Mail should be addressed to GPO Poste Restante, with the city name. Generally, mail must be claimed within two months or it will be returned to sender.

For general inquiries, visit www.post.gov .tw, or phone ☎ 02-2321 4311 or toll free ☎ 0800 099 246.

## SHOPPING

Taiwan is a shopper's paradise.

Night markets are a highlight of any trip to Taiwan. While the specialities vary from market to market, you can generally expect to find cheap clothing (though occasionally cheap in both senses), toys, homewares and trinkets. They're also among the best places to find snack food – some night markets specialise in food only.

Other good buys include traditional Chinese crafts, jade and aboriginal crafts. See the Lugang (p207), Yingge (p152), Sansia (p153) and Taipei (p103) sections for more great buys.

Electronics are widely available, including some Taiwanese brands and many international brands. However, prices may not be any better than in your own country. If there's something you've been looking for, price it before leaving home and don't be disappointed if you leave Taiwan without it. Also, make sure that the current of any item you buy is compatible with the one at home.

Areas such as Guanghua St (p104) in Taipei specialise in computers, peripherals

| Basic mailing rates | Postcard | Letter |
| --- | --- | --- |
| within Taiwan | NT5 | NT5 |
| mainland China | NT7 | NT7 |
| Hong Kong | NT6 | NT9 |
| elsewhere in Asia/ | | |
|     Australia | NT10 | NT13 |
| USA/Canada | NT11 | NT15 |
| elsewhere | NT12 | NT17 |

and components. Computer shows are also a source of good deals. Knowledgeable buyers can try shops that will assemble a computer to your specifications for about half what you would pay back home; although you won't have a name brand, the parts will be the same. See p320 for information on VAT refunds.

### Bargaining

Most shopkeepers expect you to pay the marked price and, in general, modern Taiwanese don't like to bargain as it makes them feel low class. Many merchants simply won't entertain it. Exceptions are jade and antique markets, where bargaining is the rule. That said, it never hurts to ask for a discount in casual markets, curio shops, (some) night markets and even department stores if you're buying a lot.

Moral: if you push, you may get a lower price but people won't like you much.

### Convenience Stores

More than just shops, convenience stores are a way of life in Taiwan. Sometimes it seems there's one of these brightly lit, 24-hour institutions on every block, all doing hand-over-fist business. They're popular for picking up prepared snacks from sandwiches to rice balls to chocolates, some freshly prepared dishes and an assortment of sundries. You can even get beer and bottles of alcohol selling for NT3000 – that's approaching US$100.

The ubiquitous 7-Eleven chain has the greatest range of services, from fax machines to bill payment (phone, electricity, parking tickets) for residents. Other chains include Family Mart, Circle K, Hi-Life and Nico Mart.

### SOLO TRAVELLERS

Larger Chinese restaurants tend to serve large portions meant for groups and may not know what to do with a solo traveller. Smaller restaurants are generally no problem.

Other good places for solo travellers to eat are simple tea or coffee shops with set meals (meal and drink) for less than NT150, and noodle stands. Be wary around barbecues as often the portions are set for a table or half-table.

Solo female travellers should have no problems in Taiwan if they use common

sense. Make ATM withdrawals during the day, stick to brightly lit areas by night in cities and towns and avoid obviously seedy hotels and hitchhiking alone.

If a problem arises, you'll probably find the Taiwanese very helpful.

### TAXES
#### Taxes for Residents

If you're a working resident of Taiwan, you are responsible for paying Taiwanese taxes. You can find complete information in English on the website of the **National Tax Administration** (www.ntat.gov.tw/english/03information.htm).

#### Value Added Tax Refunds

Visitors with foreign passports and others with certain ROC documents are eligible to receive refunds of Taiwan's 5% value added tax (VAT). There are catches, however. First, at the time of writing there were just a small number of shops that were registered as Tax Refund Shopping (TRS) stores; mostly large department stores and shopping malls in major cities. Second, you must make a minimum purchase of NT3000 in a single day. Third, when you leave Taiwan you must present your items with your passport along with the goods, plus an original copy of the uniform invoice to customs officers. You may claim your refund at CKS Airport (either terminal), Keelung Harbour, Hualien (airport or harbour) or Kaohsiung (airport or harbour).

For further information, contact the local tourism bureau.

### TELEPHONE

The country code for Taiwan is ☎ 886.

Taiwan's telephone carrier for domestic and international calls is **Chunghwa Telecom** (www.cht.com.tw). For detailed information on rates and services, visit the website.

#### Area Codes

Area codes throughout Taiwan are as follows. Note that you do not dial the area code when calling within an area code.

The number of digits in telephone numbers varies with the locality, from eight in bustling Taipei to five in the remote Matsu Islands. Beware of numbers beginning with ☎ 0204, which are commonly phone-sex lines – you get an extraordinary charge in more ways than one!

## Domestic Calls

From public and private telephones, local calls cost NT2 per two minutes, while long-distance calls cost NT1 per 20 seconds (35 seconds off-peak) and calls to mobile phones (beginning with ☎ 09) vary from NT0.05 per second to NT5.6 per minute, depending on the provider and the time of day. Rates are discounted from 11pm to 8am Monday to Friday, from noon on Saturday and all day Sunday.

## Fax

Most hotels offer fax services – but you'll probably pay through the nose for them. However, at 7-Eleven stores, local black and white copies/faxes cost NT15 per page; international faxes cost NT100 per page.

## International Calls

The simplest ways to make international calls are direct dial and with Chunghwa Telecom's discount E-call card. The card is sold in denominations of NT200, NT300 and NT500 and entitles users to a 30% discount on standard rates, although quality of connec-

tion is somewhat lower. For overseas direct-dial calls, dial ☎ 009 or ☎ 002 before the country code and number. If you have your own phone line in Taiwan, occasionally you use the prefix ☎ 019 to get really low rates. For E-calls, dial toll-free ☎ 0800 080 180 and your card number, and then follow the prompts (available in English). E-call cards can be purchased at Chunghwa Telecom locations and 7-Eleven convenience stores.

Overseas calls are charged per six-second unit, as follows:

| Country | Direct Dial | E-call |
|---|---|---|
| Australia | NT1.30 | NT0.96 |
| Canada | NT0.59 | NT0.40 |
| China | NT1.22 | NT0.77 |
| France | NT1.60 | NT1.04 |
| Germany | NT1.60 | NT1.04 |
| Japan | NT1.30 | NT0.96 |
| Netherlands | NT2.00 | NT1.10 |
| New Zealand | NT1.30 | NT0.96 |
| UK | NT1.40 | NT0.96 |
| USA | NT0.59 | NT0.40 |

There is a discount of approximately 5% to calls made during off-peak hours. You can dial via an overseas operator ( ☎ 100), but this will cost a bundle. For directory assistance in English dial ☎ 106 (NT3 per call).

## Mobile Phones

There are many options. Chunghwa Telecom and **FarEastone** (www.fareastone.com.tw/english) are two big carriers. Costs of handsets can vary widely, from NT680 to NT17,000. In general, expect to pay about NT1 a minute for outgoing domestic calls. Some packages charge more but give you a number of free minutes, while others offer a low monthly fee and fewer or no free minutes. Check locally or on the Web for the latest options.

You may also be able to bring your phone from home and buy a SIM card from a local carrier and a prepaid phonecard.

All mobile phones in Taiwan start with the prefix ☎ 09XX, followed by six digits.

## Public Phones & Phonecards

Calls from public phones cost NT2 for local calls of up to two minutes, NT4 for long-distance calls and NT6 for calls to mobile phones.

**TELEPHONE AREA CODES**

0836 Matsu Island

0826 Wuchiu Island

0823 Kinmen Island

02 Taipei
03 Taoyuan
03 Hsinchu
03 Ilan
037 Miaoli
04 Taichung
04 Changhua
049 Nantou
03 Hualien
05 Yunlin
05 Chiayi
06 Penghu Islands
06 Tainan
07 Kaohsiung
089 Taitung
08 Pingtung
08 Liuchiu Island
089 Green Island
089 Orchid Island

In addition to coin-operated telephones, there are two types of card-operated phone. Ordinary phonecards cost NT100, while IC cards cost NT200.

Cards are available at convenience stores. If you want to use a phonecard for an overseas call, it will probably run out pretty quickly, so you should have a replacement card(s) at the ready. When your card is about to run out, the display will flash; press the 'change card' button to insert your new card.

You can also pay cash for international calls, but you should prepare a large stack of NT10 coins.

## TIME

Taiwan is eight hours ahead of GMT; the same time zone as Beijing, Hong Kong, Singapore and Perth. This means that when it's noon in Taiwan, it's 2pm in Sydney, 1pm in Japan, 4am in London, 11pm the previous day in New York and 8pm the previous day in Los Angeles. See also p342.

Taiwan does not observe daylight-saving time. During daylight-saving time, add one hour to the local times listed above for locations outside Taiwan (eg 5am in London).

## TOILETS

While most lodgings, and restaurants in the big cities, have Western-style toilets, public facilities, many homes and any place else built before about the 1990s is likely to have squat toilets. If you haven't used these, it can be an adventure. You enter the stall, stand facing away from the door (no need to turn around), squat over the hole in the floor and do your business. If you need a Western-style toilet, try looking for a disabled sign.

Nicer toilets have toilet paper, but in remote or older toilets you are expected to bring your own (pocket packs of tissues are common giveaways on streets in the big cities). Many places ask you not to flush the toilet paper down the toilet but put it in the waste basket beside the toilet. It's a disgusting necessity; some claim that old pipes and septic systems just cannot handle toilet paper.

It's also handy to remember the characters for 'male' and 'female':

| Male *(nán)* | 男 |
| Female *(nǚ)* | 女 |

## TOURIST INFORMATION

For tourist information on provinces and national scenic areas, check out the following websites:

**Alishan National Scenic Area** (www.ali.org.tw)
**East Coast National Scenic Area** (www.eastcoast-nsa .gov.tw/en/index.php)
**Kenting National Park** (www.ktnp.gov.tw)
**Little Liuchiu Island** (www.tbnsa.gov.tw)
**Matsu National Scenic Area** (http://202.39.225.133 /NSA2002/en/matzu/index.htm)
**North Coast and Guanyinshan National Scenic Area** (www.northguan-nsa.gov.tw)
**Northeast Coast National Scenic Area** (www .necoast-nsa.gov.tw)
**Penghu Tourist Service Centre** (www.penghu-nsa .gov.tw)
**Pingdong County** (www.pthg.gov.tw)
**Sun Moon Lake National Scenic Area** (www .sunmoonlake.gov.tw)
**Taichung County** (www.taichung.gov.tw)

The following websites, while not specifically aimed at tourists, are helpful resources:

**Being Abroad** (www.beingabroad.com/resources/Asia /Taiwan/)
**Department of Transportation** (www.dot.taipei .gov.tw/en)
**Forumosa.com** (www.forumosa.com)
**Taiwan Fun** (www.taiwanfun.com)

## VISAS

At the time of writing citizens of the following countries could enter Taiwan without a visa and stay for 30 days (this period cannot be extended under any circumstances): Australia, Austria, Belgium, Brunei Darussalam, Canada, Costa Rica, Denmark, Finland, France, Germany, Greece, Iceland, Ireland, Italy, Japan, Liechtenstein, Luxembourg, Malaysia, Malta, Monaco, Netherlands, New Zealand, Norway, Portugal, Republic of Korea, Singapore, Spain, Sweden, Switzerland, UK and USA.

The **Bureau of Consular Affairs** ( ☎ 0800 085 078; www.boca.gov.tw; Taipei ☎ 02-2343 2888; 3rd-5th fl, 2-2 Jinan Rd, Sec 1; Hualien ☎ 03-833 1041; 6th fl, 371 Jungshan Rd; Kaohsiung ☎ 07-211 0605; 2nd fl, 436 Chenggung-1st Rd; Taichung ☎ 04-2251 0799; 1st fl, 503 Liming Rd, Sec 2) requires citizens of these countries to have a passport valid for at least six months, a ticket and/or seat reservation for departure from Taiwan and no criminal record.

Citizens of other countries can find information on various visa requirements via the mission in their country or on the bureau's website. The website also contains advice on procedures and requirements for changing visa status, for example from student to resident.

If you're planning to stay longer than three months and work in Taiwan, the law requires you to have an ARC. However, if you're an Australian or New Zealander aged 18 to 30, you may obtain a working holiday visa, which enables you to undertake short-term, part-time work in Taiwan for one year. This scheme was introduced in 2004; for more information, see Taiwanese Foreign Legations on p314.

## WOMEN TRAVELLERS

Taiwan is a safe country, but women should take care and be wary of walking through underground tunnels alone at night, getting felt up on crowed buses and MRT and occasionally stalked. Also, women should never take a taxi at night alone. If you have to, ask a friend to hail the taxi down (or call) and make sure you let the driver see the friend write down the taxi licence-plate number. If the driver can see that you have a mobile phone, trouble is less likely.

Although Taiwan was a male-dominated society, the women's movement that began in the late 20th century has brought great strides towards equality. This evolution

---

### TEACHING ENGLISH IN TAIWAN

Taiwan is a popular destination for EFL (English as a Foreign Language) teachers (or those who wish to become one) for a number of reasons: it's an easy place to live even without knowing much Chinese, the pay is good enough to support a comfortable lifestyle (and still save) and there is generally plenty of work available.

#### Requirements

You need a bachelor's degree from an accredited university in an English-speaking country to teach legally. It is not necessary to have TESL (Teaching English as a Second Language) certification but it is recommended, as this will only help you to teach better.

Once you sign a contract, schools apply for your visa, which entitles you to an Alien Resident Certificate (ARC) and health insurance. Pay is often only once a month, usually on the 5th, so it's a good idea to come with at least NT30,000 to tide you over until your first salary payment.

#### Where to teach?

This is really your choice. If you have time, come to Taiwan and look around. There is no need to accept a position from overseas. Housing is rarely included in a contract and is not something you should insist upon anyway, as it's easy to find your own accommodation. Generally the best times to be looking for work are at the end of summer and just after Chinese New Year.

#### How much?

This will depend on your experience and where you live. NT500 an hour seems pretty standard for new teachers. Make sure your school offers steady raises and this is written in your contract.

#### Who are you going to teach?

That depends on your school. You could teach all age groups, or just one, such as adults preparing for proficiency tests, or elementary-school kids being forced to learn English by their parents. Don't knock teaching kids, though. The experience can be extremely rewarding, especially if students study every day. You'll see great progress and feel a wonderful sense of achievement. Short weekly classes, on the other hand, can really drain your energy and make you feel displaced.

There were big changes in the air at the time of writing regarding visas, ARC regulations and just where foreigners were permitted to teach (kindergarten work was once again banned). For up-to-date information, and the latest employment and housing details, check out the websites www.forumosa.com, www.tealit.com and www.daveseslcafe.com.

can be seen in everything from the rise of a woman to the vice-presidential seat (Annette Lu, with Chen Shui-bian) to the growing number of divorces instigated by women. The number of female managers has been on the rise, although there is still a substantial difference between women's and men's salaries.

Women travelling to Taiwan for business should take care to dress modestly and conservatively (as should men). Also, although drinking and smoking are a part of Taiwanese business culture, Taiwanese women tend to smoke and drink less than Taiwanese men.

Taiwanese tourism authorities have been trying to market the island specifically to foreign women. Apart from the attention normally given to foreign travellers, women travellers should not expect any special attention.

## WORK

Taiwanese business people are known to be sharp and very tough negotiators. Not that that's a bad thing – how else does one succeed in a dog-eat-dog world economy?

If you're going to Taiwan to do a business deal, it helps to have an introduction through a government office or some other contact that does business with the other party. At least for the first meeting, modest, conservative dress is in order. This typically means dark wool suits and ties despite the country being tropical. Short sleeves are acceptable in summer.

# Transport

## CONTENTS

# GETTING THERE & AWAY

## ENTERING THE COUNTRY

Most visitors enter through Taipei's Chiang Kai-shek Airport, where the immigration procedures pose few hassles. Guards are basically efficient.

For visa information, see p322.

### INSURANCE

Please see p317 for guidelines on purchasing travel insurance.

## AIR
### Airports & Airlines

Taiwan's main international airport is **Chiang Kai-shek Airport** (TPE; www.cksairport.gov.tw), in Dayuan, 50km (40 minutes) west of central Taipei. It is locally known as CKS Airport. Taiwan's other international airport is Hsiaogang Airport (KHH) in Kaohsiung. Chiang Kai-shek Airport handles traffic from around the world, while most of the international traffic into and out of Hsiaogang Airport is from Hong Kong and Southeast Asia. There are no direct flights between China and Taiwan.

CKS Airport has two terminals, connected by a 'Skytrain'. Terminal 2 is the newer and by far the more attractive of the two, but Terminal 1 was undergoing extensive renovations as we went to press.

There is a tourist information booth in each terminal at CKS Airport. You can reach the booth in Terminal 1 at ☎ 03-383 4631, or Terminal 2 at ☎ 03-398 3341.

Taiwan has two major international airlines, China Airlines and Eva Air. While Eva Air started operation in 1991 and has had no fatalities to date, the same cannot be said of China Airlines, which is somewhat infamous for its safety record. However, an official at China Airlines assures us that since early this decade training practices and standards have been overhauled (with pilots training at US flight schools), some 80 substandard pilots have been fired and the company has a new corporate culture.

See p106 and p256 for details on transport to/from the airports at Taipei and Kaohsiung.

### AIRLINES FLYING TO AND FROM TAIWAN

If the names of the airlines listed below sound familiar but not quite right, there's a reason. Owing to agreements with China, many large international carriers operate flights to Taiwan under different names. For example, All Nippon Airways becomes Air Nippon.

**Air Macau** (NX; www.airmacau.com.mo; Taipei ☎ 02-2717 0377; Kaohsiung ☎ 07-251 0860; CKS Airport ☎ 03-398 3121; hub Macau)

### THINGS CHANGE

The information in this chapter is particularly vulnerable to change. Check directly with the airline or a travel agent to make sure you understand how a fare (and ticket you may buy) works and be aware of the security requirements for international travel. Shop carefully. The details given in this chapter should be regarded as pointers and are not a substitute for your own careful, up-to-date research.

**Air New Zealand** (NZ; www.airnz.co.nz; Taipei ☎ 02-2567 8950; CKS Airport ☎ 03-398 3018; hub Auckland)
**Air Nippon** (EL; www.ana.co.jp; Taipei ☎ 02-2501 7299; Kaohsiung ☎ 07-330 9019; CKS Airport ☎ 03-398 2968; hub Tokyo)
**American Airlines** (AA; www.aa.com; Taipei ☎ 02-2563 1200; Kaohsiung ☎ 07-566 6555; hub Dallas-Fort Worth)
**Asiana Airlines** (OZ; www.flyasiana.com; ☎ 02-2581 4000; hub Seoul)
**Cathay Pacific** (CX; www.cathaypacific.com; Taipei ☎ 02-2715 2333; CKS Airport ☎ 03-398 2501; hub Hong Kong)
**China Airlines** (CI; www.china-airlines.com; Taipei ☎ 02-2715 1212; Kaohsiung ☎ 07-282 6141; CKS Airport ☎ 03-398 2451; hub Taipei)
**Continental Airlines** (CO; www.continental.com; Taipei ☎ 02-2719 5947; Kaohsiung ☎ 07-287 3346; CKS Airport ☎ 03-383 4131; hubs Newark, Houston)
**Eva Air** (BR; www.evaair.com; Taipei ☎ 02-2501 1999; Kaohsiung ☎ 07-330 9301; CKS Airport ☎ 03-398 3006; hub Taipei)
**Far Eastern Air Transport** (EF; www.fat.com.tw; Taipei ☎ 02-3393 5388; Kaohsiung domestic ☎ 07-3371388; Kaohsiung international ☎ 07-3371353; CKS Airport ☎ 03-398 3170; hub Taipei)
**Garuda Indonesia Airlines** (GA; www.garuda-indonesia .com; Taipei ☎ 02-2560 2349; CKS Airport ☎ 03-398 2336; hub Jakarta)
**Hong Kong Dragon Airlines** (KA; www.dragonair.com; Taipei ☎ 02-2518 2700, 2772 2188; Kaohsiung ☎ 07-201 3166; hub Hong Kong)
**Japan Asia Airways** (EG; toll-free ☎ 0800 065151; www.jal.co.jp; CKS Airport ☎ 03-398 2282; Kaohsiung ☎ 07-805 1346; hub Tokyo)
**KLM Asia** (KL; www.klm.com.tw_en; Taipei ☎ 02-2772 2118; Kaohsiung ☎ 07-338 6133; CKS Airport ☎ 03-383 3034; hub Amsterdam)
**Malaysia Airlines** (MH; www.malaysiaairlines.com; Taipei ☎ 02-2514 7888; Kaohsiung ☎ 07-801 6276; CKS Airport ☎ 03-383 4855; hub Kuala Lumpur)
**Mandarin Airlines** (AE; www.mandarin-airlines.com; Taipei ☎ 02-2717 1230; Kaohsiung ☎ 07-802 6868; CKS Airport ☎ 03-398 2620; hub Taipei)
**Northwest Airlines** (NW; www.nwa.com; Taipei ☎ 02-2772 2188; Kaohsiung ☎ 0800 006070; CKS Airport ☎ 03-398 2471; hub Detroit)
**Pacific Airlines** (BL; www.pacificairlines.com.vn; Taipei ☎ 02-2543 1860; Kaohsiung ☎ 07-338 1183; CKS Airport ☎ 03-383 4131; hub Ho Chi Minh City)
**Philippine Airlines** (PR; www.philippineair.com; Taipei ☎ 02-2506 7255; CKS Airport ☎ 03-398 2419; hub Manila)
**Qantas Airways Limited** (QF; www.qantas.com.au; Taipei ☎ 02-2559 0508; Kaohsiung ☎ 07-566 6516; CKS Airport ☎ 03-398 2619; hub Sydney)

**Royal Brunei** (BI; www.bruneiair.com; Taipei ☎ 02-2512 6868; Kaohsiung ☎ 07-282 3758; CKS Airport ☎ 03-398 2451; hub Bandar Seri Begawan)
**Saudi Arabian Airlines** (SV; www.saudiairlines.com; Taipei ☎ 02-2396 3780)
**Singapore Airlines** (SQ; www.singaporeair.com; Taipei ☎ 02-2551 6655; Kaohsiung ☎ 07-805 7882; CKS Airport ☎ 03-398 2247; hub Singapore)
**Thai Airways** (TG; www.thaiair.com; Taipei ☎ 02-2509 6800; Kaohsiung ☎ 07-215 5871; CKS Airport ☎ 03-383 4131; hub Bangkok)
**TransAsia Airways** (GE; www.tna.com.tw; Taipei ☎ 02-2972 4599; Kaohsiung ☎ 07-335 9355; CKS Airport ☎ 03-383 4131; hub Taipei)
**Uni Air** (B7; Taipei ☎ 02-2518 2626; Kaohsiung ☎ 07-791 7977; hub Taipei)
**United Airlines** (UA; www.united.com; Taipei ☎ 02-2325 8868; Kaohsiung ☎ 07-273 5544; CKS Airport ☎ 03-398 2781; hub Chicago)
**Viet Air** (VN; www.vietnamair.com; Taipei ☎ 02-2517 7177; Kaohsiung ☎ 07-227 0209; CKS Airport ☎ 03-398 3026; hubs Hanoi, Ho Chi Minh City)

## Baggage Shipping

If you don't feel like dragging your luggage between CKS Airport and central Taipei, **Pinoy Express** ( ☎ 02-2591 0888; 294-2 Chungqing N Rd, Taipei) can transport it for you. Same-day service is available if the bags arrive before 9pm at the Pinoy Express counter (in the arrival hall of each terminal). To arrange pick-up of luggage from your hotel or residence in Taipei, ring Pinoy Express one day in advance.

One-way rates to/from central Taipei are NT340 for the first bag (up to 20kg) and NT300 for each additional bag. Cash only.

## Tickets

Note that the Taiwanese departure tax is included in the price of your ticket.

### INTERCONTINENTAL (RTW) TICKETS

Round-the-world (RTW) tickets give you a limited period (usually a year) in which to circumnavigate the globe. You can go anywhere the carrying airlines go, as long as you don't backtrack. The number of stopovers or total number of separate flights is decided before you set off and they usually cost a bit more than a basic return flight. With the proliferation of airline alliances (Star Alliance, OneWorld, SkyTeam etc) travelling this way is easier than ever.

If you're looking to plan a RTW itinerary, consult the airline or alliance with which you wish to fly, or a travel agent or online services such as www.bootsnall.com.

Purchasing tickets one at a time, while always an option, will cost considerably more.

'Circle Pacific' tickets allow travel within Asia, typically on the same airline group.

## Africa

**Rennies Travel** (www.renniestravel.com) and **STA Travel** (www.statravel.co.za) have offices throughout southern Africa. Check their websites for branch locations.

## Asia

Most Asian countries have direct air service from their hubs to Taipei. These include Indonesia, Japan, Korea, Malaysia, Singapore, Thailand and Vietnam.

While it is not possible to fly nonstop from mainland China to Taiwan, there are frequent flights via Hong Kong.

### JAPAN

The Japanese and Taiwanese carriers and Cathay Pacific fly between Japan and Taiwan. Sample return fares for nonstop flights are US$392 (Fukuoka), US$453 (Tokyo), US$433 (Nagoya) and US$465 (Osaka). Booking agents in Japan include **STA Travel** ( ☎ 03-5391 2922; www.statravel.co.jp) and **No 1 Travel** ( ☎ 03-3205 6073; www.no1-travel.com).

### HONG KONG

The routes between Hong Kong and Taipei and Kaohsiung are very well travelled. Hong Kong is the major transit point for travel between Taiwan and mainland China, as well as traffic to and from points in the West. Several carriers ply the skies, at rates around US$449 return.

In Hong Kong, try **STA Travel** ( ☎ 2736 1618; www.statravel.com.hk) or **Four Seas Tours** ( ☎ 2200 7760; www.fourseastravel.com/english).

### KOREA

A number of carriers connect Seoul and Taiwan, starting at about US$355 return.

### SINGAPORE

Try **STA Travel** ( ☎ 6737 7188; www.statravel.com.sg).

### THAILAND

Like Hong Kong, Bangkok is a hub of travel from the rest of the world to Taiwan.

Budget travellers tend to gravitate towards the travel agencies on Khao San Rd. **STA Travel** ( ☎ 02-236 0262; www.statravel.co.th) also has a branch in town.

## Australia

High season between Australia and Asia is late November to late January, so expect higher fares at this time. If you're looking for inexpensive tickets, browse the travel sections of metropolitan newspapers or try **STA Travel** ( ☎ 1300 733 035; www.statravel.com.au) or **Flight Centre** ( ☎ 133 133; www.flightcentre.com.au). For online bookings, try www.travel.com.au.

## Canada

Most flights from Canada transit through Vancouver. It's easy to pick up cheap tickets in Richmond or Vancouver Chinatown.

**Travel Cuts** ( ☎ 800-667-2887; www.travelcuts.com) is Canada's national student-travel agency, although you don't have to be a student to purchase through it. For online bookings try www.expedia.ca and www.travelocity.ca.

## Continental Europe

Amsterdam is Europe's big gateway city to Taiwan as KLM is the only European carrier with a direct service to Taipei. While there are no nonstop flights, KLM offers a one-stop service. Round-trip fares start at around US$1781.

Recommended travel agencies include the following.

### FRANCE

**Anyway** ( ☎ 08 92 89 38 92; www.anyway.fr)
**Lastminute** ( ☎ 08 92 70 50 00; www.lastminute.fr)
**Nouvelles Frontières** ( ☎ 08 25 00 07 47; www.nouvelles-frontieres.fr)
**OTU Voyages** (www.otu.fr) Specialises in student and youth travellers.
**Voyageurs du Monde** ( ☎ 01 40 15 11 15; www.vdm.com)

### GERMANY

**Expedia** (www.expedia.de)
**Just Travel** ( ☎ 089 747 3330; www.justtravel.de)
**Lastminute** ( ☎ 01805 284 366; www.lastminute.de)
**STA Travel** ( ☎ 01805 456 422; www.statravel.de) For travellers under the age of 26.

### ITALY

**CTS Viaggi** ( ☎ 06 462 0431; www.cts.it) Specialising in student and youth travel.

**NETHERLANDS**
**Airfair** ( ☎ 020 620 5121; www.airfair.nl)

**SPAIN**
**Barcelo Viajes** ( ☎ 902 116 226; www.barceloviajes.com)

## India

Although there are no direct flights between India and Taiwan, there are frequent connections between, for example, Bangkok and Hong Kong.

**STIC Travels** (www.stictravel.com; Delhi ☎ 11-233 57 468; Mumbai ☎ 22-221 81 431) has offices in dozens of Indian cities. Another agency is **Transway International** (www.transwayinternational.com).

## The Middle East

Recommended travel agencies include the following.

**EGYPT**
**Egypt Panorama Tours** ( ☎ 2-359 0200; www.eptours.com)

**ISRAEL**
**Israel Student Travel Association** ( ☎ 02-625 7257)

**TURKEY**
**Orion-Tour** (www.oriontour.com)

**UNITED ARAB EMIRATES**
**Al-Rais Travels** (www.alrais.com)

## New Zealand

Both **Flight Centre** ( ☎ 0800 243 544; www.flightcentre.co.nz) and **STA Travel** ( ☎ 0508 782 872; www.statravel.co.nz) have branches throughout the country.

## South America

Recommended travel agencies include the following.

**ARGENTINA**
**ASATEJ** ( ☎ 54-011 4114-7595; www.asatej.com)

**BRAZIL**
**The Student Travel Bureau** ( ☎ 3038 1555; www.stb.com.br)

**VENEZUELA**
**IVI Tours** ( ☎ 0212-993 6082; www.ividiomas.com)

## The UK & Ireland

There are no nonstop flights between the British Isles and Taiwan.

Discount air travel is big business in London. Advertisements for travel agencies appear in the travel pages of the weekend broadsheet papers, in *Time Out*, the *Evening Standard* and in the free magazine *TNT*.

Recommended travel agencies include:
**Bridge the World** ( ☎ 0870 444 7474; www.b-t-w.co.uk)
**Flightbookers** ( ☎ 0870 010 7000; www.ebookers.com)
**Flight Centre** ( ☎ 0870 890 8099; www.flightcentre.co.uk)
**North-South Travel** ( ☎ 01245 608 291; www.northsouthtravel.co.uk) Donates part of its profit to projects in the developing world.
**Quest Travel** ( ☎ 0870 442 3542; www.questtravel.com)
**STA Travel** ( ☎ 0870 160 0599; www.statravel.co.uk) For travellers under the age of 26.
**Trailfinders** (www.trailfinders.co.uk)
**Travel Bag** ( ☎ 0870 890 1456; www.travelbag.co.uk)

## The USA

Nonstop flights from Taiwan go to Honolulu, Los Angeles, New York and San Francisco. At the time of writing, round-trip fares started around US$569 (Los Angeles), US$579 (San Francisco), US$635 (Honolulu) and US$689 (New York).

Discount travel agents in the USA are known as consolidators (although you won't see a sign on the door saying 'Consolidator'). San Francisco is the ticket consolidator capital of America, although some good deals can be found in Los Angeles, New York and other big cities.

The following agencies are recommended for online bookings.

- www.cheaptickets.com
- www.expedia.com
- www.itn.net
- www.lowestfare.com
- www.orbitz.com
- www.sta.com (with discounts for students, teachers and travellers under the age of 26)
- www.travelocity.com

## SEA

Weekly ferries operate between Keelung (p127) or Kaohsiung (p256) and Naha, Japan. The journey takes about 20 hours and calls on a couple of islands en route.

For current route and schedule information, consult a travel agent or visit www.starcruises.com.

# GETTING AROUND

## AIR

CSK Airport is for international flights only, so passengers flying into Taipei and transferring elsewhere within Taiwan will have to travel to Songshan Airport (TSA). It's north of central Taipei, but the city has pretty much engulfed it in recent decades.

Considering that Taiwan is such a small island, Songshan Airport is a very busy place. Four domestic-based carriers cover the country from about 7am until 10pm, an average of about one takeoff or landing every three minutes. Destinations served include Hualien, Kaohsiung, Kinmen, Tai-

chung, Tainan and Tatung. Flights are more limited to other cities.

Songshan Airport facilities include a bank, post office, food shops and restaurants. Small/medium/large coin-operated lockers are available for NT30/50/100 per day. A **tourist information counter** ( ☎ 2349 1580; ☺ 7am-10pm) is in the main hall and you can ring **Lost & Found** ( ☎ 8770 2658).

From the city centre, bus 5 and 262 serve the airport; Songshan Airport will also eventually be a stop on the MRT extension. Several buses an hour make the run to CKS Airport, operated by Guoguang (NT110) or Free Go (aka Grey Dog; NT135).

Although Songshan is the hub and most other destinations on the island are the

**TRANSPORT**

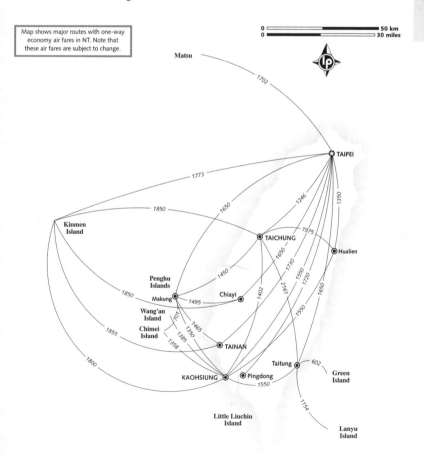

Map shows major routes with one-way economy air fares in NT. Note that these air fares are subject to change.

**AIRLINES IN TAIWAN**

**Far Eastern Air Transport** ( ☎ 0800 212 243; www.fat.com.tw)
**Mandarin Airlines** ( ☎ 02-2717 1230; www .mandarin-airlines.com) China Airlines affiliate.
**TransAsia Airways** ( ☎ 02-2972 4599; www .tna.com.tw)
**Uni Air** ( ☎ 02-2518 2626) Eva Air affiliate.

spokes, the airports at Taichung, Tainan and particularly Kaohsiung also serve multiple destinations. Because of weather, flights to Taiwan's islands can be hair-raising.

## BICYCLE

More and more towns and tourist areas are opening up bike routes and offering bike rentals. Taipei will have 100km of connected bike-only routes by the end of 2004.

Pinglin has about 25km of bike routes, and as we went to print the area around Sun Moon Lake (p214) and the east coast between Hualien and Taitung were being developed for bike travel. The stops along the Jiji Small Rail Line (p211) offer some of the nicest bike routes through the countryside in Taiwan. Kuanshan, near Taitung (p181), has become a popular cycling area. Some cyclists even bike down the South Cross-Island Hwy (p248).

Note that it's safest to bike the highways during weekdays and autumn-winter season when traffic is light.

### Hire

You can rent bikes for around NT50 an hour, or a full day might cost NT150 to NT300. There is usually no deposit required.

### Purchase

A decent mountain bike can be had for NT3000 to NT5000. High-end models for real off-road riding can cost NT20,000 and up. It's usually possible to resell.

## BOAT

There are regular ferry services between Taiwan and its outlying islands (although in recent years air transport has become more popular – though more expensive). There are also some river ferries. It can be a fun way to travel – assuming the weather cooperates and the ferries are actually running. See the regional chapters for details of schedules and prices. See also the 'Ferry Services' boxed text (below).

## BUS

While Taiwan has a long-established system of private bus companies, competition in recent years from trains, planes and automobiles has brought down the number of people using them – and standards. Add in factors such as traffic, road conditions, the general manic pace of driving in Taiwan, and a few high-profile cases in which dozens of people burned to death with emergency exits blocked to add more seating, and many expats avoid this mode of transport. Congestion is a problem on holiday weekends.

On the positive side, buses are smoke-free, at least officially.

That said, for some destinations the bus is the best – indeed the only – way to get around. Main transit points are Taipei, Taichung and Kaohsiung. See regional chapters for individual routes and schedules, but here are the major bus lines. Of these, Aloha,

**FERRY SERVICES**

| Route | Operator | Contact |
| --- | --- | --- |
| Keelung–Matsu | Taima Boat Company | ☎ 02-2424 6868 (Keelung) |
| | | ☎ 0836-22395 (Matsu) |
| Danshui–Bali & Danshui Fishermen's Wharf | Suen Fung Ferry Company | ☎ 02-8630 1845 |
| Fukang (Taitung)–Lanyu & Green Islands | several | |
| Kaohsiung–Kinmen | Kaohsiung Harbour | ☎ 07-521 6206 |
| Kinmen | | ☎ 082-329 988 |
| Kaohsiung–Makung | Taiwan Hangye Company | ☎ 07-561 3866 (Kaohsiung) |
| | | ☎ 06-926 4087 (Makung) |
| Putai (near Chiayi)–Makung | Makung Tomorrow Star | ☎ 06-926 0666 (Makung) |
| Donggang–Little Liuchiu Island | several | |

Free Go Express and Guoguang (aka Taiwan Bus Co) have the best reputation. See also the 'Bus Companies' boxed text (below).

### Reservations
Advisable for weekend travel and especially during holidays.

## CAR, MOTORCYCLE & SCOOTER
To reach certain choice areas and get around once you're there, your own transport is advisable, if not absolutely necessary; we've noted where in relevant chapters. Driving a car is not terribly difficult outside the cities, especially on weekdays. Scooters are cheap to rent (average NT400 per day).

### Driving Licence
An international driving licence (available in your home country) will be valid in Taiwan for up to three months. If you have an ARC (Alien Resident Certificate, see p323), you may also use your driving licence from your home country.

Otherwise, you will have to register for a Taiwanese driving licence. If your country has a reciprocal agreement with Taiwan, you may be able to obtain a Taiwanese licence just by showing your home licence and passport. If not, you will have to take a written test as well as a practical test on a closed course. Driving licences are issued by county. For an idea of what to expect, see the Taipei government's motor vehicles office website (http://www.tcmvd.gov.tw/en_default1.htm).

An international driving permit or Taiwanese driving licence is also valid for motor scooters up to 50cc. Any motorcycle larger than that requires a separate motorcycle licence.

### Fuel & Spare Parts
Petrol stations are everywhere, as are garages to get parts and repairs for scooters and cars.

### Hire
Car rental fees typically run between NT800 and NT1500 for a half-day, or NT1300 to NT2500 for a full day, depending on type of vehicle and rental company. Typical long-term discounts are 10% for three to seven days, 20% for eight to 20 days and 30% for longer. Ask if there is a limit to the number of kilometres you can drive. Check with local tourist information services for rental agencies in your area. Two possibilities include:

**Hertz** ( ☎ 02-2731 0377; fax 02-27766772; www.hertz.com)

**HFC** ( ☎ 0800-024550; www.easyrent.com.tw) The driver needs to have an international licence approved by Motor Vehicle Office in Taiwan.

TRANSPORT

---

### BUS COMPANIES

| Company | Contact number(s) |
|---|---|
| Guoguang Bus Corp. | ☎ 0800-010 138; 02-383 4004 |
| Free Go Express | ☎ 02-2586 3065; 02-393 1351 |
| Evervoyage Transport Corp. | ☎ 02-357 0498; 383 3801; 393 1707 |
| United Highway Bus | ☎ 02-2995 7799; 02-2995 8735; |
| Taoyuan Bus Corp. | ☎ 02-375 3711 |
| Dragon Bus | ☎ 0800-550599; 02-2571 0166 |
| Aloha Bus | ☎ 02-2550 8488 |

### Costs
Sample bus schedules from Taipei:

| Destination | Price | Duration |
|---|---|---|
| Taichung | NT220 Mon-Fri, NT260 Sat & Sun | 2½hr |
| Tainan | NT310 Mon-Fri, NT450 Sat & Sun | 4hr |
| Kaohsiung | NT350 Mon-Fri, NT500 Sat & Sun | 5hr |
| Sun Moon Lake | NT300 Mon-Fri, NT445 Sat & Sun | 4½hr |
| Alishan | NT600 Mon-Sun | 6hr |

## Insurance

Car rental fees include the required liability insurance. Comprehensive insurance (CDW in Taiwan) is optional and covers fire, theft and the like.

## Road Conditions

We strongly discourage driving within Taipei because of traffic, although outside of the city, and especially in remote regions such as the east coast, it's actually advisable.

## Road Rules

By standards of your home country, driving in Taiwan might seem just a little out of hand. Taiwan drives on the right-hand side of the road, although at times you'd be hard pressed to tell! Right turn on a red light is not allowed. There is a seat belt law, though the level of its enforcement varies. When it's enforced, fines start in the thousands of NT and can double if you're driving on a highway. Children under four must be kept in safety seats.

---

**ALL HAIL THE SCOOTER**

What the yellow taxi is to New York, the cruising bicycle is to Amsterdam and the *túk-túk* is to Bangkok, so is the humble scooter to Taiwan. There are over 10 million of them, the largest per-capita ownership of scooters in the world.

Standing on any corner, particularly in Taipei, you'll witness legions of helmeted riders (the popular colour of the moment is silver) zipping along on their Yamahas, Suzukis or Syms. Most scooters are black, but occasionally you'll spot a blue, red or green beauty. Notice the clever design of the seats, long and hinged, such that you can fit your helmet inside (helmets are required by law).

Just about any footpath, particularly the covered ones, has rows of scooters lined up on it (mostly pretty orderly). This parking practice is also a matter of law – scooters are prohibited from parking on streets unless explicitly permitted, though sometimes it seems that pedestrians' rights are being trampled.

We don't need to tell you what a scooter with flashing red and blue lights means.

---

## HITCHING

Hitching is never entirely safe in any country in the world, and we don't recommend it. Travellers who do decide to hitch should understand that they are taking a small but potentially serious risk. If you do choose to hitch you will be safer if you travel in pairs and let someone know where you are planning to go.

## LOCAL TRANSPORT

### Bus

Buses are often the only public transport in the big cities. This can pose a problem for nonspeakers (or readers) of Chinese because buses list destinations on front in Chinese only. Even if they are in English, the sign often lists both the start and end point of the bus line – difficult if you don't know which direction you're supposed to go.

Usually you enter the bus from the back and pay at the front when you leave. The driver will let you know if it's otherwise.

Fares vary by city but, for example, the fare within a single zone in Taipei is NT15. Each additional zone is an extra NT15.

### Metro

Taipei's MRT (Mass Rapid Transit) has made a huge difference to the city's environment, traffic, cleanliness and general culture (see p106).

### Taxi

In the large cities, taxi rates are NT70 for the first 1.5km or portion thereof. After that, it's NT5 per 300m, or per two minutes of waiting time (for example, at stoplights or if you're caught in traffic). The waiting time is cumulative – taxi meters are fitted with timers. Fares are surcharged approximately 20% after midnight. Surcharges may also apply for things such as luggage and reserving a cab (as opposed to hailing one).

### Train

Local/commuter trains operate like subway cars, with long benches and straps for standing passengers to hold on to. Purchase tickets at ticket counters before boarding.

## TOURS

If you're looking for a general tour of the island, **Edison Travel Service** ( ☎ 02-2563 5313; www.edison.com.tw), **Huei Fong Travel Service**

( ☎ 02-2561 5117; hf.travel@msa.hinet.net) and **South East Travel Service** ( ☎ 02-2571 3001; www.settour. com.tw) offer similar itineraries. There are about a dozen tours available including the island's most popular destinations such as Taroko Gorge and Sun Moon Lake. The companies handle everything for you, including hotel transfers and, depending on the tour, meals. On the negative side, it will cost you more, and you may find yourself spending more time in shops than you otherwise would have.

Taipei-based **Fresh Treks** ( ☎ 02-2700 6988; www.freshtreks.com; 11F-6, 237 Fuxing S Rd, Sec 2) offers something that has long been missing in Taiwan: the chance to climb the high mountains with an English-speaking guide. Run by gregarious French expat Jean-Marc Compain, Fresh Treks offers trips to Class A mountains such as Yushan (three days, NT6000) as well as purely fun outings such as horseback riding and parasailing. Travel groups tend to be well balanced between foreign and Taiwanese participants, making this a great way to meet people who share an interest in the outdoors.

## TRAIN

The Taiwan Railway Administration (TRA) operates trains on two main lines. Major stops on the Western Line include Pingdong, Kaohsiung, Taichung, Taipei and Keelung, while the Eastern Line runs from Shulin via Taipei and Hualien to Taitung. The Southern Link connects Kaohsiung and Taitung. There are also several small branch lines maintained for tourist purposes, including Pingxi (p130), Alishan (p233), Jiji (p211) and Neiwan (p141). For detailed timetable and fare information, you can pick up the Taiwan Railway Passenger Train Timetable at train-station info centres, kiosks or 7-Eleven stores, or visit www.railway.gov.tw.

Express trains are reasonably comfortable with reserved seats and carts coming through the aisles offering boxed meals (such as they are). Snacks are available on platforms at many stations, and there are always shops and convenience stores nearby.

A new high-speed rail line is scheduled to begin operation in autumn 2005.

**TRANSPORT**

## ROAD DISTANCES (KM)

| | Chiayi | Hsinchu | Hualien | Ilan | Kaohsiung | Keelung | Kenting | Taichung | Tainan | Taipei | Taitung | Taoyuan |
|---|---|---|---|---|---|---|---|---|---|---|---|---|
| Chiayi | --- | | | | | | | | | | | |
| Hsinchu | 169 | --- | | | | | | | | | | |
| Hualien | 436 | 289 | --- | | | | | | | | | |
| Ilan | 319 | 150 | na | --- | | | | | | | | |
| Kaohsiung | 92 | 261 | 344 | 411 | --- | | | | | | | |
| Keelung | 264 | 95 | 229 | 90 | 356 | --- | | | | | | |
| Kenting | 192 | 361 | 306 | 511 | 100 | 456 | --- | | | | | |
| Taichung | 86 | 83 | 372 | 233 | 178 | 178 | 278 | --- | | | | |
| Tainan | 63 | 232 | 373 | 382 | 29 | 327 | 100 | 149 | --- | | | |
| Taipei | 241 | 72 | 217 | 78 | 333 | 23 | 433 | 155 | 304 | --- | | |
| Taitung | 262 | 463 | 174 | 313 | 170 | 403 | 132 | 348 | 199 | 391 | --- | |
| Taoyuan | 215 | 46 | 243 | 104 | 307 | 49 | 407 | 129 | 278 | 26 | 417 | --- |

**TRAIN SERVICES**

| From | To | Duration/Fare *(zìqiáng)* | Duration/Fare *(fùxíng)* |
|------|------|------|------|
| Taipei | Hualien | 3hr/NT445 | 3¾hr/NT343 *(jǔguāng)* |
| Taipei | Kaohsiung | 4½hr/NT845 | 6¼hr/NT544 |
| Taipei | Tainan | 3½hr/NT741 | 5¾hr/NT476 |
| Kaohsiung | Taichung | 2½hr/NT470 | 3½hr/NT303 |
| Hualien | Taitung | 2¾hr/NT355 | 3¼hr/NT273 *(jǔguāng)* |
| Taichung | Taipei | 2hr/NT375 | 3hr/NT241 |

## Classes

There are four classes of service, ranging from the spiffy express *zìqiáng* (with dining cars) through *jǔguāng* and more ordinary *fùxíng* to short-run shuttles. All except the lowest class of shuttle have air-con.

## Reservations & Fares

For the fast trains, especially on weekends or holidays, it is advisable to buy your tickets a day or two in advance. Seats on shuttle trains are all nonreserved.

Special tourist trains offer luxury rides (special cars, big seats) to places such as Taitung and Alishan. These are packaged tours that include visits to the nearby attractions and overnight stays in hotels. You can find out more about the three such trains on the railway's website (www.railway.gov.tw).

# Health  Dr Trish Batchelor

Health issues and the quality of medical care vary significantly depending on whether you stay in Taipei or venture into rural areas.

Travellers tend to worry about contracting infectious diseases, but infections are a rare cause of serious illness or death while overseas. Pre-existing medical conditions, such as heart disease, and accidental injury (especially traffic accidents) account for most life-threatening problems. Becoming ill in some way, however, is relatively common. Fortunately most common illnesses can either be prevented with sensible behaviour or be treated easily with a well-stocked traveller's medical kit.

The following advice is a general guide only and does not replace the advice of a doctor trained in travel medicine.

# BEFORE YOU GO

Pack medications in their original, clearly labelled containers. A signed and dated letter from your physician describing your medical conditions and regular medications (use generic names) is also a good idea. When carrying syringes or needles, be sure to have a physician's letter documenting their medical necessity. If you have a heart condition bring a copy of your ECG taken just prior to travelling.

If you take any regular medication bring double your needs in case of loss or theft. In Taiwan it may be difficult to find some of the newer drugs, particularly the latest antidepressant drugs, blood-pressure medications and contraceptive pills.

## INSURANCE

Even if you are fit and healthy, don't travel without health insurance – accidents do happen. Declare any existing medical conditions you have – the insurance company *will* check if your problem is pre-existing and will not cover you if it is undeclared. You may require extra cover for adventure activities. If your health insurance doesn't cover you for medical expenses abroad, consider getting extra insurance – check Lonely Planet's subwwway (www.lonelyplanet.com) for more information. If you're uninsured, emergency evacuation is expensive; bills of over US$100,000 are not uncommon.

Find out in advance if your insurance plan will make payments directly to providers or reimburse you later for overseas health expenditures. (In many countries doctors expect payment in cash.) Some policies offer lower and higher medical-expense options; the higher ones are chiefly for countries that have extremely high medical costs, such as the USA. You may prefer a policy that pays doctors or hospitals directly rather than you having to pay on the spot and claim later. If you have to claim later, make sure you keep all documentation. Some policies ask you to call (reverse charges) a centre in your home country where an immediate assessment of your problem is made.

## RECOMMENDED VACCINATIONS

Specialised travel-medicine clinics are your best source of information: they stock all available vaccines and will be able to give specific recommendations for you and your trip. The doctors will take into account factors such as past vaccination history, the length of your trip, activities you may be undertaking and underlying medical conditions, such as pregnancy.

Most vaccines don't produce immunity until at least two weeks after they're given, so visit a doctor four to eight weeks before departure. Ask for an International Certificate of Vaccination (otherwise known as the yellow booklet), which will list all the vaccinations you've received.

## MEDICAL CHECKLIST

Recommended items for a personal medical kit:

- Antifungal cream (eg Clotrimazole)
- Antibacterial cream (eg Muciprocin)
- Antibiotics if you are visiting rural areas; one for skin infections (eg Amoxicillin/Clavulanate or Cephalexin) and another for diarrhoea (eg Norfloxacin or Ciprofloxacin)
- Antihistamine – there are many options (eg Cetrizine for daytime and Promethazine for night)
- Antiseptic (eg Betadine)*
- Antispasmodic for stomach cramps (eg Buscopan)
- Contraceptive method
- Decongestant (eg Pseudoephedrine)*
- DEET-based insect repellent
- Diarrhoea – consider an oral rehydration solution (eg Gastrolyte), diarrhoea 'stopper' (eg Loperamide) and an antinausea medication (eg Prochlorperazine)*
- First-aid items such as scissors, elastoplasts, bandages, gauze, thermometer (but not mercury), sterile needles and syringes, safety pins and tweezers*
- Anti-inflammatory (eg Ibuprofen)
- Indigestion tablets (eg Quick Eze or Mylanta)

### REQUIRED VACCINATIONS

**Yellow Fever** Proof of vaccination is required if entering Taiwan within six days of visiting an infected country. If you are travelling to Taiwan from Africa or South America check with a travel-medicine clinic whether you need the vaccine.

### RECOMMENDED VACCINATIONS

The World Health Organization (WHO) recommends the following vaccinations for travellers to Taiwan.

**Adult diphtheria & tetanus** Single booster recommended every 10 years. Side effects include sore arm and fever.

**Hepatitis A** Provides almost 100% protection for up to a year, a booster after 12 months provides at least another 20 years protection. Mild side effects such as headache and sore arm occur in 5% to 10% of people.

**Hepatitis B** Now considered routine for most travellers. Given as three shots over six months. A rapid schedule is also available, as is a combined vaccination with Hepatitis A. Side effects are mild and uncommon, usually headache and sore arm. In 95% of people three shots results in lifetime protection.

**Measles, mumps & rubella** Two doses of MMR required unless you have had the diseases. Occasionally a rash and flu-like illness can occur a week after receiving the vaccine. Many young adults require a booster.

**Typhoid** Recommended unless your trip is less than two weeks and only in Taipei. The vaccine offers around 70% protection, lasts for two to three years and comes as a single shot. Tablets are also available, however the injection is usually recommended as it has fewer side effects. Sore arm and fever may occur.

**Varicella** If you haven't had chickenpox, discuss this vaccination with your doctor.

The following immunisations are recommended for long-term travellers (more than one month) or those at special risk.

**Influenza** A single injection lasts for two months. Recommended for all travellers over 65 years of age and those with underlying medical conditions such as heart disease, lung disease, diabetes or a compromised immune system.

**Japanese B encephalitis** Three injections in all. Booster recommended after two years. Sore arm and headache are the most common side effects. Occasionally an allergic reaction comprising hives and swelling can occur up to 10 days after any of the three doses.

**Pneumonia** A single injection lasts five years. Recommended as per the flu vaccine.

**Tuberculosis** A complex issue. Adult long-term travellers are usually recommended to have a TB skin test before and after travel, rather than vaccination. Only one vaccine given in a lifetime.

HEALTH

Iodine tablets (unless you are pregnant or have a thyroid problem) to purify water

Laxative (eg Coloxyl)

Migraine medicine – sufferers should take their personal medicine

Paracetamol*

Permethrin to impregnate clothing and mosquito nets

Steroid cream for allergic/itchy rashes (eg 1% to 2% hydrocortisone)

Sunscreen and a hat

*Throat lozenges

Thrush (vaginal yeast infection) treatment (eg Clotrimazole pessaries or Diflucan tablet)

Ural or an equivalent if prone to urine infections

Indicates most commonly used items by travellers.

## INTERNET RESOURCES

There is a wealth of travel health advice available on the Internet. For further information, **Lonely Planet** (www.lonelyplanet.com) is a good place to visit for starters. The **World Health Organization** (WHO; www.who.int/ith) publishes a superb book called *International Travel & Health*, which is revised annually and is available online at no cost. Another website of general interest or up to the minute information is **MD Travel Health** (www.mdtravelhealth.com), which provides complete travel-health recommendations for every country and is revised daily. The **Centers for Disease Control and Prevention** (CDC; www.cdc.gov) website also has good general information.

## FURTHER READING

To begin with, pick up a copy of Lonely Planet's *Healthy Travel Asia & India*. Other recommended references include *Traveller's Health* by Dr Richard Dawood and *Travelling Well* by Dr Deborah Mills – have a look at the website (www.travellingwell .com.au).

# IN TRANSIT

## DEEP VEIN THROMBOSIS (DVT)

Deep vein thrombosis (DVT) occurs when blood clots form in the legs during plane flights, chiefly because of prolonged immobility. The longer the flight, the greater the risk. Though most of the time these blood clots are reabsorbed uneventfully, it is possible for some to break off and travel through the blood vessels to the lungs, where they may cause life-threatening complications.

The chief symptom of deep vein thrombosis is swelling or pain of the foot, ankle or calf. This usually (but not always) occurs on just one side of the body. When a blood clot travels to the lungs, it may cause chest pain and breathing difficulties. Travellers with any of these symptoms should seek medical attention as soon as possible.

To prevent the development of DVT on long flights you should make sure you walk around the cabin, perform isometric compressions of the leg muscles (ie contract and relax the leg muscles while sitting), drink plenty of fluids and avoid alcohol and tobacco.

## JET LAG & MOTION SICKNESS

Jet lag is most common when crossing more than five time zones; it results in insomnia, fatigue, malaise or nausea. To avoid jet lag try drinking plenty of fluids (nonalcoholic) and eating only light meals. Once you have arrived at your destination, seek exposure to natural sunlight and readjust your schedule (for meals, sleep etc) as soon as possible.

Antihistamines such as dimenhydrinate (Dramamine), prochlorperazine (Phenergan) and meclizine (Antivert, Bonine) are usually the first choice for the treatment of motion sickness. Their main side effect is drowsiness. A herbal alternative is ginger, which works like a charm for some people.

### HEALTH ADVISORIES

It's usually a good idea to consult your government's travel-health website before departure, if one is available.

**Australia** (www.dfat.gov.au/travel)
**Canada** (www.travelhealth.gc.ca)
**New Zealand** (www.mfat.govt.nz/travel)
**UK** (www.doh.gov.uk/traveladvice)
**US** (www.cdc.gov/travel)

HEALTH

# IN TAIWAN

## AVAILABILITY & COST OF HEALTH CARE

Taiwan is a relatively well-developed country and the quality of medical care reflects this. In Taipei the quality is high, however in rural areas you cannot expect to find Western standards of care.

A recommended hospital in Taipei is the **Adventist Hospital** (Map pp80-1; ☎ 2771 8151; 424 Bade Rd, Sec 2); it has English-speaking staff.

## INFECTIOUS DISEASES
### Dengue Fever

This mosquito-borne disease is becomingly increasingly problematic in Taiwan in both cities and rural areas. It can only be prevented by avoiding mosquito bites – there is no vaccine. The mosquito that carries dengue bites day and night, so use insect-avoidance measures at all times. Symptoms include high fever, severe headache and body ache (previously Dengue was known as 'break bone fever'). Some people develop a rash and diarrhoea. There is no specific treatment, just rest and paracetamol. Do not take aspirin and see a doctor to be diagnosed and monitored.

### Hepatitis A

A problem throughout the country, this food- and water-borne virus infects the liver, causing jaundice (yellow skin and eyes), nausea and lethargy. There is no specific treatment for hepatitis A; you just need to allow time for the liver to heal. All travellers to Taiwan should be vaccinated against hepatitis A.

### Hepatitis B

The only sexually transmitted disease that can be prevented by vaccination, hepatitis B is spread by body fluids, including sexual contact. People who have hepatitis B usually are unaware they are carriers. The long-term consequences can include liver cancer and cirrhosis.

### HIV

HIV is also spread by body fluids. Avoid unsafe sex, sharing needles, invasive cosmetic procedures such as tattooing and needles that have not been sterilised in a medical setting. HIV rates in Taiwan remain low by Asian standards, though case numbers are now rapidly increasing. Transmission is mainly via sexual contact in Taiwan.

### Influenza

Influenza is transmitted between November and April. Symptoms include high fever, muscle aches, runny nose, cough and sore throat. It can be very severe in people over the age of 65 or in those with underlying medical conditions such as heart disease or diabetes – vaccination is recommended for these individuals. There is no specific treatment, just rest and paracetamol.

### Japanese B Encephalitis

This viral disease is transmitted by mosquitoes, but is rare in travellers. The transmission season runs from June to October. Risk exists in all areas except the central mountains. Vaccination is recommended for travellers spending more than one month outside of cities. There is no treatment, and a third of infected people will die while another third will suffer permanent brain damage.

### Lyme Disease

This tick-borne disease occurs in summer. Symptoms include an early rash and general viral symptoms, followed weeks to months later by joint, heart or neurological problems. Prevent this disease by using general insect-avoidance measures and checking yourself for ticks after walking in forest areas. Treatment is with Doxycycline.

### SARS

In mid-March 2003 the world's attention was drawn to the outbreak of an apparent new and serious respiratory illness that subsequently became known as SARS. At the time of writing SARS appears to have been brought under control. Since the outbreak commenced, 8500 cases were confirmed, resulting in 800 deaths. The peak of disease activity was in early May 2003, when over 200 new cases were being reported daily in Asia. Taiwan had a significant number of cases of SARS.

The cause of SARS was identified as a new virus, unlike any other previously known in humans or animals. The symptoms of SARS are identical to many other respiratory in ections – high fever and cough. There is no reliable quick test for SARS so it was only by excluding other illnesses and having a relevant travel or contact history that sufferers could be identified. No specific treatment is available and death from respiratory failure occurs in roughly 10% of patients. Although many of those dying were elderly or had underlying medical conditions, a significant number of previously fit and healthy young people also succumbed. Health-care workers in sophisticated hospitals seemed to be particularly at risk. It remains to be seen if SARS will make a comeback.

## STDs

Sexually transmitted diseases are common throughout the world, and the most common include herpes, warts, syphilis, gonorrhoea and chlamydia. People carrying these diseases often have no signs of infection. Condoms will prevent gonorrhoea and chlamydia but not warts or herpes. If after a sexual encounter you develop any rash, lumps, discharge or pain when passing urine seek immediate medical attention. If you have been sexually active during your travels, have an STD check on your return home.

## Tuberculosis

Taiwan has a high rate of tuberculosis (TB) infection. While rare in travellers, precautions should be taken by medical and aid workers and long-term travellers who have significant contact with the local population. Vaccination is usually only given to children under the age of five, but adults at risk are recommended pre- and post-travel TB testing. The main symptoms are fever, cough, weight loss, night sweats and tiredness.

## Typhoid

This serious bacterial infection is spread via food and water. It gives a high and slowly worsening fever and headache, and may be accompanied by a dry cough and stomach pain. It is diagnosed by blood tests and treated with antibiotics. Vaccination is recommended for all travellers spending more than two weeks in Taiwan and travelling outside of Taipei. Be aware that vaccination is not 100% effective so you must still be careful with what you eat and drink.

## TRAVELLER'S DIARRHOEA

Traveller's diarrhoea is the most common problem affecting travellers – between 10% and 30% of people visiting Taiwan will suffer from it. In the majority of cases, traveller's diarrhoea is caused by a bacteria (there are numerous potential culprits), and therefore responds promptly to treatment with antibiotics. Treatment with antibiotics will depend on your situation – how sick you are, how quickly you need to get better, where you are etc.

Traveller's diarrhoea is defined as the passage of more than three watery bowel-actions within 24 hours, plus at least one other symptom such as fever, cramps, nausea, vomiting or feeling generally unwell.

Treatment consists of staying well hydrated: rehydration solutions such as Gastrolyte are the best for this. Antibiotics such as Norfloxacin, Ciprofloxacin or Azithromycin will kill the bacteria quickly.

Loperamide is just a 'stopper' and doesn't get to the cause of the problem. It can be helpful, for example, if you have to go on a long bus ride. Don't take Loperamide if you have a fever or blood in your stools. Seek medical attention quickly if you do not respond to an appropriate antibiotic.

Eating in restaurants is the biggest risk factor for contracting traveller's diarrhoea. Eat only freshly cooked food and avoid shellfish and food that has been sitting

---

### DRINKING WATER

- Never drink tap water
- Bottled water is generally safe – check the seal is intact at purchase
- Avoid ice
- Avoid fresh juices – they may have been watered down
- Boiling water is the most efficient method of purifying it
- The best chemical purifier is iodine. However, it should not be used by pregnant women or those with thyroid problems.
- Water filters should also filter out viruses. Ensure your filter has a chemical barrier such as iodine and a small pore size (less than four microns).

HEALTH

around in buffets. Peel all fruit, cook vegetables and soak salads in iodine water for at least 20 minutes. Eat in busy restaurants with a high turnover of customers.

### Giardiasis

Giardia is a common parasite in travellers. Symptoms include nausea, bloating, excess gas, 'eggy' burps, fatigue and intermittent diarrhoea. The parasite will eventually go away if left untreated but this can take months. The treatment of choice is Tinidazole, with Metronidazole being a second-line option. Giardia is not common in Taiwan.

## ENVIRONMENTAL HAZARDS
### Air Pollution

Air pollution, particularly vehicle pollution, is an increasing problem in Taipei. If you have severe respiratory problems speak with your doctor before travelling to any heavily polluted urban centres. This pollution also causes minor respiratory problems such as sinusitis, dry throat and irritated eyes. If troubled by the pollution, leave the city for a few days and get some fresh air.

### Insect Bites & Stings

Insects are not a major issue in Taiwan, though there are some insect-borne diseases present.

Ticks can be contracted from walking in rural areas. They are commonly found behind the ears, on the belly and in armpits. If you have had a tick bite and experience symptoms such as a rash at the site of the bite or elsewhere, or fever or muscle aches you should see a doctor. Doxycycline prevents and treats tick-borne diseases.

Bee and wasp stings mainly cause problems for people who are allergic to them. Anyone with a serious bee or wasp allergy should carry an injection of adrenaline (eg an Epipen) for emergency treatment. For other people, pain is the main problem; apply ice to the sting and take painkillers if necessary.

### Parasites

There are a number of flukes (liver, lung and intestinal) that can be contracted by eating raw or undercooked seafood, meat and vegetables in Taiwan. Such dishes should be avoided unless eating in a top class restaurant.

### Skin Problems

Cuts and scratches can become easily infected when travelling. Take meticulous care of any cuts and scratches to prevent complications such as abscesses. Immediately wash all wounds in clean water and apply antiseptic. If you develop signs of infection (increasing pain and redness) see a doctor.

Rashes can often be very difficult to diagnose, even for doctors. If you develop a rash you should seek medical advice as soon as possible.

## WOMEN'S HEALTH

In most well-developed areas of Taiwan supplies of sanitary products are readily available. Birth-control options may be limited so bring supplies of your own contraception.

Heat, humidity and antibiotics can all contribute to thrush. Treatment is with antifungal creams and pessaries such as

---

**INSECT AVOIDANCE**

Travellers are advised to prevent mosquito bites at all times by following these suggestions:

▪ Use a DEET-containing insect repellent on exposed skin. Wash this off at night as long as you are sleeping under a mosquito net. Natural repellents such as citronella can be effective, but must be applied more frequently.

▪ Sleep under a mosquito net that has been impregnated with permethrin

▪ Accommodation should have screens and fans if not air-conditioned

▪ Impregnate clothing with permethrin in high-risk areas

▪ Wear light-coloured long sleeves and pants

▪ Use mosquito coils

▪ Spray your room with insect repellent before going out for your evening meal

Clotrimazole. A practical alternative is a single tablet of fluconazole (Diflucan). Urinary tract infections can be precipitated by dehydration or long bus journeys without toilet stops: it's best to bring suitable antibiotics.

Pregnant women should receive specialised advice before travelling. The ideal time to travel is in the second trimester (between 16 and 28 weeks), when the risk of pregnancy-related problems are at their lowest and pregnant women generally feel at their best. During the first trimester there is a risk of miscarriage and in the third trimester complications such as premature labour and high blood pressure are possible. It's wise to travel with a companion. Always carry a list of quality medical facilities available at your destination and ensure you continue your standard antenatal care at these facilities. Avoid rural travel in areas with poor medical facilities and transport. Most of all, ensure travel insurance covers all pregnancy-related possibilities, including premature labour.

Traveller's diarrhoea can quickly lead to dehydration and result in inadequate blood flow to the placenta. Many of the drugs used to treat various diarrhoea bugs are not recommended in pregnancy. However azithromycin is considered safe.

## TRADITIONAL & FOLK MEDICINE

Traditional Chinese Medicine (TCM) remains very popular in Taiwan. TCM views the human body as an energy system in which the basic substances of *chi (qì;* vital energy), *jing* (essence), blood (the body's nourishing fluids) and body fluids (other organic fluids) function. The concept of yin and yang is fundamental to the system. Disharmony between yin and yang or within the basic substances may be a result of internal causes (emotions), external causes (climatic conditions) or miscellaneous causes (work, exercise, sex etc). Treatment modalities include acupuncture, massage, herbs, dietary modification and *qijong* (the skill of attracting positive energy) and aim to bring these elements back into balance. These therapies are particularly useful for treating chronic diseases and are gaining interest and respect in the Western medical system. Conditions that can be particularly suitable for traditional methods include chronic fatigue, arthritis, irritable bowel syndrome and some chronic skin conditions.

Be aware that 'natural' doesn't always mean 'safe', and there can be drug interactions between herbal medicines and Western medicines. If you are using both systems, ensure you inform both practitioners what the other has prescribed.

**HEALTH**

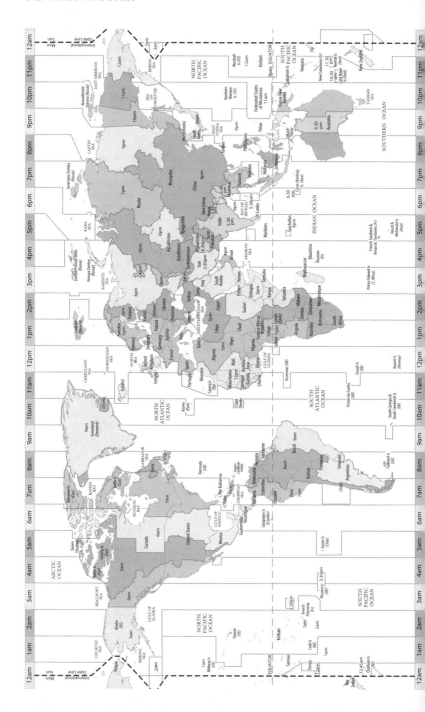

# Language

## CONTENTS

After the Kuomintang (KMT; Nationalist Party) fled China for Taiwan in the late 1940s, it promoted Mandarin Chinese as the official language for the island. At the time, however, few Taiwanese could speak it. The main languages of Taiwan then were Hokkien, usually referred to as 'Taiwanese' (also called *Minnanhua*, a name that emphasises its roots in southeastern China, where it is also spoken), and Japanese. Hakka, another Chinese language, is also spoken in some areas, and Taiwan's aboriginal tribes have their own languages, which belong to a completely separate language family to Chinese.

Although Taiwanese is often referred to as a 'dialect' of Mandarin, the two are in fact separate languages and are not mutually intelligible. Relatively little has been written in Taiwanese beyond Christian religious material, due in part to the efforts by the authorities during the Japanese colonial era (1895-1945), and later by the KMT, to suppress the language. Despite these years of suppression, the Taiwanese language has endured, and today at least half the population prefers to speak Taiwanese at home, especially in the south and in rural areas. It's too soon to know whether the government's recent creation of a Hakka-language TV station will succeed in helping revive the use of Hakka.

Travellers to Taiwan can get by without having to even attempt any Taiwanese. Virtually all young and middle-age people speak Mandarin. Many older people also know Japanese as a result of the 50-year Japanese occupation of Taiwan.

Although Taiwan's students are required to study English, few actually learn to speak it. As a result they tend to read and write English much better than they can speak it so if you need to communicate in English try writing your message down. The reason for this is that students learn English from textbooks, without any opportunity for conversation. Introductory English now begins in junior, rather than secondary school, and classes have begun to focus more on the spoken language. This shift is too recent to have had any noticeable effect on the proliferation of spoken English.

# MANDARIN

## TONES

Mandarin, Taiwanese and Hakka are all tonal languages – by altering the voice's pitch within a syllable, the meaning of a word is completely changed. Getting your tones wrong can have embarrassing consequences – *wǒ gǎnmào*, for example, means 'I've caught a cold', while *wǒ gàn māo* means 'I copulate with cats'! Mandarin has four tones, while some of the other Chinese languages have as many as nine. For example *ma*, has a number of meanings in Mandarin depending on which tone is used:

| high tone | mā | 'mother' |
| rising tone | má | 'hemp' or 'numb' |
| falling-rising tone | mǎ | 'horse' |
| falling tone | mà | 'scold' or 'swear' |

There is also a 'neutral' tone, which is usually not indicated by a tone mark.

Mastering tones is tricky for the untrained Western ear, but with discipline it can be done. Try practising the following tongue twister: *Māma qí mǎ. Mǎ màn. Māma mà mǎ.* (Mother rides a horse. The horse is slow. Mother scolds the horse.)

Don't let yourself be discouraged by the language. Apart from the problem of tones, Mandarin is not especially difficult to master. Most people in Taiwan are very friendly and will praise your linguistic skills if you manage to say even a few words in one of the island's languages.

## CHARACTERS

The greatest difficulty associated with the language is its written form: Chinese characters. To borrow from a Chinese proverb, it can take a lifetime and a little bit more to learn how to read and write Chinese. The reason for this is that, unlike most languages, written Chinese does not employ an alphabet. This has led many to the false conclusion that Chinese characters represent a system of 'idea-pictures' or ideograms; in reality, the vast majority of characters consist of a phonetic element and another element called the 'radical', which provides a semantic clue to the meaning.

Some dictionaries list more than 55,000 characters, but many of these entries are no longer used or they are variants. The 2,400 most frequently used characters account for 99% of most texts. A further complication in learning to read Chinese is that some 20% of characters have more than one pronunciation.

The sounds represented by Chinese characters are each one syllable long, but few Mandarin words are monosyllabic. As a result, many characters cannot stand alone as words, much as the the prefix 'im-' in 'impossible' is a unit of meaning, but not a complete word in itself.

Taiwan doesn't use the system of 'simplified' characters that was progressively introduced in China after the communist takeover. Instead, Taiwan has retained the use of traditional characters, which are also found in Hong Kong and in many Chinese communities abroad.

## ROMANISATION

Romanisation is the rendering of non-Roman alphabet languages, such as Arabic, Mandarin, Thai or Russian, into a form that can be read or spoken by anyone familiar with the Roman alphabet (ie a, b, c etc) and the sounds it represents. Contrary to popular belief, it is entirely possible to Romanise Mandarin, but travellers to Taiwan are unlikely to encounter much Romanisation other than for names of people, places and streets. Unfortunately, Taiwan's approach to Romanisation has been slapdash, resulting in the island's road signs and maps displaying a veritable Babel of Romanisation systems, and even outright misspellings. There are many tales of signs exhibiting a variety of spellings for the same street – even at the same intersection!

Further complicating the matter is the fact that, until recently, Taiwan tended to use the Wade-Giles Romanisation system, which most native English speakers find counterintuitive due to the use of apostrophes to represent phonetically related sounds (such as 'b' and 'p', written in Wade-Giles as **p** and **p′** respectively). This explains why English has the spelling *Taoism* for what would be represented in most other systems as *Daoism*. Although there are sound linguistic reasons for this approach, the problems for the uninitiated are obvious. To make matters worse, the apostrophes are often routinely omitted, making it impossible even for those few who are familiar with the Wade-Giles system to be able to read it reliably. Without the apostrophes, for example, what is written *Kuting* could be pronounced 'Kuting', 'Guting', 'Kuding' or 'Guding'. Although Taiwan officially switched to the less ambiguous MPS2 Romanisation system in 1986, implementation was spotty and halfhearted, resulting in perhaps even more ambiguity and confusion than before.

The good news is that after years of complaints from foreigners Taiwan has finally begun to take steps to correct its use of Romanisation. The bad news is that the new signs tend to be in one of two different Romanisation systems: Hanyu Pinyin, which is used in China (and has become the international standard for Mandarin), and Tongyong Pinyin, a home-grown alternative born in the late 1990s of the desire to help differentiate Taiwan from China. Although advocates of Tongyong Pinyin often claim that the systems are 85% the same, in reality only about half of place names are spelled the same way in the two systems.

The major differences between the two systems are as follows:

| HANYU PINYIN | TONGYONG PINYIN |
|---|---|
| zh- | jh- |
| q- | c- |
| x- | s- |
| -ü* | -yu |
| -ui | -uei |
| -iu | -iou |
| wen | wun |
| weng | wong |
| feng | fong |
| jiong/qiong/siong | jyong/cyong/syong |
| zi/ci/si | zih/cih/sih |
| zhi/chi/shi/ri | jhih/chih/shih/rih |

*ü is written u (ie without the umlaut) when no ambiguity would result. Thus, *ju, qu, xu,* and *yu* should be pronounced as if they were written *jü, qü, xü,* and *yü.*

Although the central government has declared Tongyong Pinyin to be Taiwan's official Romanisation system for both Hakka and Mandarin (but not for Taiwanese), it left local governments free to make their own choices. Taipei has selected to use Hanyu Pinyin and has applied the system consistently. In times of budget constraints, however, most local governments have priorities other than putting up new signage for the benefit of foreigners, so progress toward standardisation in any form of Pinyin is slow in most of the country.

Taipei has also introduced a system under which major roads have been assigned numbers. Although this 'nicknumbering' system might at first glance seem like a boon to visitors to the city, don't bother asking for directions to '4th Boulevard', because no-one in Taipei knows what streets the numbers are supposed to match. This system is best ignored.

To sum up the situation, signage in Taiwan can be found in MPS2, Wade-Giles (which most people also use inaccurately for spelling their names), Hanyu Pinyin (mainly in Taipei), Tongyong Pinyin (mainly on highway signs and at train stations), plus a range of other possibilites employed with varying degrees of inaccuracy.

Given such a range, what is the poor traveller to do? When something written in

Romanisation doesn't seem to make sense, a few guidelines can help you make an educated guess as to what is actually being referred to. Anything with **x**, **q** or **zh** will be in Hanyu Pinyin. Anything with **jh**, **iou** or **uei** will be in Tongyong Pinyin. Anything with **r** used as a vowel (eg *shr*) will be in MPS2.

If you're going to learn only one Romanisation system, your best bet is to learn Hanyu Pinyin and study a few of the most common differences (such as those listed below) to help you navigate through the other systems you'll likely encounter.

The following Hanyu Pinyin conversion could fairly safely be assumed where different systems are used:

| WRITTEN | HANYU PINYIN |
|---|---|
| c | q |
| ch | zh/q/j/ch |
| jh | zh |
| k | g |
| p | b |
| s | x |
| t | d |
| ts/tz | z/c |
| h (at the end of a syllable) | – (no letter) |

For example, Chihpen and Jhiben are sometimes seen for Zhiben, and Kueishan for Guishan.

## More Info on the Internet

For a list of Taiwan's city names, street names, and names of railroad stations in Hanyu Pinyin and traditional spellings, see www.romanization.com.

For loads more information on Chinese characters, Pinyin and Romanisation, including a full comparison of the main Chinese Romanisation systems, check out www.pinyin.info.

If you'd like more information on the ins and outs of Chinese characters there are many suitable books on the subject listed at www.pinyin.info/readings/. 'The Ideographic Myth' at www.pinyin.info/readings/texts/ideographic_myth.html is an extract from *The Chinese Language: Fact and Fantasy* by John DeFrancis (University of Hawai`i Press 1984). DeFrancis gives an interesting and detailed history of the widely-held belief that Chinese characters are ideographic (ie pictorial) in nature.

LANGUAGE

## PRONUNCIATION

The following is a description of the sounds produced in spoken Mandarin Chinese. The letter **v** is not used in Chinese. The trickiest sounds in Pinyin are **c**, **q** and **x**. Most letters are pronounced as in English, except for the following:

### Vowels

| | |
|---|---|
| **a** | as in 'father' |
| **ai** | as the word 'eye' |
| **ao** | as the 'ow' in 'cow' |
| **e** | as in 'her' |
| **ei** | as in 'weigh' |
| **i** | as the 'ee' in 'meet'; also as the 'oo' in 'book'* |
| **ian** | as the word 'yen' |
| **ie** | as the word 'yeah' |
| **o** | as in 'or' |
| **ou** | as the 'oa' in 'boat' |
| **u** | as in 'flute' |
| **ui** | as the word 'way' |
| **uo** | as 'w' followed by the 'o' in 'or' |
| **yu** | as German 'ü' – round your lips and try saying 'ee' |
| **ü** | as German 'ü' |

\* The letter 'i' is pronounced as 'oo' only when it occurs after **c**, **ch**, **r**, **s**, **sh**, **z** or **zh**.

### Consonants

| | |
|---|---|
| **c** | as the 'ts' in 'bits' |
| **ch** | as in 'church', but with the tongue curled back |
| **h** | guttural, a bit like the 'ch' in Scottish 'loch' |
| **q** | as the 'ch' in 'cheese' |
| **r** | as the 's' in 'pleasure' |
| **sh** | as in 'she', but with the tongue curled back |
| **x** | as the 'sh' in 'ship' |
| **z** | as the 'ds' in 'suds' |
| **zh** | as the 'j' in 'judge' but with the tongue curled back |

Consonants other than **n**, **ng**, and **r** can never appear at the end of a syllable.

In Pinyin, apostrophes are occasionally used when a syllable in the middle of a word begins with a vowel, eg *ping'an* ('ping-an') compared with *pin'gan* ('pin-gan').

## PHRASEBOOKS & DICTIONARIES

Conflicting Romanisation systems aside, reading place names or street signs isn't too difficult, since the Chinese name is usually accompanied by some form of Pinyin; if not, you'll soon learn lots of characters through repeated exposure.

Lonely Planet's *Mandarin Phrasebook* includes script throughout and loads of useful phrases – it's also a very useful learning tool. A small dictionary with English, Pinyin and Chinese characters is also useful for learning a few words.

## ACCOMMODATION

**I'm looking for a ...**
*Wǒyào zhǎo ...*      我要找 ...
  **camping ground**
  *yíngdì*      營地
  **guesthouse**
  *bīnguǎn*      賓館
  **hotel**
  *lǚguǎn*      旅館
  **tourist hotel**
  *bīnguǎn/fàndiàn/jiǔdiàn*      賓館/飯店/酒店
  **hostel**
  *zhāodàisuǒ/lǚshè*      招待所/旅社
  **youth hostel**
  *qīngnián lǚshè*      青年旅社

**Where is a cheap hotel?**
*Nǎlǐ yǒu piányì de lǚguǎn?*
哪裡有便宜的旅館?
**What is the address?**
*Dìzhǐ zài nǎlǐ?*
地址在哪裡?
**Could you write the address, please?**
*Néngbunéng qǐng nǐ bǎ dìzhǐ xiě xiàlái?*
能不能請你把地址寫下来?
**Do you have a room available?**
*Nǐmen yǒu fángjiān ma?*
你們有房間嗎?

**I'd like (a) ...**
*Wǒ xiǎng yào ...*      我想要 ...
  **bed**
  *yíge chuángwèi*      一個床位
  **single room**
  *yìjiān dānrénfáng*      一間單人房
  **double room**
  *yìjiān shuāngrénfáng*      一間雙人房
  **bed for two**
  *shuāngrén chuáng*      雙人床
  **room with two beds**
  *shuāngrénfáng*      雙人房
  **economy room (no bath)**
  *yǎfáng (méiyǒu yùshì)*      雅房(没有浴室)

**room with a bathroom**
*tàofáng (yǒu yùshìde fángjiān*   套房(有浴室的浴室的房間)

**standard room**
*biāozhǔn fángjiān*   標準房間

**deluxe suite**
*háohuá tàofáng*   豪華套房

**to share a dorm**
*zhù sùshè*   住宿舍

**How much is it ...?**
*.. duōshǎo qián?*   ... 多少錢?

**per night**
*měitiān wǎnshàng*   每天晚上

**per person**
*měigerén*   每個人

**May I see the room?**
*Wǒ néng kànkan fángjiān ma?*
我能看看房間嗎?

**Where is the bathroom?**
*Yùshì zài nǎlǐ?*
浴室在哪裡?

**Where is the toilet?**
*Cèsuǒ zài nǎlǐ?*
廁所在哪裡?

**I don't like this room.**
*Wǒ bù xǐhuān zhèijiān fángjiān.*
我不喜歡這間房間

**Are there any messages for me?**
*Yǒu méiyǒu rén liú huà gěi wǒ?*
有沒有人留話給我?

**May I have a hotel namecard?**
*Yǒu méiyǒu lǚguǎn de míngpiàn?*
有沒有旅館的名片?

**Could I have these clothes washed, please?**
*Qǐng bǎ zhè xiē yīfú xǐ gānjìng, hǎo ma?*
請把這些衣服洗乾净, 好嗎?

**I'm/We're leaving today.**
*Wǒ/Wǒmen jīntiān líkāi.*
我/我們今天離開

## CONVERSATION & ESSENTIALS

**Hello.**
*Nǐ hǎo.*   你好
*Nín hǎo.* (more polite)   您好

**Goodbye.**
*Zàijiàn.*   再見

**Please.**
*Qǐng.*   請

**Thank you.**
*Xièxie.*   謝謝

**Many thanks.**
*Duōxiè.*   多謝

**That's fine.** (ie, you're welcome, don't mention it)
*Búkèqì.*   不客氣

**Excuse me, ...**
*Qǐng wèn, ...*   請問, ...

When asking a question it is polite to start with the phrase *qǐng wèn* 請問 – literally, 'may I ask?' – this expression is only used at the beginning of a sentence, never at the end.

**I'm sorry. (forgive me)**
*Duìbùqì.*   對不起

**May I ask your name?**
*Nín guìxìng?*   您貴姓?

**My (sur)name is ...**
*Wǒ xìng ...*   我姓 ...

**Where are you from?**
*Nǐ shì cōng nǎlǐ lái de?*   你是從哪裡來的?

**I'm from ...**
*Wǒ shì cōng ... lái de.*   我是從 ... 来的

**I like ...**
*Wǒ xǐhuān ...*   我喜歡 ...

**I don't like ...**
*Wǒ bù xǐhuān ...*   我不喜歡 ...

**Wait a moment.**
*Děng yīxià.*   等一下

### Yes & No

There are no specific words in Mandarin that mean 'yes' and 'no' when used in isolation. When asked a question the verb is repeated to indicate the affirmative. A response in the negative is formed by using the word *bù*, 不 (meaning 'no') before the verb. When *bù* (falling tone) occurs before another word with a falling tone, it becomes *bú* (ie with a rising tone).

**Are you going to Shanghai?**
*Nǐ qù Shànghǎi ma?*   你去上海嗎?

**Yes.**
*Qù.* (literally 'go')   去

**No.**
*Bú qù.* (literally 'no go')   不去

**No. (don't have)**
*Méi yǒu.*   没有

**No. (not so)**
*Búshì.*   不是

### DIRECTIONS

**Where is (the) ...?**
*... zài nǎlǐ?*   ... 在哪裡?

**Go straight ahead.**
*Yīzhí zǒu.*   一直走

**Turn left.**
*Zuǒ zhuǎn.*   左轉

## SIGNS

| 入口 | Rùkǒu | **Entrance** |
|---|---|---|
| 出口 | Chūkǒu | **Exit** |
| 詢問處 | Xùnwènchù | **Information** |
| 開 | Kāi | **Open** |
| 關 | Guān | **Closed** |
| 禁止 | Jìnzhǐ | **Prohibited** |
| 有空房 | Yǒu Kòngfáng | **Rooms Available** |
| 客滿 | Kèmǎn | **No Vacancies** |
| 警察 | Jǐngchá | **Police** |
| 警察局 | Jǐngchájú | **Police Station** |
| 廁所 | Cèsuǒ | **Toilets** |
| 男 | Nán | **Men** |
| 女 | Nǚ | **Women** |

**Turn right.**
*Yòu zhuǎn.* 右轉

**at the next corner**
*zài xià yíge zhuǎnjiǎo* 在下一個轉角

**at the traffic lights**
*zài hónglǜdēng* 在紅綠燈

**Could you show me (on the map)?**
*Nǐ néng bunéng (zài dìtú shang) zhǐ gěi wǒ kàn?* 你能不能(在地圖上)指給我看?

| **behind** | *hòumiàn* | 後面 |
|---|---|---|
| **in front of** | *qiánmiàn* | 前面 |
| **near** | *jìn* | 近 |
| **far** | *yuǎn* | 遠 |
| **opposite** | *duìmiàn* | 對面 |

| **beach** | *hǎitān* | 海灘 |
|---|---|---|
| **bridge** | *qiáoliáng* | 橋樑 |
| **island** | *dǎoyǔ* | 島嶼 |
| **main square** | *guǎngchǎng* | 廣場 |
| **map** | *dìtú* | 地圖 |
| **market** | *shìchǎng* | 市場 |
| **old city** | *gǔchéng* | 古城 |
| **palace** | *gōngdiàn* | 宮殿 |
| **sea** | *hǎiyáng* | 海洋 |

## HEALTH

**I'm sick.**
*Wǒ shēngbìngle.* 我生病了

**I need a doctor.**
*Wǒ děi kàn yīshēng.* 我得看醫生

**Is there a doctor here who speaks English?**
*Zhèlǐ yǒu huì jiǎng yīngyǔ de dàifu ma?* 這裡有會講英語的大夫嗎?

**It hurts here.**
*Zhèlǐ téng.* 這裡疼

## EMERGENCIES

**Help!**
*Jiùmìng a!* 救命啊!

**emergency**
*jǐnjí qíngkuàng* 緊急情況

**There's been an accident!**
*Chūshìle!* 出事了!

**Could you help me, please?**
*Nǐ néngbunéng bāng wǒ ge máng?* 你能不能幫我個忙?

**I'm lost.**
*Wǒ mílùle.* 我迷路了

**Go away!**
*Zǒu kāi!* 走開!

**Leave me alone!**
*Bié fán wǒ!* 別煩我!

**Call ...!**
*Qǐng jiào ...!* 請叫 ...!

  **a doctor**
  *yīshēng* 醫生

  **the police**
  *jǐngchá* 警察

**I'm ...**
*Wǒ yǒu ...* 我有 ...

  **asthmatic**
  *qìchuǎnbìng* 氣喘病

  **diabetic**
  *tángniàobìng* 糖尿病

  **epileptic**
  *diānxiánbìng* 癲癇病

**I'm allergic to ...**
*Wǒ duì ... guòmǐn.* 我對 ... 過敏

  **antibiotics**
  *kàngshēngsù* 抗生素

  **aspirin**
  *āsīpǐlín* 阿司匹林

  **penicillin**
  *qīngméisù* 青黴素

  **bee stings**
  *mìfēng dīng* 蜜蜂叮

  **nuts**
  *jiānguǒ* 堅果

**anti-diarrhoea medicine**
*zhǐxièyào* 止瀉藥

**antiseptic cream**
*xiāodúgāo* 消毒膏

**condoms**
*bǎoxiǎn tào* 保險套

**contraceptive**
  *bìyùnyào*    避孕藥
**diarrhoea**
  *lā dùzi*    拉肚子
**headache**
  *tóutòng*    頭痛
**medicine**
  *yào*    藥
**sanitary napkins (Kotex)**
  *wèishēngmián*    衛生棉
**sunscreen (UV) lotion**
  *fángshàiyóu*    防曬油
**tampons**
  *wèishēngmián tiáo*    衛生棉條

## LANGUAGE DIFFICULTIES

**Do you speak English?**
  *Nǐ huì shuō yīngyǔ ma?*
  你會說英語嗎?
**Does anyone here speak English?**
  *Zhèlǐ yǒu rén huì shuō yīngyǔ ma?*
  這裡有人會說英語嗎?
**How do you say ... in Mandarin?**
  *... zhōngwén zěnme shuō?*
  ... 中文怎麼說?
**What does ... mean?**
  *... shì shénme yìsi?*
  ... 是什麼意思?
**I understand.**
  *Wǒ tīngdedǒng.*
  我聽得懂
**I don't understand.**
  *Wǒ tīngbudǒng.*
  我聽不懂
**Please write it down.**
  *Qǐng xiěxiàlai.*
  請寫下來

## NUMBERS

| | | |
|---|---|---|
| 0 | *líng* | 零 |
| 1 | *yī, yāo* | 一, 么 |
| 2 | *èr, liǎng* | 二, 兩 |
| 3 | *sān* | 三 |
| 4 | *sì* | 四 |
| 5 | *wǔ* | 五 |
| 6 | *liù* | 六 |
| 7 | *qī* | 七 |
| 8 | *bā* | 八 |
| 9 | *jiǔ* | 九 |
| 10 | *shí* | 十 |
| 11 | *shíyī* | 十一 |
| 12 | *shí'èr* | 十二 |
| 20 | *èrshí* | 二十 |
| 21 | *èrshíyī* | 二十一 |
| 22 | *èrshí'èr* | 二十二 |
| 30 | *sānshí* | 三十 |
| 40 | *sìshí* | 四十 |
| 50 | *wǔshí* | 五十 |
| 60 | *liùshí* | 六十 |
| 70 | *qīshí* | 七十 |
| 80 | *bāshí* | 八十 |
| 90 | *jiǔshí* | 九十 |
| 100 | *yìbǎi* | 一百 |
| 1000 | *yìqiān* | 一千 |
| 2000 | *liǎngqiān* | 兩千 |

## PAPERWORK

**name**
  *xìngmíng*    姓名
**nationality**
  *guójí*    國籍
**date of birth**
  *chūshēng rìqī*    出生日期
**place of birth**
  *chūshēng dì*    出生地
**sex (gender)**
  *xìngbié*    性別
**passport**
  *hùzhào*    護照
**passport number**
  *hùzhào hàomǎ*    護照號碼
**visa**
  *qiānzhèng*    簽證
**visa extension**
  *yáncháng qiānzhèng*    延長簽證
**Public Security Bureau (PSB)**
  *gōng'ānjú*    公安局
**Foreign Affairs Branch**
  *wàishìkē*    外事科
**credit card ...**
  *xìnyòngkǎ*    信用卡
  **number**
  *hàomǎ*    號碼
  **expiry date**
  *yǒu shìxiào rìqī*    有效日期

## QUESTION WORDS

| **Who?** | *Shuí?* | 誰? |
|---|---|---|
| **What?** | *Shénme?* | 什麼? |
| **What is it?** | *Shì shénme?* | 是什麼? |
| **When?** | *Shénme shíhou?* | 什麼時候? |
| **Where?** | *Zài nǎlǐ?* | 在哪裡? |
| **Which?** | *Něige?* | 哪個? |
| **How?** | *Rúhé?* | 如何? |

## SHOPPING & SERVICES

**I'd like to buy ...**
  *Wǒ xiǎng mǎi ...*    我想買 ...

**How much is it?**
*Duōshǎo qián?* 多少錢?
**I don't like it.**
*Wǒ bù xǐhuān.* 我不喜歡
**Can I see it?**
*Néng kànkan ma?* 能看看嗎?
**I'm just looking.**
*Wǒ zhǐshì kànkan.* 我只是看看
**It's cheap.**
*Zhè bùguì.* 這不貴
**Is there anything cheaper?**
*Yǒu piányi yìdiǎn de ma?* 有便宜一點的嗎?
**That's too expensive.**
*Tài guìle.* 太貴了
**I'll take it.**
*Wǒ jiù mǎi zhèige.* 我就買這個

**more**
*duō* 多
**less**
*shǎo* 少
**smaller**
*gèng xiǎo* 更小
**bigger**
*gèng dà* 更大
**too much/many**
*tài duō* 太多

**Do you accept ...?**
*Shōu bushōu ...?* 收不收 ...?
  **credit cards**
  *xìnyòngkǎ* 信用卡
  **travellers cheques**
  *lǚxíng zhīpiào* 旅行支票

**Can I pay by travellers cheque?**
*Kěyi fù lǚxíng zhīpiào ma?*
可以付旅行支票嗎?

**Excuse me, where's the nearest ...?**
*Qǐng wèn, zuìjìnde ... zài nǎlǐ?*
請問, 最近的 ... 在哪裡?
**I'm looking for a/the ...**
*Wǒ zài zhǎo ...*
我在找 ...
  **ATM**
  *zìdòng guìyuánjī/* 自動櫃員機/
  *tíkuǎnjī* 提款機
  **bank**
  *yínháng* 銀行
  **chemist/pharmacy**
  *yàojú* 藥局
  **city centre**
  *shìzhōngxīn* 市中心

  **... embassy**
  *... dàshǐguǎn* ... 大使館
**foreign affairs police**
*wàishì jǐngchá* 外事警察
**currency exchange**
*wàihuì duìhuànchù* 外滙兌換處
**hospital**
*yīyuàn* 醫院
**hotel**
*bīnguǎn/* 賓館/
*fàndiàn/* 館店/
*lǚguǎn* 旅館
**market**
*shìchǎng* 市場
**museum**
*bówùguǎn* 博物館
**police**
*jǐngchá* 警察
**post office**
*yóujú* 郵局
**public toilet**
*gōnggòng cèsuǒ* 公共廁所
**telephone**
*diànhuà* 電話
**telephone office**
*diànxìnjú* 電信局
**the tourist office**
*guānguāngjú* 觀光局

**change money**
*huàn qián* 換錢
**telephone card**
*diànhuà kǎ* 電話卡
**international call**
*guójì diànhuà* 國際電話
**collect call**
*duìfāng fùfèi diànhuà* 對方付費電話
**direct-dial call**
*zhíbō diànhuà* 直撥電話
**fax**
*chuánzhēn* 傳真
**computer**
*diànnǎo* 電腦
**email (often called 'email')**
*diànzǐyóujiàn* 電子郵件
**internet**
*wǎnglù/* 網路
*(wǎngjì wǎnglù)* (網際網路)
(more formal name)
**online**
*shàngwǎng* 上網

**Where can I get online?**
*Wǒ zài nǎlǐ kěyǐ shàngwǎng?*
我在哪裡可以上網?

Can I check my email account?
*Wǒ jiǎnchá yíxià zìjǐ de email xìnxiāng, hǎo ma?*
我檢查一下自己的 email 信箱, 好嗎?

# TIME & DATES

What's the time?
*Jǐ diǎn?* 幾點?

... hour ... minute
*... diǎn ... fēn* ... 點 ... 分

3.05
*sān diǎn líng wǔ fēn* 三點零五分

When?
*Shénme shíhòu?* 什麼時候?

now
*xiànzài* 現在

today
*jīntiān* 今天

tomorrow
*míngtiān* 明天

day after tomorrow
*hòutiān* 後天

yesterday
*zuótiān* 昨天

in the morning
*zǎoshang* 早上

in the afternoon
*xiàwǔ* 下午

in the evening
*wǎnshang* 晚上

weekend
*zhōumò* 周末

| | | |
|---|---|---|
| Monday | *Xīngqīyī* | 星期一 |
| Tuesday | *Xīngqī'èr* | 星期二 |
| Wednesday | *Xīngqīsān* | 星期三 |
| Thursday | *Xīngqīsì* | 星期四 |
| Friday | *Xīngqīwǔ* | 星期五 |
| Saturday | *Xīngqīliù* | 星期六 |
| Sunday | *Xīngqītiān* | 星期天 |

| | | |
|---|---|---|
| January | *Yīyuè* | 一月 |
| February | *Èryuè* | 二月 |
| March | *Sānyuè* | 三月 |
| April | *Sìyuè* | 四月 |
| May | *Wǔyuè* | 五月 |
| June | *Liùyuè* | 六月 |
| July | *Qīyuè* | 七月 |
| August | *Bāyuè* | 八月 |
| September | *Jiǔyuè* | 九月 |
| October | *Shíyuè* | 十月 |
| November | *Shíyīyuè* | 十一月 |
| December | *Shí'èryuè* | 十二月 |

# TRANSPORT
## Public Transport

airport
*jīchǎng* 機場

long-distance bus station
*kèyùn zhàn* 客運站

subway (underground)
*jiéyùn* 捷運

subway station
*jiéyùn zhàn* 捷運站

train station
*huǒchē zhàn* 火車站

What time does ... leave/arrive?
*... jǐdiǎn kāi/dào?* ... 幾點開/到?

the boat
*chuán* 船

intercity bus; coach
*kèyùn* 客運

local/city bus
*gōnggòng qìchē* 公共汽車

minibus
*xiǎo gōnggòng qìchē* 小公共汽車

the plane
*fēijī* 飛機

train
*huǒchē* 火車

I'd like a ...
*Wǒ yào yìzhāng ...* 我要一張 ...

one-way ticket
*dānchéng piào* 單程票

return ticket
*láihuí piào* 來回票

platform ticket
*yuètái piào* 月台票

1st-class ticket
*tóuděngcāng* 頭等艙

2nd-class ticket
*èrděngcāng* 二等艙

I want to go to ...
*Wǒ yào qù ...*
我要去 ...

The train has been delayed/cancelled.
*Huǒchē (tuīchí le/qǔxiāo le).*
火車(推遲了/取消了)

When's the ... bus?
*... bānchē shénme shíhou lái?*
... 班車什麼時候來?

| | | |
|---|---|---|
| first | *tóu* | 頭 |
| last | *mò* | 末 |
| next | *xià* | 下 |

**boarding pass**
*dēngjīzhèng* 登機證
**left-luggage room**
*jìfàng chù* 寄放處
**platform number**
*yuètái hàomǎ* 月台號碼
**ticket office**
*shòupiào chù* 售票處
**timetable**
*shíkèbiǎo* 時刻表

## Private Transport
**I'd like to hire a ...**
*Wǒ yào zū yíliàng ...* 我要租一輛 ...
  **car**
  *qìchē* 汽車
  **4WD**
  *sìlún qūdòng* 4輪驅動
  **motorbike**
  *mótuōchē* 摩托車
  **bicycle**
  *zìxíngchē* 自行車

**How much is it per day?**
*Yìtiān duōshǎo qián?*
一天多少錢?
**How much is it per hour?**
*Yíge xiǎoshí duōshǎo qián?*
一個小時多少錢?
**How much is the deposit?**
*Yājīn duōshǎo qián?*
押金多少錢?
**Does this road lead to ...?**
*Zhè tiáo lù dào ...?*
這條路到 ...?

| road | *lù* | 路 |
| section | *duàn* | 段 |
| street | *jiē* | 街 |
| No 21 | *21 hào* | 21號 |

**Where's the next service station?**
*Xià yíge jiāyóuzhàn zài nǎlǐ?*
下一個加油站在哪裡?
**Please fill it up.**
*Qǐng jiāmǎn yóuxiāng*
請加滿油箱
**I'd like ... litres.**
*Wǒ yào ... gōngshēng.*
我要 ... 公升

**diesel**
*cháiyóu* 柴油

---

### ROAD SIGNS

| 讓 | *Ràng* | **Give way** |
| 繞行 | *Ràoxíng* | **Detour** |
| 禁止進入 | *Jìnzhǐ Jìnrù* | **No Entry** |
| 禁止超車 | *Jìnzhǐ Chāochē* | **No Overtaking** |
| 禁止停車 | *Jìnzhǐ Tíngchē* | **No Parking** |
| 入口 | *Rùkǒu* | **Entrance** |
| 保持暢通 | *Bǎochí Chàngtōng* | **Keep Clear** |
| 收費 | *Shōufèi* | **Toll** |
| 危險 | *Wēixiǎn* | **Danger** |
| 減速慢行 | *Jiǎnsù Mànxíng* | **Slow Down** |
| 單行道 | *Dānxíngdào* | **One Way** |
| 出口 | *Chūkǒu* | **Exit** |

---

**leaded petrol**
*hánqiān qìyóu* 含鉛汽油
**unleaded petrol**
*wúqiān qìyóu* 無鉛汽油

**How long can I park here?**
*Zhèlǐ kěyǐ tíng duōjiǔ?* 這裡可以停多久?
**Can I park here?**
*Zhèlǐ kěyǐ tíngchē ma?* 這裡可以停車嗎?
**Where do I pay?**
*Zài nǎlǐ fùkuǎn?* 在哪裡付款?
**I need a mechanic.**
*Wǒ xūyào jīshī.* 我需要機師
**We need a mechanic.**
*Wǒmen xūyào jīshī.* 我们需要機師
**The car has broken down (at ... )**
*Qìchē shì (zài ...) huài de.* 汽車是(在 ... )壞的
**The car/motorbike won't start.**
*Qìchē/mótuōchē* 汽車/摩托車
*fādòng bùqǐlái.* 發動不起来
**I have a flat tyre.**
*Lúntāi pòle.* 輪胎破了
**I've run out of petrol.**
*Méiyou qìyóu le.* 没有汽油了
**I had an accident.**
*Wǒ chū chēhuò le.* 我出車禍了

## TRAVEL WITH CHILDREN
**Is there a/an ...?**
*Yǒu ... ma?*
有 ... 嗎?
**I need a/an ...**
*Wǒ xūyào ...*
我需要 ...
  **baby change room**
  *yīng'ér huànxǐshì* 嬰兒換洗室

**baby food**
*yīng'ér shípǐn* 嬰兒食品
**baby formula (milk)**
*yīng'ér nǎifěn* 嬰兒奶粉
**baby's bottle**
*nǎipíng* 奶瓶
**child-minding service**
*tuōér fúwù* 托兒服務
**chidren's menu**
*értóng càidān* 兒童菜單
**(disposable) nappies/diapers**
*zhǐniàokù* 紙尿褲
**(English-speaker) babysitter**
*(huì shuō yīngwén de)* (會說英文的)
*yīng'ér bǎomǔ* 嬰兒保姆

**highchair**
*yīng'ér cānyǐ* 嬰兒餐椅
**potty**
*yīng'ér mǎtǒng* 嬰兒馬桶
**stroller**
*yīng'ér chē* 嬰兒車

**Do you mind if I breastfeed here?**
*Wǒ kěyǐ zài zhèlǐ wèi nǎi ma?*
我可以在這裡餵奶嗎?
**Are children allowed?**
*Yǔnxǔ értóng ma?*
允許兒童嗎?

Also available from Lonely Planet:
*Mandarin Phrasebook*

# Glossary

See also Language (p343) for useful phrases, and Food & Drink (p48) for an explanation of Taiwanese food terms.

**aborigines** – the earliest people of Taiwan; thought to have inhabited the island from around 10,000 BC, coming from southern China and Austronesia
**ARC** – Alien Resident Certificate
**Ami** – aboriginal tribe
**Atayal** – aboriginal tribe

**bàngqiú** – baseball
**bīnguǎn** – hotel
**Bunun** – aboriginal tribe

**catty** – unit of measure (600g)
**chi (qì)** – vital energy
**congee** – rice porridge
**cūn** – village

**dàfàndiàn** – hotel
**DPP** – Democratic Progressive Party; Taiwan's first opposition party

**fàndiàn** – hotel
**Fujianese** – people originally from Fujian province in China who migrated to Taiwan

**gǎng** – harbour/port
**guānxi** – the art of giving and receiving favours; mutually supportive and cooperative relationships

**Hakka** – people originally from Hunan province in China who migrated to Taiwan

**Ilha Formosa** – the name Portuguese sailors gave Taiwan, meaning 'beautiful island'

**jiǎotāchē zhuānyòng dào** – bike path
**jié** – festival
**jiē** – street
**jīn** – unit of measure; see *catty*
**jīngjù** – see *opera (Taiwanese)*
**jiǔdiàn** – hotel

**Kaoliang** – liquor made from sorghum; made in Matsu
**KMT** – Kuomintang, Nationalist Party of the ROC
**koi** – carp

**láojiǔ** – medicinal rice wine made in Matsu
**laver** – edible seaweed

**liǎng** – unit of measure (37.5g)
**lù** – road
**lǚdiàn** – hotel

**mainlanders** – people from mainland China who came to Taiwan after WWII
**Matsu (Mǎzǔ)** – Goddess of the Sea, the most popular deity in Taiwan; one of the Taiwan Strait Islands
**mínsù** – room (ie for rent)
**MRT** – Mass Rapid Transit; Taipei's underground railway system

**One China** – the idea that mainland China and Taiwan are both part of one country: People's Republic of China
**opera (Taiwanese)** – also known as Beijing or Chinese opera, a sophisticated art form that has been an important part of Chinese culture for more than 900 years

**Paiwan** – aboriginal tribe
**píng** – unit of measure (1.82 sq metres)
**Pinyin** – the current system for Romanisation of Chinese
**PRC** – People's Republic of China
**pùbù** – waterfall
**Puyuma** – aboriginal tribe

**qiáo** – bridge
**qū** – district/area

**ROC** – Republic of China; covered all of China before the *PRC* was established
**Rukai** – aboriginal tribe

**Saisiyat** – aboriginal tribe
**sēnlín** – forest
**shān** – mountain
**sì** – temple
**Sinicism** – Chinese method or customs
**shoji** – rice paper

**tael** – unit of measure; see *liǎng*
**taichi** – graceful but powerful slow-motion shadow-boxing commonly practised as the sun rises
**Taipeiers** – people from Taipei
**Three Small Links** – the opening of cross-Strait trade between China and Taiwan's offshore islands
**tóngzǐ mǐ gāo** – sticky rice
**Tsou** – aboriginal tribe
**tuán tǐfáng** – youth hostel dormitory

**VAT** – Value-Added Tax

**Wade-Giles** – a system of Romanisation of Chinese words; widely used until the introduction of *Pinyin*
**wēnquán** – hot spring
**White Terror** – a large-scale campaign started by the *KMT* to purge the island of political activists during the 1950s; one of the blackest times in Taiwan's martial-law period

**xiàng** – lane

**Yami** – aboriginal tribe
**yèshì** – night market

**zhàn** – station
**zhāodàisuǒ** – hostel

# Behind the Scenes

## THIS BOOK

*Taiwan* was first published in 1987. The first five editions were written by Robert Storey. This 6th edition was written by Andrew Bender, Julie Grundvig and Robert Kelly. Dr Trish Batchelor wrote the Health chapter.

## THANKS from the authors

**Andrew Bender** First thanks go to Mark Tsui at the TBROC in Los Angeles, for introductions on the ground in Taipei. Christine Lai and Emily Huang made the most excellent hand-off to Edward Wu, whose patience and willingness to help know no bounds. Thanks also to Amy Shen at the Taipei City Government. Additional thanks to Shandy Ho, James Spencer, Veronica at the Beitou Hot Springs Museum, Corbett Wall, Connelie Klijn, Richard Jacobs, Margaret ten Cate and anyone else who lavished me with more time and attention than I deserved. Thanks also to Earl Wieman for his *guānxi*, Dianne Cockery for her enthusiasm and great ideas, and especially Brent Hannon for consistently spot-on advice.

Finally, thanks to Michael Day, who proves that it is still possible to be both a gentleman and a success in today's world, Rebecca Lalor for being a valuable and congenial helper, and to Julie and Robert, for their extraordinary hard work, diligence and understanding.

**Julie Grundvig** Special thanks to Yipeng for being, as always, so supportive in my endeavours. Also, thank you to Andy Corey, Katie Cohn and Molly Timmers for their suggestions on the road. A word

of appreciation to the Penghu National Scenic Area Office, Mr Zhang from the *Matsu Daily News*, Mika Chen from Peikan, and Giselle and Theresa from Lanyu. I'm eternally grateful to Marjie Bloy, John Abbey and Paul Brennan for taking over my responsibilities in Beijing so I could research this edition. Lastly, a word of gratitude to Cassandra MacLeane, Shannon Emmerson, David Jenkins, James Sherrett and Stephen Osborne for their encouragement and advice.

**Robert Kelly** Taiwan is both fast-changing and traditional. I never would have been able to keep up with both aspects without the feedback and tips from a number of people around the island. Special thanks to Yin Hui-ming, my wife, especially for her help with scripting, Brian Rawnsley for his knowledge of the north coast, Elisa Wang at the Taoyuan Cultural Foundation, Ann Wang at the Hsinchu Cultural Centre, Brian Chang in Hsinchu, Sarah Gowen for patiently listening as I rambled on about yet another 'great' place I had discovered, Mr Peng in Taian for all his insight into this mountain treasure, the Adams family, Jason Su, Ann and Ping for their help with Kenting, my Chinese teachers at TLI, Durins Bane, Tigerman, acearle, braxtonhicks, San Liu, Yin Cheng-kwen, Bi Yen-ling, Jenny Bennet, Pao-liang Chin, and Paolo and Francesca. To the staff at the various tourist offices and travel centres around the country, I send my warm thanks for helping me far beyond the call of duty. And my final thanks goes to Rebecca Lalor for introducing me to Lonely Planet.

---

### THE LONELY PLANET STORY

The story begins with a classic travel adventure: Tony and Maureen Wheeler's 1972 journey across Europe and Asia to Australia. There was no useful information about the overland trail then, so Tony and Maureen published the first Lonely Planet guidebook to meet a growing need.

From a kitchen table, Lonely Planet has grown to become the largest independent travel publisher in the world, with offices in Melbourne (Australia), Oakland (USA), London (UK) and Paris (France).

Today Lonely Planet guidebooks cover the globe. There is an ever-growing list of books and information in a variety of media. Some things haven't changed. The main aim is still to make it possible for adventurous travellers to get out there – to explore and better understand the world.

At Lonely Planet we believe travellers can make a positive contribution to the countries they visit – if they respect their host communities and spend their money wisely.

# CREDITS

This title was commissioned and developed in Lonely Planet's Melbourne office by Michael Day and Rebecca Chau. Cartography for this guide was developed by Corinne Waddell. Overseeing the project were project manager Chris Love, managing editors Dan Caleo and Martin Heng, managing cartographer Corinne Waddell and layout manager Adriana Mammarella. Editing was coordinated by Rebecca Lalor and Kate Evans with able assistance from Helen Yeates, David Andrew, Diana Saad, Andrew Bain and Charlotte Harrison. Andrew Smith was the coordinating cartographer, and he was assisted by Barbara Benson and Nicholas Stebbing. The book was laid out by John Shippick. Laura Gibb and Indra Kilfoyle assisted with layout. Quentin Frayne coordinated the Language chapter. The cover was designed by Pepi Bluck, and Brendan Dempsey prepared the artwork.

The authors and Lonely Planet would like to thank Osman Chia and Pearl Lee of the Taipei Economic and Cultural Office in Australia for their invaluable assistance. Special thanks to Henry, Betsy and Owen Lin who helped with all things Taiwanese during production and to Rebecca Lalor for her help with script, Pinyin and fact-checking, and for her continual support throughout production.

Jose Laroy, Erik Larson, Lawrence Lavigne, Jeanpey D Lean, Alix Lee, Kira Leisau, Mikelson Leong, Elton Levingston, Wilson Liao, William Lieder, Monte Lin, Jodi Lindal, Maria Lit, Jimmy Liu, Tzu-wei Liu, Einat Lotan, Artur Loza, Reed Lu, Nick Lucchetti **M** Donald Mac Donald, Paul Maslowski, Susan McLachlan, Shane McNamara, Ken Merk, Francois Mes, Bernhard Messerli, Nicole Mies, James Miller, Doug Milliken, Lauren Milner, John Mitchell, Jed Mitter, Martin Moeller, Teresa Moore **N** Terry Nakazono, DA Nelson, Blair Neufeld, Yuya Ni, Anders Nilsson, Erin Noose **O** Hans Oberlaender, Nancy Oxford **P** Joanne Paines, Karen Pao, Suzanne Perry, Wayne Peterson, Cory Pettit, Hsuan-yun Pi, Nelson Pires, Katherine Pitts, Anne Podoll, Caleb Powell, Lauren Powell, Maija Pratt **Q** Erik Quam **R** Theodore Ragsdale, Karim Rahim, Thomas Reckers, David Reid, Dave Rhenow, Chris Ridout, Millie Rivera, Paula Rogers, Jose Luis Rojas, Thomas Runte **S** Johannes Schilli, Ed Schlenk, Gil Schneider, Christine & Carrie Shaw, Hans Simon, Mike Sluchinski, Kenneth So, Karen A Stafford, Rev Brent Stewart, Eduard & Wendy Stiphout, Helmut Straner, Peter Stutvoet, Guy Summers, Yee Szemen **T** Ka Lun Tam, Gene Trabich, Karl-P Traub, Laura Truncellito, Christopher Tsai, Ian Turner **V** Dennis van de Ven, Shirley van Essen, Luca Verduci, Jerry Vochteloo, Peter Voelger **W** Megan Walch, Mei-lan Wang, Brian Webb, James Weiler, Thomas Wilken, Dave Wilson, Richard Wise, Debra Wong, Joy Wood, Cornelius Wuelker **Z** S Zangpo, Oliver Zoellner

# THANKS from Lonely Planet

**Thanks to the many travellers who used the last edition and wrote to us with helpful hints, useful advice and interesting anecdotes:**

**A** Daniel Aaron, Mark Anderson, Nike Annys **B** Christa Bennett, Jocelyn Bertheau, Kevin Bertman, Michael Bischof, Todd A Born, Joseph Bosco, Jim Boyden, David (Dick) Boyes, Jude Bradley, Bryan Brandsma, Karen Bray, Cindy & Allen Brown, Jacob Brown, Lee Burman, Heather Burns, Will Burris **C** Nicole Caissey, Andrew Cameron, Sven Carstensen, John Chambers, Jason Chang, Sophie Chang, David Chen, Frances Chen, Jessica Chen, Vincent Chen, Deborah Chen Pichler, Melissa Cheng, Yoon-Jung Choi, Tan Hui Choon, Chungwah Chow, Leigh Churchill, Barry Climate, Herb Con, William Cox, Dr Anne C Crook, Terry Crossley **D** Larry Daly, David Dayton, Frans & Mei-lan de Lange-Wang, Jan de Vries, Thomas Deas, Peter Degen, Ronny Denk, Angela Di Pietro, Sarah Downes, Philip Drexler, David Drukarz **E** Keith Ekstam, Digby Entwisle, Anat Errel, Andrew Essen **F** Alan C Fitton, Andy Foltz, Isaac Forbes, Erwin Fugger **G** Greg Garff, Dave Gauthier, Walter Gillies, Paul W Gioffi, Irene Goedhart, Esme Goss, Yves Goulnik, Francine Grandsard, Lindsay Gray, Alison Greene, Jennifer Gross, Danny, Gad & Merav Gudovich, J Guilhem **H** Jarrod Hall, Jody Hanson, Simon Hay, Moritz Herrmann, Chua Hian Koon, Patty Hill, Kimiyo Hiruta, John Holmes, Mark Holmes, Thng Hui Hong, Tony Horrigan, Jill Hsieh, Celia Hsu, Yider Hsu, David Hughes **J** Alex Jacobs, Jessica Jacob, Geir Jakobsen, Richard J Johnson, Brent Jones **K** Arlene & Alan Karpel, James Kent, Don Klein, Jochem Kramer, Nikki Kuo **L** J Lamare, Moa Largerman,

## SEND US YOUR FEEDBACK

We love to hear from travellers – your comments keep us on our toes and help make our books better. Our well-travelled team reads every word on what you loved or loathed about this book. Although we cannot reply individually to postal submissions, we always guarantee that your feedback goes straight to the appropriate authors, in time for the next edition. Each person who sends us information is thanked in the next edition – and the most useful submissions are rewarded with a free book.

To send us your updates – and find out about LP events, newsletters and travel news – visit our award-winning website: **www.lonelyplanet.com**.

Note: We may edit, reproduce and incorporate your comments in Lonely Planet products such as guidebooks, websites and digital products, so let us know if you don't want your comments reproduced or your name acknowledged. For a copy of our privacy policy visit www.lonelyplanet.com/privacy.

# Index

INDEX

INDEX

**000** Map pages
**000** Location of colour photographs

**000** Map pages
000 Location of colour photographs

368

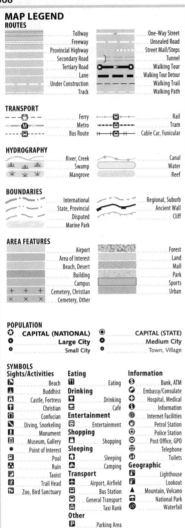

## LONELY PLANET OFFICES

### Australia
Head Office
Locked Bag 1, Footscray, Victoria 3011
☎ 03 8379 8000, fax 03 8379 8111
talk2us@lonelyplanet.com.au

### USA
150 Linden St, Oakland, CA 94607
☎ 510 893 8555, toll free 800 275 8555
fax 510 893 8572, info@lonelyplanet.com

### UK
72–82 Rosebery Ave,
Clerkenwell, London EC1R 4RW
☎ 020 7841 9000, fax 020 7841 9001
go@lonelyplanet.co.uk

### France
1 rue du Dahomey, 75011 Paris
☎ 01 55 25 33 00, fax 01 55 25 33 01
bip@lonelyplanet.fr, www.lonelyplanet.fr

**Published by Lonely Planet Publications Pty Ltd**
ABN 36 005 607 983

© Lonely Planet 2004

© photographers as indicated 2004

Cover photographs: Close up of temple dragon Taiwan, David South/
Image State Pictor (front); Perfectly sized Taiwanese family mobile,
Martin Moos/Lonely Planet Images (back). Many of the images in this
guide are available for licensing from Lonely Planet Images: www
.lonelyplanetimages.com.

All rights reserved. No part of this publication may be copied, stored
in a retrieval system, or transmitted in any form by any means, elec-
tronic, mechanical, recording or otherwise, except brief extracts for
the purpose of review, and no part of this publication may be sold or
hired, without the written permission of the publisher.

Printed through SNP SPrint Singapore Pte Ltd at
KHL Printing Co Sdn Bhd, Malaysia

Lonely Planet and the Lonely Planet logo are trademarks of Lonely
Planet and are registered in the US Patent and Trademark Office and
in other countries.

Lonely Planet does not allow its name or logo to be appropriated by
commercial establishments, such as retailers, restaurants or hotels.
Please let us know of any misuses: www.lonelyplanet.com/ip.

WARNER MEMORIAL LIBRARY
EASTERN UNIVERSITY
ST. DAVIDS, PA 19087-3696

Although the authors and Lonely Planet have taken
all reasonable care in preparing this book, we make
no warranty about the accuracy or completeness of
its content and, to the maximum extent permitted,
disclaim all liability arising from its use.